"MARVELOUS . . . HEART-STOPPING . . . MOVING . . . OFTEN ONE MUST BLINK AWAY THE TEARS"   —*Saturday Review*

They emerge from the shadows of the past—schoolteachers and laborers, conservatives and communists, soldiers and clerics, men and women from every walk of life—at times bitterly disliking and distrusting one another, yet united in their love of country and hatred of the Nazi conqueror. They formed the backbone of the French Resistance—and now their story is told in full in a monumental book that fills a vital gap in the history of World War II and fleshes out one of the great human dramas of our time. *Soldiers of the Night* magnificently recreates those dark years between the fall of France and the liberation—years in which the Resistance was born amid the chaos of defeat, fought to survive internal dissension, Nazi repression and Allied political bickering, and paid the full price in blood and pain for its eventual triumph. It stands like a beacon light for all who believe in the power of human pride, will and courage to prevail.

"Engrossing, immensely poignant and dramatic . . . chock-full of exploits, intrigues, heroisms and tragedies"   —*Publishers Weekly*

DAVID SCHOENBRUN saw the Resistance at first hand as an American intelligence agent and war correspondent in North Africa and France, and while taking part in the French liberation. He holds the French Croix de Guerre and Legion of Honor and personally knows many of the figures in this book. He was for seventeen years chief of the CBS Paris bureau, and his notable books include *As France Goes* and *The Three Lives of Charles de Gaulle*.

SOLDIERS OF THE NIGHT

THE STORY OF THE FRENCH RESISTANCE

DAVID SCHOENBRUN

A MERIDIAN BOOK
NEW AMERICAN LIBRARY

TIMES MIRROR
NEW YORK AND SCARBOROUGH, ONTARIO

NAL BOOKS ARE AVAILABLE AT QUANTITY DISCOUNTS
WHEN USED TO PROMOTE PRODUCTS OR SERVICES. FOR
INFORMATION PLEASE WRITE TO PREMIUM MARKETING
DIVISION, THE NEW AMERICAN LIBRARY, INC., 1633
BROADWAY, NEW YORK, NEW YORK 10019.

Copyright © 1980 by David Schoenbrun

All rights reserved. No part of this publication may be reproduced
or transmitted in any form or by any means, electronic or
mechanical, including photocopy, recording or any information
storage and retrieval system now known or to be invented, without
permission in writing from the publisher, except by a reviewer
who wishes to quote brief passages in connection with a review
written for inclusion in a magazine, newspaper or broadcast. For
information address E. P. Dutton, 2 Park Avenue, New York,
New York 10016.

This is an authorized reprint of a hardcover edition published by
E. P. Dutton. The hardcover edition was published
simultaneously in Canada by
Clarke, Irvin & Company Limited, Toronto and
Vancouver.

MERIDIAN TRADEMARK REG. U.S. PAT. OFF. AND FOREIGN COUNTRIES
REGISTERED TRADEMARK—MARCA REGISTRADA
HECHO EN WESTFORD, MASS., U.S.A.

SIGNET, SIGNET CLASSICS, MENTOR, PLUME, MERIDIAN AND
NAL BOOKS are published in the United States by The New
American Library, Inc., 1633 Broadway, New York,
New York 10019, in Canada by The New American Library of
Canada Limited, 81 Mack Avenue, Scarborough, Ontario M1L 1M8

First Meridian Printing, August, 1981

3 4 5 6 7 8 9

PRINTED IN THE UNITED STATES OF AMERICA

To
Noémi June Szekely,
my granddaughter.
May she know people as dedicated
to freedom and as brave as my friends
of the French Resistance.

CONTENTS

ACKNOWLEDGMENTS

A great many people gave of their time, talent, and energies to help prepare this book. Some of them I have known and worked with on this story ever since the summer of 1943 when I arrived at General Eisenhower's Supreme Headquarters in Algiers. As a soldier in the Military Intelligence Branch of the army I was assigned to an organization called the Psychological Warfare Branch (PWB), where I served for a year as desk editor and broadcaster, in French, to occupied France.

It was in Algiers that I met General Charles de Gaulle and General Henri Giraud, then co-presidents of the French Committee of National Liberation. I also met members of the French Resistance, as well as British and Russian political and intelligence officers in Algiers. I also worked closely with the American military and diplomatic officials, notably Consul General Robert Murphy, who was Eisenhower's political affairs adviser. It was there in Algiers at PWB that I met one of the principal editors of this book, William Doerflinger, of E. P. Dutton, publishers. I wish to thank by good friend Bill Doerflinger most particularly for sharing his knowledge of this period with me and for his professional skill in helping edit this book. I wish also to thank his associate at E. P. Dutton, Paul De Angelis, for his many valuable editorial suggestions.

John Taylor, one of the directors of the National Archives in Washington, was most helpful in making available the reports of American officials and officers in Washington, London, and Algiers, as well as the hundreds of field reports sent in by American intelligence agents inside France working with the French Resistance. Mr. Taylor had already offered me his hospitality by giving access to the files of his remarkable treasure-house of an institution for my book on Benjamin Franklin's years as American ambassador to France.

Special mention is due my research colleague Amy Clampitt, who spent backbreaking and eye-straining months in the National Archives poring over the thousands of documents of this period.

My wife, Dorothy, who reads and comments on every page as it comes out of the typewriter, performed her usual invaluable role as first editor of this book, as she has for every book and article I have written. Without her help, patience, tolerance, and encouragement there would be no book.

Shirley Sulat typed the manuscript, at times an almost impossible task, for I scribbled hundreds of corrections up and down and around the text. She deserves apologies as well as thanks.

In addition to these good people, there were several hundred men and women whom I interviewed for hours on end, sometimes over and over for weeks, about their role in the Resistance. I cannot name them all, but there were close to fifty of them who made an important contribution to this study and who deserve special mention.

Foremost among all the Resistance leaders who helped on this book is one of the true heroines of the struggle, Marie-Madeleine Fourcade, whose own book, *Noah's Ark*, the story of her espionage network, is one of the most exciting I have ever read. Marie-Madeleine is one of the principal characters of this story. I thank her not only for her help but also for enriching my life by knowing her.

I can say the same about her close friend Marie-Claire Scamaroni, to whom I here express my appreciation, admiration, and affection.

Jean-Pierre Lévy, chief of Franc-Tireur, one of the three largest of the democratic Resistance movements, gave generously of his own time and convened his comrades of his movement at a dinner party at his home. For six fascinating hours they recounted the drama of their lives in the underground. My thank to Jean-Pierre Lévy, to Eugène Claudius-Petit, and to Dominique Veillon, the historian of their movement.

My good friend for almost thirty years, Claude Bouchinet Serreulles, General de Gaulle's envoy to the Resistance, is, like Marie-Madeleine, a hero of France and a principal character in the cast of this drama. He shared with me his intimate, detailed knowledge of General de Gaulle's Free French movement and of the Resistance.

Anthropologist Germaine Tillion was an invaluable source of information about the movement of the Musée de l'Homme and an inexhaustible well of wisdom about France and the French.

Pierre Bertaux, chief of a Resistance band, professor of German, and former chief of the Sûreté Générale, France's equivalent of the FBI—and where but in France would one find a scholarly chief of a national police?—has been my friend since the liberation of France. Much of what I have learned about the complexities of French life I have learned from Pierre, a complicated man himself.

Finally, in alphabetic order, is the list of other men and women who made important contributions to this book and to the cause of freedom for France:

Lucie and Raymond Aubrac, Raymond Basset, Anne-Marie Bauer, Georges Bidault, Patrice Blank, Claude Hettier de Boislambert, Henri Bulawko, Michel Cailliau, Jean Cassou, Jean Chaintron, Louis Closon, José and Nicole Corti, Jean Cosson, Alfred Coste-Floret, Jacques Destrée, Geneviève de Gaulle, Gilbert Grandval, Dr. Albert Haasz, Léo Hamon, Max Heilbron, René La Combe, Joseph La Picirella, General Jean de Lattre de Tassigny, Anny Lévy Latour, Jacques Lazarus, Robert Lencement, André Manuel, Daniel Mayer, Joseph-Henri Monjaret, Robert Noireau, Alexandre Parodi, Father Michel Riquet, Edwige de Saint-Wexel, Emile Valley, Pierre Villon.

I wish to thank Claude Lévy, of the Comité d'Histoire de la Deuxième Guerre Mondiale, one of the directors of the French Archives; and Marianne Danson of the same organization, who searched out and provided most of the photographs that illustrate the text. Elizabeth Learson gave similar help in searching the archives of *Life* magazine.

Very special thanks are due Jack Macrae, president of E. P. Dutton, whose idea it was to publish a book on the French Resistance.

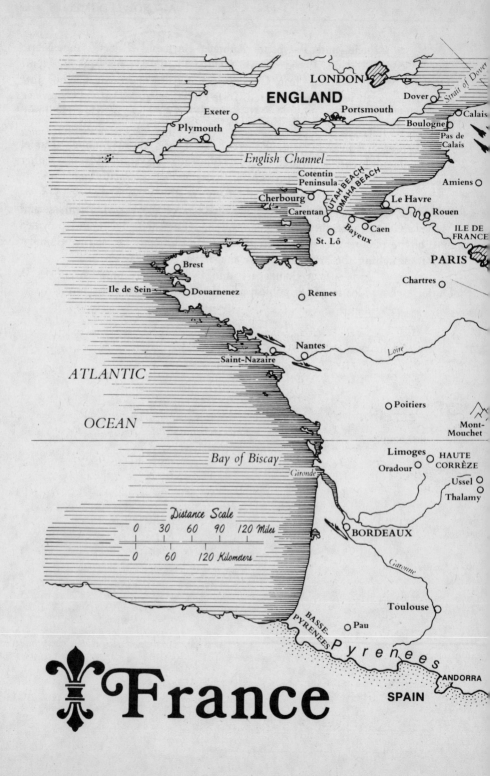

ENGLAND

LONDON

ENGLAND

Dover

Strait of Dover

Exeter

Portsmouth

Calais

Plymouth

Boulogne

Pas de
Calais

English Channel

Cotentin
Peninsula

UTAH BEACH

OMAHA BEACH

Amiens

Cherbourg

Le Havre

Rouen

Carentan

ILE DE
FRANCE

St. Lô

Bayeux

Caen

PARIS

Brest

Chartres

Ile de Sein

Douarnenez

Rennes

ATLANTIC

Nantes

Loire

Saint-Nazaire

OCEAN

Poitiers

Mont-
Mouchet

Bay of Biscay

Limoges

HAUTE
CORRÈZE

Oradour

Gironde

Ussel

Thalamy

Distance Scale

0   30   60   90   120 Miles

BORDEAUX

0   60   120 Kilometers

Garonne

Toulouse

BASSE
PYRENEES

Pau

Pyrenees

ANDORRA

SPAIN

France

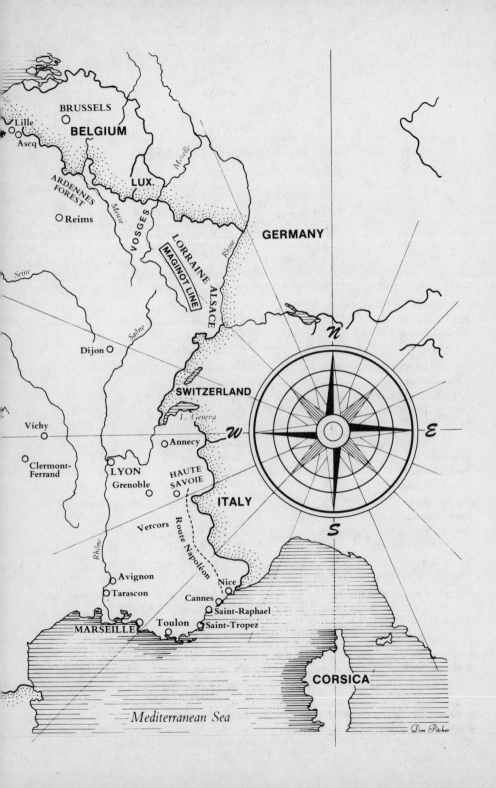

THE CAST:
PRINCIPAL RESISTANCE LEADERS

The Musée de l'Homme
Boris Vildé
Anatole Lewitzky
Paul Rivet

The Alliance
Marie-Madeleine Fourcade
George Loustaunau-Lacau
Léon Faye

Combat
Henri Frenay
Claude Bourdet
Michel Brault
Bertie Albrecht
Jacques Renouvin

Libération
Emmanuel d'Astier de la Vigerie
Raymond and Lucie Aubrac

Franc-Tireur
Jean-Pierre Lévy
Eugène Petit
Antoine Avinin
Yves Farge

Socialist Resistance Leaders
Christian Pineau
Vincent Auriol
Daniel Mayer

Gaullists
Claude Serreulles
Charles de Gaulle
Claude Hettier de Boislambert
Colonel Passy
Colonel Rémy

Franc-Tireurs et Partisans
Français; Front National
(Communists)
Pierre Villon
Robert Noireau

Conseil National de la Résistance
Jean Moulin
Georges Bidault
Jacques Bingen
Alexandre Parodi

Paris Liberation Committee (CPL)
Jacques Chaban-Delmas
Léo Hamon
André Tollet

The Secret Army; Free France; Forces
Françaises de l'Intérieur (FFI)
General Charles Delestraint
General Leclerc
General Jean de Lattre de Tassigny
Colonel Henri Rol-Tanguy

PROLOGUE

THE SURVIVORS

Ussel, Haute-Corrèze
September 2, 1977

They came from every corner of France: from fishing villages on the rock-ribbed coast of Brittany and from the apple orchards of Normandy; from sugar beet fields and textile factories in the north; from Alsace and Lorraine, which they had fought to win back for France, as their fathers and their grandfathers had fought.

Wheat farmers drove down from the Beauce, where the soil is as black and rich as the fertile plains of America. They came from the Alps and the golden vineyards of Burgundy and the green valleys of the Rhône; from the flowerbeds of Grasse and Nice; from Cassis and La Ciotat, from Marseille,* Bordeaux, and Toulouse; from Perpignan and the Pyrénées that so many of them had fled across, almost forty years before. Some had ended up in Spanish dungeons, waiting for a French or British consul to rescue them. Others had made their way down the Costa Brava, to Barcelona, then to Madrid and Lisbon and on to London to join General de Gaulle and Free France.

Then, against all odds and hopes, many made their way back to Occupied France, parachuting in by moonlight, hiding in barns until they made contact with comrades of the underground, of what came to be known as the French Resistance. These men and women had never accepted the defeat of France. At the risk of torture and death they sabotaged Nazi communications, published propaganda tracts and journals, spied out Hitler's military installations, and sent the intelligence information back to London. They were the patriots who rallied to de Gaulle's proclamation of June 18, 1940, broadcast on

---

* This is the correct French spelling; in English it is spelled Marseilles. Throughout this book the French spellings are used for names of places in France.

1

the BBC: "Whatever happens, the flame of French resistance must not die and will not die." Some rose to resist without having heard his proclamation.

The flame did not die. Those who came to Ussel on that September day of 1977 were the survivors of one of the most daring and successful of the intelligence networks of the Resistance. It called itself the Alliance. The Gestapo called it Noah's Ark because the members used animal names as their code-aliases. Its leader was a woman, Marie-Madeleine Fourcade—Hedgehog—the only woman to head a major Resistance network. It was she who called them to Ussel to celebrate their anniversary and to reconstruct one of the dramatic moments of their underground life.

Marie-Madeleine put together and led a network of thousands of secret agents, with clandestine radio receivers, secret airfields, caches of arms and funds smuggled in from England. They sent out of France, back to London, detailed maps of German fortifications in Channel ports and submarine pens, as well as sailing schedules and routes of German submarines, enabling Allied destroyers to hunt out the U-boats and save thousands of tons of shipping and hundreds of lives. The Alliance network penetrated deep into the German bases and stole the plans of Hitler's secret weapons, enabling the RAF to bomb the sites and save London terrible destruction and loss of life.

Marie-Madeleine was not only a master spy but a beautiful one, with raven's-wing black hair parted in the middle and brushed sleekly down the sides of her head, framing her large, deep brown eyes and finely chiseled features and full lips. Time has taken its toll of Marie-Madeleine. She is wracked with the pain of arthritis and would lead the anniversary parade in Ussel leaning heavily on a cane, her features drawn tight. Yet the beauty is still there in the fine bone structure, the luminous eyes, the radiant, brave smile, and in her continued leadership. It was she who arranged the Congress of Ussel, she who persuaded one of France's most important political leaders to attend, Jacques Chirac, former prime minister, leader of the Gaullist group in Parliament, rival for power of French President Giscard d'Estaing. Although Marie-Madeleine's network worked for the British, she and most of the members were and are loyal to General de Gaulle and his memory.

When war broke out in 1939, Marie-Madeleine Fourcade was a young Paris matron in her early thirties, mother of two children. She was the executive secretary of a publishing house led by a dynamic figure, Commandant Georges Loustaunau-Lacau, a World War I hero. He was a graduate of Saint-Cyr, first in his class at the prestigious war college, the Ecole Supérieure de Guerre, a fighting soldier and a scholar, fluent in five languages. He had one obsessive interest: the secret services.

When Loustaunau-Lacau left the army to publish political magazines, he set out to create an intelligence network of his own inside Germany, foreseeing the inevitability of war against Hitler and mistrusting official services. In his journal L'Ordre National, he published, on the eve of war, the battle order of Hitler's land, sea, and air forces. It had been compiled for him by a

fervently anti-Nazi Jewish friend, Bertold Jacob, an intelligence wizard who
had been tracking the advance of nazism from its beginnings.

Marie-Madeleine collated and filed their material, advance training for her mission as chief of a major Allied intelligence network. Twice she
was arrested, twice she escaped. At one time she fled France to Spain by doubling
up into a mailbag and being delivered over the Pyrénées to the French Embassy,
almost freezing to death en route. And once she fled by clandestine aircraft,
aboard a British Lysander that landed in the dead of night, picked her up, and
flew under cloud cover to England, hiding from German night fighters and
bouncing over bursts of antiaircraft flak. It was that air escape in 1943 that
would be reenacted in 1977 in Ussel.

Only one Lysander is left in flying condition, and it proved impossible to get all the clearances needed for it to fly again to France. So Marie-
Madeleine, never daunted, arranged to borrow a French air force Broussard,
very close to the Lysander in design, and have it fly in, with a British pilot
aboard, to reconstruct the wartime drama of the pickup by moonlight in
Occupied France.

It was in July 1943 that Marie-Madeleine was scheduled to fly to
London for consultation and planning sessions. She was to be picked up at the
little airstrip of Bouilhancy, near Paris.

"I shall never forget that flight. The weather was bad, I wondered
if the Lysander would get through that night. We worried about being able to
light the strip with our feeble flashlights. Then we heard a muffled motor
straight ahead, heard it before we could see a thing. Then it was there, dead
ahead of us, at two hundred feet, coming in. *Mon Dieu*, what skill, what bravery!
Those wonderful young pilots. Our carrier pigeons, our homing pigeons, that's
what we called them.

"The Lysander had caught our Morse signal, it touched down,
rolled so short a distance, a fantastic plane. Then, out jumped the pilot. So
tall, so handsome, a movie actor of an RAF pilot. He was just twenty years old,
had been flying in and out of France for a year, right under the noses of the
Luftwaffe and the Gestapo. His name was as typecast British as his tall, slim,
elegant figure: Peter Vaughan-Fowler."

Marie-Madeleine laughed with delight, stretched out her arms,
and shouted her joyous greeting: "And here he is, back with us again, our
handsome hero, Peter Vaughan-Fowler."

He stepped out of the small hotel, where we all were staying, right
on cue, with a shy smile but holding out both hands to Marie-Madeleine. Peter
Vaughan-Fowler was now a colonel, fifty-four years old, but he was as slim,
elegant, and graceful as the twenty-year-old boy-pilot whom Marie-Madeleine
had described. He looked like a young actor who had had to powder his hair
and paint in just a few lines around his eyes and lips to appear old enough for
the third act. Under the gray hair and behind the few lines on his face, the
youth he was still lived and smiled out at us.

Just a few steps behind Vaughan-Fowler came another Englishman, equally tall, equally slim, graceful, and boyish. He was in his mid-fifties. Marie-Madeleine caught sight of him over Vaughan-Fowler's shoulder. "Captain Verity! Welcome, welcome, oh, how good to see you here." She turned to us and said, "Captain—no, now he is a colonel—Hugh Verity was the squadron commander of the Lysanders. It is he who assigned the missions and ran the operations. And he himself flew two dozen flights in and out of Occupied France. And somehow we were all spared to live to see this day."

It was quite a day, September 2, 1977, the thirty-fifth anniversary of the first flights out of Ussel in 1942; in fact quite a long weekend of celebration, of nostalgia, of tears for those who had fallen and cheers for those who had survived. We all gathered at the Monument des Morts on the village square. Bronze plaques, fixed to a stone pedestal, carried the names of soldiers and civilians who had fallen in past wars. Every village in France has its monument to the dead. A color guard presented arms, and Marie-Madeleine, leaning on her cane, stood as straight as she could and began to lead the survivors of her network in the "Chant des Partisans," the "Marseillaise" of the Resistance. It begins with the stirring quatrain:

> Ami, entends-tu le vol noir
> Des corbeaux sur nos plaines?
> Ami, entends-tu ces cris sourds
> Du pays qu'on enchaîne? *

We stood at attention, bareheaded, sang the "Song of the Partisans" and then deposited our flowers at the base of the monument. Then, France being France, we all marched off to a splendid lunch of country sausages, ham, boiled potatoes, thick slabs of country bread, creamy mounds of butter, all washed down with a hearty red *vin du pays*, strong enough to stand up to the salty, spicy dish of *potée Limousin*.

The next day, convoys drove through the fragrant countryside, blooming with wild flowers, heading for the field of Thalamy, some fifteen miles outside Ussel. The trees were still heavy with green leaves in September in south-central France. As the road climbed, plane trees gave way to the first mountain firs, standing straight and tall. And then through the trees we saw the clearing, as long and wide as a soccer field, carpeted with grass, surrounded by the sentinels of tall trees. The trees had given cover to the Resistance teams that had guarded the field to protect the passengers and crew of the planes that would come swooping down to disembark passengers, load on others, and take off again in less than ten minutes.

Marie-Madeleine took her place at the end of the field, the long

---

* Friend, do you hear the black flight
  Of the crows on our plains?
  Friend, do you hear the mute cry
  Of our country in chains?

end, where the plane would taxi up. She held tightly to the strong arm of Colonel Vaughan-Fowler, who had flown into that field more than three decades earlier. He squinted as he looked up into the sun, scanning the sky for the Broussard, which would be carrying his old squadron commander, Colonel Hugh Verity.

And there it was, suddenly cutting down out of the sun. Its lights began to flash, in Morse, M-M-M-, the signal agreed in advance for identification. On the ground a survivor of the network, who had lived through this drama with German troops all around Thalamy, came forward, in daylight this time. In his hand a flashlight blinked its own recognition code, C-C-C-, and the Broussard, wagging its wings in confirmation, swooped down almost at treetop level and came in for a bouncy landing on the grass.

Marie-Madeleine embraced Colonel Verity and then turned to give her hand to the man who had risked his life over and over again to hide resistants coming in to Ussel or waiting to fly out. Jean Vinzant was, in 1942, a merchant in coal and wood and leader of the Resistance movement in Ussel. It was in his house that Marie-Madeleine and so many others, French resistants and Allied airmen, had hidden out. She had given him the code name Great Dane. He had given her network a hideout that he had built in his cellar and a radio-reception center in his attic. His survival, like that of many of his comrades, was a miracle of luck and bravery.

One day Vinzant had been finishing a radio circuit with London when his doorbell rang imperiously. He peered out the window to see who was punching the bell and his heart almost stopped as he saw two Gestapo officers in their dread black uniforms.

He had no time to put his radio set away and hide all the wires, batteries, and papers. He did the best he could, sweeping them off the table, piling them up on the floor, and throwing a rug over the heap. Not much of a hiding place if the Gestapo had come to search.

Downstairs he went and saw his maid opening the door. She was clutching her apron piled high with string beans. He rushed to the Gestapo officers, apologizing for his simpleminded maid and her inelegant service. Nervously he made them welcome, asking if they would like a drink.

They smiled politely and said they would.

He called the maid and she came ambling in still clutching her apron full of *haricots verts*. He shooed her out of the room and served the officers himself. The maid went clumping upstairs muttering about *les Boches*. He was furious at her imprudence and vowed to deal with her later, praying he would get the chance.

The Gestapo officers, still correctly polite, informed him that they had information he was using a radio and would have to search his house. He protested it was untrue and that a search was an insult to his honor. Still smiling, the Gestapo officers took him by the arms and pushed him forward. They began in the cellar.

The cellar was clean. There were no resistants or Allied airmen there that day. All through the house they went, and finally, Vinzant's heart beating so loudly he feared they would hear it, climbed up to the attic, passing on the way his simpleminded maid who scowled at them as they passed and turned sideways so that they could squeeze past her swollen apron in the narrow corridor.

Into the attic for the moment of truth, the end of the long road for Jean Vinzant. He could not talk his way out of the evidence, and a shortwave radio and code book meant, at best, execution by firing squad, at worst torture and deportation to a concentration camp in Germany. What Jean Vinzant feared most, what every resistant feared, was that under torture he would talk, that he would blow the network.

The Gestapo officers looked everywhere. They were clearly disappointed and puzzled. Someone had tipped them off to the radio setup. They were sure of it. Yet there was nothing there, just an old cluttered, innocent attic.

Jean Vinzant was stupefied. He had given himself up as dead. He staggered out of the attic, accompanying the Gestapo officers down to the front door and protesting their search, reaffirming his loyalty to the marshal, to collaboration, to the New Europe, whatever his numbed brain could bring to his trembling lips.

Alone at last, he collapsed against the door, drained by fear, soaking in cold sweat.

"The *sales Boches* have gone?" he was asked by a voice behind his back. It was the maid, still, incredibly, clutching her apron sack. She grinned at him and hefted the apron up and down. "Your radio, it's heavy, Monsieur, heavier than the *haricots verts*."

As he relived that moment thirty-four years later, Jean Vinzant again had to wipe sweat from his brow. "I had always thought she was a simple country girl. My brother and I believed we were so careful when using our radio, that no one knew what we were doing. Well, thank God she knew, and that she had the wit to go to the attic, to get the radio and clean up the mess I had made. She saved my life, as so often the lives of many of us were saved by simple, brave citizens everywhere in France."

The Alliance of Marie-Madeleine Fourcade was only one of a hundred and more such organizations. The specialty of Noah's Ark was espionage and that is why it was called a *réseau*, a network of spies. There were other *réseaux* that furnished the Allies with valuable intelligence on the enemy, and in the course of this story of the French underground war against the Germans and against their own pro-Nazi regime of collaborators we shall meet them and follow their exploits.

There were also representatives in Ussel of the many movements that provided the main body of troops in the underground war. A *mouvement* did not specialize as a *réseau* did. The Resistance movements created a number of groups assigned different tactical and strategic functions, much as a regular army does, but without artillery, tanks, or planes. They fought with knives and pistols, grenades and dynamite. They did not have the rigid structures and collective discipline of an army. Living a clandestine life in hideouts, changing hideaways every few days, along with changes of clothes and names, does not permit a military discipline. This would become a problem as the Allied armies, and even the Free French of de Gaulle, tried to work with and understand the men who fought in the underground. The movements were very different from each other in character and composition. There were democratic movements and Socialist movements, Catholics and Communists across the political spectrum.

Clusters of people began to gather in the street outside the small hotel where Marie-Madeleine and a few of us were staying. They had converged on Ussel in every kind of vehicle, and from every social class. A Rolls-Royce Silver Shadow, with a Paris license plate, was parked next to a Renault 2-CV, with a Lyon license plate, the most expensive and the cheapest car in the world. The men wore mechanics' blues or Guy Laroche cardigans; the women were dressed in smart Paris *tailleurs* or home-sewn frocks. Rich, middle class or poor, they were all one, greeting each other with the traditional triple kiss, left cheek, right cheek, left cheek, a hand-squeeze on the shoulder, a tender caress, a hearty slap on the back—each to his own style, but all delighted to greet a fellow survivor of Noah's Ark. Fox hugged Great Dane, Hedgehog embraced Ram.

Associates from other networks greeted those with whom they had worked in the Alliance. "Bob"—Robert Lencement—was everywhere hailing everyone. He was the second agent whom London had parachuted into France. So thin that he looked as if he had just emerged from prison, Lencement had a wiry strength that surged through his firm handclasp. He was one of the very few Frenchmen to have heard General de Gaulle's call to resistance on June 18, 1940. He heard it because he was a radio engineer of the French Broadcasting System and he was monitoring the London wavelengths. And he became one of the first to rally to that call. He formed, in Ussel, a Resistance network that he called Copernic. It was he who discovered the field at Thalamy and told London to use it as a pickup point. He had two associates at the outset: a politician, Dr. Henri Queuille, who became an almost perennial prime minister of the postliberation Fourth Republic; and a handsome, daring young Corsican, Fred Scamaroni.

For young Fred, it was not only an honor to fight for his country but to carry his arms in Ussel, where his father, before the war, had been subprefect of the department. Fred was called to London, to take his training there and to get a new assignment as the delegate of Fighting France to his native island of Corsica. There he organized an underground network. And there he was betrayed by a member of General Giraud's anti-Gaullist secret service, taken prisoner, and turned over to the dread OVRA, Mussolini's Secret Police, as barbaric as Hitler's Gestapo. He was cruelly tortured but he refused to answer any of their questions. They threw his broken, bleeding body into a cell, promising him they would make him talk the next morning. He knew he would not be able to hold out. When they came back for him, he was dead. He had taken his own life rather than risk giving the names of his comrades. His memory was very much alive in Ussel, his martyrdom invoked by Marie-Madeleine in an address to the assembled survivors.

Standing among them, her eyes shining and bright, applauding the name of her beloved brother was his sister, Marie-Claire Scamaroni, today the mayor of the Third Arrondissement of Paris, during the war a young married woman, with a newborn baby girl, who became the courier of her brother's network. Tiny in stature, she is a dynamo of energy and strength, her deep black eyes always aflame. In her small apartment in Paris she serves hot Corsican sausages and spicy Corsican cheeses, and everywhere there are pictures and mementos of Fred.

These men and women of the French Resistance were quite ordinary men and women. They never planned to be heroes, did not yearn for greatness, as did a man like Charles de Gaulle. They were average people, a young matron of upper-middle-class society, a working girl, a magazine editor, a lawyer, doctor, teacher, a merchant, accountant, bureaucrat, an engineer, a pastrycook. There was a not-so-simpleminded maid who could hide a radio in her apron and laugh at the Gestapo. Ordinary people who did extraordinary things.

The story of the French Resistance is the story of these commonplace people who under circumstances that none had foreseen began to do things they never would have imagined possible. They were not consciously trying to save the honor of France, although that is what they did. They simply refused at risk of their lives to accept dishonor and degradation of human values. Although they themselves talk of networks and movements and the maquis, although they did function through such structures, and those developments need to be traced, the real story is one of individual actions often taken impulsively to the astonishment of the actors themselves.

PART ONE

THE
FALL

1
THE
PHONY WAR

It was particularly hot that August, and August is traditionally the month when all France goes on holiday. Most citizens knew that war threatened in that year, 1939, but they did not believe that Hitler would dare take on France. The French army was the largest and the best in the world. Everyone knew that, not only in France, but in America. The regular dispatches from the Paris bureau of the *New York Times* and the analytical pieces in the special Sunday magazine described the might of the French army and the long experience of its professional staff, still led by the conquerors of Germany in the last world war.

There were those who had their doubts about French army might and general-staff professionalism, particularly those who had read the books and articles of a young officer named Charles de Gaulle. De Gaulle had called for new strategies and tactics based on mobile strike forces, tanks and planes working in tandem, armored units massed as full divisions rather than as cavalry backups for infantry. De Gaulle and others had severely criticized the Maginot Line, not only for its static concept, but its incompleteness. If it were not extended north to the English Channel, it would simply leave a gap through which the German armor could pour without bothering to test the Maginot defenses. Spirited debates had filled the French papers, but most people were reassured by the testimony of Marshal Pétain, the hero of Verdun. Pétain had stated that the Ardennes forest was impenetrable and no German units could attack through that sector, so it had not been necessary to extend the Maginot Line.

A career officer named Captain Henri Frenay was in the Maginot Line in one of the units of the Forty-third Army Corps. He was proud of the emplacements, which he felt were impregnable. The big guns could blast an enemy miles before he could get to the Line. Should any small units infiltrate, the fields of fire of the machine-gun nests in the Line would mow them down. Frenay approved of the standing orders to resist all attacks vigorously and never to retreat from the Line. He came from a family with a long military tradition. His mother revered Marshal Pétain, and from his earliest days he had been brought up with tales of the glory of French arms.

Had anyone told Captain Frenay that the Maginot Line would be bypassed and enveloped so that he and all the defenders would have to fall back in rout, he would have certified him as insane. Nor could he have imagined for an instant that his hero, Pétain, would, before a year had passed, be called to the highest post of France, while he, Frenay, was destined to become one of the first and foremost of the Resistance leaders.

As the dog days of August drove almost everyone to the beaches, storm clouds rolled up in the east of Europe. Soviet Foreign Minister Vyacheslav Molotov signed a nonaggression pact with Hitler's foreign minister, Joachim von Ribbentrop. The worst fears of diplomatic observers had come true: Nazi Germany had wooed Stalin away from the West, which had been slow to offer Stalin the security guarantees he had been demanding. Observers guessed accurately that Hitler must have made a secret deal with Stalin for the partition of Poland. It was the twenty-fourth of August.

The foreign minister of France, Georges Bonnet, who feared communism more than nazism, and who thought he would get along with Hitler, did nothing to counter the move. Nor did Britain's Prime Minister Neville Chamberlain react, although he knew that his country, as well as France, had promised to protect Poland from a Nazi invasion. Now the specter of a joint Nazi-Soviet invasion loomed over the eastern plains, yet neither France nor Britain girded for action.

French Premier Edouard Daladier did make a nationwide broadcast warning that France would stand by her commitments. But he was more concerned about the threat of the French Communist party than he was about Hitler. In the last week of August, instead of taking action to put the French army on a combat-readiness alert, Daladier issued a decree banning all Communist papers, while his police launched a campaign of terror against all Communist party headquarters. Communist members of Parliament were arrested in violation of their parliamentary immunity. French Communists were taken into custody while on military service, without any charges against them. The head of the party, Maurice Thorez, alerted to what was happening, deserted his army unit, fled to Belgium and then made his way to Moscow, where he would spend the war years.

The hero of the Battle of Verdun, Marshal Pétain, was in Madrid as French ambassador. He kept a close watch on the war clouds, sensing that the time was rapidly approaching when he would have a role to play. The old conqueror in World War I was not worried about the Germans this time. Like many French military men, and like most of the French bourgeoisie, Pétain hated and feared communism and Stalin. He sent a note to Count René de Chambrun, the son-in-law of Senator Pierre Laval, a former premier, who also feared communism and was committed to making a deal with Hitler rather than coming to the defense of Poland. Laval had been making speeches calling for a "strong man" who would cleanse France of Communist and Socialist traitors. Pétain knew that Laval and other spokesmen of the Right looked upon him as that providential strong man.

On September 1, 1939, at 4:45 A.M., Nazi troops and Nazi armor struck across the borders of Poland while in the skies a new war weapon, the Stuka dive bomber, screamed down in vertical dives with a wail that startled Polish defenders and sent their horses into a frenzy. Horse cavalry against Stukas and Panzers! The Battle of Poland would not be much of a contest.

Premier Daladier called his Cabinet into session at 10:30 A.M. to inform them that he had received a telegram from the Polish government calling upon the French to honor their commitment to go to war alongside the Poles. The Cabinet agreed to call for general mobilization and to convoke Parliament the next day to ask it for war-credits.

Daladier did ask Parliament for the credits, but put great emphasis in his speech on the need to achieve a conciliation and restore peace. His words of conciliation received the loudest applause, and it was apparent that neither the premier nor the Parliament was eager to go to war. However, they could not, without dishonoring France, renounce their commitment to Poland. Daladier instructed his ambassador in Berlin to deliver an ultimatum to Von Ribbentrop: Beginning at 5 P.M. on that day, France would fulfill its commitments to Poland. Daladier also instructed the commander in chief of the French armed forces, General Maurice Gamelin, to begin hostilities at the stroke of 5 P.M. He had given Hitler six hours to come up with a proposal.

Hitler did not even deign to reply. His invading forces were cutting deeply into Poland.

General Gamelin, on his own initiative, issued secret instructions to his army, navy, and air commanders to delay opening hostilities for twelve hours. A Cabinet minister, Anatole de Monzie, noted in his diary: "France at war does not believe in the war." The British government was no more keen to go to war than the French, but Prime Minister Chamberlain, like Daladier, was obliged to honor Britain's commitment to declare war in defense of Poland.

By September 8, with French mobilization just barely complete, before British troops and armor in real strength had joined the French, the Nazi blitzkrieg had swept away the hopelessly outgunned and outarmed Polish infantry, artillery, and cavalry. German Panzers were breaching the lines at the outskirts of Warsaw and only remnants of Polish units were still holding out.

Daladier panicked. He had assured his colleagues that the gallant Poles would hold off Hitler's forces. He could not believe that the Poles could be destroyed in one week's time. In his panic he sent a desperate appeal to old Marshal Pétain, the symbol of steadfastness, the man who had said before Verdun, "They shall not pass!" and who had held off the mass of the Kaiser's elite troops in attack after attack, for seven long months until finally the Germans fell back.

Daladier implored Pétain to join his government as a sign to the French people and to Hitler, who had been a soldier in the German defeat of World War I, that France was committed to the battle and would again triumph. Apparently it did not occur to Daladier that an old, feeble man in his eighties would not be a frightening menace to Hitler.

The search for a symbol in the person of an octogenarian was an absurdity that underlined the bankruptcy of the ruling circles of France. Later, when catastrophe struck, the leaders of France and many of its citizens would blame it on the Left, on the pacifism of the Popular Front, on Socialist and Communist refusals to increase military budgets. The more rabid rightists would rail against Jews, Freemasons, and Communists. But the truth is that in September 1939, the French army had as many guns, as many tanks and planes, as many fighting soldiers as the Germans. There was no sabotage, no treason. There was, instead, a lack of the will to fight.

One of the French leaders most lacking the will to fight Hitler was Marshal Pétain. He certainly wanted no part in Daladier's War Cabinet. Daladier had collaborated with the Socialists in the Popular Front of 1936. Pétain did not consider him reliable, nor did he feel the time was ripe for him to play a major, perhaps the principal, role. He came to Paris to refuse the premier's offer and also to confer with friends and supporters, including Laval. Then he returned to Spain to wait for his hour to strike.

On September 17, France was shocked to learn that the Soviet Red Army had invaded Poland from the east. The total dismemberment of that tortured land was only days away. Hitler, sensing the French and British reaction to the Soviet invasion of Poland, promptly announced in a speech in Danzig that he had "no war aims against Great Britain and France." He was still hoping that the anti-communism of the West would triumph over their fears of Germany and leave him a free hand to deal with Stalin.

Daladier denounced the Russian invasion and issued a decree dissolving the French Communist party, a decree that violated the basic tenets of the French Constitution. He had not ordered an offensive against Hitler at the front but he was waging a fierce offensive at home against French citizens who were Communists. He charged that Communists were loyal to Moscow, therefore they must logically be held to account for Moscow's villainy in raping besieged Poland.

British forces, totaling four infantry divisions, 158,000 men, made their way into France and took up positions alongside French troops in northern France. Then, like the French, they dug in and did not move. Colonel Charles de Gaulle, commander of tanks of the Fifth Army, was disturbed by the High Command's static strategy. He addressed an urgent communication to headquarters arguing that French tanks, then widely dispersed in support of infantry battalions, should be put together in an armored division with its own battle orders, free to strike powerfully in any direction needed. He had been urging this tactic for years, but only the German High Command had paid him attention and were putting his proposals into action in Poland.

French and German artillery exchanged salvos from time to time, but the front was quiet all along the line. People began to talk about the *drôle de guerre*—the phony war.

Suddenly the front did come alive. Not the western front, but the northern front of Europe. On November 30, to the astonishment and fury of the French, Soviet forces struck against Finland. Almost overnight, the war in the west and Hitler were both forgotten. Brave little Finland's defense against Russia was the main event for the Western world, and Stalin replaced Hitler as public enemy number one.

Daladier's hatred for Communists and for the Russians now knew no bounds. At a meeting of the Supreme Allied War Council, Daladier, whipped ahead by the screams of the rightist press, recklessly proposed a complete rupture with the Soviet Union, even if it meant hostilities with the Russians.

The British were shocked. They shared France's anger at the Soviet attack but knew that it was not in the interests of the Allies to react emotionally. The main enemy was Hitler. He was the one with powerful forces on the western front. The principal aggressor in Europe, since the *Anschluss* with Austria and the destruction of Czechoslovakia and Poland, was Hitler. It could also be argued that Stalin was acting in self-defense. He needed a buffer zone in Poland against Nazi power. Finland directly menaced Leningrad and northern Russia, particularly if Hitler moved in there.

Communists and their friends did use such arguments to defend Stalin's moves. The British were certainly no friends of Stalin or the Communists, but they were eminently practical and felt they could not afford a rupture with Russia while fighting a war against Germany. They finally persuaded Daladier not to break with Stalin and mollified him by agreeing to join France in shipping aid to the Finns.

A young Alsatian, Roger Ginsburger, was watching these events. He read the right-wing press, with its demands to root out Communist traitors. He listened to Daladier's speeches denouncing the Russians. He became certain that rightists, appeasers of Germany like Daladier and Pétain, could not possibly lead France into battle with Hitler and win the war.

Ginsburger, born and educated in Strasbourg, the son of a rabbi, was a middle-class intellectual, a student of architecture at the Ecole des Beaux Arts in Paris. During the Depression, in 1932, angered by the failure and lack of compassion of capitalist governments, he had joined the Communist party. By 1939 he had given up his profession to become a fully employed militant of the Communist party.

When war broke out, Ginsburger was exempted from service because of weak lungs. Then, when police terror hit the Communists, he went underground, living in friends' houses, moving constantly to avoid police detection. He became the editor of the Communist party paper, *Humanité*, which had also gone underground. Ginsburger then adopted the alias of Pierre Villon.

The Paris police, looking for Villon and other Communists, were running around like Hollywood's Keystone Kops, on orders from Daladier to suppress all activities of the Communist Third International. They had no real idea, however, what the Third International was, as Villon discovered one day.

He was working in a bookstore in the Rue Monsieur le Prince, with false papers in his pocket. A commissaire de police led a raid into the shop. At first Villon feared they had received a tip that he was there. But it turned out to be a raid to ferret out the Third International.

"The first thing the inspector did," Villon reminisced in a talk in Paris in 1977, "was to seize the complete works of Lenin." Villon laughed. "I told him that the Third International, an organization designed to organize Communist parties around the world, was created in 1920, *after* Lenin's works had been written. It didn't stop him. He was after Communist books. The idiot even seized the novels of Gorki. I warned him that the whole world would condemn France and put our country in the same category as the book-burning Nazis. Well, he wasn't too bad a fellow, that *flic*. He put Gorki back on the shelves."

The phony war dragged on without action as 1939 drew to an end. The year 1940 did not dawn brightly for the country of the Rights of Man. Seven Communist members of Parliament, who had been at the front, came back to the Chamber in Paris to protest in uniform the police war launched illegally against their party. They were bodily assaulted on the floor of the Chamber of Deputies and a law was rushed through canceling all the mandates of the Communist party parliamentarians. The illegal police terror was made legal.

Even the Supreme Allied War Council was more obsessed with Communist Russia than with Hitler. At a February meeting in Paris, the High Command discussed the Finnish-Soviet war. The French wanted to send forces to Petsamo to fight the Russians alongside the Finns. The British talked them out of going alone and proposed a joint Anglo-French expeditionary force for Finland. Their real objective was to use Finland as a pretext for invading neutral Scandinavia. They planned to capture the southern Norwegian port of Narvik and then seize the Swedish ore railway before proceeding to Finland.

While this planning was going on, Russian forces were driving back the Finns and penetrating deeper into that country. On March 12, 1940, the Finns capitulated. The brave little nation was, after all, much too small to stave off giant Russia any longer. The fall of Finland deprived the British and French of what little excuse they had to invade Norway. Nevertheless the Allies went ahead with their plans. So did Hitler. Each side hoped to outflank the other in the north before meeting head on on the western front.

The Russian victory over Finland further inflamed the anti-Communists in Parliament in Paris. Senator Henri Lemery, a friend of Marshal Pétain, proclaimed in the Senate: "We are at war. We need not discriminate between our enemies except to ask ourselves which is the most vulnerable, in order to defeat it first. There is no doubt. It is the USSR. You had in Finland an almost miraculous opportunity to vanquish the Soviet Union. You let it slip by. France weeps over it! Her heart bleeds!"

A week later, in a secret session of the Chamber of Deputies, rightist politician Pierre-Etienne Flandin shouted at Premier Daladier: "I defy you to explain why you make war against Germany and not also against Russia!" The deputies then cast their ballots on a confidence vote. The results were 230 for Daladier; 1 against; 300 abstentions. Affirmative votes thus counted for less than the majority of the Chamber. Daladier had no choice but to resign.

With a war on, even a "phony war," a new government had to be voted in quickly. And so the next day, March 21, a majority chose a veteran politician, a moderate Conservative named Paul Reynaud, as the new premier. Reynaud was an assertive little bantam cock of a man. He exuded an air of self-confidence and competence, of energy and cunning. He did not walk, he strutted, as so many small men do to try to make themselves seem taller.

Reynaud was an admirer of Charles de Gaulle, whose theories of aggressive tank tactics appealed to his own fighting spirit. He asked de Gaulle to help him draft his speech to the Chamber. The speech was a clarion call for all-out, total war and a strong vote of confidence in the new government. Reynaud had misread the defeatist mood of the politicians. The vote was 268 to 156 with 111 abstentions. A tally of those who voted for him and those who did not vote for him came to 268 to 267, a margin of one. Not exactly a vote of confidence for total war.

Pierre Laval, who had persuaded his friends not to vote for Reynaud, telephoned one of his supporters, General Jacques de Chambrun, to tell him, "Reynaud's resignation is inevitable." He sensed that it would soon be time to call in Marshal Pétain; Laval hoped to rule as the Gray Eminence behind the old man.

To bolster up his slim margin, Reynaud decided to appeal to the anti-Communist fervor of the Chamber. Communist deputy Florimond Bonte and many others were sentenced to long prison terms. Top party leaders Maurice Thorez and Jacques Duclos also received severe sentences, but in absentia. Thorez was in Moscow; Duclos and others had gone underground and would organize the strongest of all Resistance movements. Communist resistance did not begin as an anti-German movement, but as a reaction to political and police repression.

On April 8, while the British and French were still drawing up plans to invest the Norwegian ports, Hitler struck first. Thousands of German assault troops trained in amphibious commando actions hit Norway's principal ports, with the biggest units striking at Trondheim and Narvik. By nightfall the Germans had achieved their objective in another blitzkrieg success. They had captured the major seaports and airfields of Norway. The next morning the French War Cabinet met in urgent session and decided that the Allies must retake Trondheim and Narvik at once. But when the ministers came out of their meeting they were handed dispatches informing them that the Germans had captured Oslo, the Norwegian capital, without a shot being fired. Some nine thousand Germans had conquered Norway. Thousands more were being rushed in and it had become apparent that only a major Allied offensive could dislodge them.

Admiral Darlan, the French naval chief, told Reynaud it would be wiser to take advantage of Germany's preoccupation with the northern front and move strong Allied forces into Belgium to block the German's main line of invasion into France. The proposal was sent to London and accepted by the British, who immediately asked the Belgians to authorize the Allies to set up new defense lines around their country. On April 11, to the dismay of London and Paris, the Belgians refused permission for Allied troops to cross their borders.

Reynaud, under heavy political pressure, conferred with former Premier Daladier, whom he had taken into his own Cabinet as defense minister. They agreed to try to recapture some of the Norwegian ports. They asked the British to join them, or at least to furnish naval transport and convoy protection. Neville Chamberlain's government promised to do everything possible, but did nothing. The French would have to go in alone.

On April 20 French troops began landing on the coast of Norway at small ports or on beaches not yet occupied by the Germans. Less than a division strong, the French forces were not capable of penetrating in enough depth to defeat the entrenched Germans in Norway. Again the French called urgently for British help. But the British once again refused, arguing that it was impossible to do anything against the enemy's superior air power. Having captured all Norwegian airfields, the German Luftwaffe controlled Norwegian skies and would be able to destroy any landing parties big enough to be effective. The French had to pull out, and by early May all their troops had been withdrawn.

Sensing that his hour was striking, Marshal Pétain left Spain and returned to Paris. The fiasco in Norway had doomed Reynaud's chances to remain in power for long. To make things worse, Reynaud came down with the grippe and a high fever. His mistress, the Countess de Portes, took over the management of his affairs and decided that the time had come to get rid of the army commander, General Gamelin. While spooning medicine to Reynaud, she urged him to fire Gamelin. The last days of the phony war had degenerated into a theater of the absurd, with the affairs of France in the hands of an ailing premier's mistress.

2
THE
DEBACLE

Spring, with its annual promise of new life and new hope, had turned Paris green, from the Bois de Boulogne at its western gates to the Bois de Vincennes in the east. The chestnut trees on the Champs-Elysées were budding early in the first week of May 1940. The weather was perfect all through the country whose neighbors had always envied it. The Spaniards, looking at France across their rocky, lunar landscape, sighed and called it "the garden of Europe." The Germans, in their black woods and sooty, industrial valleys, peered across the border and muttered, *"Freulich wie Gott im Frankreich"*—happy as God in France.

But in that verdant spring the French were not happy in France. Spring brought no new hope and no new life. Instead, a desiccated old man in his eighties with an unmerited reputation that would soon enough be shattered, was called in by Premier Paul Reynaud for advice on the deteriorating situation at the front.

Premier Reynaud appealed to Marshal Pétain to join his Cabinet. He felt that if Pétain, who was an idol of the Right, accepted a portfolio, this might disarm the opposition in Parliament. Former Premier Daladier, General Gamelin, and Admiral Darlan did not readily accept Reynaud's authority, but they might not dare stand up to Reynaud and Pétain together. Pétain listened to Reynaud's plea and then replied that he would not refuse a call to duty if the situation required it. It was an ambiguous reply, for a call to duty could come from Reynaud or from a Chamber that voted no confidence in Reynaud. The marshal also reserved judgment on whether the situation required him to respond to a call.

On May 9, having been persuaded finally by his mistress, Reynaud called a Cabinet meeting to propose replacing General Gamelin as commander in chief. Defense Minister Daladier opposed the motion, openly challenging the authority of the prime minister. With powerful German forces massing on their borders, the French were engaged in suicidal games of politics.

Reynaud told the Cabinet that in view of his conflict with the defense minister, he would have to consider his government in crisis and inform the Chamber that he had resigned. The day was spent in political maneuvers, with Laval and his agents preparing to call for the appointment of Marshal Pétain as prime minister. General Gamelin, to his credit, refused to ally himself with the plotters and sent a note to Reynaud saying he was ready to be replaced but would remain vigilant at his post until Reynaud named a new commander in chief. Late that night all the principals went to sleep hoping the new day would bring new counsel.

The new day shattered all their plans. At 5 A.M. the duty officer called General Gamelin with news that German columns were moving through Luxembourg in the direction of Sedan, a traditional invasion route into France. Then an hour and a half later the entire Cabinet was awakened with the shocking news that the Germans had invaded Belgium and Holland and were racing along a wide and deep front. Too late, the Belgian government wanted the French to move in to stem the German tide.

General Gamelin sent orders to General Alphonse Georges, in command of the northern front, to advance at once into Belgium. But there were no orders, no plans to meet the kind of coordinated air, infantry, and armor attacks that were the hallmark of the German blitzkrieg. The general staff had failed to heed the warnings or adopt the tactics that Colonel de Gaulle had been urging for years.

De Gaulle had at last won permission to form an armored division and had been given command of the new Fourth Armored. But the Fourth Armored existed only on paper at HQ. De Gaulle had to contact scattered unit commanders and begin scraping together his new command while strong German forces advanced on his front.

The German blitzkrieg exploded all along the front from the North Sea down to the Ardennes forest. By May 14, the Germans had crushed the Dutch army and the next morning the government of Holland formally surrendered. The Belgian army was still fighting under heavy pressure. Even at that last desperate moment King Leopold turned down a government proposal to rejoin the Anglo-French alliance from which he had withdrawn his nation five years earlier.

At two-thirty in the morning of May 16, General Gamelin, still waiting to be replaced as commander in chief, awakened Premier Reynaud to warn him that the Germans were advancing rapidly and that the government must prepare to leave Paris. Reynaud called one of his ministers, Anatole de Monzie, asking him to arrange a truck convoy to evacuate government files. Monzie replied that he had only a few trucks and no trains.

Senior ministers panicked and began to burn their papers in the courtyard of their ministries. Parisians en route to work saw the bonfires and turned around, rushing home to pack and flee Paris. Trains to the Riviera were jammed and tickets for Biarritz were sold out. The rich were running.

In London the defeatist government of Neville Chamberlain had resigned with the news of Hitler's invasion of Luxembourg, Belgium, and Holland. The most outspoken opponent of appeasement, Winston Churchill, had been named prime minister. On the morning of May 16, with the French panicking, Churchill flew to Paris to stiffen Premier Reynaud's resolve for the fight. He arrived just as the bonfires were roaring along the Seine. Churchill watched in dismay as officials pushed wheelbarrows of archives into the flames. Rushing to the Hotel Matignon, Churchill told Reynaud that four new squadrons of British fighter planes were coming to help the French. By the end of the day Churchill had pledged six more squadrons, leaving a thin screen of only twenty-five in all to defend the British Isles.

Commandant Loustaunau-Lacau had been watching the phony war from his command post in eastern France. Then he saw German units go into action exactly as his analyst Bertold Jacob had foreseen, and as he had predicted in his journal, *L'Ordre National.* He began to denounce the general staff publicly and finally accused the High Command of treason. Loustanau-Lacau was arrested and brought to trial on the charge of demoralizing the army under the wartime emergency decree that authorized the death sentence by firing squad for that offense.

Marie-Madeleine Fourcade and other associates and friends of the man they now called Navarre rushed to his defense with articles alerting public opinion. Hundred of admirers of the fiery patriot pressured their political representatives to save his life. On May 10, the very day of the German offensive he had so accurately predicted and that had caught the general staff sleeping, an examining magistrate confirmed the validity of Loustanau-Lacau's charges of extreme negligence of the military leaders. Navarre was severely reprimanded, however, for excessive zeal in accusing his superiors. Charges against him were dropped and he was told he could have a new command and fight the Germans if he would cease his attacks on the French High Command.

Loustaunau-Lacau was given command of a Zouave battalion in eastern France. Before going to his new post he told Marie-Madeleine: "It is hopeless. Your best way to escape the Germans would be to take the roads that run through central France. Then, head southwest. Rendezvous ultimately at my place in Oloron-Sainte-Marie in the Pyrénées." Navarre and Marie-Madeleine, without thinking of it in those terms, had taken the first step on the road to a Resistance network.

Premier Reynaud sought to reassure the nation on May 17, announcing that Marshal Pétain had joined his Cabinet as vice-premier. He told the people of France in a nationwide broadcast the next day: "The victor of Verdun, Marshal Pétain, will now be at my side. . . . He will remain there until victory is won!"

Reynaud did not know that on leaving Madrid, Pétain had told dictator Franco that France was already beaten and that he was going back to get ready to sign an armistice. Pétain, refusing to admit any of the errors of the High Command, blamed the defeat of France on "thirty years of Marxism."

If Reynaud did not know that Pétain had already written off France as defeated, Pétain, himself, did not know that only the day before Reynaud had told a startled Winston Churchill: "We are beaten." Or that General Gamelin had informed the government: "We have lost."

On May 19, General Maxime Weygand, a protégé of World War I hero Marshal Ferdinand Foch, flew back to France from his outpost in Syria to be named commander in chief, replacing Gamelin. At seventy-three, Weygand was not exactly young blood. He was admired, however, for the role he had played as chief of staff to Foch, and was revered by the Right for having directed the defense of Warsaw in 1920 against the Red Army of the Soviet Union. He had led Poland to victory over the Communists. Weygand was an intimate and ally of Marshal Pétain. Reynaud was underwriting his own overthrow by bringing both these arch reactionaries into his government.

Churchill, apprised of the Cabinet changes, flew immediately to Paris to get a reading of their significance. His meetings with Reynaud went badly. Reynaud complained about British failures and evaded Churchill's questions on French plans to meet the critical situation at the fronts. He flew back to London deeply disturbed.

On May 23, German pressures increased as the Fifth and Seventh Panzer divisions pushed back British General Lord Gort's two infantry divisions on both sides of Arras. Gort had to order his divisions to withdraw. He did not confer with the French about this move and Weygand did not hear about it until the next morning. He was furious. He promptly used the incident to justify calling off a French counteroffensive that he himself had already delayed despite promises to the British. This led to a bitter Anglo-French controversy over the disaster that was looming in the north.

General Erwin Rommel's Seventh Panzer division swept past Arras and headed for the seacoast. Boulogne was bypassed as the Germans closed a giant net around thirty French divisions and the totality of the British Expeditionary Force.

In Paris the government received the news from the north and even the most optimistic saw that the end was near. The minister of finance of the earlier Daladier Cabinet, Lucien Lamoureux, had already given orders to transfer the gold of the Bank of France to seaports in the south and west of the country. As the Germans were taking Arras, Pierre Fournier, the governor of the Bank of France, decided to move the gold out of the country. A high official called in a newly appointed director of the Exchange Control Office, Charles Moreton, and asked him to take control of a plan to form a convoy of French gold coming from ten bank vaults en route for the southwestern port of Bordeaux.

Moreton was told to leave for Bordeaux immediately. He was given a list of the gold freight-wagon numbers, told to reassemble them in Bordeaux and form a new gold train to be shipped from the port of Verdon. He would be told what ship to load with the gold and the ultimate destination of the shipment.

Moreton had been an official of the Ministry of Finance in Longwy and in Boulogne. It was a tranquil life he had led, dealing mainly with dossiers, reports, economic and fiscal studies for the bank, conferences with prefects about the economic situation of the department. Nothing in his experience and training had prepared him for an adventure of this kind. In Bordeaux he received a top-secret document informing him that the gold he was in charge of was destined for Halifax, Nova Scotia, where it would be stored and earmarked for the Bank of France. The inventory list he was given showed a total of 758 heavy cases and 3,080 sacks containing 212 tons of fine gold, with a market value of 4,240,000,000 French francs, something close to a quarter of a billion dollars.

Moreton found his gold train at the Saint-Louis station in Bordeaux and made contact with Captain Aubert, the naval commander who would guide him toward the embarkation docks at Verdon. Moreton carried an official note to the captain of his transport ship, the *Ville d'Oran* of the Algerian lines, a new steamship that had been refitted as an auxiliary cruiser for the transport of the gold.

He found the loading dock without trouble but was appalled at the filth everywhere. Only a few hours earlier the navy had unloaded a Canadian vessel carrying horses and mules assigned to the French cavalry. The air stank with the fumes of manure, and Moreton cursed as he walked ankle-deep through the muck, muttering to himself, "My God, do they expect mules to stop German armor and tanks!"

As Moreton finally got through the path of manure, two customs agents suddenly appeared before him and ordered him to halt.

"What are you loading onto that ship?" they asked.

"It's a state secret," Moreton replied.

"That's no answer. We want to know what you're loading."

"Dammit, can't you see that this train is guarded by French soldiers, in uniform, and armed? Can't you see that we are loading onto a French naval vessel? You must understand that this is a transport ordered by National Defense."

"Maybe it is. But regulations require that you tell us what you are loading," the two customs men sang out in chorus.

Moreton, fed up, decided there would be no harm in telling them.

"It's the gold of the Bank of France."

"Aha! Gold! Do you have an authorization from the Exchange Control Office?"

"I'm the director of the Exchange Control Office!"

"You'd better prove it."

Moreton pulled his letter of nomination to the post out of his pocket and showed it to the customs officials.

"This is only a letter of nomination, it does not prove that you were officially appointed to the post. And it does not authorize you to load gold for export. You have not conformed with regulations and we forbid this loading. Stop at once!"

To Moreton's bewilderment the two customs officials pulled their revolvers out of their holsters and took up positions as armed guards in front of the loading platform.

Moreton looked up at Lieutenant Eyglier, deputy commander of the transport vessel, and raised his eyebrows questioningly.

Commander Eyglier winked back at Moreton and signaled to him to stand by. He then motioned to two enormous sailors standing beside him. They grinned, vaulted lightly over a railing, landing almost on the backs of the customs men whom they grabbed in a bear hug.

The customs officials were disarmed, tied up, and thrown into a nearby shed. Moreton, who had never done anything in his life more violent than breaking string on a package, was amazed at the change in himself. Cool and detached, he walked to a telephone, called up the director of customs and told him: "We have two of your clowns locked up here. Send someone to fetch them; we're taking off."

The loading of the gold then went on with dispatch, except for one moment that almost turned Moreton's hair white. The sacks containing gold pieces were old and worn and suddenly a number of them broke and gold Napoleons began falling all over the place. Fortunately, the sacks had broken over the hold and not over the decks. None of the pieces fell into the sea. Later, when the ship was off-loaded, all the gold coins, a bit more than a hundred, were found in the hold.

Moreton understood, of course, that the government had given up any hope of victory in the Battle of France. But he himself did hope that the movement of the gold was evidence that the French were planning to fall back to strong positions in the empire and had enough gold to pay for the continued fight and battles ahead. Or so he thought, as he sailed with his precious cargo aboard the *Ville d'Oran*, heading first for Casablanca, then for Canada.

As the gold of France was moving south, so were the German armies. On May 24 German divisions on the northern front, striking westward, suddenly wheeled around and veered to the south, straight at Belgian defense lines. The heavy German armor and screaming Stuka dive bombers simply overwhelmed the Belgians, who were completely unprepared for the blitzkrieg attacks. By evening the German Sixth Army had broken Belgian defenses on both sides of Courtrai on the Lys and had opened a new threat of encirclement against the British Expeditionary Force.

The Belgian government met with King Leopold, urging him to

fly at once to London to set up a government-in-exile to carry on the war rather than risk becoming a German prisoner or a German puppet under occupation. King Leopold rejected their proposal. The ministers were furious, and upon leaving the meeting, they drove to the port of Dunkirk and took ship for England where they themselves would set up the government-in-exile. The Battle of Belgium, already lost in some ten days, was drawing to a close.

Meanwhile two French officers whose paths would later join met each other on the war front. At the outbreak of the war, First Lieutenant Claude Hettier de Boislambert had commanded a cavalry company assigned to reconnaissance patrols in front of the Maginot Line. In the winter of 1940, there was an urgent need of English-speaking French officers to assign to the British. De Boislambert was transferred to the British Second Armored Reconnaissance Brigade on the Belgian frontier. His brigade fought valiantly through the battles of Tirlemont and Louvain, suffering heavy losses.

In the course of battle de Boislambert got to Forge les Eaux, where he contacted the British First Armored Division and met a man who would play an important role in his future, Brigadier Bill Morgan, a career officer who would become an aide to Winston Churchill. From Forge les Eaux de Boislambert went on to the Somme and joined the newly formed Fourth Armored, commanded by Colonel de Gaulle. During the Battle of the Somme in northern France, de Gaulle asked de Boislambert to sleep at his command post and serve as his liaison officer to the British. The two men became comrades-in-arms, one of the rare occasions when de Gaulle permitted himself a close friendship. They would meet again in London, where de Boislambert would become the first French officer to rally to de Gaulle's call for resistance. But in the last days of May they separated, de Boislambert falling back with the British, de Gaulle falling back with the French.

On May 25 Premier Reynaud called a meeting with France's senior military men—Marshal Pétain, General Weygand, and Admiral Darlan. While they were describing the situation to the premier, a messenger from the First Army arrived to report that only three of its divisions were still capable of fighting and that the First Army had only one day's reserve of ammunition left.

Reynaud convoked the War Cabinet to an afternoon conference to plan new strategy in the light of the German advances. General Weygand, bearing responsibility for the French failure, sought to shift the blame. He charged that "France has committed the immense error of going to war without having the matériel or the military doctrine which was necessary." His statement about the lack of matériel was factually incorrect. France had what was needed to wage war, as the records showed; he was correct in saying that military doctrine was missing, but that was mainly because of the very men in the room that day. Proper doctrine was not in fact lacking, it had been ignored.

Reynaud, disheartened by the day's meetings and the defeatism of the military, agreed to call off a planned counteroffensive in the north. He sent off a midnight order to the three Allied armies to regroup to form a bridge-head that would cover the port of Dunkirk. The new plan was aimed at holding off the Germans long enough for the bulk of the Allied troops to escape the trap by sailing from Dunkirk to England.

On May 26, General Weygand introduced a new concern into the calculations of the government: He had come to the conclusion that the French army had to be saved so that it could put down anarchy and revolution at home. Weygand had conjured up a phantom Red Menace, although the Communist party had been hounded and persecuted for almost a year and was in no position to launch a revolution—even if such a plan existed. Certainly Weygand had no such evidence and did not even bother to try to document his wild charges. With France's once "invincible" army collapsing and a debacle looming on the fronts, generals and politicians began looking for scapegoats.

General Weygand, Marshal Pétain, and politician Camille Chautemps began meeting privately in Paris, forming a cabal to bring about an end to the fighting and a way out of the war. They discussed the possibility of Pétain taking over the Cabinet from Reynaud. Pierre Laval was advancing the same ideas in his circles, so that soon there was a kind of shadow Cabinet operating in the wings of the Reynaud Cabinet, waiting to take over. If there was any real threat of a coup or a revolution, it came from these men of the Right and not from any imaginary Red Menace.

Directors and executives of the powerful Worms Bank met privately in Paris. They had all come to the conclusion that Germany had won the war, that Paris would soon fall, and that a puppet French government would be formed. The meeting discussed how the Worms Bank could get along under such conditions. Thus, while some Frenchmen wondered how to continue the fight and to resist the enemy, others pondered the modalities of doing business under Hitler, how to collaborate with the enemy. Resistants and collaborators, who would divide France between them in a desperate civil war for the next five years, were lining up and choosing sides in the last week of May 1940.

The Worms Bank was not the only organization preparing to do business with Hitler. There were many whose contempt for democracy and admiration for fascism made them ready collaborators of the "New Order" in Europe. Some were World War I heroes, like Pétain. Some were journalists, like Marcel Déat, or ex-Communists turned fascist, like Jacques Doriot. At the outset, and for some time to come, a great many more men and women would be ready to accept defeat and collaboration, at least passively, than to risk resistance.

The king of the Belgians was one only too ready to accept defeat. Just before midnight on May 27, King Leopold yielded to Hitler's demand for unconditional surrender and proposed a cease-fire for 4 A.M. the following day.

As the Belgians put down their arms on May 28, the mass

evacuation of British and French forces from Dunkirk got under way, while last-ditch Allied troops held off the Germans. They fought magnificently and permitted the bulk of the Allied armies to be saved. They sacrificed themselves, knowing that the Germans would kill or capture them, but they did it so that the others could escape.

On the last day of May Winston Churchill flew to Paris again, hoping against hope to stiffen the backbone of the French government and persuade the French to go on fighting. The French Empire, like the British, was huge, with vast resources. Churchill never doubted that the final outcome would be an Allied victory. He did everything to transfer his own faith and courage to the French.

He reported that 165,000 men had already been taken off the beaches at Dunkirk, some 15,000 of them French. He declared that "today will be French Day and French troops will be given absolute priority over the British." He pleaded and stormed about the need to carry on the fight. "Even if one of us is struck down, the other will not abandon the struggle. It must not put down its arms until its friend is on his feet again. . . . The British people will fight on!"

His words rang hollowly through French corridors empty of courage or faith. Only one Frenchman obstinately refused to yield ground. Colonel de Gaulle, commanding his Fourth Armored Division, surprised the Germans by launching a counterattack south of Abbéville, with all other units in retreat. Astonished, the Germans fell back. But as de Gaulle knew, it was a meaningless gesture. Superior German armor and air simply regrouped, caught its breath, and halted the counterattack. De Gaulle's division was then forced to fall back. In a desperate attempt to stem the tide, de Gaulle went to Weygand's headquarters to urge that the remaining tanks be deployed into two groups, one north of Paris, the other south of Reims. "At least," said de Gaulle, "we would have a battle instead of a debacle."

Weygand, already thinking of an armistice, paid no attention to de Gaulle's proposal.

By the morning of June 4 the evacuation at Dunkirk had come to an end. According to official British records 338,226 troops had been rescued. The exact figure of French troops was not known but was estimated at 115,000 to 120,000. The British defenders of Dunkirk, men of the First Army whose mission it was to save the others, were overrun. Forty thousand of them were rounded up and sent to prisoner-of-war camps in Germany. The Germans now controlled all of Belgium. The Battle of France was to begin.

On June 5 the Germans smashed at the French lines on the Somme.

In Paris, Reynaud finally dismissed Daladier from his Cabinet. Although he did not immediately name his new minister of defense, he did name an undersecretary, the newly promoted brigadier general, Charles de Gaulle. De Gaulle told Reynaud, "If this war is lost, there is another to be won." He strongly recommended to the premier that the government should prepare to fall back to French North Africa and, with the empire behind it, carry on in strength. Reynaud said that that was his intention.

Reynaud's vice-premier, Marshal Pétain, however, was openly talking of peace. De Gaulle ran into Pétain at army headquarters. They had not seen each other since the early thirties when they had worked closely together and admired each other.

Pétain said: "Well, here you are a brigadier general. I don't congratulate you. What good are promotions in time of defeat?"

De Gaulle, towering over the little marshal, at almost six feet eight from his polished toes to the crown of his stiff kepi, looked down upon him coldly and said: "But you yourself, Marshal, received your first star during the retreat in 1914. Afterward came the victory of the Marne."

Pétain stiffly replied: "There is no connection between the two." He could not have said more clearly that this time there would be no victory "afterward." Pétain had already surrendered.

On June 7 General Rommel's Panzer Division broke through the French lines, advancing toward Rouen and the Seine. Rommel's attack split the French Tenth Army into two parts, cutting four divisions off from the rest of the army. Other units of the Fifteenth Panzer Corps widened the breach in the French lines. French troops were falling back from the Somme and the Germans were approaching the lower Seine. The French retreat was becoming a disorganized rout. By the night of June 9 the Germans occupied the river Seine, from Rouen to Vernon. Advance German patrols were only forty miles from Paris. Many French troops broke and ran. Parisians would see them—dirty, ragged, beaten—staggering in across the Seine bridges on the west of the city. They would provoke a hysterical mass exodus from the capital.

When the Germans reached the Marne at Château-Thierry, near Paris, Marshal Pétain sent a formal demand, in writing, to Premier Reynaud proposing that he ask Germany for an armistice. Reynaud replied, "No honorable armistice with Hitler is possible." He added that it would be both unwise and dishonorable to seek a separate peace after pledging to the British that France would not desert her Allies. The marshal sharply replied: "The interests of France must come before those of England. England got us into this situation. . . . Let us try to get out of it."

Reynaud again refused to seek an armistice. With the Germans so near Paris, he decided that the government would have to leave the next day. He chose Tours as a temporary refuge for the Cabinet.

On June 10, while all French ministries and officials were on the road to Tours, Mussolini declared war on France. President Roosevelt, in a nationwide broadcast, charged that the "hand that held the dagger" had plunged it into "the back of its neighbor." Premier Reynaud sent Roosevelt an urgent appeal for help, calling for him to send "a cloud of planes."

The premier stated: "We shall fight in front of Paris; we shall fight behind Paris; we shall close ourselves in one of our provinces to fight, and if we should be driven out of it, we shall establish ourselves in North Africa to continue to fight."

Observers in Washington noted with interest that the premier did not say that the French would fight *in* Paris. This time there would be no taxicab army to the Marne, no fight to the death for the French capital. General Weygand had already told Reynaud: "Paris is an Open City." The general said that to "preserve its character as an Open City, it is my intention to avoid any defensive organization around the city." This decision was not published that day, June 10, nor was it even communicated to the military governor of Paris, who called in the police chiefs and prefects of the Seine Department and told them, "The capital will be defended to the last."

By then all the people of Paris knew that the Germans would soon be in the capital. They could see the smoke of gas and oil depots that the army was destroying. Newsstands were empty, for all papers had ceased publication, with editors, reporters, and printers rushing south. French soldiers, battle-shocked, eyes glazed, uniforms dirty and torn, were stumbling across the bridge at Saint-Cloud. All railway stations were mobbed with frantic Parisians trying to force their way onto overcrowded trains. Children screamed, mothers sobbed, and fathers cursed as they tried to claw a path through the crowds. Two million Parisians were fleeing their capital in panic. Every type of vehicle jammed the roads: cars old and new, bicycles, horse carts laden with household goods.

A few Parisians did not join the fleeing mob. Some stayed, mainly the poor, the workers, because they had no place to go and no transportation. Some stayed because it was their job and they knew it had to be done, under the Germans or not. They were the police, the gendarmerie, gas, electric, and water workers, telephone company operators and technicians. Paris was almost empty and easily policed by a public order force of some twenty-five hundred men. There was no looting by the fleeing mobs, nor would there be any by the Germans when they arrived. The Germans would be very "correct."

On June 12 Reynaud presided over a Cabinet meeting at Tours. He told Pétain and Weygand: "You mistake Hitler for Wilhelm I, the old gentleman who only took Alsace and Lorraine from us. But Hitler is a Genghis Khan." General Weygand warned the premier that "if an armistice is not immediately demanded, disorder will spread to the armies as it already has to the population." He was still threatening the government with his fantasies of a Red Menace.

On June 13 the Cabinet met again in Tours, in the Château de Ohissay. The premier presided under the attentive eyes of his mistress, the Countess de Portes, who had the audacity to join the ministers in the dining room. One junior minister was too worked up to remain at table. General de Gaulle paced up and down with giant steps, muttering to himself, and marshaling up new arguments for his latest proposal: to pull all French troops back into Brittany and establish a redoubt that the Germans could not break. Of course, no one paid any attention to de Gaulle, not even his great admirer, the premier.

Reynaud again appealed to London, and once again Winston Churchill flew to France. He arrived in Tours early in the afternoon. To bolster up the French premier, Churchill spoke to him of the vast resources of the United States and the possibility of immediate and massive American aid. Reynaud told Churchill that Roosevelt had failed to respond to his plea for planes, but he agreed to send another urgent cable to Washington. Both men knew that isolationist America had starved its armed forces and had almost no arms or planes to spare, but they were desperate and hoped for a miracle.

While Reynaud conferred with Churchill, the Cabinet ministers, who had been called to a 3 P.M. meeting, had to stand by and wait. The meeting was finally called at 6 P.M. There was an outburst of protest when Reynaud walked into the room alone. The ministers were hoping that Churchill would attend the meeting. Many, particularly Georges Mandel, the strongest and bravest man in the Cabinet and a Jew already marked down on German lists for arrest and imprisonment, had hoped that Churchill's presence would give the Cabinet courage to carry on. Mandel was the most fervent protagonist of moving the government to North Africa to carry on the war. Reynaud was willing to follow that lead if a majority of the Cabinet would support it. But the ministers were greatly influenced by Pétain and Weygand. As civilians they did not feel competent to overrule France's most illustrious soldiers.

General Weygand shocked the Cabinet by announcing that the Communists had taken over Paris and installed Maurice Thorez in the Elysée Palace in the president's office. By then the commander in chief must have been mad or deliberately sabotaging the government, for there was not a word of truth in his report. Mandel called Roger Langeron, the prefect of Paris, to ask him what was happening, and Langeron, surprised, replied: "Why, we are just quietly waiting for orders." When Mandel told this to the Cabinet, Weygand stalked out of the room saying that Mandel was trying to make a fool of him. Weygand told friends later that it was Pétain who had told him the Communists were taking over.

Pétain, stating that the Americans would do nothing, and that Britain, as always, would defend her own interests, told the Cabinet that only an armistice could satisfy the necessary conditions for the perpetuity of an eternal France. The solemn tones of the old marshal impressed the Cabinet ministers. Reynaud knew, without a formal ballot, that a majority of his Cabinet now favored an armistice.

On the morning of June 14 the Germans moved into Paris. They did not come in as combat troops on the attack. Paris, Open City, offered no resistance. The conquering Germans paraded into Paris. Their uniforms were neatly pressed, their boots shined to mirror brightness. They rode their motorcycles and tanks like blond gods, knowing well the impression they were making on the Parisians, who stood and watched like rabbits paralyzed by the eyes of the weasel. A great many Frenchmen and women stood and wept, tears rolling shamelessly down their cheeks. Others stared with interest, even admiration. The Germans waved at young girls who giggled and smiled until a father's slap wiped the smile from their faces.

German armored vehicles clanked around the Arc de Triomphe and advanced down the Champs-Elysées. A detachment turned right at the Rond-Point, moved down toward the Seine and the bridge of Alexandre III. They were heading for the Invalides on the Left Bank. By surrounding it they would cut off General Dentz, the military governor of Paris, and his small staff, who were waiting to hand Paris over to the Germans.

By eight o'clock that night the Germans held all bridges and all key points in Paris. German headquarters had been set up in the Place de la Concorde, in the luxurious Hôtel Crillon, next door to the American Embassy. By nightfall the Germans had flown a giant-size red flag with a huge swastika from the Arc de Triomphe. German flags flew from all French public buildings, from the Chamber of Deputies, the Senate, all the ministries and the principal hotels.

All around the Etoile armed German units were in position. Machine guns were aimed down all the avenues, backed up by four cannons that covered the Champs-Elysées, the Avenues Foch, Victor Hugo, and Marceau. Although French officers who had met with the Germans at the gates of Paris at dawn had promised that there would be no resistance, the Germans were making sure by an impressive show of strength and firepower.

The Germans found it hard to believe the total passivity of Paris. They knew the revolutionary history of Paris, the readiness of Parisians to tear up their streets, erect barricades, and defend their city. The complete calm of Paris startled the Germans. They sent loudspeaker trucks through the city, warning the people to remain calm and orderly, though they hardly needed the warning. The High Command posted threats: Any act of aggression, any hostility or sabotage of any kind would be instantly punished by death. By advertising their own fears the Germans were planting suggestions as to what the French might do.

German propagandists, carefully trained and prepared for this moment, took over the Paris broadcasting studios and told the people in perfect French that the Germans wished them no harm. They had been deceived by their own leaders, the Germans said. France had been poorly led and had obeyed directives from the Jews and Freemasons who had betrayed France. The British who had led France into the war would be beaten in a few weeks' time, just as soon as France made peace with Germany.

The Germans were on their best behavior. They gave up their seats in the Métro to old people and women. They smiled at young girls but made no attempt to fraternize with them. They were everywhere with their cameras but always respectful. Before taking pictures at the Tomb of the Unknown Soldier, the Germans snapped to attention and saluted the tomb. And they pasted a poster on the walls of Paris showing a handsome German soldier holding a boy in his arms, with two little girls clinging to his sturdy leg. The caption read: "Abandoned people, have confidence in the German soldier."

There were some Parisians who decided at once to grant the Germans the collaboration they had asked for. Their voices could be heard over Radio Paris, spreading German propaganda to the French. They could be seen fraternizing with soldiers in the streets or the cafés. But there were other Parisians who could not tolerate the sight of the Germans in Paris. One of them was a noted French surgeon, head of the American Hospital in Neuilly, Dr. Thierry de Martel.

He went to see the American ambassador, William Bullitt, who was chairman of the board of the hospital. Dr. Martel asked the ambassador for permission to leave his post and to leave Paris. "Don't make me witness this spectacle," he pleaded with Bullitt.

The ambassador brushed aside his entreaty. He told the doctor that the hospital had a vital mission and that men of Martel's skill were badly needed in the operating room. "I myself am staying to try to ease the sufferings of this unfortunate city," said Bullitt, arguing that a patriotic French doctor could not do less. He said that Martel must stay on.

The surgeon asked quietly if that was an order. Bullitt smiled, patted him on the shoulder, and said: "If you wish, but the friendliest one in the world."

"All right," said Dr. Martel, "I will stay."

Two days later, the doctor's chauffeur brought the ambassador a note. In it, Dr. Martel said that he had promised to stay in Paris, but had not said whether he would stay dead or alive. The note was signed "Adieu, Martel." Early that morning Dr. Martel had injected strychnine in his veins.

During the same day more than a dozen other Parisians committed suicide.

Other Parisians, while risking death, had chosen to fight. Graffiti began to appear on the walls of Paris, even scrawled across German posters. "Nazis assassins," "Nous Vaincrons," "Les Boches au poteau"—words of defiance to the German firing squads. Some brave souls in the Jewish section of Paris, in the Rue Vieille du Temple, had scrawled Mogen Davids, the six-pointed Jewish star, across the face of the German soldier on the poster. Small acts, perhaps, of no real danger to the Germans, but the very first acts of resistance under the occupant's guns.

In the Louvre Museum an official was working furiously to save art treasures, fearful that Nazis would loot the museum. Jean Cassou had been named assistant curator of the Luxembourg Museum when war broke out. He was then sent to be curator of the Château de Compiègne, with the mission of overseeing the packing and shipping of its paintings and furniture after its curator had fled in fear of the German advance. When German armor did reach the outskirts of the town, Cassou locked up the château and drove down to Paris, where he was reassigned to the Louvre. He was there when the Germans entered Paris. Most of the Louvre's treasures had already been evacuated, so the director sent Cassou on a mission to the Loire and the historic Château de Chambord to organize its masterpieces and see that they were properly packed and put underground. He was also responsible for receiving and safeguarding the furniture from the Palace of Versailles, en route to Chambord on trucks.

On June 14 the French government moved farther south, to Bordeaux, a logical port from which the government could sail for North Africa. De Gaulle was putting pressure on Premier Reynaud to set up the government in Algiers. Reynaud agreed and asked de Gaulle to set the project in motion. General de Gaulle, still believing in miracles, told Reynaud that he would leave for London to arrange for British shipping to help with the evacuation. First however, de Gaulle was to drive all through the night to Brittany to see what ships and matériel could sail from its ports to England. De Gaulle arrived in Rennes early in the morning of the fifteenth and conferred with the generals commanding Brittany. The Germans, in a rush to take Paris and demoralize the French, had kept away from the twisting roads and strong defenses of Brittany. De Gaulle proceeded to the port of Brest, where in the afternoon he boarded the destroyer *Milan,* scheduled to leave for Plymouth. He met aboard the vessel a group of chemists with army bodyguards who were keeping a tight watch over some mysterious flasks. The flasks contained something called "heavy water." They told de Gaulle it was precious and would be used in "atomic experiments." Concentrating on other urgent matters, Charles de Gaulle paid no attention to talk of atoms, so remote from the imperatives of the war. He arrived in London on June 16.

While Reynaud and de Gaulle were planning a governmental flight to Algiers, Pierre Laval arrived in Bordeaux and set up an office at the Hôtel de Ville. It rapidly became the center for intrigues against Reynaud, designed to force his resignation in favor of Pétain, who was already in town. Laval cast himself in the role of prime minister in a government theoretically held by a senile President Pétain.

Weygand arrived and immediately went into a meeting with Admiral Darlan. After the meeting, he went to see Reynaud. The premier informed his commander in chief that the government would move to Algeria. He asked Weygand to arrange a cease-fire with the Germans. Weygand defied him and flatly refused to carry out his order. He told the premier that the government could not leave France, adding that he would not carry out even a written order. It was more than just insubordination. Theoretically, Reynaud could have had him shot, except that the premier of France did not control his own armed forces.

Former political supporters of Reynaud began to call him in the afternoon of June 15 to urge him to abandon his plan to move to Algiers. Cabinet ministers added their pressure. Meanwhile Pierre Laval kept sending emissaries to Marshal Pétain urging him to take over the government. Reynaud's own political spies knew what Laval was doing and they kept the premier informed. The more he received reports of growing opposition to his plans and growing support for Pétain, the weaker he became in his resolve.

Reynaud had received a message of sympathy and friendship from President Roosevelt, but the U.S. Congress and the mood of the nation were still isolationist. Reynaud, now desperate, drafted a message to Churchill asking him to agree to a French armistice with Germany. If Churchill held Reynaud to his pledge of no separate peace, then Reynaud would have no alternative but to resign from office. He had lost the majority support of his own Cabinet. The French army had all but disintegrated and members of Parliament were scattered all over the roads of France.

The next morning, June 16, Marshal Pétain came to the Cabinet meeting with a written letter of resignation. He had decided that the time was right to force Reynaud's hand. Reading from his letter, he told the Cabinet that he could no longer stay in a government that contemplated leaving the soil of France and that had refused to bring to an end the hostilities that were destroying the nation. He finished reading, turned to Reynaud, and said: "Here, then, is my resignation."

Reynaud refused to accept it. He told the marshal that he had asked Churchill to authorize him to sue for an armistice. The least that Pétain could do would be to await Churchill's reply. Pétain agreed and asked to be informed the moment the reply from London arrived.

A few hours later Churchill's message was received. His government would give consent to an armistice in France provided—but *only provided*—that the French fleet sail forthwith for British harbors, pending negotiations.

General de Gaulle called from London with another, later message. A group of Frenchmen in the Economic Mission in London, headed by the remarkable Jean Monnet, had proposed a Declaration of Union between Great Britain and France, with all citizens to share citizenship in both countries. Winston Churchill, despite initial doubts about the revolutionary proposal, had accepted it and was offering it to Reynaud. De Gaulle, a chauvinistic Frenchman, had also swallowed his doubts and endorsed the plan.

Reynaud, ecstatic, assured de Gaulle that he was prepared "to die defending these proposals." De Gaulle told him that he would fly immediately to Bordeaux to bring the premier a copy of the declaration.

At 5 P.M., the Cabinet met for the second time that day. Reynaud had the proposals in hand and read them to the assembled ministers. An ominous silence engulfed his reading and when he had finished there was not a sound in the room. Reynaud knew then that he was finished.

The talk turned at once to the main topic of the moment: an armistice. Georges Mandel clarified the situation by stating: "The question is really quite simple. There are those here who want to fight on and others who don't want to."

No sooner had Mandel made this statement than a messenger arrived from General Georges, in command on the northern and central fronts. He reported that the overall military situation was worsening, that food was lacking, maneuvers difficult or impossible. He said that it was imperative that a decision be taken without delay to call for a cease-fire or the entire front would collapse in a rout.

That did it. Those who wanted to move to North Africa to continue the war had lost.

President Lebrun summoned the two leaders of Parliament, President Jules Jeanneney of the Senate and Speaker Edouard Herriot of the Chamber, the men involved when a change of government impended. They went into a closed session. Everyone knew that when they came out later that night it would be with the name of Marshal Henri-Philippe Pétain as the new premier of France, and that his very first act would be to ask the Germans for an armistice.

General de Gaulle arrived from London at nine-thirty at night on the sixteenth and went to see Reynaud, carrying the Declaration of Union. A beaten Reynaud sadly told him what was happening. De Gaulle, not at all surprised, made arrangements to return to London in the morning and to have his wife and children sent to England from Brittany, where they had been staying with his mother, who was too old and ill to leave.

Black clouds began to roll in over Bordeaux on the morning of June 17, as though the weather itself had gone into mourning for the Republic of France. As President Lebrun announced that he had asked Marshal Pétain to take over the reins of government, the clouds thickened and rumbles of thunder echoed over the port. Pétain drew up his Cabinet list, dismissing de Gaulle and many other members of the Reynaud Cabinet, most particularly his critic Georges Mandel, and others who had talked of continuing the war. Then, at 12:30 P.M., the old marshal sat down before a microphone to address the nation. At that instant a violent storm erupted, thunder and lightning lashing Bordeaux.

The old marshal began talking in a high-pitched, quavering voice. Many thought that he was in the grip of a deep emotion. Those who knew him were aware that his trembling voice was simply the voice of an old man. But there is no doubt that as he spoke the entire nation of France was gripped with deep emotions, varying from fear to fury, tempered in many cases with relief, relief that the nightmare was over. The French did not yet know that it was the war alone that was ending. The nightmare was only beginning.

"I offer to France the gift of my person that I may ease her sorrow. It is with a heavy heart that I tell you that we must halt the combat. Last night I asked the adversary whether he is ready to seek with us, in honor, some way to put an end to the hostilities."

While Pétain's words of defeat were still echoing through the air, the Resistance had already begun.

3
BIRTH OF
THE RESISTANCE

Among those listening to Marshal Pétain on that fateful seventeenth of June 1940 was General Gabriel Cochet, commander of the Fifth Army Air Force and former chief of the Deuxième Bureau, the Intelligence section of the French army. Cochet knew the Germans from his years of intelligence work. He did not share the view of Marshal Pétain that an armistice with honor could be won from the Germans. Within two hours of the end of Pétain's radio address, General Cochet called together his staff officers.

They had all been fighting together, suffering heavy losses, and retreating constantly for weeks. The general's voice was hoarse with fatigue and cracked with emotion and anger. He told his men that Pétain was wrong. There was no hope of an honorable collaboration with Hitler. "We must learn to hide what we are doing, to camouflage our movements and our arms. We must, at all costs, continue the struggle against the enemy."

General Cochet's orders to his staff constituted the first official acts of resistance, although the word itself was not used. The word *resistance* would be heard for the first time the next day, June 18, on the wavelengths of the British Broadcasting Corporation. But even before that historic event, acts of resistance were being carried out throughout France, as many men and women of every social class reacted in anger and even disgust to Pétain's capitulation.

An old lady in the village of Luray, Madame Bourgeois, was so infuriated when Germans came to requisition and occupy her house that she shouted and shook her fist at them. Two soldiers grabbed her and tied her to a tree in her garden and assassinated her before the eyes of her horrified daughter. They told her daughter to leave the body tied to the tree for twenty-four hours, as a warning to all as to what would happen if anyone resisted German orders.

News of the cold-blooded murder of the old lady reached the desk of the prefect of the department of the Eure-et-Loir. His name was Jean Moulin. Moulin called German headquarters to protest the murder of Mme. Bourgeois and to demand that action be taken against the guilty soldiers. That night two German officers came to see Moulin and told him that their general had an important communication for him. Moulin immediately accompanied them to German headquarters.

There Moulin discovered that there was no communication for him and no general waiting to see him. Instead, a lower-grade officer ordered him to sign a "protocol," an official document attesting to the "fact" that Senegalese riflemen in a French battalion had committed a horrible massacre in a nearby village, raping and killing women and children.

Jean Moulin was stupefied. No such massacre, no incident of any kind involving Senegalese soldiers had occurred. As prefect he would have been notified immediately of any such crime. He asked the Germans for proof of their charges. Their "proof" was a rifle butt across his jaw, loosening his teeth and knocking him bleeding to the floor.

For hours the prefect was brutalized, insulted, and badly beaten for refusing to sign the protocol. Late that night his torturers led him to a cell, jeering: "Since you love niggers, we've given you one to sleep with." As Moulin stumbled forward into the cell he saw a Senegalese soldier, crouched in the corner. He too had been beaten by the Germans.

Moulin sat in the darkness brooding. "I know," he recalled later, in a book called *Premier Combat*, "that today I was tested to the very limits of my resistance. Tomorrow, if the torture is renewed, I will finish by signing. This was my dilemma: sign or die." Moulin concluded that to sign would be to dishonor both the French army and himself. As for dying: "From the start of the war I had accepted the risk of death, along with thousands of other Frenchmen."

Moulin looked around the cell. He saw that the floor was covered with shards of glass from windowpanes shattered by air attacks of the past few days. "I knew at once what these fragments of glass could do. They could cut a throat as easily as a knife could."

A few hour later a German guard, making his rounds, found the body of Jean Moulin in a pool of blood spreading through the cell. He sounded the alarm and men came running, thinking that Moulin had escaped. In a way he had: They were forced to take him to the hospital. They could not prevent hospital attendants from learning the story and spreading it through the village. After so many humiliating months of retreat and defeat, the people had found an authentic French hero overnight. Moulin escaped with his life in that first test, but further confrontations with Nazi torturers awaited him.

While Moulin was being tormented by the Germans, Captain Henri Frenay was retreating on the eastern front along with the entire Forty-third Army Corps. No formal authorization to lay down their arms had yet reached the armies in the east. Up until June 22 General Weygand failed to order the cease-fire. Some scattered units in the Maginot Line would go on fighting for a week after that. But the order to abandon the Maginot Line had been given by Weygand on June 12. Frenay could hardly believe what was happening. "We, the defenders of the Maginot Line, had received the incredible order to retreat. Nothing had prepared us for such a move, neither our individual equipment, nor our permanent armored emplacements, least of all our garrisons' standing order to hold the Line at all cost."

Frenay knew that German armor had cut his unit off from the French hinterland. In the bright blue June skies, the Luftwaffe was virtually on an excursion flight. There were no French planes in sight. Frenay and two fellow officers turned on their radio on June 17, not for battle news—they knew only too well what it would tell them—but for news from France. Their commanding officer, General Lescanne, had already told them: "The situation is critical but there's still hope: Marshal Pétain has taken charge."

Frenay knew that the government was in Bordeaux and that Bordeaux was the gateway to the French Empire. He kept twisting the dial of his radio while telling his fellow officers that everything would be all right.

"Suddenly, through the static on the radio, we heard the words 'The marshal speaks.'"

The three officers listened in silence. "Only those who like myself heard it through the thunder of artillery can still recall the sorrowful gravity of those words," Frenay recalls today. "For what seemed endless moments we remained speechless. With clenched jaws I averted my eyes from those of the others, knowing that I would see tears like those I felt on my own cheeks."

"It's impossible. Impossible!" cried one of the officers. "In one month we cannot have been totally beaten."

"I can't understand it," said another. "Well, at least the marshal is there. He'll demand respect from the Germans. After all, he is Marshal Pétain."

"Yes," said Frenay, "Pétain is a great name. And yet . . ." A doubt had crept into his mind. Would a great man have capitulated so quickly, so unconditionally, leaving a vast empire out of combat? It would take Frenay— a traditional military man, a man of the Right—a long time to realize the defeatism of Pétain's position and his hatred for the Republic. But it did not take Frenay more than a few weeks to understand that his duty was to fight for the ultimate liberation of France.

Frenay drew up a personal manifesto, which he would later show to friends. In it he wrote: "Our struggle is by no means over. It is first and foremost the struggle of the human spirit against barbarism and paganism, while we prepare for the day of our armed liberation." Today Frenay smiles ruefully as he recalls the last sentence of his manifesto: "May Marshal Pétain live long enough to see the day when success crowns our efforts." Pétain did live long enough, but he did not celebrate the success as Frenay had once imagined. Frenay understood at once the significance of his manifesto: "It was my first clandestine act."

Marie-Madeleine Fourcade was en route with friends to the Pyrénées, to Loustaunau-Lacau's home, when she turned on the radio for the midday news.

"When Marshal Pétain's bleating voice uttered the fatal words, they did not surprise us. On that lovely summer Sunday the imminence of the armistice burst upon our consciousness. . . . Women smiled. People kissed one another. In the cafés the crowds drank the health of the old marshal. . . . Hitler's raving in *Mein Kampf* arose in my memory to cancel out the instinctive feeling of relief that I, like everyone else, felt at the first news of the cease-fire. An immense wave of anguish swept over me: It was disaster now and uncertainty in the future." She pushed on toward her rendezvous with Commandant Loustaunau-Lacau, now also known as Navarre. She was certain that something had to be done to prevent Pétain from making France a Nazi satellite. Loustaunau-Lacau would know what to do.

Loustaunau-Lacau at that moment was fighting to stay alive. He had been seriously wounded in action: A bullet had penetrated his neck, bounced off his shoulder bone, and zigzagged down his back. He had lost a lot of blood, but no vital organs had been hit and he was strong. In a POW hospital he willed his strength back, plotted his escape, and planned what he would do to rally his countrymen to continue the fight.

In London, General de Gaulle had heard about Pétain's speech, but was more concerned about drafting his own radio talk to the French people. The British had already given him permission to speak at 6 P.M. the next day, June 18, right after an important speech by Winston Churchill in the House of Commons. Sir Edward Spears escorted de Gaulle to Downing Street for a meeting with Churchill. The prime minister had already met de Gaulle in France in the last critical weeks, was familiar with his military works, and knew that he was committed to carrying on the war. He received him in the garden under a hot, brilliant sun. Their first meeting in London was warm and cordial— though this would not be the climate in which they would continue to meet.

After conferring with de Gaulle, Churchill sent personal messages to Pétain and Weygand: "I wish to repeat to you my profound conviction that the illustrious Marshal Pétain and the famous General Weygand . . . will not injure their allies by delivering over to the enemy the fine French fleet." Churchill had already been informed by Naval Intelligence that two new French battleships, the 35,000-ton *Richelieu* and the *Jean Bart*, were still anchored in the ports of Brittany, a province being overrun by the German army.

That same afternoon Pétain received a cable from President Roosevelt declaring that, in the opinion of the United States government, failure to keep the French fleet out of the hands of the Germans would fatally impair the eventual restoration of French independence. Roosevelt sternly warned that in such an event "the French government will permanently lose the friendship and goodwill of the government of the United States." FDR's note to a friendly country could not have been more severely worded. It was meant to put powerful pressure on Pétain and was understood as such.

Admiral Darlan, sensitive to the Anglo-American power play,

immediately sent orders to the *Richelieu* and the *Jean Bart* to steam out of their Brittany anchorages and to sail to Casablanca, Morocco, far from German hands. They sailed the next morning, June 18. Meanwhile in Morocco General Noguès, resident-general and commander in chief of the North African theater of operations, sent a message to General Weygand informing him that French North Africa was prepared to resist the Germans. Since Weygand and Pétain were anxiously awaiting Hitler's armistice terms, this was not the kind of message they wanted: General Noguès would have to be removed from his command.

After hearing Pétain's speech, Senate President Jeanneney and Chamber Speaker Herriot felt guilty about their role in investing him. Calling upon him the next day at 5 P.M., they told him that, after all, the government should leave Bordeaux and carry on in North Africa. They pointed out that fighting was still going on, that German troops were advancing toward Bordeaux, and that the government could be captured.

Pétain announced that he "would never leave France," managing to put a patriotic cast upon his capitulation to the Germans. Weygand said he would stay on with Pétain. But it was agreed that all Cabinet ministers and parliamentary leaders should leave for North Africa. The meeting in Pétain's office ended just as de Gaulle in London was sitting down to a microphone of the French Service of the BBC. It was 6 P.M. on June 18, 1940, a date that would live in French history.

The tall, thin French general, sitting ramrod-stiff in his chair, directed a piercing look through the glass partition of the studio at the BBC engineer sitting behind it. It was the engineer's duty to signal to the general when it was time to speak. He was so fascinated and intimidated by the grim-faced French giant that, when the time came, he gave the hand signal to talk but forgot to depress the needle on the turntable next to his console. Thus, General de Gaulle's broadcast of June 18 would never be recorded.* But his words would not be forgotten, for in the years that would follow they would be printed and read and repeated, not only in French but in many tongues around the world. They were a call to action and to honor that was universal.

"Is the last word said? Has all hope gone? Is the defeat definitive? No. Believe me, I tell you that nothing is lost for France. . . . This war is not limited to the unfortunate territory of our country. This war is a world war. I invite all French officers and soldiers who are in Britain or who may find themselves there, with their arms or without, to get in touch with me. Whatever happens, the flame of French resistance must not die and will not die."

---

* In the mid-fifties, Edward R. Murrow was preparing a "Hear It Now" album of famous speeches. As the CBS News Paris correspondent, I was asked to get a copy of de Gaulle's broadcast of June 18, 1940. I flew to London, discovered it had never been recorded, and was told why. I then saw de Gaulle, who confirmed the story. I asked him if he would record the talk for the record. De Gaulle refused: "It would not be authentic history to record the appeal now."

Very few Frenchmen or women heard that message of June 18 *on* June 18. They had not yet developed the habit of listening to the BBC, and they did not yet know who General de Gaulle was. Besides, his appeal was not primarily addressed to the people inside France: It was an invitation to Frenchmen who were in England, particularly military men, to rally to his flag.

Charles de Gaulle was a professional soldier. He thought in terms of soldiers, not civilians. He did not envisage an internal French resistance movement—that was too revolutionary a thought for him. He was authoritarian in temperament and he mistrusted, despised politicians. A civilian resistance would be political; he could not call for one. He sought simply and directly to rally Frenchmen in the empire, outside of France, to keep France in the war at the side of its Allies. He thought not only of French honor, but of the need for France to continue fighting if France was to participate in the final victory, claim a place at the peace table and a rightful place among the first-rank powers of the world. This was de Gaulle's main objective, from first to last.

Some of the men who became de Gaulle's closest associates, and some who became the leaders of the Resistance movements inside France, did not hear about the speech of June 18 until later, in some cases much later.

Captain André Dewavrin, who later, as chief of de Gaulle's Intelligence Service, would be known as the famous—some would say infamous—Colonel Passy, was in Brest on June 18. He had sailed back to France from Glasgow, Scotland, to which port he had been brought by the British navy, which had evacuated the French from their aborted invasion of Norway. Captain Dewavrin was a graduate engineer and officer who had stood high in his class at the Ecole Polytechnique, France's elite school of engineers and mathematicians. In his late twenties, he was strong, self-confident, combative as a soldier and as a man. He was as authoritarian as de Gaulle, as cold in his passions, determined to have his own way, fiercely patriotic and contemptuous of the weak, corrupt parliamentary system of the French Republic.

Dewavrin tried to get a ship to North Africa to rejoin the French army there, but he wound up first in Southampton, then in the regroupment camp at Trentham Park with hundreds of other French Chasseurs and Légionnaires who were being interrogated and pressured by representatives of two governments. The representatives of Pétain urged, indeed ordered all French officers and troops to return to France. British recruiting officers appealed to them to stay in Britain and carry on the fight against the Germans.

"Every now and then," Dewavrin wrote later, "someone would mention the fact that a French officer, with Churchill's agreement, had called on all French military men to join him, under the French flag, to resist the enemy. Some British officers confirmed this as a fact but of no great significance. I never did catch de Gaulle's name until the twenty-fifth of June (when de Gaulle once again spoke over the BBC, as he would do all through the war). Then I heard, on the radio, a high-pitched nasal voice calling for resistance.

It seemed to me logical to fight on under a French banner and a French general, so I made my way to London and, with some difficulty, found de Gaulle's office and joined up."

A French filmmaker, Gilbert Renault-Roulier, a bright, ambitious dynamo of a man, was getting ready to make a film in Spain on Christopher Columbus when France fell. He hurriedly found a safe place for his family to stay, while he immediately sought passage to London to be out of the hands of the Germans and have time to decide what to do next. Like so many men and women, Renault knew he had to do something. He would not surrender. Sitting on the deck of a cargo ship on which he had obtained passage, he was handed a copy of a local paper by the ship's captain, who told him to look at page two. There he found a report warning the French people against an appeal from London by a General de Gaulle. The captain asked Renault: "Did you hear him?" And when Renault said he had not, the captain replied, "That's a pity. It was good."

On arrival in England, Renault set out to find de Gaulle. He found him, joined the Free French movement, and, as Colonel Rémy, became de Gaulle's top secret agent inside France.

Claude Hettier de Boislambert, the former French liaison officer with the British Expeditionary Force, who had spent some time at Colonel de Gaulle's headquarters on the Somme, was in Brest on June 16. He was trying to decide whether to make his way south to join the French in North Africa, or to take ship to London and fight on with the British. He had a letter from a British general giving him clearance to sail. "There was a Canadian brigade in Brest," de Boislambert recalls, "that had just arrived. It had not been able to get into the war and now had to be evacuated. That's how swift the German breakthrough was. Well, I went with the Canadians. I didn't trust our own generals or our own government to fight on."

De Boislambert crossed the Channel and then caught a train to London. On the train ride he heard a British general's wife say that a French general had just made a broadcast, in London, calling on all officers and men to come to him to carry on the fight against Germany. His name, she said, sounded very prophetic: de Gaulle. "The man of Gaul—fancy that for a name!" she laughed.

De Boislambert was overjoyed. "It was my old friend of the Fourth Armored, the best general of our army. I made up my mind at once to join him. In London I went first to the French Embassy. There was no one there but the janitor. But he told me where de Gaulle was: Seymour Place. I rushed there and was let in by a tall girl, Elisabeth de Miribel, his secretary. A few minutes later de Gaulle's aide, Captain Guy, came in, also very tall and very slim. I smiled to myself and wondered if de Gaulle only took on tall, thin people. Well, I need not have wondered. De Gaulle saw me at once and gave me the warmest greeting. He too remembered our days at the front together.

"De Gaulle put me on his staff at once. My first assignment was to help him rally Africa to our colors. He had remembered my twenty-five years of experience there. We could make a strong comeback from defeat with our African resources in matériel and men. Thus I became the first officer to join La France Libre, the Free French of General de Gaulle—on June 19, 1940. I didn't have to hear him or Pétain to make up my mind."

Joseph-Henri Monjaret is today an executive of a corporation in Paris involved in the supermarket business. M. Monjaret is a neatly groomed man and has a neat and orderly office: the very image of an efficient executive. He would not stand out in a crowded room; it is hard to imagine him as an adventurer who parachuted into France under the code name Hervé to serve as underground operator for de Gaulle's delegate to the Resistance, Jean Moulin.

Monjaret was a student when war broke out. He was finishing his studies for the dread baccalaureate examination, the demon that makes life miserable for all French youth. A student who does not pass the "bac" cannot go on to university work, and without a university degree, a Frenchman or woman is almost condemned to a mediocre career. Monjaret was determined to pass his bac. He was a good student. But like all young men his age at that time the real crisis of life was not an exam, not a career, but the war. He had been born in 1920, and was ready to be called up as soon as he passed his exam.

"I had been a keen student of history and politics," Monjaret recalls today, "and had closely followed events in Germany, particularly the rise of Hitler and nazism. My own family was Catholic and conservative, if not right wing—more worried about communism. I took the opposite position, disagreeing with my parents and my teachers at the Catholic lycée I attended. I heard Pétain and knew at once that this feeble old man would not be able to stand up to Hitler. If I stayed in France, I would become a Nazi subject. I knew I had to get away.

"I had a younger brother, only seventeen. We talked it over. He felt the same as I. So we decided to try to get to Canada, thinking that since they spoke French, we would find it easier to fight in their army. We were living in Brittany, knew the coast very well, and were good sailors. We made contact with fishermen who would be taking to sea on the night of June eighteenth. They agreed to take us with them. The next morning we landed at Falmouth. There we were told of de Gaulle's speech the night before. We decided we did not have to go to Canada after all.

"We went to London, to Empire Hall, where we found French Embassy people meeting with soldiers and officers of the Chasseurs and the Legion, who had just returned from Norway. The French diplomats were telling everyone to return to France at once. Many did go back. My brother and I refused. We went to find de Gaulle. We did. I was, at last, fighting for my country."

On June 18 Geneviève de Gaulle, niece of Charles de Gaulle, was en route to a family home in Brittany with her grandmother, Charles's mother. Just twenty years old, Geneviève de Gaulle was a graduate student at the University of Rennes. Raised in the de Gaulle family tradition of the glory and grandeur of France, she could not believe the collapse of the French army in four short weeks. The day before she had heard Pétain's broadcast. "I was outraged," she recalls today, "outraged and sickened by his whining voice, by the dreadful image of 'the gift of his person.' I wanted to weep but was too angry to do so."

Then, the next day, she saw her first German soldiers. They were *motards*—motorcycle troops. "They looked so strong, so competent, so conquering in their impeccable black uniforms. Ah, they were truly the Gods of War. It was awful to see unarmed French officers milling about them, in total disorder, and French troops in dirty uniforms just wandering about, not knowing what they were doing. It was humiliating to see the contrast with the Germans and even worse to listen to the Germans telling them to go back to their camps and to be orderly."

Geneviève de Gaulle (today Madame Paul Anthonioz) smiled, then began to laugh as she remembered what happened next in that Brittany village square on June 18, 1940.

"A village priest, a *curé*, came running out of a café from across the square, all excited. A crowd gathered around him and he said: 'I just heard a young French general talking from London. He said the war isn't lost, that victory will be ours. He said the flame of French resistance must not die. Oh, he was magnificent! His name was something like Gaule.'

"My grandmother got all excited. She grabbed the *curé* and she shouted, 'Why, that's Charles! That's my boy! That's my son who said that!'"

Geneviève laughed again. "Ah, what a day that was! I may not have heard my uncle speak on the radio, but I heard about it in extraordinary circumstances, and I saw how his words electrified a crowd that had been bowed in defeat and despair only moments earlier. As for myself, my own resolve to resist had already been taken the day before, when Pétain infuriated me. But my uncle's appeal reinforced my decision, gave me additional courage and strength. I think it was that way, or became that way for many of the resistants."

The de Gaulle women continued their trek to their home at Paimpol. One month later de Gaulle's mother died there. Geneviève recalls that the Germans censored the obituary notice and made the papers drop the name de Gaulle. The death was listed as that of Jeanne Maillot, his mother's maiden name.

"They fooled no one. Everybody in the region knew that de Gaulle's mother was being buried and they came by the hundreds, bearing flowers and wreaths. They came by car and by country cart and by bicycle. They came to pay their respects not only to Grandmother, but of course to Charles de Gaulle. And by doing so they were defying the Germans. It was in its way an early act of resistance, a spontaneous act of ordinary people."

Hitler had not been in any hurry to reply to the French armistice request.

The former World War I corporal, who had been wounded, gassed, humiliated by Germany's defeat and by the harsh terms of the Versailles treaty, was enjoying his victory. Hitler was in Paris, on the morning of June 18, reviewing troops in the Place de l'Etoile, then sightseeing, enjoying particularly the spectacular view from the esplanade of the Palais de Chaillot, between the museums which faced the Seine, the Eiffel Tower, and the Ecole Militaire. Audiences in America would later laugh at a newsreel view of Hitler doing a stiff-legged jig of joy with the Eiffel Tower in the background. It became a famous scene.

In fact Hitler never did do that jig. John Grierson, a clever Canadian moviemaker with a sense of humor, had got hold of newsreel shots of Hitler at the Chaillot and had tricked the jig footage.*

After his sightseeing tour of Paris, Hitler flew to Munich for a meeting with his Axis partner, Benito Mussolini. They would discuss both German and Italian armistice plans. Mussolini, despite a show of bravado, knew that he was a partner in name only and that Hitler, whose armies had won the victory, would define the armistice terms.

About 6 A.M. on June 19 Pétain, in Bordeaux, received the German reply to his request for an armistice. It would be granted, but on condition that an armistice be concluded with Italy also. The ambassador of Spain delivered the message, and then relayed Pétain's agreement back to the Germans and Italians. At a Cabinet meeting, Pétain called for volunteers to the armistice delegation. There were no hands. Pétain, with a sigh, named General Charles Huntziger to head the delegation and set it up.

Pétain called in the Spanish ambassador to inform him of the steps he had taken and to ask the Germans, in view of the impending armistice, to stop their advance toward Bordeaux. Whether the Germans got the message in time is not clear, but their heavy bombing raid on Bordeaux the night of June 19 killed 63 people and injured 180.

Pétain had to go on the air the next morning to tell the French people of the moves he had made to bring about an early armistice. He also announced that the government was leaving for North Africa, with members of Parliament and the chief of state, President Albert Lebrun. However he, Marshal Pétain, as chief of the government, was staying at his post. He would not leave France.

At Pétain's request Admiral Darlan had put a ship, the *Massilia*, at the disposal of the members of Parliament. It was scheduled to sail on the twentieth for Morocco. The president and the Cabinet ministers were instructed to drive, via Perpignan, to Port-Vendres, from whence they would sail on the twenty-first, in a navy destroyer, for Algiers. All arrangements had been approved by the government and the military chiefs.

---

* Grierson was at the time an executive of the U.S. Office of War Information, working with such famous producer-directors as John Houseman. All of us who worked in that madcap establishment enjoyed a number of propaganda hoaxes dreamed up by a brilliant but not altogether responsibile staff. Hitler *did* perform a jig at the armistice ceremony at Compiègne.

Rafael Albert, a newly appointed minister of justice and security and a leader of the Right, was angrily opposed to the departure of the government. He was convinced, probably correctly, that once in North Africa the stronger men of the government and Parliament would take over and make plans to continue the war, leaving Pétain and all those inside France to be German puppets without power or prestige. He was determined to sabotage the departure. Unknown to Pétain, he forged the marshal's signature on an order to all government ministers to remain at their lodgings until 8 A.M. the following morning, June 20. He called President Lebrun, who was just leaving his office to drive to Perpignan, and told him, "There are new developments. Pétain has called a special meeting. Stand by." President Lebrun, not imagining a lie, dismissed his driver and went back to his desk.

General de Gaulle, in London, received a summons from Weygand after his speech of June 18, ordering him to return immediately or be charged with desertion. As commander in chief he had the right to issue such an order. De Gaulle sent a message back informing Weygand that he would return at once, on condition that "an armistice is not signed."

On June 21, after a day's delay, the *Massilia* steamed out of port en route to Morocco, carrying twenty-six deputies of the Chamber and one senator, Tony Revillon. These men had not received any order to stay in France. Alibert's false order had been issued too late to reach them. On board were Daladier, Pierre Viénot, Georges Mandel, Jean Zay, and Pierre Mendès-France. The latter three were Jews, aware that they faced a special threat. Former Premier Léon Blum and Speaker Edouard Herriot had decided to go with the government to Algiers and were, therefore, not on the *Massilia*.

Pierre Viénot, Jean Zay, and Mendès-Frances were still in uniform, still on active duty. However, as members of Parliament, they were sailing with the official consent of the government, including the military chiefs. That did not prevent the army from calling a court-martial, charging them with desertion and finding them guilty. Right-wing parliamentarians who remained behind charged all passengers on the *Massilia* with illegal flight and treason.

On the afternoon of the twentieth, Pierre Laval burst into the office of President Albert Lebrun and, in a violent scene, warned him that if he left France, he would be accused of defection and treason. Lebrun, who had voluntarily obeyed Alibert's false call about a Pétain meeting, was outraged and threw him out of his office. Laval went to Pétain and asked him to stop Lebrun from leaving. Pétain, with no legal authority as prime minister to give orders to a president of the Republic, assured Laval that if Lebrun tried to leave he would arrest him.

On June 21, the French Armistice delegation was being escorted to an unknown destination to meet with the Germans to sign an armistice. There had been no negotiations. The armistice terms would be dictated to the French without discussion.

When he arrived at the meeting place, General Huntziger paled and felt his stomach turn over. It was the railway siding at Rethondes, in the forest of Compiègne, the historic monument symbolizing France's victory over Germany in World War I. It was there on November 11, 1918, that a young officer named Weygand had dictated surrender terms to the Germans in the name of Marshal Foch, generalissimo of the Allied armies. On that hallowed ground, in that same railway car, General Huntziger would have to bow to the terms of the victorious Germans.

A former corporal would not miss this opportunity to gloat. Adolf Hitler arrived at 3:15 P.M. to dictate the terms personally. Hitler told Huntziger that a million and a half French prisoners of war were to remain in German hands until the conclusion of a peace treaty. The French fleet was to be demobilized and put into mothballs. The most humiliating condition, a grave violation of human rights, provided that the French turn over to the Nazis all anti-Nazi refugees in France. That would mean rounding up all the German and Austrian Jews who had fled persecution and handing them over to the death camps, along with a great number of non-Jews who had fled Germany in opposition to nazism. There were other conditions, splitting French territory in two, but they would not be known publicly for a few days.

When Pétain received the German terms, he summoned his Cabinet at 1 A.M. on June 22. President Lebrun, virtually a prisoner of Pétain, sat in on the meeting, his head in his hands, his shoulders bowed. He raised his head for an instant when his name was called, and said, "These terms are totally unacceptable." Then he relapsed into his shell, knowing that all was lost.

There were several hours of fruitless proposals for amendments, but the French had been beaten and there was no way to persuade the Germans to change their terms. The armistice was signed at 6:50 A.M. in the railway car at Rethondes. Two days later another armistice was signed, *pro forma*, with the Italians. It meant nothing. The Germans were the masters of defeated France.

By order of Marshal Pétain, General de Gaulle was stripped of his rank and a court-martial convened on June 23. It would find him guilty of desertion and treason and condemn him to death.

Pierre Laval was invited to join Pétain's Cabinet, not as a minister with portfolio but as a minister of state, without function. This would permit him, without departmental responsibilities, to freewheel and intrigue with the Germans.

Hitler, fresh from the signing of the armistice, returned to Paris for another tour. This time he chose the Tomb of Napoleon and had himself filmed by German newsreels in meditation at the bier of the Corsican, who, like himself, had risen from the rank of corporal to become the master of Europe. Two corporals together—no one could miss the symbolism that Hitler wished to project.

While Hitler was communing with Napoleon, Archbishop Suhard conducted Sunday mass at Notre Dame Cathedral, calling upon the faithful to remain calm and orderly. The High Church had already accepted the inevitability of collaboration, but a number of lower-ranked clergymen and nuns would refuse to follow their superiors.

One of these priests who rejected Pétain and the Nazis was Father Michel Riquet. At age forty-one, in 1939, Father Riquet was called to arms as an adjutant-chief of an infantry battalion, and its unofficial chaplain. In May 1940, he finally was officially named chaplain. "I was in the Ardennes when the Germans broke through. We fell back to Reims and to the Marne. I was taken prisoner by the Germans on June seventeenth, the day that Pétain offered the gift of his person to the nation."

The Jesuits intervened with the authorities and obtained Father Riquet's release on June 27. From that day on, in 1940, his main work was to improve the situation of prisoners of war and to work with the underground, running escape networks to Spain. He worked to save not only soldiers but also Jews and anti-Nazi refugees. Word soon got around: If in trouble, go see Father Michel Riquet, the partisan-priest.

The armistice became official on June 25, but on that day there was still sporadic fighting between Germans and pockets or fragments of French troops. On the eastern front, where Captain Henri Frenay commanded a company of the Forty-third Corps, his corps commander, General Lescanne, refused a German order for unconditional surrender under the armistice terms.

"If you refuse," warned the German commander, "we shall resume our attack tomorrow morning, and here is a summary of the strength, condition, and stations of the forces which will storm your positions." He handed over a full battle order that showed the hopelessness of the French opposition.

General Lescanne stood up to end the discussion and said calmly but firmly: "Sir, as you know, my means are greatly inferior to yours, but I shall still kill a great many of your men."

The German could not help but admire his French opponent. He felt it would be tragic and useless for so many men to be killed over some petty argument of protocol. He asked Lescanne what he really wanted and Lescanne replied that he sought basic and traditional military respect. He demanded that each French officer be permitted to keep his side arm, a mark of his rank and commission, and that each officer be kept in command of his own unit, even as a prisoner. The unit would keep its regulation equipment and part of its field gear, except for its weapons. All German orders would be transmitted through French officers.

The German general agreed and threw Lescanne a snappy, full-dress salute, complete with clicking heels.

The Forty-third Corps had held out until the very last moment. It held the northernmost point of the French front, and had fired the last cannon shot by French forces. In his last active order, General Lescanne said:

"Be proud! Be confident! Be loyal to one another! The days of mourning shall come to an end."

The French soldiers cheered. Then Frenay, with a feeling of shame and horror, watched his men throw down their arms, shuck off their field packs, and begin folk-dancing in the road, shouting with joy, destroying the dignity and discipline of their commanding general. "In the faces of the young German soldiers who passed by, I read astonishment and contempt."

Frenay was shocked not only by the behavior of the troops, but by the lack of spirit among his fellow officers. They all talked in a friendly fashion with their German opposite numbers, who assured them that they would not be long in captivity. After all, said the Germans, what could we do with more than a million French prisoners whom we could not even feed?

Frenay was not at all convinced by German reassurances. He had heard that they were going to be transported to Strasbourg. Why all the way to the German border? It seemed suspect to him. He decided to escape and began to sound out fellow officers. "I found not a single officer willing to join me," Frenay noted later in his memoirs. "It was a noncom, Adjutant Bourguet, who became my companion."

The very day that General Lescanne was demanding that the Germans grant him dignity in surrender, a group of fishermen on the Ile de Sein, a small but strategic island off the west coast of France commanding the Pointe du Raz, were meeting to decide what to do. The Germans had reached the nearest mainland village, Audierne. Many of the Seinans were already on active duty, either on warships or in the Merchant Marine. But 130 men, available for duty, were on the island that day, June 24. Some of them were already in uniform and were home on a brief leave. They met at a town hall meeting. The entire island community reached a unanimous decision: Their men must not be taken prisoner; they must not capitulate; they should sail to England to carry on the fight.

Feverishly the fishing boats were made ready to sail: the *Arzenith*, the *Rouanez Armor*, the *Corbeau des Mers*, the *Velleda*. The men—all 130 of them—jumped aboard. The oldest among them, Jean-Marie Menou, was sixty; the youngest, the choirboy, Jean Morsmoguer, was only twelve. As they moved silently out of the harbor without motors or lights, the women, the oldest men, and youngest children of the island stood on the beach, watching them with eyes and faces made old by squinting through a hundred storms and winds. No one knew that day how the community would survive without the fishermen, who were the sole industry and support of the island. Every affection, every asset the islanders possessed sailed with the fleet to England.

When the Germans arrived the next day and expressed their surprise at seeing the men in black suits and the women wearing black coifs, the Seinans told them quietly: "We are in mourning for France." It was June 25, the armistice was official. France had surrendered.

Almost a million French soldiers were taken prisoner. A half-

million more had already been captured. More than 100,000 had been killed
and 250,000 wounded. A line of demarcation running roughly through the
center of the country from west to east, would divide France into two zones,
one in the north, with a population of 25 million, occupied by the Germans;
another unoccupied zone in the south, a so-called Zone Libre, with 14 million
people. To travel across the line from one zone to another, a French citizen
would have to ask for a German pass, an *Ausweis*. Any attempt to cross without such a pass would be severely punished. In Paris all clocks were moved
back an hour to conform to German time. Pétain announced on the radio:
"A New Order begins."

The fishing boats from the Ile de Sein crossed the Channel
and reached the English shore at Portsmouth. Some of de Gaulle's Free French
agents, alerted by radio, rushed to the beach to greet them and tell them,
"Today, you are half of France." That is what their 130 men represented for
the thin ranks of de Gaulle's forces on the twenty-fifth of June.

De Gaulle in those early days was a lonely figure in London.
Some of the most important personages of the French Republic would not
join with him. Jean Monnet, head of the Economic Mission, who would play
a major role in the war, mistrusted de Gaulle and all generals. He believed
that Frenchmen should concentrate on cooperating with the Americans—theirs
was the only power that would win the war. André Maurois, the distinguished
biographer; Pertinax, France's Walter Lippmann, its most influential and
widely read columnist; Georges Gombault, another important journalist—
these men had little confidence in de Gaulle. Many believed he was a right-
wing militarist of dangerous personal ambition. Some would later prejudice
President Roosevelt against de Gaulle. Nor would de Gaulle help his own
cause with his haughty manner, his defiance and criticism of his Allies, his
evident contempt for many of his own compatriots.

Undaunted by his problems, General de Gaulle went back to
the radio to warn the French people again not to trust Pétain. "The armistice
is dishonorable," de Gaulle told the French on the same day that Pétain was
promising a New Order.

Admiral Darlan sent out a coded message to all navy unit commanders to scuttle their ships immediately in the event that either Germany
or Britain should make an attempt to seize them.

On June 27, not trusting the French to keep their fleet out of
German hands, the British High Command decided upon an operation code-
named Catapult whose purpose was to seize, control, disable or, if necessary,
destroy all of the French fleet that the British could reach. The target date
for Operation Catapult was July 3.

Pétain decided on June 29 to move his government from Bordeaux to Clermont-Ferrand, in central France.

In Paris, a group of men began to collect civilian clothing to
smuggle to French prisoners of war, so that they might cover their prison
uniforms when escaping. Safe-houses were being found and mapped for the

escape route. One of the men who organized this project was a manufacturer named Le Faurichon. Others were Jean Volvey, president of the Society of Escapees of World War I, and a friend, Marc Turenne. They did not think of it as such but they had organized an early Resistance movement in Paris. So had a medical doctor, a general practitioner named Jacques Destrée.

Dr. Destrée had not been mobilized because of a bad leg, injured in an accident. He practiced in Paris, where doctors, during the war, were in short supply. He knew nothing about de Gaulle and not much about Pétain. His patients kept him too busy for politics. But then the Germans came to Paris. Dr. Destrée was appalled by the collapse of France and even more dismayed when he read the terms of the armistice.

As he made his rounds, he began to sound out his patients. "What do you think we should do?" "Is anyone taking any action?" "We can't just sit still, can we?"

In the same apartment in central Paris where he lived in those days, and where Germans were later to arrest him, Dr. Destrée today reminisces: "You know, that is exactly how the Resistance started. First one would sound out friends, people we felt were reliable. We were all careful about what we said, but soon caught on when the spirit was there. Then, we would take greater risks, talk to strangers. In a café, at a newspaper kiosk, in the Métro or a bakery. It was dangerous, but one learned how to play the game, what key words to use that were, on the surface, innocent enough, but sent out signals.'"

Destrée stretched out and rubbed his bad leg. "There were small beginnings but important, and they grew. Some friends told me they were members of a movement called 'Valmy,' mainly in the Fifteenth Arrondissement. They printed and distributed mimeographed tracts, exposing the lies of Pétain, publishing news of de Gaulle, appealing to the French to resist. It was very small in those early days. But, as the story unfolds, you will see, it grows. Our little tracts became a regular paper, called *Résistance*, with a circulation of one hundred twenty thousand."

Far south of Paris, in Brive, a group of young Catholics working in social service teams had the same idea as Doctor Destrée and his friends. Using a mimeograph machine, they produced tracts that they distributed in June 1940. Some historians of the period credit the leader of this young group, Edmond Michelet, with having produced the very first propaganda tracts of the Resistance. That may well be true, although it is today difficult to determine the exact date that the first underground sheets appeared. One thing is certain: Sometime at the end of June, about the time of the armistice, an embryonic Resistance "press" was coming into being—in Paris, in Alsace, in the Pas de Calais, and in Toulouse, where a young Jew wrote out the first underground brochure of the Jewish Resistance movement.

His name was David Knout. He and his wife were independent Zionists, not members of any official Zionist organization, but Jews believing that the ultimate salvation of their people would be found only in the Jewish homeland of Palestine. He quoted the old, bitter exclamation of the precursor of Zionism, Pinsker, who had said: "Our eternal tactic is flight." David Knout did not believe that that was the good solution. In his brochure, a woman asks, pleadingly, *"Que faire?"*—what is there to do?

That was the title of his brochure—*Que Faire?*—typed out painfully in many copies. Knout did not even possess a mimeograph machine. He offered as answer to the question "what to do" two slogans: *"Partout Présent"* and *"Faire Face."* Be Present Everywhere and Stand Up. As his brochure went to a few Jewish friends, they would recopy it and distribute it to others. It made its way like a chain letter throughout France, giving comfort and courage to a persecuted people organizing its self-defense.

Propaganda was not the only activity of the early resistants of France. In the department of the Seine, the Pas de Calais, the Côte d'Or, and the Nord, in dozens of villages and towns, Frenchmen were cutting telephone lines used by government officials and by the Germans. It was a crime punishable by death and several died when caught.

On June 20 a young man named Etienne Achavanne, acting on his own, not a member of any network or movement, cut the lines between the German Feldkommandantur and the airfield at Boos. It probably, almost certainly, was the very first act of sabotage of the French Resistance, and it was a very successful one. Boos was without communications when an RAF bomber raid hit the field hard. Eighteen German planes were destroyed on the ground and twenty-two German soldiers were killed.

Etienne Achavanne was caught and brought before a court-martial in Rouen, where he was found guilty and condemned to death. He was the first martyr of the Resistance.

Achavanne's act was spontaneous, impulsive, as were the first acts of Dr. Destrée and David Knout. They were only a handful, these few precursors of the Resistance in June 1940. There was, as yet, no real movement, no structure, no organization except for the Communist underground, and the Communist party did not organize any resistance at first, though individual Communists did.

Robert Noireau was an infantry soldier in the 213th Dépôt de Guerre on the Italian front. He was a northerner, born near the Belgian frontier in a working-class family. His father was a miner. At fifteen Noireau became an ironworker, at a low salary for a backbreaking ten-hour day. Like most of his friends he became a Communist.

"Although a Communist, trained in the Communist party school for union organizers, I was also a Frenchman, born on the Belgian border in 1912. My father, the whole family, lived through the German invasion and I was brought up to hate the *Boche.* I could not understand the Soviet-Nazi Pact, although I still put my faith in the party.

"But, Pétain—contemptible. An old fool. I was enraged. So were all my comrades in the army. We were talking about what we were going to do when somebody said that a general named de Gaulle, in London, said we must fight on. Well, I didn't know him and I didn't trust generals, but I agreed with the idea. As a Communist, I knew they would be after me anyway, so I deserted from the army and went to Paris to contact the underground. I was a skilled worker, a machinist. They gave me false papers and a job in a factory and told me to wait for action orders."

Robert Noireau would become one of the most effective of the underground fighters. He was known, later, in the maquis, as Colonel Georges.

The Communists were tightly organized, they had been persecuted and chased by police for more than a year. They took to clandestine life more readily, more efficiently than others and they would, after the Nazi invasion of Russia, build a Resistance movement that became the biggest and strongest in France. But the Communists never fully cooperated with other movements of the Resistance: They neither fully trusted nor were fully trusted by most other Frenchmen.

A few hundred, even a few thousand individuals acting spontaneously, do not add up to anything that could be called a national resistance. But like a new-born baby, which is at first a tiny, helpless thing, the Resistance movement was born and was alive as early as June 1940. At the moment of defeat and humiliation, the seeds of a renaissance and an ultimate liberation were implanted in French soil, while across the Channel one lonely but determined man, with a small following, was holding high the banner of France in the ranks of the Allies.

At the outset the flag of France flew in London more by tolerance than by true force. But the force would grow throughout the French Empire, and the Allies would learn, with some pain, to respect a new symbol on the French banner, the Cross of Lorraine, personal symbol of Charles de Gaulle. France would have two Resistance movements, the Resistance of the Interior and the Resistance of the Exterior. At times they opposed each other and their Allies almost as passionately as they fought their common enemies, the regimes of Marshal Pétain and the Germans.

4
DEATH OF
THE REPUBLIC

On June 30, 1940, at a meeting in Clermont-Ferrand—the last to be held there before moving on to his final seat of government in Vichy—Marshal Pétain conferred with Pierre Laval and his principal henchmen about how to put an end to the French Republic.

Rafael Albert, an outspoken fascist, suggested to the marshall that he adjourn Parliament for six months and rule alone by decree. That was not enough for Pierre Laval, who rejected the proposal as a "half measure." He said that he would go to see President Lebrun and persuade him to give his consent to a convocation of Parliament for a revision of the Constitution. Laval, counting on the marshal's age to permit Laval himself to run the government, wanted to create a dictatorship for Pétain. Pétain promised Laval an early answer on his proposal.

The next day, July 1, the government moved to the resort town of Vichy, site of the famous spa and the world-renowned Vichy water. The reason for the move was the availability in the famous resort of a greater number of well-equipped hotels, all of them empty because of the war. These hotels had been occupied by French army headquarters during the retreat to the south. They had been requisitioned by Lieutenant Claude Serreulles.

Claude Serreulles was a young man of good family and excellent education, destined in normal times for a career in the French diplomatic service. His father was a well-to-do businessman with useful political connections. Claude was tall, slim, attractive, intelligent, and well liked by all. He did well in his law classes, was admitted to the prestigious Institut des Sciences Politiques, the breeding-farm of the Quai d'Orsay, the Ministry of Foreign Affairs.

On graduation, Serreulles was sent to the French Embassy in Berlin as a junior attaché. He stayed there for eighteen months, from 1937 to 1938, seeing firsthand the brown-shirt terror of the Nazis and the war preparations of the German general staff. He had no doubt that war was coming soon and that he would have a role to play.

But in the fall of 1939 Claude Serreulles had been just another young Frenchman called up in the general mobilization. He was given an active commission as reserve lieutenant and assigned to the general staff of the Army of Brittany. Fluent in English as well as German, Lieutenant Serreulles was named liaison officer between General Alphonse Georges's HQ and the HQ of General Lord Gort, of the British Expeditionary Force. He had been evacuated with the British from Dunkirk but made his way back to France in a small boat, hoping against hope that the French army would halt the German attack.

Serreulles recalls today: "It was a terrible moment in our lives, running like rabbits, chased by the German wolfhounds. I thought we might dig in at the Loire, but again we received orders to retreat. I was asked to find a suitable place for HQ. I thought of the hotels of Vichy and went there on June sixteenth. It was there, on June seventeenth, that I heard Pétain's call for an armistice. I was sick with rage and shame, not only because of Pétain but because most of the officers at HQ were defeatist and agreed with Pétain. I told them of my experiences as a young diplomat in Berlin, about Hitler and the horrors of nazism, but they would not listen."

Serreulles left Vichy on June 18 for Bordeaux, where he obtained passage at the last minute aboard the *Massilia*. Because he was young and a low-ranking officer, because he had arranged his departure so hastily and without attracting public notice, Serreulles was overlooked by the Vichy police who were maintaining surveillance on all other *Massilia* passengers. In Morocco, police plainclothesmen trailed behind former Premier Edouard Daladier and former Interior Minister Georges Mandel, the two men whose influence Pétain feared most. Mandel was the prime target, for he had openly displayed his contempt for the marshal. When Mandel went to visit the British consul general in Rabat, Morocco, he was immediately arrested, although the British were still nominally allies of the French. Lieutenant Serreulles, however, was ignored. It was an oversight that Vichy would later regret.

Most of Serreulles's fellow officers had stayed on in Vichy and felt highly honored when the hero of Verdun, the new chief of government, moved his Cabinet and the general staff there. Pétain installed himself and his closest collaborators at the Hôtel du Parc, which would become the nerve center of the Pétain regime and an extraordinary beehive of intrigue and espionage for the rest of the war.

On July 1 the British had sent out secret signals from London to all navy commanders, informing them that Operation Catapult—the plan to seize or knock out French naval units—was on, and that the target date was July 3.

Well before dawn on July 3, British troops swarmed over the docks at Plymouth and clambered aboard the French warships anchored there: two battleships, four light cruisers, eight destroyers, a number of smaller craft, and several submarines. By 3:45 A.M., they were all securely in British hands and twenty thousand French sailors and officers were told that they could decide to join General de Gaulle's Free French forces or elect to return home to France. Only nine hundred would rally to de Gaulle's Free French flag.

Meanwhile British warships, which had been zigzagging along erratic routes and patterns for days in order to escape detection and to co-ordinate the attack on July 3, steamed within range of the French naval base at Mers-el-Kebir in Algeria. Without warning, their cannons opened fire on an unsuspecting, sleeping French fleet. It was a slaughter. French battleships exploded in flames and sank or were crippled: the *Bretagne*, the *Provence*, the *Mogador*, and the *Dunquerque*. The death toll of French personnel was 1,297. Another 341 men were wounded. Damage to the British fleet was minor.

A cry of rage emanated from the Pétain regime in Vichy. Pierre Laval and Admiral Darlan, long an Anglophobe, demanded an immediate dec-laration of war against Britain. François Mauriac, the Catholic novelist and columnist of the newspaper *Le Figaro*, wrote: "Churchill has arrayed against England—for how many years?—a unanimous France."

Mauriac was a writer with style and power, but he was not, then or later, the most reliable of political analysts. All of France was not unan-imously arrayed against Britain. Mers-el-Kebir did come as a shock and many French citizens were angered or dismayed by the attack of a wartime ally. But many also understood Britain's fear of Pétain's capitulation to the Nazis and Pétain's failure to take the necessary steps to assure the British that the French fleet would not fall into German hands.

Pétain rejected Laval's and Darlan's hotheaded call to arms. But on July 4, he did accept the proposal of his foreign affairs adviser, Paul Bau-doin, to break off formal diplomatic relations with Britain. At a Cabinet meet-ing, Laval then put to the ministers a project already approved by Pétain: to convene the Chamber of Deputies and the Senate in a joint session, as a National Assembly, on July 10. The purpose: to abolish the Constitution of the Third Republic of France.

On July 8, the day after an order to intern foreign Jews, Pierre Laval dropped all pretense and drafted a resolution denouncing the Republic and calling for the creation of a government based upon the model of Nazi Germany. He circulated his resolution as a kind of petition among members of Parliament and on the first day obtained seventeen signatures of endorse-ment, including those of several members of the French Socialist party, sup-posedly the champion of a democratic Left.

Former Premier Paul Reynaud, the man who brought Pétain into his Cabinet as vice-premier, easing his way to power, arrived in Vichy. He had been in the hospital after having been injured in an automobile acci-dent on June 28. His mistress, the Countess de Portes, had been killed.

On July 9, on the eve of the convocation of the National Assem-bly, President Lebrun presided over what proved to be the last Cabinet meeting of the Third Republic of France. Pétain was present but it was Laval who did all the talking in favor of a constitutional revision that would abolish the Republic and institute a new French State. Not one Cabinet member rose to oppose Laval. The Cabinet members were paralyzed by a "panic of fear," according to Socialist party leader Léon Blum, who wrote about the meeting later. Blum believed that Laval did not so much convince or bully the deputies, but rather that he "infected" them with the fear either of German intervention or a military coup by General Weygand. Some of the deputies present at the meeting did not have to be infected. They were men of the extreme right wing who had long despised the Republic. One of them, Pierre Tixier-Vignancour, introduced a resolution calling for the trial and punishment of those responsible for the disaster.

On the morning of July 10, Tixier-Vignancour's idea was picked up by Senator Charles Reibel, who proposed a law to punish those responsible for the war, for France's lack of preparation for the war and for its continuance in the face of certain defeat. In his mind, those who wanted to fight on against the Germans were traitors.

The morning session of the National Assembly was a secret session, closed to the public. Laval took the podium and read a letter from Pétain authorizing him to speak in his place. He made it clear that Pétain was not merely asking for a revision of the Constitution of 1875. What Laval demanded was its outright abrogation and the creation of a new, different constitution to be drafted by Pétain. There would be no constitutional convention, no debate. Pétain would create a new French State modeled on Germany and Italy.

Laval did not hesitate to praise Hitler and Mussolini. He told the members of the National Assembly that the Fascist and Nazi dictatorships had restored "love of country" and "order" in their nations. Veteran politician Pierre-Etienne Flandin followed Laval to the podium and nailed down the coffin of the Republic by endorsing Laval's remarks. The closed session was adjourned and members were asked to return at 2 P.M. for the public session and the vote on an article of law granting Marshal Pétain authorization to promulgate a new constitution of the French State.

When the National Assembly returned, Senate President Jeanneney was in the chair. Chamber of Deputies Speaker Edouard Herriot asked for the floor and demanded the right to read into the record a telegram of protest from the members of Parliament who had left on the *Massilia* for North Africa, with the full consent of the government, and who were now being harassed and held there and were unable to come to Vichy to vote in the National Assembly that day.

Chairman Jeanneney told Herriot that all discussion was limited to the article of constitution before the Assembly and that no other subject might be introduced. Furthermore he ruled that there would be no debate. He declared Herriot out of order and called for the balloting to proceed.

The final tally was: 569 in favor of a new constitution; 80 opposed; 17 present but abstaining. There were a great many deputies and senators who were physically absent from the vote: the twenty-six deputies and one senator who had sailed to Morocco on the *Massilia*, others still in the army, and, above all, the members of the Communist party, who had been outlawed.

The largest percentage of the eighty who had refused to vote for a fascist state was Socialist. Thirty-six members of the Socialist party (twenty-nine deputies and seven senators) had won themselves a special place in French history, and the special hatred of the Pétain-Laval clique, by refusing to grant Pétain constitutional powers. Venerable party leader Léon Blum was one of the thirty-six, as was Vincent Auriol, a future president of a restored Republic.

Thirty-six out of eighty represents 45 percent, giving the Socialists by far the honor of the largest contingent of defenders of the Republic. The next largest group, the Democratic Left, totaled only fourteen names. But when one considers that the overall parliamentary strength of the Socialist party (one hundred and fifty-six deputies and ten senators) totaled one hundred and sixty-six, then the figure of thirty-six votes for the Republic against dictatorship is strikingly low.

No one felt the shame of July 10 more keenly than a Socialist journalist and social worker, Daniel Mayer. Mayer had spent most of his life as a militant fighter for the Ligue des Droits de l'Homme. He had joined the League of Rights of Man in 1927, when he read with rising anger the French press reports on the Sacco-Vanzetti case in the United States, reports tending to assert their innocence and the villainy of the American prosecution. Mayer was only eighteen years old then, finishing his baccalaureate studies and working as a runner at the Paris Bourse, the Stock Exchange of Paris.

Daniel Mayer has been a Socialist all his adult life, the kind of social democrat who professed Marxist economic theories but insisted on democratic principles for politics and government. Like many French Socialists of his times, he regarded the Communists as dangerous rivals and did not believe their protestations of democratic commitment. But he was appalled by the Daladier decrees and the police terror launched against the Communists during the war against Hitler. Daniel Mayer was a soldier in an infantry regiment stationed in the Ardennes in 1939. He could not comprehend French policy. Hitler was the enemy, not the French Communists. "I knew it would all end badly and that I would have to follow the Communists into the underground. Our government and general staff were bankrupt."

Thirty-seven years after July 10, 1940, sipping tea in the salon of the Hôtel Lurétia, Daniel Mayer recalled with sadness the degradation of the politicians of France in 1940. "It was not that I was surprised by the vote," Mayer said, "for I had expected something like it since Daladier's capitulation to Hitler in Munich, when the democracies abandoned Czechoslovakia to the Nazis. It was more like the terrible day they first told me my wife had terminal cancer." Mayer's eyes filled with tears as he recalled the tragedy: "That day, I knew I had lost her. That day I suffered the ultimate shock. Her death later was an anticlimax. So in the same way was the death of the Third Republic an anticlimax in 1940. It had died in September 1938 in Munich."

Mayer's answer to the death of the Republic was to take a personal vow to fight on to restore a healthy, democratic Socialist party. He took this assignment upon himself. The party was fragmented, decimated, split into opposing factions. Mayer began to travel through France contacting party members of the rank and file, telling them to stand firm, to await word from him, that the party would be re-created along with the French Republic.

"I went south to begin my search," Mayer recalled. "First I saw one of our leaders, Marx Dormy, to ask him what to do. He told me he did not know what to do, but 'As for you, Mayer, you're a Jew. You can do less than others. You are in danger and must be prudent.' Then I went to Toulouse, thinking I might make my way to Spain and London. There Suzanne Buisson, whose husband was an official of Léon Jouhaux's staff in the Labor Confederation, told me to stay on. She was Jewish too, but thought we should not run. Then we found Léon Blum, who was staying in Colomiers, near Toulouse. Blum told us: 'You're not soldiers or sailors. What can you do in London? Stay here and reorganize a clandestine party.' Since this was exactly what I had already intended to do, I was delighted with Blum's advice. From that day on, I went underground and began to organize Socialists in the Resistance."

Since the Communist party was not present at the National Assembly on July 10, their votes were not recorded. For almost forty years now a controversy has been raging over what their vote might have been, and what, in fact, their policy line and action were on that historic day.

Those who were in Paris on July 10, 1977, witnessed the rebounding of a historic quarrel. The Communists put up a poster quoting the "call to resistance of Maurice Thorez and Jacques Duclos on July 10, 1940." Friends and foes of the Communist party have had a longtime passionate debate about that "call," said to have been published in the party paper, *Humanité*, on the day of the National Assembly vote. Copies of the paper in the archives show that there is no date on its masthead. And the issue carrying the appeal by Thorez and Duclos is not numbered. A full collection of the paper shows Number 60, dated July 7, 1940, followed by Number 61, dated July 13, 1940. There is nothing in between, no issue of July 10.

Even the most faithful Communist party members do not claim to have seen the issue in question before the month of August. Nor, in the text, can one find anywhere the word *résistance*. Pierre Villon, who was an underground editor of *Humanité* at the time, explodes with anger today when anyone questions the veracity of the claim that this issue was a call of resistance. Sitting in his modern office in the new wing of offices assigned to deputies of the National Assembly, Villon insists that "it is simply bad faith to argue that it was not a true call to resistance. The statement includes a phrase to the effect that the French people were not a people of slaves, affirming the fact that there would be a struggle for liberation and that the true road to salvation would be found by the working classes. That, in effect, is a call to resistance."

The quarrel reflects current politics more than historical debate. The Communists want the French people to believe that their struggle started at the very beginning, despite the Hitler-Stalin Pact. Critics of the Communist party want the French people to remember that no organized party action took place before the Nazi invasion of the Soviet Union. There is evidence that in the beginning, in 1940, the Communist party did make some attempts to collaborate with the Germans and that the official party line did not call for determined resistance to the Germans or to Vichy until the Russians were attacked.

While July 10 was making history in France, the Luftwaffe made its first move to back up Marshal Goering's boast that he would break the back of the British and win the war for Germany. He sent his bombers out on their first mass raid on England. The Battle of Britain had begun.

On July 11, as the acts creating the new State of France were promulgated, its officials moved to demonstrate that it would, indeed, be modeled on Germany and Italy. Prefects began rounding up those accused of "jeopardizing national security," a charge so vague that it could include anyone who had ever made a remark criticizing Pétain or Laval, or calling for a continuation of the war. The new constitutional acts named Marshal Pétain as the chief of state, replacing President Lebrun.

The next day Pétain promulgated another constitutional act naming Pierre Laval as his successor. It was the ultimate triumph of Laval's long months of intrigues and plots against the Republic.

Later in July, on the thirtieth, still another constitutional act was promulgated, creating a special Supreme Court at Riom to try those accused of mismanaging the affairs of France and bringing disaster upon the nation. That same day General de Gaulle was condemned to death. De Gaulle, not impressed with the death sentence, sent an appeal to all governors and administrators of the French Empire to rally to the cause of Free France and break with the new fascist state of Pétain. Earlier that month, New Hebrides and the Ivory Coast had sent de Gaulle messages of support.

Among those observers watching with dismay the disintegration of the French Republic was a naturalized Frenchwoman, Jewish-born and raised in Austria, Anny Latour, née Lévy. A graduate of the University of Graz, Anny Lévy was a historian. She came to Paris, married, and became French. In Austria, as in France, the Jews were highly assimilated into the national culture. It could almost be said that in Austria the Jews *were* the national culture. Certainly the Viennese theater and the publishing houses were dominated by Jewish intellectuals, writers, and artists. Most of them would never have believed that the barbaric anti-Semitism of Poland and Russia, then of Hitler, could infect the gay, carefree *gemütlichkeit* of Vienna—not Vienna, the city of Mozart and Beethoven, Vienna of Strauss and the Blue Danube, of chocolate cakes and the rose gardens of Schönbrunn Palace.

Anny Lévy Latour witnessed what could happen. At the moment

of the Anschluss in 1938 she was in Vienna on a trip home. She saw the charming Viennese turned into savages. She stood almost paralyzed in the street, watching a distinguished doctor, head of a famous clinic, prostrate in the roadway, a brute's foot on his neck, lapping up dirty, ammoniated water from the gutter. Crowds of well-dressed Viennese stood by and cheered and shouted, "Dirty Jew." Finally the doctor, gagging and weeping, was pulled to his feet while his torturer shouted at him: "Very good, *Herr Doktor,* now come back tomorrow at the same time and bring your wife with you." The crowd roared with laughter. Anny Latour, cold with horror, ran quickly away, packed, and returned to Paris. One year later, she saw the signs of barbarism arise in Paris, even before the fall of France and the German occupation. On May 14, the Reynaud government in a panic ordered the roundup of Jews from Germany, Danzig, and the Saar—the rationale given was the fear of a German fifth column. The men were taken by police to Buffalo Stadium, the women to the Vélodrome d'Hiver. Today Anny Latour recalls: "I saw them, the women, with their children, huddled on the floor, while the idiots in nearby cafés were shouting, 'We caught the Hitlerites!' Imagine, Jewish refugee Hitlerites!"

Anny Latour remembers the seventeenth and eighteenth of June 1940. "On the seventeenth, I heard Pétain and cried in despair. On the eighteenth, I heard de Gaulle, and cried for joy. As a Jew, I feared we would be in for very bad times. I packed and left Paris with my son, making my way south. Before deciding what action to take, I had to have a safe place for my child, and time to think." Anny found a place for her son, and found her place in a special Resistance: false papers and escape routes for Jews. In the next five years, Anny Lévy Latour and her friends would save some five thousand lives. Her first efforts were directed toward helping the Jews who had taken refuge in France: the Germans, Poles, Czechs, and Austrians. It was essential to get them new identities. Pétain's government issued its first anti-Semitic decree on July 7, a forerunner of what would come later. It ordered the immediate internment of foreign Jewish refugees in France. Within the year some twenty-five thousand Jews would be rounded up and interned. French concentration camps would be built in Le Vernet, Argelès, Rivesaltes, Gurs, and many other centers. The poet Aragon, writing about Gurs, called it "that peculiar syllable that sounds like a sob caught in the throat."

On July 17 Pétain's government decreed that all foreign-born Jews and the children of such Jews, even if native-born French, were excluded from holding official posts in the public administration. The high clergy of France did not react; instead the three senior cardinals of France—Gerlier, Baudrillard, and Suhard, the archbishop of Paris—addressed a note to Marshal Pétain asking him to abrogate the laic laws of the old Republic and promulgate new laws to provide state subsidies for religious schools.

On July 22 came a new decree revising the nationalization law of 1927. The decree provided a review of every nationalization since that date, with each individual case to be decided on its current merits. As a result some ten thousand Jews who had been French nationals for more than ten years were suddenly deprived of French citizenship, and thus subject to Hitler's anti-Semitic laws. Many of them rushed to obtain new identity cards or went into hiding, as had Anny Latour.

Another Jewish Resistance leader was a man named Jacques Lazarus, former lieutenant of infantry, a patriotic Frenchman born and raised in France, member of a family that had served France as soldiers since the Revolution. Jacques Lazarus had always thought of himself as a Frenchman first, a Frenchman of the Jewish faith, exactly the same as Frenchmen of the Catholic faith. He was, as most French Jews were, a thoroughly assimilated Frenchman.

Lazarus knew, of course, that most German Jews had felt exactly about Germany as he did about France. Never had they expected the savage attacks, the barbaric persecutions launched by Hitler. That sort of thing happened to Poles, to Russians, not to Germans. So they had thought. So too thought Joseph Lazarus. "It just cannot happen here, it can't, it can't," he muttered to himself, wondering for the first time whether it could.

Many Jews were to play a prominent role in various Resistance movements and networks. But Lazarus and some French Jews, particularly sensitive to the infamous charges that Jews were cowards and would not take up arms, preferred to fight in an exclusively Jewish fighting underground, the Organisation Juive de Combat, the OJC. Lazarus, patriotic Frenchman, officer of the French army, took that path when an anti-Semitic decree of the Pétain government stripped him of his commission and discharged him from the army.

There was another group besides the Jews that had a natural reason for rejecting the dishonorable terms of the armistice, and it was also highly capable of carrying on both public and clandestine missions of resistance: the French army. An army is not a revolutionary organization. The French army was one of the most conservative institutions of French life. Above all it had been trained to obey its superiors, and most officers revered Marshal Pétain. Nonetheless there were a number of French officers, like General Gabriel Cochet of the Fifth Army Air Force, who could not stomach Pétain's armistice broadcast and who hated the Germans enough to risk resistance to the supine capitulation of Pétain and Laval.

One such officer was a colonel named Rivet, who was in a particularly appropriate post to organize clandestine action: He was in charge of "Special Service," a euphemism for Intelligence and Counterespionage. In an article he wrote later for the "Special Services Bulletin," Rivet explained that "the first instructions we gave defined our general mission: The fight must go on, whatever happens. Not one voice on our team was raised to contest the sacred character of that mission."

Colonel Rivet stated that Intelligence and Counterespionage were necessary preludes to France's reentry into the war later on. In the meantime the information would go to the British and the American high commands, there being no doubt, in his mind, that America would soon enter the war. The intelligence information from his section would also go to the head of the Deuxième Bureau of the French general staff.

Counterespionage activities would be hidden under the cover of two sections: one called Menées Antinationales (MA, antinational activities) and one called Travaux Ruraux (TR, Rural Works). Their mission was to ferret out crimes of espionage and of treason, crimes against the state. There were, of course, organizations in Pétain's government and in the national police set up to do exactly that kind of work, but their definition of espionage and crimes against the state did not at all correspond to Colonel Rivet's definition of the same crimes.

Parallel to the clandestine activities of Rivet's group was another nucleus within the French army whose mission it was to prepare for a renewal of the armed struggle. It was set up by Colonel Mollard and called itself the CDM, the initials standing for Camouflage du Matériel. Even before the armistice was officially declared, the men in this group were preparing the camouflage of French matériel, arms, and even of tanks. This project began in the southern Alps, where the French army faced the Italians, a far less formidable foe than the Germans. Its purpose was to cache weapons for the day the French army could support an Allied landing.

The rudiments of an Allied Intelligence service began to function in the last days of June both outside and inside the French army. Foreign soldiers and officers who had been working with the French army, and refugees from Czechoslovakia, Poland, Austria, and Belgium who were German-speaking and, in some cases, had obtained employment with the Germans, gathered information on German troop movements and army, air force, and naval bases. They began passing that information on to London, either via Swiss business contacts or friendly diplomats accredited to the Pétain government but favorable to the Allies. The very first spy network, called Alibi, was created by Georges Charaudeau, a Frenchman with personal contacts with the Franco regime in Spain that permitted him to cross the border easily.

American diplomats, who had been working in the embassy of the United States in Paris, had moved with the French government from Tours to Bordeaux to Vichy. They made contact with a number of French officers and bureaucrats who opposed the new fascist French State of Marshal Pétain and were ready to work with the British and the Americans to subvert the regime. Their reports convinced Washington that Vichy would be an important listening post and espionage center and that it would be useful to build up a strong American presence there.

President Roosevelt, deeply concerned about the rapid collapse of the French, had sent an envoy to find out what had happened and to report back to him on the situation in England and on the Continent. The man he sent would later become the chief of the American Secret Service in the war, the organization called the Office of Strategic Services, OSS. He was William Donovan, one of America's most decorated soldiers of World War I. "Wild

Bill" was a nickname from his youth; he was anything but a wild man. At fifty-eight, stocky, gray-haired, William Joseph Donovan was a millionaire Wall Street lawyer, a conservative Republican and devout Irish Catholic. Some thought him a strange choice to direct America's operations in espionage, sabotage, guerrilla warfare, and all kinds of subversive activities.

Donovan's investigation of the European situation resulted in an alarming report to Roosevelt. He concluded that Hitler's blitzkrieg conquests of Poland, Norway, Belgium, Holland, Luxembourg, and France were "military masterpieces." Donovan explained the German strategy of mechanized, lightning war. He felt that German power and methods had made all other armies "obsolete."

Even more alarming was his finding that it was not German military superiority alone that produced German's lightning victories. Donovan concluded that it was internal political weakness that had brought down the European nations. He felt that France, with a great military tradition and a powerful armed force, was a tragic case in point. The French nation, Donovan told Roosevelt, had "cracked morally." Donovan reported that "new defeatist leaders sought to purchase the German's mercy, if not his respect, by supine submission to France's conquerors."

Donovan charged that France's high-ranking officers, wealthy industrialists, and prominent politicians had ceased to believe in democracy and freedom. They had lost faith in the Republic, preferring authoritarian regimes like Germany and Italy. They were more concerned about defending their privileges of wealth and power than the defense of France, preferred to make war on Russia rather than on Germany. All this had led to "one of the most contemptible surrenders on record."

Donovan's analysis of the fall of France corresponded almost exactly to the theories that had been put forward by French Communists and by many French liberal democrats who blamed the Right for the fall of France. These same accusations, coming from Donovan, a man of the Right, were taken seriously in Washington. His report deeply affected Roosevelt's views of France. The president came to believe that France was morally corrupt and decadent, and that most French high-ranking officers were fascists and potential dictators. It caused him to have little or no concern about a role for France in postwar Europe and colored his antagonism to General de Gaulle.

Roosevelt, despite Donovan's charges that Pétain's regime was pro-fascist, decided it would be useful to establish diplomatic relations with Vichy. He rationalized the move as one providing a useful "listening post" inside Nazi-occupied Europe. American diplomats could work with the French underground and pass vital military secrets on to the British. Churchill concurred in this view. British diplomats had been expelled when Pétain broke relations after Mers-el-Kebir.

Roosevelt also hoped that the Americans could stiffen Pétain's backbone and persuade him to make fewer concessions to Hitler. This was the rationale given to anti-fascist Americans who denounced Vichy inside the

United States and protested American diplomatic relations, particularly on a high level. Roosevelt would appoint a personal friend and high-ranking officer, Admiral William Leahy, as ambassador to Pétain. Leahy was anathema to American liberals who knew him to be a deeply conservative ideologue, suspected by the liberals of having fascist sympathies.

General de Gaulle and his followers were infuriated when the United States recognized Vichy as the legitimate government of France and refused to extend any recognition or direct aid to the Free French in London. Other captive European nations had governments-in-exile in London, with Allied recognition. Only France lived in isolation with a general who had no governmental authority and was thoroughly dependent upon British arms and British credits.

As the month of July drew to an end, the first month in the life of the new State of France, the Germans began expelling French citizens from Alsace and Lorraine and confiscating French assets in those provinces. Within a year some two hundred thousand French residents of Alsace-Lorraine would be expelled and take refuge in unoccupied France. The University of Strasbourg was reconstituted in Clermont-Ferrand by faculty members who had fled the German occupation. Clermont-Ferrand would become an important center of the French Resistance.

On August 1, the new "Grand Inquisitor" of the Vichy regime, the fascist-minded Minister of Justice, Rafael Albert, persuaded Pétain to sign a decree ordering the trial of those who had committed "crimes and those who had later aggravated the consequences of the situation thus created." "Crimes and offenses" were not defined, nor was there any definition of what was meant by a betrayal of duties. But the most monstrous charge was the last one: the charge of having "aggravated the situation." It would permit the prosecutor to charge anyone who had been in the government or the army during the war.

Those charged with these and other offenses included former premiers Paul Reynaud, Léon Blum, and Edouard Daladier, and former commander in chief General Gamelin. Former ministers Georges Mandel, Jean Zay, and others would also be brought to trial. Some would be court-martialed, charged as military men with desertion, particularly those who had gone to London. It was at this time, on August 2, that the court-martial declared General de Gaulle guilty and sentenced him to death.

De Gaulle received the news while he was negotiating with Churchill for a combatant status for his forces. On August 7, La France Libre —Free France—would become La France Combattante—Fighting France.

Pétain's police conducted a series of raids against clandestine groups. In the month of August they arrested 871 and charged them with clandestine activities, and seized thirty-five mimeograph machines and printing presses.

The more the fascist French and the Germans struck at the embryonic underground, the more rebels joined up. The end of the summer of

1940 and the last months of the year would see the embryo maturing. Henri Frenay would lay down the basic cellular structure of the movement that would become Combat. Georges Loustaunau-Lacau and Marie-Madeleine Fourcade would find each other again and create their remarkable espionage network. And on the broad esplanade of the Trocadéro, facing the Eiffel Tower across the Seine, a remarkable group of men and women on the staff of the Musée de l'Homme, the Museum of Man, were organizing the first resistance movement of intellectuals, scholars in arms.

PART TWO
UNDER THE NAZI BOOT

5
SCHOLARS
IN ARMS

Slowly, cautiously, by the hundreds, then the thousands and tens of thousands, the hordes of refugees who had fled Paris at the approach of the Germans began to come home. The rich, or those with substantial families south of the river Loire, stayed in that unoccupied zone of France policed by the regime of Marshal Pétain. But those who could not afford to build a new life, uprooted and lost without their familiar homes and jobs, began to move back to the capital despite their fears of living under German occupation.

In the summer of 1940 the Germans were still on their best behavior, except for some isolated instances of brutality. Stories of beatings and executions swiftly made the rounds and Parisians were careful to do nothing to provoke the Germans. There were, of course, exceptions to public prudence. Students wrote pro-de Gaulle slogans and anti-Nazi challenges on walls and posters. Mechanics punched tiny holes in gas and oil tanks on German vehicles. Sabotage was sporadic, but each successful coup encouraged others to greater efforts. These first acts of resistance were fragmentary, inchoate, but also inspirational, giving courage to those who watched with dismay the jackbooted Nazis parading through Paris.

Someone had printed little stickers and affixed them to the bumpers of German cars or on walls near German installations. They would say: "Back away from the Nazis." Subway riders would pick up a copy of a morning paper of the collaborationist press, with articles calling for participation in the New Order of Europe. But, inside, they would find mimeographed copies of de Gaulle's speech of June 18 calling on the French to resist.

One day toward the end of summer two retired colonels of the French army, Dutheil de la Rochère and Paul Hauet, heard that the Germans had destroyed, with sledgehammers and pickaxes, a statue of a World War I hero, General Mangin, who, they charged, had rounded up German women in special brothels for African soldiers. The two colonels went to a small square behind the Ecole de Guerre to view the wreckage.

They met at the pedestal of the broken statue and began to talk about the fall of France and the shameful capitulation of Pétain. A friendship immediately flowered. So did a common purpose: a resolution to resist the Germans. They knew an anthropologist, a certain Germaine Tillion, and went to talk of their newfound purpose with her. She promptly agreed to join with them to seek out other patriots willing to resist: Her mind immediately turned to the anti-Nazi scholars of the Musée de l'Homme. In fact there was already a blossoming movement in the Musée.

The Musée de l'Homme, the Museum of Man, was essentially the creation of anthropologist Paul Rivet, an authority on the American Indians, a celebrated personality, and an official of the city of Paris. The Musée de l'Homme was a complex of four museums: a navy museum, a museum of national monuments, another of popular arts and traditions, and, finally, its most prestigious museum, the heart and soul of Rivet's dream, the Musée de l'Homme. The complex is housed in two graceful pavilions separated by a vast open esplanade with a spectacular view of the Seine and the Eiffel Tower with the Ecole Militaire framed in its curved legs. Rivet and his scientific colleagues were anti-racist and anti-Nazi. All their teachings vigorously refuted the spurious Nazi theories of Aryan superiority.

Anthropologist Germaine Tillion was not a member of the staff of the Musée de l'Homme, but she did work with its members in seminars and knew of their contempt for the Nazis. She had attended meetings of an organization that Paul Rivet had created to fight Nazi propaganda. He called it the Vigilance Committee of Anti-Fascist Intellectuals. Among those intellectuals were some of his closest associates in the Musée de l'Homme: Anatole Lewitzky, Leo Kelley, Yvonne Oddon, and Boris Vildé.

Anatole Lewitzky worked closely with Paul Rivet and functioned as deputy director of the museum, although his official title was chief of the European-Asiatic Department. He was an expert on many aspects of Eurasian cultures in the fields of economics, sociology, religion, and law. He was also the world's foremost authority on Siberian shamanism. He himself was Russian-born and baptized in the Orthodox church. He had accompanied his family to Switzerland when they fled the Bolshevik Revolution. He then went on to Paris and, like so many "White Russians," earned his living by driving a taxi-cab. But he drove only at night and completed his university education by day. He took his degrees with honors, completed his military service, and became a French citizen and distinguished scholar.

Leo Kelley, whose nickname was Pat, was a big, amiable bear of an American from southern Illinois. "Pat" Kelley had been an American soldier in France in the First World War. Back home in Illinois, he became a successful bond salesman and made a fortune, which permitted him to pursue his true passion: prehistoric studies. He worked with France's master scholar in the field, Abbé Henri Breuil, achieved a reputation of his own, and became the Musée de l'Homme's expert on the Paleolithic period.

Yvonne Oddon ranked as one of France's leading specialists in a comparatively new field: modern library science. She had graduated from a pioneer American library school, that of the University of Michigan, at a time when few French people ever went to study at an American university, particularly in the Middle West. Yvonne Oddon, a tiny person in physical stature, like her equally tiny friend Germaine Tillion, was, like Germaine, a big brain with a big, brave heart. She was appointed head librarian of the Musée de l'Homme when it opened its doors. She would be a key figure in its fight against the Nazis.

Finally, there was Boris Vildé, a handsome young man, a gifted linguist, who would emerge as the leader of the museum's Resistance movement. He was a protégé of Anatole Lewitzky, and like him, Russian-born. A passionate anti-Nazi, Vildé was, ironically, the ideal "Aryan" type: tall, blond, with bright, clear blue eyes and fair skin. At thirty, his gracefulness, his warm smile, his easy self-confidence attracted men as well as women and made him a natural leader.

Vildé had been born in St. Petersburg and had gone to school there. In his youth, he organized, only as a joke, a so-called separatist movement for Livonia province. The Stalinist officials had no sense of humor. Vildé was imprisoned for anti-Soviet activity. He was released in 1930 and left Russia for Berlin. There he was active as a young, radical anti-Nazi, and was again arrested and imprisoned. He left Germany in 1932, foreseeing Hitler's rise to power.

Lewitzky and Vildé soon became fast friends and confidants. As Russian émigrés, with more knowledge than the other scholars about the political situation in Europe, they were drawn together in a mutual hatred of both Stalin and Hitler. They were certain that war was coming and that France would be drawn into it. Vildé, more the man of action than Lewitzky, told his older friend that they must plan for action when war broke out, particularly to counter the demoralizing propaganda of the French Right. They knew that their director, Paul Rivet, was a fervent anti-Nazi and that he would help them. However, Rivet had gone off to Colombia, whose government had asked him to create for them a museum of ethnography. Any action by the Musée would have to await his return. Meanwhile preparations could go forward.

Vildé knew that in the cellar of the Musée de l'Homme there was a mimeograph machine that Rivet had used to put out manifestos distributed by the Vigilance Committee of Anti-Fascist Intellectuals. He put it to work again to turn out single sheets denouncing nazism and supporting democracy. He was helped by Yvonne Oddon, Pat Kelley, and other colleagues. Lewitzky drafted and corrected the sheets. The war had not yet broken out, and they could work in the open; it was good training for the work they would later do underground.

Working as a part-time typist in the secretarial pool of the Musée de l'Homme was a young woman in her twenties named Jacqueline Bordelet. She was fragile but elegant, with huge, violent eyes. Men wanted to put their arms around her and protect her from a harsh world. The American, Leo "Pat" Kelley, had passed her in the hall and immediately turned around and set off after her.

Pat had a large apartment in Paris that he offered to share with the Bordelet family when Jacqueline told him that her mother was terrified of German air raids and their house had no cellar. Pat's apartment house had everything the Bordelets needed, while he, himself, only needed and wanted Jacqueline.

When the Germans arrived at the gates of Paris, Pat Kelley took the Bordelet family and conducted them all to safety in the south. It was then that he discovered that his visa to France had run out. He rushed to Vichy to obtain new papers and was turned down. He had to leave France. His parting from Jacqueline was brief and unemotional, for he was certain he would obtain a new visa and return soon. He was wrong. He would not return until the war was over.

In the summer of 1940 Jacqueline returned to her secretarial job in the museum. Boris Vildé and Anatole Lewitzky had not yet returned from the front. Yvonne Oddon had long since moved out of her apartment in central Paris and was living in Anatole Lewitzky's basement office, where she slept on a couch. The director, Paul Rivet, had returned from Colombia and resumed his post. Before long, Jacqueline began to wonder about the strangers who kept coming in to ask Yvonne Oddon to give them English lessons. Jacqueline knew full well that Yvonne had never been an English teacher. She particularly noted the frequency of visits by two American women, Josie Meyer and Penelope Royall, who were on the staff of the American Embassy. They were not doing research at the library, but they were certainly holding many private meetings with Yvonne. The American Embassy was officially neutral in the war, but individual diplomats were not.

Jacqueline remembered conversations she had had with a friend and neighbor, the anthropologist Germaine Tillion, who had told her that "something must be done against the German occupation." She wondered whether that was what Yvonne was doing, some kind of anti-German clandestine activity.

She went to Yvonne and said she would like to help in "your other work." Yvonne at first pretended she did not understand what Jacqueline was talking about, then, finally, told her that she was too young. Jacqueline, indignant, told Yvonne that she was twenty-seven, even though she looked eighteen. Yvonne would not deal with her, but Jacqueline would find others who would, until finally her colleagues at the Musée de l'Homme would bring her into their network.

Vildé returned to Paris in July and moved back into his basement office next to where Yvonne Oddon was living. He was immediately aware of her strange phone calls and meetings, and long absences from her desk. He walked in on her, smiling, and said: "Would you like to give me English lessons?" She smiled back and held out her hand to him. They talked for hours about ways and means of making contact with London, of collecting military information that could help de Gaulle and the British. They discussed plans to write, print, and distribute propaganda tracts denouncing the French collaborationists and the German occupants. The movement of the Musée de l'Homme entered its first planning phase with Vildé and Oddon. They began sounding out others on the staff, while impatiently awaiting the return from the army of their friend and mentor, Anatole Lewitzky.

A good friend of Yvonne Oddon, historian Agnès Humbert, who had been sent to Limoges to store valuable artifacts, returned to her post at the Musée des Arts et Traditions Populaires—also in the Palais Chaillot—in July. She was sickened by what she found. Books by second-rate German writers were on her library shelves. Books by first-rate Jewish writers had been mutilated or removed. The museum offices and corridors were swarming with society ladies talking of their intimate connections with the Pétain regime. They hailed a "rejuvenated" France—oblivious to the irony of rejuvenation by an octogenarian leader. The Musée des Arts director received and entertained German officers; posters announced that the visit to the museum was free to German soldiers. Agnès Humbert cured her sickness at this scene by a strong dose of rage. She was determined to take some action against this shame.

She went to tell her troubles to an old friend, Jean Cassou, former director of the Luxembourg and Compiègne museums, recently appointed director of the Museum of Modern Art, not associated with her museum but a close colleague in the field. Cassou had replaced the former director, who had been promoted to head all national museums in place of a Jew who had been removed for "racial reasons." Cassou's wife was Jewish and he felt his own days were numbered. He had discussed the situation with an educator, Marcel Abraham, and with his old friend Claude Aveline. The three of them had decided to form a group to write and distribute anti-Nazi and anti-Vichy propaganda, and had asked Agnès Humbert to join them. Claude Aveline was a Jew, a writer of poetry and children's books. He had been a close friend of Anatole France and was well known in literary circles.

Aveline, Abraham, and Humbert were all enthusiastic about Cassou's plan. They knew they would have a hard time, for it was very difficult to get typewriters, mimeograph machines, paper, ink. The Germans, already aware of the existence of clandestine tracts and papers, were keeping a close watch on all sales of materials that could be used for propaganda. But the four learned plotters decided to call in six more friends, into a group of ten, who would pool ideas and resources and find the way. In addition to propaganda tracts they planned to put out an underground newspaper, to be called *Résistance*, and assigned Claude Aveline to do the planning and to be the editor.

As a cover for their activities they formed a literary club, which they called Les Amis d'Alain-Fournier. Alain-Fournier's classic books were published by the Emile-Paul brothers, who were also publishers of Aveline's works. The publishers allowed them to meet and to work in their offices. Since they spent a lot of time listening to the BBC and particularly to Maurice Schumann and the broadcasters of the Free French in London, Aveline dubbed his group the "Free French in France." Although they were serious people, and their actions risked prison and death, they looked upon it also as a lark, a gay adventure for cultured men and women who had always led a cloistered life. Cassou and others would say years later: "We did not slink about in cloaks and daggers, looking grim. We laughed a lot and felt younger than we had in years."

Early in August, Anatole Lewitzky was discharged from the army and came back to Paris and the Musée de l'Homme, moving back to his basement office next to Vildé's. Yvonne moved back to her library. The three of them became the closest of friends as they discussed plans for anti-German action.

Without any particular thought about it, Yvonne told them one day that the museum had donated furniture for a French soldiers' club in the Grand Palais and that the arrogant Germans had moved in and taken over the club for their own troops.

"Maybe we ought to get it back," Lewitzky remarked, more in jest than in seriousness.

But Vildé thought it an excellent idea. "Let's go," he said, jumping up excitedly. They ran downstairs, got the museum's panel truck, and went racing down to the Grand Palais.

With grim faces and a solemn air of authority, knowing the German submissiveness to authority, they strode into the club, dressed only in sports shirts and slacks but behaving as though they were in full-dress uniform. A few German soldiers were sitting about the lounge, reading magazines, listening to the radio.

Vildé, who spoke fluent, Berlin-accented German, bellowed out "*Achtung!*" with all the flair of a Nazi majordomo.

The German soldiers jumped out of their chairs to stiff attention.

"Take the furniture out to the truck. This table. That chair." Vildé strutted around, gesticulating as he gave instructions. The Germans knew an officer with a commanding presence when they heard one, in civvies or not. They jumped to obey Vildé's orders, and in minutes the job was done.

Vildé and Lewitzky drove off in their loaded truck, exploding with laughter.

It was a fool thing to do, a silly prank that could have cost them dearly without any real result. But it did serve a major purpose. It opened up a valve, letting them blow off their deep frustration and resentment at what had happened to this France they loved and that had given them refuge in freedom. Once the steam had blown off, they could settle down to a more sober assessment of what had to be done. They trusted each other, made an excellent team. It was time then to put the team into action.

The three friends and colleagues drew up a program for action. In addition to anti-Nazi propaganda, they would collect information on German military installations and the political situation in France. They would learn how to sabotage German operations and French collaboration with the Germans. They would not only organize their own movement with their own friends, but would cast out lines to other groups and unify their efforts for maximum effect.

It was understood without discussion that Vildé would be the chief of the movement, with Lewitzky and Oddon as principal aides. Their precise functions would define themselves in action.

One of their first recruits was a colleague at the museum, René Creston. He introduced them to an old friend, Albert Jubineau, who had formed an antioccupation group at the Palais de Justice, composed of attorneys, judges, and law clerks. Jubineau and Vildé agreed to coordinate their activities. The movement was growing rapidly.

René Creston made three trips to Brittany to attempt to find a way to contact London. In the course of his trips, he recruited friends in Saint-Nazaire who had access to the German submarine base. They drew up plans and maps of the port and base, particularly of a water-locks system vulnerable to British bombing. Creston passed the documents on to the Musée de l'Homme. Vildé had found British agents and Frenchmen en route to England who carried the documents to London. Inevitably, the Germans intercepted some of the couriers and the Gestapo began looking for the group that had obtained the secret information.

Paul Rivet's secretary, Marie-Louise Joubier, agreed to be the typist and mimeograph operator for the clandestine operations of the group. She had to work secretly in the basement, for German soldiers and officers were constantly trooping through the corridors or wandering into the offices of the museum.

They found an excellent "letter box" in the shop of one Madame Templier, in Auteuil. She sold religious books and articles, most innocent-looking. At least it had become innocent after Penelope Royall of the American Embassy walked by and saw a picture of General de Gaulle in the window. She rushed in and warned Madame Templier that what she was doing was dangerous and useless. Instead of an empty gesture, she would be able to protest the paganism of the "unchristian" Nazis, whom she hated, by receiving letters, messages, and documents left by agents of the movement. It was just the right place for undercover operations.

By early fall, Vildé had his own organization staffed and structured, with connections to other groups, including Jubineau's at Justice and that of Colonels Hauet and de la Rochère, whose contact was Germaine Tillion.

Colonel de la Rochère had needed a place to work quietly on intelligence reports that he, Colonel Hauet, and other resistants were putting together: German military plans, maps of air bases and seaports, new German construction projects, key generators and cable lines. It had to be a place where the Germans would not think of looking. Someone told him to go to see a woman with a most promising name, Espérance—"Hope"—Blain, who worked at the Office of Special Instruction of the city school system. The colonel was told that she would certainly be helpful.

She was. Madame Blain was one of the first and most effective of French Resistance rebels against the New Order.

Her work had begun shortly after the armistice, when a young man came to ask her for help. He had deserted from his army unit to avoid being taken prisoner and needed a false identity card. He had brought with him a blank form that he had bought at a department store. Citizens were supposed to fill out the cards with name, address, and photo and get them stamped at a police station. He had his ready, all filled out, and with his picture attached, but he did not dare go to the police with a false identity. What he needed was an official stamp. A friend had told him that Madame Blain was resourceful and patriotic.

Madame Blain obliged. She took the stamp of the director of primary education and twisted it as she pressed it on his card, just enough to blur the letters. Then she took it to a police station and said she had found it in the street. They looked at it, thanked her for turning it in, and promised to give it to the owner when he showed up. She watched carefully as they checked the card, noting that they accepted the false, blurred stamp. That was what she wanted to know. From then on she satisfied a big demand for false cards.

Soon Madame Blain was falsifying demobilization papers for soldiers. Then she recruited a team of ten dear old ladies, sweet and innocent as cotton candy, who became the most proficient thieves of ration cards at the town halls of Paris. It was, after that, no problem for Madame Blain to enter Colonel de la Rochère's name on the ledger as an inspector general of instruction, obtain a building pass for him, and give him a small room, where each day he would copy out his intelligence information and then pass it on to a network of couriers carrying documents to Switzerland and Spain.

It was inevitable that Espérance Blain would be caught. Practically everyone in the Resistance was eventually arrested by the French police or the German Gestapo. Some escaped and carried on, but the majority suffered torture, deportation, concentration camps, and death. Madame Blain was one of the lucky ones. A French judge, sympathetic to the cause, had arranged to have a doctor certify her as mentally disturbed and not responsible for her acts. She was dismissed and told to cease her activities. She went to live with a friend and was never questioned again. Her work was taken up by others, including the Musée de l'Homme group, which was particularly active in false identity cards.

Other writers and scholars were producing propaganda sheets and pamphlets. Essayist Jean Texcier wrote a brochure giving the French advice on how to behave under occupation. It was witty, sharp, and sarcastic and enjoyed an immediate success. People read it, copied it, and sent it around like a chain letter. Political wit is particularly effective in France and it is a very special gift to make people laugh in the most desperate of days.

A number of jokes and pranks made their way around France. One had Hitler desperate to find a means to cross the Channel and invade Britain. Someone told him that a rabbi knew the secret of Moses and how he led the Hebrews dry-shod across the Red Sea. Hitler summoned the chief rabbi of Berlin and demanded to know if the secret did exist. The rabbi assured him it did. It is, he said, a magic wand that God gave Moses. Where is it, shouted Hitler? Tell me where I can get it and I'll release a thousand Jews. It is, said the rabbi, in the British Museum.

A bookstore on the Avenue de l'Opéra indulged its sense of humor and contempt for Vichy somewhat dangerously. It put in its window a framed portrait of Marshal Pétain, with a sign attached: *"Vendu,"* Sold Out. Yet another bookstore displayed pictures of Hitler and Pétain and then put next to the portraits two volumes of Victor Hugo's famous work, with a big sign, *"Les Misérables."*

Students at the Sorbonne began to write and distribute propaganda tracts denouncing Vichy and the Germans. Young Roger Morais posted handwritten pamphlets on the walls of the university and its library. Christian Rizo, a Communist student, began printing and distributing anti-German tracts. The police caught him and sentenced him to two months in prison. On leaving prison, he went underground and founded a movement that became one of the major organizations of the French Resistance, the Communist-led Francs-Tireurs et Partisans Français.

In many cases motivation for Frenchmen and women to oppose the Germans came at first from the plight of French and British prisoners of war. In the summer of 1940, before the Germans were able to organize trains to take the prisoners off to Germany, it was relatively easy to escape from loosely guarded detention centers. The real problem was not to break out of internment, but to get civilian clothes and false papers that would enable the escapees to remain at large. In the case of the British, it was necessary to find English-speaking guides. Rescue missions were therefore created to help the thousands of men escaping from the centers.

One of the most successful of these rescue teams was located in the town of Béthune and was headed by a woman, Sylvette Leleu, owner and manager of a garage. The business had been built by her husband, who had been killed while flying a reconnaissance mission over the German lines during the *drôle de guerre*. Madame Leleu had grown up hating the *Boche*, for Béthune had been occupied by the Germans in the First World War. In this, the second one, her husband had been killed by them, leaving her widowed with two small sons. She would do anything against the Germans.

Sylvette sent her sons to live with their grandmother. She turned her house over as a shelter to prisoners on the run, and used cars from her garage to transport escapees. She worked closely with a nun, Sister Marie-Laurence, who was an Irishwoman from County Cork, and with Madame Angèle Tardiveau, a café owner in town. Sister Marie-Laurence was a nurse with official access to the prison camp. Madame Tardiveau supplied food for the escapees. Sylvette drove them on to other contacts who would move them south to Spain. It was an efficient operation that rescued hundreds of men.

Working as a bookkeeper in Sylvette Leleu's garage was a young man named René Senéchal. He was eager to go to London to join General de Gaulle. Madame Leleu gave him the name of a man in an automobile agency in Paris who might, she thought, tell him how to get to London. Senéchal went off to Paris, met the man, who said he did not, himself, know how to help, but he gave René the name of another man who definitely would know. The man was Boris Vildé, the language specialist of the Musée de l'Homme.

Vildé told René that he could get to London via Madrid, but that meanwhile there was work to be done in France. He tested him on a few missions, found him reliable and brave, and began using him as a guide to escort French, British, Dutch, and Polish soldiers and agents across the demarcation line between the occupied zone in the north of France and the unoccupied zone in the south. Senéchal forgot all about going to London. He was proud to work in an escape net and delighted to have introduced and brought together the two people he most admired, Boris Vildé and Madame Leleu.

All these men and women, individually and in separate but cooperating movements, were working to counter the German occupation in that year of defeat, 1940. Boris Vildé extended his connections from Paris down to Vichy, Toulouse, Bordeaux, and Marseille. Conscious of the need for secrecy, he wrote nothing down, keeping all names and addresses in his remarkable brain and keeping them to himself. If anyone else were picked up and questioned by the police, they could tell nothing.

Vildé took on the code name of Maurice. Lewitzky became Chazalle.

Director Paul Rivet felt the need for action as keenly as any of his staff at the musée. He risked his position, even his freedom, by sending Marshal Pétain an open letter, with copies to leading politicians and newspaper editors. In it, Rivet warned the chief of state that he was deceiving himself in the belief that the country was completely behind him. Pétain did not reply and Rivet was fortunate that there was no reaction.

As director of the Musée de l'Homme, Rivet thought it more prudent not to work closely with his own staff in Resistance activities. Rivet, without telling Vildé at first, was busy working with Claude Aveline and his friends in their group, the "Free French in France." In September, Museum of Arts Director Jean Cassou and his wife held a meeting of the group in their home. Marcel Abraham told them that he expected to be fired from his teaching position in a purge of Jews. He brought them a packet of American and Swiss papers that he had picked up at the American Embassy, along with a number of documents, flyers, slogans, and stickers to be copied and reproduced in various forms. Agnès Humbert was there, along with the publishers, the Emile-Pauls, and Claude Aveline.

Cassou told the group of his meetings with Rivet at the Musée de l'Homme. He said they could use Rivet's mimeograph machine, on which he had already run off one hundred copies of Rivet's open letter to Pétain. Cassou had also finally met and been impressed with Vildé. He proposed to his small group that they cooperate with Vildé's. They agreed and named Agnès Humbert to be liaison agent to her neighbors across the esplanade.

Meanwhile Vildé's group had recruited a few more agents, including a fisherman in Brittany who was able to sail the Channel. By now they also had a safe-house on the way to Spain, and a radio link to London. Vildé and the Musée de l'Homme resistants were ready for a major effort.

6
SECRET AGENTS
AND STUDENT REBELS

In the summer of 1940 the Germans began digging in powerful occupation forces in the north of France and particularly all along the Channel coast facing England. In the south, the old marshal was setting up his satellite regime in Vichy. Both General de Gaulle and Winston Churchill knew that it was urgent to move secret agents into France before the Nazi grip would be too tight to break. But instead of coordinating with each other, they made separate plans to set up their own intelligence services, each wanting to control the vital information that the agents would ferret out.

On July 16 and 17, each man made his move in a rivalry that would provoke bitter conflicts all through the war. On July 16 Winston Churchill asked his minister of economic warfare, Hugh Dalton, to set up an organization for espionage and sabotage against Vichy and the Nazis. On the very next day, General de Gaulle gave orders to send his first agent into France.

Dalton created an organization that he called the Special Operations Executive, SOE, for overall European intelligence activities. It included a French section headed up by a resourceful businessman, Maurice Buckmaster, former manager of Ford, France. Buckmaster set up a training school for spies and saboteurs in the English countryside. He recruited many Frenchmen who wanted to fight on against the Germans, but who for one reason or another did not want to serve under de Gaulle. He also recruited a great number of French-speaking Englishmen. Within a few weeks Buckmaster sent a mixed Anglo-French team into France with instructions to set up a Resistance network of their own. His agents would soon find Commandant Loustaunau-Lacau and Marie-Madeleine Fourcade and recruit their services for the SOE. Loustaunau-Lacau had been a classmate of de Gaulle in Saint-Cyr, and his "defection" to the British would infuriate the proud leader of Free France.

Buckmaster's student spies and saboteurs were housed in a stately country house in the green fields of Kent. A high fence and armed guards kept prying eyes from scenes of men attacking each other on the lawn once used for cricket. Paired off into attack and defense duos, the student-agents smashed at each other with clubs, slashed with wooden knives, punched, kicked, and rolled around like wrestling bears. Tough sergeants ran them around the lawn in thick wool uniforms in the July heat, with twenty-pound packs on their shoulders. One by one, men would fall exhausted or faint in the sun. They would be doused with a bucket of cold water while the sergeant screamed: "Defend yourself or you're dead." Then, barely able to stand up, they would be marched off to the showers and be told to be ready in ten minutes for classroom work. Until late in the night they would learn the mysteries of Morse telegraphy, of secret codes and invisible inks, and the care and use of carrier pigeons.

General de Gaulle owned no country houses in Kent. He had no training fields and no corps of tough combat sergeants to beat his recruits into shape. Indeed de Gaulle had almost no facilities at all, and none that were his own. He had first lived with his wife in the elegant but very civilian Hotel Connaught, where he could fly no flag and show no visible signs of authority. Later Churchill would make a small house available to him. De Gaulle's offices in Carlton Gardens were located in a small town house, very old London, with dark wood paneling, library shelves, a billiard room, a tiny garden in the rear —a handsome dwelling for a couple doing the London season, but not the kind of setting that corresponded to the notions of grandeur and dignity of the man named Charles André Joseph Marie de Gaulle. His very name was too big to fit into his office.

De Gaulle depended totally upon the British for everything. His communications were run by the British. His office expenses and the salaries of his aides were paid by a British stipend that Churchill had provided for Free France. This dependency served to reinforce his determination to remain politically independent of his ally. Despite his poverty of means, in fact *because* of his weakness, de Gaulle became each day more obstinate, more intransigent in his dealings with the British. Years later when Anthony Eden, Churchill's foreign secretary, who admired de Gaulle, asked him why he had never been flexible enough to yield on any point, de Gaulle replied: "We were too weak to yield. Only the strong can afford to bow their heads."

De Gaulle was not the only man in the Free French group who was proud, self-centered, arrogant by temperament and by necessity. Claude Hettier de Boislambert, de Gaulle's chief of Cabinet, absorbed into his psyche his leader's courage and indomitable spirit.

All the men around de Gaulle were combat-blooded, fiercely patriotic, and willful men. General Jacques-Philippe de Hautecloque, who took the name Leclerc to protect his family still living inside France, was a lean, dry, and dour man of powerful inner resources. De Gaulle would name him later to train and command an armored division for the invasion of France. Never for a moment did de Gaulle or Leclerc doubt that the Allies would mount a tremendous force to breach Hitler's Atlantic Wall and liberate France.

Among the war veterans was the former commando from the ill-timed invasion of Norway, Captain André Dewavrin. Tall, blond, with eyes the color and coldness of steel, Dewavrin was physically strong and fearless. He had a sharp, quick mind and a ruthless personality. He would let nothing and no one stand in the way of his goals. He would become one of the most influential and most hated men in de Gaulle's service, feared by his own colleagues, constantly in conflict with the men of the Resistance, to whom he would send orders as though they were private soldiers in an army in which he was a commanding general.

In mid-July de Gaulle selected Dewavrin as the officer for the all-important Deuxième Bureau of his command. Dewavrin created an agency that would be the rival of the British SOE and that would engage in competition with his Allies and with his fellow countrymen inside France in the Resistance movements. He called the agency the Bureau Central de Renseignements et d'Action, the BCRA. In his mind "Renseignements" meant espionage and "Action" meant sabotage, the same mission given to Buckmaster and his SOE.

Dewavrin's first recruit was Gilbert Renault, the moviemaker. Renault knew more about espionage and sabotage than his chief, Dewavrin. He had toured the coastal villages of the Channel and the Atlantic in June, had noted German units at anchor. Renault had taken down the names of men who might serve later as the eyes and ears of an espionage network. Before leaving Madrid, where he had gone to shoot a movie, Renault had talked to an old friend who functioned as consul of France. The friend agreed at once to become a "letter-drop" for confidential communications. Renault believed it would be necessary to create a network of people whose occupations gave them justifiable reasons to travel through France and to move from the occupied to the unoccupied zone, people who could obtain official passes and become underground couriers. He knew a prominent Paris lawyer, with clients throughout the country, who agreed to play that role.

Dewavrin eagerly offered Renault an assignment to be his secret agent in France and to create the networks needed. The first code name he was given was Raymond, but it was soon changed to Rémy and it was as Colonel Rémy that Renault would carry out his exploits. Sir Claude Dansey, one of the chiefs of the British Secret Service, called Rémy "the greatest secret agent I have ever known," high praise from a man against whose own networks Rémy would be competing for the next five years.

Renault went into specialized training, learning codes and struggling with the chemical mysteries of invisible ink—a skill he would never quite master. While he was training, another agent was chosen to become the very first to go to France from headquarters in London. His name was Jacques Mansion—code name Jack. He had been chosen because of his detailed knowledge of the Brittany coast.

Jack set out on the seventeenth of July, but conditions were not right and he could not land at his target site. Two days later French fishermen who had sailed over to Britain under cover of night joined up with the Free

French "Navy." They agreed to make another attempt to put Jack into France. They sailed in their frail craft and with no difficulty at all dropped him off near the Cap de la Chèvre, in Brittany. Jack's pockets were stuffed with a hundred and more questions that Dewavrin and the Deuxième Bureau had prepared for him. They wanted to know everything, from the price of herring to the location of German submarine pens. He would return to London in September, his pockets and briefcase bulging with answers.

In the weeks that followed, during the most beautiful summer in decades, French agents sailed regularly to the coasts of Brittany and Normandy. The weather was perfect, the stormy Channel was for once calm; French fishing boats provided an excellent cover and German patrols were not yet familiar with the coastal waters and not yet alerted to the existence of a spy network.

At the end of the month of July, Churchill, suspecting that the first Luftwaffe mass air raids were the opening round in a German campaign to invade England, became alarmed at the almost total lack of information his own agents were providing about German preparations. The invasion would almost certainly have to come from the Normandy coast, which was close to Britain and offered the best harbors and beaches for the launching of an invasion fleet. Churchill asked de Gaulle if the Free French could find out what was happening.

General de Gaulle was delighted. This was exactly the kind of request he had long been hoping for, a chance for Free France to demonstrate its usefulness as an ally. He instructed Dewavrin to get the information that Churchill wanted, and he made it clear that the mission was of the greatest importance for the future of Free France.

Dewavrin called in a comrade-in-arms from the Norway campaign, a powerful giant of a man named Maurice Duclos. A native of Ouistreham, he had sailed the waters of the Norman coast all his life, and knew every cove, every strip of beach of the coast of Normandy. Duclos said that he would carry out his mission to explore German preparations on the coast, but that then he would like to go on to Paris. He claimed he had many patriotic and brave friends there who would join him in setting up a Free French network in the capital and in surrounding departments.

Dewavrin, eager to get his espionage networks into operation, agreed to Duclos's plan. However, since Churchill needed the intelligence on German preparations urgently, another soldier, who had been in the Norway campaign with them, was assigned to accompany Duclos. His name was Boris Beresnikoff. He was instructed to return to London by speedboat with the information, while Duclos would go on to Paris. Duclos proposed that their code names be taken from stations of the Paris subway system, the Métro. Duclos became Saint-Jacques. Beresnikoff became Corvisart and Captain Dewavrin became Passy.

For the next three days, the new secret agents "went to school," learning how to code and decode messages, how to mix and apply invisible ink and how to make it visible; finally they were given a flock of homing pigeons, which they would use for sending daily intelligence back to England.

The mission ran into trouble as soon as it reached the French coast at dawn on August 4. The speedboat that had dropped them off in a rubber dinghy about two miles off the coast at Saint-Aubin had been spotted by a coastal patrol. Saint-Jacques and Corvisart managed to row to the beach, sink their dinghy, and escape inland before the patrol could catch them. But in the haste of their escape they abandoned the cages of homing pigeons, hastily hiding them behind a big rock.

In London everyone waited anxiously for the first pigeon to arrive. None came. Later they learned that Saint-Jacques came back every day to recover the pigeons, but was stymied each time by a guard patrolling the beach near the rock where he had hidden the birds. Meanwhile he had been busy during the day and night making his way along the Normandy coast, observing German bases. He had compiled a detailed map of enemy emplacements and personnel, exactly what Churchill wanted. He gave it to Corvisart to take back to London when the speedboat picked him up.

On August 8 Passy sent the speedboat to get Corvisart. For once the weather, otherwise perfect that summer, turned against the Allies. Fog rolled in and smothered the Norman coast. They tried again and failed again the next day. Passy was now convinced that his agents had been caught. But he kept sending the boat at scheduled intervals. Corvisart was there each time; he even heard the motor of the British launch, but could not see its signals through the nightly fog. By the thirtieth of August Passy gave up and wrote the mission off as a failure. By then, Churchill had received a detailed set of reconnaissance photos of the coast and a number of reports from other espionage sources.

The failure of the Saint-Jacques mission did not discourage Passy. Duclos in fact had not failed; he had gone on to Paris where he had set up a central command post for an underground network. He had recruited agents in Rouen, in various Norman cities, in the Pas de Calais and the Somme. He had also contacted a major who had excellent personal relations with officers of the Gendarmerie. Messages were getting through to London, not by carrier pigeon but by fishermen, or by businessmen traveling to Geneva or Madrid.

French journalists in London watched closely as de Gaulle put his staff together, guessing at his operation, trying to decide whether to join, to ask others to join, or to remain aloof. They were disturbed by the presence of men like Maurice Duclos and Captain Pierre Fourcaud in Passy's service. They were prewar members of a French fascist organization called La Cagoule. The "Cagoule" was a hooded cape, very much the same kind of symbol used by the American Ku Klux Klan. Its leaders cooperated with Mussolini's secret police and the Cagoule was responsible for assassinations and other crimes in France during the thirties. Duclos made no secret of and no apology for his membership in the Cagoule. His wing of the organization had always been anti-German, even though another wing was fanatically and notoriously pro-Nazi. Passy cared nothing about their politics so long as they hated the Germans and were not Communists.

Liberal reporters, suspicious of de Gaulle, angered by the presence of Cagoulards in Free France, spread damaging stories about Passy's secret service and his headquarters at the "Little House on Duke Street," where, it was alleged, French patriots were tortured, even killed if they refused to join de Gaulle. There was absolutely no evidence to back these charges, but they damaged de Gaulle's movement severely and gave President Roosevelt and Secretary of State Cordell Hull reasons to refuse to recognize de Gaulle as the leader of a French government-in-exile.

While General de Gaulle and his staff were struggling for recognition in London and for an implantation of its networks in France and in the empire, Marshal Pétain, by a series of fascist decrees, was beginning to alienate even some of those who had so long revered his name. The outrageous behavior of Vichy and the Germans made it easier for the first resistants to recruit new volunteers for clandestine action.

The Vichy government pushed forward a campaign to indict former leaders of France for the disaster of the war and the defeat. The special Supreme Court at Riom, created for that purpose, opened its hearings on September 5, with the prosecutor demanding the indictment of Guy La Chambre and Pierre Cot, former ministers of the air. The next day police imprisoned former Premier Paul Reynaud and Interior Minister Georges Mandel. By the end of the month Léon Blum had been arrested, while Edouard Daladier and General Gamelin were also cited by the prosecutor, who called for their indictment.

Meanwhile new fighting broke out. The British navy, with Free French units participating, staged an attempted landing at the port of Dakar on September 23. The Anglo-Free French assault was beaten back by French defenders. It was a serious setback for General de Gaulle, in an ill-conceived project that had been strenuously opposed by his own African expert Claude de Boislambert. On that same September 23, the Japanese attacked French outposts in Dong Dang and Than Moi in Vietnam and overran them. Three days later the invaders captured Lang Son and landed two thousand commandos in the port of Haiphong. French Indochina was falling into Japanese hands.

On September 27, the Rome-Berlin-Tokyo Pact was signed in Berlin. In Washington, President Roosevelt conferred with members of the Joint Chiefs. He feared that America could be cut off by Japan in the Pacific and by the Nazis in the Atlantic, isolated inside a giant global pincers.

Socialist party leaders Vincent Auriol, Jules Moch, and Marx Dormoy were arrested and interned on September 26. The French State was rapidly becoming the fascist state that Pierre Laval had called for in his speech to the National Assembly in July. Laval himself was becoming the Gray

Eminence behind Pétain's throne in Vichy. Each arrest of a prewar leader would provoke a number of Frenchmen to join a Resistance movement. Posters began appearing in the Paris region warning the public of severe punishment for sabotage. The threats did not stop constant cutting of telephone cables in the Paris region.

The Germans in the occupied zone issued a decree on September 27 prohibiting all refugees in the unoccupied zone from returning to their homes in the north if they professed the Jewish faith or had more than two Jewish grandparents. Vichy, a week later, followed in the steps of its Nazi masters by depriving all Algerian Jews of French citizenship. Many of these families had been French for half a century.

Colonel Passy kept sending agents over to France. He was not, however, the only one of de Gaulle's men engaged in this activity, although he thought he was and logically should have been. But a number of strong-willed men on de Gaulle's staff had ideas of their own. One of them was de Boislambert, who took it upon himself to dispatch an agent without informing Passy— a major error, for, if queried by the Resistance, Passy would not be able to validate the agent, who might be taken for a Vichy spy.

The man de Boislambert chose was André Weil-Curiel, code name Dubois. He was a lawyer, accredited to the bar of Paris. He was a militant Socialist on the left wing of the party, but also an enthusiastic follower of General de Gaulle and his concept of a Free France in the Allied ranks. Like de Boislambert and Serreulles, he had been a liaison officer with the British and had been evacuated at Dunkirk. The mission given him by de Boislambert was to find out how many Gaullists there were in France, and to recruit and organize patriots for service to de Gaulle.

To have a better cover for his activities, Weil-Curiel decided not to enter France by clandestine means but rather officially. He opted for repatriation, professing to have had a change of heart and wanting to leave de Gaulle's ranks. It was a risky procedure, and he would always be suspect in Vichy. But he felt it was less risky and certainly more practical than trying to operate underground. He arrived in the south of France in August and immediately made a number of important contacts.

In Toulouse, Weil-Curiel found Suzanne and Georges Buisson and Andrée Marty-Capgras, loyal Socialist militants. They were deeply suspicious of de Gaulle, who seemed to most militants of the Left to be a man of the Right, a general on a white horse with the aristocratic *de* before his name, a militarist and a royalist, not a democrat. Weil-Curiel told them that de Gaulle could be trusted, the more so if enough Socialists and democrats joined his movement and exercised influence on him.

Weil-Curiel then went on to Muret where he saw veteran Socialist leader Vincent Auriol, a few weeks before his arrest. He had no trouble convincing Auriol to join. Auriol had endorsed de Gaulle from the moment of the appeal of June 18. In Sète, Weil-Curiel saw trade union leader Léon Jouhaux and was assured of his goodwill. He also found the energetic young

Parisian lawyer René Sanson, who had located the safe-house in the Pyrénées for Boris Vildé. Sanson, who had been in the Deuxième Bureau of the army, was just the man to be the Gaullist agent in Vichy. Sanson agreed at once. Weil-Curiel, well satisfied with his first contacts in the south, then headed for Paris and the occupied zone.

He arrived in Paris at the end of August. One of the first men he went to see was an eminent attorney, Léon-Maurice Nordmann. He, too, was a left Socialist. He had been active in support of Léon Blum during the Popular Front and had been an outspoken critic of the appeasement at Munich. He was a Jew, well aware of the catastrophe of French collaboration with the Nazis. He had volunteered for active duty in the army but had not been sent to the front because he was severely nearsighted. The army had, however, given him a commission and assigned him to the meteorological service in Paris. Nordmann was embarrassed by his plush office in the luxurious George V Hotel, and was anxious for direct action against the enemy.

Weil-Curiel's most audacious move came when he decided to renew a prewar acquaintance with Otto Abetz. In August 1940, Hitler had appointed Abetz as his ambassador to Paris, a singular post, for there is no normal diplomatic appointment to a city. But Hitler was anxious to promote Franco-German amity and felt that Abetz was the man to achieve it in the occupied capital. Abetz spoke fluent French, was married to a Frenchwoman, and was well known as a Francophile.

Otto and Suzanne Abetz were old friends of Weil-Curiel. They had organized lectures and conferences in Paris before the war, had gone on a walking trip through the Black Forest, had sat together during the 1936 Olympic games in Berlin, with Weil-Curiel as a guest of the Nazi party. It was an aberrant relationship between an extreme right-wing Nazi and a left-wing French Socialist before the war. It would have been even more aberrant during the occupation, as a friendship between Hitler's and de Gaulle's delegates.

Weil-Curiel thought he could gather valuable intelligence information about the occupation, about collaboration, about German tactics and strategy if he could only renew his old ties with Abetz, keeping secret the fact he was de Gaulle's envoy. He telephoned and wrote to the German Embassy and to the Abetzes' residence, but received no reply. He wondered whether his messages were not getting through or whether Abetz was deliberately avoiding him.

Meanwhile Weil-Curiel called upon many old associates at the Palais de Justice, and then dropped by to attend a lecture by Paul Rivet at the Musée de l'Homme. Both Weil-Curiel and his contact, Léon-Maurice Nordmann, were old friends of Rivet. Rivet sharply denounced racism in his lecture, despite the presence of German officers, proponents of the superiority of the Aryans. After the lecture, Rivet revealed to Weil-Curiel the existence of the Musée de l'Homme group, at that point mostly a propaganda group. Weil-Curiel replied that more direct action than just producing tracts was needed. Rivet introduced him to Boris Vildé, with whom Weil-Curiel discussed the need for some dramatic public act.

While Weil-Curiel was trying to conceive a ground strategy, a number of actions were undertaken by individual Frenchmen. In Brittany, a naval officer, Gabriel Lejeune, put together a commando of sailors and raided a warehouse filled with German military equipment and destroyed the matériel and the warehouse. Throughout France German soldiers were attacked on guard duty. Telephone lines were cut in four departments and someone succeeded in cutting German army communication cables.

October also saw a great increase in the number of clandestine tracts and papers. It was in October that *Pantagruel* appeared, printed in offset by the music publisher Raymond Deiss. Some historians believe it was the very first printed underground newspaper. It was the organ of a new movement that called itself l'Armée Volontaire. Five or six other sheets appeared, most of them destined to a short span of circulation. The best organized and most widely circulated clandestine paper was the official Communist party organ, *Humanité*, issued in local and regional editions and distributed by loyal party members.

On October 13 German wall posters in Paris threatened, for the first time, the death penalty for anyone harboring English soldiers. The notice informed Parisians that they must report to the German Kommandantur before October 20 any information on English military personnel being sheltered. Anyone after that date who gave refuge to an Englishman would be shot.

All Jewish businesses were ordered to register with the prefecture and all Jews were required to report their ownership of stock before October 31.

On October 28 the London radio reminded French citizens that Armistice Day was approaching and asked them to be ready to demonstrate on that traditional holiday commemorating the victory of France and the Allies over Germany in World War I. London suggested a peaceful manifestation, with patriots gathering at the Arc de Triomphe to lay flowers at the Tomb of the Unknown Soldier and also midway down the Champs-Elysées, to put wreaths at the foot of the statue of the "Tiger of France," Clémenceau.

The police prefect of Paris, Roger Langeron, warned his staff to be prepared for student demonstrations on November 11. He had already received reports from his agents that rebellious students had been incensed by a meeting between Pétain and Hitler at Montoire and the marshal's appeal for collaboration. More and more de Gaulle stickers, flyers, and graffiti were appearing on the Boulevard Saint-Michel and all the streets surrounding the Sorbonne. Incendiary gas bottles were being dropped from rooftops on German vehicles. The Latin Quarter of the Sorbonne and student lodgings were heating up.

The Communist paper *Humanité* dated October 31 carried a strong condemnation of the Montoire meeting. It said in an editorial: "In the same way that our party opposed the imperialist war waged for the benefit of British High Finance, just so does it now oppose the entry of France into a war for the so-called New Order of Europe, which can only lead to the vassalization of France." This Communist denunciation of Pétain and Hitler and of collaboration increased the opportunities for cooperation between the Communist resistants and the other resistance movements, although they remained suspicious of each other.

Tempers began to flare and tensions mounted on November 3 when a fight broke out at the Café d'Harcourt, on the Boulevard Saint-Michel, between Sorbonne students and German soldiers. In reprisal, German authorities ordered the café closed down. Serious trouble was signaled when the Union Nationale des Etudiants put out a leaflet protesting the arrest of the famous physicist Paul Langevin (a Jew who was charged with exercising a pernicious influence on young people), calling on students and teachers to defy the police and attend a protest rally at the Collège de France. Hundreds showed up in the first public demonstration against the Germans since the occupation.

Gustave Roussy, rector of the University of Paris, received instructions from the authorities to keep classes open on November 11, and to warn all students of the gravity of an absence on that day. Schoolwork was not to be interrupted, but brief ceremonies could be held within each school in memory of the dead, in the presence of teachers only. There were to be no public demonstrations or mass appearances by the students. He passed on these instructions to all the inspectors of the academy and all school directors.

On November 10 the Paris press carried the following communiqué: "Public administration offices and all private establishments will work normally on November 11 in Paris and in the department of the Seine. Commemorative ceremonies will not take place. No public demonstration will be tolerated."

It was apparent that the first trial of force between the people of Paris and occupation authorities was impending.

Resentment of the occupation and anger at Vichy's supine capitulation to nazism were boiling over among the youth of Paris. In the lycées and collèges, even more than at the university, young men and women were seething and looking for a fight. They had received their instructions to attend class all day on November 11, and so they spread the word from class to class spontaneously, without leadership or planning, to turn out in force at the Etoile at 5 P.M.

Meantime André Weil-Curiel, anticipating that November 11 would present a great opportunity—perhaps the dramatic public act that he had discussed with Boris Vildé—had been busy drafting and circulating tracts and stickers calling for a big turnout at Clémenceau's statue and asking all patriots to come with flowers. A friend of Weil-Curiel ordered a big wreath, while Weil-Curiel himself, working with Léon-Maurice Nordmann and other friends at his apartment, made a gigantic calling card, one yard long, wrapped in a blue-white-red ribbon, and bearing the legend in thick capital letters: *"Le Général de Gaulle."* Early on the morning of the eleventh they put the giant card into a Citroën truck, drove to the Place de la Concorde, then up the Champs-Elysées to Clémenceau's statue, where they deposited their wreath and de Gaulle's *"carte de visite."*

The police soon saw the card and took it away, but not before a number of Parisians had seen it too and had begun to spread the story all over town. The prank was a huge success. An even greater success was the overwhelming turnout of Parisians bearing flowers to the statue of the unconquerable Tiger. Police guarding the statue did not interfere, as all day long thousands of Parisians paid homage to another France.

The manifestation of the adult population went off peacefully, from the statue of Strasbourg on the Place de la Concorde to the statue of Clémenceau and the Tomb of the Unknown Soldier. As the day wore on and more and more people arrived, police inspectors became nervous. Orders came in from higher up telling police to break up the crowds milling about the statues. Policemen began to bark out orders: "Move on, move on, no demonstrations allowed." Then a police commissioner began circulating up and down the Champs-Elysées warning all agents that the Germans were getting angry and wanted all demonstrations ended at once. Armed German soldiers had started patrolling the Champs-Elysées. It was almost five o'clock and nerves already frayed on police lines when the lycée and university students began to pour out of the Métro and up to the Etoile.

Many of the students unrolled the tricolor flag of France and began to unfurl their banners for a parade. Thousands of students jammed into the Place de l'Etoile and around the Arc de Triomphe in a matter of minutes. Then, without warning, and no one knows from where or why, shots rang out and students began to scream. German soldiers charged into the crowds. Army cars and trucks ran right into the middle of the mob, scattering fleeing students from their path. Sirens sounded, students fell bleeding on the pavement. When comrades ran to pick them up, police charged with batons flying.

Just down the hill from the Etoile another group had formed, mostly students, but with a number of war veterans. They were massed together at the angle of the Avenue Georges V and the Champs-Elysées. A roar came up from their ranks: *"Vive la France! A bas Pétain! A bas Hitler! Vive de Gaulle!"* Then, arm in arm, students and veterans began to sing "La Marseillaise."

Whistles shrilled the alarm and SS troops poured out of the Biarritz cinema, where they had been stationed expecting a riot. Convoys of German soldiers shot out from the side streets, slowing down at intervals to permit machine-gun crews to jump out and set up their positions. German soldiers, holding guns chest-high, charged the students and war veterans and began clubbing them with rifle butts. A grenade exploded and someone screamed in anguish. More shots rang out and the students broke ranks and began to run in all directions, with German soldiers in pursuit. German patrols were still chasing and searching for demonstrators well into the night.

More than 100 students were arrested. No one knows exactly

how many were wounded or killed. London broadcast the accusation that 11 youths had been shot down. The Vichy government denied this in a communiqué on November 15, insisting that no one had been killed during the demonstration and that no one had been executed after it. It admitted, however, that 123 persons had been arrested, among them 90 lycée students and 14 university students, and that, furthermore, 4 persons had been slightly wounded. The communiqué was put out by Pierre Laval. It was clear proof that Vichy was seriously alarmed and that all France was talking about the extraordinary demonstration in Paris in defiance of the German occupation.

Vichy then made the mistake of compounding the repression by dismissing the rector of the university, closing the university down, and obliging all students to report every day to the police station in their neighborhood. But perhaps the most stupid of their errors on that historic day, November 11, 1940, occurred when Jean Moulin, the courageous prefect of Eure-et-Loir who had defied German torture and cut his veins open to prevent himself from talking to his inquisitors, received a letter from the Ministry of the Interior informing him that he had been removed from his post as prefect. Moulin went underground, establishing false identities, planning to escape to London to join de Gaulle.

Edwige de Saint-Wexel, born in Paris in 1923 of an aristocratic family with considerable wealth, was a seventeenth-year-old student, preparing for her baccalaureate at a lycée during this troubled period. Today she is an executive at a Paris bank, a woman of grace and dignity. She wears her hair in a smooth pompadour, her face only lightly touched with cosmetics, a discreet necklace of pearls around her throat over a high-necked blouse, and a smartly but conservatively tailored suit. Only after hearing her story does one know why she always wears a high-necked blouse or a foulard: to cover scars on her upper chest, a memento of November 11, 1940.

"On November tenth," she recalled, "our teachers informed us that there would be no celebration of Armistice Day. Classes would be held as usual and attendance taken. However, any student who had lost a parent in the war could request special permission to go to the Tomb of the Unknown Soldier.

"After class we all met to decide what to do. A majority voted to defy the ban and to buy a wreath, which we would deposit at the tomb. Students at the Lycée Saint-Louis would inform other students at the Facultés des Lettres and also Médecine and ask them to join us. We all agreed that we would dress neatly, be dignified and calm in accordance with the solemn spirit of the day and give the police no pretext for attacking us."

Madame de Saint-Wexel smiled and twisted her pearl necklace as she thought back to that extraordinary day in her life. "We really were very naïve to think we could defy a police ban with impunity, no matter how well behaved we would be."

The students had agreed to meet as they got off at the Arc de

Triomphe subway stop to form ranks and then go up to the Place de l'Etoile to-gether. In her case, they ignored the general consensus that it would be better to wait until five in the afternoon. Edwige and her friends had always been taught that the First World War had ended with an armistice at 11 A.M. on November 11, and that this had always been the traditional time to com-memorate the event. So they went in the morning, about one thousand strong.

"When we got to the Tomb of the Unknown Soldier, a few German soldiers were there. It was not clear whether they were guards or simply there as tourists. I've always felt they were off-duty tourists, for one of them had leaned his bicycle against a pillar of the tomb. He would not have done that if a sergeant had been there on military duty. In any case it infuri-ated some of the boys with us. They were all worked up emotionally anyway, and one of them announced that the bicycle was an insult to the honor of France. So we picked the bicycle up and carried it away.

"The German soldier who owned it saw us and started to shout angrily, ordering us to put it down. He and his friends charged into our group and a fight broke out. One of the Germans began to yell for help and German guards heard him and came running over.

"We started to walk away from the island of the tomb, in the middle of the Place, but all the avenues leading away from the Etoile were now blocked by German troops and by police. We did not know where to go or what to do. An officer came up to us, in the middle of the roadway, and told us to go back to the sidewalk in front of the tomb. Instead we pushed forward. Nobody knows why. We were not going to fight the German army. It was just the sort of thing that happens in an uncontrolled mob, particularly of inexperienced and hotheaded youth.

"A fusillade of shots rang out, mostly, I think, over our heads. But someone off to the left of me fell down. We panicked and began to run in all directions, squirming through the army and police lines. I saw an opening into the Avenue Kléber and scurried through like a mouse into a hole in the wall. I ran down the avenue, dodged into side streets as though demons were after me. I've never been so frightened."

Edwige's face was flushed as she relived the awful moment. But her voice was steady as she went on to explain that the next morning notices were posted in the school, instructing all students to go to the Commissariat de Police of their *quartier* and register, or there would be severe sanctions imposed not only on them but on their families.

"Once again we met after class. Now what should we do? We decided that to protect our parents we had better report in to the police. So, I went to my *quartier*, the Eighteenth, near Montmartre, where my father had given me a *garçonnière* to live in. That enabled me to avoid giving my parents' address. They lived in the Sixteenth.

"The police gave me a '*cahier d'écolier*,' and had me fill in my name, birth date, school, home address, and religion. I was shocked. It was the first time that any official state document asked for a French citizen's religion. I was disgusted.

"The really dangerous question concerned my actions and whereabouts on November eleventh. I chewed my pen and then wrote down that I was at the Bibliothèque Sainte-Geneviève, studying for my course on the history of art. I knew that one could consult the art history books there without filling out a form, so no one could prove that I was not actually there."

The desk officer looked at her card and her answers and then told her to come back again the next day.

The next morning, November 13, Edwige went back to the police station, was given a clean form, and told to fill it out again. She did. Then she was told to sit down on a bench at the end of the hall. Puzzled, she went and sat down. Two hours went by. She asked permission to leave for lunch and said she would be right back. "No, you just sit right there," was the order. She sat.

"At two-thirty P.M., German officers entered the police station, accompanied by soldiers. The commissaire pointed to me and the German soldiers came over and told me to stand up. I was under German arrest. Nobody told me why. Nobody said a thing to me. I was taken, trembling, to the Cherche-Midi prison. There, a German officer, speaking perfect French, began to interrogate me, asking me where I was on November eleventh.

"I repeated the story of being in the library. He told me I was a liar. The librarian had said that no students came in that morning. Furthermore they had searched my apartment and had found English tracts saying that the war was still going on and that one must resist the occupant. They had also found my personal diary, filled with anti-German sentiments that had spilled out of me as I wrote at night.

"I denied everything. I was proud, defiant, angry, resenting the arbitrary arrest, the bullying questions.

"Then two big brutes came in—SS men. Without a word they began beating me with their fists. Their silent, cold brutality was even more terrifying than the beating itself, although they were hurting me cruelly. They tore my wool coat off my shoulders, ripped open my dress. Then they lighted cigarettes and pressed the burning ends into my chest and my temples, just above the ears."

Edwige de Saint-Wexel turned her head to the side, pushed back her hair, which she wears brushed forward over the ears. "You can still see the scars." They were dark blemishes in her fair skin. She then undid just one button on her blouse and exposed the scar tissue high on her chest.

"They knocked me down, my face cut, bruised, and bleeding, and picked up my legs and began pulling me around the room. I screamed again and again when I felt something snap in my ankle. They had dislocated it."

Edwige fainted. The Nazis picked her up and carried her down to the cellar where they threw her into a solitary, damp, cold cell. She woke up in the cell, looked around, and saw a straw mattress and a pot in the corner. She ached all over and her ankle was swollen and excruciatingly painful. She rolled up into a ball, clutching herself and crying without stop until she almost choked on her sobs.

For the first three days she was given only one bowl of watery soup and a crust of hard bread a day. Then they increased her ration to two bowls of soup, morning and late afternoon. Guards came in on the fourth day, tried to pull her up, but her ankle would not hold her and they just let her drop where she was.

She was feverish and feared her wounds would be infected when at last, on the fifth day, a doctor came in to examine her. He washed off her face and put some antiseptic lotion on her cuts and bruises. Then, suddenly he grabbed her ankle and pulled sharply on it. She screamed in agony, something snapped again, and this time the ankle went back into place. It was still swollen and terribly tender, but the doctor had fixed the dislocation.

"They kept me there in that cellar from November through February 1941. It was three months, but I had no concept of time. I lived like an animal, unwashed, famished, lapping up my soup, no one to talk to, no idea what was happening, no orientation beyond my cell. It was like living in a cold, black hell. I was less than human.

"I had never been charged with a crime, never brought to trial. Finally towards the end of January an officer came, carrying a stool. He sat down on it in my cell and said to me: 'You know you are ridiculous. You are a member of the elite class and should understand that the French and Germans should work together in mutual interest.'"

Edwige listened in astonishment in her stinking rags, while this elegant officer told her how well behaved the Germans had been in their occupation of Paris, how they had shown the French every courtesy, given them every chance to be friends. Then he asked her whether she regretted her attitude. She protested that she had done nothing to deserve this torture. He then asked her who could vouch for her. She gave him her parents' names. But he brushed her answer away. "No, I mean a German or someone in the French government."

Edwige thought back and called to mind two German students who had come to study in Paris before war broke ou. Her classmates had been rude to the Germans and she could see that they were lonely and disoriented. She had gone to them and asked if they would like a coffee or something and had spoken kindly to them a few times. It was a long shot. They had gone back to Germany. But, in desperation, she gave the Gestapo officer their names.

A few days later the Gestapo officer came back to her cell, smiling. The two German boys who had studied in Paris were now officers attached to the Kommandantur. They remembered Edwige and confirmed the story of her kindness to them. They said they would stand as guarantors for her. The Gestapo officer told her: "You're free now. We'll drive you home. Behave yourself. Don't get in trouble again. It will be much worse next time."

She asked if she could clean up before going home. He looked at her as though she were mad. "You'll clean up at home. Now, don't bother me. Get along."

A police car was outside the prison. A sergeant put her in it, gave her parents' address to the driver, and the car took off. It was February 8, almost exactly three months since she had seen or been able to communicate with her parents. She was filthy and she stank, but she yearned to be in her family's arms and then in a steaming hot tub. Her foot still hurt and she limped when she walked, but the ankle was healing and she felt she would be fine with a little rest.

She rang the bell and the maid let out a scream when she saw and smelled her. She hastily called out that Edwige was home. Her father came into the entrance hall, looked coldly at her, and said: "I knew you would be back. Had you been dead, they would have sent me your clothes. Now you had better wash up." He then turned and walked away. She stood there grim-faced, then limped off to the bathroom. She scrubbed herself clean, asked the maid for a change of clothes, then let herself out and went back to her own room.

A family friend was a professor of medicine. He came to examine her and said that she would need an operation on her ankle but was too weak for the moment. He gave her shots for her swollen legs. As for her burns, he said they had scarred over and healed. She could have a skin graft later for cosmetic reasons if she chose, but there was no danger.

"I was on crutches for weeks. I needed some emotional wounds, too, after the scene with my father. I knew there were people who wanted no trouble with the Germans and who disapproved of student militancy. The same thing happened in families in the United States during the Vietnam War, parents and children turning on each other. It is very sad. Many of my comrades had been arrested after November eleventh, but none had undergone the torture I had suffered. It must have been the subversive material they found in my room and my refusal to confess.

"I knew by then what I was risking, as the Gestapo officer had said, but I was determined to get revenge against the Germans. I finished my bac, went on to take my license in law and in letters. At the same time, I joined a Resistance movement called Allié, whose chief was Yves Helleu. Our main objective was to save English pilots who had been shot down. We had a series of safe-houses and moved them from one to the other. We also had a rescue mission for Jews, using the same network down through France to Spain.

"In 1943 my chief decided I should go to London. I was engaged then to a French officer, a Basque, Max d'Almendare de Mongelos. He was also assigned to go to London with me. We made our way out through Spain and Portugal. In London I was sent to the 'Patriotic School,' the training camp run by 'Buck' Buckmaster of the SOE. My fiancé went on later to Indochina, where he was killed in 1945. I was prepared to parachute back to France, but they wiped me out of para school when they saw my weak ankles could not support a drop.

"I came back through Spain and reentered the Allié network, working on escape routes. A great many of my comrades were caught, shot, or sent to concentration camp, where most died. I was lucky. I was caught only once, on that incredible day, November eleventh. Once was quite enough."

While Edwige was lying in her solitary cell in the Cherche-Midi prison, about one hundred other students were undergoing imprisonment in Paris. The very youngest of them were released on November 20, with a warning to their parents to keep a tight rein on them or suffer punishment themselves. A bloc of forty-three more were let out on December 4. And the rest, with a few exceptions like Edwige, were released in time for Christmas.

In the first week in December, mayors and municipal councils of thirty-one towns were dismissed for refusal to carry out Vichy's programs, evidence of widespread opposition to the new Etat Français. Indications of even graver difficulties at the highest level of the new state came on December 13, when the vice-president of the council, Pierre Laval, official successor to Marshal Pétain, was arrested and dismissed from his post. No public explanation was made, but American diplomats in Vichy sent a report to Washington saying there had been an inside power struggle and a plot against Laval by the interior minister, Marcel Peyrouton, and the justice minister, Rafael Albert. They were supported by Colonel Groussard, an ex-Cagoulard, violently anti-German, who had a position of great power in Vichy as head of Pétain's personal praetorian guard, the Groupe de Protection.

The Germans, seeking to mollify the French by a generous gesture, decided to return to Paris the ashes of Napoleon's son, L'Aiglon, the duke of Reichstadt, who had been buried in Vienna. On December 15, the massive coffin was carried in a torchlight procession to the Invalides. Parisians, unimpressed by the ceremony, ridiculed the gesture and with their usual mordant wit said that, in the dead of winter, they would have preferred coal to ashes.

It was on the same Sunday, December 15, that a clandestine paper called *Résistance* appeared in Paris. The first word of its editorial was "Resist!" It was the first time, in the occupied zone, that a paper spoke directly of resistance and how to carry it out. It was a mimeographed sheet and had been run off on Paul Rivet's machine at the Musée de l'Homme. The "operators" of the machine were Boris Vildé, Anatole Lewitzky, and Marie-Louise Joubier. The group of the Musée de l'Homme was now ready to extend its activities. And another group in the south, led by Commandant Georges Loustaunau-Lacau and Marie-Madeleine Fourcade was in the process of creating one of the most successful and daring espionage networks in the underground war.

7
THE CRUSADE

Waiting anxiously at Loustaunau-Lacau's home in southern France, Marie-Madeleine Fourcade* had suddenly received a message: "Navarre" had escaped from prison camp and had crossed the demarcation line into the free zone on August 20. He was on his way home.

He arrived exhausted, in great pain from his still unhealed war wound. He had lost forty pounds and could barely stand up. But his spirit was strong as ever, and he was eager to renew the struggle against the Germans. When Marie-Madeleine argued that one could not re-create an army in a country swarming with the conquerors' troops, in towns full of fifth columnists and informers, and that they must act quickly to make their way to London, Loustaunau-Lacau promptly disagreed.

"It's not a practical proposition for forty million Frenchmen to cross the mountains and the sea. We shall have to get ourselves sorted out and show what we can do, for help to come from outside," said Navarre. "For the moment Hitler controls France, with Marshal Pétain at the head of affairs. He's fed up with our concerns. It's just what we need to get a foothold in Vichy."

"Vichy!" Marie-Madeleine spat out in disgust. "That place is a phony capital."

Navarre smiled and shook his head at Marie-Madeleine. "Of course Vichy. Marie-Madeleine, you'll have to get in the habit of deceiving people. If you want to get information, you must go to the source of power, and to act you must make outside contacts. Quite apart from being the source of power, Vichy is the diplomatic center, the place where foreign embassies are. It is only when we know all the facts that we'll be able to persuade other people to act."

---

* Marie-Madeleine's name at the time was Méric. She later divorced and married Fourcade. She has been Madame Fourcade for so long, and is so well known, that for convenience we have called her Fourcade throughout.

Commandant Loustaunau-Lacau had chosen deliberately to start his resistance activities in the heartland of collaboration with the Germans. He called his project the Crusade and his associates Crusaders. Later the network would be called the Alliance, and dubbed by the Gestapo Noah's Ark.

Never in its heyday as a spa for French colonials suffering from liver complaints was Vichy as busy and as gay as in the summer of defeat in 1940. The weather was glorious and a holiday atmosphere reigned in the resort town. Endless queues formed in front of restaurants and there was a fierce competition to obtain entry to the Hôtel du Parc, Pétain's headquarters, where the elite gathered in the ornate dining room.

Monarchists regarded the marshal as the stepping-stone to the return of a French king; industrialists had joined Pétain's Cabinet and there was a scramble for contracts. Opportunists among the intellectuals, educators, and the sporting set mingled with racists and *commissionnaires*. Marie-Madeleine, in her description of this scene in her memoirs, wrote: "Those people were the aristocracy of defeat. Anyone who was not a member was a pariah."

Navarre was not worried about being treated as a pariah. He had an excellent reputation, was respected by everyone, even by those who did not share his views. He had some money available and had an air of authority about him that impressed all bureaucrats. No sooner had Navarre arrived in Vichy, where the smallest room was at a premium, than he had rented a small hotel, the Hôtel des Sports. He went directly to Marshal Pétain's aide and told him that he intended to set up a reception center at his hotel for demobilized soldiers and escaped prisoners who were pouring into Vichy with no one to look after them. He wanted a financial subsidy and official endorsement from Pétain. The answer was positive, and Commandant Loustaunau-Lacau was appointed general delegate of the newly formed Légion des Combattants, a veterans' organization under Pétain's sponsorship. Some patriotic Frenchmen thought that Loustaunau-Lacau had become a collaborator.

Navarre came back from his meeting with officials at the Hôtel du Parc to see Marie-Madeleine, who had come to join him. "I'll pick out the best elements among the veterans," he told her, "the ones who want to put up a fight. I can send them, as patrols, throughout France." He paused, puffed on his cigarette, blew up a cloud of smoke, and then pointed the cigarette at her: "And *you*, you will organize the underground side."

Marie-Madeleine has never forgotten the shock of that moment. Seated in her elegant Paris apartment overlooking the Seine, near the Alma Bridge, looking more like a society lady than a Resistance leader who had defied the Nazis and escaped from jail, Marie-Madeleine recalled her first reaction: "But Navarre, I'm only a woman; who will obey and follow me?"

Navarre brushed away her objection. "That's a good reason to use you. Who would suspect a woman? As for myself, I've got to mix with these ninnies, see the marshal, and let the old hypocrite know what I'm doing for his 'dear old soldiers.' I must be above suspicion. So I'll leave all the secret stuff to you. It'll be a tough job."

She shook her head. "I can't do it."

"Navarre then fixed me with a piercing glance, and in a sarcastic tone of voice he said: 'Poor Marie-Madeleine, you have every right to give it all up. You won't be the only one to give up.'"

His words stung Marie-Madeleine, as they were intended to. He was sure she would rise to the challenge. But to his surprise she didn't. In a low voice, and with a solemn face, Marie-Madeleine said: "I'm very afraid I won't be able to live up to what you expect of me, Navarre. This job is terrifying. I'm hardly thirty and you're asking me to command hardened old campaigners like yourself. I know your friends; they aren't easy. I'd rather serve in the ranks."

There was a long silence. Then Navarre put on his glasses, picked up a pen, pulled up a notepad, and turning to Marie-Madeleine said: "If you haven't the strength to do the job, I won't give it to anyone at all. I'll do it myself. I've been betrayed so many times. I must make a clean sweep and start from scratch."

Marie-Madeleine, her heart beating fast, her cheeks flushed, sat and watched him as his pen flew across the paper. She had no idea what he was writing. She could hardly think clearly for the pounding in her head. She looked at the back of his neck and saw the still unhealed scar at the top of the wound that zigzagged down the whole length of his back from the bullet that had struck him during the battle on the Meuse. She thought of all the battles he had fought, political as well as military, single-handedly, unmindful of danger or the damage to his career. She felt ashamed of herself.

"You don't think that someone else . . . ?" she asked timidly.

"No, I can't trust anyone."

"Thank you. I'll try not to let you down. I accept," said Marie-Madeleine.

Navarre nodded his head, and kept on writing. Then he handed the paper to her and said: "These are my intentions and your orders. Learn them by heart. I told you before France fell that the means at Hitler's disposal are neither infallible nor eternal. We're going to nibble them away."

All the time he had been writing, he knew that she would yield. Marie-Madeleine realized then that they could not fail. Navarre's monumental gall would carry them through. She could not know that it would not be Navarre's gall but her own inner resources that would make her the leader of the network. But she would later pick an apt code name for herself, Hedgehog, an animal soft and warm inside, all prickly and sharp outside, a tough little animal that even a hungry lion would hesitate to bite.

Marie-Madeleine read Navarre's instructions nervously, wondering if she would be able to carry them out. He had noted down the need to divide up the unoccupied zone into sectors and to set up "patrols," or teams, in each sector. Their mission would be to observe the enemy, note his movements, his facilities, his equipment. An analysis of intentions would be made on higher levels as information was collated, cross-checked, and verified. On the operational level what was important was data, the physical facts. In each sector each team would need couriers for the delivery of their data. Eventually they would need radios and operators.

A southwest sector was already functioning, with crossing points established along the demarcation line and channels of communication down to Spain. Marie-Madeleine would have to recruit and set up patrols to operate to Switzerland and to Italy, and an important one in Marseille to keep an eye on the Mediterranean. Then she would have to go north, set up sectors in the occupied zone, and create patrols with extensions into the forbidden zones of the north and the east. She and Navarre worked over a map of France, tracing out in red ink sectors selected for subversive activity.

Marie-Madeleine checked out the arrivals at the Hôtel des Sports, looking for recruits. A great many escaped prisoners were coming in, but there were also some who did not seem to be genuine. Marie-Madeleine suspected they were spies. One in particular caught her eye. "He was a character who might have stepped straight out of a Tolstoi novel. He intrigued me because of his habit of looking out of the corner of his eye, and he had a strange, overelaborate way in which he adjusted a leather jacket with abnormally large pockets."

She went to ask Navarre about him. He laughed and said, "Oh, him, that fellow in the leather jacket? Why, that's Captain Fourcaud, the first of General de Gaulle's special envoys to this zone. He's going to pass on the information we get. I've got another channel, too, a brave Canadian diplomat here in Vichy. But, to be safe, I'll need a personal ambassador to London. I don't want to depend on other men's agents alone."

Marie-Madeleine told him that her brother, Jacques Bridou, married to an English girl, was planning to go to London. She would bring him to Navarre and they could make a deal for him to be a delegate of the Crusade to General de Gaulle.

Despite the similarity of the names Fourcaud and Fourcade, the captain was less than a favorite of Marie-Madeleine, who told Navarre that the arrival of de Gaulle himself could not be more of a bombshell than Fourcaud's. Navarre clapped his hands and said, "Excellent! Bombshell! We've been looking for a code name for Fourcaud. That will be it. He's going off to Spain now but he'll be back to help us. Don't worry about him, he's all right."

Marie-Madeleine's brother arrived in Vichy, met Navarre, and agreed to carry out the mission to London, to establish contact with de Gaulle. "But only this one mission, that's all," said Jacques Bridou. "Your underground intrigues are too involved for me. I'm going to join de Gaulle's forces as a military officer. But I will take your questions to him and bring you back his answers."

Navarre wanted to assure General de Gaulle of his complete and eager willingness to cooperate with him in continuing the struggle. He said nothing about accepting de Gaulle's authority or putting his network under de Gaulle's command. Navarre explained that he would, at the start, "march with de Gaulle in parallel." He considered it essential to maintain an underground command in France, to make decisions on the spot, hour by hour, according to changing circumstances. He was eager to transmit his information directly to the British, who were waging war on their own, and to avoid any waste of time in transmission of intelligence information. Nonetheless, Navarre explained, he wanted his enterprise to be purely French in character and, therefore, hoped that "the means of taking action would reach him via the Free French services."

Captain Fourcaud was preparing to return to London. He asked Marie-Madeleine to get together all the intelligence information available. He promised that he would return with radio transmitters and money that the network needed badly. She locked herself into a room with him and then wrote out, in invisible ink, all the messages that he was to take out through Spain. She confirmed her brother's mission to de Gaulle and Navarre's message.

Air Force General Baston, who had left the service and become a dealer in Armagnac liquor, joined the Crusade and became supervisor of the reception center. A navy engineer, Henri Schaerrer, also joined them and put Marie-Madeleine in touch with one of his former officers, Commandant Jean Boutron, who wanted to participate in action against the Germans. Schaerrer said he had excellent friends in Marseille who could form the patrol there. Marie-Madeleine went off to Marseille to meet with them.

One was Gabriel Rivière—thickset, solid, strong as a bull. The other was Emile Audoly, slender, refined, and reserved, who moved with the grace of a bullfighter. Marie-Madeleine thought they made a good team, despite an awkward moment when they had greeted her in the station buffet by shouting: "Good God, it's a woman!" Apparently Schaerrer had only told them they were meeting the chief of the network. But the moment passed rapidly and they immediately saw Marie-Madeleine's authority and command of the situation. Rivière would eventually become "Wolf" and Audoly "Fox."

Rivière needed a cover. He proposed that the network purchase a small wholesale vegetable business, which his wife would run. The warehouse would be a useful hiding place for men and matériel and he would have a good cover to move about the port and the region. He knew of one available for forty thousand francs, not a huge sum of money but enough to give Marie-Madeleine pause. Audoly worked for grain dealers, an excellent cover in itself, for it gave him access to the docks and the railway stations. He had ships' manifests and could check on cargoes. He was a valuable recruit.

Marie-Madeleine assigned the Marseille sector to Rivière. Audoly would concentrate on intelligence for the Mediterranean area, above all naval movements. She inspected the greengrocery business and arranged with Navarre to buy it. Commandant Boutron was appointed supervisor of the patrol.

On her return to Vichy, she found Navarre worked up about the news that anti-German officers around Pétain had arrested Pierre Laval. "The Germans will demand his release," he told Marie-Madeleine. "They're going to strengthen their positions in this zone." He decided that the reception center was no longer a safe cover. He said he would close it down, liquidate the Hôtel des Sports, and rent a floor in the Hôtel du Grand Condé. "You must take care to disperse your people," he told Marie-Madeleine.

By Christmas 1940, the Crusade, which had begun in September with only six people, had now grown to a total of some fifty "patrollers." The roots of the network had been laid down. They hoped to get the radios, radio operators, and money they needed to step up activities and increase personnel. It would have to come from the Free French in London after Jacques Bridou and Captain Pierre Fourcaud had delivered their messages.

Marie-Madeleine, Navarre, and a member of their team, Maurice Coustenoble, who would later become "Tiger," decided to go to Paris to set up the network's base in the occupied zone. A friend named Dubidon whom they called Twister, a collaborator willing to serve as a double agent, procured them the necessary *Ausweis* for the occupied zone. Navarre was a bit uneasy about traveling, for his name was posted as an escaped prisoner of war. But when the train reached the demarcation zone, it was only Marie-Madeleine who was challenged.

Nazi women auxiliaries of the Gestapo, whom the French called "the gray mice" because of the color of their uniforms and because they seemed to pop out of the walls, searched Marie-Madeleine thoroughly and took notes on her luggage. It was obvious that they had her name on a list. But she had a good alibi: She was really going to Paris on a business trip to arrange the sale of Indochinese rice to Spain. She had set the deal up as a cover but to her surprise, in Paris, it developed into a genuine sale and the contracts were drawn up.

When she was cleared, and the train crossed the line, Navarre said to her teasingly: "Not bad, not bad. You were immediately suspected of being a spy. That's a good start."

Coustenoble saw nothing funny in the incident. "There must be something fishy. Just how sure are you of your friend Dubidon, the Twister?"

To limit the risk, the three of them split up as soon as the train arrived in Paris. The two men had safe-houses set up in advance. Marie-Madeleine, under suspicion, acted out in the open. She went to the offices of the paper that she had edited for Navarre, *L'Ordre National,* a logical place for her to go. She was greeted by a white-faced concierge who told her the Germans had come looking for her and for the Jewish military expert, Bertold Jacob.

"That's fine," said Marie-Madeleine. "Now, give me the keys. I'm staying here. The Germans will never guess that I have come back."

Coustenoble then came to the office with an old, true friend of Marie-Madeleine's, a member of the Secret Police, Pierre Dayne. He too would join the network, under the code name Ant. He agreed to get Marie-Madeleine's belongings from her old apartment and fix her up in the office with the facilities needed to establish a pied-à-terre that could serve as a resting place and meeting room for agents passing through Paris. He further agreed to protect the hideout by sending through an innocuous report to the police.

Marie-Madeleine called on her best friend in Paris, Nelly de Vogüé, who promised at once to help. Henri Champin, an executive with the important Compagnie Française des Pétroles, was still on the job in Paris and had influential contacts who, he told Marie-Madeleine, were at her disposal. She met an Armenian industrialist who lived in a house on the Avenue Foch, the avenue of millionaires. He gave her the key to an unused maid's room on the sixth floor. She had another "safe-house" for her network. Marie-Madeleine left Paris a few days later, satisfied with having built a solid structure for the Paris base. Back in Vichy she found two full-time agents to run it.

Henri Schaerrer had found the new recruits. He was an invaluable asset to the Crusade in those first days. There were men like Schaerrer in every budding Resistance organization—men who seemed to be everywhere, to know everyone, ready to take on any job and get it done. Some, like Schaerrer, were exactly what they seemed to be. Some, unfortunately, turned out to be Gestapo informers. They would bide their time, take part in dangerous and highly effective anti-German actions so as to win the confidence of the movement. Then they would turn over complete lists and addresses to the police, and an entire movement, group, and network would be debilitated. It happened to all of them.

Marie-Madeleine and Navarre were at that most dangerous phase of operations, the beginning, where risks had to be taken to build up the personnel. She was constantly concerned about loose security. One day she went to visit the network's chief of intelligence, Colonel Charles Bernis, who had set up a headquarters near the Spanish border at Pau, in the Basses-Pyrénées. He was an ex-officer of the Deuxième Bureau. "Tell me, Colonel," asked Marie-Madeleine, "is there any way to avoid being taken in when recruiting people?"

"Apart from their ability," he replied, "I can't see anything to judge by. How do *you* set about it?"

"It's all a hodgepodge, Colonel. The loftiest ideals and most naïve goodwill are all mixed up. I'd like to welcome everyone with open arms and I'm ashamed of suspecting people."

"My dear girl, I pity you. Experience alone will teach you how much credibility you can place in each person."

Marie-Madeleine had no choice at the moment but to judge people by what seemed to be their enthusiasm, brightness, and apparent ability. She thus welcomed Schaerrer's new recruits for the Paris operation. One, Armand Bonnet, was a regular army noncom, a man who radiated the competence of a professional sergeant. With him as his adjutant was Jean Toeuf, one of the spahis, African cavalry, who had fought valiantly against overwhelming odds during the German advance on Lyon. He was tough and hard, a veteran fighter.

Meanwhile Navarre had extended activities to North Africa, turning that area over to an extraordinary air force officer, Commandant Léon

Faye, who would rapidly become a leader of the network. "We called him Eagle, for he was a high-flyer, sharp-eyed, fearless," Marie-Madeleine explained. He was brought to them by General Baston, who told Navarre: "I've had the greatest difficulty stopping him from having a showdown with Pétain. He could be pacified only by assuring him that he would find here the same kind of fools as himself."

Faye excited them by reporting that a plot was being hatched for a rebellion in North Africa. "The air force groups in Tunisia have all agreed. Algiers is easy. We're making headway in the navy. The army needs to be worked on more." General Baston threw up his hands: "What have I done? With you two, all hell will break loose."

Navarre told Faye to let him know if a rebellion really looked as though it were on. I'll go myself." They shook hands and from that day until the day he was killed in a German prison, Faye was one of the most successful operators of the intelligence network.

Fourcaud returned from London as promised, and showed he merited the code name Bombshell. First he flipped back the lapel of his jacket and revealed a badge, featuring the Cross of Lorraine. It was the badge of the Free French of General de Gaulle. Then he laughed and said: "You can't imagine what an effect it has on people. It's magical. Everybody asks for one." He had been going around Vichy flashing his de Gaulle badge right under the noses of Pétain's people.

Navarre snapped at him: "For safety's sake you'd do better to pin on the marshal's Frankish ax." Navarre's face was flushed with anger, not only because of Fourcaud's indiscretion, but because of a letter Fourcaud had handed him. It was handwritten and, according to Marie-Madeleine, was signed "Charles." Marie-Madeleine took it from Navarre and saw that it was very brief. The point was made curtly in its final sentence: "Whoever is not with me is against me." *

Marie-Madeleine, then and still today a Gaullist, was taken aback by de Gaulle's harsh reply to Navarre's suggestion that they work in "parallel" and that the Free French supply Navarre's network with facilities. She was even more dismayed when she heard the answer to her question: "What about the money and help we've been expecting?" Navarre said: "Captain Fourcaud has been forbidden to help us. He may help only those who agree to wear the Free French label." Navarre's jaw muscles flexed as he turned to Fourcaud and snapped out: "Let Charles come over here and see how easy it is to get people to accept it."

The controversy between Navarre and de Gaulle was typical

---

*Those close to de Gaulle in London decry the notion that de Gaulle would ever sign a memo or letter with the name "Charles." He never used his first name by itself. In his memoirs de Gaulle made no reference to any personal quarrel with Loustaunau-Lacau.

of early quarrels between the leaders of the interior and exterior forces of France. De Gaulle and his people in London did not have a good grasp of the conditions under which the Resistance movements inside France were forced to operate. The Resistance leaders inside France, living in isolation, had no idea of the difficulties de Gaulle was facing in trying to establish an independent Free France while begging his allies for money and supplies.

Fourcaud shook his head at Navarre's display of temper. Then he wagged a finger at him and said: "Keep your shirt on! There's one thing that's very important for you. The British agree; they admit your complete independence. . . . They'll send someone to meet you. You can straighten things out with de Gaulle later. Meanwhile I'm going to share my money with you. Here are half a million francs."

What Fourcaud had done was typical of the developing situation. Men on the spot would make deals on their own initiative that administrative chiefs, jealous of power and engaged in political infighting, would never agree to.

Navarre and Marie-Madeleine now had operating funds and the hope, at last, that the British would provide the one thing missing from making their network fully operational: radio transmitters. They sent Henri Schaerrer to discuss this need with British agents in London. They knew they had to set up a more direct and rapid system of communications with London than the courier system they were using to Switzerland and Spain. And their appetite for a transmitter had been whetted when the incredible Fourcaud took them to his room and pointed dramatically to an armchair on which was lying a large leather case. "That is Roméo," Fourcaud proclaimed.

Roméo was the code name for a radio transmitter, and somehow Fourcaud had smuggled the dangerous contraband into Vichy. A shortwave transmitter was a weapon of war, strictly outlawed, and its illegal possession could bring one before a firing squad. Marie-Madeleine was furious: "You're crazy leaving this thing lying around. What if someone came in?"

Bombshell laughed. "Nobody knows what it's for yet. The police on duty asked me what I was carrying and I said, 'You can see quite clearly —a radio set.' All they said was 'Get along.' I suppose they thought no one would be fool enough to flaunt it."

Marie-Madeleine, still upset, looked more closely at the case and saw streams of plastic-coated wires of every conceivable color trailing out of it. She turned toward Fourcaud: "Why is it losing its innards?" He grimaced and answered: "It was dropped. I hope nothing vital has been damaged."

"We'll give it to one of our maintenance boys," said Marie-Madeleine. "Meanwhile if you'll allow me I'll hide it under my bed; it'll be better for its health and perhaps for yours."

Marie-Madeleine's technicians were able to repair the set. Fourcaud then called Marie-Madeleine to his room and told her that he was ready to communicate with London. Before her astonished eyes, a radio operator began the transmission and received London's acknowledgment—all in a few minutes. She knew that she would not rest until she had a set of her own for her network.

Marie-Madeleine went on a field trip to set up communication channels. She first stopped off at the Jesuit school where her eleven-year-old son was boarding. She had not seen him for months and felt the time had come to tell him what she was doing. She decided to take him with her as she made her way down to Toulouse. When she told him about her activities, he asked if it was dangerous and she replied: "No more than what all Frenchmen do in time of war." Then she added: "You're the son of an officer, the grandson of an officer." Her son said nothing, but he squeezed her hand.

Later on the trip Marie-Madeleine said to him: "I'm giving you a funny sort of holiday, darling." He grinned at her and said: "Don't worry, Mother, it's as funny as being at the circus, except that *we* seem to be the clowns." Marie-Madeleine knew then that her son would be all right.

They were staying at a hotel when the phone rang in her room, jolting her out of a moment of brooding over the difficulties she was encountering on communications. It was her naval engineer aide, Henri Schaerrer. "We've had our Lisbon meeting with the British. They've come to our help. We've got a transmitter!"

Marie-Madeleine packed hastily and ran for the train to Pau, where Navarre had taken the transmitter to give to Colonel Bernis, the chief of the network's Intelligence Service. She was met at the station by her long-patient radio operator, Lucien Vallet. One glance at the broad grin on his face told her that all was well. She said to him: "So, you've got your 'piano' at last!" He grinned back at her: "Four transmissions a day on KVL. The British are very pleased. They received me QS5. I'm really living at last."

"KVL, QS5? What's all that jargon mean?"

"KVL is our call sign. QS5 means 'receiving you loud and clear.'"

The Crusade now had everything it needed: men, money, communications. And it could provide the most precious of all commodities: the intelligence information London so desperately needed. Colonel Bernis had already sent to London a complete, detailed map of all French and Italian naval bases, facilities, and operational units along the Riviera east and south down to Genoa. The Marseille patrol sent daily data on ship and cargo movements in and out of the port. Marie-Madeleine's spies were watching the port of Bordeaux. Engineer Schaerrer was on his way to explore the Gironde estuary and check on the German submarine pens. Soon KVL would transmit a full list of German submarines.

The transmitter was not the only miraculous rabbit that the British had pulled out of their hats for Navarre at the Lisbon meeting. He smiled broadly as he told Marie-Madeleine: "They've given me five million francs."

Marie-Madeleine gasped: "But that's far too much."

"No, it isn't. I've got to send a wad to Faye in North Africa. And we've been given a lengthy questionnaire requesting data on everything happening in France: ports, airfields, troop movement, freight trains, truck convoys, new construction. We must increase our agents. We must spare no expense. Britain is fighting alone, her back up against the wall. Hitler won the ground war in Europe. The air war is hanging in the balance. Britain must hold on at sea, where she is strongest. Everything depends upon Atlantic and Mediterranean lines of communication. We've got to help Britain hold those lines by watching every move the enemy makes. I'm planning to go to Algiers. I'm leaving the entire intelligence operation in your hands for the moment. The money is yours. Use it where it is most valuable."

Schaerrer had also brought back from Lisbon a new code system and a new method of designating the members of the network. The code was based on a series of books, held in identical editions by the leader of each patrol. London would send out or receive from Pau a message consisting of a number of digits: 20 3 15. The digit 20 meant twentieth page, 3 meant third paragraph. And 15 meant fifteenth word. It was a code that could not be broken by the Germans.

The personal designations were by letters and digits. They signified nothing and could be understood only by someone who had the master list. Marie-Madeleine would be known as POZ 55. Navarre as N1. They had not yet begun to use animal names, nor had they yet settled upon a definitive name for their network. But the net was already operating and feeding into London a steady flow of vital intelligence information that astounded and delighted the British.

8
BETRAYAL OF
THE MUSÉE DE L' HOMME

Boris Vildé had moved the Musée de l'Homme operations into higher gear. He had created escape routes over the mountains to Spain and prospected other escape routes across the sea to England. One such attempt to get across the Channel was to prove the undoing of him and his entire movement.

One day in the late fall of 1940, Vildé's associate, Léon-Maurice Nordmann, met with de Gaulle's agent, André Weil-Curiel, at a café near the Panthéon. They were discussing lists of possible financial contributors to their movement when suddenly a woman's voice was heard: "Why, André, what good luck to run into you!" It was Suzanne Abetz, wife of Otto, the German ambassador, the old friend he had been trying so hard to contact. Otto waved to him and he got up. Nordmann took the hint, bowed, and left. Outside, the three old friends, now representing Hitler and de Gaulle, began to chat and to make appointments to meet again the following week. Weil-Curiel hoped that somehow his old relationship with Abetz could be turned to the advantage of the Resistance. But nothing came of it and he finally felt he had gone far enough on this mission, possibly too far, and that he had better think about getting back to England. He spent most of his time in the days that followed his meeting with Abetz exploring possibilities for his return. The Channel was pretty well bottled up. To cross into Spain required sure contacts. Who would have them? Then, he remembered what Nordmann and Paul Rivet had told him: Boris Vildé had the best connections.

Vildé was only too happy to oblige. Of course he knew somebody who could get Weil-Curiel to England. An architect in Brest would handle all arrangements. Vildé, helpful as ever, told Weil-Curiel that he would send along an escort who would help with arrangements, a young man in whom he had complete confidence, Albert Gaveau. Gaveau was an aviation mechanic who had been recommended to Vildé by a pilot. He hated the Germans, was eager to help, and was, Vildé felt, an excellent, all-around troubleshooter.

Weil-Curiel went to see Léon-Maurice Nordmann to tell him of his departure and to leave with him the names and addresses of friends and sympathizers that he had found in Paris and the Paris region. Nordmann was not the best choice that Weil-Curiel could have made as a depository of names and addresses, as he was a Jew, subject to increasingly anti-Semitic decrees. He was not physically strong, nor young, although he was a man of the highest integrity and reliability.

False identity papers were obtained for Weil-Curiel. Then Vildé came to Weil-Curiel's apartment with Gaveau. He found Gaveau to be sturdy and bright, radiating confidence. Vildé gave them the names of Henri Waquet and Auguste Dizerbo as contacts in case he needed help after seeing the architect in Brest. Weil-Curiel then called a young man, Philippe Engelmann, who had been recommended to him by several lawyers he knew well. Engelmann had told him he wanted to go to England to join de Gaulle, and Vildé had endorsed the idea, saying it was better to travel with someone young and resourceful than to try to escape alone.

The three men, Weil-Curiel, Engelmann, and Gaveau, set off together just before Christmas. Their journey was uneventful and Weil-Curiel's false identity card stood up to inspection when Germans boarded the train to check the passengers.

But the architect in Brest was a disappointment. Whatever he had told Vildé, he certainly had nothing arranged for passages to England. Weil-Curiel decided to go to the small port of Camaret and asked Gaveau to go to Quimper to contact Dizerbo, to see if he had any ideas.

On the quay, in Camaret, Weil-Curiel met François Salaun, who owned a fishing boat and was preparing to sail to England. However he had already agreed to take twenty young Gaullist volunteers across. He thought a moment, decided he could make room for Weil-Curiel and Engelmann, and told them how much it would cost for the trip. He promised to pick them up in Quimper.

Weil-Curiel and Gaveau met back at their hotel in Brest. Gaveau had not found Waquet or Dizerbo in Quimper. But that did not dampen Weil-Curiel's excitement. He had found a boat for England. He asked Gaveau to return to Paris and gave him the names of Nordmann and René Etienne, another lawyer, who would help. He was sure that they would provide the cash needed to pay Salaun for the voyage. It was Christmas Eve and Weil-Curiel was sure he'd spend New Year's Day in London.

Weil-Curiel and Engelmann went to Quimper the next day and easily found Dizerbo there. Weil-Curiel wondered why Gaveau had not located him. Dizerbo said he knew Salaun and that he was a reliable skipper, although he talked too much. Practically everyone along the coast already knew that Salaun was taking a number of men to join de Gaulle. Dizerbo feared the Germans would hear the gossip soon enough.

The days went by and Salaun kept telling them that the group of Gaullists had not yet made arrangements to come to the port. Gaveau had returned from Paris with the money from Nordmann, and Weil-Curiel was impatient to leave. New Year's Day had come and gone.

Salaun called to say that all was ready at last. He would sail empty from Camaret on January 3, to avoid arousing any German suspicions. Then, out of sight of the port, he would change course and head for the harbor at Douarnenez, where he would pick up his passengers at dusk. He told Weil-Curiel to go to Quimper and catch the train there for Douarnenez. He would find the twenty young Gaullists on that train.

Gaveau was helpful, although he frequently left Weil-Curiel to go on side trips to visit relatives in the region. He was part Breton. Weil-Curiel rather liked the easygoing young man, although it was all but impossible to engage him in conversation. Gaveau had almost no interests and very limited education and knowledge. Weil-Curiel thought it strange that someone so militant about the Resistance should have no interest at all in politics. Still, it was good of him to take great risks to help Vildé and his friends.

On the train for Douarnenez, Weil-Curiel was uneasy when he heard the twenty young volunteers for Free France talking loudly about going to England. He became even more nervous when he went to the café rendezvous point and saw that the port was crowded with Germans. His nervousness increased when a cyclist came to the café to report that Salaun would be delayed and would not sail in until the next day, January 4.

Weil-Curiel and his companions took rooms above the café. He noticed that his young friend, Philippe Engelmann, had made good time with the café waitress, whom everyone called Mimi la Blonde. His flirtation turned out to be more than useful the next day.

Late on the afternoon of the fourth, Salaun sailed his craft into Douarnenez. Weil-Curiel had asked a friend to stand lookout on the quay and signal them the all clear. They waited anxiously in the café.

The lookout came on the run to tell them that the Germans had been waiting for Salaun and had boarded his vessel as soon as he moored it to the quay. He had been taken away in handcuffs. The Germans had searched the boat and had found Weil-Curiel's suitcase, which he had given Salaun a few days before.

Mimi la Blonde took Weil-Curiel, Engelmann, and Gaveau out of the café to a private house where they could hide out safely. Mimi told them that the police had rounded up most of the young Gaullists and that one of Salaun's crew had confessed that they had planned to sail to England. Weil-Curiel's own chances of getting out were now nil. He would have to try again, somewhere else.

While Weil-Curiel was in Brittany over Christmas and New Year's, the Musée de l'Homme team was working hard on the second issue of their paper, *Résistance*. It now had six pages and carried news either suppressed or distorted in the censored French press: news of British bombings of Germany, of battles in the North African desert, of French Empire territories rallying to the flag of General de Gaulle's Free French. The paper told of the reelection of President Roosevelt and of his pledges of aid to Free France. The paper reported the details of the German economic pillage of France and the conscription of young Alsatians into the German army.

Stencils of the papers were taken by a group member, pilot Daniel Héricault, to an Aero Club in Aubervilliers, just outside Paris, where additional copies would be run off on a mimeograph machine located there. Members of the club were waiting to help in the mimeographing and packing of the papers, giving up their New Year's Eve to do so. After all, there was not much to celebrate and no food and drink available for a party, so they worked all through the night of December 31.

A neighbor, with sharp eyes and a long nose, kept watch on all the young people working late and carrying mysterious packages in and out of the house. Suspicious that it was some kind of a black-market ring, he called the police. They came at once. Searching one of the young men, they found a list of names and addresses where the newspapers were to be delivered. Among the names were those of Paul Rivet, Léon-Maurice Nordmann, and two lawyers, Albert Jubineau and René Etienne.

The Gestapo, which kept a close check on French police activities, read the report of the arrests at Aubervilliers and secured the list of names and addresses. They passed the data on to SS Captain Doehring in Paris. He was already on the trail of the Musée de l'Homme and had seen earlier reports drawn up in Berlin about the dangerous intellectuals in that institution. He increased surveillance of the group and sat back, waiting for the moment to break up the entire movement.

The French police, ambivalent toward the Resistance and knowing that the Germans had picked up something important, quietly tipped off everyone on the list that the Germans now had their names and addresses and would be watching them.

When Nordmann, the Jew, learned that the Gestapo had his name on a list he was quite properly alarmed and decided he had to leave Paris. He asked Vildé for a hiding place and an escape route.

Vildé called the woman who had turned over her house in the Pyrénées to be used as a safe station on the movement's escape network to Spain and England: Elisabeth de la Panouse, Countess de la Bourdonnaye, called Dexia by her friends. She agreed immediately to shelter Nordmann, no questions asked. She gave him a bedroom, brought him his meals, did not question him, did not know his name or ask for it. When she saw Germans in the courtyard of her Parisian town house, she warned Nordmann and showed him how to slip out the back entrance. He spent the day at the public bath and returned in the dark of night.

Meanwhile, in Brittany, Weil-Curiel and his associates were hiding out, in the private house of Mimi la Blonde. Gaveau was nervous and kept telling Weil-Curiel that he had to get back to Paris to report what had happened to Vildé. When he peeked out of the window and saw a funeral procession passing by, he saw his chance. He slipped out of the house, stepped into the procession, bowed his head as a mourner, and walked away. From the cemetery he went on to the railway station and caught the train to Paris.

In the capital, Gaveau told Vildé about the failure of the mission to England and blamed it on "loose talk in town." Vildé then told Gaveau that Nordmann, who had given him the money for Weil-Curiel, was now on the run himself. Despite what happened in Brittany, Gaveau told Vildé that he would take Nordmann to Douarnenez, and that he was sure Weil-Curiel would finally come up with a passage to England. Vildé, extremely worried because Jubineau had already been called in by the Germans for interrogation, felt that Nordmann had to get away.

He went to Dexia's house, told Nordmann that Gaveau was willing to accompany him to Brittany and help look for an escape route. Nordmann jumped at the chance and told Vildé he was ready to leave at a moment's notice.

Gaveau came for Nordmann with false identity papers on January 13. They went to the Gare Montparnasse and boarded the train for Douarnenez. As the train approached Versailles, Gaveau excused himself and went to the toilet. At that moment the train arrived at the station and German police came rushing in. They entered Nordmann's compartment and arrested him, taking him off the train. They did not think to check the toilet and Gaveau escaped as the train pulled out of Versailles.

Arriving in Douarnenez, Gaveau saw Weil-Curiel at the station. The Free French agent had decided that he had to return to Paris to pick up clothes, since the Germans had seized his valise on Salaun's boat. He would then go south to Sète and try to get to England by the southern route.

German police in Paris, not knowing that others had already arrested Nordmann on the train, went to his apartment, and when his brothers and sisters told the Germans that he had left, they arrested his older sister Antoinette and took her to the Santé prison. They locked her in a cell, still not knowing that he was in another cell in another wing of the same prison. That same night other Germans picked up lawyer René Etienne and took him to prison. The Germans found on Nordmann the full list of people that Weil-Curiel had recruited for Free France.

A few days later the police arrested Daniel Héricault, the pilot who had mimeographed the paper at the Aero Club. Vildé's closest friends and associates, Anatole Lewitzky and Yvonne Oddon, told him that he had to leave Paris at once. It was too dangerous for him to stay on. Reluctantly he agreed, and officially requested sick leave to care for his knee, which had been damaged during the war. On January 20 Vildé went south, far from the German police.

While Vildé was in the south, the Germans were still investigating the activities of his group. They had found in Salaun's pocket the name of Auguste Dizerbo. They arrested him and interrogated him about his relationship with Vildé. He denied that he knew anyone of that name. They put him in a cell and told him that if he wanted to get out he would have to freshen up his memory.

In Paris, Anatole Lewitzky took charge of the movement. He shifted the mimeograph machine to a new apartment and then worked with Claude Aveline and Jean Cassou in the apartment of another member of the group, Simone Martin-Chauffier. Lewitzky took the copy they had written and delivered it to another site to get it run off. On January 31 it appeared as the third issue of *Résistance*. Knowing full well that a police net had been thrown out for them, they courageously continued their clandestine activity.

This third issue contained quotations from a message sent by President Roosevelt to Pétain in answer to the marshal's message of Christmas greetings to the Americans. Roosevelt replied that "it is for France that my heart beats and I pray that the people of France will soon recover peace with liberty, equality, and fraternity." Roosevelt's message was a deliberate slap in the face of Pétain, for the old fascist had abolished the Republic's traditional slogan and had replaced it with the slogan of the new State of France: Work, Family, Fatherland.

The paper also reported the tragic death of one of France's most eminent writers and scholars, Nobel Prize winner Henri Bergson, recipient of the Grand Cross of the Legion of Honor. Bergson, a Jew, received no pension, no help in his old age. He died alone in an unheated room, of cold and malnutrition.

Early in February the German police arrested Albert Jubineau. To his astonishment, they did not bring up his activities with the Musée de l'Homme group, but accused him of being the chief of a paramilitary group of seventy-five thousand men in Paris, heavily armed with machine guns and cannon. Jubineau was flabbergasted and at the same time relieved, for the charge was insane. He challenged the police to search his home, his cellar. Where were his guns, his ammunition? Where were seventy-five thousand men, armed with cannons, hiding out in Paris? The Germans booked Jubineau and put him away to await trial.

Working on the staff of the Musée de l'Homme was Jubineau's childhood friend from Saint-Nazaire, René Creston. He had received the mission to go to Saint-Nazaire and establish an intelligence group to keep a watch on that strategic naval base on the Atlantic coast. He instructed group members to seek out means of communication with London and to spy out every move the Germans made in the base. His spies had been highly successful in obtaining from friends and workers inside the base detailed plans of the base itself, the submarine pens, and, above all, German improvements in the water locks that controlled entry into the pens. The locks would be vulnerable to British bombers if they had accurate plans of the base. The espionage team delivered these plans to Creston.

Early in January the plans, which Creston had brought to Vildé, were reproduced in several copies at the Musée. One copy was given to Yvonne

Oddon. She passed it on to Alice Simmonet, a graduate student at the Sorbonne and a friend of Vildé's wife. Alice entrusted it in turn to a woman named Erouchkowski, a White Russian employee of the Musée, whom everyone called Ski. Ski had told them that she was close to a London undercover agent who would get the plans to England. Alice and Ski rendezvoused in an apartment on the Champs-Elysées with the undercover agent, who turned out to be a handsome, charming Baltic baron, a kind of White Russian James Bond. He fascinated Alice. She had no way of knowing that the "Baron" was an agent for the Gestapo.

That very day, February 10, Paul Rivet, the director of the Musée, who had been dismissed from his post after he had been accused of anti-Vichy sentiments, packed his bags and left his apartment atop the Palais de Chaillot. He had decided to accept an invitation he had received months earlier from the president of Colombia, to return to that country and supervise the building of the ethnographic museum. A friend procured Rivet a passport and another group member said he could conduct him across the demarcation line. Since he had to catch an early train, and transport in Paris was difficult, Rivet decided to spend the night before his departure in a small hotel near the station, so that he could walk to the train in the morning. By that routine decision he barely escaped the German police who descended on his apartment that night to arrest him.

The net closed in quickly that night of February 10. Agents surrounded the Musée de l'Homme and broke into Rivet's apartment. They picked up Alice Simmonet at dinner in a restaurant, found Professor Robert Fawtier's name and address in her pocketbook, and sent a squad to seize him. He was jailed in the Cherche-Midi prison. At midnight SS Captain Doehring and Gestapo agents arrested Yvonne Oddon and Anatole Lewitzky. They then seized Ski, who lived just above Yvonne.

The next day Creston surrendered himself to the police. He was one of the lucky ones. After four months in jail Creston was released; partly due to lack of any hard evidence against him, partly because Yvonne Oddon and Lewitzky kept to a previous plan in case of arrest and separately told the same stories, including a deliberate denunciation of Creston as a worthless, inept scamp who could not be trusted. The Germans told him he could no longer work at the museum and could not stay in Paris. They banished him to Rennes and made him check in at a police station every day. He did as he was told, kept quiet throughout the rest of the war and the occupation. But his main job had been done: Several copies of the Saint-Nazaire papers had been sent on to London and the RAF was using them in preparations for bombing the base out of existence.

Nordmann and the youngsters who had been turning out the clandestine paper at Aubervilliers were brought to trial before a military court. He freely admitted that he was part of a group distributing the paper, but claimed he had no idea at all who the people were who put it out. He also told the officers of the tribunal that the youngsters of the Aero Club were completely innocent of any political crime. They were just a couple of kids running a machine for fun and a few francs' pocket money. Nordmann himself was a skilled attorney and he had an excellent defense attorney helping him. They managed to convince the tribunal of their arguments. The youngsters were given a few months in jail, while Nordmann, to his great relief, was given two years. As a Jew, he had feared the firing squad.

Claude Aveline received a message from Vildé warning him to get out of Paris. He took off at once. Jean Cassou and Agnès Humbert, seeking a new editor in chief to replace Aveline, approached Pierre Brossolette, a prewar journalist and radio commentator who with his wife was now running a stationery store. They urged him to run their paper. After some hesitation and pessimistic grumbling, Brossolette agreed. Brossolette could not know that by this decision he was signing his own death sentence.

Early in March Vildé went to Lyon where he met Paul Rivet and Claude Aveline. The two older men were planning to leave France. Vildé astonished and dismayed them by saying that he would return to Paris where the resistance group of the Musée de l'Homme, decimated by arrests, needed him badly. They protested that his name was on the Gestapo lists, that he would never last in Paris. He simply said he could not live in safety in the south while his comrades risked everything under the German occupation. He shook their hands, wished them well, marched off, and boarded the train for Paris.

Agnès Humbert could not believe her eyes when she opened her door and saw Vildé standing in the hall. She told him that he would be arrested and jailed, and he sadly replied that no doubt they would all end in jail. By then a good many of his comrades had been arrested, the latest victim having been Countess "Dexia" de la Bourdonnaye.

At a meeting at another house that night Vildé welcomed a new friend whom he had met in the south and whom he admired greatly, Pierre Walter, known as Didier. Vildé told the others that if anything happened to him, he would want them to accept Didier as their new chief. Simone Martin-Chauffier went over to Vildé and asked him if he had returned from the south with reliable new papers. He confessed that his papers were not good and asked her if she could procure better ones. She said she had an excellent source and they agreed to meet the next day at a café on Place Pigalle, where he would give her a new photo and tell her what false name and address to use.

The next day, March 26, Simone went to the café, arriving a few minutes before their three o'clock meeting time. No sign of Vildé at three. Nor at three-thirty. At four Didier came in and sat near her. He whispered a question about Vildé and she whispered back that he had not shown up for the rendezvous. Didier shook his head sadly and told her that Vildé had lunched with him, just across the square, and had left at two minutes to three, saying he was going to meet her. He must have been picked up. Simone could not believe it, for the police would have normally followed him to grab him with anyone he was meeting.

The next day the news was out. Vildé had been arrested while walking across the Place Pigalle.

Meanwhile, young Albert Gaveau had gone south to meet Weil-Curiel in Toulouse. He was all excited, for he had found out about a departure for London the day after next from Nantes. He said he had also found a safe crossing of the demarcation line. Weil-Curiel was skeptical and hesitant, but Gaveau finally won him over by telling him that a member of Jubineau's group was waiting to see him in Tours the next morning.

Weil-Curiel packed his things and got into a car with Gaveau and a young man who was serving as Gaveau's driver. When they got near the demarcation line, Gaveau pointed out a farm to Weil-Curiel. It was on the unoccupied side of the demarcation line. About a hundred yards farther on, through the trees, was another farm, which was on the occupied side. By moving quietly from farm to farm, Weil-Curiel could get across the line. There were no guards or patrols between the farms. Meanwhile Gaveau, with official passes, would drive across and meet Weil-Curiel along the road when he came out of the fields.

Praying that Gaveau knew what he was talking about, Weil-Curiel made his way cautiously across the fields from farm to farm. Gaveau was right. No patrols, no guards. He emerged from the fields, walked out on the road. He saw no car, but, in the distance, a man approaching on foot. It was Gaveau. The car had broken down and was being repaired in a garage in town. He said it ought to be ready by the time they got there.

Once again Gaveau was right on the ball. When they reached the village garage the car was ready. Gaveau got into the front seat, next to the driver. Weil-Curiel went to the rear. As he sat down, his head turned toward the rear, Weil-Curiel saw a black Citroën pull up behind them. It was a model favored by the police, but Weil-Curiel relaxed as he saw a man and a woman in the car. He looked ahead down the road and then saw another identical Citroën parked at a crossroad. This car pulled out, blocking the road, signaling to Weil-Curiel's car to stop. He was now trapped between the two cars. They were German police. They ordered Weil-Curiel into one of their cars, Gaveau into the other. As they arrived in Tours, Weil-Curiel noticed that the car with Gaveau had dropped out of line and disappeared.

They took Weil-Curiel to Paris, to Gestapo headquarters in the Rue des Saussaies. He was interrogated by Captain Doehring. They asked him to write about his relationships with Lewitzky, Agnès Humbert, Nordmann, and many others. Doehring said he was completing the file on the "affair of the Musée de l'Homme." Weil-Curiel wrote out answers that stated, truthfully, that he had never met Lewitzky or Humbert. So far as he knew, Nordmann was only slightly involved in distributing some underground paper. Jubineau had a vivid imagination but had never done anything Weil-Curiel knew about. As for Rivet, yes he was anti-Vichy, even anti-German, but had always counseled against direct anti-German action.

One day, Weil-Curiel was escorted by guards down a corridor

to the glass door of an office. The guards pointed proudly inside, where Weil-Curiel saw Boris Vildé. The Germans seemed very proud to have captured him. Doehring called him the ringleader of the bandits of the Musée de l'Homme. He said he had broken up the ring and would now arrest the remnants of the band who were still at large.

The police picked up Agnès Humbert, the historian of the Musée des Arts. They had found stencils of the paper *Résistance* on Vildé when they arrested him, and they were covered with Agnès's fingerprints. They also had her typewriter and confirmed that its keys had typed the stencils. They took her to Cherche-Midi.

Sylvette Leleu was arrested in her garage in Béthune and taken to Cherche-Midi.

Jacqueline Bordelet, the violet-eyed secretary at the Musée de l'Homme, had finally found a man who did not think she was too young, too inexperienced to participate in underground activity: Pierre Walter Didier, the new chief of the group now that Vildé had been arrested. Didier had decided she could be a valuable addition to the group as it attempted to reform— she could provide a cover for him by playing at being his fiancée. They made themselves conspicuous in public by holding hands, acting the role of lovers. He told her if they were ever arrested to deny any knowledge of his activities.

Didier had introduced her to Albert Gaveau, who had been released by the Germans in Tours. Jacqueline had taken a liking to Gaveau, as did almost everyone. He had become a sort of right-hand man for Didier as he had been for Vildé. In mid-April they all met at a small hotel where the three of them were to meet another contact. As they entered the dining room, Gaveau said he was not feeling well and excused himself. Didier and Jacqueline sat in an alcove to await their contact. Then Didier, feeling uneasy, said he would take a look around the lobby.

As soon as he stepped out of the dining room, four huge men moved in on him, pulled out revolvers, and snapped handcuffs on his wrists. Then they hustled Didier out to a car at the curb. The whole scene did not take three minutes. Two other men went quickly into the dining room over to Jacqueline's table and said: "Mademoiselle Lise?"

Jacqueline was startled. Lise was her code name used by Didier. She wondered how the police could possibly know it. They took her arm gently—she was so young and fragile—and led her to the car, where she saw Didier sitting, handcuffed. She got into the back and burst into tears. As she pulled out a handkerchief, she also slipped out of her pocketbook small pieces of paper on which were written names and addresses. She bent over, sobbing, and behind the handkerchief, began stuffing the bits of paper into her mouth. She sobbed, cried, and chewed all at once, until finally she had swallowed all the bits of evidence. The Germans patted her on the back sympathetically as she almost choked on the wads of paper. As they wrote down her name at the Cherche-Midi prison, she wondered once again how they had come to use the name Lise.

All the principal participants in the Musée de l'Homme had been arrested and jailed. The fisherman, François Salaun, was tried in Brittany. At first condemned to death, his sentence was reduced to ten years. In June 1941 he was deported to Germany to a work camp, where he died. Auguste Dizerbo got hard labor for life and Henri Waquet ten years, in the Brittany trials.

In Paris, Weil-Curiel was offered a strange proposition by Doehring. Would he go to the unoccupied zone and return every fortnight with a review of the press? Doehring would pay his expenses and a salary and cancel his prison sentence. Weil-Curiel thought it was an extraordinary opportunity for him to get away. He agreed, went south, and began asking everyone he knew for a way to get to Spain. He kept coming back to Paris and giving Doehring the press reviews he wanted. It was all public information and Weil-Curiel could not understand why he wanted it. Doehring was, in fact, hoping to turn him into a double agent.

By the end of 1940, André Weil-Curiel finally found the contact he had sought and made his way across the Pyrénées and on to London. His mission was finished. But so was the movement of the Musée de l'Homme. Members of the group in Paris were kept in jail all through 1941, for their trial which would not begin until January 1942.

Meanwhile Nazi and Vichy repression would grow more severe every month of 1941. In the month of March alone, American observers in Vichy reported to Washington that there were sixty-two death penalties meted out by German courts and twenty-two executions by firing squad.

On March 29 the Vichy regime created a Commissariat of Jewish Affairs. An extreme right-wing lawyer and former deputy, Xavier Vallat, was named to head it. The Commissariat promulgated a new definition of a Jew: anyone with three Jewish grandparents, or two Jewish grandparents if currently married to a Jew.

Nazi occupation authorities issued a decree on May 13, ordering all foreign-born Jews to report to police precincts the following day, with their wives and other members of the immediate family and two days' supply of food and clothing. Some five thousand Jews reported as told. Many fled, asking French friends to hide them and escort them to the south. It is impossible to know how many did manage to get away, but of those who reported to the police, all five thousand were sent to internment camps in France and then transshipped to extermination camps in Poland.

On May 20 the Germans invaded Crete and announced the news with proud headlines in the Paris press. On June 1 the British and Greek defenders evacuated fifteen thousand troops from the island in a mini-Dunkirk defeat. But the British and the Free French struck back on June 8, in an Allied invasion of Vichy-held Syria. Admiral Darlan, now vice-premier and designated successor to Pétain, made a speech calling for closer collaboration with the Germans. But he made no mention of an earlier pledge not to turn the French fleet over to his new friends. On June 21 Free French and British troops entered Damascus.

On June 22 Germany invaded the Soviet Union.

The invasion of Russia would be the first major turning point of the war, with worldwide consequences and with a particular impact on France. The invasion ended all confusion, controversy, and hesitation in the Communist camp, and clarified relations between Communist and non-Communist Frenchmen, bringing about almost instant unity of purpose. The basic mistrust between the Communists and non-Communists continued in both camps, but now some cooperation and coordination of efforts became possible.

Communists, mainly on an individual basis, had played a role in the Resistance before the invasion of Russia. The Front National, an effective Resistance movement, with wide acceptance among all classes of Frenchmen, had been completely endorsed by the Communist party. But there was no clear party line as long as the nonaggression pact of Hitler and Stalin remained the official policy of Germany and Russia. With the invasion the pact was broken.

The Communists threw themselves into resistance activities with all their strength, courage, and skilled organization of clandestine activities. A great many Communists had received their military training not only in the French army but also in the war against Franco in Spain. Many were highly trained soldiers and officers. They were anti-German and anti-Nazi and had been for years, despite the pact Molotov had negotiated with von Ribbentrop. And so the very first consequence of the news of the invasion was an outbreak of violence all through the occupation zone. The Communists were the first, the only resistants to adopt a policy of execution of German soldiers and officers. The killings were senseless, for they did not substantially weaken the power of the German army, while they infuriated the Germans and brought more severe repression upon the French. For the first time, the Germans announced that prisoners would be considered to be hostages and that for every German soldier killed, the French would pay with the lives of hostages. First it was five to one, then ten to one. It would end in massacres of hostages. General de Gaulle denounced the individual killings, called for an end to them, and an increase in more substantial sabotage, the destruction of rail lines and communications, the blowing up of electric stations, industrial sabotage—all more effective than the shooting or knifing of an individual soldier.

The Communists did, of course, carry out traditional acts of underground activity, but they continued to attack German soldiers on the grounds that German repression in retaliation would further alienate the French people and add to the ranks of the Resistance. The Germans themselves knew that their policy of repression was not working. General Otto von Stülpnagel, German commander in Paris, estimated that four out of five people in the occupied zone were pro-Gaullists. He did not favor the policy of shooting hostages and he moved slowly on suggestions that he unleash a reign of terror to crush the Resistance. By the end of the year 1941 he was removed from his post and his cousin Heinrich von Stülpnagel sent in his place.

This increase in terror and violence came at the worst possible moment for the group of the Musée de l'Homme, for their trial would be held in the heat of the bloody combat. It was the worst of luck for Léon-Maurice Nordmann, who had thought he had got off with a light sentence of two years. A sadistic Nazi, an anti-Semite and a bully, Captain Gottlob, had been appointed prosecutor of the large trial. He insisted on bringing Nordmann to trial again, an illegal act even under Nazi concepts of justice. The presiding judge of the court, Captain Ernst Roskothen, a young German in his thirties who spoke fluent French, detested Gottlob and did not hide his feelings of admiration for the prisoners, whom he characterized as brave patriots. But he did not have the authority or the courage to buck the Nazi prosecutor, and he did not halt the retrial of Nordmann.

Gottlob tried to dirty Nordmann's name during the trial when he suddenly charged that Nordmann had denounced Dexia de la Bourdonnaye for having sheltered him. Nordmann's lawyer intervened to deny the calumny and Gottlob, red-faced with anger, turned on him and tried to shout him down for having interrupted. Judge Roskothen rapped on his gavel, brought the court to order, and then told Gottlob that the defense attorney was right. Nordmann had not turned in Dexia; she had been betrayed by an informer, for blood money. Courtroom spectators began to wonder who the informant was.

Germaine Tillion remembers how she found out.

"I was meeting regularly with Wilhelm, the defense attorney, when one day he rushed in and shouted: 'It's Gaveau. Gaveau is the traitor.' He had just come from a meeting with Captain Roskothen, who had told him that all the information the Germans had on the accused was given to them by Gaveau, who was an agent of Gestapo Captain Doehring. Roskothen said that the newspapers should not be calling the trial the Vildé Affair, but the Gaveau Affair."

Gaveau had betrayed Weil-Curiel to the Germans and had arranged the ambush at the demarcation line. Gaveau, on his "side trips" in Brittany, had been meeting with the Gestapo, not with relatives. He had told them all about the plans of fisherman Salaun to take the Gaullists to London and had had him arrested on arrival in Douarnenez. He had had Dizerbo and Waquet picked up and had arranged for the arrest of Nordmann on the train at Versailles, while he had hidden in the toilet. By telephoning lawyer Etienne to warn him that his name was on a German list, he had established the fact that Etienne was at home and had tipped off the German police to pick him up. He had betrayed everyone; and even after the trial he continued to work as a German informant. Resistance leaders were unable to find him and he continued his dirty work all through the war; no one could ever determine how many people he betrayed to the Gestapo.

Gaveau retreated into Germany when the Allies liberated France, and when the war ended, he managed to find his way back to France. He had accumulated a lot of blood money. He bought himself a house in Normandy and lived there quietly. He almost got away with it. No one knew where he was. But a former police commissioner, Jean Pradon, who had learned what Gaveau had done, had sworn to bring him to justice. He spent years on a personal manhunt and managed to track Gaveau to his house in Normandy. Gaveau was arrested and brought to trial in Paris in 1949. It was learned then that his mother was German and a distant relative of Captain Doehring's secretary. Surviving members of the Musée de l'Homme came to testify against him, as did the former judge, Ernst Roskothen, who came from Germany to bear witness against Gaveau. He was found guilty and sentenced to life imprisonment.

Speaking of the Gaveau Affair decades later in her house in the Parc Saint-Maur, Germaine Tillion remembered: "It was impossible to protect a group or network from a traitor. How does one recognize a traitor?

"I carried on my resistance work until August 1942, long after the Musée de l'Homme had passed away. And then, I, too, was betrayed to the Germans by a traitor in our midst, a priest, the Abbé Alesch, vicar of the parish of la Varenne. He too was found and arrested after the liberation, but he was executed for his treachery."

Germaine and her mother were deported to Germany. Her mother died in concentration camp but Germaine survived. That remarkable woman maintained her spirit in camp and bucked up the morale of all the other women she worked with in Ravensbruck. During the day, in the short breaks in a work party she was in, building a road, Germaine gave the women a course in the history of man. And at night, in her cell, using the broken end of a spoon, Germaine Tillion scratched into the wall her plan for a reorganization of primary education in France after the liberation.

"I never doubted that the Allies would defeat Hitler and that France would be liberated. I never doubted that the Republic would be restored." Germaine's eyes twinkled and she laughed: "And I knew, beyond doubt, that our educational system would need revision." Aside from the loss of her mother and her comrades of the Resistance, Germaine's greatest personal sorrow was the loss of her masterly and unique study of the Berber peoples of the Aurès Mountains. The Germans had seized all of her papers when she had been arrested. They were never found again.

Germaine Tillion did everything possible to win clemency for her friends of the Musée de l'Homme. She haunted the office of the archbishop of Paris. She was shocked by his behavior. He raved and ranted, accusing her of persecuting him, saying that everyone was after him, that they would all kill him. She tried to interrupt his tirade to ask him to write a letter to Hitler to grant clemency to the accused. He shouted at her: "Herr Hitler? I do not know any Herr Hitler." She thought he must be mad. Finally he promised her that he would write the letter. His niece, acting as his personal secretary, whispered to Germaine that she would see to it that he would send the letter.

The next day Germaine came back. But the niece had taken ill and was in the hospital. She discovered that Cardinal Baudrillard, head of the Catholic Institute and a rabid pro-Nazi collaborator, had appointed the infamous Canon Tricot as the archbishop's secretary. Tillion knew that Canon Tricot was a traitor and a sadist. Germaine shuddered as she recalled what he did. "He smiled at me—a beaming, happy smile, almost an angel's smile—but he talked of death and execution. There was no hope for the prisoners. They would die. He seemed to suck on the word *die* as though it were a juicy fruit." Germaine paused, then continued. "I was to see that unctuous death-smile once again, at Ravensbruck, on the face of the officer who selected women for the gas chamber."

Despite Germaine's effort, despite hundreds of letters that poured into Paris from the leading personalities of France pleading for clemency, despite the openly expressed sympathy of the German judge, the Nazi prosecutor demanded maximum penalties.

Judge Roskothen went to Saint-Nazaire to check out Gaveau's report about the plans of the base being stolen. He asked naval authorities about it and they confirmed the fact that the plans had been stolen, that they were accurate and important. He could not get around the fact that an important act of espionage had been committed, and that the sentence for espionage was death.

On February 17, 1942, the prisoners, many of whom had been held for a year, were brought into the courtroom and were directed to seats in accordance with the severity of the sentences that had been decided upon. Jacqueline Bordelet was given the first chair—which meant the lightest sentence—and Boris Vildé was given the last chair. As he sat down, he knew that he was a dead man.

Judge Roskothen, pale and tense, opened proceedings by saying that his duty was a difficult one. He admired the men and women he was about to condemn. He then read the verdicts:

Jacqueline Bordelet	——acquitted and to be released
Albert Jubineau	——acquitted and to be released
Daniel Héricault	——acquitted and to be released
René Etienne	——acquitted and to be released
Henri Simmonet	——released, arrested by mistake, because of his wife
Elisabeth de la Bourdonnaye	——six months in prison, for sheltering a fugitive, but to be released in view of time already spent in jail
Jean-Paul Carrier	——guilty of being a liaison agent, three years

Emile Muller	——various crimes, five years prison in Germany
Agnès Humbert	——anti-German crimes, five years in Germany
Léon-Maurice Nordmann	——serious anti-German crimes, death by execution
Georges Ithier	——serious anti-German crimes, death by execution
Jules Andrieu	——serious anti-German crimes, death by execution
René Senéchal	——serious anti-German crimes, death by execution
Yvette Oddon	——espionage, death by execution
Alice Simmonet	——espionage, death by execution
Sylvette Leleu	——espionage, death by execution
Pierre Walter	——espionage, death by execution
Anatole Lewitzky	——espionage, death by execution
Boris Vildé	——espionage, death by execution

Of all the outrages committed by the court, the verdict against Léon-Maurice Nordmann was the most outrageous. He had done nothing more than René Etienne. He had given Gaveau money for Weil-Curiel and he had distributed a few newspapers. René Etienne was acquitted and freed, Nordmann condemned to death for the same actions. It was Gottlob, the Nazi prosecutor, who had insisted on execution for the Jew, and no one on the court, not even the sympathetic judge Roskothen, had had the courage to stand up to the prosecutor. Roskothen told friends later that after the verdicts were read and court adjourned he went to the toilet and vomited. His vomit did not save the life of Nordmann.

The death sentences on the women were commuted to prison sentences on appeal, and they were deported to Germany. The death sentences of the seven men were upheld. They were taken to the Fort Mont Valérien, atop a hill just outside Paris. Captain Gottlob was there to identify his victims and read the judgment of the court before execution. The German officers and doctor present were amazed at the calm of the accused, who chatted and joked with each other.

In the courtyard there were only four execution posts for the seven men. Who would go first, who last? Vildé spoke up and said that, as chief, he would go last, along with Walter and Lewitzky. The Germans agreed. The three men stepped back to watch their comrades be tied to the posts, and a red cardboard pinned over their hearts as targets. They all refused blindfolds.

As the officer commanding the firing squad gave his first order, the four men at the posts began singing "La Marseillaise." The shots rang out, they slumped on the posts, and the doctor, checking each corpse, stated: "This man is dead." Vildé, Lewitzky, and Walter watched the procedure, then walked to the posts for their turn.

Even the Nazi prosecutor who had vilified them during the trial, was impressed. He said: "They all died as heroes." Then, as though he could not believe it of a Jew, Gottlob added: "Even Nordmann." Throughout France some dozen other Jews died that same day, February 23, 1942, and each day would bring a new toll of Frenchmen of all faiths.

Claude Aveline and Jean Cassou stayed in France and worked with Resistance groups in the south.

The Countess de la Bourdonnaye survived the German occupation and the many risks she took to rescue Jewish children by manufacturing identity cards and various false papers.

Yvonne Oddon and Agnès Humbert survived the German concentration camps and came back to Paris. Sylvette Leleu also survived and returned to Béthune. The graduate student Alice Simmonet came back to her husband.

Jacqueline Bordelet continued to work with Resistance groups, and she was in Paris on August 25, 1944, when General Leclerc led the Free French troops into the capital. She was one of the first to greet him and to help set up a provisional, free French government. Paul Rivet returned from Colombia after the war and took over again as director of the Musée de l'Homme. He welcomed back the American, Pat Kelley, who rejoined his staff, and soon everyone celebrated the wedding of Pat Kelley to the woman he had not forgotten during the war, Jacqueline Bordelet.*

---

*An extended version of the story of the Museum of Man may be found in *The Vildé Affair*, by Martin Blumenson See Bibliographical Notes.

PART THREE
MEN OF THE SHADOWS

9

REBELS ON THE RIGHT

The scholars of the Musée de l'Homme were mainly liberals and Socialists, the kind of men and women one might expect would rebel against extreme right-wing militarists like Marshal Pétain and the fascists around him in Vichy. But France is a country that seems to revel in political fratricide, where Left fights Left and Right fights Right often as single-mindedly as Left and Right fight each other.

At the moment of Pétain's surrender to the Germans a number of French officers, who revered Pétain as a great hero of World War I and who shared his distaste for democratic politics, nonetheless turned against him and prepared to work arm in arm with liberals, even Socialists and Communists, against the greater common enemy, Nazi Germany. They were not only anti-German, but also proud Frenchmen and they bitterly resented the shameful capitulation of Pétain and the loss of French honor in the surrender.

Commandant George Loustaunau-Lacau was one of those career officers of the Right who planned to resist the defeat and find a way to go on fighting even when he was bound in pain to his hospital bed with a wound that almost took his life. At the very same moment Captain Henri Frenay was doing his own planning. While Loustaunau-Lacau had had to wait impatiently to recover enough strength to escape from the hospital, Frenay had already rejected his commanding officer's order to surrender and had made his escape through the forests of the Vosges in eastern France.

For weeks Frenay made his way through the forest, hiding from German patrols, stopping at isolated farmhouses to seek food and water and a change of clothes. Along the way he heard and was shocked by the news of France's total capitulation, by Germany's annexation—once again, as in 1871—of the ancient provinces of Alsace and Lorraine. At one farmhouse he learned with dismay of the British attack on the French fleet at anchor in Mers-el-Kebir. And then he was warned that France had been cut in half by a demarcation line that he would have to cross as he made his way south, a dangerous undertaking without a German pass. Frenay's world of France, one of the great powers of the world, had crumbled so fast that he could not believe what had happened.

He crossed the demarcation line in a truck, hidden under a mound of boxes, and then drove on toward Lyon. His driver told him: "The war is over, and now the Germans are helping our people. We're not afraid of them anymore. After all, they're human beings like us."

Frenay shuddered and wondered if all Frenchmen were as naïve as his truckdriver. Frenay wanted to tell him what Hitler and the Nazis were really like. "But, I hadn't the heart," Frenay recalled later. "I was free, in the unoccupied zone, and I would have to find out for myself what the next step was."

Despite his escape, Frenay was still a disciplined, traditional officer. He headed at once for general headquarters in the Place Carnot, in Lyon. He was greeted by a desk officer who commented coldly, "So you escaped. Why didn't you remain with your regiment? Here, take this slip; tomorrow you'll be assigned to a new unit."

Disgusted by the reception at headquarters and by the question of why he had escaped, Frenay decided not to return for his new assignment. Instead he telegraphed his mother that he would be coming to her home in Sainte-Maxime, on the French Riviera, for a visit and rest. He had no idea what he would do next, but he knew he needed time to think and bring his body back to health.

On the train south, Frenay listened in silent dismay as an old, retired officer in his compartment sounded off on the defeat. The officer wore the rosette of the Legion of Honor in his buttonhole. He must have served with valor and been a patriot, but he stated that the French fully deserved their fate. France had been betrayed by the Republic, by the Jews, by the Freemasons, the schoolteachers, the deputies. The old man and his fellow passengers seemed to be secretly pleased with the French defeat.

In his memoirs, Frenay stated: "A gulf separated me from my fellow travelers. I still lived in the prewar world, when France was strong. . . . I had not assimilated defeat. I could not even understand it; it was utterly foreign to me. I had evaded defeat when I escaped from Donon. I was free, but they, my neighbors, were not. They were defeated; I was undefeated."

Frenay had separated himself from the majority of the French, and above all from Marshal Pétain, who had already embraced defeat. But it would take Frenay some time to realize this, for he still revered the marshal and kept inventing all kinds of excuses for what the old hero was doing. After resting at his mother's home, he returned to Lyon and received a notice assigning him to the Marseille garrison. He took off at once.

Marseille is the second city of France, after Paris, with a population of some 660,000. It was founded many centuries ago as a trading post called Massilia by Phocaeans from Asia Minor and is today one of the busiest ports of the Mediterranean, France's gateway to Africa. It is a city of fragrant and pungent aromas and colors, of bougainvillea, yellow jonquils, and red roses on almost every balcony. It is the home of bouillabaisse, and of a black-haired, olive-skinned, stocky people who rarely converse in anything less than a shout.

Marseille, always an international port, was, in August 1940, teeming with Czechs, Poles, Belgians, Dutch, and Jews of many nations fleeing from Nazi persecution. A great many French had also fled from Alsace-Lorraine and the occupied cities of the north, seeking refuge there. Frenay knew and loved Marseille. As he jumped off the train he breathed deeply, savoring all the odors of the port. His thoughts were directed to an old friend who had done prewar military service with him in the Third Alpine Infantry, a doctor, Marcel Recordier. The Recordier family greeted him warmly and listened to the adventure of his escape, his experiences in the Maginot Line, and his comments on the defeat. Dr. Recordier asked Frenay what he intended to do about it, and Frenay, expecting the question, pulled out of his pocket the manifesto he had written for himself weeks earlier, stressing the need to fight on to national liberation. He intended to organize a resistance group that he would call the Mouvement de Libération Nationale.

Dr. Recordier read the manifesto aloud to his wife and daughter, then turned to Frenay and said: "You are right. If you need us, you know you can count on us."

Frenay had won his first recruits. The Recordiers played an important role from then on. Their apartment in the Rue de Rome became a safe-house for Frenay, who would hide out there when the Gestapo was after him. The other members of the movement would sleep over, get changes of clothing, or food and money when they were on the run. It is easier to hide in a big city than in a town or village and that is why Marseille, like Lyon and Paris, became a principal center of Resistance activity.

The "blitz" was wreaking its havoc on England, with waves of German bombers inflicting heavy damage and loss of life. German submarines were blockading Britain, taking a heavy toll of transports, particularly food convoys. German troops in France were undergoing landing exercises and it seemed as though Hitler would carry out his boast to invade Britain. Frenay knew he would have to move quickly if he was to have any chance to take action against the Germans.

On August 15, at the officers' club, he met a young lieutenant of the colonial infantry home on armistice leave. His name was Maurice Chevance. He had served several years in Africa, in the Camel Corps, and was an enthusiast of the French Empire. He planned to stay in Marseille, get demobilized, and open a travel and freight transport agency for Africa.

Frenay was impressed with Chevance's energy, ambition, and physical strength. "With his broad shoulders and thick neck, he was a powerful force of nature . . . and a profoundly decent human being." Frenay asked him what would become of his plans if the Germans won the war and conquered England. Chevance replied that Germany would not win the war. Frenay sensed that he was anti-German and that he could risk an approach to him. He would have to take such risks if a movement was to be created.

He took out his manifesto for the second time. And for the second time a man looked up from it and said, "You're right. You can count on me." Chevance would set up his agency and use it as a cover for intelligence activities. A travel and freight agent is in an ideal position, in a major port like Marseille, to keep close track of all military activities and shipments, and to provide transportation to all militants in the movement, in and out of France. Chevance was a key recruit.

Frenay's disillusion with the Pétain regime grew as he learned of the arrival in Alsace and Lorraine of German gauleiters, in open violation of the armistice terms, with no protest from Pétain. He read German communiqués in the French press and on the radio, recounting the tremendous blows the Luftwaffe was striking against England. But the French people knew nothing about the high price the Luftwaffe was paying for the raids, as the young fighters of the RAF rose to the challenge and started shooting the Germans out of the skies. Frenay heard BBC broadcasts and saw confidential French army reports on the Battle of Britain. He burned to make all this news available to the public. He knew that he would have to organize an underground paper and clandestine espionage and information-gathering services as the first objectives of his movement.

As a professional officer, Frenay had been trained not to proceed with any project without an organizational structure. He began, at summer's end, to put his ideas into structural form.

First he created a unit that he called the ROP—Recrutement, Organisation, Propagande. "It was a sort of induction service through which each new rookie had to pass, either to remain in ROP work, or, in accordance with his aptitude and desires, to be transferred to our Intelligence Service or to Choc, our paramilitary cadres.

"ROP and Choc were further to be divided into six-man and thirty-man cells. Each chief of a six-man cell would know only his five subordinates and his immediate supervisor in the thirty-man cell. This would provide both security from mass arrests and a useful division of labor."

Over and above the basic cellular structure, Frenay provided for an administrative superstructure, with units assigned to cantons, arrondissements, and departments, parallel to the French public administration divisions.

His structures clearly in mind, Frenay then thought about the first urgent steps to be taken to form an active organization, beyond recruiting friends and sympathizers. "What we really needed immediately was money. And there was only one solution: to put the bite on each and every friend, every militant and sympathizer. Whenever I met anyone I would start talking about England and Hitler, stating my conviction that Germany would lose the war, and then wait for a reaction. If the reaction endorsed my views,

I would go further and begin to hint about 'men in the shadows'—that is, the Resistance.

"If the answer was positive, I'd push ahead, tell them about our organization and invite them to join. I'd give them a contact name and then ask for a contribution to our treasury."

Frenay was proceeding in a manner very different from Vildé when he moved to create the Musée de l'Homme group. Vildé cautiously approached people in his own milieu—fellow workers, intellectuals, scholars, people who knew each other and shared the same views. He did of course branch out beyond his own kind, as he had to, but only after his group had been well established on a person-to-person basis with some knowledge of where he was going and whom he was approaching. Frenay, on the other hand, approached strangers from different milieus.

Frenay was playing a dangerous game, but he had little choice. He was an officer in the Armistice Army, under Pétain's command. He did not know his fellow officers well. He could not go to fellow workers as Vildé did. It was a miracle, and a tribute to the character of the people he met, that no one informed on him and that the police did not immediately pick him up. If the French had been as generally collaborationist as some historians and some moviemakers later charged, Frenay would not have lasted a month, and his movement, Combat, would never have come into existence.

Frenay, however, was profoundly disappointed by "the general drift of public opinion." He felt that "people had made themselves comfortable in defeat and there was not a hint of the spirit of revolt aside from the few friends and sympathizers we had recruited. The principal public worry was food. Supplies were dwindling. By the end of September ration cards for bread and meat were issued."

Despite his disappointment, Frenay kept finding people willing to join his movement and to await instructions for action. They were willing, too, to pay their dues, and his treasury began to prosper, rising from a thousand francs to fifteen thousand francs in a few months' time; not a great war chest, but a good start in hard times.

Frenay's faith in Pétain received a severe jolt on October 25. He opened his morning paper and learned that Pétain had just gone to meet Hitler in a little town called Montoire. The paper said the meeting would be "beneficial for France" and that the marshal would shortly address the nation. Frenay could not imagine how any meeting with Hitler could be beneficial and he was distressed that Pétain had met him almost surreptitiously in an out-of-the-way place. His instincts told him it was a bad development.

On October 30, in Dr. Recordier's apartment, Frenay heard the marshal speak about Montoire.

"It is in a spirit of honor, and to maintain the unity of France . . . that I enter today upon the path of collaboration. This collaboration must be sincere."

Frenay sat bolt upright and glared at the radio set.

"Collaboration with Hitler's Germany! Only yesterday the marshal had said we must not harm our ex-allies. Today honor seemed to require collaboration with the enemy! More dejected than disgusted, I could not fathom this new turn. Then, the next day, the newspapers published a photo of the marshal shaking Hitler's hand."

Several days later, the Marseille garrison received orders to make arrangements for an official visit of Pétain to the city, set for December 3. When the day came, Frenay watched Pétain tour the port in an open motorcar. As he watched, his mind was torn with doubts. "That hand, waving to us, was it not the one that had shaken the hand of Hitler? Was he fooling the Führer or fooling the French? Just what was that old man up to?" Frenay found it more and more difficult to find excuses for the official fascist policies of the Pétain regime. Whatever Pétain was up to, Frenay was now determined to carry out his own plans to resist the Germans.

Chevance had launched his agency and was doing well. Recordier was setting up a whole network of correspondents around the port of Marseille. Frenay had recruited a chemical engineer, Jean Gemahling, who became his chief of Intelligence Service, and had met a young officer, Pierre de Froment, whom he attempted to recruit to set up the movement in the north.

In the first week of December Frenay received an appointment to the Deuxième Bureau, the Intelligence Service of the army general staff, in Vichy. This would give him the chance to infiltrate right into the brain center of the Pétain regime.

Winter was coming on. It was apparent to Frenay that Hitler had lost the Battle of Britain. There would be no invasion. The Italians, fighting in Greece, were being set back by a brave, tough band of Greeks. Roosevelt had been reelected president of the United States and was sending his close friend, Admiral Leahy, to Vichy as ambassador, Frenay hoped that Leahy would provide a counterbalance to the pro-German Pierre Laval. Frenay felt the tide would soon turn. He intended to play a double game when he took on his new assignment in Vichy, pretending to go along with collaboration while secretly setting up his Resistance movement. He kept hoping against hope that Pétain was also playing a double game with Hitler.

Frenay turned responsibility for the Marseille area of his movement over to Maurice Chevance, with Dr. Recordier as his deputy. They were greatly encouraged to receive in the mail a new "newspaper." They did not know who sent it or who printed it. Its title was *Liberté*. It was less a newspaper than a glorified pamphlet. It had been slipped into the letter box and had not cleared the post office. It was, they immediately saw, an underground paper. Someone else was thinking as they had been thinking and had beaten them to action. But they were overjoyed. "We were not alone! Others, though faceless, were working alongside us in the shadows. We would look for them and one day soon we would meet!"

As Frenay was packing his bags to leave for Vichy, on the morning of December 14, there was a thunderbolt of news: Laval, the constitutional heir to Pétain, had been dismissed from the government and arrested. There was no official comment or explanation at that time. Pétain was silent. It was in this atmosphere of government crisis that Captain Frenay left Marseille, on December 16, on the train to Vichy.

Things began to look up for Frenay as soon as he reported in to his new assignment at the Deuxième Bureau. Its chief, Colonel Louis Baril, had Frenay's dossier in front of him. One of the first things he said was, "Tell me, Frenay, about the Centre d'Etudes Germaniques at Strasbourg. What did you get out of your work there?"

Frenay decided to take his chances and find out at once where his new chief stood.

"Colonel, I learned German and German history and philosophy. In brief, I regard its present philosophy as the greatest monstrosity of the twentieth century, the negation of every spiritual and religious view I hold dear." Frenay held his breath as he awaited his colonel's reaction.

Colonel Baril gave him a long, intense look. "It's a pity your view is not shared by France as a whole—especially by Vichy."

Frenay recalled later, in his memoirs: "I was transfixed. Baril was anti-German, hence anti-collaborationist. But his reference to Vichy was ambiguous. Whom did he mean to criticize? The government? The marshal? In any case, the Deuxième Bureau was apparently in good hands."

Frenay left his chief's office greatly encouraged. He was excited about the assignment he had been given by Baril: to brief the Foreign Ministry on the intelligence analyses prepared by the Deuxième Bureau and to receive, in return, the intelligence gathered by the diplomatic service. The Foreign Ministry was on the first floor of the Hôtel du Parc. Pétain's office was on the third floor, the vice-premier's on the second. Frenay, who would not accept defeat, was working in the very heart of the defeated Vichy regime. He worked alongside Colonel Rivet's Intelligence Service, the most anti-German unit inside the army. Frenay would get all the information he needed for an underground paper.

His decision to go ahead with this project was uppermost in his mind when he received a surprise visit from a dear friend, Bertie Albrecht, an elegant Frenchwoman of Swiss origin who had married an English financier. Her husband lived in London, which Bertie had left in 1934, homesick for France. They had two children in their teens. Bertie had many friends among French intellectuals on the political Left. She had invited Frenay, a man of the Right, to meetings in her apartment in Paris that were rallies for Republican Spain. She wanted to educate him about the political realities of the day.

Although a military man, brought up in the traditions of the Right, Frenay was personally committed to democratic principles of justice and human rights. He had been deeply suspicious of Hitler's aid to General Franco and saw in it a threat to France, the threat of encirclement by Nazi Germany, Fascist Italy, and Falangist Spain. Then, at Bertie's apartment, he had met a number of Jews fleeing Nazi persecution. He heard their horrifying stories of the barbarism of Hitler's regime. Because of that he had asked the army to transfer him to the Center for Germanic Studies in Strasbourg.

He told Bertie what had happened to him since they had last met in Paris, how he hated the Germans and was now profoundly suspicious of the Vichy government. He revealed to her his projects for propaganda and intelligence-gathering. She hugged him and said how happy she was that he had turned out to be a rebel. "I've seen so much apathy, so much cowardice."

When Frenay asked her if she would join him in clandestine activities, she agreed at once. She told Frenay that she would give thought to the project of a clandestine paper and be back to him with a plan.

Just a few days before the end of the year, Colonel Baril told Frenay that a certain Lieutenant de Froment was passing through and wanted to talk with him. It was Pierre de Froment, whom Frenay had met and tried to recruit in Marseille. Hoping that de Froment had decided to participate, Frenay went off to see him. The young lieutenant told him at once that he had thought seriously about what Frenay had said and had concluded it was the right thing to do. He had himself initiated a program of information, propaganda, and the recruitment of action groups in the occupied zone.

De Froment and his friends made detachable inserts that they pasted into books. They had distributed pamphlets and organized crossings of the demarcation line. One of his associates, Jean Monmousseau, owned vineyards in Touraine. It was part of his business to ship wine casks throughout France, and in those casks he had stowed away men escaping from the police. He also transported matériel and documents in his casks.

De Froment said his group had accumulated a number of intelligence reports on German troop bases and movements. He did not know what to do with the reports and had decided to come to see Frenay, remembering their talks in Marseille.

Frenay decided to take de Froment to Colonel Baril and ask for his help. It was a gamble but Frenay thought a good one in view of the way Baril had reacted to his comments about the Germans. Frenay had not miscalculated. Baril gave them a warm welcome and the names of contacts for passing on information, a Swiss, an Englishman in the British Consulate, and another contact in the American Embassy in Vichy.

That night de Froment was introduced to Bertie. Frenay briefed him on the need for a cellular structure and general methods of security. De Froment told them the best ways to cross the demarcation line. They agreed upon the need to keep in touch with each other. De Froment went north as Frenay's delegate.

The next night Bertie told Frenay that she had come to a conclusion about their propaganda organ. "We must design it to contain lots of raw news and information, with a minimum of editorializing. I'll type it myself, with several carbons. But to whom shall we mail it?"

Frenay thought it a good idea to avoid editorials, at least at the outset. He did not want to risk antagonizing different political factions, either among his readers or in his movement. It was more important to inform people, to get to them the truth about the war, about the intrigues of Laval and Darlan, about the evils of collaboration. In answer to Bertie's question about the mailing, he decided to try it out first on a limited number of people whom they already knew. "We'll keep our authorship secret and sit back and observe their reactions. They'll be our guinea pigs."

Frenay sat down, sorted out and classified his intelligence files, which were considerable. He selected war news, German troop behavior, the situation in Alsace-Lorraine, early acts of resistance, as the basic news items for his first edition.

Bertie typed up "Information Bulletin No. 1," with eighteen copies. Ten copies were addressed to people living in Vichy whom they knew well. The copies were dropped in their letter boxes. Other copies were sent to friends and associates such as Chevance and Recordier in Marseille. Just eighteen copies—it was not much. But it was a start, and it would lead to one of the most important clandestine papers of the French Resistance, and one that remained a force in liberated France for many years after the war.

Modest as the first effort seemed to them, it exploded like a bombshell. People carried the bulletins around and showed them to friends. Frenay was asked by a number of people whether he knew where the bulletin came from. Everybody wanted more of them. There was always someone else, someone powerful and important who had to see the bulletin. Frenay knew he had hit upon the right formula. He and Bertie began putting the newsletter out twice weekly. Day after day new addresses were added to their lists in Vichy and many other cities.

Frenay was delighted to learn that more and more groups were springing up and printing underground bulletins just as he and Bertie were doing. A friend coming south to Vichy from Paris, just after the turn of the new year 1941, showed him a typewritten sheet that called itself *Libération*. It was drafted by two trade unionists in the Paris region, both Socialists: Christian Pineau of the Federation de Banque et de Bourse, representing workers in the banking and stock market firms, and Robert Lacoste of the Federation des Fonctionnaires, the civil servants of the government. Both men went well beyond the parochial interests of syndicalism when they published a manifesto denouncing anti-Semitism and repression of human rights. Frenay decided that he would have to meet Pineau and Lacoste and the men behind the earlier sheet he had seen, *Liberté*, in order to exchange ideas and coordinate their efforts.

In mid-January, Frenay met an old friend who was passing through Vichy. He confided in him that he was trying to build up a clandestine movement to alert the French people against collaboration with the Germans and, eventually, to organize an armed resistance. The friend, a certain Captain Gouyou, who had served in the French military mission in Prague at the time of Hitler's invasion of Czechoslovakia, confided to Frenay his own disgust with Vichy's policy of collaboration. He advised Frenay to meet with General Fornel de la Laurencie, who had been dismissed from his post as delegate-general of the government in Paris. He felt sure that de la Laurencie would want to help and would be in a position to help. The general had many contacts with all the foreign missions and particularly with the Americans.

Frenay lunched with General de la Laurencie and the men exchanged views openly. The general said that he bore no grudge against Pétain but that his contempt for the Vichy regime around Pétain was "absolute." This coincided with Frenay's own ambiguous feelings about the marshal he respected and his regime, which he detested. When he spoke of Admiral Darlan, General de la Laurencie's contempt escalated to a deep hatred. The general then told Frenay: "Let's stay in touch. I want very much to help you, and I believe that I shall be able to do so. But, above all, please be careful."

Frenay went back to work, collecting his intelligence information from the Deuxième Bureau, BBC broadcasts, and Swiss papers and selecting items for bulletins that Bertie would type up. On January 19, 1941, a decisive event set Frenay permanently on a new course. He opened his paper and read that Marshal Pétain had conferred with Pierre Laval and had "dispelled" the misunderstanding of December 13.

Frenay had rejoiced when he had learned in December that Laval had been ousted and arrested. He had discovered in Vichy that Laval's disgrace had been engineered by anti-German patriots who were vying for power with the fascists around Pétain. He knew, too, that the marshal had openly expressed his hatred for Laval after the arrest. Now apparently Pétain was preparing to take Laval back into the government. It was evident to Frenay that Laval had appealed to his German masters, who had forced Pétain to take him back. In his memoirs, Frenay commented: "So! Darlan was dancing to Hitler's tune, while Pétain met with Laval. The cards were on the table. I asked Colonel Baril for a short leave, for my morale had plummeted."

At his mother's home in Sainte-Maxime, his traditional refuge, Frenay brooded about the old marshal and his own sense of loyalty and duty. "Clearly the government, firmly under German control and ruling only half of France, was no longer its own master. In the shadow of the doddering marshal various clans now jockeyed for power. . . . I began casting about for an honorable way to quit. I couldn't just disappear one fine day without telling anybody, including Baril. That would be the same as deserting. London was out of the question, for I wanted to stay in France and continue my resistance work. To resign was impossible for an officer in wartime, and France was legally still at war; an armistice is not a peace."

Frenay found the way in a frank talk with Lieutenant General

Desbordes of the general staff, whom he had met in 1938 and whom he trusted as a patriot. He confided in him his Resistance activities and the troubled state of his conscience. Desbordes thanked him for his confidence and told him that there was a special ministerial form that would permit him to leave the army honorably. Frenay went to the personnel office and found the form. A few weeks later, toward the end of February, Colonel Baril called him in and gave him the approved papers confirming an honorable "armistice leave" from the army. It was not a discharge but only put him on the reserve list pending a peace treaty, which, Frenay guessed, would mean forever. Frenay put away his uniform and prepared to devote himself full time to the Resistance. "But in the pit of my stomach it was fear that I felt. The fear of a young boxer the first time he enters the ring."

Early in March, Frenay set off for Lyon. He knew by then that Lyon was a major center of Resistance activities. He also knew that the Deuxième Bureau, the Intelligence Service for which he had worked in Vichy, had set up, under cover of a commercial firm, a special "German section" to collect information on the German army and German occupation activities. He knew some of the officers in the unit and went to see them to establish contacts for his Resistance work. They received him with open arms, completely approving his plans. Enthusiastically, he sent a message to his dearest comrade, Bertie Albrecht, asking her to join him in Lyon, which she promptly did.

By then, Frenay had heard a good deal about other Resistance groups inside France and also about General de Gaulle and Free France in London. He kept hoping that de Gaulle would set up underground activities in France and would send him an emissary, but communications were poor in the first springtime after the fall of France.

Frenay made trips to Paris where he conferred with his delegates, Lieutenant de Froment and an old classmate of Frenay's at the Ecole de Guerre, Captain Robert Guédon. Guédon had created an intelligence-gathering network of his own in the winter of 1940–1941, and this spring, he merged his network with members of Frenay's group. One day, they came upon a clandestine paper that called itself *Les Petites Ailes du Nord et du Pas de Calais.* As its name implied, it was spreading its wings through the strategic department that bordered on the Channel. Guédon and Frenay thought it could be a very useful propaganda device for undermining German occupation of that important area but that it could also serve well for all ports and strategic centers. Guédon persuaded the editor to let them try to make it into a national paper called *Les Petites Ailes de France,* in two editions, one edited by Guédon in the north, the other by Frenay in the south. Frenay promised to make a substantial financial contribution to the paper.

Frenay returned to Lyon where he received word that a number of groups all through France—in Tours, central France, Champagne, eastern France, and Caen in northwestern France—had offered to affiliate with his movement. He had, at last, selected a name for his groups. He called his organization the Mouvement de Libération Nationale, the MLN. By the late spring of 1941, Frenay's MLN had units in four departments of the south and another four departments in the occupied north.

Pierre de Froment sent word to Frenay of successful talks with officers of the army's camouflage service, who had passed on to him a stockpile of 150 tons of weapons and ammunition. Frenay was overjoyed, for he did not want to remain forever engaged in propaganda and espionage activities. As a soldier he dreamed of the day when he would once again fight the Germans alongside France's allies, Britain and America. A stockpile of arms was just what he needed to prepare for that day; he might also use some of the arms for guerrilla attacks on the Germans.

Frenay soon met a mysterious person who introduced himself as Captain Besson. He never did discover what service he was in or who had sent him. Clandestine activities often left gaps of knowledge and understanding and demanded big gambles with strangers. Captain Besson introduced Frenay to a businessman who was the director of a big construction firm, with offices on the Avenue de Saxe in Lyon. The firm had two furnished rooms, separate from the main office but on the same floor. The offices had a working telephone. Frenay could have the rooms for an office; all he had to do was invent a false name for the door. Having just seen a movie starring Victor Francen, he decided to call himself Henri Francen, to be consistent with the initials H.F. inside his hatband. It was to be the first of many aliases that Frenay would use. He and Bertie moved their files into their new office.

Some few weeks later, in mid-June, Bertie startled Frenay by bursting into the office, shouting: "I've got one!" When she calmed down, Bertie told Frenay that she had found a printer, named Martinet, who had agreed to provide enough paper for ten thousand copies of their underground bulletins now called *Les Petites Ailes*. He would run the copies off on his presses. *Les Petites Ailes* was about to be born as a newspaper, no longer a mimeographed bulletin.

Frenay was not by any means the only officer or government official who found that he could not go on serving the German puppet regime of Marshal Pétain. One of the bravest of French officials, Jean Moulin, the prefect who had cut his own throat with a shard of glass rather than yield to Nazi demands, had been fired from his service some time after he left the hospital, his wounds scarred but healed. Moulin had made his way into the underground escape channels of France, seeking passage to London, where he intended to offer his services to General de Gaulle.

In mid-June 1941, Moulin was in Marseille, asking about guides who might take him across the Pyrénées to Spain, en route to London. He met an American, a Reverend Howard, one of the leaders of an American relief organization. Howard had met Frenay some months earlier in Marseille and remembered his talk about forming a Resistance movement and helping people escape to Spain. He thought that Moulin ought to meet Frenay. He called

Frenay and told him that a high French official was about to leave for England and it might be a good idea to see him.

Frenay noted in his memoirs that this seemed to him to be a good chance, at last, to establish a liaison with London. "I say London because I made no distinction between de Gaulle and the British government." Frenay's words indicate more than a little lack of respect or appreciation for de Gaulle's Free France. Frenay would come to have a clearer idea of what de Gaulle represented, but he never fully accepted de Gaulle's authority over the men fighting inside France. He came to view de Gaulle as a valuable source of financing and arms, even as a symbolic leader incarnating the spirit of the French Resistance, but not as his superior officer or the overall leader of France.

Jean Moulin and Henri Frenay met on June 15 in the Rue de Rome apartment of Dr. Recordier in Marseille, the safe-house of Frenay's Mouvement de Libération Nationale.

Frenay explained to Moulin: "There are many clandestine activities of which I am not aware and many more that are springing up. But we must guard lest such a proliferation lead straight to anarchy. Efficiency, logic, and even security all require some minimal coordination of our efforts." Frenay had become convinced that the ultimate success of the Resistance depended on overcoming individual differences on policies and conflicting egos, and that would require a symbol outside the Resistance, with a remoteness and federal authority acceptable to all. He told Moulin that "only the Cross of Lorraine and de Gaulle can play such a role."

Frenay said that the Resistance needed access to de Gaulle. "It's pathetic," he told Moulin, "that we have no means of transmitting our information directly to London. And we have serious financial problems." Moulin took notes all through their talk and promised Frenay that his words would be heard in London. Moulin agreed with his views and would, therefore, he told Frenay, "have no trouble in being your advocate." He expected to be in London by the end of the summer and to return to France as soon thereafter as possible. He did not ask Frenay about escape routes, since he had already found a means of getting to London.

Shortly after this meeting Frenay, back in Lyon, came strolling into his apartment house humming contentedly—all was going well. It was about eleven at night and he was surprised to see his concierge sitting at her table in her loge, long after her normal lights out. She was waiting for him. She told him about two men who had claimed to be friends of his, who had come around earlier asking questions. She had a hunch they were police.

Frenay smiled and told her not to worry—they really were friends of his. Still he thanked her for her concern and her warning. He then said he had forgotten to buy a paper and would be right back. He left the building whistling gaily, and of course never set foot in it again. He had long suspected that the police must have been suspicious of his activities, but they had never made a move for him. Now that they had shown up at his door, it was time for him to go completely underground.

He instituted a series of security measures and procedures and insisted that his close friends in the movement adopt them, too. First, a frequent change of pseudonyms to confuse the police. He was successively "Francen," "Molin," "Maurin," Tavernier," "Cervais," "Lefebvre," "Xaintrailles." Second, he insisted on the use of false papers, as inspection-proof as possible. His agents would walk along a street until they saw someone who looked like the man or woman for whom they needed false papers. They would stop the person with the sharp command: "Police!" and demand to see identity papers. They would scrutinize the legitimate identity card, memorize the details and return it to its owner with a salute, then go off and give a clandestine forger of the movement all the correct details for a false card. In this way police records would verify exactly the information on the forged card.

Frenay shifted meeting places constantly, used code numbers or code letters in communications, arrived early at rendezvous and cased the area. On trips in and out of Lyon, he would take the tramway two or three stops beyond the railway terminal before boarding a train and would leave the train three stops before Lyon. He changed his hat and coat often, changed his hairstyle even more often. Sometimes he wore spectacles, with different types of rims, sometimes he did not wear them. He did everything to avoid falling into any kind of a recognizable pattern or image and, almost alone among Resistance leaders, Henri Frenay was never arrested.

But he was almost always just a step ahead of the police and sometimes he was very lucky, as on the day when a voice he did not know called to say that the chief of police would be visiting him the next morning. He received the call in the Avenue de Saxe office that almost no one knew about, or so he had thought. Someone obviously did know. He hurriedly packed his files and every scrap of compromising paper and material. The next morning the police raided his abandoned office. Frenay never discovered who his anonymous tipster was.

He told Bertie Albrecht they would have to change their names and identities again and that it would be a good idea to change the name of their paper. He firmly believed that name changes confused the police and kept the trail cold. They decided to call the paper *Vérités*, on the theory that in the era of the Big Lie, truths must be told. He also remembered a statement that Pétain had made in a speech in 1940 after the fall of France: "I hate the lies that have done us so much harm." It appealed to Frenay's sense of humor to use the Pétain statement on the front page as the motto of his new paper *Vérités*.

The editorial committee that worked with Frenay decided to make *Vérités* much like an ordinary aboveground newspaper, more entertaining, more complete than their first clandestine paper. It would cover world events. Father Pierre Chaillet would write a religious column. There would be a "Truth about . . ." column and an editorial by Frenay under the pen name Veritas. It would have six pages, be published every ten days, and the first issue would have a run of five thousand copies.

Vérités was a considerable undertaking, but not the only one. Always the professional soldier, Frenay decided to make an administrative map of the unoccupied zone, divide it into regions and departments, the better to issue instructions to his agents for their activities and particularly to avoid duplication and overlapping. His map coincided with the divisions of the Vichy government, an arrangement that gave him real advantages. His breakdown of the southern zone was:

R.1—chief municipality, Lyon	10 departments
R.2—chief municipality, Marseille	7 departments
R.3—chief municipality, Montpellier	6 departments
R.4—chief municipality, Toulouse	9 departments
R.5—chief municipality, Limoges	9 departments
R.6—chief municipality, Clermont-Ferrand	5 departments

Frenay's group used his administrative map until the end of the war. It was also adapted by all the major Resistance movements, and by the English and French services in London. Within each of these administrative districts there were many different units of Frenay's movement: distribution of the paper; fund-raisers; armed commandos for attacks on Vichy centers and collaborationist papers and organizations; secret radio monitoring posts. There was, of course, much overlapping. Some men and women had double or triple duties. There were not enough forces for strict specialization or compartmentalization, and this would later lead to bitter disputes with de Gaulle's delegates.

Frenay's relations with his friends of the Quai Saint-Vincent, the Vichy Intelligence Service office in Lyon, had become strained early in June in an argument over the combined British-Free France invasion of Syria. The ancient land of Syria had been put under French mandate by the League of Nations after World War I. From its air bases, planes could attack ships in the Mediterranean or even threaten the Suez Canal. The threat to the canal became urgent when the Germans, with the connivance of Vichy, dispatched warplanes to Syria. Admiral Darlan had met Hitler in Berchtesgaden and had ceded Syrian air bases to him. The British, anticipating the threat to the canal, had decided to attack Syria and take the bases away from the Vichy authorities and Nazi squadrons. General de Gaulle, fearing that imperial Britain would gobble up Syria as a colony if there was no French presence in the invasion, had insisted on sending Free French forces. As a result de Gaulle's troops were fighting Pétain's troops in a French civil war in Syria.

Army officers in Lyon were furious about the British invasion of Syria "with those Gaullist bastards in tow." Frenay, anguished by the fratricidal war, was at first angry with de Gaulle for sending Frenchmen to fight Frenchmen, but he told his fellow officers: "Don't forget, the Germans are in Syria too. Doesn't that make the whole issue difficult to judge?" Frenay was still in the state of mind of trying to forgive Vichy while not quite trusting de Gaulle. But events were forcing him to a complete break with the Armistice Army.

Early June had been a trying period for all those who hoped for an Allied victory. On June 1 the German High Command announced that its troops had captured the island of Crete and taken eight thousand British and four thousand Greek prisoners of war. There were staggering losses of Allied convoys in the Battle of the Atlantic and Britain's food supply was in jeopardy. The battleship *Hood* had been sunk by the *Bismarck*. The British had a chance to cheer when their fleet caught up with the *Bismarck* and sank the German warship off Brest. But, in the Mediterranean, the Luftwaffe sank four British cruisers and six destroyers, while severely damaging the aircraft carrier *Formidable*.

Then came one of the great explosions of the war, Operation Barbarossa, the Nazi invasion of the Soviet Union. Hitler, tearing up his non-aggression pact with Stalin, sent his Panzers and Stukas in a blitzkrieg assault on the Russian lines on June 22, 1941. Henri Frenay knew nothing about that turning-point event of the war the day it happened. Those living underground sometimes had difficulty getting access to radio or to the press. Frenay recalled, in his memoirs, that it was on the morning of June 23 that he saw people clustered around the news kiosks on the Rue de la République in Lyon. He pushed his way through and bought a copy of the paper *Le Progrès*. "I couldn't believe my eyes: German troops had entered Soviet territory the day before, driving back the Red Army, which appeared to be in full retreat."

Frenay wondered about the "real value" of Soviet troops, which, he recalled, had not fought with great success against little Finland. But uppermost in his heart and mind were feelings of "hope and joy." Russia, he told himself, was immense, its troops numberless. Above all, the attack would lift the threat against England. Frenay was certain that Hitler could not fight on two fronts. Frenay was cheered up further by the enthusiasm of the ever-cheerful Bertie Albrecht. She told him: "Hitler will never defeat the Red Army. He has just signed his death warrant." Then Bertie added, with keen political sense, that this news would be a boon to the Communists, who could now join forces with all French patriots in a united front against the Nazis. As she and Frenay were discussing this development on June 23, 1941, Churchill announced in London that Britain would send aid urgently to Russia.

Frenay, himself, suddenly became the recipient of badly needed aid in that turning-point month of June 1941. A friend, Jean Batault, called him and arranged a meeting at a little bistro in the marketplace of Lyon. Batault shook hands and slipped Frenay a long envelope. He whispered in his ear, "Here's a hundred fifty thousand from the general. He'll get you two hundred fifty thousand more shortly, and will provide it each month."

The general was de la Laurencie, who had not forgotten his meeting with Frenay and his promise to help him. Frenay, overjoyed, promptly dispatched eighty thousand francs by courier to Robert Guédon in Paris to finance expansion of the movement in the north.

In August Frenay himself went to Paris. He found that Guédon had developed some extraordinary contacts and made a number of important recruits. Among his "contacts" was the writer Jean Luchaire, the best-known collaborationist of the day and an unwitting source of important information. He had also won the cooperation of Father Michel Riquet, the Jesuit, who helped spread the word and encouraged people to join up. The biggest recruit was Claude Bourdet, prewar managing director of Poste Parisien, an important broadcasting station. Bourdet had agreed to be managing editor of their paper. Guédon also arranged for Frenay to meet with Captain Touny, one of the chiefs of the Organisation Civile et Militaire, the OCM, one of the most effective and militant of the Resistance movements in the occupied zone.

On his return to Lyon, Frenay found his mother waiting for him, pale and tight-lipped. She told him that she finally realized that he had been plotting against the marshal and that he was probably a Communist or a sympathizer. She said: "I love you dearly, but I believe that patriotic duty comes before maternal love. I'm going to denounce you to the police. I must stop you from doing evil and, yes, from doing yourself harm as well!"

Frenay was "more stunned than indignant." He told his mother that if she did this, it would "cause an irreparable breach between us. I respect your conscience; please try to respect mine. But if you insist on doing what you've just threatened to do, don't bother to call for me on your deathbed, for I shall not come."

Frenay remembers that he bent down and kissed his mother good-bye and left. "We didn't meet again until after the liberation. I was by then a member of the government. She had not denounced me."

Frenay heard about a new group operating in Tarbes, near Spain in the Hautes-Pyrénées, which had not only been distributing tracts and leaflets, but had carried out direct action, in particular burning down the depot of Vichy's Légion des Combattants. Frenay checked the group out, discovered it was led by an engineer of the Hispano-Suiza works named Henri Garnier. He called on him, told him about his Mouvement de Libération Nationale and persuaded him to join up.

Frenay then called on one of his militants named Jaquinot. He doubled as an agent for Frenay and for the French general staff, stockpiling arms for the latter. Jaquinot had also just recruited an employee of the Messageries Hachette, Henri Devillers. Devillers had a valid pass for the demarcation line, routinely renewed. His delivery van was always loaded with Hachette books and periodicals and he crossed the line once a week. German guards knew him so well that they waved him on. He was the ideal courier for a clandestine organization and Frenay was overjoyed at his luck in finding him.

Unfortunately, just as Lady Luck was patting Frenay on the head, she gave him a sharp and painful kick in the rear. He received word that General de la Laurencie wanted to see him at the home of a Lyon businessman. Frenay had received funds from the general through the summer and the month of September and was looking forward to another contribution, perhaps from the mysterious people he was told he would meet there.

On entering the meeting place, Frenay was introduced to two

Americans who called themselves Mr. Smith and Mr. Scott. To his dismay, de la Laurencie introduced Frenay as "my agent here." The general then launched into a diatribe against Vichy and said that Pétain was powerless to halt the most servile collaboration with the Nazis. He then dumbfounded Frenay by saying: "There is only one way to reverse this policy of collaboration, and that is to get rid of the present government. Believe me, all France will rejoice at the replacement of the Vichy regime by a provisional Resistance government. It is just such a government that I desire to form."

Frenay could not believe his own ears. How in the world did de la Laurencie intend to overthrow the Pétain regime? With what troops? With the Germans only a few days' march from Vichy? And who had elected or selected General Fornel de la Laurencie to be the chief of a Resistance government? Frenay began to suspect that the man was mad. He was also astonished to see "Mr. Smith" carefully taking notes. The same Mr. Smith asked him how much money he needed for his movement. Frenay gulped and replied that he could use a million francs right away and about a dozen two-way radio sets, plus a long list of light weapons and explosives. Mr. Smith kept nodding and noting down what was being said. Later, Frenay would learn that Mr. Smith was Colonel Legge, the American military attaché in Berne, Switzerland. Mr. Scott was none other than Allen Dulles, chief of the American secret service in Europe and the future first chief of the CIA.

Frenay was "mad as hell," as he noted in his memoirs. De la Laurencie had no right to call Frenay his agent, nor had he any right to propose himself as chief of the Resistance. The Americans had also angered Frenay with a number of caustic, hostile remarks about de Gaulle and Free France. Frenay felt that he would have to have another meeting with de la Laurencie and thrash out the incredible situation; but he did not want to make any decisions alone and felt he needed support from other Resistance leaders. Earlier he had discovered that the man behind the clandestine paper Liberté, which had impressed him, was a distinguished professor of law, François de Menthon, who had started a movement with other law professors and Catholic militants. He got in touch with him to ask his views about General de la Laurencie. He also contacted Emmanuel d'Astier de la Vigerie, whose aristocratic family was even more eminent than the family of de la Laurencie, and who was the head of the southern branch of the Resistance movement Libération.

Toward the end of October Frenay set up a meeting with de la Laurencie and d'Astier in Valence, south of Lyon. De Menthon could not make it. D'Astier told de la Laurencie that the British had already recognized de Gaulle as the leader of French freedom fighters. D'Astier and Frenay were seriously considering enlisting their own movements under the Gaullist banner in the interests of French unity with the Allies. De la Laurencie brushed de Gaulle away with a wave of his hand. Frenay protested: "You can't just ignore de Gaulle." To Frenay's and d'Astier's astonishment, General de la Laurencie nodded his head and commented, "Of course, I'll grant him amnesty."

D'Astier and Frenay left the meeting in disgust. Despite their need for funds, they would have nothing further to do with General de la Laurencie. Later they would learn that de la Laurencie was being manipulated by the Americans, who were giving him money and trying to get him to woo the Resistance away from de Gaulle.

Frenay's bad luck grew steadily worse.

One of Frenay's contacts in the Intelligence Service was a Captain Garon, who provided him with data for his paper. At the end of October, making his rounds in Vichy, Frenay was told by Garon that the file was "not ready." Frenay, knowing the army's punctiliousness about reports, knew it was not true. He asked Garon to level with him and Garon told him bluntly that "*Vérités* was showing Gaullist tendencies. Was it true?" Frenay replied that he did intend to join up with de Gaulle as soon as he could establish sure contacts and that all French patriots must unite against the common enemy, Germany. Garon exploded: "In that case we have nothing more to say to each other. You are a Gaullist—we are not! We are loyal to the marshal. You are no longer welcome at the Quai Saint-Vincent." Frenay's principal intelligence source had dried up.

Disaster followed disaster.

The police arrested Jean Gemahling, Frenay's espionage chief in Marseille. They also arrested the technician in charge of radio and telegraph monitoring in Vichy, plus other members of the movement. The most crushing blow for Frenay was the apprehension of his dear friend Bertie Albrecht. She had been taken to police headquarters in Lyon, questioned for hours, mainly about Frenay, and finally released. He felt "the net tightening around us."

Frenay had been meeting as often as possible with François de Menthon and d'Astier de la Vigerie to talk of unity of action. The latter's movement, Libération, was Socialist and trade unionist, definitely on the Left, whereas Frenay was a rightist, with an amalgam of militarists and middle-class bourgeois in his movement. De Menthon's people, in Liberté, were left-Catholics but not at all as leftist as Libération. De Menthon was much closer to Frenay and they made progress in their talks.

Early in November, de Menthon agreed to merge his group, Liberté, with Frenay's Mouvement de Libération Nationale. The organization and cellular structure of the MLN would be extended to the united movement. There would be a governing committee of six, three from each group. From the MLN Frenay designated himself, Maurice Chevance, and Claude Bourdet. From Liberté there would be Pierre-Henri Teitgen, Alfred Coste-Floret, and de Menthon, all three militant Catholics and eminent professors of law. Later they would be joined by a lycée history teacher and journalist, another left-Catholic, Georges Bidault. They agreed to scuttle their two separate newspapers, *Vérités* and *Liberté*, and publish a new joint paper. Frenay, after some thought, hit upon the title *Combat*. He added an epigraph from Clémenceau: "In war, as in peace, the last word belongs to those who never give up." To throw the police off the track, they decided to pretend that it was a brand-new movement and make no mention of any merger of older groups. They called the new group the Mouvement Pour la Libération Française, MLF. Eventually the title of the paper *Combat* would become the final title of Frenay's movement.

As soon as their merger meeting in Lyon had broken up, de Menthon drove home to Annecy, where he was living with his family. On the road home he was stopped and arrested. The police transferred him from Annecy, in the corner of eastern France near Switzerland, to Marseille, where they incarcerated him in the Prison des Baumettes. He had no idea what was happening to him or why, for the police told him nothing.

De Menthon was then taken from Marseille and driven to Vichy, to the office of Commandant Rollin, chief of the feared DST, the Direction de la Surveillance du Territoire, a counterespionage police group. There, to his surprise, de Menthon was subjected to a lecture about his "antinational" attitude, based mainly on Rollin's glorification of Marshal Pétain. He told de Menthon that he was strongly anti-Nazi and could understand resistance against the Germans, but not against France's revered old hero. He then let de Menthon go, with a warning about engaging in anti-Pétainist activities. De Menthon went right back to his Resistance activities, ignoring the warning.

As winter closed in, Frenay visited all the six regions of the south. He met with Coste-Floret, the new chief of R.6, and with the well-respected Edmond Michelet, another devout Catholic and democrat, the new chief of R.5. He was most impressed in Montpellier, R.3, with two men running that region, Pierre-Henri Teitgen, the Catholic militant from *Liberté*, and René Courtin, a Protestant. They both taught in Montpellier University and their classes were famous for the anti-Nazi and anticollaborationist speeches of the two professors.

Also in Montpellier, Frenay met an extraordinary new recruit who would take over armed combat and commando operations for his movement. His name was Jacques Renouvin. He was a prewar member of a fascist organization called Les Camelots du Roy. In ancient times a *camelot* was a combination of a crier and a street hawker; the name was used by the fascists to convey the impression of men speaking out against the Republic in a royalist and antidemocratic movement. The Camelots du Roy were an extreme rightist wing of a larger royalist organization called Action Française. Renouvin was tall, powerful, a street brawler. Although a fascist, he hated the Nazis, for they were Germans, and Renouvin, despite his contempt for the Republic, was a French patriot who loved his country if not its government.

When rightist politician Pierre-Etienne Flandin sent Hitler a telegram of congratulations after the Munich Conference of 1938, Renouvin was furious. He followed Flandin to a ceremony at the Arc de Triomphe, and when Flandin leaned over to deposit a wreath on the Tomb of the Unknown Soldier, Renouvin reached across intervening shoulders and rocked Flandin's head back with a meaty slap from his ham-size hand.

Frenay had heard that Renouvin, demobilized after the armistice and at loose ends in Montpellier, had been recruiting a band of street fighters

Hitler on esplanade of the Palais de Chaillot,
June 23, 1940. (Heinrich Hoffman)

Nazi SS in front of their headquarters,
Rue des Saussaies, Paris. (J. Delarue)

ABOVE LEFT
*Marshal Pétain and Pierre Laval
in Vichy.
(Collection Comité d'Histoire)*

ABOVE RIGHT
*General de Gaulle presiding over a
meeting of the French National
Council, Carlton Gardens, London.
(Comité d'Histoire)*

LEFT
*Winston Churchill wearing the Cross
of Lorraine, symbol of de Gaulle's
Free French movement in London.
(AGIP—Robert Cohen)*

LEFT
Claude Hettier de Boislambert,
one of de Gaulle's aides in London.
(Private collection)

RIGHT
Colonel Rémy (Gilbert Renault),
foreground, right, in liberated village,
August 5, 1944.
(Comité d'Histoire)

BOTTOM
Colonel Passy (middle, facing
camera) with Colonel Eon of the
F F I, during an action at Kerien
(Côtes du Nord), August 6, 1944.
(Comité d'Histoire)

LEFT
Paul Rivet, Director of the Musée
de l'Homme, 1946.
(Keystone)

BELOW
Boris Vildé, leader of the Musée
de l'Homme Resistance movement.
(Comité d'Histoire)

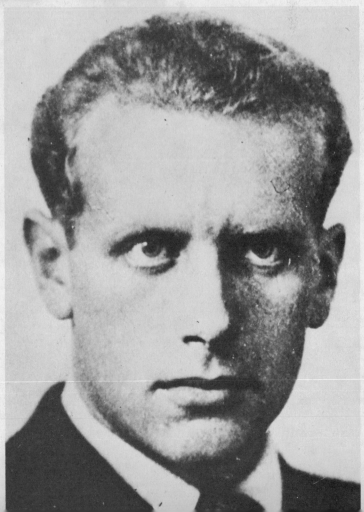

Commandant Léon Faye, one of the
leaders of the Alliance.
(Courtesy M-M. Fourcade)

Commandant Loustaunau-Lacau,
founder of the Alliance Resistance
group. (Private collection, courtesy
M-M. Fourcade)

Henri Frenay, chief of Combat.
(Polpress)

Marie-Madeleine Fourcade, chief
of the Alliance, 1940.
(Courtesy M-M. Fourcade)

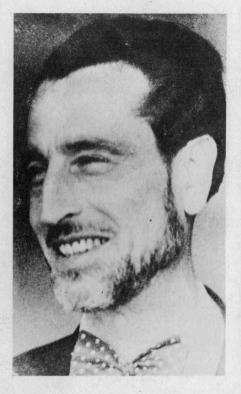

ABOVE LEFT
*Emmanuel d'Astier de la Vigerie,
chief of Libération, 1942.
(Comité d'Histoire, courtesy
Mme. d'Astier)*

ABOVE RIGHT
*Jean-Pierre Lévy, chief of
Franc-Tireur, 1940.
(Private collection, courtesy
M. Lévy)*

OPPOSITE
*Jean Moulin, chief of the CNR.
(Comité d'Histoire)*

ABOVE
Admiral François Darlan (l.) and
General Henri Giraud in Algiers,
December 18, 1942.
(ECPA, Army Photographic Service,
Ivry)

RIGHT
Robert Murphy represented the
United States as Consul General
in North Africa during World
War II.
(Courtesy U.S. Department of State)

TOP
*Chamber of Deputies, Palais Bourbon, Paris,
with Nazi swastika on the rostrum.
(Comité d'Histoire)*

BOTTOM
*French resistants being arrested by the Gestapo, Paris.
(March of Time/Time Inc.)*

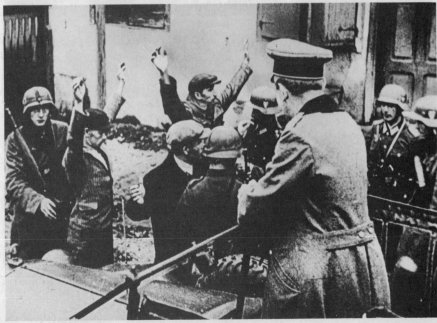

RIGHT
Underground printer.

BELOW
Pulling copy from the clandestine press.

Close-up of underground paper of the Combat movement.
(Photos: March of Time/Time Inc.)

LEFT
Resistant sabotaging rail line.
(Archives Documentation Française)

BELOW
Resistant taking gun from secret
cache of weapons.
(March of Time/Time Inc.)

OPPOSITE TOP
Claude Bouchinet Serreulles in his office at General de Gaulle's headquarters at Carlton Gardens, London, circa 1941. (Private collection)

OPPOSITE BOTTOM
Georges Bidault, president of the CNR; photo taken in 1945 when he was named foreign minister of France. (Presse Libération)

RIGHT
Maquis camp in forest. (March of Time/Time Inc.)

BELOW
Maquis group in forest camp. (Carl Mydans, Life Magazine © 1944 Time Inc.)

Members of the National Council of the Resistance at the liberation. (LEFT TO RIGHT) *M. Debu-Bridel (Fédération Républicaine); Pierre Villon (Front National); Gaston Tessier (Conféderation Française des Travailleurs Chrétiens); M. Chambeyron (Secretary); Pascal Copeau (Libération-Sud); M. Laniel (Alliance Démocratique); M. Lecomte-Boinet (Ceux de la Résistance);* (IN FRONT) *Georges Bidault (Parti Démocratique Chrétien);* (BEHIND BIDAULT) *M. Mutter (Ceux de la Libération); M. Ribière (Libération-Nord);* (IN FRONT) *Daniel Mayer (Parti Socialiste);* (BEHIND MAYER) *Jean-Pierre Lévy (Franc-Tireur); P. Bastid (Radical); M. Gillot (Parti Communiste); M. Neunier (Secretary); M. Saillant (Conféderation Générale du Travail).* (Musée Carnavalet)

like himself to act as commandos in raids on collaborationist sites. This was just what Frenay wanted and needed for his movement. Up to now he had recruited mainly intellectuals, journalists, or soldiers used to disciplined combat. He needed men suitable for guerrilla warfare and clandestine operations and Renouvin and his gang were just the ones the situation demanded. Frenay was not concerned about Renouvin being a fascist. What better job to give a fascist than the mission of street brawling attacks on collaborationist news kiosks, printing presses, meeting halls? Frenay and Renouvin hit it off well together, agreeing on the need to fight Vichy and the Germans. Frenay suggested that Renouvin call his commandos Groupes Francs, a name connoting guerrilla activity. Renouvin became the chief and set about creating a national organization. They soon left a trail of shattered, smoking cinemas, newsstands, and French-German social centers across France.

In his initial concept of a Resistance movement, Frenay had provided for paramilitary units, trained to launch armed attacks on occupation troops. He had given that future structure the name Choc. In the year of organization, 1941, he had managed with difficulty to put together several six-man and thirty-man cells of commandos. He had been afraid to give them the signal for any action, for they were not yet ready. And he had come to realize that there had to be two types of paramilitary organizations: one, direct-action commandos, which were needed immediately; and the other, a larger, more military group, for long-range action to liberate the country. The first group came into being with Renouvin, the Groupes Francs. The second had to be set up. He decided to call it L'Armée Secrète.

Frenay was in his room on a bitter cold December 7, when he heard the radio announce the Japanese attack on Pearl Harbor. "It was wonderful news! It didn't even occur to me to think about the terrible American losses, about those burned-out hulls in Hawaii. Only one thing mattered: America, the great and powerful America was now on our side."

On December 15 Frenay received word that things were going badly in the occupied zone. Robert Guédon's wife had died, and he was stricken with grief. The Gestapo was hunting for him and he lived from day to day, on the run, in Normandy. He had to be replaced as chief, and the whole movement needed reorganization. Frenay went north to see what could be done.

He met with his friend Guédon for a frank discussion, then launched an investigation of his own. He met with key members of the movement in the occupied zone, with Jeanne Sivadon, Elisabeth and Paul Dussauze, with Father Riquet and his friend André Noël of the Pax Romana group, and with the Abbé Vallée. They all agreed the movement needed a general staff, a hierarchy of command, a tighter structure.

Elisabeth Dussauze convened a team meeting for Frenay. He spoke to them at length about the history of the movement, the current situation, and the need to throw their lot in with de Gaulle. Then they set up a steering committee of the northern zone, headed by André Noël and Elisabeth Dussauze. The meeting broke up and Frenay left. None of them could know it, but a terrible threat was hanging over them and they would never see each other again.

It was at the end of the year 1941 that Frenay met a man named Michel Brault, known as Jérome. He was an international law expert, with important connections in London and Washington. The British Intelligence Service had asked him to set up an intelligence and action network in France and he was engaged in that activity when he met Frenay. He told Frenay that he would like to work out a reciprocal exchange of information and explained that he had all the means to get the information to London. Frenay was devoured with jealousy when he heard that Jérome had "many two-way radios" and rapid, direct communication with London. Frenay was still trying to get a set after a year and a half of operations.

Jérome offered to help Frenay and provide him with the matériel he needed. "All I had to do," Frenay later recalled, "was to say yes and our whole position would improve enormously." But he understood it would mean working with the British, not de Gaulle. It would mean breaking the unity of the Resistance he had been trying to forge. He told Jérome that his answer was negative. He could not make the deal with him.

The year 1941 ended. Frenay and Bertie, who had come to meet him in Paris, finished their work in the north and headed back to Lyon right after the new year had been ushered in. On his return he received an urgent note from Dr. Recordier, his old friend in Marseille: "Come to Marseille immediately. The high official whom you met in my house last July has returned. He has been staying with Georges and he wants to see you."

In their code, "Georges" was London. And the high official Frenay had met in Marseille was Jean Moulin. Moulin had returned from London. Frenay was eager to see him. He wondered: Would he have money and radios for me; would there be a permanent liaison with de Gaulle? Frenay felt the answers to those questions would make or break the unity of the Resistance and Free France.

10
REBELS, LEFT AND CENTER

France is a country of paradoxes where the opposite of any generalization may be as true as the generalization itself. Frenchmen and women are dedicated Catholics and France prides herself upon being the "elder sister of the Church." Many Frenchmen and women are also dedicated Communists, and through most of the postwar years were the most faithful followers of Moscow. The French are visionaries and cynics, poets and peasants, their heads in the clouds, their feet deeply stuck into their fertile earth.

The Frenchman with the very French name of Emmanuel d'Astier de la Vigerie encompassed in his being almost all of the French contradictions. He was descended from one of the most ancient, aristocratic families of France. One of his brothers was a general, another an ambassador, and yet another a freebooting adventurer. "Manny," as his friends called him, was a journalist and a naval officer, a Catholic who rarely went to church, and who sought out Communists as comrades-in-arms. But, before the war he had been a member of the rightist movement Action Française and had been antidemocratic and anti-Semitic. To be sure, later in the Resistance d'Astier's best friends and closest companions were Jews and Communists, and as a former naval officer, the man he detested most was the French navy chief, Admiral François Darlan.

D'Astier was so lean, his skin pulled so tight over his facial bones that he looked like a victim of the concentration camps. His finely chiseled features, deep-set eyes, and high flush made him look like an ancient doge of Venice. All he would need to step out of an Italian canvas would be to wear a high-necked ruffled shirt—which indeed he sometimes did.

All who knew Emmanuel d'Astier de la Vigerie were impressed with his singular mix of idealism and black cynicism, of enchantment and disenchantment. One might easily envisage d'Astier sitting comfortably at a meeting of the College of Cardinals in Rome, after having cordially conferred with the chief of the Communist party. It was not that he was an opportunist, lacking any personal conviction, but rather that he thoroughly enjoyed and entertained a great many convictions. D'Astier de la Vigerie was a Renaissance man and an incurable romantic, exactly the kind of man that one might expect to find in an underground revolutionary movement.

As soon as he was demobilized in the summer of 1940, d'Astier went to visit a number of trusted friends living along the Riviera and the southeastern slopes of the Alps. He told them that the French people had to be alerted to the dangerous illusions of collaboration with Hitler and then, once informed, organized to fight again for the honor of France. It was exactly the same reasoning reached independently by so many other French patriots.

D'Astier proposed that they begin with a simple tract, a one-sheeter they could then expand. He gave it the title *La Dernière Colonne*, a takeoff on the phrase the fifth column. He gave copies to friends in a number of places and told them to carry on, while he toured about, looking for new people, new ideas, seeking some grand enterprise. He spent a few days in Vichy, was disgusted by the gloomy defeatism of the Pétain entourage, and left at once for a place that he had heard was fermenting a revolutionary brew, the city of Clermont-Ferrand in central France, not far from Vichy. Clermont-Ferrand was the site of a huge Michelin tire plant, with thousands of militant Socialist and Communist workers. D'Astier, the wealthy aristocrat and former rightist, had begun to believe that the best recruits to fight the defeatist marshal and his Nazi masters might well be the leftist workers of France.

On arrival in Clermont-Ferrand, before he could make any contact with union leaders, d'Astier discovered a vigorous center of hostility to Vichy and the Germans in the exiled faculty of the University of Strasbourg. One of the first men he met was Professor Jean Cavaillès, a professor of philosophy. With Cavaillès was a young woman who had brilliantly passed the highest examinations of the French academic system, the *agrégation*. To be an *agrégé* was to win the top competitive rank in the university and it entitled the winner to a university teaching appointment.

Lucie Aubrac was an *agrégée* in history and geography. D'Astier —who had a flair for dramatic exaggeration in his writing style, tending to the florid and often cruel—described Lucie Aubrac as an *"amazone agrégée d'Histoire,"* giving the impression that she was a large, muscular, aggressive female. Those who know her would not accept that description. Madame Aubrac today, serving a visitor a Scotch and soda on the terrace of her apartment overlooking Montparnasse, is a graceful, chic Parisienne. She is highly cultured but does not flaunt her learning. She speaks warmly and admiringly of d'Astier and her comrades of the Libération movement that emerged from their meeting, as she recalls how she came to be a resistant.

"My family was a peasant family in Alsace. We worked the vines. They wanted me to have an education and rise above the fields. I studied at the University of Strasbourg and passed my *agrégation* examinations before the war. From 1937 to 1939 I taught history and geography at the university. Just before the outbreak of war I won a scholarship, the David Weill Scholarship for study in America. I was scheduled to leave in September 1939 on the *Ile de France.*

"I was in Saint-Nazaire. My trunk had already been put aboard, when war broke out. I was engaged at the time to Raymond Samuel, an engineer in the Department of Bridges. He was a Jew and I knew there would be trouble. I ordered my trunk to be taken off the boat and canceled my passage."

Raymond Samuel later took the Resistance name Aubrac, the name the couple legally uses today. (Many men and women kept their Resistance names for the rest of their lives.) At the outbreak of war, Ray Samuel was mobilized as an engineer officer in Alsace. Lucie took a temporary appointment as a history teacher in a lycée. Among her pupils was a young girl named Kaminsker, whom the world would later know and admire as the great French actress, Simone Signoret.

"After the Germans broke through the French lines in the spring offensive, I learned that Ray had been taken prisoner. As a professor of history, I knew all about nazism and Hitler. I had carefully followed the events of the thirties, and I knew I would never see Ray alive again if he did not find a way to escape from prison camp.

"On August 25, 1940, I received permission to visit him in his camp. I had been waiting impatiently for the call and I was ready for it. I carried in my bag a box of pills, called Pinatra. It was a hormone that women took to lose weight. They would give a man a high fever. I slipped a few to Ray, explaining to him what they would do. He swallowed them after I left.

"The next day Ray had a raging fever. The Germans transferred him at once to the hospital, fearing a contagion that would spread through the prison. They wanted those prisoners for a work force and for blackmail of the French government. I called and got permission to see my husband in the hospital. This time I smuggled in workman's *bleus*—a kind of blue-jean uniform. I had a car parked outside the hospital wall and went there, anxiously waiting for Ray to climb over. When I saw his blue pants coming over the wall, I shouted with joy and started my motor. He flopped down, ran over, and we were away rapidly.

"I drove straight to Lyon in the unoccupied zone. We had a moment of anxiety crossing the demarcation line, but controls were not yet as rigid as they would soon become and Ray's name had not yet been posted as an escaped prisoner. He had no difficulty being demobilized in Lyon and getting a job as an engineer. He had an excellent record in the Department of Bridges and Highways and there was a shortage of experienced engineers.

"I had to go to Clermont-Ferrand, where the University of Strasbourg had located, to seek a new teaching assignment. As an *agrégée* with a few years' experience, I had a high rank and felt I would have no difficulty. I had been a member of the Jeunesse Communiste and supported the Popular Front and one day they might dig that out of my past. But I had not been a militant, had held no party post. I was, by then, just a left individualist, not a Marxist, not even a Socialist, but not an anarchist either.

"I was willing to work with others, to build a better society and to fight for the rights of man. I was anti-Nazi, anti-Pétainist, antiracist. Strangely, I was not anti-German, not at that time. Later, when I saw the horrors of the Nazis and the failure of the Germans to mount an effective resistance against their monstrous leaders, well, then I became anti-German. But, despite all these 'anti' motivations, which we all shared, we were positively motivated to restore the Republic and basic human rights."

It was in Clermont-Ferrand that Lucie Aubrac met d'Astier de la Vigerie and agreed to join his movement, La Dernière Colonne. As with most early Resistance movements, its first activity was the production and distribution of tracts criticizing Vichy policy and denouncing the German occupation.

The Germans were beginning to loot France officially. They gave their troops a special scrip and set an artificial exchange rate for it. Then they simply printed as much scrip, and later marks and pfennigs, as they chose to print. With that money German officers and men soon started clearing out French jewelry shops and clothing stores. Even more serious for the health of the French people, occupation authorities began buying up milk, butter, meats, vegetable oils, fats, and flour. Bread, meat, and fats were rationed in France and each month the rations would be cut or the products would disappear from the shelves.

Lucie Aubrac remembers that there were also early attempts at sabotage. "We did not yet have guns or explosives, and what we did was in a way childish. We risked our lives stupidly and Ray was furious with us. For example, we learned that a sugar train was coming in from Spain, headed for Germany. We found out from friends in the marshaling yards where the Spanish freight was being parked. Then, at night, armed with oil cans, we crawled up like Indians and surrounded the sugar train, broke open the freight doors, and began injecting oil into the sacks of sugar. I suppose it was infantile, but it made us feel good to be taking direct action and it showed us what we were capable eventually of doing. We discovered a will, a courage and daring that we did not know we possessed. We were after all just middle-class people, teachers, journalists, shopkeepers, quite ordinary people."

Lucie laughed as she recalled a series of passwords that d'Astier gave them. As one agent approached another the first would say: "*Sous le pont de Mirabeau.*" The second agent would respond: "*Coule la Seine.*" * It was not very professional in the fall of 1940, but within a year the Germans would learn to respect the amateurs of the French Resistance.

While d'Astier was recruiting for La Dernière Colonne, he was already thinking ahead to a much larger movement that would bring together all the trade union members of the unoccupied zone. He was certain that the workers could be organized. He knew that they were completely fragmented and lost in the fascist State of France. The principal prewar trade unions, the

---

* "Under the Mirabeau Bridge runs the Seine."

Confédération Générale du Travail (CGT), mainly Communist and Socialist, and the CFTC, the Confédération Française des Travailleurs Chrétiens, the Catholic trade union, had suffered heavy losses in the war and then had their leaders replaced by Vichy stooges and German collaborationists. Many of the top trade union leaders of France had gone into hiding.

Trade union leader Léon Jouhaux and his wife were living in a small villa in Sète, where the Socialist journalist Daniel Mayer found them on a tour of France. Daniel was in the process of seeking out Socialists to rebuild the party. Jouhaux told him that the CGT would also have to be rebuilt. Later they met with d'Astier and listened to his ideas on a trade union Resistance movement. Meanwhile two CGT officials, both members of the Socialist party, were working in Paris to organize trade union action: Christian Pineau, of the Fédération de Banque et Bourse, and Robert Lacoste, of the Fonctionnaires.

Pineau had begun to organize some elements of the trade unions into a movement called Libération-Nord. He did not believe that he and Lacoste had the personal authority and credentials to reconstitute the CGT but rather to bring together a nucleus of comrades who were committed to maintaining the true principles of French syndicalism. Pineau and Lacoste drafted a manifesto condemning repression and anti-Semitism, pledging allegiance to the fundamental principles of liberty and justice. It went much beyond professional principles of syndicalism and was meant to. They obtained signatures from Catholic as well as Socialist trade unionists.

As with other movements, the first action decided upon was to publish an underground paper. On December 1, 1940, the first issue of *Libération* appeared in the occupied zone. Its opening circulation was modest in the extreme: seven typewritten copies. But it would grow to the thousands and would be printed on regular presses. Even the minimal seven copies mushroomed rapidly as they were recopied and recopied again by trade unionists throughout the northern zone.

D'Astier was thinking exactly along the same lines in the south. Although he had very few adherents to his group, he also decided to launch a new clandestine paper. Independently of Pineau, he called it *Libération*. Its first issues appeared in January and February 1941. By July he had found a printing press and the first printed issue of *Libération* appeared.

Daniel Mayer, Christian Pineau, and other union leaders conferred on the advisability of setting up a strictly trade union Resistance movement, or joining forces with d'Astier, the Aubracs, and other professionals and intellectuals. They concluded, finally, that a man like d'Astier with an eminent name, a naval rank, friends in many milieus, would make an excellent leader and act as a shield against those critics of the worker organizations who still blamed Léon Blum and the Socialists for the pacifism of the Popular Front. An umbrella like d'Astier was also needed for left Socialists like the Aubracs, who were not Communist party members and did not want to work in Communist ranks. The time would come, Mayer felt, when the Socialists would be able to emerge and act in their own name. At the start, d'Astier was just the leader they needed.

D'Astier was an energetic and persuasive recruiter for his movement, Libération. He won the adherence of a number of outstanding members: the former deputies Pierre Viénot, Marcel Poimboeuf, and Augustin Laurentin. Louis Martin-Chauffier, the journalist and husband of a prominent member of the Musée de l'Homme group, became the editor of the paper *Libération*. Their sabotage groups struck almost daily against production in factories, on the railways, and in postal communications. Léon Jouhaux endorsed Libération, wrote articles for the paper, and urged trade unionists to join the movement. This enabled d'Astier and de Gaulle's envoy, Yvon Morandat, who worked with him, to bring about much needed cooperation between Libération-Sud and Libération-Nord. The members of the movement in the occupied zone were almost exclusively trade unionists and former members of the Socialist party.

Finally, every effort was being made to cooperate with still another movement, whose clandestine paper had appeared for the first time in December 1941: *Franc-Tireur*. As in the case of Libération and Combat, the paper would give its name to its movement. There would be a good deal of overlapping among members of these three movements. Some men, at times, were working for all three in one capacity or another. In every city it was generally the same men and women who first began to resist and it was some time before all of them got sorted out among the movements and then coordinated the work of the movements themselves. Each movement grew in numbers and strength until they had formed the Big Three democratic movements of the Resistance: Frenay and Combat on the right; d'Astier de la Vigerie on the left with Libération; and in the center, a remarkable young man and group, Jean-Pierre Lévy, chief of Franc-Tireur, founded and headquartered in Lyon.

Lyon, the third city of France, is located in the east central part of the country at the confluence of the rivers Rhône and Saône. It is almost equidistant between Paris and Marseille, and in more ways than just geography.

When one hears the word *Paris*, images of beauty and brilliance flash across the memory: the gold leaf dome of Napoleon's Tomb under the arc lights at night; the world's most majestic square, the Place de la Concorde, with its stone horses guarding the entry into the broad Champs-Elysées. Almost all the history of France can be seen in the streets of Paris. Paris is living theater. It is the capital of France and in some ways of the world.

Marseille is the sweaty, earthy body of Mediterranean France. If Paris is the elegant woman of fashion, Marseille is elemental Woman. On the Arc de Triomphe is the magnificent statue of a warrior-woman by Hude, her head high, charging forward, shouting a battle cry. Hude called her *La Marseillaise*, the woman-symbol for France's stirring national anthem.

Unlike either Paris or Marseille, Lyon is solid, reliable, and sober

—the city of the successful, prudent bourgeois. Its buildings are made of cut and chiseled blocks of stone that look as though they will last forever. Paris and Marseille are female. Lyon is a middle-class, middle-aged man. When one thinks of Lyon, one sees in the mind bolts of the finest silk and plate upon plate of the most succulent foods. Lyon is the fabric and culinary capital of France, home of the world-famous Lyonnaise potatoes, sliced thin, sautéed with browned onions. Shimmering silks and simmering potatoes, that is Lyon. It is hardly the place one would expect to become the principal center of an underground war.

But Lyon was the most logical place for the Resistance to take root and grow. It is a big city, whose many buildings, cellars, and warehouses offered a warren of safe hiding places. It was south of the demarcation line, free, at the outset, of German occupation. Above all, Lyon is the hub of the principal rail lines and national highways of France. And its stolid, sober, conservative way of life was the best cover for revolutionary activities.

Not every resident of Lyon was a bourgeois conservative. Among workers and intellectuals there was a strong, if small group of Socialists, Communists, and dedicated liberal democrats. Among them were two former Communists: Elie Péju, a white-collar worker, and Jean-Jacques Soudeille, a small businessman, owner of a moving van company. Both had quit the Communist party early in 1930, in a break with "Stalinism." Although they had left the party, both remained men of the Left, committed to fight for a democratic Republic of France.

These men had seen the decline of democracy all through the thirties. They asked themselves: What will the future bring down around our heads? They decided they could not passively wait to let it happen.

They went to see Georges Vavasseur, a bookseller. For the past fifteen years he had been the spark plug of a club called the Tribune du Rhône, a free discussion group where speakers of all political tendencies had the right to take the floor. Meetings were lively at the club and most of Lyon's intellectuals and public opinion leaders attended and participated in the discussions. Péju was certain that Vavasseur would be the man to understand the need for united action.

Vavasseur was interested, as were others who had been in the Tribune group: Antoine Avinin and Auguste Pinton, particularly, were discussion leaders. Auguste Pinton was a teacher in a lycée, a member of the centrist Radical party, and a municipal councillor of Lyon. Avinin was a merchant who had joined the movement called Jeune République, a group of liberal Christian Democrats. Avinin was well known and liked in Lyon and was able to attract the sympathies of his fellow members in the Catholic group.

One of the first things that Avinin had done on his own when France fell was to organize an escape network for war prisoners, particularly the British who had not got out at Dunkirk. He had set up a reception center at Mâcon and a series of safe-houses down through France to Perpignan on the Spanish frontier. Pinton had already begun to organize resistance to Vichy and the Germans after the Vichy government had illegally dissolved the municipal council of Lyon.

Noël Clavier, an industrial engineer, also conducted regular meetings to discuss what to do. Attending the meetings were Georges Vavasseur and Jean-Jacques Soudeille. They discussed their affairs, as all the other groups did, not knowing what each little circle was up to.

Early in November, Avinin and Pinton met at the Café du Moulin Joli with Maurice Rolland, an ex-municipal councillor, member of the Executive Committee of the Radical party, a lawyer and journalist well known and respected in Lyon. The three men agreed that discussion groups did not go far enough, that a clandestine organization must be created for direct action against Vichy and the Germans. They agreed to meet regularly at the Café de la Poste, whose owner was one of them and could keep an eye out for police spies. They were quickly joined by Noël Clavier, Jean-Jacques Soudeille, Elie Péju, plus several others. They were a mix of social classes and professions: merchants, office workers, industrialists, engineers, lawyers; also an amalgam of political tendencies: Communists, Socialists, radicals, Christian Democrats.

A few of those meeting at the Café de la Poste formed an inner circle and met again at Clavier's house. They felt the larger group was still bogged down in the talking phase. They wanted to put out propaganda, tracts, pamphlets, brochures, perhaps a newsletter, to expose the lies of the collaborationist press and the Vichy radio. They also wanted people to know the truth about Pétain. One member of their group had found documents charging that Pétain had actively worked for the defeat of France to bring about the fall of the Republic and his seizure of power. Another associate had procured a copy of a secret report called the Doyen report, named after its author, Paul Doyen, chief of the French delegation to the Franco-German Armistice Commission. It revealed German plans for the annexation of Alsace and Lorraine and a drastic revision of France's northeast borders. They had sent these documents, via Switzerland, to General de Gaulle and were electrified one night to hear Maurice Schumann, the Free French spokesman in London, broadcast details from their documents.

In the late fall of 1940 they formed themselves into a group and gave it the title France-Liberté. Their first venture into direct action was a *papillon*—literally a "butterfly," a small piece of paper that could be used as a sticker for walls, backs of trucks and buses, with just a few words on it. *"Vive de Gaulle"* was a popular papillon slogan, as was Churchill's victory sign, *V*, or de Gaulle's Cross of Lorraine. The group also distributed typewritten tracts, limited to a small circulation among sure friends.

The Resistance activities of France-Liberté did not advance very far until, in the late fall of 1940, a new recruit joined them. His name was Jean-Pierre Lévy.

Today Jean-Pierre Lévy is an official in the Ministry of Health. Looking back to the last months of 1940, he says: "You must know, first, that

I was born in Strasbourg. As an Alsatian, I was, in 1940, fiercely anti-German. Second, you know that I am Jewish, a double reason to hate the Germans. And, of course, I am French, enough reason to despise the traitors and collaborationists of the Vichy regime. From the day I was demobilized from the army, I was burning to take action against the Germans and against Vichy."

Jean-Pierre was twenty-nine years old in 1940. He was tall, strong, self-confident. He had taken his *licence* in law and his diploma from the Institut de Commerce Supérieur. He was a reserve officer, a lieutenant in the artillery, the 124th Regiment, on the Somme. His unit had to fall back under the pressure of German armor, but Jean-Pierre fought valiantly and was decorated with the Croix de Guerre.

Jean-Pierre speaks in a low voice, but all his authority and commitment to a cause can be heard in the intensity rather than the volume of his speech. "I had read *Mein Kampf*, in 1933. Seven years later, I saw that Hitler had done what he said he would do. I did not, therefore, doubt that he would try to carry out all the ravings in *Mein Kampf*. I knew he would try to exterminate the Jews, that he would turn on the Russians, that he would liquidate all human rights for all peoples."

After the armistice Jean-Pierre Lévy decided at once that he would find a way to continue the struggle. First, however, he had to find a job and a cover for his activities. Before the war he had been a salesman in the Lyon area, for a jute factory. He had risen to the position of administrative chief of the enterprise just before war broke out. The owners of the firm were Jews and had taken refuge in Marseille. When the armistice was signed they offered Jean-Pierre the position of director of their Paris office. He told them they were crazy to ask a Jew to work under the German occupation of the capital. They agreed to send him back to Lyon, from which the Germans had withdrawn when the demarcation line was drawn to the north of it.

"It was in Lyon that I met Antoine Avinin. He introduced me to friends who had created a group called France-Liberté. The first meetings were held in October-November 1940. I felt that we ought, at once, to create chains of distributors of our propaganda material, starting with students at the university. As a salesman I traveled a lot and was able to meet many people and sound them out, from Lyon to Marseille, and could extend our distribution.

"I soon realized that typing and copying tracts would never provide enough copies. We had to get a mimeo machine. But the Germans had already put controls over the sale of such machines and also of stencils. Luckily I found a friend in the sewing machine business who had a mimeo and a supply of stencils. Instead of six copies at a time, on carbon paper, we could now turn out two hundred copies at a time on stencil. Do you know how thrilling that was?"

No American, living safe from invasion in our continental fortress, can truly feel and appreciate the emotions, fears, anxieties of the French living under occupation. Jean-Pierre explained: "When you hold that tract in your hand, it is your life, all your hopes that you are holding. You Americans revere your Constitution, as you should, and you live free because of your Bill of Rights. But when a nation is defeated and oppressed by a cruel enemy and a shameful government, then no Bill of Rights is meaningful. What means something infinitely precious is that piece of paper that you have typed and mimeographed yourself. It is your personal Bill of Rights, your defiance of evil, your very own life that you risk when you dare print a few words of defiance."

Later, when Jean-Pierre and his comrades strengthened their movement and were able to go from one-sheet tracts to four- and six-page newspapers, printed underground, their danger multiplied. The papers often were literally printed underground, in cellars, with blankets piled up around the windows to keep out light and sound from the eyes and ears of patrolling police. Sometimes, daring printers at official papers would run off a few thousand copies of a clandestine paper between or after runs of the public paper they were working on. At all times, the Resistance movement had to station their own patrols and watch guards, armed with revolvers at first, later with submachine guns, to protect the printers from an overzealous patrolman nosing around, or from a sudden raid by the Gestapo. The Gestapo had its spies everywhere and many an underground printer paid with his life for his commitment.

Jean-Pierre continues: "My sister Denise, who lived in Roanne, started a chain of distribution there. I began to think of this not only as links in a chain, but as antennae, curling out across the country, picking up and sending out messages to fellow Frenchmen. It was an exhilarating moment. I buttonholed almost everyone I could to work for us. I had a cousin in Toulouse, Pierre Lipschutz, who sold cloth. He had friends who were willing to participate. One was a pharmacist, Frank Arnal, who showed me a copy of an underground paper called *Les Petites Ailes* and another called *Libération*.

"I didn't know then that the *Petites Ailes* was put out by Captain Henri Frenay and his friends in a movement called Combat and that *Libération* was the organ of a movement by the same name headed by a fabulous personality, Emmanuel d'Astier de la Vigerie. But although I did not know these men or anything about their movements, it was enormously encouraging and challenging to know that we were not alone, that others were already fighting against Vichy and the Germans. It spurred us on to greater efforts."

Early in 1941, the key formative period for all groups, Jean-Pierre Lévy met a man named Pierre Eude, a fellow Alsatian, secretary-general of the Chamber of Commerce of Strasbourg, who had fled from the Germans and established himself in Lyon. An immediate bond of affection, respect, and common purpose linked the two men: Eude was a walking encyclopedia of economic information that Jean-Pierre could use for tracts. He was also in touch with the thousands of Alsatian refugees in Lyon. Some seven thousand were being lodged in temporary dormitories in the Palace of the Lyon Fair. Each of them cleared through Pierre Eude on arrival. They were a powerful nucleus of resentment and opposition to the regime, and when France-Liberté put out a tract denouncing the rape of Alsace, they flocked to sign up to help the organization.

Pierre Eude and Georges Boll, son of the director of the paper *Journal d'Alsace*, had the idea of producing a postcard of the Cathedral of Strasbourg, with the caption FRANCE in bold letters, under which was quoted the message of President Roosevelt of June 18: "The government of the United States will not accept the validity of any attempt to diminish by force the independence and territorial integrity of France." Jean-Pierre and his associates distributed these cards by the hundreds.

One day in 1941 Benjamin Roux, a technician at the Berliet trucking plant and a friend of Jean-Pierre's, called him to report, "I have found a printer who will help." Jean-Pierre rushed over to meet him. The printer's name was Henri Chevalier. "He had a plant on the street appropriately named Cours de la Liberté," Jean-Pierre recalled. "He agreed to print an underground paper for us."

Jean-Pierre called a meeting of his most trusted friends in the movement: Avinin, Gayet, Pinton, Soudeille, Péju, Clavier—the men who had founded France-Liberté. He told them the good news. They immediately approved the project of an underground paper except for Gayet, who was violently opposed. He wanted military action. He quit the group.

After some discussion, it was agreed to use a time-honored revolutionary name for an independent fighter: *Franc-Tireur*.

The name *Franc-Tireur* had been proposed by Jean-Jacques Soudeille. It referred back to the irregular army of republican soldiers, without uniforms or any official backing, that had formed spontaneously during the terrible days of 1870–1871 in the Franco-Prussian War. They were all volunteers who rallied together to defend the Republic and their country when all else was lost. It seemed an appropriate name for an underground Resistance movement, without uniforms, opposing the official and puppet government. They also felt that the independent ring to the name Franc-Tireur made it clear that they were not working for de Gaulle or the British.

The leaders recognized two enemies: Germany and fascism. The Germans would have to be driven out, but so would Vichy and its fascist ideology, so that a new Republic could be reborn. Its first editorial, in December 1941, had stated its objectives: "We want to found after the war a new regime, a synthesis between authority and liberty, a true democracy cleansed of the bumblings of political parties and the domination of the trusts and the financial powers. We want neither a military dictatorship, nor a religious dictatorship, nor a proletarian dictatorship, nor a capitalist dictatorship."

Union linotypists agreed to put out the paper without charge, and the printer, Henri Chevalier, also volunteered his services. Paper was bought at the factory price and the entire expense of the first edition was only ten thousand francs, which the leaders of Franc-Tireur scraped together. They had been offered financial backing by a British Special Operations secret agent but had turned it down. They would not accept outside help until they met Yvon Morandat, de Gaulle's delegate. He offered to help them, with no strings attached. They trusted him and worked with him.

In order to relieve Henri Chevalier of a heavy burden and to share the risks, Jean-Pierre Lévy and his friends looked about for additional printers. They found the brothers Rey and Eugène Pons. Rey was already printing issues of *Libération* for d'Astier, but he agreed to take on *Franc-Tireur*, too. Eugène, a militant Catholic democrat, a good friend of Antoine Avinin, also agreed to print *Franc-Tireur*. In addition he worked with Combat and *Témoignage Chrétien*, the underground Catholic journal. He was eventually caught by the Germans, deported, and died in concentration camp.

The leaders of Franc-Tireur, unlike Frenay and d'Astier, came to the conclusion that they needed the most professional help to turn out a first-rate paper. They would be responsible for its propaganda and political line, but outstanding newspapermen had to be found to edit it properly. They struck pure gold when they contacted two of the top editors of the paper *Le Progrès de Lyon*, Georges Altman and Yves Farge. Their regular jobs were perfect covers for clandestine journalism and they both jumped at the chance to put out *Franc-Tireur*. They split up the duties, Altman as day editor, Farge as night editor. Their offices had two entrances and exits, one for the public, the other through the composing room, past the printing presses.

Franc-Tireur had more trouble increasing its forces and contributions than some other movements because it was the first of the movements to denounce Vichy and Marshal Pétain directly and by name, at a time when the old marshal was still revered by a great many people who were otherwise sympathetic to the Resistance. Franc-Tireur, mainly Jean-Pierre Lévy, would accept none of the theories about Pétain's playing a double game. The paper attacked Pétain directly as a defeatist and a fascist. It cost Franc-Tireur a lot of support but won it the admiration of those who saw the truth. The circulation of the paper rose from six thousand in December 1941 to fifteen thousand in the period January to April 1942. It reached thirty thousand by the end of the year and one hundred fifty thousand by the time of the Allied liberation campaign in 1944.

"As a traveling salesman I could go everywhere," Jean-Pierre recalled, "but I always came back to Lyon. One can hide better, disappear into the crowd in a big city, and Lyon had facilities of all kinds to offer, so it remained our headquarters."

The group soon found an ideal meeting place in Lyon: a shop called La Lingerie Pratique, owned by two women, Mesdames Péjot and Denisetti. "These women gave us not only their shop but their apartment nearby on the Place des Jacobins. We were able to function on their premises until late in October when we were denounced to the police. One of our men, in a bizarre mix-up, had picked up the wrong valise in a station. Someone else got his, and in his valise was incriminating material and—the idiot!—a list of names and addresses. It was on October 24, 1941, that the police came to the apartment on the Place des Jacobins. France Péjot and I were there, along with my secretary Micheline Eude.

"Micheline managed, somehow, to tear pages out of her notebook and swallow them. France Péjot threw herself on my lap and began kissing and hugging me, telling me with sobs: 'Oh, darling, I'm in the Resistance.' She pretended to be my mistress and wanted the police to think that I was ignorant of any Resistance activities. I caught on and acted as though I was shocked by her behavior. Then Pierre Eude came in looking for his daughter. The police must have thought we were a bunch of circus clowns. It would be difficult to imagine that we were leaders of a major Resistance movement.

"We were all taken to the Commissariat of Police where we spent the night. Then one by one we were released, except for the two women, France and Micheline. They were given sentences of three weeks and three months. The police searched my house and Clavier's but found nothing. Poor France Péjot was later deported to Germany. She offered her life to save mine."

In addition to Jean-Pierre, the Executive Committee was composed of Antoine Avinin, Elie Péju, Auguste Pinton, Noël Clavier, and Jean-Jacques Soudeille. Jean-Pierre reported all major developments to the committee, but, for security reasons, he shared details, such as names, addresses, depots, printers, with only one other member at a time. Some of the members resented his obsession with secrecy and their pique would lead to an internal crisis when, in the spring of 1942, Jean-Pierre received an invitation to meet with General de la Laurencie, who was still seeking a lever on the Resistance.

Not wanting to go alone, he invited Fleury Boucher to accompany him. They were warmly received by de la Laurencie, who told them he had a plan: to overthrow the Pétain regime and unify the Resistance to form a new government, with the aid of the Americans. When Jean-Pierre asked him about de Gaulle, de la Laurencie was sharply critical of the man who 'fled France.' Jean-Pierre was deeply mistrustful of everything he said, particularly when the general told him that he had already met with d'Astier and Frenay, without adding that they had both turned him down, which Jean-Pierre had already decided to do.

Upon his return to Lyon, Jean-Pierre reported on this meeting to his *comité directeur*. Jean-Jacques Soudeille, who had already been critical of Jean-Pierre's leadership, burst into a violent denunciation of the entire proceeding and said he should never have gone to see the general. He then announced his resignation from the committee. The others approved Jean-Pierre, reconfirmed his leadership, and tried to talk sense to Soudeille. He refused to rejoin the committee, but he continued to work for Franc-Tireur, with his close friend Elie Péju. This clash of egos was typical of the conflicts that plagued the Resistance movements.

Then, since bad news always seemed to come in clusters, the bookseller Georges Vavasseur was arrested, in May, followed at once by the arrest of Antoine Avinin, charged with editing and distributing tracts. Fortunately his sentence was extremely light, very different from punishments handed out by the Germans in the north: He got three months in the Saint-Paul prison. The arrests caused Jean-Pierre to cancel committee meetings. He would take on all responsibilities working with Péju and Clavier. Fortunately he obtained the help of two first-rate men: Georges Altman, the editor, and Eugène Petit, alias Claudius, who became his number-two leader of the movement.

Jean-Pierre Lévy had been impressed with Henri Frenay's concepts of organization of a clandestine movement and tried, up to a point, to use his methods. He felt that the first objective must be to organize a successful propaganda section, before going on to develop intelligence and military sections of his movement. Once the paper *Franc-Tireur* was well developed, Jean-Pierre began to create other services, notably: political, economic and military intelligence, security, and paramilitary units, commandos and reserves for a long-range Secret Army.

Although he never was able to duplicate the extraordinary penetration of the public administration that Claude Bourdet had created for Frenay, Jean-Pierre did succeed in recruiting very useful secret agents inside the Lyon police, telecommunications and post office systems, and Justice Department. A police inspector, Charles Bassauer, whose job it was to hunt out persons of "Republican sentiments," met Benjamin Roux of Franc-Tireur and decided to join with them, a most valuable agent, for he was often able to tip off resistants on an arrest list. He, himself, was eventually arrested in the fall of 1942.

In Lyon, a young telephone line-checker, Emile Bontoux, joined Franc-Tireur. He was in charge of maintaining surveillance of German telephone lines and monitoring stations. Marie Roure, an employee of the central Lyon switchboard, was another agent of Franc-Tireur. Dozens of engineers, technicians, and workers in the highly industrialized region of Lyon were recruited. Many were able to form sabotage teams to destroy German orders. A handful of sand in the gearbox of a truck, a slight error in measurement on a finely calibrated machine, could wreck a military order.

Jean-Pierre set about creating Groupes Francs, as Jacques Renouvin had done for Frenay. Their objective was to attack and terrorize Vichy propagandists and the collaborationist press. Benjamin Roux was appointed chief of this operation. He recruited young men for this dangerous mission. His biggest problem was getting arms and explosives. He took his problem to Jean-Pierre. Jean-Pierre went to see an agent of the British SOE, Georges Dubourdin, who had offered them help in 1941. The help had been refused at that time, for Franc-Tireur wanted to be independent of a foreign power. Dubourdin, known as Alain, told Jean-Pierre he would furnish him with arms and explosives and ask nothing in return, thus preserving the movement's independence.

Jean-Pierre thanked Alain and told him that Franc-Tireur would want to help in picking up the matériel when it was parachuted. Alain agreed. The first parachutage took place on May 28, 1942, near Port-Galland. A Franc-

Tireur team was at the site, picked up the drop with speed and efficiency. Alain was impressed and promised Jean-Pierre more arms and aid whenever possible. Jean-Pierre and Roux set up training schools for their "terrorists," with professionals teaching them how to use and manipulate the new plastic explosive, incendiary pencils, time fuses, detonators, and the whole panoply of sabotage weapons.

Groupes Francs were formed in Lyon, Roanne, Clermont, Limoges, Vichy, Nice, and Toulouse. They used Frenay's six-man cell structure. They received more and more arms, including Bickford fuses, grenades, and light machine guns. As soon as they were trained, sometimes during training itself, they were given real "field exercises." In Lyon, Benjamin Roux led a team of six in attacks on newsstands carrying Vichy papers and on the shops of members of Vichy's militia. Arms depots were set up throughout the city. So successful were Jean-Pierre and his comrades in stockpiling arms that Combat and Libération came to him and asked him to set up depots for them.

Claudius-Petit talked the guardian of a park into hiding arms in a hothouse for plants. In five days' time, in November, Claudius brought him eight tons of arms to hide. The chief of a garage gave them the trucks for transport. Arms were also hidden in the home of Jean Roure, in a store that sold equipment to fishermen, and in various warehouses. They also stocked gas for the movement, thanks to a former Army Intelligence officer who took over a tank-reservoir in an arsenal in Roanne.

In addition to the Big Three democratic movements of the south, spreading their own influence to the occupied zone of the north, there were a great number of independent movements and networks in the occupied zone, as well as the special networks set up by the British and by Colonel Passy, Rémy, and other Gaullist agents. The coalition of military men and rightist intellectuals known as the OCM, the Organisation Civile et Militaire, was one of the most powerful of the movements in the north.

The biggest of all the movements, in both zones, were Communist-controlled, a direct result of the long-term clandestine organization of the Communist party, always a kind of pariah in French society. The two principal Communist organizations were the Front National and the Francs-Tireurs et Partisans Français, FTPF. Front National, as its name indicates, was a front organization, run by the Communists but including many liberal and conservative elements who were persuaded to join the Communists in the name of national unity and also with the promise that the skill of the Communists in clandestine activities would make them all more efficient resistants to the common enemy. Finally, there was the organization that was constantly confused with Jean-Pierre Lévy's Franc-Tireur movement. The Communist party, not wanting to create a movement in its own name, chose the name Francs-Tireurs et Partisans Français. They liked the ring of Francs-Tireurs, as Lévy and his men did, and for the same reasons. But they also added the name Partisans, which was the name the Russians used for their own guerrillas. And they added Français to underline their argument that Communists were good Frenchmen and not servants of Moscow.

All of these various movements were ready for an active extension of their activities in 1942, hoping that within a year the Allies would launch an invasion and then they could all join in for the final struggle to drive the Germans out of France. But, at the end of 1941, they were not yet supplied with enough arms for much direct action. Above all, they had only just become aware of each other and of their many duplications of efforts and lack of coordination. The next step, in many ways more difficult than the creation of the first movements and networks, would be the task of unifying them inside France and also with the forces of General de Gaulle and Free France across the Channel.

11

A CHIEF FOR THE RESISTANCE

Jean Moulin, the former prefect in Chartres, had made his way south during the course of 1941, with the hope that he would find a way out of France across the Pyrénées.

He had read underground papers and listened to the radio broadcasts from London, becoming more convinced daily that General de Gaulle and Free France were the hope of the future. He did not fear de Gaulle as a "man on horseback," a potential dictator, as some resistants did. He had taken careful note of some of the men around de Gaulle whom he knew personally to be dedicated democrats. De Gaulle had rejected defeat, had denounced collaboration with the Germans, and, above all—a critical point for Moulin—de Gaulle would return to France in the wake of the British and American armies. Britain and America, Moulin was convinced, would not tolerate a dictatorship in liberated France. So de Gaulle was his man. His problem, he reasoned, was to make himself de Gaulle's man so that he could play a role in creating strong ties between the internal Resistance movements and Free France in London.

Moulin felt he had to inform himself thoroughly about Resistance strengths, weaknesses, and needs before escaping to London. This reasoning had led him to a first meeting with Henri Frenay, among others. In weeks of questioning everyone who knew anything about Resistance activities, Moulin had concluded that Frenay's Combat movement was the largest and most effective group in the Resistance. After his meeting with Frenay in the summer of 1941, Moulin redoubled his efforts to arrange passage to London.

A friend of Moulin's, Major Henri Manhès, obtained a false passport for him, issued by the *sous-préfecture* in Grasse, the city of roses and perfume near the Riviera. In it he was described as Joseph-Jean Mercier, professor of law at New York University. He took the passport to the American consul in Marseille, Hugh Fullerton, telling him that he wanted to go to London to join the Allied forces. Fullerton promptly issued Moulin an American visa. Armed with the American clearance, Moulin quickly obtained transit visas from the Spanish and Portuguese consulates in Marseille.

By September 12, with all papers in order, "Professor Mercier" crossed the French-Spanish frontier at Cerbère. He took the train to Lisbon. In Lisbon, Moulin went to see the British consul and asked for a visa to Britain. There he ran into his first difficulty. The British were suspicious of all travelers, even with the best-looking credentials. Many Nazi spies, drawn from the conquered nations, had infiltrated into British services posing as anti-Nazi refugees. Moulin, raging with impatience, had to wait a full month in Lisbon before the British Secret Service signaled the consulate that he was genuine.

Moulin arrived in the English port of Bournemouth at the end of October, hoping for an early meeting with General de Gaulle. De Gaulle himself had been alerted by messages from France that Jean Moulin was en route to offer him his services and was anxious to take him on. Moulin's dossier in the prefectoral service had been forwarded to de Gaulle by his spies inside Vichy and was filled with "most excellent" evaluation reports, stressing his administrative and organizational ability and leadership qualities. This was the kind of high-level recruit de Gaulle needed for his still thin ranks in the fall of 1941.

De Gaulle wrote to Anthony Eden, Churchill's liaison officer for all exiled groups in London, asking him to send Moulin to him as soon as he arrived in London. But Eden, alerted by his own services that this was a valuable man and a potential British agent for France, had no intention of turning Moulin over to de Gaulle.

Moulin was astonished to find the British overwhelming him with kindness and flattery and keeping him tied up in meetings and interrogations about what was happening in France. They never quite refused to let him go to London to see de Gaulle. They kept him so busy in Bournemouth, and then at various camps to which he was conducted on a guided tour of British services, that he never could get a car or a ticket to go to London, despite his daily appeals. The British offered him top jobs and used every means of seduction to win him away from de Gaulle. After a month of this game, they finally understood that Jean Moulin was as fervent a French patriot and nationalist as de Gaulle himself. Reluctantly they gave in and sent him on his way. It was November before Moulin arrived in London and was granted an appointment not by de Gaulle at first, but by the head of de Gaulle's Intelligence Service, Colonel Passy.

Passy, of course, had his own full dossier on Moulin, and was most anxious to take him on as his envoy to the French Resistance. He had only recently become aware of the true potential of the Resistance. De Gaulle and the men around him had concentrated from the start on recruiting Frenchmen in England or persuading Frenchmen to escape to England to join Free France. Their aim was to build a large enough force to be able to resist Allied efforts to turn them into friendly puppets; they were convinced that this was the aim of both Roosevelt and Churchill. As for the internal Resistance, it was still too small to attract full attention from de Gaulle and his men.

But by the late fall of 1941, reports sent back from France by de Gaulle's principal agents, Rémy and Yvon Morandat, had convinced Passy that the Resistance was growing and would become a major force. It was imperative in his view that this force not be a power rival to de Gaulle but become an arm of Free France, under the control and orders of de Gaulle, and, of course, of Passy, himself, whose own importance would grow as the forces under his command grew.

Jean Moulin's report strengthened Passy's conviction that the Resistance had to be harnessed by Free France. Passy felt that Moulin should be sent back to France as the envoy of General de Gaulle, with the mission of coordinating all Resistance activity through a central command. Moulin would, of course, report to Passy, whose organization, then called SR (Service des Renseignements), was in charge of all intelligence activities for Free France. Passy was already planning at that time to change the name of his organization in order to broaden its scope and power. The name he had in mind was Bureau Central de Renseignements et d'Action (BCRA). There were two key words in this title as he conceived it: *Central,* which meant that all intelligence, political and economic as well as military, would be centralized under his command, through Moulin; and *Action,* which would broaden his authority to include operations as well as intelligence. It was an ambitious plan that would make Passy second only to de Gaulle himself as a leader of Free France. Providing of course that both de Gaulle and the internal Resistance would accept it. The big first step would be to win Moulin's approval.

Moulin, who had come up through the ranks of the political jungle of the French governmental bureaucracy, where infighting was the daily bread and wine of life, saw clearly what Passy was attempting. He was wise enough not to discuss any of the power aspects of the proposal. He could deal with that later. He concentrated on the substance of the plan, the idea of centralizing inside France all Resistance activities under his leadership. With no political ambitions of his own—he was a career civil servant already near the top of his profession—Moulin saw instantly the wisdom of centralizing political, economic, and military operations under one High Command. He knew how closely related all these activities were, any one of them influencing the others, so that they should not be rigorously compartmentalized. He enthusiastically endorsed that aspect of Passy's plan, winning for himself Passy's own support for his assignment to a key role.

Toward the end of November, Moulin was finally ushered into the presence of General de Gaulle. He was impressed by the strength and self-confidence that radiated from his bearing, as were all who met the general. Even in a crowded room de Gaulle always seemed to be alone, taller than all around him, his head held high, his eyes looking at some distant object, untouched by those around him. Moulin felt de Gaulle's hauteur but was not awed by it. He had enough strength of character and self-esteem of his own not to become a sycophant of another man.

De Gaulle asked for his report on the situation in France and listened carefully without interruption. Used to delivering reports to high government officials, Moulin was crisp, clear, and brief. De Gaulle complimented him and then began to question him on his evaluation of the situation and his recommendations on how to deal with events in France, most particularly, how to deal with the Resistance, for de Gaulle had come to realize that he could no longer concentrate on recruiting for his forces in England and the French Empire. He had to have a commanding position inside France.

General de Gaulle told Moulin that he would see him again in a few days for further discussion. Moulin left his office pleased with the results and set about meeting other staff members of Free France, confident that he could win support for his plan to return to France to organize the Resistance under de Gaulle's banner. One of the first men to endorse Moulin was Claude Serreulles, de Gaulle's chef de Cabinet officer, who hoped that eventually the general would release him from his administrative duties so that he, too, could return to France and work with Moulin. Serreulles, as chief aide to de Gaulle, had constant access to him and was a valuable new ally for Moulin.

De Gaulle called Moulin back at the end of the week. He had decided to send him to France as his personal envoy with the mission of organizing, coordinating, and controlling a Resistance High Command loyal to de Gaulle and willing to accept orders from London. Moulin was delighted but he warned de Gaulle that it would not be easy. The Resistance leaders, particularly Frenay, had created their movements by themselves without any help from London. They were proud and independent men, living dangerously under the Nazis, and could not be expected to follow orders as soldiers would in a traditional army command structure. Moulin said that the success of his mission would depend greatly on de Gaulle's ability to persuade the British, who held the purse strings and the keys to the armories, to send all the help that the Resistance needed. The Resistance could be made dependent on this aid and thus more likely to accept orders.

De Gaulle said he understood and would do what he could. Then, to Moulin's surprise, he said that he wanted him to meet with André Diethelm, a major prewar political personality whom de Gaulle had appointed commissioner of the interior in the new Conseil National Français (CNF) in London. Diethelm, said de Gaulle, was in charge of all political questions for Free France and would be the one to whom Moulin would report on political issues. On military questions, Moulin would report to Passy.

De Gaulle seemed to be setting up exactly the kind of separation of political and military affairs that Moulin felt would not work. A military man all his life, de Gaulle always insisted that the military must be kept out of politics, an ironic position to adopt since he, himself, was the political leader of Free France. Moulin was further startled when de Gaulle went on to tell him that in Moulin's own command structure he would be both the political and military chief, in fact the overall chief of the Resistance, with everything centralized in his person and organization. Moulin would centralize everything in France but would report to different and separate authorities in London. Moulin knew it was a hopeless administrative structure, but one did not argue with de Gaulle when he announced a decision. Moulin, anxious to be away and get on with his mission, agreed to the terms. De Gaulle told him that in a few days he would be given his credentials and specific descriptions of his authority.

Passy was furious at having his authority cut in half, but there was nothing he could do other than to try to circumvent de Gaulle's decision in his communications with Moulin. He was relieved to learn that Moulin's authority was limited to southern France, to the so-called free zone not occupied by the Germans. That gave Passy a free hand to step up the activities of his own agents north of the demarcation line. He was obliged by the decision to make yet another change in the name of his own organization. It would now become the BCRAM, the Bureau Central des Renseignements et d'Action Militaire, since de Gaulle insisted that he handle military affairs and Diethelm political affairs. He knew it could not work and there would be friction and rivalry between him and Diethelm and their staffs.

Moulin busied himself with plans for his return to France. He had recruited two men to accompany him: the twenty-two-year-old Joseph Monjaret, code name Hervé, as radio operator, and a thirty-year-old teacher, a reserve lieutenant named Raymond Fassin, code-named SIF, who would be his liaison officer to Frenay and Combat. They were due to fly to a target area in southern France, near Moulin's birthplace, where there were many friends and safe-houses to hide in after the parachute drop. The date of departure was symbolically important: January 1, 1942, the beginning of a new year and a new life for Jean Moulin.

At two in the morning, when revelers in southern France were still celebrating the new year, a British Armstrong-Whitley bimotor was circling at a low level trying to find the drop zone. People wending their way home, who had had too much to drink, were astonished to see a British plane flying around their houses. The clearing that Moulin had chosen was an open space between the rivers Rhône and Durance. It was a clear night and there should have been no difficulty about finding it, but somehow the pilot had got off course. As leader, Moulin had decided to jump first. He seated himself in the open bomb bay, his legs dangling in space, looking for the clearing.

Moulin never saw the clearing, but he did get the jump signal and promptly pushed himself off. He landed in a swamp, thigh-high in reeds and mud. It took him more than half an hour to extricate himself. He was shaking with cold, his clothes soaked through. He whistled for his companions and heard an answering whistle off to his right. It was dark, several hours before dawn, and he could see nothing. Continuing to whistle and to shake with a chill, he made his way to the echoing whistle. It was Hervé. Moulin had lost his pistol in the swamp and was relieved to recognize his radio operator.

Moulin then discovered that he had also lost his compass in the swamp and that a package of sandwiches for their supper had become a sodden mess. Hervé told him that he did not know where SIF was and had not seen where the container with the radio equipment had landed.

The two men set about to search for their comrade and the container. It was five in the morning and dawn was near. It would be risky to be out in the open when daylight arrived. Suddenly they saw a shadow move ahead of them. It was SIF. He was digging a hole preparing to bury the radio and his parachute. Joyfully Moulin ran ahead and embraced SIF. Hervé jumped on his precious radio and inspected it. It was intact. The container had protected it. The three men set out for their first hiding place, a shepherd's hut that Moulin had marked on their maps. They agreed to go singly in order not to make too much noise and attract attention. Moulin went first and SIF followed him, about a hundred yards back. Hervé was to go last.

Hervé will never forget that moment. "When it came my turn to go, a pair of gendarmes materialized in front of me like ghosts in the pale dawn. They had seen the three of us huddled together and were intrigued to watch us break up and begin to walk on singly. They asked for my papers. Fortunately London had done a perfect job giving me false identity and ration cards." The gendarmes looked his papers over carefully, asked him a few questions, told him he had better get home, and then left. Hervé, fearing that they were setting a trap, stayed where he was. He did not want them to follow him and catch the others. He waited an hour until he was sure the gendarmes had left. He knew it was then too late to join Moulin and SIF. He walked until he reached a main road and then took the bus to Marseille.

Moulin and SIF waited a half hour for Hervé and then, afraid that he had been caught and that the police were looking for them, they took off to find the hut. Once there they threw themselves down exhausted and fell into a deep sleep. In the afternoon, refreshed, they set off for Montpellier where Moulin wanted to visit briefly with members of his family. From there, Moulin went to Marseille to meet with Dr. Recordier and set up a meeting with Frenay. Meanwhile, Hervé headed from Marseille to the village of Bargemon. Moulin had told him that if anything went wrong he was to go there and contact Major Manhès, who had been so helpful in getting Moulin false papers for his escape from France. Moulin had telephoned to his sister Laure, telling her to start looking for Hervé at the addresses he had given him. Laure found him a few days later and called her brother to report that his precious radio operator, his vital link to London, was safe and sound.

Recordier told Moulin that Frenay was anxious to see him and that a meeting had been arranged at the home of Agnès Bidault, the sister of the Catholic militant Georges Bidault. Maurice Chevance, whom Frenay had named chief of Combat for the Marseille region, came to the meeting with Frenay. Frenay and Moulin rushed to embrace each other. Frenay, famished for news about London and de Gaulle, begged Moulin to tell him everything in every detail, bombarding him with questions.

Moulin first described London and the bravery of the British under the devastating Luftwaffe blitz. He told him about the men of the RAF who had shot the Luftwaffe out of the skies night after night. They could not prevent terrible destruction in London, but they had dealt the Luftwaffe fatal blows. "The Germans will never succeed in invading Britain. Hitler has lost his chance. The only invasion will be that of the Allies and it will succeed. We will survive. We will be liberated," Moulin vowed.

"And de Gaulle? What is he like? Tell me all about de Gaulle," Frenay shouted.

"He is magnificent," Moulin replied, "a true son of France, indomitable. He will lead us to victory and liberation." Moulin went on to describe de Gaulle's fierce independence, his courage in standing up to Churchill, his refusal to be an Allied puppet. Frenay grinned. This was just what he wanted to hear. Then Moulin drew a matchbox out of his pocket and extracted some strips of microfilm. He took a magnifying glass out of another pocket and said to Frenay: "Read this."

Frenay, puzzled, took the film and the magnifying glass and began to read. It was just a short paragraph stating that Moulin's mission was to "bring about the concerted action of all elements that resist the enemy and the collaboration." It further stated that Moulin was to report directly to de Gaulle.

Frenay's first reaction was positive. He noted later in his diary: "Here at last was what we had so long awaited: contact with Free France, miraculous contact on the highest level."

Frenay told Moulin that he had met with François de Menthon and the leaders of Liberté, who had agreed to merge their groups with Frenay's in a larger new movement, which they had agreed to name Combat. He went on to say that he had not been able to work out any agreement with d'Astier de la Vigerie and his Libération movement or with Jean-Pierre Lévy and Franc-Tireur, although he was sure that something could be done to arrange an overall coordination. He also told Moulin that he had gone north and met with leaders of Resistance groups under the Nazi occupation, principally the strongest of them, the Organisation Civile et Militaire (OCM), the coalition of military officers and conservative intellectuals. "These men are fighting the Germans directly. They are not inclined to rally to de Gaulle. They say they resent the men who fled France. The real fight is here, they argue, in the internal Resistance."

Moulin was not worried about this development. His mission had been limited to the territories south of the demarcation line; he told Frenay they would get to the problem of the north later. Meanwhile, Moulin would serve as the Resistance intermediary with London. He had a radio, an operator, and an airtight code. He promised that he would be able to help Frenay with important aid. On the spot he pulled out of his pocket a thick wad of notes totaling two hundred and fifty thousand francs, and handed it to him. Then, he said: "From now on you will call me by my code name. It is Max. You must give me code names for yourself and your principal lieutenants." Frenay smiled and said: "Pleased to meet you, Max. I am Charvet. And this [pointing to Chevance] is Bertin."

Frenay's wide grin was soon to disappear. Moulin continued to pull objects out of all his pockets, like an amateur magician; he handed Frenay new rolls of microfilm. Frenay began to read very precise instructions, covering every possible operational question down to the tiniest details. As he read, it dawned on him that these instructions were in fact orders. Frenay was not one to take orders for Resistance operations from a remote headquarters unfamiliar with conditions in France. In fact Frenay, who had shaken off the habit of army discipline in the active months of independent activity, was not the one to take orders from anyone. He had labored hard and long and risked his life every day to build his movement. He was eager to cooperate with de Gaulle and his men: He needed money and arms and radios from them. But he was not about to jump to his feet, salute, and take orders.

Moulin, either oblivious or indifferent to his reaction, went on to tell Frenay that Colonel Passy, chief of de Gaulle's intelligence and action service, was "very upset" about the techniques and tactics of the Resistance, particularly the "intermingling" of political, intelligence, and propaganda services. The various functions would have to be separated out and compartmentalized.

Bertin immediately objected. He argued that London's view was correct in terms of military orthodoxy. But in the field it was completely impractical. "We have commando squads at our disposal. How can we possibly forbid them to receive and distribute *Combat*? How can we possibly order them not to transmit some important intelligence report they receive?"

Frenay then added that these activities were the only plausible role for a Resistance movement in the unoccupied zone. The men had to have something to do while waiting for D-day. If units were to stay together and be combat-ready, they had to take daily risks and have regular operations. Aside from commando attacks on collaborationist institutions, what could they do other than distribute propaganda and gather intelligence? The argument continued through the night and would not be the last between the forces of the interior and the forces of the exterior.

Frenay assigned Henri Aubry as liaison and facilities aide to Max. He also said he would arrange for Moulin to meet de Menthon and d'Astier. The meeting with de Menthon took place a few days later, but d'Astier met with Moulin separately, without Frenay. Max told Frenay to check out sites for parachute drops, and said he would be back to him soon. They were to meet almost weekly in the months to come.

The differences that Moulin and Frenay ran into in their first meeting presaged many conflicts to come. Christian Pineau, the Socialist trade unionist, was the first resistant from the interior to get to London to see de Gaulle in March 1942. Writing about his meeting in his book *La Simple Vérité*, Pineau expressed his astonishment at de Gaulle's almost total lack of appreciation of the Resistance inside France. "He mentioned the Free French, the troops in Africa, as if they were the sole representatives of the French Resistance. . . . He put me not a single question about the Resistance, not a single question about my activities. Perhaps it seemed too humdrum to him to ask if I'd had a good journey to London, but in my eyes it had been no ordinary journey, and it merited some small word of acknowledgment."

Frenay called a meeting, at Nîmes, of his movement's steering committee and informed them in detail of his talk with Max and the troublesome attitudes and directives of London. They all agreed it was a serious dilemma. To accept London's directives would be to place Combat under the command of de Gaulle. To refuse would be to risk losing the money, transmitters, and arms that only London could supply. They finally agreed to try loyally to carry out Passy's instructions.

"All during the year 1942, we tried our utmost to accomplish this," Frenay wrote later. "It was so much wasted effort. Though it was possible to separate our political arm from our military arm on the national, regional, and departmental levels, as we approached the rank-and-file membership the resultant dislocation seemed appalling. In the last analysis, it was simply impossible to bring about the required political/military articulation."

Just before the meeting at Nîmes, Bertie Albrecht took Frenay aside. "Henri," she burst out, "if what I've heard is true, our Hachette messenger, Devillers, is a German spy."

Frenay gasped: "A German spy? Are you out of your mind, Bertie? Who in God's name has been handing you such nonsense?"

Bertie told him that his former agent in Toulouse, Jean-Pierre Lien, had come down from Paris to tell her about Devillers. In Paris, he frequented a restaurant where a number of Germans also ate. Lien, an Alsatian, understood German and listened in to their conversations. One day he heard some plainclothesmen at the next table talking about Combat and Frenay. Pretending to be a collaborator, he joined their table and ordered champagne.

They were Abwehr undercover men assigned to maintain surveillance on Frenay and the movement. They knew all about Frenay and an upcoming trip of his to Paris and were planning to arrest him as soon as they had learned more about the movement. One of them, half-drunk, said that they knew every move that Frenay and his people made, because "the guy who works as their messenger between Paris and Lyon is one of our boys."

Frenay was in a state of shock. Devillers had carried all of their messages once a week for months. If he was really an Abwehr spy, they certainly knew every detail of the movement. Lien caught the train back to Paris to alert Jeanne Sivadon and the others. He promised to get word back quickly. No word was ever received from Lien and he did not return to Lyon. Devillers, the messenger, also disappeared. Frenay felt a crisis approaching and redoubled security measures.

One night, a few nights after having heard about Devillers, he accompanied Bertie most of the way back to her hotel; for security reasons, they split up just before coming to it. He stayed in the shadow of trees and watched her cross the street in front of the Hôtel d'Angleterre. As she proceeded on to the Hôtel Dubost, where she was staying, Frenay saw three motionless silhouettes forty yards ahead, facing the hotel lobby. It was the German police. He had to make an instant decision, to walk on or to turn and run. He suspected that they were not after Bertie but were tracking her to find him.

Deciding that they would hear his footsteps if he ran for it, Frenay continued to walk deliberately toward them. It was a cold night, so he rubbed his hands, coughed, and pulled up his coat collar. As he came abreast of the figures in the shadows, he coughed again, bringing his hands to his mouth, shielding his face, while striding ahead. He heard one of them say: "Is that him?" He kept on walking at the same pace, fighting with all his strength to resist the temptation to run. He reached the Cours de Verdun, slipped behind a streetcar stationed there, and then raced as fast as his legs could move to the Gare Perrache, where he caught a train to the suburbs and a safe-house there.

The next day, calling one of his agents, he learned of an avalanche of arrests that had hit his movement.

A member of the Combat movement, André Koehl, had been stopped in the streets of Clermont-Ferrand carrying a suitcase stuffed with issues of *Combat*. In his pockets, in violation of security rules, he had a long list of names and addresses. It was a windfall for the police.

A number of leaders—including his two top aides and closest friends, Maurice Chevance and Bertie Albrecht—had been arrested. In all, the police had rounded up forty members of the movement. After interrogation, they were transferred to prison in Clermont-Ferrand.

Frenay's gloom at the disaster deepened when he received a note from Robert Guédon. Guédon had pulled out of the north and, with a new wife, was making his way toward the Spanish border. He sent Frenay a list of names of new regional chiefs in the north and wished him luck. Frenay wondered what had provoked the precipitate pullout.

He decided to consult with de Menthon and drove to Annecy, near the Swiss border, where he halted for the night before going on to Menthon-Saint-Bernard in the morning. And there in the lobby of his hotel, was an unexpected, a miraculous sight. It was Bertie! She was free; she was not in prison after all. He rubbed his eyes and ran to embrace her.

They sat at the bar and she told him her story. She had been taken from prison for interrogation by officers of the DST, the Vichy counter-espionage source in Lyon. There, the police commissioner had told her that, acting on a tip, they had picked up the traitor Devillers at the demarcation line. The officers were anti-German and sought every opportunity to counter the Abwehr. They had discovered that Devillers had been a POW in Germany and had been released from prison camp to become an Abwehr spy. Devillers was put on trial by a Vichy military tribunal, found guilty of treason, and shot at Fort Montluc, just one day before Pierre Laval, who had been promoted back into power, demanded his release from prison. Laval was constantly countered by French officers and police authorities who despised him and the Germans while making excuses for Marshal Pétain.

Bertie had been taken from Lyon to Vichy, where she met the same man who had earlier talked with de Menthon: the chief of the DST, the pro-Pétain, anti-German Commandant Rollin. Rollin told Bertie that he would release her from prison so that she might contact Frenay and persuade him to come to Vichy for a meeting. He promised safe-conduct for Frenay to and from the meeting.

The next morning de Menthon told Frenay that he should accept Rollin's offer and try to arrange for clemency for the movement's prisoners. But Max and the steering committee had to be notified first. On January 27 the committee met and agreed that Frenay should go to Vichy, and try to find out more about Rollin and men like him—Vichy officials who hunted down and arrested German agents as well as resistants. It was a strange situation, with Rollin apparently playing a double game against both sides.

In Vichy, Frenay had a long talk with Rollin, who complained about the Resistance as a bunch of ill-advised troublemakers. He tried to convince Frenay that the Vichy regime was doing everything possible to help the French people obtain better conditions from the Germans and to prevent more repression. He told Frenay that he ought to meet with the new interior minister, Pierre Pucheu. Frenay was taken aback. Pucheu was an all-out collaborator, a vicious anti-Semite and fascist. The mandate from the steering committee had authorized him to meet Rollin, but Pucheu was well beyond Frenay's clearance. It might also be dangerous, for Frenay had vilified Pucheu in his columns in *Combat*.

However, Frenay decided that it was important to know what Pucheu might want, and that it would be no more compromising to see Pucheu than to have seen Rollin. So he agreed to a meeting. The meeting with Pucheu led nowhere. Frenay was treated to the same kind of harangue he had already heard from Rollin about the goodwill of the Pétain regime and how loyally it was working for the French. Pucheu told Frenay that the Resistance would have to show signs of understanding the government's true policy. "I am simply giving you a warning before proceeding to repress your organizations with extreme severity."

Frenay reported back to his steering committee, which endorsed his actions and discussed ways of exploiting the double game that Rollin and some others were playing. The committee agreed that Vichy officials were opportunistic and would always try to be on the winning side—and the Resistance should convince them it was the Allies who would win.

But others did not look kindly on Frenay's talk in Vichy. D'Astier de la Vigerie was outraged and began waging a campaign of criticism of Frenay and the entire Combat movement. Moulin arranged a meeting between them at the Hôtel Terminus in Lyon, but the meeting went badly, with d'Astier accusing Frenay of "serious errors" and "grave compromises." Moulin tried to reassure Frenay later that he understood what he had been trying to do. The quarrel between these two strong-minded, vain, and ambitious leaders did nothing to facilitate Moulin's mission.

Frenay's mood was not at all improved by news of a disaster that had struck his comrades in Paris. The traitor Devillers had done his job only too well, turning over lists of names to the Gestapo. On February 4, Jeanne Sivadon, a key agent, and her secretary had been picked up. Then, rapidly, the police arrested Elisabeth Dussauze and André Noël, Combat's regional chiefs in Paris, along with Elisabeth's husband, Paul, his colleague Tony Ricou, and many others. The full list of arrests reached forty-seven.

The Parisian resistants would suffer as the men and women of the Musée de l'Homme had suffered. They were thrown into Santé prison, interrogated harshly, then transferred to Fresnes. From Fresnes, they were sent on to Saarbrücken, where they were given the grim designation NN, "*Nacht und Nebel*," the designation of "Night and Fog" invented by Hitler himself for prisoners so dangerous that they were to be cut off from all contact with the outside world.

As in the case of the Musée de l'Homme resistants, the German judge was impressed with the courage of the accused, with their dignified bearing and patriotism. He conceded publicly the virtue of their motivation. But again, the public prosecutor was severe and unbending. He demanded the death penalty for twenty-three of the defendants. The court was embarrassed when André Noël arose and said: "It was one of your own writers, Fichte, who told German youth during the Napoleonic occupation: 'Always preserve your dignity before the occupier and do not slacken your resistance.' We have simply followed his counsel."

But the sentence was death for the twenty-three, seventeen men and six women. Others among the accused received long prison sentences. The sentences of the women were commuted to life imprisonment. But four of them died in concentration camps. Only Elisabeth Dussauze and Jeanne Sivadon survived. The men died horribly—in prison in Cologne, where they were decapitated with an ax.

Long before the tragic end to their story, Henri Frenay and his associates of Combat were faced with the challenge of rebuilding their movement, so shattered by the arrests in both the south and the north. Moulin, in turn, was deeply troubled, not only by developments in France but also on other battlefronts.

Moulin and the Resistance leaders, despite their faith in an ultimate Allied victory, were shocked to hear the BBC admit that the Japanese had captured the Crown Colony of Hong Kong. Far more seriously, the Japanese stunned the world by conquering the "impregnable" fortress of Singapore, taking prisoner the garrison of eighty thousand troops. Tojo's minions had also occupied Java, while in the Indian Ocean, the British had lost an aircraft carrier and two warships.

There was also bad news from the Russian front. The Nazi drive into Russia had been stopped by winter's blizzards and ice, but by the spring of 1942 the Panzers were rolling again and the Russians were dropping back. The only good news came from America, which was gearing up for total war. American soldiers had not yet proved themselves in combat, but American factories were turning out vast amounts of weapons that were being rushed to the British for use in Asia and for storage against the day when the Allies would invade Europe. Production news was not, however, any match for the news of reversals in Russia, Asia, and on the oceans. Nineteen forty-two was a gloomy year for occupied France, torn by arrests, executions, severe rationing of food, clothing and fuel, and a lack of coordination and unity among hard-hit Resistance movements. Combat was the hardest hit of all, but it was also, by far, the largest. It would recover and grow.

Colonel Passy was able to report to de Gaulle considerable progress in the north. His secret agent Rémy had created his own network, to which he had given the name Confrérie Notre-Dame. It replaced earlier groups that he had formed and that had been hit hard by police raids. Rémy had recruited some outstanding men. François Faure, code-named Paco, son of the art historian Elie Faure, was brought to him by Pierre Julitte, one of his closest associates. Rémy had long been looking for someone of authority and leadership quality whom he could designate as his successor should he be arrested. He offered the assignment at once to Paco, who accepted without hesitation.

Rémy then recruited a giant of a man, named Jacques Robert, a lieutenant in a tank company who had been decorated with the Croix de Guerre on the battlefield of Rethel, where he had fought valiantly. He would become Denis. Max Petit was taken on and coded as Poucet, a name reflecting Rémy's sense of humor, for *petit* means little in French, and *petit poucet* is the French translation of Tom Thumb. One of his most important recruits, who would play a significant role in his operations, was Roger Dumont, an air force officer. Dumont, dubbed Pol, became his specialist for intelligence on aviation and would furnish London with information that would lead to spectacular raids on German installations.

It was Pol who spotted a pylon the Germans had constructed on the coast and had alerted the British to new German antiaircraft devices. He had also personally explored a strip of coast at Theuville at the request of Passy, who, in turn, had received the request from the British. They wanted precise details on composition of the beach, on barbed-wire emplacements, on mines, machine-gun nests on the beach, and on the cliff overlooking it.

Pol had been able to get every detail down to fine measurements, such as the thickness of barbed-wire emplacements. It was the best espionage report the British had received, and it permitted them to plan a dramatic operation. By an extraordinary coincidence, Rémy was picked up in a Lysander and flown to London just as the operation for which his network had provided the basic data was launched. He enjoyed the greatest satisfaction that a secret agent can experience when a friend handed him the front page of the

Evening Standard with the headline "BRITISH PARATROOPS FOLLOWED BY INFANTRY WRECK NAZI RADIO EYE ACROSS CHANNEL. ARMY, NAVY, RAF RAID N. FRANCE IN DARK." The British, thanks to Pol's information, had knocked out the radio-electric eye that had been alerting the Luftwaffe and coastal batteries to departures of British bombing squadrons.

Rémy had also brought to London new models of miniaturized transmitters made portable by building their three principal components so that they could be carried separately: the power supply, receiving and sending units. The British said it was impossible until Rémy showed the model built by his agents to Colonel Snook of the Intelligence Service. Pierre Julitte had created a transmission unit no bigger than a brick. Colonel Snook stared at it as though he were hypnotized. Rémy was rewarded with the promise of ten new sets and spare parts. British scientists were also excited by a new alloy that Rémy brought with him, the latest creation of German metallurgists.

Rémy wore two hats in France. He was the delegate of de Gaulle in the north and he was also the head of his own network. His mission was quite different from Moulin's. He was not called upon to unite the northern movements under de Gaulle's banner. Chances of doing that were too slim in any case. He maintained liaison with the major movements, OCM, Libération-Nord, and several others. And he concentrated on his own intelligence-gathering operations.

Despite all the difficulties in the south, notably the personal feud between Frenay and d'Astier, Moulin kept sending in optimistic reports to London. Meanwhile he was busy creating a number of indispensable services for what would eventually be the unified command. He divided the volunteers he recruited into groups for liaison, communication, landings, and parachute drops.

Moulin had two other ideas of great importance. One was the creation of a Comité Général d'Etudes, a consultative commission of eminent jurists who would draft a plan for the political, economic, and administrative structures of France immediately after the liberation. Such structures would have to be put in place rapidly to avoid chaos as the Allied troops drove Vichy and the Germans out of power. The other idea, which could be set up much more quickly for immediate functioning, would be a central press agency for the Resistance, to furnish clandestine writers and editors with all the information they needed for their journals.

Moulin was given this idea by his associate Yvon Morandat. He approved at once and gave it the name BIP, Bureau d'Information et de Presse. It would furnish the Resistance with information and propaganda themes from London and also transmit material back to London from France. It would prepare articles for the British, American, and world press. Moulin recruited Georges Bidault, left-Catholic prewar editor in chief of *L'Aube*, to be chief of the BIP. Bidault put together a first-rate team of men, most of whom became prominent in postliberation France: Rémy Roure, Louis Terre-noire, Pierre-Louis Falaize (who would become Bidault's chief of Cabinet when Bidault was named foreign minister after the war), Yves Farge, Emmanuel d'Astier, and the brilliant young Communist writers Pierre Courtade and Pierre Hervé.

Moulin in France and his associates in London were less enthused about another development that took place in April 1942. It concerned d'Astier and the British secret services, the SOE. One of their agents, Francis Basin, known as Olive, was in touch with an eminent personality of the Côte d'Azur, Dr. Lévy of Antibes. Lévy had earlier arranged meetings between Olive and Generals de la Laurencie and Cochet. He then called in Olive to meet d'Astier.

Olive was immediately subjected to a flood of d'Astier oratory. D'Astier could talk Niagara Falls to a halt when he was at the flood tide of his own conversation. His purpose was to persuade Olive to provide him with a means of transport to London. Olive did have a submarine at his disposal, but it was not to be used except for the most urgent reasons. And he was not convinced even by d'Astier's oratory that he rated a submarine.

To try to dam up the flood, Olive told d'Astier that he ought to call a meeting of all the Resistance movements of the south and have them designate one man to speak for them to de Gaulle. A man with those credentials would rate space in a submarine. D'Astier clapped his hands and promised to carry out Olive's proposal.

Two weeks later, an excited d'Astier de la Vigerie contacted Olive and announced that the convention of the Resistance had taken place and had designated him, d'Astier, to go to London to represent all of them. Suitably impressed this time, agent Basin arranged for a submarine to surface off the beach of Antibes and pick up d'Astier. D'Astier was thrilled to be off at last. His excitement was somewhat dampened when he learned, on board, that the sub had another mission in the Gulf of Genoa, and d'Astier would have to spend two weeks under the seas before being dropped off in May at Gibraltar, where he caught a plane for London.

Olive came under heated attack when other Resistance leaders discovered what had happened. D'Astier had never contacted them. No meeting had been held. D'Astier was not designated to speak for them, but had invented the entire scenario. Frenay was frothing with anger. Basin hastened to cable London, warning his people that d'Astier spoke only for himself, not for others, and asking whether he ought to send Frenay on too, to placate him. But London replied: "No thanks, one of these fellows is quite enough."

Frenay's rage was well justified. What d'Astier had done was inexcusable if not dishonorable. Combat was much bigger and more important in every way than Libération. Frenay had conceived the basic cellular structure copied by the other groups, and he was far ahead in every aspect of clandestine operations. If anyone should have been designated to go to London, it ought to have been Frenay, particularly since Moulin had treated him as the most important of the Resistance leaders.

D'Astier cared nothing for these reasons. He was a willful, swashbuckling, ambitious adventurer. He was convinced that Frenay, for all his merit, was essentially a dull military fellow and an obstinate, oversensitive prima donna who would infuriate everyone in London and hurt the Resistance. On the other hand, he regarded himself as a skilled and imaginative diplomat. He convinced himself that he could best represent Resistance interests in London. D'Astier was not all wrong about his self-estimate, somewhat exaggerated though it was. He was a charmer, a persuasive talker with a keen understanding of relationships among the Free French, the Allies, and the Resistance.

D'Astier made many friends in London and even impressed General de Gaulle, no mean feat. It was d'Astier who persuaded de Gaulle to introduce the theme of restoration of the Republic into his speeches and his radio broadcasts. De Gaulle was obsessed with the idea of the grandeur of France, eternal France, and did not think of talking about the French Republic. D'Astier explained that many resistants suspected him of Bonapartism and that it was necessary to refer frequently to Republican freedom for the French. That was perhaps his greatest accomplishment in his London sojourn. To try to protect himself from the anger of other leaders back in France, d'Astier also told de Gaulle, Passy, and Diethelm that it was necessary to invite Henri Frenay and Jean-Pierre Lévy to London as soon as possible. It would be months, however, before that was done.

Jean-Pierre Lévy, unlike Frenay, was not at all angry about d'Astier's solo visit to London. Lévy, a solid, stable man, had no ego problems or personal ambitions. He was suspicious of de Gaulle. Lévy had been frank to tell Jean Moulin when they met, soon after Frenay's talk with Moulin, that the Free French movement in London seemed to be oriented toward military goals only and that made him uneasy. Moulin had personally reassured him of de Gaulle's commitment to democracy and the Republic of France, saying that he would not have come back to France as de Gaulle's representative if he had thought otherwise.

Lévy reported Moulin's words to the Central Committee of Franc-Tireur and a heated controversy broke out at once. Georges Altman, their most professional journalist and a left Socialist, had no use for de Gaulle and his *coterie militaire*. He opposed any move that would make the Resistance dependent upon de Gaulle and the men in London. Jean-Pierre understood his objections but believed that Franc-Tireur had no choice but to work with London. That was where the money and arms would come from. That was Allied headquarters and the liberation of France would have to come through the Allies. The Resistance could not grow in strength if it remained isolated.

Jean-Pierre also reminded his comrades of the extent of overlapping already taking place. In many communities and regions, the rank-and-file member of Franc-Tireur was also either a member or associate of Combat or Libération. So there was already considerable unity in the rank and file of the Resistance. Would it not be more practical to accept the notion of a general unity while insisting that each movement maintain its own identity?

Founding member Antonie Avinin, on return from prison, along with Péju and Clavier, supported Jean-Pierre's arguments, and he was able to tell Moulin that Franc-Tireur was ready for unity, whenever the others indicated they were ready to proceed. Moulin, grateful for Jean-Pierre's cooperation, assigned his radio operator Hervé to Franc-Tireur as a permanent liaison officer to Moulin and to London. Hervé would prove an invaluable addition to Franc-Tireur until his own arrest and deportation to Mauthausen a year later.

Hervé was so favorably impressed by Jean-Pierre and his teams that he kept singing their praises to Moulin. Since Jean-Pierre was also the most cooperative of the Resistance leaders, Moulin was already sympathetic to his requests. Thus he agreed when Hervé asked for a special sabotage instructor to be parachuted along with another radio transmitter for Franc-Tireur. He arrived in November 1942. His name was Gilbert Mus, known as Marin.

Marin formed a special commando team that operated in the region of Roanne. Their major exploit was carried out on Christmas Eve, when they blew up the France-Rayonne factory, which was producing for the Germans. It was knocked out for three months.

Jacques Rasmuny, or Moutiers, to whom Jean-Pierre had entrusted the mission of preparing a Secret Army, had begun organizing his cells. They collected army maps and marked off all strategic points that would have to be seized when the signal for the insurrection would be given: town halls, prefectures, police stations, post offices, crossroads and bridges, rail lines. Frenay and d'Astier had long been working along the same lines, although Libération lagged behind the others in forming commando groups. D'Astier's own interests were political. He had first-class propaganda writers in his two Communist aides, Pierre Hervé, the philosophy teacher, and Pierre Courtade, journalist. Raymond and Lucie Aubrac were daring and efficient in planning sabotage of bridges and railroads. But Libération had no one to match Jacques Renouvin of Combat or Rasmuny of Franc-Tireur. However, they had organized and were training Secret Army units in some twenty towns in small groups. All told they had about two hundred armed men available.

In September 1942 after many meetings and discussions and constant urging by Jean Moulin, the three movements agreed to unite their paramilitary formations, including all their Groupes Francs, into a single Armée Secrète. It was the first important step toward the complete unification that Moulin sought.

It was not a decision that was easily reached. Henri Frenay argued that he was uniquely qualified to be the commander of the united Secret Army. His arguments were cogent. The very idea had been his from the start. Combat had more men in paramilitary units than the other two movements combined. The movement would, in fact, provide about 80 percent of the personnel and trained cadres of a unified Secret Army. He argued that he could not turn over to a stranger thousands of men who risked their lives because of their trust in him.

Jean-Pierre agreed with Frenay and was willing to accept him as the unified commander. But Frenay's old rival, d'Astier de la Vigerie, just back from London, would not budge on the issue. He insisted that the head of the Secret Army could not be a leader, not even a member of any of the three movements. He had to be a completely independent man with no partisan attachment to any one movement. Moulin agreed with d'Astier and reminded everyone of London's insistence that the paramilitary outfits of the Resistance be rigorously separated from the political. D'Astier and Jean-Pierre concurred on this point.

Frenay went back to his steering committee to submit the proposal to his colleagues. To his surprise and disappointment, they all counseled him to go along with d'Astier and Jean-Pierre toward a unified Secret Army with a new and independent commander. Frenay was badly hurt. "To my eyes, the decision was unfair, and it evidenced rank suspicion born of the purest jealousy, jealousy that I had in no way incited."

Frenay at least had the satisfaction of finding the man to head the Secret Army: General Charles Delestraint. Delestraint, code name Vidal, was in his early sixties, still youthful and energetic. As a divisional commander, he had once had a young colonel named Charles de Gaulle under his orders. He told Frenay that he admired de Gaulle and would have no compunction about serving under him. "But if I accept to take over the Secret Army," he said, "I must have my appointment endorsed in writing by de Gaulle himself."

Moulin informed London, de Gaulle instantly agreed and sent back the order that Delestraint had requested and a new, unified Secret Army, with a professional general at its head, came into being. It was a giant step forward toward unity for the Resistance and for Free France. The Resistance now had a military commander.

12
THE ALLIANCE OF THE ANIMALS

The escalation of activities by French Resistance movements stressing propaganda, sabotage, and the training of assault troops was paralleled by the growth of British-directed networks specializing in espionage. Of all the espionage nets reporting to the Special Operations Executive in London, the biggest and most efficient was the network that, in the spring and summer of 1941, still called itself the Crusade, but was about to change its name to the Alliance. Although it reported to the British and received its funds and equipment mainly from the British, it was French-led and staffed almost exclusively by the French. After its founder Loustaunau-Lacau (Navarre) turned over direction of operations to Marie-Madeleine Fourcade, the only woman to head a major Resistance organization, he himself pursued grandiose schemes for a major strike against the Vichy regime.

Marie-Madeleine and Navarre were together in Paris late in April 1941, meeting with their agents there, when a message arrived by courier from Algiers. It had been sent by one of Navarre's earliest agents, Commandant Léon Faye, code-named Eagle. Eagle had gone to North Africa to recruit fellow officers for one of Navarre's schemes, an uprising to seize power in Algiers and oust Pétain's officers there. The message reported that all was ready for the coup. Navarre told Marie-Madeleine that he would leave at once and advised her to get out of the occupied zone and back to relative safety down south.

Navarre and Marie-Madeleine traveled south together. Navarre seemed to have gained thirty pounds overnight; he wore a Homburg, and a heavy wool suit and vest, with a thick gold chain stretched across his huge "stomach." He grinned at her and told her that he was disguised as a M. Lambin, a prosperous wine merchant. His friends in Army Intelligence had issued him false papers in that identity and travel orders to Algiers to negotiate the purchase of the new wine crop. "The next time you hear from me, I'll have taken over Algiers," Navarre boasted.

Navarre arrived in Algiers on May 5 and met immediately with his co-conspirator Eagle. With Eagle was a Captain André Beaufre, an officer in the Cabinet of General Maxime Weygand, who had been transferred to the Algiers High Command by Marshal Pétain, mainly as a means of getting him out of Vichy where he could have become a troublesome rival for power. Beaufre's presence in the conspiracy demonstrated that Eagle had planned well and had found men in high places. Navarre had also turned up a high-ranking name whom he believed would join them in their plot. It was a classmate of his at Saint-Cyr, a colonel nicknamed "Hare Face." He was deputy chief of staff of the Nineteenth Army Corps in Algiers. Navarre had been in touch with Hare Face in Vichy during the winter and thought that he could trust him.

Captain Beaufre told Navarre that he had been in close touch with a number of American observers in Algiers. Though officially America had good diplomatic relations with Vichy and was sympathetic to Marshal Pétain, unofficially some American agents were hoping to find French officers more committed to the Allies. Beaufre thought they would back a pro-Allied coup.

While they were talking, Navarre's old classmate Hare Face arrived. He had been out of town the night before when Navarre called him. Navarre was delighted to see his old friend and plunged right in to explain the planned uprising to Hare Face. By seizing power in the name of the French Republic, Navarre and his group could welcome the Allies as free men, and forestall any Allied plan to occupy North Africa as conquered territory when they landed. The liberation of France must spring up from French soil, planted and nourished by Frenchmen. Hare Face listened intently, then got up and said: "You can count on me, old man. Come and see me this evening and I'll put your identity papers in order here and we'll talk about the next step."

Navarre, Eagle, and Beaufre congratulated each other and broke for lunch. They met again in the afternoon. Eagle spread out a map of army locations and a series of tables listing personnel they could count on, estimating the number of men, weapons, and planes needed for the coup. At that moment the doors burst open and uniformed police surged into the room, led by a police superintendent wearing the tricolor sash of office. He produced from a briefcase a series of warrants for search and arrest. Navarre, Eagle, Beaufre, and several other officers who had joined their meeting were hustled off to the police station. The Great North African Uprising has come to a sudden, inglorious end.

Marie-Madeleine, back in one of her offices in Marseille, was busy transmitting messages to London. Three days had gone by without any message or sign of any kind from Algiers. She knew how impetuous and imprudent Navarre could be.

As she brooded over her fears, her friend Gabriel Rivière came running into her apartment, where radio operator Lucien Vallet was tapping out a message to London, and shouted: "You'll have to clear out at once. First, some nitwit has told the police that he had heard strange noises here . . ." Vallet interrupted: "Yes, it's my key, it's very noisy." Rivière continued: "Second, they've all been arrested in Algiers. The Deuxième Bureau just tipped me off."

Captain Fourcaud, de Gaulle's representative, who happened to have stopped by the office to see Marie-Madeleine, told Vallet to interrupt his transmission and send an urgent message to London reporting the news. Marie-Madeleine thought of Colonel Bernis and her intelligence headquarters in the city of Pau. It had been agreed by all of them that if any leaders were arrested, they would have to dismantle their headquarters at once and move all offices to new sites. Bernis had to be warned and helped to set up a new operation. Marie-Madeleine said she would catch the next train to Pau. Fourcaud, always gallant, said: "It's too risky to go by train. I'll drive you to Pau."

En route, they checked into a hotel for the night. Fourcaud got a room for their chauffeur, Guy, and signed himself in with Marie-Madeleine as husband and wife, to avoid any questions about a woman traveling alone with two men. At breakfast, he laughed when he saw her and said: "You should have seen the waiter's face when he came into Guy's room with morning tea, and found me in bed with him." Marie-Madeleine thought: "So much for security."

In Pau, Marie-Madeleine told Colonel Bernis of Navarre's arrest. He wanted to stay where he was, but Marie-Madeleine insisted that he leave. "No matter how brave and tough you are, if the Gestapo gets you, you'll talk. They can make a wall talk." Bernis had no choice but to pack up and go to Monte Carlo, where a fallback position had been planned. Marie-Madeleine said: "I'll tell the British you'll run the operation from there." He understood that she intended to go on with the network, and nodded assent: "Just give me a sign, I'll get cracking again."

Marie-Madeleine left Pau for Marseille to arrange her own affairs. She covered her head in a broad-brimmed hat that threw shadows on her face. She had not eaten for two days. She was hot, tired, dispirited. The book she had bought was a bore and the journey seemed endless.

A traveler who had entered her compartment annoyed her by sitting next to her and then slyly pressing his feet against hers. She kicked his foot away. He pressed back again, then a third time. Two other passengers were watching and smiling. In a rage, Marie-Madeleine spun around to confront the rude masher. She saw that he was loudly dressed, in checked trousers under a black jacket, with a purple rosette in the buttonhole and an enormous tie, such as poets wore in Montmartre. And on his head, above a florid face, he wore a grotesque Stetson. She did not know whether to slap him or burst out laughing. She looked more closely and almost choked. It was Navarre!

Not a muscle on his face moved. She buried her face in her book, trying to regain her composure while her head whirled. How did he get out of an Algerian prison and turn up on her train? She could not believe it, and peeked out at him again. Yes, it truly was Navarre.

He got up, took a cigar out of his pocket, bowed to her, and left the compartment to smoke in the corridor. After a few minutes she got up and followed him.

He whispered around his cigar: "I got out of jail with the help of a police commissioner, an old pal. The boys told me you'd be on this train."

"You were betrayed?" Marie-Madeleine asked.

"Yes." Navarre made a wry face. "My old classmate, Hare Face, rushed off the moment he left us."

"The others?"

"They were free on parole when I left. There'll be consequences."

Navarre decided that they should go back to Pau. "They'll never believe I went home and will be looking for me elsewhere."

The Vichy government had Faye and Beaufre transferred to jail in Clermont-Ferrand to await trial and issued arrest warrants for Navarre. Though threatened with arrest, Navarre carried on. A marked man, he should have gone to London. But he had resolved to fight in France against all odds. He established a contact inside the Abwehr itself. He made connections with the extraordinary Belgian clandestine organization, "Dame Blanche," which moved escaped prisoners south and sabotaged German installations.

Marie-Madeleine supervised the patrols, which now exceeded one hundred. Their couriers came and went smoothly from Paris to Lyon to Marseille and Pau. The British sent over three new transmitters: BAY for Bernis in Monaco, MED for Audoly in Marseille, and LUX, which Marie-Madeleine held in reserve. They had been received by their comrade Jean Boutron, the Vichy government's deputy naval attaché in Madrid.

Boutron had been an officer on one of the French warships sunk by the British at Mers-el-Kebir. Vichy naturally thought he was anti-British. In fact he was anti-German and he made immediate contact with the British after he had been sent to Madrid. At the same time, he arranged with the French Embassy to let him carry diplomatic bags on his trips back to France. He put secret messages and equipment for Marie-Madeleine into the bags and brought them over the border with a diplomatic seal. He went back to Madrid with a Vichy seal, carrying all Marie-Madeleine's secret intelligence information to the British. It was an incredibly successful system.

Marie-Madeleine was warned that the police were closing in on Navarre. She went to see him to ask him to move: He had been in Pau too long. He agreed, but said he had to wait one more day, for he had to see his wife and child one more time before moving on. Marie-Madeleine was appalled at his violation of every security tenet. "But the police will follow your family. They are the best lead to you." Navarre brushed aside her objections. "My wife will go to the church, then slip out and take the shortcut to the house. There's nothing to worry about. Besides, we'll watch to see if the police are tailing her."

The next day Annick Loustaunau-Lacau, who had been staying with her family in another village, arrived in Pau and made her way to the church. Guards posted on the way saw nothing that looked like police, although a large group of more than a dozen men in black suits came in behind her. They thought they must be mourners. But they were not, they were police traveling in a large group deliberately in order to confuse spotters on the lookout. Annick slipped out of church and the police followed her to the pension where Navarre had been hiding. Navarre was grabbed and taken to Pau prison to await transfer to Clermont-Ferrand.

Choking back her sobs, Marie-Madeleine, now the sole chief of the network, sat down and coded her message to London about the arrest of N1. She signed with her own code POZ 55. In a few hours London acknowledged and asked who was taking over. She replied: "As planned, I am. POZ 55." London said OK. They did not yet know that POZ 55 was a woman.

With the capture of Navarre in Pau, that village would become a safe place to operate—at least for a time. The police would not expect Navarre's associates to return. Marie-Madeleine arranged for some agents who had left Paris to rent a house in Pau. She installed an operational office there, while maintaining other operations in Marseille. Her operations were, however, seriously curtailed and she had to be very careful about her own movements.

But there was good news too. The British were parachuting in an agent named Blanchet who was a specialist in new ciphering and transmission methods. Marie-Madeleine called in her own cipher men to be ready to "go to school." When finished in their area, he would go on to Normandy where he would set up an independent sector. Blanchet's code name was Bla. He came down safely and was whisked away to Marie-Madeleine's Villa Etchebaster in Pau, where she awaited him. As they shook hands, Marie-Madeleine's chief of staff, Maurice Coustenoble, put on a gramophone he had rigged up and it blasted out at full volume "God Save the King" and "La Marseillaise." It was comic theater.

Marie-Madeleine burst out laughing when she looked closely at the English agent. They had dressed him up to look like an Englishman's idea of the perfect Frenchman. "He was attired as if for a village wedding—short jacket, waistcoat, striped trousers, a spotted cravat, a stiff shirt with cutaway collar, a little goatee beard, a pair of pince-nez and, as a crowning glory, a bowler hat. The boys burst into roars of laughter."

Marie-Madeleine felt sorry for the Englishman standing in the circle of guffawing Frenchmen. She began to say a few words of welcome in English, but he cut her off and said in fluent French, but with a strong Cockney accent: "Don't bother, madame, I've spent most of my life in France." They all laughed together and Bla was offered a hot bath, a shave, and a complete change of clothes. Absurd though he seemed, he had been sent from London; therefore he must be tops at his job.

Antoine Hugon, another agent from Paris, appeared a few days later in Pau, proudly wearing Germany's Iron Cross on his lapel. He had been awarded the cross in World War I when he saved the life of a German soldier who had fallen into a canal and was drowning. "I hate the *Boche*," he explained, "but a human being drowning, well, one must save him." The Iron Cross turned out to be the most useful shield an agent could have. He stood in front of his friends and began to get undressed, tearing off his jacket, tie, and shirt. Wrapped around his body was a huge map of all the U-boat pens the Germans had built in Saint-Nazaire, reproduced to scale, down to the last inch, by the engineer Henri Mouren. It was a great coup for Marie-Madeleine and London was overjoyed to receive it.

But it was followed by bad news from Paris. Inspectors in the post office division had become suspicious of activities around Box 118, the box of the network. They searched the postal premises and in a disused cloakroom found compromising documents and weapons. They recognized the handwriting of a postal worker who was in the network, and shadowed him until other Resistance agents came to visit him. Radio operator Lucien Vallet was caught in the trap, along with three other agents who had just returned to Paris.

Annie, the girl friend of André Hugon, managed to escape with a precious transmitter, the OCK set.

From Clermont-Ferrand came the verdicts in the trial of Navarre and Eagle. Loustaunau-Lacau got two years' imprisonment and confiscation of his present and future property. Commandant Faye was given five months and Captain Beaufre two months. Since they had been charged with "an attempt against the external security of the state and of inciting North Africa to revolt," very grave charges, their sentences were almost ludicrously light. It was an indication that Vichy was not sure of the sentiments of the army and was afraid to punish too severely three highly respected, patriotic officers. In the fall of 1941, authorities in Vichy were not sure of themselves. Pétain had dismissed Laval and given new powers to Admiral François Darlan, and no one was sure just who was loyal to whom.

With Navarre put away for two years, and with Faye forced to remain quiet when he came out, it was clear that POZ 55 would have to continue to function as chief of the network. Marie-Madeleine advised her fellow agents of the sentences and announced that she would carry on. They all continued to accept her leadership—a considerable achievement for a young woman in a country where males were not used to taking orders from females.

The British informed Marie-Madeleine early in September that there would be a big parachute drop coming up with everything she had asked for: money, radios, and another radio operator. There would be three million francs in one parachute, while another three million were being sent to Commandant Boutron in Madrid to be delivered to her in Pau. An additional four million were to be deposited in an Intelligence Service box in Barcelona, to be held in reserve, a total award of ten million francs—solid proof of the value of the network to the British. Six new radio sets would come floating down in perfect condition to be stored in Maurice Coustenoble's house in Toulouse.

And Julien Bondois, the radioman, would arrive on schedule, although in the jump he sprained his foot slightly.

Marie-Madeleine loved her house in Pau, an ancient village in the foothills of the Pyrénées, founded in the eleventh century. It was the home of the kings of Navarre and the birthplace of Henri IV. Nestled in the trees, it is watered by mountain streams and is an idyllic, peaceful village in normal times. But there was no normalcy in Marie-Madeleine's life in the underground.

Several of her agents had taken off for the north, along with her mother, who had insisted on making the trip across the demarcation line despite warnings from Marie-Madeleine that it was dangerous. The Germans were tightening controls in the fall of 1941. Old friends whom she had not seen for a long time, Jean-Philippe Salmson and his wife, who had been scheduled to go to Paris with the mission and had canceled out, came bursting in to tell her: "They've all been arrested, along with your mother! We've come to get you out of the way."

They drove out of Pau just minutes before the police came for Marie-Madeleine. On the road they stopped to call Commandant Boutron to tell him what had happened and to ask him to get Marie-Madeleine out of France until the pursuit cooled down. He gave them a rendezvous location and when they met he told Marie-Madeleine that he would smuggle her across the border to Spain inside his diplomatic mailbag. He told her that he was also smuggling British intelligence agent Jean Schoofs, who would be hidden in the trunk of his car. He laughed and told her that the car was her own Citroën, which she had given to him when he had agreed to act as a courier for the network.

Just before they got to the station, Schoofs got into the trunk and Marie-Madeleine was folded up and pushed into the mailbag on the rear seat of the car. Boutron drove the car up a ramp to a platform on the train. He wanted to stay in the car to be near them and take care of them, but the stationmaster would not hear of it. "Far too dangerous; you must go to your compartment." Boutron, uneasy, left his passengers where they were, one in the trunk, the other in the sack in the car.

The train ran into difficulties and delays and was unbearably slow. Marie-Madeleine was doubled up painfully in the bag for nine unending, torturous hours, frozen stiff and suffering almost unendurable pain in her neck and hips. Four new tires, piled on the seat to camouflage the appearance of the sack, had shifted position and were cutting into her neck, already pressed down by the seal on the bag.

Schoofs managed to get out of the trunk and open the seal on her bag so that she could get out, suck in fresh air, and stretch, but as each station drew near, she had to double up again inside the bag, which was only four feet long by two wide. At five feet six, Marie-Madeleine had trouble fitting into the sack. If she had not lost a lot of weight she never would have made it. She almost didn't, for when Boutron got to the other side, he had to drive for a stretch before stopping, and Marie Madeleine fainted. When he opened the sack he thought for a moment that he had a corpse. When she opened her eyes, Boutron sighed with relief. "We'll have a decent cigarette now and then on to Madrid," he said.

The British had planned to bring POZ 55 on to London, but Marie-Madeleine had notified them that POZ 55 had to return to France as soon as possible and could not afford the time for London. Instead they agreed to send an SOE agent, Major Richards, to Madrid for a meeting there. Richards had no idea that POZ 55 was a woman and was startled to find Marie-Madeleine. But he soon got over the shock and complimented her on her fine work.

Richards told her of disaster that had struck her network. The police had caught her right-hand man, Maurice Coustenoble. He had been stripped naked, forced to kneel on a metal yardstick, while his torturers passed burning paper up and down his body. Several other agents had been caught. Those who had been arrested by the French in Paris had been turned over to the Abwehr and were in Fresnes prison.

The British agent then told her that one of their men, a certain Gavarni, had been caught and was trying to strike a deal with Rollin in Vichy: a transmitter and two million francs in return for the release of the prisoners. He had tried to persuade Rollin that the network had been broken up and was no longer a threat to security. He had sent a message via Marseille and wanted to know if Marie-Madeleine would approve the deal with Rollin. Rollin was still playing his double game as a Vichy official, loyal to the marshal but opposed to the Germans and sympathetic to non-Communist resistants.

Marie-Madeleine agreed to turn over the LUX transmitter and two million francs for the release of the prisoners. It would mean virtually the end of fourteen months of hard work, constant sacrifice, and danger. And the entire network would have to be rebuilt from the fragments left in Marseille, Nice, Grenoble, Vichy, Pau, and some subsectors. She felt she would be able to do it and had no choice but to try.

The worst of it for Marie-Madeleine would be the trip back to France inside the mailbag. She shuddered at the memory of her torture. But Boutron promised the return journey would be much better. The train they had taken out had missed its connection and had thus been delayed many more hours en route than needed. He told her the truth, but the return journey was painful and long nonetheless.

On her return, Marie-Madeleine learned that the deal had been made and her comrades, including Coustenoble, released from prison. Her mother was also safe. And Léon Faye—Eagle—had also been released. She promptly asked him to stay on as her chief of staff and he agreed. Faye and Coustenoble would help her rebuild the network. Later she would discover that Gavarni had given Vichy the transmitter and eighty thousand francs, not two million, keeping the difference for himself.

Marie-Madeleine's troubles were not quite over. Her brother-in-law, Commandant Georges-Picot, who was well connected in Vichy, came roaring in to see her, shouting: "Who is ASO 43? Who is PLU 122? What's all this about killing Darlan?" Georges-Picot, a member of a wealthy, illustrious family, was a conservative, well-placed in ruling circles. He was no collaborator but not a resistant, either, and he disapproved of Marie-Madeleine's activities.

The police had found some papers with code numbers on them and a scribble about Darlan being shot that Coustenoble had written over and over again one night, when he had claimed he was receiving prophetic messages. Marie-Madeleine thought the pressure of underground work had got to him; still, she presumed he would recover. But the "prophecies" were not all that Vichy knew about. Georges-Picot told her the police knew she had gone to Madrid and that she had been smuggled over the border. "You've made the marshal look ridiculous. Everyone's furious with you. You'd better come to Vichy with me. Commandant Rollin wants to see you."

Wearily, Marie-Madeleine agreed.

In Vichy she told Rollin about Coustenoble's "prophetic vision," denying that there was any assassination plot. He believed her and called Admiral Darlan's office to let him know he could relax. He told her: "You know the admiral's not been sleeping ever since we picked up that note." Rollin then gave her the same scolding and warnings he had given Frenay, advising her to give up her troublemaking ways. "Go back to your children and behave yourself. You've done enough. I'm going to spread my protective wing over you." He promised to release the rest of her friends from prison.

She left Vichy, thinking Rollin had given her good advice and that a few weeks' rest would do her good. She was yearning for her children and her family and release from the constant tension of running from the police. She knew she would regain her strength and rebuild the network. And she had a new idea for codes. No more numbers. She had, in a moment of fatigue, seen them all in her mind as hunted animals. Animals were survivors. They had outlasted the Flood, hadn't they? So, from now on, all her people would have animal names. She would be a Hedgehog and no one would be able to touch her. All her airmen would be birds. Marie-Madeleine laughed, feeling better already. A new network would be born, the Alliance of the Animals.

After some six weeks of inactivity Marie-Madeleine and her animals were again hard at work. Commandant Faye—Eagle—was operating again early in 1942, bubbling with new ideas, arms full of new recruits. Colonel Kauffman, an old air force pilot, farming his property in Sarlat, agreed to take over the Dordogne sector in the southwest. A young pilot, Pierre Dallas, and his friend Lucien Poulard, in their mid-twenties, joined the team. High-ranking officers on the Armistice Commission, even the general staff, came into the network: Colonel Morraglia, Colonel René de Vitrolles, Commandant Felix Cros.

More and more officers had become disillusioned with Marshal Pétain by the end of 1941. They realized that Admiral Darlan was powerless to prevent the Germans from commandeering most of France's wheat, butter, milk, eggs, and meat. Rations had been cut to a bare subsistence level. French machine tools were shipped off to German factories. France was being systematically looted.

One of the most useful new recruits for Marie-Madeleine's network was a wealthy aristocrat and scion of a famous family: Maurice Mac-Mahon, the Duke of Magenta. He was descended directly from the General MacMahon who had led French troops to victory over the Austrians in the Battle of Magenta, a town in northern Italy, in 1859. Napoleon III had granted the general the title of duke of Magenta. The present duke's nickname was Sloughi, the French word for the elegant, swift greyhound, which is called saluki in English. It was an ideal code name for one of Marie-Madeleine's "animals." Sloughi set up posts in Normandy, Burgundy, and Paris.

Marie-Madeleine received a message from the radio operator Lucien Vallet telling her that he had investigated the arrests and was certain that the British Intelligence agent, Blanchet, whom they called Bla, was the traitor who had turned them in to the Germans. He reported that Bla's own team in Normandy had all been arrested. Marie-Madeleine sent an urgent message to London with the report but was told in a sharp reply that she was quite mistaken: Blanchet's transmitter in Normandy was operating fully and sending through excellent information.

Two days later an urgent message came in from her contact Richards, in London. "You were right. Bla a traitor. We are issuing execution order."

The British had discovered that Blanchet had been a member of Sir Oswald Mosley's Nazi party in Britain, the Brown Shirts, and had been working for the Gestapo from the day he had arrived in France. Everyone was shocked: The first British Intelligence agent to be sent to the network was a German spy! His father had worked in Germany and in France before the war and it was as a youngster that Blanchet had learned French. A message was sent to Bla in Normandy, ordering him to report to one of Marie-Madeleine's aides in Lyon, but he naturally failed to show up.

The network was rapidly approaching peak activity again early in the winter of 1942. Marie-Madeleine was concerned about the lack of emergency withdrawal and evacuation areas, safe places to hide people, and safe landing fields for pickups by air or for parachute drops. Just as she was most worried about it, help came unexpectedly from a redheaded giant.

He walked into her office early in April 1942 and announced that he had been sent by Tiger-Cat. That was the new code name for the network's lawyer, Louis Jacquinot, who had defended Navarre. Jacquinot had also defended this new recruit when he had been arrested earlier. Marie-Madeleine dubbed him Gulliver because of his Herculean physique. Later, to be consistent with the other animals, she called him Ram. She never used or revealed his real name. Some of her agents demanded anonymity.

Ram had had a group of his own, engaged in gunrunning. He

wanted to get started again after his arrest and agreed to join the network if Marie-Madeleine would help him. He said that his native department of Corrèze in south-central France was ideal as an emergency hideout. His partner in the arms business, Jean Vinzant, lived there, in Ussel, and had a whole circuit of hiding places in the Auvergne Mountains, and a perfect landing strip in the fields of Thalamy, outside Ussel. She asked him if he would work for her first in Vichy, under her patrol leader there. He growled: "Depends on who it is." When Marie-Madeleine said it was General Camille Raynal, who had been introduced to her by British Intelligence, he grinned in recognition, held out his huge hand, and said: "I'm in." Gulliver the Ram became one of the most useful animals in the menagerie, along with Jean Vinzant, Great Dane. Many men and women would owe their lives to his hiding place in Ussel. And Lysanders would soon be flying in to land on the grassy plateau at Thalamy.

The big excitement in Vichy in the spring of 1942 was the resignation of Admiral Darlan's Cabinet, on April 17, and Pétain's announcement that he had recalled Pierre Laval and made him chief of government. Laval would not even bother to hide the fact that he was Hitler's man. Laval was a Nazi puppet. Darlan, with his tremendous influence in the navy, was kept on as commander of the military forces.

President Roosevelt called Admiral Leahy home from Vichy for consultations in Washington. U.S. planes carried out a successful air raid on Tokyo shipyards and other military objectives around the Japanese capital. The Russians were still holding out in Stalingrad, despite constant German announcements that they had broken through and were soon to capture the city.

Marie-Madeleine's spies had helped the Allied cause by providing precise information on the location and construction of German naval bases all along the Atlantic coast and the Channel, as well as pinpointing German arsenals, warehouses, troop transport movements, and French factories turning out products for the German war machine. The spring and summer of 1942 were productive, rewarding months for the Alliance.

Not so for the other major Resistance movements. Combat, Libération, Franc-Tireur, and many others in the north, particularly the Communists, were decimated by arrests. They lacked funds and weapons and hit a low point in this period. They were shaken by the return of Laval and knew it signaled a new wave of repression and persecution.

Spirits perked up in July with a cheering demonstration by masses of ordinary citizens. Radio London had asked French citizens to come out peacefully on July 14 and celebrate the traditional Republican holiday, Bastille Day, to show Vichy that they were not dupes of the puppet State of France.

In Lyon alone some one hundred thousand people came out, carrying tricolor banners. The crowds were so huge that the prefect of the district sent a telegram to Vichy saying that the police were overwhelmed and he had called out the troops. He asked whether they could fire blanks at the crowd. Vichy messaged back: no shooting of any kind!

The Resistance movements had taken the leadership in getting the crowds out and in confronting the police. Their Groupes Francs, ready and armed for action, had charged police lines and set up security patrols to protect the public. They had come from Combat, Libération, and Franc-Tireur in a magnificent example of united action. It was a victory for Jean Moulin, who had insisted on uniting the commandos, and above all, it was a victory for the entire national Resistance. They sent messages to all police stations telling officers that their behavior was not patriotic, that they were servile to a rotten regime, and that they were being warned to change their attitude toward true patriots or they would be held responsible "in their assets and in their persons" for their behavior. The messages were signed "The Movements of the Resistance."

In August, Frenay got word from Jean Moulin that he would be taken to London along with d'Astier, who had returned to France but would go back again. Moulin believed that when they had met de Gaulle together it would help facilitate his efforts to persuade them to resolve their differences. Moulin was highly optimistic because of the tremendous success of the Bastille Day demonstrations.

Moulin had made real progress, too, in setting up the structure of his General Delegation whose mission was to function as the top policy-making, unifying organ of the Resistance. He had his own communications with London and began placing his delegates as liaison officers with each of the three principal movements of the Resistance: Lieutenant Raymond Fassin with Combat, Hervé (Joseph Monjaret) with Franc-Tireur, and Paul Schmidt with Libération. He gave Georges Bidault a monthly budget of one hundred and fifty thousand francs for his Information and Press Bureau, BIP, and set in motion the machinery of the Comité Général d'Etudes, which was drafting the new Republican laws to be proclaimed as soon as Vichy was defeated.

Moulin began to hear that messages were coming in to the Resistance members about a planned Allied invasion of North Africa. René Capitant, Combat's representative in Algiers, had asked for and received a special budget of one hundred thousand francs so that he might intensify his efforts in view of a possible Allied landing there. Colonel Passy sent through messages to France to explain the importance of the role to be played by the Resistance in the ever-increasing likelihood of major action in the Mediterranean. Marie-Madeleine received urgent messages to obtain all possible intelligence on Vichy and German strength in the Mediterranean. If the Germans did not know by the early fall of 1942 that the Allies were planning an invasion in either southern France or North Africa, they were the only ones who did not know.

13
THE AMERICANS SEARCH FOR A NEW FRENCH GENERAL

There was one man who knew exactly what was happening in North Africa in the fall of 1942, for his spies were all over the territory, from Morocco through Algeria to Tunisia. He was America's superspy, appointed by President Roosevelt to create and staff a worldwide intelligence-gathering organization.

Roosevelt had called this man to the Oval Office in the summer of 1941. As a conservative Wall Street lawyer and a Hoover Republican, William Joseph Donovan was anything but a New Deal admirer of FDR. Roosevelt knew all about "Wild Bill" Donovan's politics, but it did not bother him. He wanted the best man available to head up an American Intelligence Service, and his advisers told him that Donovan was just the man for the job.

Donovan was one of the best informed Americans on European affairs. He had publicly railed against isolationism and had not hesitated to criticize America's hero, Colonel Charles A. Lindbergh, "Lucky Lindy," a leader of America's isolationist forces. After touring Europe, Donovan had predicted to Roosevelt that the Luftwaffe would fail to drive the British to their knees. Having witnessed the success of the Nazi fifth columns in penetrating European countries, he kept up a barrage of memos to Roosevelt urging the creation of an American international secret service to meet the Nazi challenge.

In July 1941, almost six months before Pearl Harbor would precipitate America into the war, FDR gave Donovan the green light to create an agency for espionage, sabotage, propaganda, guerrilla warfare, and any other subversive activities. Donovan would conjure up some incredible stunts: incendiary bats, phosphorescent foxes, and other unlikely schemes that his staff might propose. Donovan checked out every bizarre proposal; his slogan was: "I ignore nothing—you never can tell."

Donovan first created an innocent-sounding planning staff, the Coordinator of Information, or COI, in Washington. Heading up the COI's New York office was another unconventional figure: the towering playwright and presidential speechwriter, Robert Sherwood. Whereas Donovan was a right-wing devout Catholic, Sherwood was an irreverent liberal, an anticlerical intellectual. He staffed his office with New Deal enthusiasts, left-wing journalists, and famous writers, such as Thornton Wilder and Stephen Vincent Benet.

Sherwood and Donovan were irreconcilable personalities and they were doomed to separate. About midway through 1942, Sherwood's division split off from the COI and became the OWI, the Office of War Information, housed on Fifty-seventh Street in New York. Devoted to propaganda, the OWI created the Voice of America, our equivalent of the BBC. Donovan's COI became the OSS, the Office of Strategic Services, the international secret service and all-around department of dirty tricks and subversive activities that Donovan had so often recommended, and forerunner of the CIA.

The OSS developed into a curious amalgam of conflicting ideologies, from extreme right to extreme left, from multimillionaire capitalists to hard-core international Communists. This created controversy inside the organization and confusion in the ranks. Columnist Drew Pearson criticized Donovan for choosing right-wing "Red-baiters" among his top personnel, while young left-wingers and liberals recruited also by Donovan performed "some of the most heroic work of the war." Donovan had no compunctions about using Communists. When the FBI complained that one of his agents was "on the Communist honor roll, Donovan dryly retorted: "Maybe so, but he sure is on the honor roll of the OSS." Inevitably this kind of grab-bag, no-rules, no-holds-barred organization would kick up a storm wherever it went to work, and this is what happened in North Africa and France.

Before the OSS began to operate in France, the principal American agent there was Robert Schow, military attaché in Vichy, who enjoyed close relations with the Resistance and conducted successful espionage operations for Washington, lending some credibility to the U.S. policy of keeping a post in Vichy. Our principal agent in North Africa was the State Department consul in Algiers, Robert Murphy. Murphy reported to Secretary of State Cordell Hull, whereas Donovan reported directly to President Roosevelt. Murphy's policies were frequently in conflict with Donovan's, and their agents competed and often clashed. De Gaulle's men and Resistance leaders never did understand the confused relationships of American agents and this would cause considerable trouble.

In February 1941 Murphy negotiated an economic accord with General Maxime Weygand, then Vichy governor of Algeria. The agreement provided American supplies to North Africa in return for permission to send a special team of American diplomatic observers to Algeria, Morocco, and Tunisia. It was a real coup for the United States, initiated by the War Department. Our chiefs of staff were understandably nervous about growing German influence in North Africa. American "food control officers" could use that cover to perform much needed intelligence and espionage duties and to advance American propaganda, along with anti-Nazi propaganda. Seen by General de

Gaulle in London, however, the American agreement appeared to strengthen the pro-Vichy faction, particularly since America would not extend any but the most limited recognition to de Gaulle. De Gaulle's antipathy toward Murphy would only increase when his agents reported that Murphy frequented the most reactionary, militarist Vichy elements in Algiers.

Wallace Phillips, an expatriate American businessman in London with a good deal of experience on the Continent, put together a team of about a dozen Americans to act as "food control officers." Selected from the army and the navy, they were men of culture and elegance who could speak French well and would impress the French. They were appointed as "vice-consuls" to assist Murphy in his own espionage network. They arrived in North Africa in the summer of 1941, before Donovan's men got there, and found themselves plunged into an exotic world of Gestapo agents, Italian spies, paid informers, prostitutes, and a handful of legitimate diplomats. It was frequently difficult to tell one of the players from another.

The Germans, believing their own Nazi propaganda, refused to take the young Americans seriously. Gestapo spies sent back uncomplimentary reports about American social climbers, sexual degenerates, and decadent and corrupt democrats, congratulating themselves that they had nothing to fear from such incompetent enemy agents.

The Nazis were wrong in their assessments. Not that the Americans were not socially and sexually active—they were—but they were also diligently doing their job. Pillow confidences were not an insignificant element of espionage. Murphy's "disciples," as they were called in Washington, were soon sending through a thick file of political, economic, and military information on North Africa and the Mediterranean theater.

After Pearl Harbor, Winston Churchill flew to Washington to confer with Roosevelt. Near the top of their agenda was North Africa. They thought they ought to try to find a pro-Allied French officer who could control the conservative colonial army. The British had had their agents contact General Weygand earlier. Weygand had put them down hard, proclaiming his loyalty to the Pétain regime and his opposition to any North African uprising.

Roosevelt told Churchill that he did not like and would not support his protégé, General de Gaulle, whom he accused of entertaining dictatorial ambitions and being either unknown to or unpopular with the French people. Churchill defended de Gaulle, but he had his own problems with the haughty and touchy leader of Free France and was not going to quarrel with his most important ally. The two leaders agreed to ask their field agents to continue the search for a pro-Allied French general.

Murphy and his "vice-consuls" were consorting with a nucleus of French army officers, officials, and businessmen involved in a series of whispered conspiracies, men like Captain Beaufre and Commandant Faye, or the vegetable-oil millionaire Jacques Lemaigre-Dubreuil, an opportunist who managed to be friendly with Vichy, the Nazis, and the Americans all at the same time.

Donovan was planning to take over espionage and subversive activities in North Africa as soon as he could get trained men in. By the fall of 1941 he had found the men for that mission: Robert Solborg and William Eddy, two extraordinary characters typical of Donovan's early cloak-and-dagger recruiting. Solborg was commissioned as a lieutenant colonel and Eddy as a colonel.

Robert Solborg was a Pole, born in Warsaw, son of a Polish general in the army of the czar. In World War I, Solborg received his first commission, as a czarist cavalry officer. He was gravely wounded, then assigned to a Russian military purchasing mission in New York. When the Bolshevik Revolution broke out, Solborg applied for and received American citizenship on enlisting in the American army.

Speaking fluent French, he was assigned as military attaché in the American Embassy in Paris. After his army service, Solborg became an executive of the Armco Steel Company and by 1939 was managing director of Armco for France and Britain. Under this cover, he traveled through Germany and gathered intelligence information for the British. He then joined U.S. Army Intelligence and was sent to North Africa by the War Department, still under cover as an Armco executive. He spent eight months traveling all through North Africa, seeking out French Resistance elements as potential allies of the Americans.

In the fall of 1941, Donovan asked Solborg to head up a Special Operations section of COI and sent him to London to study the structure and operations of the SOE there. By then the British Special Operations Executive had had a year's experience in dealing with European Resistance movements. Solborg returned to Washington after his study mission and was then sent on to open Donovan's operations center in Lisbon, the key espionage capital of Europe. From Lisbon, he was to coordinate his activities with Murphy in secretly contacting French and Arab underground organizations.

Colonel William Eddy, Donovan's second agent, was sent to operate inside North Africa after Pearl Harbor from another key espionage center: the international zone of Tangier.

Eddy, like Solborg, was not American-born. He was born in Syria, of American missionary parents. He was an American intelligence officer in the First World War and had become an instructor in English at the American University in Cairo. In 1941 he returned to the military as U.S. naval attaché in Cairo. He spoke fluent Arabic and good French and was an ideal agent for Donovan to send to Morocco.

Eddy was briefed by Murphy on a plot brought to him by the millionaire French vegetable-oil magnate, Jacques Lemaigre-Dubreuil. Lemaigre-Dubreuil was a right-winger, some said a member of the infamous Cagoule, the "hooded ones." He was on the best of terms with the leaders of Vichy, whose ideas he shared, and they, in turn, had warmly recommended him to the Nazis as a valuable collaborationist. His German connections had permitted him to transfer his oil business to North Africa and he traveled freely between

France and Algiers. A shrewd opportunist, he was anxious to sell himself to Murphy as pro-Allied, so that no matter who finally triumphed he, Lemaigre-Dubreuil, would be in the winning camp.

Lemaigre-Dubreuil had been in touch with Faye and Beaufre and knew about their aborted coup. But he told Eddy that it was still possible to mount a coup that would establish a pro-Allied government in North Africa. He claimed to be in touch with a number of dissident officers who could pull it off. For the plot to succeed, he argued, it would need American arms and money, which could be secretly supplied. French officers supplied Eddy with a list of their arms requirements. In March 1942, he sent his report on this plot back to Donovan, after having already passed it on to Murphy.

Donovan was not favorably impressed. He thought the arms request extravagant and out of all proportion to an operation that could only succeed if it were speedily successful and virtually a bloodless coup. A heavily armed operation would be tantamount to a French civil war in Algeria and would serve no useful purpose. It might even give the Germans a pretext to intervene.

Undaunted, Colonel Eddy sent through a new request a month later, for a half-million dollars and massive arms shipments, including thousands of motorcycles, tanks, howitzers, and heavy equipment needed for a war, not a coup. Lemaigre's friends had frightened Murphy and Eddy with talk of an impending German intervention. Eddy, angry, told Donovan that if he and Murphy could not be trusted with a few million francs, he ought to be recalled and replaced by someone else. Donovan shrugged off Eddy's pique. It was not the money that made him hesitate—Donovan would spend much more on other schemes—it was the massive arms request, and Donovan's own distrust of the reliability of the military plotters. Donovan also received an unfavorable reaction from the Joint Chiefs of Staff, whom he had queried. They too questioned the reliability of the Lemaigre group and worried about the arms eventually falling into German hands. They decided to send only money and to advise Eddy to use it to build up a guerrilla Resistance movement.

Meanwhile, the American press and public were pressing the administration to break relations with Vichy in reaction to the reinstatement of Laval as chief of government. Laval had promptly broadcast his desire to see a German victory, and instituted new anti-Semitic decrees. French Jews were required to wear a yellow star and, to sharpen the shame, to yield six precious textile ration points to pay for the star. Laval also called for French conscript labor for Germany.

The State Department had to recall Admiral Leahy for "consultations," and expressed its displeasure to the French Embassy in Washington. But it would not break relations with Vichy. It was a painful dilemma for Roosevelt, who despised Pétain and Laval but could not publicly explain that his diplomats in Vichy were really useful spies. Private attempts to explain to selected correspondents did not succeed, for feelings were running very high against any kind of "appeasement" of fascist France.

Donovan and Ambassador Leahy had already been feuding, for the ambassador would not let American undercover agents send espionage messages over embassy communications lines. Leahy had also objected to Bob Schow's increasing relations with the French Resistance. Donovan managed to get his objections to the attention of President Roosevelt, to let him know that conservative, hidebound old Admiral Leahy was not the right man to represent America in the kind of complex, revolutionary situation that existed inside France.

Army Intelligence was also proving to be way off the mark in its reports on France. General Sherman Miles, assistant chief of staff, G-2, had sent through a highly inaccurate report to the chief of staff on the Free French movement late in 1941, and subsequent reports continued in the same vein. In OSS document 5274, General Miles reported that the Free French movement did have a current psychological value of "maintaining the French flag in the field," but that it was "unlikely that this value would extend over the postwar era." He added that the leadership was made up of "a group of unknowns and discontented politicians," of Gaullists "whose sole value is that of publicity." General Miles stated that the "only group worth recognition, if it can be reached" was the "vast mass now living and suffering in France."

General Miles's concluding sentence stated: "It is safe to assume that no one now connected with the de Gaulle movement will be accepted by the long-suffering French in France as a leader when peace comes." It is truly difficult to imagine a report that could have been more wrong, except for dozens of other incorrect reports and analyses sent to or made by Washington's various French desks. It was official policy laid down on high by Roosevelt himself that de Gaulle was the wrong man to lead the French and this prejudice colored most of the intelligence reports on de Gaulle. This strengthened the determination of Robert Murphy and other American agents to find or invent a French rival general to replace de Gaulle.

There were, however, some sophisticated and reliable observers among the woolly-headed. One was an attractive, cultured young American writer, lecturer, and world traveler, thirty-two-year-old Colonel Nicol Smith of the OSS. Donovan was generous in giving exalted rank to his young officers. Smith was assigned, with State Department consent, to the post of cultural attaché in Vichy. That would be his cover for his espionage work. But his cover was blown before he even got to Vichy by a State Department official who virtually admitted to the French Embassy in Washington that Smith would function as a spy. Many orthodox State Department men resented and mistrusted the OSS agents using their diplomatic posts, and often undercut their missions.

Smith reported back that Vichy was "mad," a kind of "Graustark" or other fabled kingdom. On all sides he saw Gestapo agents—at bars, restaurants, at the opera. "You expect to find them in your bed and perhaps you would not be wrong." He soon observed that hotel servants were busy eavesdropping and were paid spies. He received anonymous letters telling him to blow up various places. Traps were opened before him everywhere. "Foreign ladies of a type never to have noticed me in the past now find me irresistible."

Smith found considerable pro-Allied sentiment in the unoccupied zone and learned soon enough to appreciate the force that the Resistance movements represented. But since he was in Vichy, he also discovered a hard-core fascist minority, and was alert enough to realize that it was, for the most part, an opportunistic minority and in no way representative of France.

Donovan was getting a most useful file of military intelligence information from Murphy and the vice-consuls. He won State Department and War Department backing to keep all agents at their posts as observers and to send them funds. But the Joint Chiefs of Staff remained hostile to Murphy and his requests for large arms shipments. They would also later be hesitant to parachute arms to the Resistance in France. Orthodox soldiers—whether American, British, or French—had come up in grade slowly over twenty years, imbued with classic theories, and were suspicious of the notion of dropping arms to civilians.

Murphy was having trouble with angry French military dissidents who protested his shipments of money instead of arms. They finally returned the money to him and sent him an ultimatum: All plans for a coup would be dropped if they did not get a guarantee of American military aid by May 20, 1942.

Suddenly Murphy received a new communication from his army "resistants." On May 22 they asked for more American funds. Encouraged by this move, Colonel Eddy decided to go to Washington and present their case for arms in person.

Murphy sent a confidential memorandum to the OSS saying that he had developed a new "lead," a new "white hope" among the French generals—someone who could get France back into the war again on our side, the kind of leader who could take over and then ask the Americans to come into North Africa.

He was nervous about revealing the identity of the general he had in mind, fearful of leaks back to Vichy. He told Donovan that he had to give his word as an officer that he would not pronounce the general's name to anyone but General George C. Marshall. The conspirators feared that the Americans would give the general a big buildup and then "blow" him before he could act. Murphy, whose sense of security was always pitiful, and who could not quite keep his own mouth shut, added in his note: "Suffice it to say that he is in France and a very able rope climber for his age." Since General Henri Honoré Giraud had escaped from Koenigstein Fortress only a month earlier by climbing down a rope from his cell, and since his escapade had been written up by practically every major paper in the world, no one could possibly be in any doubt about the true identity of the general whose name Murphy had sworn never to pronounce except before the chief of staff.

General Giraud outranked de Gaulle by two stars. He had a fine combat record in the First World War and also in the Riff campaign in

Morocco in the twenties. He was as tall as de Gaulle and as fearless, and his remarkable escape from a German fortress had added prestige and widespread publicity to his name. Desperate for a rival to de Gaulle, Murphy was sure he had found one at last in Giraud.

Wheeler-dealer Lemaigre-Dubreuil had been to see Giraud in Lyon and had heard some of his new madcap schemes for uprisings against the Germans in France. Others who had talked to Giraud characterized his plans as "strategic delirium." At that time Giraud would not listen to talk of an uprising in North Africa; some OSS officers wondered just why Murphy considered him to be a "white hope."

Murphy was not the only one counting on Giraud. Robert Solborg, Donovan's man in Lisbon, looking for more direct action, had his own sights aimed at Giraud. The British wanted him too. Some right-wing members of the Resistance also wanted him, until he demonstrated his almost total lack of common sense or any form of political perception. To paraphrase what Churchill would say later about genuine heroes, rarely had so many counted so much on so little.

Solborg flew to London to see de Gaulle. De Gaulle did not impress him. Americans consistently underestimated de Gaulle or took a sharp dislike to him. It was easy enough to dislike de Gaulle, but there was no excuse for underestimating him. Yet Americans did so regularly, except for a coterie of Gaullists in OSS and OWI who had to be very circumspect about their opposition to official policy. Solborg and others in OSS made the error that more than one observer had made, be he spy, diplomat, or journalist: He took his own predilections for reality. Since he felt that Giraud was the man to back, he convinced himself that everyone in London thought the same thing. It was an aberration for Solborg to report to Donovan that de Gaulle enthusiastically endorsed Giraud and that he was the one man whom de Gaulle would accept as his superior. There was not a jot of truth in this report, which grew out of a simple remark of de Gaulle to Solborg that Giraud was a good soldier. By 1942, Charles de Gaulle was so firmly established as the head of Free France, so deeply committed to his mission, that there was not the slightest question of his yielding leadership to anyone else, let alone another general who was cooperating with Vichy at the time.

Solborg decided to go to North Africa to check out the situation there, although he had been forbidden by the State Department and by his own office to cross the Mediterranean. State feared that Solborg was so well known as an intelligence operative that he might compromise Murphy if he came into his territory. But there was considerable conflict and confusion among the various agencies claiming authority in intelligence operations, and somehow Solborg obtained permission from army's G-2 to make the trip.

Murphy did not order him back to Lisbon. Instead he approved a meeting between Solborg and the ubiquitous Jacques Lemaigre-Dubreuil. Lemaigre, an audacious if not a practical conspirator, proposed a rebellion, setting up a new government in North Africa to be financed with Lend-Lease funds. All the Allies had to do, he suggested airily, was to arrange some "provocatory action" by the Axis that would give the French an excuse to ask the United States to send in soldiers "to protect the country." Lemaigre was sure that the military in North Africa were "in the mood" to follow the rebels in an uprising.

Solborg said that some kind of deal might be worked out on condition that the French produce an outstanding leader who could call for American aid at the right time and swing the colonial army to the American side. He had Giraud in mind and so did Lemaigre. Lemaigre said he would go to Vichy to sound out Giraud. Solborg said he would await his return in Algiers.

Lemaigre arrived in Vichy and paid his compliments first to Laval, before going on to see Giraud. He was playing every side of the game, as was his style. Giraud still preferred a revolt in France but thought it might be a good idea to stage simultaneous revolts on both sides of the Mediterranean, with himself as commander in chief of a united Resistance. None of these amateur conspirators checked out the Resistance to ascertain what its leaders thought of Giraud or whether they would accept him as commander in chief.

While Solborg and Lemaigre were dreaming of revolts, Donovan had learned of Solborg's insubordination and meddling. He sent him a "rocket" ordering him out of North Africa and back to Lisbon at once. Solborg flew to Lisbon and then on to Washington to face out his problem with Donovan.

Donovan was so angry that he would not even see Solborg when he arrived. Solborg sent him memo after memo, arguing that the time was ripe for revolt in North Africa and that Giraud was just the man to lead the army into the Allied camp. Donovan, who felt that the future of his new OSS would depend upon its success or failure in North Africa, would not risk his organization's chances on the dubious proposals of a Lemaigre-Dubreuil, or the changing scenarios imagined by Giraud. He was, also, enraged by Solborg's flouting of discipline and impetuous behavior. He fired Solborg, one of the rare occasions when an OSS officer was severely punished for an unauthorized initiative. Solborg did stay on in the Lisbon embassy as military attaché. After the war, he returned to his post as president of Armco Steel in Europe.

Meanwhile, Colonel Eddy had had more success pleading his brief in Washington. He told the Joint Chiefs that he and Murphy controlled some ten thousand Arab irregulars in Morocco, under the direction of two American agents. His information was inaccurate, but there was no way the Joint Chiefs could verify the complexities of Arab politics and the various games being played by the clever Sultan of Morocco, an experienced conspirator. Eddy's talk about an Arab "underground" also ran counter to State Department instructions to keep away from Arab dissidents for fear of alienating the touchy French, who resented any foreign interference in their zone of influence.

The British had already angered the French by talking of independence for Syria and Lebanon, which France ruled under a League of Nations mandate. Morocco was a French "protectorate" and Eddy was playing with dynamite there. Murphy himself must have known better. The French military dissidents with whom he dealt were all committed French nationalists and imperialists. They would not for a minute tolerate any interference in French territory.

Murphy's associates understood the situation. One of the vice-consuls sent through a report denying that there was any desire to make trouble for the French in North Africa. "Whatever our private opinions, as Americans, about imperialism, we were in North Africa as guests, and really as allies of the French people in all but name. We were not there to preach democracy or independence."

OSS men had little sensitivity to State's diplomatic considerations. They felt they were at war with Germany and were prepared to launch any kind of attack that would win the war, without regard for political or diplomatic consequences. Some OSS agents had, for example, conceived the idea of bringing back the Riff rebel, Abd-el-Krim, who had been exiled to Reunion Island, and supporting him in leading a revolt of Moors in Spanish Morocco if General Franco of Spain opposed an Allied landing. This was only one of a number of harebrained schemes that OSS men would put forward. Murphy opposed the plan and Donovan killed it.

Colonel Eddy bombarded Washington with warnings of a rapidly deteriorating situation in Morocco. Pierre Laval, under German orders, was replacing pro-Allied and anti-German French officers with collaborationists. The Vichy police in Morocco had arrested some three hundred French officers who had supported underground movements. French fascists were rapidly taking over key positions in North Africa and chances were increasing that they would fight against Allied landing forces. French coastal defenses in North Africa were formidable and a landing would be costly if the French there opposed it.

Murphy and Eddy were disappointed to hear nothing from Solborg after he flew back to Lisbon. They knew nothing about his trip to Washington and Donovan's decision to fire him. The French officers in Algiers were pressing Murphy for money and arms and he had very little to give them.

Eddy flew off to London in July to try his luck with the British, a foolish move that would have drawn lightning from Donovan had he succeeded. But an assistant director of OSS there invited him to a dinner party with top American brass: Generals George Patton, James Doolittle, and George Strong, who had just been appointed chief of G-2, Army Intelligence.* Strong was Donovan's most bitter rival in Washington and it was incredible that Donovan's representative in London would bring his North African agent to a meeting with Strong and two top generals, both noted for their tough and independent characters.

---

* Later, as G-2, General Strong plucked this writer out of Fort Dix and sent him to Camp Ritchie, the army's Military Intelligence Officer Training School. From Camp Ritchie, I was assigned to General Eisenhower's headquarters in Algiers, where I had a front-row seat on that "intelligence" circus. Earlier I had been an editor and broadcaster in the OWI Overseas Division in New York.

Eddy had dressed for the occasion in his marine uniform, with five rows of World War I ribbons. He walked in slowly, limping noticeably from old wounds. General Patton laughed and shouted: "The son of a bitch's been shot at enough, hasn't he?" Eddy grinned back, did not comment. It was a good start for his pitch to them about needing arms for the underground. He briefed them on the situation and assured them that if they endorsed his plan, American invasion troops would meet "only token resistance."

Eddy flew back to Algiers and told Murphy that the generals had seemed interested in the plans. Murphy kept up his contacts with French officers and with Lemaigre, who kept flying over to France for meetings with Giraud. Giraud's own strategic concepts kept shifting, the only constant being that he must be the leader in any of the plans. Eddy went back to London in August for further talks, and submitted his and Murphy's estimate of the number of pro-Allied officers who would take over North Africa.

The American and French plotters were electrified when Murphy was called back to Washington and told that plans had been finalized for an invasion of North Africa, under the command of General Eisenhower, toward the end of the year. The Murphy–Lemaigre conspiracy to overthrow Vichy and clear the way for American landings was no longer a remote possibility. It was swallowed up in the planning for America's first major offensive action of the war, Operation Torch.

One of Murphy's early recommendations had been taken into account by the planners: his warning that the French in North Africa were anti-British and would resist British landings. Churchill had agreed that Torch would be almost exclusively an American "show," with the British very much in the background, not only in respect to combat troops but also for secret service activities. North Africa would be Donovan's "theater" and the SOE would stay back in the shadows, letting the OSS run underground operations. It would be America's first great test in every sphere—military, diplomatic, economic, political, and subversive.

At the same time another decision was taken that would have the gravest consequences for French-American relations for decades to come. It would be no exaggeration to say that its shock waves are still being felt in France today. It was Washington's decision, recommended strongly by both Murphy and Eddy, that General de Gaulle and his Fighting French be excluded totally from the operation. Lemaigre told Murphy that de Gaulle might be "capable of treachery" if he were even to know about the plans. Just what Lemaigre meant by that was never explained. Who in his right mind could believe that de Gaulle would warn Vichy or the Germans?

General de Gaulle never forgot and never forgave. It was not only that he had been excluded from the operation. Although angered, he might have accepted the explanation that he and Free France represented a red flag to the conservative military of North Africa. But to be not only excluded but also blacked out, snubbed, and mistrusted—that was unforgivable. Those of us who knew de Gaulle and saw him over the years were left in no doubt about his feelings. One could not pronounce the name of Murphy in his presence without provoking a tirade. He considered him incompetent at best, malevolent at worst. As we shall see later, de Gaulle also believed Murphy to be guilty of plotting assassination when anyone got in the way of his policies.

Most of the pro-Gaullists in the American services were working in the OWI in New York. Those of us who were specialists in French affairs, who broadcast in French to the French, and who followed closely what was happening inside France, knew that the Resistance, after some hesitations and doubts, had rallied to de Gaulle. The best elements in France were Gaullist. Some of the worst elements were behind men like Giraud. It is true that the Gaullists seemed to have an evil genius for making the worst of every opportunity. They wrangled among themselves and acquired a bad reputation as troublemakers both in London and in Washington. But, to be fair, everyone wrangled in London.

De Gaulle himself, faced with the awesome power and willfulness of such egotists as Churchill and Roosevelt, had to fight for his life to keep Free France from being totally dominated. His natural temperament was cold and haughty and the struggle to survive only served to stiffen his already rigid neck. But none of that was justification for the wrongheaded policies of the White House, State Department, and the OSS. They may not have liked de Gaulle, but they ought to have realized that it was up to the French people, not the Americans, to determine whom they wanted as a leader.

De Gaulle never disliked Donovan nor did he consider him malevolent, as he did Murphy. He would say, in private talks, that Donovan was a man of goodwill, *"un brave type,"* if not exactly very bright. He thought that Donovan and most Americans did not understand the French situation and, as in Murphy's case, seemed to think that France was "the people with whom he had dinner." Colonel Passy had excellent relations with some of the OSS men in London, and a number of Gaullists, like Claude Serreulles, were friendly with Americans and remained friendly over the years. But on top levels, and particularly in North Africa, de Gaulle and the Americans were on a painful collision course.

The Gaullists did have a few powerful friends, even in Washington. Arthur Roseborough was one of them. A Rhodes scholar and a lawyer who had worked forty years in the prestigious law firm of Sullivan and Cromwell, the firm of Allen and John Foster Dulles, Roseborough spoke fluent French and was well briefed on French affairs. He headed up the western European desk of the OSS in Washington.

Roseborough appreciated the importance of the Resistance and understood that the men in the Resistance, along with Charles de Gaulle, would be the force to reckon with in France not only for the balance of the war but in the postwar world. He tried to tell Donovan that American policy was tragically mistaken, but he was drowned in the flood of on-the-spot reports from Murphy and his disciples. Moreover, the president of the United States shared Murphy's views, and that was too much opposition for any American Gaullist.

Roseborough was delighted to welcome to Washington, to plead his cause, one of the leaders of the French Resistance, Emmanuel d'Astier de la Vigerie, chief of Libération. D'Astier, after conning the British into taking him to London as the "spokesman" of the united Resistance, made the best use of his time once he got there. He had had long talks with de Gaulle and had urged him to introduce into his broadcasts and speeches the theme of reconstructing a new Republic after the war. Many resistants were still suspicious of de Gaulle as a militarist and royalist. Free France had dropped the slogan "Liberté, Fraternité, Egalité," and had substituted the Army slogan "Honneur et Patrie." De Gaulle had been impressed with d'Astier's ideas. It had been agreed to send him directly to Washington to try to convince the Americans of the importance of the Resistance and its allegiance to de Gaulle.

D'Astier was an impressive man; he could enchant an audience with his stories and his arguments, particularly in his exquisite French. But his act did not go over in Washington. They thought he was a somewhat comic character—in some ways he was—and refused to take him seriously. He recognized his failure and commented that the State Department regarded him as a "sort of little Highland chieftain, who had been seduced by an adventure and a symbol." D'Astier returned to Paris in the early summer of 1942. He then returned to London with Henri Frenay of Combat in September 1942 for a series of meetings with de Gaulle and his staff to conclude tentative agreements reached between the men of the Resistance and Jean Moulin on the creation of the unified Secret Army. While there, they met with representatives of the OSS. They told the American secret service agents that the Resistance was implacably opposed to Vichy and anyone connected with Vichy. They explained that Laval was the most abject and servile puppet of Hitler and would never win support of the French people. His bootlicking had already destroyed the myth of Pétain's "double game." They told the OSS representatives that every wing of the Resistance, from right to left, supported General de Gaulle, and that the union of Free France and the Resistance was the most powerful and only legitimate force in France.

Arthur Roseborough, reporting to Donovan on the London meeting, warned him that de Gaulle had now become the very "symbol" of French resistance. The French would never accept the leadership of a man like General Giraud who, on escaping from Germany, had come to Vichy to pledge his allegiance to Marshal Pétain. Giraud had never seriously cooperated with the Resistance and had limited his interest to demands that he be proclaimed the chief of the Resistance for all Europe. Men like Lemaigre-Dubreuil, carefully maintaining his ties with Vichy, with Laval, and with the Nazis, were not the kind of men who could speak for democratic France.

All the arguments for a sensible, realistic, and democratic policy toward France were doomed, mainly because of Roosevelt's unbending dislike and mistrust of de Gaulle, plus the influence of two of his most respected and right-wing advisers: Murphy and Leahy. Murphy's arguments about the French army in Algeria being anti-Gaullist and anti-British were potent arguments. Roosevelt was also impressed by Admiral Leahy's accusations of poor security in the Gaullist camp. There is no doubt that security was not as tight as it ought to be, but it was ironic that Leahy and Murphy should raise the issue, since security in Leahy's embassy in Vichy was deplorable and Murphy in Algiers had no security system at all. Nevertheless, Roosevelt and Churchill not only agreed to exclude Fighting France from the landings, but FDR insisted that de Gaulle not even be informed of Torch until after the landings were physically under way. And Roosevelt endorsed Murphy's suggestion that they conclude their search for a rival to de Gaulle by backing Giraud.

PART FOUR
THE TURNING POINT

14
WAITING
FOR GIRAUD

Marie-Madeleine Fourcade had first read the name Giraud in April 1942 in an urgent, confidential code message from London: "Have learned heroic escape of General Giraud stop repeat Giraud stop believed to have fled to Lyon stop would be most happy you contact him to discover his intentions stop would he serve again stop if so where stop end."

Marie-Madeleine, who was completely apolitical, saw her network as exclusively committed to espionage against Vichy and the Germans. She had grave doubts about getting involved in any way with General Giraud. She wondered what was behind the message. Was Churchill looking to set up a rival for the troublesome de Gaulle?

When Eagle came by the next day, she asked what he thought about it. "You're off the beam," he told her. "If the Allies need Giraud, it's for a North African landing. A general from France would oil the wheels. I learned to my cost that the African army is not Gaullist."

Eagle recommended that they send the Duke of Magenta to contact Giraud. Marie-Madeleine concurred at once. "His dash, his martial bearing, the secrecy with which he surrounded his activities, guaranteed success, at least of the part I was asked to play. I informed London."

The meeting between Magenta and Giraud, in Vichy, did not go well. First, Giraud said he could not understand why the British were interested in him, and, in any case, he would not go to London. Then he went on to say that he was ready to become the chief of the entire European Resistance, that is, the Resistance in every country occupied by Hitler. He suggested the British send him money and help introduce him to the Resistance chiefs in Europe to facilitate his task.

Marie-Madeleine sent London a watered-down version of this absurd notion of Giraud's. She said he wanted to stay in France and head up the Resistance. She also said that Eagle would try to help him and she suggested that London avoid any publicity about Giraud on the BBC.

Giraud saw Laval, who tried to persuade him to return to Germany. Laval did not dare arrest him or turn him over to the Germans. Resistants in the French army, led by Lieutenant Colonel Gonzalez de Linarès, had helped Giraud escape from Germany and there would have been a revolt if Laval had dared act against him. Giraud had already announced his allegiance to Marshal Pétain, so no one dared make a move.

In Lyon Henri Frenay, who wondered what Giraud was up to, asked François de Menthon to see Giraud and try to find out. De Menthon returned from the meeting with a most unfavorable impression of Giraud. Giraud was strongly anti-German but unduly respectful of Pétain and was "idiotically self-important," de Menthon reported.

Claude Bourdet, one of Frenay's top aides in Combat, then went to see Giraud, who had left Lyon for Cannes. On his return he reported: "If I had to sum up my conversation with him, I'd say that on all available evidence he's setting up a broad military action against Germany. He's got some important backing, probably American, which has bolstered his confidence. . . . He knows nothing about the Resistance and wants nothing to do with de Gaulle. . . . The general seems utterly impervious to political reasoning."

Giraud had been living in Lyon, had briefly visited with Marshal Pétain in Vichy, and then gone on for a rest to a family home in Cannes. There he had received messages from Pétain asking him to return to Vichy after a good rest and to be available as a general consultant and confidant for the marshal and his top military men until some special post might be found for him. Giraud did not think it at all inconsistent to work with Vichy while proposing that the Allies back him for chief of all European Resistance movements. Giraud was a French patriot who hated the Germans. He was willing to make allowances for Pétain's collaboration as a necessity to save France from an even crueler German occupation. Giraud wanted an important combat post in the war against the Germans; he knew the Allies were unhappy with de Gaulle and he intended to make them pay a big price if they wanted to use him against de Gaulle.

In Vichy, Giraud had the opportunity to meet often with American diplomats. He alternated between telling them he ought to be named chief of the European Resistance and that he be named commander in chief of an Allied landing on the Mediterranean coast of France. He had decided that a landing on the Atlantic or Channel coasts would be too difficult and that it was unnecessary to invade North Africa, for a landing on the beaches of the Riviera would bring the Allies directly into France. There the people would rise up in support of the Allies and rally to the invading troops led by Giraud.

Marie-Madeleine had heard no more from London about working with Giraud after the first message and was going ahead with her regular espionage activities, stepping up spy missions all along the Mediterranean in the expectation of Allied actions there. She moved back and forth between her headquarters in Pau and Marseille but spent most of her time in the fall of 1942 in Marseille because of its prime importance as a Mediterranean port.

Late in October, Marie-Madeleine received a warning to get out of Marseille from a most unexpected source: the English traitor Bla. Marie-Madeleine's men had been looking for him for months when one of them spotted him in a bar in Marseille. They followed him out, grabbed him, hustled him into a car, and took him to Marie-Madeleine.

Marie-Madeleine and others interrogated Bla, who finally broke down and admitted his treachery. He told them that he was a Nazi sympathizer, did not share their political views, and had done what he felt he had to do. Marie-Madeleine left the room when Eagle told her that the interrogation was going to get rough. She was not present when Eagle told Bla that they had received orders from London to execute him and asked whether he had any last thing to say.

Bla said: "Tell your chief that it must be terrible for a lady to do all the things she's obliged to do. And I want my last act to be of help to her." He paused, swallowed, and said: "Tell her to get out of Marseille. The Germans will invade the free zone on November eleventh."

A few days later, Alliance men executed Bla and threw his body into the sea.

Eagle went to Vichy to see Captain Beaufre, who had been one of his fellow conspirators in the aborted uprising of Algiers. Beaufre was back in Vichy with the army, and had excellent contacts with the Americans there as well as with friends in North Africa. He told Eagle that a North African landing was imminent and that Bla might have been right about the German reaction. He added that he had heard the Alliance might have to make arrangements to take General Giraud to Algiers, where he could take command of French troops. Beaufre was getting his information from pro-Allied spies in Army Intelligence.

Eagle came back to tell Marie-Madeleine that Giraud and a number of high-ranking officers were scheduled to take a submarine to Algiers and that the Alliance network had been designated to make the arrangements. He said he had been told to call the operation Minerva. He added that Giraud knew the submarine would be British, for there were no American subs available, but that he insisted the crew would have to be American, because most of his officers were anti-British. Marie-Madeleine began to wonder if she was dealing with lunatics. All this had been arranged in London and the information relayed to Vichy and to Giraud, but she, chief of the network responsible for the operation, had been told nothing. As for Giraud's insistence on an American crew for a British submarine, well, she thought, he must be thoroughly "bonkers."

Eagle had also told Marie-Madeleine that he had met with Lemaigre-Dubreuil, who had been active plotting with dissident officers in North Africa in anticipation of an Allied landing. He had made close contact with such men as General Mast, who held a key post commanding troops in Morocco, and with Captain Henri d'Astier de la Vigerie, a brother of Emmanuel d'Astier de la Vigerie. Henri was a high-born cutthroat, with a flair for dramatic action. Eagle also saw Marie-Madeleine's own agent in Algiers, Commandant Barjot. Lemaigre-Dubreuil had been working so closely with the Alliance that Marie-Madeleine had given him the not very flattering code name of Tripe. Lemaigre professed to be delighted with the name and had cracked that he hoped that all tripe in France would be cooked with his very own vegetable oil.

Lemaigre told Eagle that he had learned—probably from Murphy or his people—that the Americans had decided to land in Morocco and Algeria and were willing to give Giraud an important role in the invasion if he could persuade the French commanders there not to oppose the Allied landings. Giraud, he said, had agreed to work with the Americans, but, true to his madcap ideas, was trying to persuade them to combine their invasion of North Africa with a simultaneous landing on the French Mediterranean coast, bringing down personnel from Ireland and equipment from Gibraltar.

Murphy had told Lemaigre-Dubreuil that the Americans were opposed to any Gaullist or British intervention in North Africa. His information was that French commanders in North Africa were violently anti-Gaullist and anti-British, particularly because of Mers-el-Kebir. Tripe seemed to know everything, which did not say much for Murphy's discretion. He told Eagle that the Americans had amassed a giant armada of five hundred thousand troops, two thousand aircraft, and a hundred supporting warships, including carriers. Lemaigre-Dubreuil told Eagle that he would go to Algiers and tell Murphy about Giraud's demand for a submarine with an American crew, and would work out the arrangements. Marie-Madeleine sent all this "information" on to Major Richards in London, requesting urgent confirmation and instructions.

While all this was going on in October 1942, "Wild Bill" Donovan began to make his own moves to get in on the show. Sensing the opportunity for the OSS to star in North Africa, Donovan gave Eddy another two million dollars as a war chest for subversive action. The Joint Chiefs approved his plans but instructed him to clear all subversive activities with the supreme commander, General Eisenhower, through his staff. Eddy "obeyed" this injunction by clearing his projects through the friend he had made at dinner in London, General Patton. Unfortunately, Patton did not think it necessary to inform Eisenhower's chief of staff. As a result there was a big flap in London about unauthorized OSS action, until it was established that Patton was at fault, not Eddy.

Eddy was working on a number of bizarre plans. One involved the father of a boy whom the Germans had shot in Paris, and who was burning to avenge his son's death. Someone sent him to Eddy, who hired him to assassinate the Nazi military staff in Algiers as soon as the landings began. Eisenhower's staff men were horrified and killed the project immediately. The staff officers were conventional West Pointers, straight as a ruler, and would hear nothing about unorthodox warfare. They would become more sophisticated later on as they gained combat experience and began to understand some of the complexities of European politics and "total warfare."

Eddy, undiscouraged by the turndown, found a British-educated black African, an elegant gentleman, who was fond of quoting Shakespeare and mixing potent Mickey Finns, which he assured Eddy he would drop into the drinks of the Nazis when the time came.

Murphy, in Washington for conferences, met one of Donovan's more expert assistants, an able journalist, Edmond Taylor, who had worked in Europe for some years for the *Chicago Tribune*, no mean trick for a liberal reporter having to cope with the arch-reactionary owner of the paper, Colonel McCormick. Taylor had written a perceptive book on Nazi psychological warfare and he was excited by Murphy's idea of an uprising of the North African underground under command of General Giraud. He had some doubts about the exclusion of de Gaulle from the plans but was aware of the Gaullophobia that reigned in Washington and was circumspect in stating his views. Taylor would play an important role in North Africa.

Murphy assured President Roosevelt that he could count on the administration, police, and army not to oppose the American landings if the Giraud–Lemaigre plotters were recognized as the provisional government of North Africa. America would have to promise them, he reported, to leave the French territories in French hands, under French control, and they would do the rest. Roosevelt felt that was a very good bargain for winning North Africa almost bloodlessly for the Allies.

Actually Murphy was not in a position to give the president such assurances. He did not know whether the Lemaigre-Dubreuil conspirators were sufficiently numerous or powerful to seize control. The earlier attempt by Navarre had failed miserably. But President Roosevelt had been favorably impressed by Murphy, who, it must be said, possessed considerable personal charm. Tall, graceful, with bright blue eyes and a quick intelligence and wit, Bob Murphy became a highly regarded top American diplomat. He made mistakes, some of them serious, but survived them all. In fact, he rarely was blamed for the mistakes made by him or under his authority. His early support of General Weygand had failed; he had not accomplished anything remarkable in North Africa, but Roosevelt promoted him from consul in Algiers to the highly responsible post of political adviser to General Eisenhower. He also put Murphy in charge of all OSS activities in North Africa, while Eddy was made titular chief reporting to Murphy, outflanking Donovan. As a result of those decisions, Eisenhower would be getting political advice from one of the most conservative, if not reactionary, of American diplomats. The New Deal president seemed to have a special penchant for appointing right-wingers to key policy positions in international affairs.

Murphy returned to Algiers in October to get his planning ready for the invasion scheduled for November. His vice-consuls did an excellent practical job of mapping the beaches, harbors, and coastal defenses. Murphy's contacts among the officers who would participate in the uprising were informed that an invasion was imminent, although the date was withheld, as elemental security required. At that moment, a new element erupted that threatened to change all plans.

Officers known to be close to Admiral François Darlan, chief of Vichy's armed forces, now that he had been supplanted by Laval, let Murphy know that he might be ready to switch camps and join the Allies. Since Darlan was a magic name of authority for the French navy, who would provide the principal opposition force to a landing, Murphy was being offered a real prize as an alternative to General Giraud. The trouble was that Darlan was an even bigger fascist than Giraud. It would be a political hot potato for Eisenhower's political adviser, and for Eisenhower himself. Murphy understood at once that Darlan was seeking to desert a sinking ship and get on board with the winning Allied side. Could he sell this to Eisenhower and the American press?

Near the end of October, Giraud's representatives in Algiers requested a top-level meeting to work out joint strategy for the invasion. Eisenhower agreed to send General Mark Clark to meet secretly with them at a beachside villa on the Algerian coast. Clark was taken in by submarine to a point near the coast, then onto the beach, where Murphy was waiting to escort him to the villa.

Giraud had given his usual stiff conditions to his delegates. As always, he demanded that he be named supreme commander of Torch. It is interesting to note that the Americans were always angry with de Gaulle for being "demanding," but did not hesitate to support egomaniacs like Giraud and, later, totally corrupt dictators in China, Korea, Vietnam, and South America. Apparently de Gaulle was the only difficult man American leaders would not tolerate, although his patriotism, honesty, and courage were never in question.

General Clark told Giraud's representatives that he was not authorized to discuss top command questions and that Giraud himself would have to work that out with Eisenhower. As to Giraud's second condition, an uprising in Vichy following landings on the Riviera, Clark ruled that out at once. There would be no simultaneous landings in France. The target of Torch was North Africa and that was quite enough at one time.

Clark would not give Giraud's men the specific date of the landings, but the huge armada that would be needed for the invasion had already gone to sea as they were talking, on October 23. The slowest ships in the convoy had to leave early, and German reconnaissance would begin to spot them. When the armada could no longer be hidden, on November 5, Murphy informed his fellow conspirators in Algiers of the date, November 8. They protested that it did not leave them enough time, but, when queried, Eisenhower replied he could not change the timing. He instructed Murphy to tell Giraud to keep on the alert. He would soon get a signal for him to come to an urgent meeting with Eisenhower.

As October drew to a close, Supreme Commander General Dwight D. Eisenhower set out from London to new headquarters in Gibraltar, not far from the planned invasion beaches of North Africa. As Eisenhower was getting out of his car on the tarmac of the London airfield where his plane was waiting

to take him to Gibraltar, via Scotland and Northern Ireland, the circuitous
route used to avoid Nazi fighter planes, an elegant Englishman raced breathlessly up to the supreme commander waving a batch of messages in his hand.
"It's Giraud," the high-level messenger exclaimed. "We've just heard from one
of our networks in France [Marie-Madeleine]. He is ready to leave France but
wants a submarine commanded by an American."

Eisenhower smiled, nodded his head. "Winston has agreed to
send a submarine. Tell Giraud one of my officers will be on board. I shall
expect to see him in Gibraltar."

In Marseille, Eagle and Marie-Madeleine sat staring at their radio set, willing
it to start tapping out a message. Contact time came and went, along with the
fifteen minutes' grace period. Nothing. They stared and waited for the next
hour. Tringa, their operator, had scarlet ears from pressing the phones too
tightly against them in his tension. Then he shouted: "WCS. WCS—They're
calling!"

"For God's sake, answer, acknowledge!"

Tringa worked his key, sent his call sign, said he was ready to
switch over to receive. As his pencil moved and the groups took shape, Marie-
Madeleine copied them down to prepare the grid and decode the message. It
was difficult work but her fingers flew.

London told them a submarine would cruise in the vicinity of
the beach she had earlier designated, at Le Lavandou, from November 4 on,
looking for the appropriate shore signal. An American officer would be on
board. Giraud would be taken by sub out to sea, where a seaplane would pick
him up to take him to see Eisenhower in Gibraltar. Recognition signals were
then given, followed by the name of the sub, the *Seraph*, commanded by
Lieutenant Commander N. L. A. Jewell. This message still did not tell Giraud
the date of the invasion, only the date the sub would take him to meet Eisenhower in Gibraltar.

Eagle raced out of the room to call the message in to Giraud.
Marie-Madeleine encoded an acknowledgment to London. In minutes Eagle
was back, frowning. "Giraud says that one submarine is not enough. He needs
two subs and more than four places. He's taking his son, his aide-de-camp, his
personal body guard, and several other generals."

Marie-Madeleine gasped: "Where in the world are they all coming from?"

"They'll be streaming into Marseille and I've arranged for them
to use Beaver's bar as a rendezvous."

"It's unthinkable," Marie-Madeleine exploded. "I'll take care of
Giraud, but the rest will have to fend for themselves. I'm not running a public
transport firm."

On November 3, Lemaigre-Dubreuil returned crestfallen from
Algiers. General Mast had informed him that the landings would take place

during the night of November 7–8. He thought such haste was ill-advised and there would not be enough time to make necessary arrangements to inform and win over key army and navy commanders in North Africa.

Tripe had told Giraud what he thought and that high-handed gentleman had immediately announced a change of mind: He would not take the submarine. He would not leave France.

Marie-Madeleine blew up again: "That bunch are going to drive us loony with their politics! Don't they know that police patrols are already out looking for Giraud, and with his tall, thin figure, there is no way to disguise him!"

Marie-Madeleine refused to send a message to London on a change in plans. Let Giraud miss the sub or take the sub, it was his responsibility.

By nightfall, Giraud had changed his mind again. He wrote out a proclamation of liberation for the army and gave it to Lemaigre, to take to Algiers by the next plane.

Colonel Bernis, Spaniel, drove from Monte Carlo to Le Lavandou to the safe-house to which he had told Marie-Madeleine to direct Giraud and his party, the villa of Maritou Brouillet, known as Bee in the network. They sat around all day on the fourth, knowing the sub might then be cruising off the beach, wondering if the temperamental General Giraud would show up. At ten at night, two cars pulled up: Giraud, his youngest son, Captain Beaufre, Lieutenant Louis Viret, an aide-de-camp whose name no one knew, and Eagle.

Giraud went to bed, while an odd couple, sixty-eight-year-old Colonel Bernis of the Alliance and a twenty-six-year-old lieutenant pilot, Pierre Dallas, went to the beach to send out flashlight signals to the sub.

At 3 A.M., the outside limit the admiralty had given them for recognition on that date, they left the beach and went back to the villa. The whole operation had to be postponed to the night of November 5–6.

The next night a terrible wind battered the coast. The fishing boat to take them to the sub could not leave harbor. The old colonel and the young pilot kept watch on the cold and windy beach. Finally, near midnight, the wind died down. Giraud and his party came to the beach and got into the boat to be ready. Pierre Dallas flashed his signal and shouted with joy when, out at sea, confirmation flashes came from the sub. The boat left at once. Dallas and Bernis stood on the beach watching anxiously. When Giraud and his retinue climbed out of the fishing boat onto the deck of the sub and then disappeared into its belly, they sighed with relief. It was a triumph, at last, to get him off and be rid of him.

Marie-Madeleine and Eagle went back to headquarters in Marseille to transmit to London. A second submarine had been scheduled for the following night, but the admiralty had to be warned that it could not surface in Le Lavandou, for Bee had sent a message that the beach was "blown." The sub had to go to a secondary site at Cros-de-Cagnes. The radio operator, Tringa, had made contact with London and was tapping out his message when suddenly a crash shook the house, and someone was yelling: "Police!"

Marie-Madeleine looked out of the window and saw that they were surrounded. Escape was impossible. She ran into the office, saw Tringa holding a cigarette lighter, trying to burn his schedules, while a man with a gun ordered him to stop. Another man, in a leather coat, a Gestapo officer, was searching the drawers. Marie-Madeleine, in a rage, screaming insults inspired by twenty-four months of underground tensions, threw herself at him, clawing at his face. Astonished by her wild attack, the policeman grabbed his spectacles, pulled back, and lifted a chair to defend himself like a wild-animal trainer facing a tigress. Hedgehog was not the appropriate name for a furious Marie-Madeleine.

She rushed back to her room, grabbed up her secret notes, crushed them, and stuffed them in her mouth. The man she had attacked stuck his head cautiously around the door and started to shout: "She's swallowing paper. Stop her!"

A small, wiry man came bounding through the door and gripped her throat.

Her mouth full of paper, choking from the grip, Marie-Madeleine, beside herself, managed to growl: "*Boche!* Dirty *Boche!*" She chewed, swallowed, and grunted again: "Disgusting *Boche!*"

The man loosened his grip on her throat, whispered in her ear, "I'm not a German. I'm a Breton. My name's Goubil. I'll help you."

They took Marie-Madeleine back to the living room. Tringa shouted at her: "QS5! QS5!" The Gestapo agent smashed him in the face. Marie-Madeleine understood the message. QS5 was radio code, meaning: received OK. London had received Tringa's message warning off the second submarine from Le Lavandou.

Eagle was in the bathroom calmly shaving when the police found him. He laughed at the French detectives and said: "The Germans are coming in and you'll be in the same cell with us." The police looked nervously at each other. Were the Germans really going to invade the unoccupied zone? Many of the Vichy police and army officers were anti-German, and ambivalent toward the Resistance. They had arrested German spies, like Henri Devillers, and shot them. Was Eagle right? What should they do with these Allied spies?

When pale dawn crept into her dismal, vermin-infested cell the next morning, Marie-Madeleine awoke at the sound of footsteps. It was a police inspector, with a broad grin on his face. "I shouldn't really tell you, but it's absolutely marvelous! They're landing in North Africa, in all their glory."

Marie-Madeleine gave the policeman a mighty hug. "It's too wonderful for words. What a splendid November eighth! And it's my birthday. What a fantastic birthday present!" She laughed, then screamed and dug her nails down her neck to squeeze a louse enjoying her blood.

They were taken from jail to the police station for interrogation. There, a superintendent of police told Eagle that if the Germans crossed the demarcation line, he would let them escape. A few moments later another superintendent arrived to take Eagle into custody. They all broke out into roars of laughter, for the superintendent, Cottoni, was code-named Alpaca. He was one of their own animals.

One of the inspectors came to Marie-Madeleine to tell her that they had contacted her agents in town to tell them the route of a police van that would be taking her back to prison. She would be under the guard of two Corsican inspectors and a Corsican driver, all of whom were in on a plot for her rescue from the van.

The van arrived in the morning of November 11, a November 11 that would have the most dramatic consequences for France. When Marie-Madeleine's comrades surrounded the van and demanded her release, the three Corsicans not only let her go immediately but asked if she could help them escape from France. She agreed at once and arranged for them to go to Ussel and be picked up there by a Lysander plane to take them to London. She did not want them arrested and shot by the Germans for letting her escape.

She would have to find a new safe-house for herself. She left Marseille wondering if Giraud had finally met Eisenhower and was playing a part in the invasion.

15
THE AMERICAN LANDINGS IN NORTH AFRICA

The war had gone badly for the United States in the theater in which Americans were in combat, the Pacific. The Japanese had invaded the Philippines and swiftly captured Manila. General Jonathan Wainwright regrouped his forces on the Bataan Peninsula, with a last-ditch garrison on the fortress island of Corregidor just off Bataan. The Battle of Bataan lasted three terrible months of a brave but hopeless fight against overwhelming odds. Wainwright fell back to Corregidor but in another month of heavy fighting and severe casualties his positions were finally overrun in May 1942. The gallant Wainwright, who had fought on against all odds, was beaten down as the Japanese stormed over Corregidor. Wainwright was captured, ordered his troops to cease fire, and, with a breaking heart, signed the surrender of his forces, the first surrender of American troops to a foreign army in the history of the United States.

Americans were ashamed and infuriated, vowing to wipe out the humiliating defeat. The navy called for an all-out top priority buildup in the Pacific. But General George C. Marshall, army chief of staff, was convinced that the fate of the United States and of Western civilization depended on the defeat of Hitler and the defense of Europe. He told President Roosevelt that Europe was the only theater in which all the Allies—America, Britain, and Russia—were fighting together, able to bring their maximum forces into action against the enemy. He insisted that a second front had to be opened up in the west to relieve Nazi pressures on the embattled Soviets in the east. Once Hitler had been stopped, it would be time to mount all-out action in the Pacific against Japan. Until then, first priority was the west.

Prime Minister Winston Churchill reinforced Marshall's arguments, as did the European theater commander, General Eisenhower. Roosevelt accepted their strategic recommendations and ordered a massive buildup of American strength in England in preparation for the second front. Churchill then startled Marshall and Eisenhower by saying that Britain would not be ready in 1942 or even 1943 to attempt to breach Hitler's Atlantic Wall defenses. Despite arguments from Marshall and bitter protests from Stalin, Churchill stood firm. The British, in 1942, would have had to provide almost all the combat strength of an invasion. American forces were not yet strong enough or experienced enough to lead the way. Yet it was essential to take some action and to give the Americans the combat blooding they had to have for the critical invasion of Europe. It was to solve this problem that Torch, the invasion of North Africa, was planned.

Torch would be a first, major test for the supreme commander, General Eisenhower, who was as green in combat experience as his own troops. Eisenhower had spent the First World War in the planning division back in headquarters and had never commanded so much as a platoon in combat. Torch, with a half-million soldiers, sailors, and airmen under his orders, would be Eisenhower's first combat command. That is why the North African landings were so important. They were vital psychologically to the Americans and also to the French. The liberation of French North Africa would be seen by the captive people inside France as the first step toward their own liberation. It would be a desperately needed shot in the arm to the Resistance, reeling from the shock waves of arrests all through 1942. That is why Marie-Madeleine and many other resistants, in vermin-infested cells, facing torture, deportation, and death, shouted for joy on November 8, forgetting their own plight in the news of the American landings in North Africa.

The landing forces moved in during the night of November 7–8 on the beaches of three major ports: Casablanca, Morocco, on the Atlantic, and Oran and Algiers, on the Mediterranean coast of Algeria. The man commanding the landing operations was General Mark Clark, the same officer who had earlier come in by submarine for a secret meeting with Murphy and French officers to work out a deal for French defenders to welcome in the Americans without opposing the landings. General Giraud was supposed to send word to his supporters to be ready to launch an uprising to overthrow the Vichy authorities and seize power in time for the American invasion. But everything went wrong with those plans.

General Giraud had finally got to Gibraltar to meet the supreme commander. But to Eisenhower's dismay, Giraud told him right off that he, General Henri Honoré Giraud, must be named forthwith supreme commander of all Allied forces, and that a landing on the French Mediterranean coast must immediately be ordered to coincide with the North African landings.

"Ike," a genial man who could get along with just about the crustiest and most egomaniacal of generals—men like Britain's feisty Montgomery and his own arrogant American two-gun cowboy, George Patton, even the haughty Charles de Gaulle—could not budge Henri Giraud. Eisenhower thought Giraud must be mad as a hatter to tell him to turn over his Supreme Command and launch a Riviera invasion when he barely had the ships and men for North Africa. Eisenhower pleaded with Giraud, telling him that at that very moment on November 8, American men were hitting the beaches. Frenchmen were firing on them. Frenchmen and Americans, allies throughout their history, were now killing one another. Giraud must act, he must broadcast to North Africa at once calling for a cease-fire. Ike also had a plane ready to fly him to Algiers, where he could take command and lead the planned uprising.

Giraud would not budge, would not act until his demands were met. Eisenhower, his face brick-red with anger, stalked out of the meeting, muttering that he would see Giraud later, warning him curtly to reconsider his position.

Eisenhower went to his war room to read dispatches from General Clark and Robert Murphy, and a sheaf of radio messages from Fleet Command. The supreme commander was not worried about the ultimate outcome. He knew he had enough force to breach French defenses and overcome any opposition. What he was worried about was the showing his American forces would make. They had to win quickly, smartly, efficiently to demonstrate American combat worthiness. And above all Eisenhower wanted to avoid, as much as possible, bloodshed between the French and Americans, which would make the eventual invasion and liberation of mainland France much more difficult. For that, he counted heavily on Murphy and the American agents inside North Africa.

Frenchmen hostile to Vichy and the Germans did go into action as they had promised Murphy they would. The pro-Allied commander of the French army in Morocco arrested the Vichy governor on the morning of November 8. In Algiers, some government buildings and strategic locations were seized by groups of young patriots, most of them Gaullists. The element of surprise caught the Vichy police off-guard, giving the anti-Vichy forces a chance to hold on until the Americans arrived.

Unfortunately, everything was going wrong with the landings. The British navy, unfamiliar with the coast and the port and insufficiently briefed, mainly because of the Allied refusal to cooperate with de Gaulle's naval experts in London, landed the American troops in the wrong places. There were difficulties and delays in getting the troops and their equipment up onto the shore, then orienting them properly once there. Many precious hours were lost, eliminating the advantage of surprise and giving the Vichy "loyalists" in the armed forces and the police time to organize counterattacks.

In Morocco, Vichy police regrouped and arrested pro-Allied officers, setting the governor free. Vichy coastal batteries opened fire at point-blank range on the Allied landing boats, while army units and police raked the beaches with fire and patrolled the streets, bridges, and crossroads. The young patriots in Algiers were driven out of all the places they had occupied. They only had light arms, since Washington had refused to send them the machine guns and explosives that Murphy had promised to deliver them. Casualties were heavy in Allied ranks in the first hours of the invasion.

In the midst of all this confusion, Murphy suddenly got word that Admiral François Darlan, commander of all the Vichy armed forces, had arrived in Algiers. Murphy was taken aback by the news and did not know, at first, what to do. Since the approach by Darlan's men a few weeks earlier, no deal had been made. Now the top Vichy commander was physically present in Algiers. Murphy wondered just what the scenario was and how it would be played out. It was generally assumed in all camps that Darlan, a schemer and opportunist, had come to Algiers to switch sides and join the Allies, who would be the eventual victors in the war. In fact, for once Darlan was not scheming. He was in Algiers on that day as a result of one of those unpredictable quirks of fate: The admiral's son, Alain, had been stricken with poliomyelitis and taken to the hospital in serious condition. Darlan had flown over urgently to be at his son's side.

Although Murphy had no idea why Darlan was there, he assumed, logically, that it was to make a deal and come over to the Allies. American men were dying on the beaches, Englishmen were being blown out of the water, all was confusion. Giraud had not come to take charge. Darlan seemed like a life preserver to Murphy. He picked up his phone, ordered his aides to contact Darlan and ask him to take over and bring about a cease-fire. It was made clear to Darlan by General Clark that the Americans were prepared to pay a high price for his cooperation.

Contrary to the assumptions of those who thought that Darlan had schemed for weeks to jump at the right moment, he was indecisive when the moment came. He communicated with Pétain in Vichy and with fellow officers in Algiers. Pétain sent an order to resist the landings. Officers in Algiers were divided in their views, but most favored a cease-fire. While Darlan consulted and tried to make up his mind, hundreds of men were dying on the beaches and in the ports. Finally, late in the afternoon of November 8, Darlan decided to order his troops to cease fire and asked Murphy to pass the same order on to the Allied commanders.

Fighting stopped at once in Algiers but not throughout North Africa, for it took time for the orders to reach other ports and to be debated by the commanders. There was prolonged fighting in Oran and in Casablanca, Morocco, while in Tunisia, to the east of Algeria, a German expeditionary force moved swiftly to occupy all strategic places. Any hope of capturing Tunisia in addition to Algeria and Morocco was lost in the early hours, mainly because of the surrender of the Vichy commanders there to Nazi troops that had been dispatched to the scene just before the American invasion. It would take some six months of hard fighting and thousands of casualties before the Allies could drive the Germans out of Tunisia.

General Mark Clark kept calling Darlan to get him to impose the cease-fire throughout North Africa and not just in Algiers. But Darlan kept stalling him, telling him that communications were uncertain and that he had to check on conditions inside France as well as in North Africa. Finally, late on November 10, Darlan agreed to call a halt to fighting on all the fronts. It was November 12 before General Clark would be able to tell reporters that all fighting had finally ended. Not the most elegant of gentlemen, Clark growled that the "yellow-bellied sons of bitches" had made a deal.

The deal that had been made would become a national scandal

back in the United States when the terms became known. Young American war correspondents would become coast-to-coast personalities overnight as they told the people back home just what was being done in their name by Robert Murphy and American leaders in North Africa. One of the young men, who would become one of America's best-known and highly respected broadcasters, was Charlie Collingwood of CBS News. Several times a day his cool, clear voice would detail the scandal of the deal with Darlan and the installation of a fascist French regime in North Africa, covered by the American flag.

Robert Murphy and General Clark agreed to accept Admiral Darlan as the top political authority for North Africa. He could function at the same time as the personal representative of Marshal Pétain! Furthermore, all the French officers who were anti-Vichy and pro-American, and who had worked for Murphy and the Americans during the landings, would be removed from their commands; Darlan could maintain his Vichy commanders at their posts.

General Giraud, who had finally decided to go to Algiers, arrived on November 10 and went to see Murphy. Murphy offered Giraud— who had done nothing but refuse to help the Allies at the critical moment— the post of commander of all French forces in North Africa. Murphy, in the name of General Eisenhower, had turned over all political authority to an infamous collaborator and all French military commands to a fatuous fascist.

The uproar in the United States when the details of the deal were reported obliged President Roosevelt to assure his fellow citizens that the arrangements in North Africa were only "a temporary expedient" undertaken because of the pressures of combat. The president promised that a new, permanent arrangement would be worked out as soon as peace and order were restored in North Africa.

Meanwhile inside France a terrible blow against the people and the Resistance had been struck by the Germans. Just as the Nazi agent Bla had warned Marie-Madeleine, the German army, in full battle array, came across the demarcation line between the occupied zone in the north and the so-called free zone in the south. They marched on November 11 as Bla had said they would. On that grim Armistice Day all of France came under German occupation.

Resistance leaders, now confronting heavier German repression, were appalled to learn what the Americans had done in North Africa. They had waited so long for the weight of America to swing the scales to their side in the war, they had counted on Roosevelt as the Galahad of democracy, the hope of freedom in the world. They knew that FDR did not like de Gaulle and they hoped that somehow this problem could be solved. But they could not abide the thought that the American army could be installing fascists and collaborators in North Africa.

Henri Frenay and Emmanuel d'Astier de la Vigerie had heard about the invasion in London and cheered with delight at the news. Then, when they learned what Murphy was up to in North Africa and that the

Germans had invaded the unoccupied zone, they made all haste to return to France to rally their forces. On November 18, a Lysander took them over the Channel to a landing field near Lons-le-Saunier. The men on the ground had been alerted to their flight by a code phrase on the BBC: *"Les courgettes sont cuites."* * Waiting for them to descend so that they in turn could get in for the return flight to London were Yvon Morandat and General François d'Astier de la Vigerie. Emmanuel asked his brother François if he had any news of Henri, who was in the thick of the plots in Algiers. News of his troubles there would only arrive later.

Morandat told them that he had received a report from Jean Moulin on the reaction of their movements and other Resistance groups to events in Algiers. He was taking the report to de Gaulle. In it was a telegram, dated November 9, that had been sent to the British and American governments in the name of Combat, Libération, Franc-Tireur, and a number of labor unions and political parties. The telegram congratulated the Anglo-Americans on their liberating actions in North Africa and expressed the hope that the day would come soon when an armed Resistance could fight alongside its Allies against the common enemy. It went on to say that the Resistance was united behind General de Gaulle and that the new destiny of North Africa must as soon as possible be put into his hands. The message warned sternly that no last-second switch of sides by those responsible for political and military treason would be tolerated as an excuse for past crimes—a very clear reference to Darlan and Vichy officers. Morandat delivered the message in London, but American military censors killed it and stopped the BBC from carrying it in broadcasts.

The leaders of the French Armistice Army in France had known that a crisis was approaching. Intelligence had informed General Verneau, chief of staff of the army, and General Revers, chief of staff of Admiral Darlan's overall command, that the Germans had a plan—Operation Attila—to invade the unoccupied zone soon after the Allied landings in North Africa. They had devised their own counterplan to pull all troops out of their garrisons and away from the main arteries of communication, to make it difficult if not impossible for the Germans to order the disarmament of the French armed forces. They had about fifty thousand to sixty thousand men, ill-armed, without tanks or heavy artillery. They could not have put up much of a fight against the powerful forces that General von Rundstedt was massing beyond the demarcation line, but they planned to fight if they had to.

In fact, no fight developed at all. Only one top commander ordered his troops out of garrison and onto the roads: General Jean de Lattre de Tassigny. But orders were then sent out informing all unit chiefs that de Lattre had been removed from his command and was to be apprehended. De Lattre ended up in jail in Toulouse, his honor intact but his body imprisoned. He would later make his way out of jail to North Africa on his way to be-

---

* "The squash is cooked."

coming commanding general of the First French Army in the southern landing of 1944.

But on November 11, 1942, when von Rundstedt's troops crossed the demarcation line and occupied all of France, General de Lattre was in jail, while most of his fellow officers were cooperating politely with their German conquerors. Von Rundstedt noted in his field report that the French army was "loyal" and "aided our troops." He added that the French police hastened everywhere to show goodwill to the Germans. German occupation decrees announced that the French administration would remain in place, proof enough that Pétain and Laval had become lackeys of their German masters. It was not long after, on November 27, that Hitler issued his order demobilizing the French army. There would be no buffer of any kind left between the Resistance and the Nazis, no clandestine military help for the Resistance.

All the elements of the Resistance understood instantly that they had to put aside their personal quarrels and rivalries to present a united front to Roosevelt and Churchill. The three principal democratic movements, Combat, Libération, and Franc-Tireur, were not the only ones to send messages similar to the telegram of November 9 that Moulin had sent on to de Gaulle. Two of the most powerful opposition forces in France, the Communist party and the Communist-led Resistance movement, Francs-Tireurs et Partisans Français, FTPF, also made their voices heard. It was in the last days of November that de Gaulle's delegate in the north, Rémy, was taken through a circuitous route to the hideout of Fernand Grenier, a member of the Central Committee of the Communist party. Rémy was honored to meet a brave Resistance leader. Grenier had been arrested by the Germans and had suffered horribly before escaping from the camp at Chateaubriant. He handed to Rémy two documents signaling the tightening of ties between the Communist Resistance and the Fighting French of London in the wake of the Allied invasion of North Africa.

The Central Committee of the Communist party, taking note of what had happened in North Africa, expressed its regrets that "the names of the Forces Françaises Combattantes and of General de Gaulle had not been pronounced by the American government" and drew the attention of that government to "the grave danger" that such behavior might have.

Similar statements were issued to the effect that the Communist party and the FTPF movement were solidly united with General de Gaulle and Fighting France. And, at the same time, five well-known democratic members of Parliament of the Third Republic of France, including Pierre Mendès-France and Félix Gouin, sent a joint letter to President Roosevelt, telling him that they had come to London to join de Gaulle and Fighting France, informing him that all patriots and all organized political parties were firmly united under the banner of La France Combattante. The Americans could not thereafter claim ignorance of the stand taken by the most important elements in France actively resisting the Germans.

None of this French reality seemed to have any influence on the illusions nurtured by Murphy, who continued to give his support to Darlan, despite the warnings and the protests of the French Resistance and the outcries of liberal groups in America. Conditions inside North Africa, under the American flag, were shameful. Jews had to wear the yellow star and were barred from professions and many ordinary jobs. They could not even be insurance agents, for some unexplained reason. Concentration camps were filled with victims of political persecution by Vichy. The Vichy generals and admirals who had given the orders to fire upon the American landing troops were still at their posts openly boasting about installing a Pétainist regime in Algeria.

The only group of Americans in Algiers that dared openly and loudly to express their criticism of the Darlan deal and the Vichy fascists in power was an unorthodox team of former OWI men who had been put into a new organization called the PWB, the Psychological Warfare Branch. It was a mixed bag of about sixty Americans and Englishmen, civilians and military, the brightest, wittiest, most dedicated men that anyone could ask to serve with. Bill Tyler, a Harvard instructor in fine arts and an expert on French cathedrals, born in the Ile Saint-Louis in Paris and speaking a better French than the French, was there, along with his close friend Mike Bessie, an editor of *Look* magazine before the war. Bill Doerflinger, an editor at E. P. Dutton, publishers, was then a respected editor of the PWB. The war editor of the *New York Post*, Bernard Frizell, who was this writer's barracks-mate at the G-2 school for intelligence officers, came later to Algiers with me to serve in PWB.

Most of the PWB personnel were billeted in a hotel, high on a hill, called the Cornouailles. We had dubbed it the "Cornwillie." It was a combination billet, brothel, and refuge for Gaullists on the run from the Vichy police. It was the dissident center of all rebels opposed to Murphy, the State Department, Darlan, Giraud, and practically everyone in authority. The PWB office was in the Maison Agricole on the Boulevard Baudin, and our "boss" was a West Pointer, Colonel Hazeltine, who did not understand what in the world we were up to and tried to make us conform to regulations and respect authority, knowing all along it was a losing battle.

Edmond Taylor was the chief of the Intelligence section of PWB and known to be a severe critic of the Darlan deal. Taylor and most of the PWB men went out of their way to cultivate French officers and let them know that there were some Americans who would not make immoral deals and abandon their friends for the sake of "expediency."

Henri d'Astier de la Vigerie, brother of Libération chief Emmanuel d'Astier de la Vigerie, was in Algiers embroiled in the kind of adventure on which he thrived. He was at one and the same time chief of police of Algiers, appointed by Darlan, and a leader of the anti-Vichy, anti-Darlan underground. D'Astier had put together an incredible group of conspirators including Communists, Gaullists, and monarchist supporters of the Comte de Paris, Bourbon pretender to the throne of France. Henri was said to have been a prewar member of the Cagoule, the extreme rightist movement, and was equally at home with the Right or the Left, a not uncommon dichotomy in complex French politics. Darlan had taken on Henri knowing full well that Emmanuel and François were dedicated resistants. More than one family was divided against itself, so Darlan was ready to believe that Henri was opposed to his brothers.

Although Police Chief Henri d'Astier secretly supported de Gaulle and despised Darlan, his policemen searched out and arrested Gaullist supporters. When a group of young de Gaulle enthusiasts went through Algiers painting pro-Allied and anti-Darlan slogans on the walls, a flying squad of police raced to catch them. Four of them escaped the police net and came running into the "Cornwillie" seeking protection. Ed Taylor hit upon the solution of turning them over to American military police, who treated them well and kept them out of the hands of the Vichy police who would have meted out severe punishment and jail sentences.

Tensions increased in Algiers as reactionary French officers, fascist and pro-Nazi businessmen and journalists infested the streets and the government bureaus. D'Astier had no real power as chief of police; it was a mere title. Besides, he was spending most of his time on all kinds of absurd plots, including a scheme to seize power and put the Comte de Paris in charge of the government. The count must have believed him, for he suddenly showed up in Algiers.

A new crisis broke out on the day before Christmas when a young Frenchman, twenty-year-old Fernand Bonnier de La Chapelle, shot and killed Admiral Darlan. No one was quite sure just who La Chapelle was or whether he had killed Darlan as a personal act or as the agent of a power or a group. Early rumors around Algiers made him out to be a royalist, a supporter of the Comte de Paris; still others said he was a Gaullist, although the Gaullists said he was an independent patriot striking a blow against fascism. Everyone looked forward to the trial to find out just who the youngster really was.

There was no trial, at least no public one. Bonnier de La Chapelle was hauled summarily before a court-martial in closed session, and condemned to death on Christmas Day. The sentence was carried out by a firing squad at dawn on December 26. The whole Western world was shocked by the secret, hasty, kangaroo-court aspect of the affair. What were the authorities trying to hide? If young La Chapelle was a Gaullist, as alleged by the French authorities and by Murphy's office, why not hold a public trial and prove it?

Washington was determined to convince everyone that it was a plot of de Gaulle's. They tried to make much of the fact that General François d'Astier de la Vigerie had flown in to Algiers carrying large sums of money to fund the Fighting French movement. It was alleged that La Chapelle was a member of the pro-de Gaulle "Corps Franc," although other sources said he was a member of the right-wing Chantiers de la Jeunesse. The French Resistance acclaimed La Chapelle as one of their own because he killed the odious Darlan, but there was no evidence of any connection to any Resistance group. Much later, in 1945, an appeals court in Paris rehabilitated La Chapelle as a patriot, and no one ever really discovered why he had done what he did. La

Chapelle is a French mystery, equivalent to the mystery of Lee Harvey Oswald in America, and for the same reason: He was shot before he could talk.

In his *Mémoires de Guerre*, General de Gaulle called La Chapelle a patriot who had acted on his own initiative, and then added, strangely, that no individual had the right to kill outside of a battlefield. It was a strange comment from a man whose supporters in the Resistance were killing a great many Germans and French traitors in individual acts well outside of battlefields. De Gaulle deplored the "hasty and truncated procedures" used in rushing La Chapelle to the firing squad, but he did not suggest in his *Mémoires* that there was any conspiratorial reason for doing so.

Many years later, in the late fifties, after General de Gaulle had returned to power following the collapse of the Fourth Republic, he took another position. It came at a time of a crisis in Tunisia in which American conciliation had been requested. The State Department named Robert Murphy, by then one of our most senior and eminent diplomats, to carry out our "good offices." I was the CBS News correspondent in Paris then and, from time to time, had the privilege of "conversations" with President de Gaulle. The president of the French Republic did not give "interviews" to the press, so my meetings with de Gaulle were always dubbed "conversations." I was permitted to make use of information gathered in the talks but never could I quote de Gaulle or indicate the source of the information.

It was during one of those conversations, at the time of the Murphy appointment, that de Gaulle told me that Murphy was not the right man to be a "good officer" in North Africa. De Gaulle said: "Murphy arranged the assassination of Darlan and the hasty execution of Bonnier de La Chapelle. Darlan had become an embarrassment to American policy and had to be disposed of. When La Chapelle did the disposing, they promptly killed him too, to keep him quiet."

I knew from my own experience in Algiers and afterward that de Gaulle hated Murphy, but this accusation seemed wild and irresponsible. De Gaulle had never hinted anything of the kind in all the intervening years. Nor did he offer any new evidence beyond his own words of accusation. President de Gaulle's charge was, of course, passed on confidentially through the American Embassy in Paris to President Eisenhower, and a decision was taken not to appoint Murphy again to any position within the orbit of Charles de Gaulle. The charge itself, without any supporting evidence, was not made public.

Darlan had, before his death, created an "Imperial Council," a high-level consultative body of commanders in his regime. One of them was the commander in chief of the armed forces, General Henri Giraud. As soon as Darlan was shot and killed, the Imperial Council met and "elected" Giraud high commissioner for North Africa to succeed Darlan. The "election" was virtually dictated by Robert Murphy.

The elevation of Giraud to top authority proved to be even worse than the deal made with Darlan. If anyone had any lingering doubts left that

Giraud was a fascist, they must have been dispelled when an explosion of violent repression signaled the nature of his regime. The most reactionary pro-Nazi officers unleashed flying squads of police to arrest every officer or civilian merely suspected of Gaullist sympathies. Police broke into the homes of known Gaullist leaders, handcuffed them, and virtually kidnapped them in police vans that took them to concentration camps in the south of Algeria. They were charged, with no evidence at all, of conspiracy to assassinate Giraud and Robert Murphy. They were thrown into concentration camp without interrogation, without trial, without permission to see lawyers, family, or friends. It might just as well have been the Nazi Gestapo in action instead of the "liberated" French "Allies" of the United States.

Chief of Police Henri d'Astier de la Vigerie was tipped off that his own police had been ordered to shoot him on sight. He fled to the PWB sanctuary of the Hôtel de Cornouailles, where he hid out for a few days, until he thought it was safe to leave. As soon as he left the hotel, he was grabbed by waiting police, hauled off to jail, and charged with complicity in the murder of Darlan. Great pressure was brought to bear on Murphy and d'Astier was finally released.

Ed Taylor called Murphy about the Gaullists who had been hauled off to concentration camps and told him that most of these men had been his, Murphy's, own fellow plotters before the landings. He certainly would not abandon them to brutal imprisonment on false charges, thought Taylor. But Murphy thought otherwise. He blandly and coldly told Taylor that he could not interfere in an internal French affair. Murphy was not the only American official to close his eyes to fascist persecutions of patriots. Eisenhower's own staff had its share of men with Nazi views.

Right after the Darlan assassination and the Giraud succession, OSS agent Arthur Roseborough, an outspoken critic of America's pro-Giraud policy, arrived in Algiers to replace Ed Taylor who had been kicked upstairs to the planning staff. He arrived in January 1943 from London and learned that the Gaullists who had been hauled off to concentration camp were still languishing in their desert prison without being charged or tried. Roseborough was furious. He called Eisenhower's headquarters and raised Cain about the persecution of French patriots who had supported the Allies at the risk of their lives. One of Eisenhower's top staff officers told Roseborough to pipe down and suggested, "Art, old fellow, if you have nothing better to do in Africa than to worry about those Jews and Communists who helped us, why don't you go home?"

Roseborough was undaunted by such obscene rebuffs. He found out about nineteen French soldiers at Oran who, on the day of the Torch landing, had cut the communication wires to their officers' quarters and dismantled the artillery guns so they could not be used against the Americans. It was a clear-cut case of Frenchmen acting to help the Americans land safely. But a Military Tribunal, set up under General Giraud, had sentenced them to long prison sentences. Outraged, Roseborough called General Patton and asked him to intervene. Patton brushed him off, saying, "They got what they deserved. It was treason, wasn't it?"

As the year 1943 dawned, all interest was centered on North Africa. On January 14 Roosevelt and Churchill met at Anfa, a suburb of Casablanca. Before coming, Roosevelt had cabled Churchill that he wanted to arrange a meeting between Giraud and de Gaulle. Roosevelt said that he would bring Giraud as the "bridegroom" if Churchill would provide de Gaulle as the "bride," and they would perform a shotgun marriage of the French rivals.

De Gaulle at first flatly refused to go with Churchill. He was furious with Roosevelt for many slurs and insults and outraged by the American's deal with Darlan, compounded by the elevation of Giraud. De Gaulle also did not much trust his "friend" Churchill, knowing Churchill to be subservient to Roosevelt, and suspecting that Churchill was, himself, not overly fond of de Gaulle. But he finally had to yield. He could not defy the men who were his sole support.

The meetings went badly. American secret service bodyguards were certain that de Gaulle would try to assassinate Roosevelt, so they hid behind the curtains when the men met. De Gaulle was infuriated when he saw their big feet sticking out from under the draperies. He tried, without success, to make Roosevelt understand that the French people were behind him and that he ought to be recognized as the leader of the French. FDR told him that the French people were in chains and would only be able to elect a true leader after liberation. De Gaulle replied that there were times in the history of a people when a patriot would arise from the ranks in times of crisis to assume leadership without election. He mentioned Joan of Arc as an example.

Roosevelt understood quite well that de Gaulle was simply making a historical argument, but FDR, who had a malicious sense of humor on occasion, turned it against de Gaulle by telling the story to reporters in such a way as to suggest that de Gaulle actually thought he was Joan of Arc. This was the origin of the oft-repeated charge that de Gaulle had a "Joan of Arc complex." De Gaulle's feelings were not spared by anyone. When Churchill was asked what he thought about de Gaulle being Joan of Arc, he raised his huge head, his eyes twinkling as he rumbled: "Yes, I know and the trouble is my bloody bishops won't let me burn him."

Roosevelt and Churchill forced Giraud and de Gaulle to appear before the press and shake hands to symbolize "French unity." The two very tall French generals, towering over everyone and glowering at each other, were almost comic figures as they stiffly held out their hands and turned up their noses as though they smelled something very rotten, which was, of course, exactly how they felt. There was no French unity created at Casablanca.

Giraud retained command in North Africa, slowly and grudgingly yielding to pressure to get rid of Lemaigre-Dubreuil and other unsavory elements around him. The American services were badly split between pro- and anti-de Gaulle factions with the anti-de Gaulle group the larger and more influential. Murphy continued to support Giraud as the leader of the French.

De Gaulle went back to London more determined than ever to push ahead with unity of the Resistance. He knew that would be his only hope to overcome Giraud and force the Americans to accept his leadership. That would be the primary objective for 1943, that and the most important of all objectives for the Resistance: surviving under the total German occupation of France.

16
PROGRESS TOWARD UNITY

Nineteen forty-three would start out as a terrible year for the Resistance as the Nazis tightened their controls throughout France. No longer could Resistance movements count on a sympathetic Vichy police playing a double game, or an anti-German French Armistice Army anxious to help.

Army dissidents had to commit themselves to underground action and form a Resistance movement of their own. They called it ORA, the Organisation de Résistance de l'Armée. A few brave men did stay on in Vichy, pretending loyalty to the marshal, in order to spy in his regime. But former officers like Frenay, Navarre, and Eagle, had lost their best contacts in Vichy.

Nineteen forty-two had already ended on a grim note of civil war between French armed forces. Admiral Estéva, in Tunisia, remained loyal to the marshal and even to Hitler, for he welcomed the arrival of a German expeditionary corps that had been sent by Hitler with Laval's consent. Admiral Derrien had turned over the strategic port of Bizerte to the Germans, with its garrisons and ships. But General Barre established liaison with French troops under the Allied High Command in neighboring Algeria, and on November 19, at Medjez-el-Bab, the first shots of the campaign of Tunisia were fired, with the French in the German camp shooting at the French in the American camp.

In Toulon, both the Allies and Hitler were shaken by the blast waves of a gigantic suicide. Officers of the French fleet sabotaged their ships. One hundred warships were blown up. The Allies would salvage only three submarines, which sneaked out of the harbor to join them in North Africa. The consolation was that Hitler did not get his hands on the French fleet.

Hitler, in a rage, sent a long tirade of abuse to Pétain in an eight-page letter, followed by the order demobilizing all units of the French army. Otto Abetz warned Laval that any military resistance would be ruthlessly crushed.

Despite the terrifying presence of the German army and the

Gestapo in the south as well as the north, despite the lack of food and fuel, the Resistance was ready for the trials of 1943, for now there were two powerful Allies nearby, the British across the Channel, and the Americans across the Mediterranean. Resistance leaders in North Africa had seen the firepower of the Americans with their own eyes and knew it was just the beginning of American production. Resistance leaders in London had seen the courage of the British under the "blitz" and the ingenuity of British "boffins," the scientific wizards who were busily devising a new arsenal of cunning weapons for underground warfare.

Before returning to France on November 18, 1942, Henri Frenay and Emmanuel d'Astier de la Vigerie had discussions with de Gaulle's staff and the British and had visited a British "factory" for special weapons to be used in clandestine warfare. They had been amazed by the array of pen-pistols, pen-fire bombs, land mines shaped like camel turds, poison darts of all kinds in the shape of cigarette holders or other innocent forms. They had been most impressed by a new gun, the sten gun, which would later be furnished in large amounts as the principal weapon of the Resistance. Although they had quickly seen the tensions and conflicts between the British and the Free French, as well as the rivalries inside the French camp, they felt that real progress had been made on their trip and they looked forward to tightening up their own union inside France on their return.

At their farewell dinner with General de Gaulle, the men talked about the two great events of recent days: the American landings and the German invasion of the unoccupied zone. They agreed that the landings in North Africa and the machinations of Darlan and Giraud made it imperative for the Resistance to take on a more representative character so that the Allies might be impressed with its authority in speaking for the people of France. Since the Resistance by its nature was secret, the names of its leaders were virtually unknown. Something had to be done to popularize the Resistance and enhance its prestige.

Someone suggested it might be a good idea to create inside France a counterpart of the organization that de Gaulle had created outside France: the Comité Français de Libération Nationale (CFLN), generally referred to by Americans as the French National Committee. Why not such a committee for the Resistance to include all movements, groups, and political parties? General de Gaulle thought it a capital idea, and so did Passy and d'Astier. Henri Frenay however was instantly opposed to the project.

"I'm opposed," he said, "for several reasons. First, with the exception of the Communists, all the prewar political parties—the Socialists, the Radical Socialists, the Democratic Alliance, and so on—have virtually disappeared. To give official representation now to these all but defunct parties would be an invitation for them to reconstitute themselves and thus to create the Third Republic all over again." Frenay went on to detail further arguments against the plan.

According to an account that Frenay wrote later, de Gaulle

countered his arguments by saying: "We'd just have to try to find a way to work things out." When Frenay asked him what he would do if he failed to find a way, de Gaulle was said to have coolly replied: "In that case, I'd just issue orders." As Frenay recalled it later, "A pall of silence fell over the table."

Frenay, never one to take orders easily, at least not arbitrary orders, came right back at de Gaulle. "We are resisters, free to think and do as we choose. Our freedom of choice is an inalienable right. It is up to us to decide whether, in the political domain, we shall carry out your orders or not."

General de Gaulle remained silent for a few moments. Then, using one of Frenay's code names, he said quietly, "Well, then, Charvet, it seems that France must choose between you and me."

Frenay knew that de Gaulle had thrown down a gauntlet. He also knew that this would lead to a clash between himself and de Gaulle's delegate in France, Jean Moulin, when the new council was created, as it undoubtedly would be with the endorsement of de Gaulle, Passy, and d'Astier. In fact, it would take some three months for the Conseil National de la Résistance (CNR) to come into being. Meantime, there was a great deal of work to be done inside France to solidify unified command of the Secret Army.

Frenay and d'Astier left London together, but only physically together. They could not stand each other and would clash often.

Frenay and d'Astier had brought back with them important new agreements to set up a Coordinating Committee of the Resistance and to define precisely the functions of the Secret Army. The Coordinating Committee would be composed of four members: Jean Moulin, chairman, plus the chiefs of the three principal movements, Frenay for Combat, d'Astier for Libération, and Lévy for Franc-Tireur, with each maintaining its autonomy. They sought unity but not integration to the point of losing their identities. The head of the Secret Army would be an observer on the Coordinating Committee. In the political domain, the French National Council (CNF) in London would be required to consult the Coordinating Committee prior to all decisions relative to the Resistance. All existing study groups in France were to come under control of the Coordinating Committee. That, at least, is the way it was all laid out on paper. It did not quite work that way in the field.

The Secret Army was given three major functions: to knock out industrial targets, to wipe out the enemy's rear communications on D-day, and, after the Allies had landed, to harry the enemy's columns relentlessly. It was estimated that the Secret Army would need roughly a thousand tons of weapons and explosives to be parachuted monthly. The request was turned over to the British. The Resistance never was told what decision the British had finally reached, but during the early months of 1943, Frenay and the others were deeply disappointed to receive only a "dribble" of arms.

Back in France, Frenay and d'Astier met with Moulin and turned over to him the new instructions from London, plus a war chest of twenty million francs they had brought back with them. The meeting was warm and cordial, although all three men knew that no one of them fully trusted or liked the other two.

In no time at all, Frenay and Moulin had a serious quarrel. Moulin suggested to Frenay that he become an official emissary of the CFLN, a paid agent of the highest rank, with a monthly salary deposited to his name in London. Moulin meant it as a compliment and an honor. Frenay took it as an insult. He told Moulin that he and his comrades had formed a Resistance movement at the risk of their lives without being paid by London. They were free men, not paid agents of anybody. They had rallied to de Gaulle freely. "We want to be soldiers, *while remaining citizens,* and citizens cannot become agents." Frenay told Moulin that London simply did not understand and appreciate the difference between networks, *réseaux,* which worked for London, and movements, like Combat, which were independent and free.

Moulin told him that *he* did not seem to understand that they were all at war, and that "in war it is necessary to have one supreme commander, and our commander is General de Gaulle."

Frenay snapped back: "Militarily, yes; politically, no. To put the Resistance at de Gaulle's political disposal would be to go out of our way to confirm the charges of the anti-Gaullists that de Gaulle is an apprentice dictator. I must decline."

Moulin flushed with anger and the two men parted on a sour note.

The Coordinating Committee finally did meet on November 27 in Lyon. Attending were Jean Moulin, Henri Frenay, Emmanuel d'Astier de la Vigerie, Jean-Pierre Lévy, and General Charles Delestraint.

First, d'Astier and Frenay delivered an account of their mission to London, outlining the functions and powers of the committee, as well as de Gaulle's written confirmation of General Delestraint's appointment as head of the Secret Army and the pledge that there would be more parachute drops of arms in the weeks ahead.

Frenay told the others that he had argued for a "fusion" of the movements but had been overruled in favor of a "coordination" of the movements. Since that meant maintaining the autonomy of each movement, he conceded that a coordinator would be needed from outside the movements. Obviously "Max," Moulin, was the ideal man for the job. Frenay, despite his doubts about Max, agreed to his nomination as coordinator on condition that he strictly limit his functions to those of an impartial arbiter and not interfere with activities inside each movement.

It was clear that a number of fine lines had been drawn in London and inside France and that it would take a miracle of tolerance to prevent those fine lines from becoming entangled. In any case, there were several agencies that could not have an autonomous life or be coordinated. They had to be fused and ruled by a single hand. One was the Secret Army. All of the Secret Army cadres of the three movements came under the control of the army's commander, General Delestraint. He could not coordinate with Frenay and the others. He had to have all the soldiers under his orders or there would have been no army at all.

Another agency that came under a single command, the command of Jean Moulin, was known as SOAM, the Service des Operations Aériennes et Maritimes. This was the agency that scheduled and controlled all air and sea operations to and from France. The principal officers of SOAM were Moulin's delegates to each of the three movements: Raymond Fassin, delegated to Combat, Paul Schmidt to Libération, and Joseph Manjaret (Hervé) to Franc-Tireur. As delegates to the movements, these men had at first functioned individually for each movement. But for SOAM they broke down the separations and set up a unified organization based upon the six geographical regions: Fassin took charge of all operations for all the movements in R.1 and R.2, Lyon and Marseille; Monjaret took R.3 and R.4, Montpellier and Toulouse, and Schmidt took R.5 and R.6, Limoges and Clermont-Ferrand. Each one set up a team of his own for SOAM operations, each team reporting to and taking orders from the triumvirate command.

Moulin was not the only one to come under attack by Frenay. Frenay's own choice for chief of the Secret Army, General Charles Delestraint, was found wanting by him. Of course, Frenay had thought from the first that he himself should have been named chief of the Secret Army. At the Coordinating Committee meeting he delivered an analytical criticism of Delestraint's weaknesses.

The general, he asserted, was an orthodox military officer with no experience in clandestine operations. He did not yet know his troops personally nor was he familiar with the regional structures of the Resistance. Obviously the committee would have to appoint a permanent representative to the Secret Army to handle some of these functions, such as recruiting, structuring, and arming the regions. Obviously that permanent representative should be Henri Frenay, innovator of the Secret Army, the man most familiar with it. He further sought to strengthen his position by the appointment of a Combat associate, François Morin, as chief of staff.

Frenay got his way. The committee endorsed his proposal and the appointments. So did General Delestraint, who was glad to get Frenay's formidable assistance, while knowing full well that Frenay might try to steal the show from him.

Frenay, having been in London, away from his movement for many weeks, went on a trip to renew his contacts with all his comrades. He found the Marseille region still to be the best organized of the six regions. He learned that Maurice Chevance had managed to implant Combat units in Corsica in his absence.

Three of his regional leaders—Coste-Floret, Teitgen, and Courtin—had gone into hiding, with the Gestapo after them, but had been replaced by able men. A new team had expanded the work of the propaganda section and new printing presses were in operation in Crémineux, Nice, Villefranche, and

Toulouse. They had added a photography studio to the plant and now used photographic plates instead of letterpress foundry type.

Claude Bourdet, Frenay's second in command, one of the brightest and bravest of the men of the Resistance, had come up with an inspired idea that was well under way. He called it NAP, Noyautage de l'Administration Publique. It was simply a plan to infiltrate all the public administration offices of France with resistants who would be perfectly placed for espionage and sabotage by being in key places in the post office, the police, the railways, and so forth. He had set up a NAP-Rail, for the railways, and a NAP-Police. The direction of the section Sabotage-Rail had been entrusted to René Hardy, known as Didot. Hardy had been a schoolteacher who had then gone on to railway management. He had been the stationmaster of the Gare Montparnasse in Paris and was an expert on the rail system. He would become the central controversial figure in one of the most tragic events to shake the Resistance.

The NAP-Police was already rendering the most valuable services. Its infiltrators had advance lists of arrests and would tip off movement members to go into hiding well before a police raid on their homes. Inside personnel had connections with city halls and other administrations to provide the movement with false papers, ration cards, official stamps, and all the paraphernalia of the bureaucracy. Bourdet's idea would be copied by the other movements and become one of the mainstays of the Resistance.

Life went on even in the shadows of underground war. As the end of 1942 drew near, Frenay was able to celebrate two joyous events with the two women who were closest to him, his most beloved friend and associate Bertie Albrecht, and Dr. Chilina Ciosi, whom he had met in Paris, where they had become lovers.

Bertie's daughter, Mireille, had come to see Frenay to tell him that her mother, desperate to get out of prison, had successfully feigned insanity and had been transferred to the psychiatric hospital of Lyon-Bron. Mireille had visited her mother and had taken careful note of the common room in which she was permitted to sit by day, and her private chamber by night, on the second floor of an annex to the main institution. A friendly nurse had given the girl a wax duplicate to the keyholes of the annex doors. It was up to Frenay and Combat to rescue Bertie. It was a challenge they accepted with joy.

Frenay went to the hospital to case the grounds. He saw that the retaining wall around the buildings was only ten feet high and easy to scale. He noted that the doors were bolted after dinner, but he had been assured by Mireille that the keys she had given him would unlock them. And chances were that vigilance would be relaxed for Christmas. He told Mireille to inform Bertie that she should be ready for the rescue on Christmas Eve.

A member of their team, André Bollier, set up the rescue operation. He carried a ladder to the wall at the stroke of midnight on Christmas Eve. He and an accomplice scampered over the wall and unlocked the annex doors. One comrade, revolver in hand, took up position in front of the night watchman's room. Bollier and another resistant opened the doors and made their way up to Bertie's second-floor room. They handed her clothes that Mireille had given them. Grinning silently, she speedily dressed and followed them down. They carefully locked all the doors behind them. The night watchman snored away his Christmas dinner and wine and they all clambered up the ladder, down the wall to the other side and freedom in a safe-house in Vernaison, a village south of Lyon. The next morning, Frenay and Bertie embraced in their first meeting in seven months.

Then Frenay heard from the woman he loved, Chilina Ciosi. She had narrowly escaped the Gestapo, who had got her name from the traitor Henri Devillers. By an extraordinary coincidence, Dr. Ciosi had at the time diagnosed her own chest pains as tuberculosis and had gone off to a sanatorium in the south just before the Gestapo had broken into her apartment. Her disease had responded to treatment and did not require surgery. She had improved and been appointed to the staff of a hospital near the Spanish border, treating patients afflicted with bone tuberculosis. And she had managed to set up an escape route through the Pyrénées for resistants fleeing France.

She had found out where Frenay was and had sent him a note bringing him up to date. He had not seen her for a year and asked her to meet him in Toulouse. They embraced and he told her that he loved her and asked her how she would feel "if God wished us to have a child?" She kissed him and said that she would be "the happiest woman in the world." In his memoirs, Frenay noted: "Little Henri was born on October 6, 1943, while I was still in Algiers. For the safety of the mother and the child, he was declared to be of unknown parentage and placed in a foundling home until the end of hostilities. After the liberation, we had no trouble recognizing him legally." Life did go on in the shadows, but it was not exactly routine.

Discussing the poignant story of Frenay and Dr. Ciosi at a dinner party in the home of Jean-Pierre Lévy in the fall of 1977, one of the Franc-Tireur veterans said: "It is important to tell this story and others like it to your American readers. Despite the Germans and the terrible risks of the Resistance, life did go on, you know. People fell in love and had children, even resistants on the run. What was most striking about it all, as I recall, was that we had a sense of high adventure and thoroughly enjoyed ourselves. The movies give you the impression of men and women wrapped in cloaks, slinking about. Most of the time it was not like that at all. We moved about like ordinary people. We met in restaurants and café terraces. Once in a while we would go to the movies, or even a dance. Life was grim and often tragic, but we were not."

Love could, however, prove to be the undoing of a resistant. Frenay was thoroughly alarmed by the reckless behavior of Edmond Michelet, one of his most successful regional chiefs. When Frenay stopped off to see him in Brive, he discovered that he had been sheltering resistants in his own home. His activities were bound to be noticed by the police. Frenay told him it was imperative that he go underground to escape arrest. But Michelet protested:

"I just can't leave my family. They need me." Michelet's love for his family was his undoing. The Gestapo came, as Frenay had predicted, and Michelet was arrested and deported to Germany. It would be years before he would return to his loved ones.

Frenay had a special interest and concern in his heart for deportees and for French prisoners of war. Despite his difficult personality, he was a humanitarian, a man with a big, warm heart. Later, General de Gaulle would call him into his government and make him a Cabinet minister in charge of the problems of deportees and prisoners. It was natural for Frenay to seek out men working in this area, and shortly after his return from London, he did meet two young men, former French war prisoners, who were working to build a Resistance movement out of returned prisoners. One of them was Michel Cailliau, a nephew of General de Gaulle, son of de Gaulle's sister, Marie-Agnès; the other was an obscure youngster of twenty-two, of whom France would hear a great deal for many years to come. His name was François Mitterand.

Mitterand had worked as an official of the Vichy Prisoner of War Commission and had been decorateed with a Pétainist award, the "Francisque," an enameled buttonhole pin in the shape of a Frankish ax. It was worn mostly by fascists in the service of Pétain, but Mitterand had earned it by his devotion not to the marshal but to their fellow French soldiers who had suffered in captivity and needed help to rehabilitate to civilian life.

According to Frenay, the two of them—Cailliau and Mitterand—detested each other. "Since each wanted to create his own movement, their rivalry was intense." Michel Cailliau, questioned about this in an interview, laughed and said: "Well, we were rivals, that is true, but Frenay exaggerates when he says that we 'detested' each other. We were young, ambitious, strong-minded, self-confident. And each wanted to run his own show. That's about it."

Cailliau, seated at a desk overflowing with papers in his office behind the Gare Saint-Lazare, recalled vividly what they were attempting to do. "Vichy had built up an entire organization based on the prisoners, with a well-defined infrastructure. It was all there ready to be used. I believed I could set up a prisoner movement, that is, an ex-prisoner movement, to combat the insidious fascist propaganda of Vichy. I thought that some of these former prisoners would make excellent fighting men of the Resistance. And I also believed that we could set up a chain of communications back to the camps in Germany where something like a million eight hundred thousand of our men were still being held."

Michel Cailliau already had experience in clandestine action. It began when he was captured by the Germans. "We were packed into a train and sent off as prisoners to Germany. As soon as I was strong enough, I volunteered for a work gang so that I could escape. I fled through the forest, but was caught in the Siegfried line and sent back to prison. I escaped again with a friend and again was recaptured, in a railway yard trying to sneak into a freight car for France. This time they put me into a disciplinary cell in· a prison in

Hanover. There were four thousand prisoners in our camp and in the area there were one hundred thousand *commandos de travail*, slave laborers for the Nazis.

"I began to organize a Resistance group in that camp. I became the secretary and interpreter for the camp doctor. I obtained a dictionary and studied medical terms. I hoped to get myself reclassified as a *grand malade* and repatriated. Meanwhile, I talked with prisoners who were being sent off to work in factories and we worked out methods of espionage of German production. I also got men sent home by mashing up a pill for constipation called *grains de vals* and spreading the paste on their eyes. It gave them a bad eye infection, an advanced conjunctivitis, and the doctor marked them unfit for duty and eligible for repatriation.

"When the doctor I was working for got orders to go to the Russian front he left behind his medical forms. I took one and made it out for myself, listing myself as having incurable maladies of the liver and kidneys that put me into the *grand malade* category. I forged his signature, and his replacement did not think to check my papers carefully. He countersigned and I was released and sent back to France."

One of the tricks that Cailliau had pulled in prison was to organize French prisoners to pick lice off Russian prisoners who had been brought to their stalag. Cailliau had told German guards that they would not get sent to the Russian front if they were bitten by lice and got infected. He offered to sell them the lice they needed. "First I sold lice one by one, but business became brisk and I sold them by the *flacon*. Before long, typhus broke out in the German ranks and an entire division, scheduled for the Russian front, was quarantined and confined to camp for two months."

Once back in France, Cailliau went to Lyon and called on friends whom he had known in the army and in prison. He set about creating two organizations: an independent Resistance movement that he called Charette, a code name he had taken for himself, and a prisoner organization that became known as the MNPGD, the Mouvement National des Prisonniers de Guerre et des Déportés. Cailliau recalls his meetings with Frenay and a number of disagreements with him, as Frenay wanted to take over the movement and Cailliau wanted to be independent.

In his memoirs, Frenay claimed that he talked about Cailliau and Mitterand to the Coordinating Committee and that all agreed they ought to be aided. He began to furnish some money to them at the start of 1943 but admitted it was "too slender to suit them," particularly since Cailliau and Mitterand, unable to agree on anything, had started two separate ex-prisoner organizations. They would all meet up again later in 1943 in Algiers, after Charles de Gaulle had set up his provisional French government there. Cailliau talked to his uncle about the problem of ex-prisoners. So did Frenay. De Gaulle had been favorably impressed with the need to organize the former prisoners.

D'Astier had sent a number of his best young people from Libération to give muscle and brains to the staff of General Delestraint, chief of the Secret Army, among them Raymond and Lucie Aubrac and Maurice Kriegel (Valrimont). The lycée teacher of philosophy, brilliant, handsome Pierre Hervé and his attractive wife, Annie, had joined the press bureau, the BIP. Frenay later would discover that most of them were Communists and would charge that "they were the harbingers of the infiltration of the Resistance via Libération." This charge of Communist "infiltration" was part of his vendetta against d'Astier de la Vigerie, not a real objection to working with the Communists, which Frenay agreed was necessary.

One of the members of SOAM, the agency for air and sea services, was a remarkably brave young Alsatian woman of Jewish origin, Anne-Marie Bauer. Anne-Marie, a survivor of Ravensbruck, lives in Paris today, with her memories and her faithful violin. She remembers her assignment for SOAM, and her work in the Libération movement.

"I was driving trucks and ambulances when my brother, Etienne, asked me to join him in a movement called Libération. I went to work at first in Montpellier, distributing tracts and telling young Frenchmen not to yield to the labor draft for work in Germany. Then I met Paul Schmidt and Gérard Brault, who was called Kim. They asked me to join them and help in organizing parachute operations and landings of Lysander planes. My job was to scout out good landing fields, flat enough and of the right length and width, and far enough from populated places or enemy observation.

"At first, I found what I thought were excellent locations around Grenoble, but there were objections because the terrain was mountainous. Later, when more experienced they were able to use those sites, but not at first.

"When Jean Moulin came to Lyon they assigned me to help him with coding and decoding of messages and I did so, but it was boring and I pleaded to get back to spotting terrains. They agreed. It was then that I met Claire Chevrillon who said she had friends in the Corrèze who wanted to participate in the Resistance.

"I went to the Corrèze and met Geoffroy de Chaume and the Condamine family. They were the greatest find. They owned a hotel and a small bus and transport company. We not only found many, many landing sites, but also set up a team of smugglers. I took dozens of photos and measurements and brought it all to Schmidt, who gave it to Moulin.

"They were delighted with my work and congratulated me, but when, a month later, a paradrop was scheduled for my field, they wouldn't let me go. Said it was too dangerous for a woman. They sent my brother, Etienne, instead. I was enraged and told them that I'd go to the next drop or they wouldn't get any more locations from me. They gave in, and I did go to the next operation."

Anne-Marie showed them what a woman could do when Gérard Brault was caught and incarcerated in Castres prison in Toulouse. She took on the assignment to rescue Brault. She put together a team of Boy Scouts who were experts in climbing and using ropes, in order to get over two walls around the building in which Kim was being held. Then, with the help of a guard sympathetic to the Resistance, and needing money for a sick mother, they slipped sleeping pills into the wine of the other guards.

"I was supposed to be supported by an armed Groupe Franc, from Libération. They didn't show up. So we went over the wall anyway, hoping no police or Gestapo would be waiting for us when we came back. The guard had done his part and knocked out the others with the pills I had given him. We found Brault, who was very weak. It was awful getting him over the wall, and we almost didn't make it. Marguerite Losier was waiting on the other side in a truck that Libération had given us, and we took off to the house of a friend in the Dordogne, who had agreed to hide Brault until he was well enough to care for himself."

Anne-Marie was finally arrested in July of 1943. Her interrogator joked with her about her Alsatian name and suggested she ought to be working with the Germans, not against them. "I was so angry that I did a really stupid thing. I told him that I was Jewish and that I wouldn't work with them. In fact, I came from a Jewish family and was raised as a Jew. Jewish or not, it was insane to tell that I was Jewish. I thought I could shame them!"

She paused, as though wondering how to go on, then said: "I refused to answer any more questions. They smiled, tied my hands behind my back, and then strung me up by my hands. Then they pulled off my shoes and stockings and began to burn the soles of my feet with matches. I screamed. They stopped and asked me whether I had changed my mind about answering questions. I begged them to cut me down and told them I'd answer any questions. They cut me loose and asked me about my Resistance movement. I began to tell them a story I invented about my chief 'Victorine.' Knowing the Resistance as I did, it was not difficult to spin a yarn that sounded genuine."

The Gestapo took her out of jail, in the company of Nazi women guards, who walked ahead and behind her, to a café where she said she met her comrades. "There was no one there, of course, but I made believe I was looking. Then, I went out and waved my hat, as though signaling. When nothing happened, I told the Nazis that my friends had smelled a trap and ran. A Nazi Amazon put a machine-pistol to my neck and said: 'You dirty Jew liar, you'll die now.' I was, believe me, relieved. No more torture, just a quick, clean death with a bullet in my neck. I put my head down and she pulled the trigger. I heard the shot and fell to the pavement. I thought I was dead, but I woke up and saw the Nazis laughing. She had fired a blank and I had fainted. They took me back to prison, to a solitary cell, then on to Ravensbruck. You know what that was like, you've heard the story from so many victims."

Anne-Marie's brother, Etienne Bauer, was critical of the agents from London. Historian Henri Noguères quotes him as saying: "We had a lot of fights with London and with Moulin's staff. Most of the London agents were rightists, even extreme rightists, and I was a man of the Left. We had all kinds of fights about arms caches, money, and combat. They wanted us to wait for a major offensive on D-day. We believed in daily operations. We didn't want to cache our arms, we wanted to use them."

Colonel André Manuel, a deputy to Colonel Passy in London, was disturbed by the constant friction and tension between the Resistance and de Gaulle's people. Although more than thirty years have gone by, he remembers it well. Sitting in his office in Paris on the Boulevard Haussmann, Manuel looks like the successful business executive that he is, and, as so often with men and women who were in the Resistance of Fighting France, it is hard to imagine him parachuting down into Nazi-occupied territory. He is the director in France of an American firm, Compton-Knowles. He started working for them, as a young man, in the 1930s, in Worcester, Massachusetts, after his family, who had owned a big textile mill, went bankrupt in the Great Depression. Manuel had been angered by Pétain's capitulation and fled to London, where he was one of the first to join de Gaulle.

"It was a pity that our common cause had to be weakened by so much internal quarreling, much of it petty. But it was inevitable, I suppose, for those of us in London, concerned with a military buildup of our forces, to fail to understand completely an armed civilian Resistance. It really was not difficult for me, for I was a civilian basically and only became an officer in time of war. But how could you expect professional soldiers like de Gaulle or Passy to put up with the kind of chaos produced when one and the same man performs political, propaganda, intelligence, and military functions.

"I must say that I myself was quite taken aback by conditions I found in the field in France when I parachuted in on November 22, 1942. I had been given the mission of checking out the real strength and potential of our action and information networks and to give them the directives that would put them under London's control and serve London's needs. I'm talking about the networks that our own agents sent over from London and had created, and not about the groups and movements that had emerged in the Resistance. Those came under Moulin and were outside my authority. London had hoped that since I was coming in fresh I might also help Moulin, but I was so overwhelmed by my own mission and so green in the field that there was little I could do for Moulin. I knew, of course, that he was having trouble persuading all the Resistance movements to work together. He was butting heads with Henri Frenay. At times it seemed as though everyone was butting heads with Frenay."

On December 31, 1942, Henri Frenay celebrated a snowy New Year's Eve with his five closest associates: François Morin, chief of staff of the Secret Army; Pierre de Bénouville, his "ambassador to Switzerland"; Claude Bourdet, his number-two man, chief of the NAP; Henri Aubry, one of the early founding members of Combat, a member of General Delestraint's staff; and, finally, "Jérome," Michel Brault, who had replaced Jean Gemahling as the chief of intelligence for Combat.

As they were meeting, a messenger from one of their associates, Marcel Peck, came in with news for Frenay. A number of young people, mainly from the Paris area, had revolted against the STO, the Service du Travail Obligatoire. This was a forced labor draft instituted by Pierre Laval as part of what he called *la relève*, the relief program, a swindle in which young Frenchmen were to go to work for German industry in return for which a certain number of French war prisoners would be released and sent home. According to the message from Peck, the young Parisians had fled Paris before they could be drafted, had come south, and were now hiding out in an Alpine woods. They were reported to have revolvers and to be prepared to shoot it out if the police came for them.

Frenay remembered later that Michel Brault had commented: "In other words, they've taken to the maquis." It was, Frenay wrote, the first time he had ever heard the word *maquis* used in that fashion. A maquis is a scrub-wooded upland, but it came to mean a new form of resistance: armed camps in the woods, ready for combat. As the maquis grew, it needed arms, training, leadership, food. Michel Brault would become one of the national leaders of the maquis.

With bad news from all the fronts, the Germans in France were becoming more vicious in their bloody repression of the Resistance. The Vichy collaborators had dropped all pretense and committed themselves totally to the Germans. They created a Nazi-like "Milice," an armed force that functioned like the Gestapo, appointing as its director a French Nazi, Joseph Darnand. Laval took over the Ministry of the Interior and the police ministry, and made Darnand his secretary of state at the interior.

This repression by the Germans and Vichy was both a danger and an encouragement to the Resistance. Police raids caught a number of patriots and the Resistance suffered in other ways from the new pressures. But the terror also brought the Resistance new recruits, particularly the thousands of youths who refused to answer the draft to work in Germany. The Germans were demanding a new quota of 250,000 French workers, including 150,000 skilled workers, to be delivered by March 31. They had already taken 240,000 workers in 1942, in addition to the more than 900,000 French war prisoners they had put to work in Germany.

All the movements of the Resistance, including the Communists and the trade unions, decided, at the turn of the year 1942–1943, that the time had come for a direct confrontation with the French and German Nazis on the issue of the labor draft. They chose as battleground the city of Montluçon, where a number of workers had been taken from their homes on December 27 and packed off to trains by the police. A similar roundup was scheduled for January 6 and the Resistance decided to oppose it in a united effort.

In Montluçon, flying squads of painters, carrying pots of liquid tar, went all over town swabbing strike slogans and instructions on the walls, particularly of the big Dunlop tire factory. All workers were told to be at the railway station at 1 P.M. for a protest meeting. A huge crowd of about six thousand turned up, composed of young men and young women and the parents of the youths called to the draft, in addition to the many workers. The police kept the crowd away from the platforms of the trains, allowing only those carrying a labor draft card to enter the quays.

Suddenly, as often happens in such circumstances, the crowd began to push against the police lines, or the police tried to push the crowd back, and a number of fights broke out. The Gardes Mobiles, an armed police force, began hitting people with rifle butts. A number of angry workers pulled the rifles out of the hands of police and began punching them. The demonstrators broke into the main hall of the station and began to sing "La Marseillaise" and "L'Internationale." Shouts rang out: *"Vive de Gaulle! Vive l'Union Soviétique! A bas Laval! Pas de Français pour l'Allemagne!"*

A number of young men who had been put on the train jumped off and ran away. The stationmaster signaled the engineer to pull out before he lost more passengers, and he twisted his throttle. But, to their astonishment, the locomotive pulled out all alone. Some demonstrators had uncoupled the cars of the train.

They finally got the train under way, but after rolling a hundred yards it came to a halt. Railway workers, armed with wrenches and sledgehammers, had sabotaged the tracks. A tremendous roar arose from the crowd, sensing victory. The police, outsmarted and outnumbered, gave up and left the station. Troops of the Wehrmacht, bayonets affixed to their rifles, came running up, but it was not before nightfall that the train was able to leave, and most of its labor draftees had long since escaped. A Nazi official, reporting to headquarters, said that only twenty of one hundred eighty requisitioned youths had gone to Germany. A good number of the others had gone on to the maquis.

A number of maquis mushroomed across the southern zone from January 1943 on, growing greater each month. Some developed also in the north, but not with the speed or number of the southern zone, above all in the eastern and central wooded areas and mountain sectors. One place in particular began to build up and would become an issue of tragedy and controversy for years: the Vercors, a plateau in the southeastern Alps where some men had the idea of creating a fortress redoubt.

As the year dawned, the principal armed groups were still the Groupes Francs. They were not nearly as well armed as they should have been. Neither the British nor de Gaulle, in England, nor the Americans, in North Africa, were yet willing to send a mass of arms to underground groups they did not truly command. They knew, however, that they did have to send some amount of arms if they were not to lose the faith and cooperation of the Resistance. The arms drops were, therefore, carefully "dosed," just enough to keep the Resistance from rebelling, not enough to make the Resistance a potentially dangerous independent armed force.

Combat, Libération, and Franc-Tireur all received "drops" at the turn of the year: sten guns, machine-pistols, ammo, grenades, plastic explosives, radio tubes and crystals, detonators and fuses. The arms and explosives permitted the Resistance to carry out an impressive series of attacks on factories working for the Germans, on rail lines, and on telecommunications. The Germans realized that they were no longer faced by irregular "terrorists" but by a formidable clandestine army. The Gestapo received urgent new orders to ferret out the leaders of the Resistance movements and to make every effort to liquidate this dangerous enemy in the new year, 1943.

The repression launched by Vichy and the Germans strengthened the Resistance in general. Only by a tightening of the organization and an eradication of duplications could the movements successfully meet the new Nazi menace. D'Astier and Jean-Pierre Lévy decided in the course of talks during January that they would fuse their movements with Frenay and Combat. The decisive meeting took place on January 26, at the end of which a note was circulated to all members at all levels of Combat, Libération, and Franc-Tireur. This fusion went well beyond the coordination of independent movements in the Conseil National de la Résistance under Moulin. The note explained that the new police repression required new vigilance and new activities based upon a "total union of all the forces of the Resistance." Therefore, a comité directeur would be formed as a single directorate of a new organization, called the Mouvements de Résistance Unis, MRU.

Later, someone realized that the acronym MRU could not be pronounced and had no clear meaning, whereas if the name were changed just a bit to read Mouvements Unis de Résistance, the acronym would become MUR, not only easily pronounced but in fact the French word for "wall," an excellent symbol. The organization quickly became known as MUR from then on.

The members of the Directing Committee were the same as they had been on the Coordinating Committee: Jean Moulin, Henri Frenay, Emmanuel d'Astier de la Vigerie, and Jean-Pierre Lévy. But this was not merely a change of name with the same players in the same roles. Now there would be new, unified functions. Frenay would become the commissaire for military affairs, d'Astier the commissaire for political affairs, and Lévy the commissaire for intelligence, security, and supplies.

Each one, in his sphere, would command the respective staffs of all three formerly independent and separate movements. In each region where before there had been a chief for each movement, there would henceforth be only one chief of MUR, commanding them all. The only completely distinct symbols that would remain visible would be the newspapers of the movements, *Combat, Libération,* and *Franc-Tireur,* which had their own loyal readership and their own orientations. It would have been quite impossible to have brought out one paper of the Resistance, if only because no one editorial and one writing staff could be found to which everyone would subscribe.

The Secret Army would be subordinated to and controlled by the directorate of MUR.

The directorate would administer SOAM, the air and sea operations unit, and control the radio transmitters, although each of the leaders of the original three movements would maintain a personal radio at his disposal.

In actual practice, Moulin, chairman of the directorate, would maintain the control he already had of air, sea, and radio operations.

Needless to say, not everyone was happy with the new arrangements, not even Frenay, who had long demanded them. Frenay's first complaint was that d'Astier and Lévy demanded equal representation for their movements and themselves in the composition of the new committee and the various tasks and functions that were to be allotted. Frenay expected them to do so, since it is only human to demand equality. But, in fact, the movements were not equal. Frenay was quick to point out that Combat had more members than the other two put together. Moulin had given Combat a five-million-franc budget in February, against one and a half million for Libération and nine hundred fifty thousand for Franc-Tireur. That was a proportion of six to two to one.

Frenay knew he could not hold them to so rigid a formula, but he thought that in all fairness the distribution should have been two for Combat to one for the others combined. D'Astier and Lévy exploded, and a bitter debate threatened the unity of the Resistance before it was even achieved. They demanded full equality or no fusion of efforts. Anything else would in effect make Henri Frenay the chief of the united movements, and no one would buy that, for Frenay was simply too abrasive and controversial.

Frenay went back to the steering committee of Combat, as he had on previous occasions, and, as had happened before, his own steering committee did not back him up. They turned down his two-to-one proposal and agreed to accept equality of allocation of authority, insisting, as all finally agreed, that all final policy decisions must be made collectively by the directorate and not by the individual commissaires alone.

Frenay accepted the decisions, for he had no other choice, but he never reconciled himself to them. Thirty years later, in his memoirs, he wrote that "we made a terrible mistake." And in the 1970s, long after Jean Moulin had become a revered martyr of French history, Frenay was locked up in his room furiously writing a book denouncing Jean Moulin.

Frenay was not alone, however, in criticizing certain aspects of the new MUR. In fact, he himself was the object of at least one objection. It came from General Delestraint, chief of the Secret Army, who was unhappy to learn that Frenay had been named commissaire for military affairs. This made Frenay Delestraint's boss, and since Frenay had been free in his vocal criticism of Delestraint, the general felt there would be serious tensions and conflicts between them. Since Delestraint had been appointed by General de Gaulle, he felt it would be more logical and wiser if he reported to de Gaulle or his delegate, Moulin, not to Frenay. It was clear that a conflict was unavoidable.

Socialist and trade union militants had been unhappy ever since the first Coordinating Committee had been set up. They had loyally joined the Resistance through the movement Libération, as Léon Jouhaux had urged them to do, and had been given an important voice in the movement by d'Astier. But now, with MUR, they would have no voice at all. They had tried to get the others to give a seat on the directorate and a share of the posts to a group of the Socialist party called "Veni." They were flatly turned down. None of the Resistance leaders would hear of giving a top place to one of the prewar political parties. Moulin and de Gaulle's intelligence chief, Passy, were equally opposed to any party "resurrection." Socialist leaders protested bitterly and repeated their demands. The question of granting any representation in the Resistance to the political parties seemed to Moulin so serious and so important an issue that he would have to inform and consult with General de Gaulle personally. He cabled for a Lysander to come to pick him up, along with General Delestraint, who would have his own problems to discuss in London.

The trip to London of Moulin and Delestraint would prove to be crucial, particularly since it would coincide with a number of other trips. André Manuel, who had finished his investigative exploration of the Resistance, notably of Fighting France's own networks, was on his way back to London. At the same time Rémy, the principal delegate of de Gaulle in the north, would be flying to London with the delegate of the Communist party, Fernand Grenier, who spoke for a vital, if unintegrated, element of the Resistance. Colonel Passy and Pierre Brossolette would leave London on a mission to the northern zone.

Despite all the disharmony and the personal conflicts that would continue, as they do in any form of collective human endeavor, the creation of MUR, like the creation earlier of the Secret Army and SOAM, represented real progress toward unity of the Resistance. Although none of the leaders could see it clearly, since each was concerned with the constant difficulties and challenges of the movement, the early stages of unity greatly enhanced the effectiveness of the fight against the French and German Nazis. Nineteen forty-three would be the year when the Allies began their counteroffensive against the Axis and the Resistance became an effective fighting force inside France.

PART FIVE
DARKNESS BEFORE THE DAWN

17
THE TRIUMPH
OF JEAN MOULIN

Still as lean and wiry in 1977 as he had been when serving as de Gaulle's envoy thirty-five years earlier, Parisian industrialist André Manuel leaned back in his chair, ran bony fingers across his totally bald pate, gazed at the ceiling, and thought hard about answering my question about his report to de Gaulle on the state of the Resistance in 1942.

"My report came as a surprise, even a shock to everyone in London, particularly to my immediate superior, Colonel Passy, chief of the BCRA. He had sent me over on de Gaulle's instructions to check on all the technical questions of communications, radio transmissions, espionage techniques, subversive actions, and so on. Nothing else. It was not my mission to get involved in the politics of the Resistance or the general political situation inside France.

"I did what I was asked to do, but I could not help but go beyond the terms of my mission. For a French patriot it was not possible to ignore the bigger picture beyond techniques. I was impressed with the job that Jean Moulin was doing to persuade the individualistic Resistance leaders to work together and appalled by all the difficulties he was facing. I learned quickly that although we, in London, particularly Passy, chief of our intelligence operations, thought we knew all about the Resistance and what was happening in France, we simply didn't."

Manuel paused, marshaled his thoughts again, and went on to say: "My happiest discovery was the fact that the number of active collaborators with the fascists Laval, Darnand, Déat, and company, and with the Nazis, was a very small percentage of the population. There was a handful of traitors at the top in Vichy under Pétain, but they were not followed by the people of France. France, I tell you, and I told everyone in London, was not a collaborationist country. That was important to discover."

Manuel also conceded that the Resistance, the militant Resistance, the men and women who had given up their normal lives and their homes to fight in the underground, was also small. "They counted for about five percent of the population. But that is a very high figure if you understand what it means to give up everything, your job, your home, your family, your security, and live like a hunted animal. I also found out that at the end of 1942 as many as forty percent of the people had the potential for active resistance and another fifty-five percent for passive resistance. Active resistance meant to me just what the word implies, committing an *act* of resistance. That could be anything from hiding a Jew or an Allied airman to pouring sand into a gasoline tank or cutting a telephone line. If forty percent of the people committed only one or two acts, that would result in millions and millions of acts against the enemy. Passive resistance meant tipping someone off that the police were after him, or reading an underground paper or listening to the BBC—a hundred and one different ways of expressing sympathy for the Resistance and refusing to help in any way the traitors of Vichy or the Nazis. The majority of French people behaved in that fashion. Without them, the Resistance would have been wiped out before it had gone very far."

Manuel's thoughts about the French people and their attitude on resisting or collaborating correspond exactly with the conclusions reached by Germaine Tillion and many others, who were most critical of a film made many years later by Marcel Ophuls, called *Le Chagrin et La Pitié* (*The Sorrow and the Pity*), a brilliantly produced documentary that had a powerful impact on public opinion in France and in the United States. Tillion felt that the documentary greatly exaggerated the collaboration of the French and failed to present the full power and the glory of the Resistance. She was particularly critical of the fact that the film had been shot mainly in Clermont-Ferrand, a hotbed of Resistance activity to which it did not do justice. This argument about how many French collaborated and how many resisted will never be settled, but the report of a man like Manuel, who was not a man of the internal Resistance, must be accepted as an essential element of the historical record.

Manuel's study went on to examine the political factors of the internal situation. He found that the leaders of the Resistance were showing signs of antidemocratic tendencies. This was a charge put forward by leading personalities of the traditional political parties and trade unions of France: the Communists, the Socialists, the CGT, the CFTC. Although most of the parties and leaders had fallen into disrepute because of the defeat of France and their craven capitulation to Pétain and Laval on July 10, 1940, a good number of men had retained their reputations and influence and could not be shunted aside as Henri Frenay, for one, and Colonel Passy, for another, were insisting. Democracy cannot function without free, diverse political parties, a fact that General de Gaulle, himself, never understood.

Since many of the 40 percent of potential resistants, as seen by Manuel, were members of traditional political parties and did not belong to any other organizations, it would seem wise to utilize the influence of party and trade union leaders, particularly since they had already rallied behind General de Gaulle. To exclude their organizations from sharing in the direction of the Resistance would be to exclude the representatives of 95 percent of the people. This, essentially, was the important and highly controversial conclusion of the Manuel report. It endorsed arguments put forward by Jean Moulin and rejected by Colonel Passy for increasing the representation of the political parties in the Resistance.

Socialist Daniel Mayer met with Manuel in France early in January 1943. Mayer had been working hard to reconstitute the Socialist party. Many Socialist trade unionists had joined Libération and that movement had agreed temporarily to put out the official Socialist party paper, Le Populaire, until the party could do so itself. Mayer cooperated closely with leaders of the Resistance, but he did not agree that they should replace the traditional parties and build something completely new. The traditional Socialist party, he argued, must and would have its role to play in the Resistance and in postliberated France.

Sipping his tea, in the salon of the Hôtel Lutetia in 1977, Mayer looked back through the years to 1943. "We Socialists had three main objectives: to fight until France was liberated; to support a strong government, led by General de Gaulle, but committed to democratic and Republican principles; finally our own particular concern, to advance the cause of socialism and of social justice for all peoples as soon as a free government of the Republic had been put into office and been able to handle its first priorities of rebuilding a war-torn nation. I made all this quite clear to de Gaulle's delegate, Manuel. As for Jean Moulin, he knew exactly how we felt and what we were fighting for, and he was on our side."

Mayer stressed his commitment to de Gaulle and added that to carry out his mission objectively and successfully, de Gaulle must have the full backing of the complete spectrum of French opinions, from far right to far left in a national union of citizens. Then, on the day of liberation of France, the Allies would find General de Gaulle supported by and acclaimed by an almost unanimous French population. Anything less would lead to political machinations, intrigues, chaos, and anarchy. There had to be, said Mayer, a union of the movements of the Resistance with the patriotic elements of the political parties and trade unions, all linked to Fighting France.

Jean Moulin, Secret Army chief General Delestraint, and André Manuel all decided to go to London early in 1943 to put their cases to de Gaulle. Meanwhile, Colonel Rémy, de Gaulle's chief delegate in the northern zone, was escorting Communist party spokesman Fernand Grenier to London. Grenier never forgot the harrowing experience, not only crossing the Channel in a small boat under the noses of the Nazi coastal guards, but doing so in the company of the flamboyant Rémy, a modern version of the Scarlet Pimpernel.

The Gestapo kept a close watch on every boat that left a Channel port and often conducted sudden, unscheduled inspections. Grenier and Rémy were well hidden under false planking in their boat, but what terrified Grenier was Rémy's mad insistence on taking along a three-foot-high azalea plant, beautifully wrapped in gift paper by an exclusive florist on the fashionable Avenue Paul Doumer. There was no way to hide the plant. It looked ludicrous in its chic wrappings in the stern of a smelly, commercial fishing vessel, and it was sure immediately to catch the eyes of the Gestapo if they were to come on board. The plant was a gift that Rémy had decided to bring to Madame de Gaulle in London, a very gallant but insane gesture that risked the lives of all on board.

Rémy laughed about it in his memoirs, but Grenier, who had very little sense of humor to begin with, and became deathly seasick aboard, did not think it was at all funny, particularly since Rémy had warned him to take nothing with him but a toothbrush. General de Gaulle was not forgotten either, for Rémy had brought some New Year's gifts for him, too: a little box of earth from Lorraine, and a rare bottle of 1816 cognac obtained from the collection of an old White Russian general.

Before leaving, Grenier had consulted the three top leaders of the Communist party in France and they had given him a triple mission to perform in London.

First, he was to persuade de Gaulle to bring about a national union by creating a national council of the Resistance in which each party, group, and movement of the Resistance would have its representative—precisely the plan that Henri Frenay opposed so bitterly. Grenier's second objective was to try to work out a compromise between the Gaullists and the Giraudists, to get the two haughty and arrogant generals to work together for the common cause. The Communists wanted to see one French government of national unity installed in Algiers to deal efficiently with the Allies. The trick would be to get one of the generals to accept the other as the chief of a united government. Grenier had no specific proposals to make on how to achieve this, but the Giraud-de Gaulle split had started to affect the Resistance inside France adversely and had to be mended. A Giraudist secret service had been created, and Giraud was also supported by army officers of the ORA, the Resistance organization formed by the Armistice Army when Hitler demobilized it. True to its right-wing orientation, the ORA became pro-Giraud, leading directly to a conflict with the newly united Resistance directorate, the MUR. The worst situation was in Corsica, where the right-wing Giraud organization had become dominant. Gaullists believed that the Giraudists were betraying them to the police.

Grenier's final mission was to convince de Gaulle and the Anglo-American services in London to furnish the Resistance with the arms it needed to carry on its fight against the Germans. He also wanted Radio London to begin lending its voice to a call for sabotage of enemy installations, to tell the French people it was their patriotic duty to fight. Until then, London wanted mostly intelligence information from France, not fighting and not sabotage, at least not on a full scale until the Allied troops had landed. One of the main reasons was the powerful influence and great numbers of the Communist party. No one wanted to arm the Communists, and they knew it. Grenier, putting forward his plea for arms, sensed how delicate the issue was. "Everywhere," he noted, "there was a panicky fear of a people in arms."

At the same time the people who were responsible for getting Giraud to Algiers, the Alliance network of Marie-Madeleine Fourcade, had become involved in the power play. Giraud wanted them to become part of his armed command of North Africa, but Marie-Madeleine insisted on avoiding political rivalries. She managed to preserve good relations with the Giraudists and to improve relations with the Gaullists. De Gaulle and Passy had not forgotten Loustaunau-Lacau's irritating messages to them and they resented the fact that the network worked for the British, but Marie-Madeleine was not the abrasive leader that Navarre had been and her intelligence was invaluable in helping the Allied cause. She managed, therefore, to keep her lines open to her French compatriots while continuing to work for the British—no mean trick. She also had new and terrible tragedies to contend with in devastating Gestapo raids on her network.

Marie-Madeleine was staying in a safe-house in Cahors, some sixty miles north of Toulouse, at the end of January 1943. She knew from news of arrests made earlier that the network was in danger, and began sending out warning signals to her agents. Two of them, Griffin and his son Zebra, had come to see her and she had instructed them not to go home to their apartment, for the police were on their trail. Disregarding her instructions, they went home to get some things and were promptly picked up by the Gestapo.

Then the news came in of a widespread disaster: Gestapo agents had caught her people in Toulouse, Pau, Marseille, and Lyon, closing down those important radio transmitters. And the Italian secret police, the OVRA, had raided her stations in Monaco and Nice. Marie-Madeleine gave her chief radio operator, Magpie, a coded message to send to London informing them of the catastrophe, asking them to transmit on the BBC a message that "Marie-Madeleine has arrived safely in London and sends her affectionate greetings." The message would confuse many of her agents, who mistakenly thought she had gone to London, but she did it so that the Gestapo might also hear the message. She hoped they would stop torturing their prisoners to find out where she was.

Major Richards in London sent a message to Marie-Madeleine telling her she really ought to leave France at once and come to London for safety and consultations. She replied that she would first have to determine the extent of the damage to the network and then take steps to rebuild what had been destroyed.

The situation revealed by her investigation was bad, very bad, but not hopeless. Her principal transmitting stations in the south had been wiped out and some of her best operators and operatives had been taken. But she still had stations functioning in Vichy, central France, and Grenoble, and many of her intelligence agents had escaped and were waiting for new stations to be set up. She had a nucleus of trained and dedicated "animals" still with her. Her espionage network and transmitting stations in the north were all operating at full efficiency and had escaped Gestapo detection. One of the stations, at Brest, was the delight of the Royal Navy, sending it accurate information on the movements of German U-boats, which British destroyers were sinking as they left the submarine pens.

The source of the espionage information on the subs in Brest was a tiny, innocent-looking and pretty young seamstress who worked inside the German base. Her job was to repair Mae West life vests for the sailors. She knew as soon as the sailors brought her their life vests for urgent repair and verification that they were getting ready to ship out. By listening carefully to their chatter while she sewed their Mae Wests she would learn the designation of the U-boat and its time and date of sailing.

On February 2, the Allies received joyous news: Marshal von Paulus surrendered the Sixth German Army at Stalingrad. The valiant Soviet defenders had taken more than ninety thousand prisoners, including twenty-four generals. The Nazis had lost all told more than three hundred thousand men. The day before that battle ended, the Americans had driven the Japanese out of Guadalcanal. Before February was over, the Americans would have defeated Rommel at the Kasserine Pass in Tunisia, and sunk and disabled another dozen Japanese warships in the Pacific. On all fronts the Axis was suffering crippling and humiliating defeats.

The one front where the Allies were being badly hurt was the Battle of the Atlantic, where U-boats took a terrible toll of supplies and sailors, sinking tens of thousands of tons of shipping. Both Roosevelt and Churchill had announced that the Allies would launch their liberation campaign in Europe within a year. To mass the men and supplies needed to invade Hitler's Europe would require every ton of shipping the Allies could muster. The submarine front became the critical front of the war. That was why London put heavy pressure on Marie-Madeleine and every intelligence net it commanded for constant, rapid, accurate information on the U-boats.

Marie-Madeleine had an extraordinary secret agent in the Nazis' huge naval base at Kéroman in Brittany, built by the Todt organization. She did not even know who it was. The agent had been recruited by one of her members, Triton, Joel Lemoigne, but Triton had promised the man he would not reveal his name. The documents he had given Triton to deliver to Marie-Madeleine in Cahors were a treasure-house of espionage information. He had listed the exact number of U-boats in the base, with their fleet numbers and individual signs—a fish, a siren, etc.—their operational rosters, the losses they had sustained in action. It was a complete picture of the entire base.

Marie-Madeleine told Triton she absolutely had to know who the spy was and how he got his material, or she could not vouch for it when she sent it to London. Triton tried to put her off, but she would not be denied. She told him: "My old chap, your agent's work is useless if I don't know more about it."

"He's a naval engineer," Triton confessed, "an Alsatian who speaks fluent German. He has gained the Nazis' confidence so completely

that he is hated by the whole staff at the Lorient base. He has had a key post there ever since the Germans marched in. Everything passes through his hands: operational orders, U-boat movements. . . . He's the only Frenchman who's been able to get into the Kéroman base. He debriefs the U-boats on their return from operations. A young Breton friend of ours takes him out in a launch and together they photograph the various units in their lairs."

Marie-Madeleine immediately saw the enormous value of her agents in this area and promptly created a new section of the network, reporting to her, but operating autonomously in its own sphere. She called it Sea Star. Her radio chief, Magpie, began drawing up a list of new transmitters to bring into action, and Triton devised a coding system based on the names of marine creatures—for Brittany: Narwhal, Dab, Bleak, Conger, Medusa, Smelt; for Bordeaux-La Rochelle: Cod, Lobster, Turbot, Loach; and for Marseille-Toulon: Shad, Sole, Beluga, Halibut, Murena. It took a long time to discuss and work out all arrangements. The organization meeting was finally broken up by one of the "animals," Ladybird, who came blinking into the room, sniffing at the stink of cigarettes. Ladybird shouted: "You're all mad. Hedgehog, it's light, go to bed at once. You've been up all night!"

As he left the room, Triton slipped Marie-Madeleine a piece of folded paper. When she got to her bedroom, she saw he had written: "The naval engineer's name is Jacques Stosskopf."

Marie-Madeleine sent a message to England, telling the British she was still too busy on vital projects to come to London. The work of her network was so highly valued that they gave her her head and told her to let them know when she could come to see them.

London was already busy enough with the visitors they did have from France. De Gaulle had taken careful note of the reports and proposals that he had received from Communist party delegate Fernand Grenier. He had also carefully studied the thought-provoking report of André Manuel. The only key man with whom he had not yet discussed the political problems of the Resistance was his own key delegate to France, Jean Moulin, for Moulin had not yet been able to get a plane to London.

On the twenty-seventh of January, Moulin and General Delestraint, the Secret Army commander, had gone to the Château de Villevieu in eastern France, near Lyon, on whose spacious fields a Lysander was supposed to land to pick them up. The château belonged to three remarkable old ladies, whose story is one of the most charming and inspiring vignettes of the French Resistance, illustrating what André Manuel was referring to when he wrote about the "active potential" of the French population.

The three old ladies who owned the château were sisters: Mlle. Marguerite Bergerot, Mlle. Cécile Bergerot, and Mme. Suzanne Bergerot-Wurtz. Their château was located just outside a little village in the Jura Mountains. The three old ladies were patriots, hated the Germans and despised

Marshal Pétain. Like so many French citizens in the confusion that followed the defeat, they wanted "to do something," but were quite at a loss to discover what three elderly *châtelaines* could do.

They decided to ask their cheese merchant, Paul Marillier, who made an excellent Gruyère, which they appreciated. He seemed a strong and intelligent fellow. By happenstance, Marillier was the local Resistance chief in charge of landings and parachute drops. He was delighted to obtain permission from the Bergerot sisters to use their fields.

Later, according to "Jannick," Geneviève Fassin, who worked for SOAM, the sisters' fields would be incorporated into a new agency, SAP, Section Atterissages et Parachutages, organized by a London agent, Paul Rivière, whom Jannick would marry.

Paul Marillier had a narrow escape from the Gestapo due to his own quick wit. He was in his shop working late to finish preparing a mold of Gruyère. His wife and daughter had gone to visit friends while waiting for him to finish work. It was late and dark when he left his cooling shed. He saw a car parked in the shadows and knew it was Gestapo. He whistled, locked up, made a lot of noise, as an innocent man would, and walked along a path that would take him right by the Gestapo car, guessing it would be better to show no suspicion and no fear.

As he came by, still whistling, a Gestapo officer stepped out of the shadows, stopped him, and asked if he knew where the "cheeseman" lived. "Oh, Marillier?" said Marillier. "Why, yes, he lives right over there." He pointed to a house well behind him and far from his own. The Gestapo agent thanked him and stepped back into the shadows. Marillier strolled along until he could turn a corner into another lane, then ran full speed to the house of his friend, picked up his wife and daughter, and drove off to safety.

It was in that village, in the château of the Bergerot sisters, that Jean Moulin and General Delestraint awaited their Lysander for London. It did not come that January night. They had to return to Lyon, then come back on February 12 to the Jura, where, this time, the SOAM had a plane to pick them up. In fact, not one but three planes arrived. The first took "Vidal," General Delestraint. When the second landed, Henri (Frédéric) Manhès, Moulin's deputy in the northern zone, whom he had sent on an earlier mission to London, got out. He tried to tell Moulin not to go, but, according to Moulin's sister, Laure, one of Moulin's associates shoved Manhès aside and pushed Moulin into the plane. The third plane was for another agent who did not show up. It never became clear why Manhès tried to stop Moulin. In any case Moulin had wanted for a long time to go to London. The visit became a personal triumph for Jean Moulin.

Four days before Moulin arrived, de Gaulle had already made up his mind to give him important new functions, and had sent him a personal letter. It is not known whether Moulin ever received the letter. Suffice it to know that he heard everything he wanted to hear once he got to London. He had been nervous about London's reaction to proposals he intended to make.

He had reached the same conclusions as Manuel: that the political parties and trade unions had to be brought into a united Resistance. Moulin did not know that Manuel's report had already won de Gaulle to the cause they espoused.

Moulin was reassured by Manuel himself on his arrival. He also had the support of the commissaire of the interior, André Philip. The one powerful man utterly opposed to the project was Colonel Passy. But Passy, about to leave on a mission to northern France, was in the minority. In any case, General de Gaulle, like Abraham Lincoln, was the kind of man who makes up a "decisive minority" all by himself, and de Gaulle favored the proposal.

De Gaulle met twice with Moulin in long sessions that produced a final document on February 21, 1943, creating a single Conseil National de la Résistance (CNR) for the ensemble of the metropolitan territory of France, to be presided over by Moulin. As the representative of General de Gaulle, Moulin, also known as Max and Rex, would be the permanent delegate in both the south and the north, the sole representative of London's Comité National for metropolitan France. He had the authority to designate deputies responsible to him. "Arquebuse" (Colonel Passy) and "Brumaire" (Pierre Brossolette) were instructed to work out with Rex the establishment of the council. De Gaulle knew that Passy and Pierre Brossolette, Passy's assistant, were strongly opposed to giving so much power to one man, so he named them in the decree, which served as an order to them to comply. They would not argue with a direct de Gaulle order. They could try, however, to make it difficult for Moulin to impose his authority and attempt to undercut his mission.

The council was defined by de Gaulle as the "embryo" of a national delegation that would advise him politically on his arrival in France. At that time, new members, named by political parties and trade unions, would be added to it, drawn from those active forces of the nation not represented at the time. Rex, as the delegate of de Gaulle, would serve as intermediary between the council and the Secret Army, the Comité Général d'Etudes (which was to draw up proposals for the future government of France) and the Bureau d'Information et de Presse (BIP).

All these detailed provisions left absolutely no room for discussion or misunderstanding. Jean Moulin had been given tremendous powers over all the Resistance everywhere in France. It was everything he could have asked for, a complete victory. De Gaulle also made him a member of Free France's Conseil National (CNF), thus elevating him to the rank of minister, the top rank in the Gaullist hierarchy. Then, to put candles on the cake, de Gaulle awarded Moulin his highest and most coveted decoration: La Croix de la Libération.

This "beatification" took place in London. Moulin would not be hailed as a saint on his return to France.

While Moulin was in London, his troublesome "comrade," Henri Frenay, was not idle in France. They had had a bitter quarrel just before Moulin left over the fact that Moulin had been obliged to cut Combat's budget from five million francs a month down to three million. It was a severe slash, necessitated partly by London's cutting Moulin's overall budget and partly because of new demands on Moulin, notably from Yves Farge, who was involved in establishing the new maquis of the Vercors, a project of the eastern region of Franc-Tireur.

Frenay desperately needed funds to take care of his comrades and their families. Help came suddenly and unexpectedly when Frenay heard about a new source of support: an American lawyer named Max Shoop. Shoop was working for OSS, the American secret service, and told a Frenay agent that he could furnish money and military assistance if he could get a good report on the Secret Army, the Groupes Francs, and the maquis.

Members of Combat drafted a report for the Americans, and Pierre de Bénouville, who had established close ties with Allen Dulles of the OSS, was told to go to Switzerland to make a deal with the Americans. Frenay cautioned him to tell the Americans that they were Gaullists and that they distrusted Giraud. They would also not offer or accept any political quid pro quo in exchange for American help. The help must be given with no strings attached.

Pierre de Bénouville was a man of the extreme Right, a member of the prewar fascist movement, Action Française. Like many French rightists he was a patriotic nationalist and a bitter foe of the Germans. He had rejected Pétain's call to capitulation and collaboration and had gone into the underground in a British espionage network. By the end of 1942 de Bénouville had left the British operation and had joined up with Frenay and Combat.

In mid-March 1943, de Bénouville returned from Switzerland with an American deal in his pocket. He had been to Berne and had seen Allen Dulles, the mysterious "Mr. Scott" whom Frenay had met a year and a half earlier in his conference with General de la Laurencie. Dulles ran the western European OSS operations out of Berne and was ready to help. He offered three million francs in cash. De Bénouville had not brought it with him, for it was too bulky and he also felt they needed Frenay's approval first.

The Americans had offered to send money and arms regularly and to let Frenay's men use their embassy radio-communications to London, directly to de Gaulle. What Dulles wanted in return, with no political strings, was an agreement by Frenay to share his movement's military intelligence reports with the Americans. He also suggested that Frenay send him a permanent representative to maintain liaison between Berne and Lyon, a kind of Resistance ambassador to the Americans. He did not mention that Count Pierre de Leusse, an experienced and able diplomat, was already in Switzerland as the ambassador of Fighting France, de Gaulle's organization in London.

Frenay approved the deal instantly. He told de Bénouville to make it clear to the Americans that he was not representing Combat or Frenay. He and his associates would be the representatives of the MUR, the united movements of the Resistance. This was a cover on Frenay's part, for he planned to distribute the money as he saw fit, and he did not wait to consult the directorate of the MUR before acting. He also told de Bénouville that he would be their "foreign minister," again on his own initiative without consulting his fellow committee members.

Knowing that he was in for another confrontation, Frenay finally went to see d'Astier and Jean-Pierre Lévy and told them what he had done. That was not exactly the same thing as consulting them, which he would allege later. The two men were waiting to go on a London mission and he told them to inform Moulin when they got there.

Jean-Pierre was dubious about the idea of giving intelligence to the Americans without a clear understanding and agreement with de Gaulle. His close associate and friend, Claudius-Petit, who would fill in for him during his absence, felt the same way and told Frenay he did not like the way the affair had been handled. D'Astier thought it was a big mistake. Frenay, convinced as ever of his righteousness and brilliance, put their objections down to mere jealousy. "I sensed in them," he wrote, "an unmistakable frustration over Combat's new initiative." And one can sense Frenay's wry smile as he added: "Yet their frustration was nothing compared to Moulin's on his return from London."

The confrontation with Moulin would not be long in coming, for Moulin returned on the night of March 21–22. But before that, Frenay was shaken by news of disaster. The Gestapo had arrested and savagely tortured Henri Garnier, the engineer of Hispano-Suiza, one of his best fighting men. Frenay had already lost, a few weeks earlier, the chief of his Groupes Francs, the strongest and toughest of his men, Jacques Renouvin. Renouvin would be deported to Mauthausen concentration camp, where he would die. And three more of his top men had been arrested: François Morin, chief of staff of the Secret Army, Valrimont of the Secret Army staff, and Ravanal, who had replaced Renouvin as chief of the Groupes Francs. Dozens of other arrests followed. Frantically, Frenay set about changing all their pseudonyms, codes, and letter boxes. It was at that moment that Moulin returned.

Jean Moulin told the MUR committee of the decisions taken in London: the creation of the CNR, the Conseil National de la Résistance, with Rex at its head; the regrouping of political parties, trade unions, and the Resistance movements in the new CNR; and the removal of the Secret Army, the Comité d'Etudes, and the Press Bureau from the jurisdiction of the steering committee of MUR. The CNR would head the Resistance as a whole, north and south.

Frenay blew up. He shouted that they would never let the Secret Army be "sealed off" from the rest of the Resistance. He would not accept the CNR as the top authority of the Resistance and would not permit the "resurrection of the political parties on an equal footing with ourselves." He turned to Moulin and said: "Max, I refuse to be associated with this rotten business. Never will I sit in your CNR!"

Frenay recalled later that Moulin shouted back at him: "Charvet, the CNR shall be created whatever you say! You're free to join it or not to join it—as you wish. But you're not free to contact the Americans without notifying me! Or to ask them for money, with God only knows what strings attached!"

Moulin was confident that he would have the backing of d'Astier and Lévy when they returned from London and that he would be able to impose the CNR upon Frenay. Moulin was also sure that he would be able to put a stop to Frenay's potentially dangerous dealings with Dulles and the Americans, who were hostile to de Gaulle. Relations with the Americans were vital, but only if negotiated by and through de Gaulle. Otherwise the Americans, who were supporting Giraud, could use Frenay as a wedge to break the united front of the Resistance. Frenay was foolish not to see the danger in his separate dealings with Dulles.

Sure that he could control the situation in the south, where he had in fact been in control since his arrival on New Year's Day, Moulin needed urgently to turn his attention to the north. Rémy had been in charge there, not Moulin. And Moulin's rivals, Passy and Brossolette, opposed to the CNR setup, were already in the north working hard. Moulin suspected that a lot of their hard work was involved in turning the movements against his leadership of the Conseil National de la Résistance. He made haste to go to Paris to counter them.

Moulin's political instincts were more than accurate. Passy and Brossolette had, indeed, been busy organizing the north as they thought it ought to be organized. Passy set about creating a special service for air and sea operations and for transmissions, sectors that Moulin had always jealously and zealously kept for himself, for they were important power bases. Passy also moved to create a Secret Army of the northern zone and to tighten up the structure of the general staff of that zone.

There had been a good deal of controversy involving the selection of a chief for this general staff. Everyone had agreed that Colonel Touny, chief of the OCM, the Organisation Civile et Militaire, was the best man for the job. The OCM was, apart from the Communists, the biggest, most effective movement in the north. Unfortunately, at the end of 1942, the underground magazine of the OCM had shocked the entire Resistance and scandalized London with an article that was openly anti-Semitic. The OCM was a coalition of conservative to rightist army officers, writers, and politicians.

A right-wing editor named Maxime Blocq-Mascart had written that the "Jewish minority" was insufficiently assimilated into French society. Jewish successes, he said, excited fear and envy. Jews were too active and visible in political, intellectual, and financial circles. People were jealous of the achievements of the Jews in commerce, finance, law, and medicine. As for their great leader, Léon Blum, prime minister in 1936, "it is revealed that this Jew only has Jewish friends and has confidence only in Jews." Blocq-Mascart later commented that this article was "perhaps" a political error.

Whatever Blocq-Mascart may have thought, it was clear that General de Gaulle thought it more than a political error. It was a scandal of immense proportions for a Resistance publication to repeat the most odious

Nazi allegations about French citizens of the Jewish faith. Although Colonel Touny himself knew nothing about this publication, de Gaulle decided that, as chief of the movement, Touny was responsible for it, and could not be appointed at the head of the Etat-Major of the northern zone.

Passy and Brossolette had a tough job explaining this to Touny and soothing all the hurt feelings that the incident had provoked. They also had to calm down other movements that resented the arrogance of the OCM in insisting on its superior force. The OCM and Touny were a bit like Combat and Frenay, ready to lord it over other Resistance movements. De Gaulle's delegates had their work cut out for them in trying to unify the northern Resistance in such a way that it would not be under Moulin's direct orders.

Rushing to finish their work before Moulin could arrive in Paris, Passy and Brossolette called a plenary meeting of northern movements for March 26.

Present were the chiefs of the five principal movements of the north: OCM, Libération-Nord (representing the Socialist Action Committee and the trade unions CGT and CFTC), Front National (the Communist front group, with many eminent non-Communists in their ranks), Ceux de la Résistance, and Ceux de la Libération. They debated the issues that Passy had brought from London and adopted a unanimous position on a text to be sent to London as their reply.

Libération-Nord, while an independent organization, had good relations with the Libération movement of d'Astier in the southern zone. Front National, which had elements in the south as well as the north, was virtually Communist-run, despite many eminent non-Communists in the ranks. The non-Communists had joined to demonstrate their willingness to back up their belief in the need for national unity of all ideologies. Ceux de la Résistance and Ceux de la Libération, the smallest of the northern Big Five, were essentially democratic movements committed to the restoration and renovation of a French Republic. They were not Gaullists but were not hostile to de Gaulle.

The text they drafted contained long paragraphs affirming their dedication to democratic freedoms, their determination to destroy all dictatorships, and their resolution to continue their "armed struggle." London understood the prod behind the words *armed struggle,* for the northern resistants were engaging in armed clashes with the Germans and constantly appealing for arms.

The most important passages in their reply to Passy's projects could be found in some key points:

- representation in the CNR of "nuances of the French spirit of Resistance, namely, communism, socialism, free thought, Catholicism, and nationalism"
- a rejection of the permanent Executive Committee proposed by London
- creation in the northern zone of a Committee of Coordination to exclude a hasty fusion of the two zones

▪ acceptance of a Comité Général d'Etudes, but only if the Resistance movements were to be closely involved in its work.

No one of these positions would be insuperable obstacles to Moulin's mission, but all together they represented sizable obstructions. Moulin was certain that Passy and Brossolette, although they would not directly and openly counter an order of de Gaulle's, were working behind his back to make it difficult or impossible for him to carry out his mission. He knew a confrontation could not be avoided and might well be salutary in clearing the air, so soon after arriving in Paris he called for a meeting with Passy and Brossolette. The meeting was set for March 31, and Moulin was ready to explode as soon as they showed their hand.

The showdown came early. Brossolette told Moulin that the Resistance movements in the northern zone had voted almost unanimously (except for the pro-Communist movement) to exclude the political parties from the CNR. It was the same issue that Frenay had raised, the very same issue that had been debated for weeks and finally settled by de Gaulle in favor of including all the parties. Moulin exploded in anger. How many times did they expect him to fight the same old fights? They knew full well what de Gaulle had decided. Why didn't they fight it out with the movements and prepare the way for Moulin? What was the point of telling him that the movements were opposed? He knew it, they knew it, but what he wanted to hear was what they had done about it. Furthermore, Moulin had been told by his people that Brossolette had been bad-mouthing him and calling him overly ambitious.

Now it was Brossolette's turn to blow up. Who dared say that he had talked against Moulin? He demanded to face his accusers. And so forth and so on and furthermore! It was the kind of open-ended, finger-pointing session that could get nowhere. The men parted on the worst of terms, but agreed to a cooling-off period until their next meeting with the representatives of the movements to agree on the composition of the CNR. Moulin knew he could not at that point get everything that London had asked for, but he was determined to win approval of the essential inclusion of the parties and his own authority as chief of the CNR. On all the rest, he would make real compromises and even sacrifices.

The meeting convened on April 3 in Paris, under tight security by armed guards, for top northern leaders were present. Moulin agreed to yield to the opposition of the northern movements to the proposal to create a permanent commission, which was perceived as a. dangerous executive power. Moulin was also conciliatory on the way the political parties should be included and gave up the rather rigid formulas that had been established in London. He insisted, however, on the inclusion of the parties, and was supported at last by Passy and Brossolette, who could not publicly disavow de Gaulle.

An agreement was reached to create a CNR composed of sixteen members: eight delegates from the Resistance movements; two labor representatives (CGT and CFTC); and, finally, six representatives of political parties and political "tendencies."

There were loose ends to wrap up, names to be found and endorsed to fill the posts agreed upon, but what was most important was that an overall agreement had been reached, unity achieved, with difficulty at first but certain to strengthen as men learned to work together in a common cause.

Returning to the south, Moulin would face an enraged Frenay and some others of the MUR who, like those in the north, did not want to see many of the old political parties reconstructed and brought into the Resistance—except perhaps for the parties already fighting hard against the common enemy, the Communists and the Socialists. D'Astier and Jean-Pierre Lévy had doubts about the wisdom of opening the CNR to all parties but would go along with Moulin.

The disagreements were not only political. Frenay accused Moulin of looking at the Resistance through a wide-angle lens and not close up. He said that, in fact, Moulin wanted to be the chief of the Resistance but really did not know how the Resistance functioned on the operative level. And now that he had been named national chief, for the north as well as the south, the chances were he would not have the time to learn what the Resistance was all about. It was a severe, insulting attack upon Moulin's credentials as a leader. It was obvious that Frenay thought that he was far more qualified than Moulin to be the chief of the CNR. Technically he probably was, but what he did not understand was that leadership required qualities of diplomacy, statesmanship, objectivity, and political perception, which Moulin had and Frenay did not.

Among all the arguments that Frenay advanced, the one that led to the most bitter controversy was his reminder to Moulin that his budget had been severely cut, and that he had had to take steps to make up the losses. Moulin had investigated and discovered that Frenay had appointed de Bénouville "foreign minister" of the Resistance and was taking money and giving intelligence material to the Americans in Switzerland. Whether this was advisable or not could be debated, but Frenay's unilateral, independent actions were not tolerable.

Moulin demanded that Frenay call back de Bénouville and his other representatives in Switzerland and end his dealings with the Americans. Frenay asked him just where he was going to get money for the thousands of young men fleeing the forced labor draft of the STO and hiding out in the maquis. The Americans had the money and the arms that Moulin and London were not providing. Moreover they were making available excellent communication channels and not asking for a look at the intelligence information until forty-eight hours after it had gone to the intelligence office of the Fighting French.

Moulin, Passy, and the others were convinced that Dulles was using his money to bait a trap for Frenay, a plot to strengthen the hand of General Henri Giraud. Dulles denied this, and Frenay told Moulin that he had told

Dulles clearly enough that the Resistance was Gaullist and opposed to Giraud. But agents of the Gaullists in Berne discovered that the U.S. military attaché had arranged a meeting between two of Frenay's emissaries and agents of General Giraud's secret service, called the DSR/SM.* According to London's spies, the Americans were trying to get Frenay's people to go to work for Giraud's secret service. Whether true or not, it sounded convincing to Passy, who sent Moulin an urgent message to crack down on Frenay's freewheeling money dealings.

Yet Moulin himself had to admit that Frenay had raised a very important point: The credits allocated by Fighting France to the internal Resistance had been consistently insufficient to meet its needs and, with the flood of young refugees from the draft into the maquis, London's funds had become woefully inadequate. Frenay might have been high-handed, arrogant, and insubordinate, but, as was often the case, he was fundamentally right and had raised a vital issue. His actions would force London to augment its aid to the Resistance.

The most immediate problem concerned the camps in the Vercors in the eastern Alps. By April 1943, there were several hundred men there, assembled into nine different encampments. The Vercors maquis would grow to many more camps and thousands of men. Early on, arguments were developing on how it ought to evolve. Some saw the Vercors as a great fortress redoubt that could hold out against any force the Germans would want to throw against it. Others saw it not as a fortress but as a training ground for all the French maquis. They thought it ought to lie low, limited to training, until the Allies landed in the south and were near. These arguments would continue until the denouement.

Even before money and arms were procured, the maquis of the Vercors received a considerable boost in morale and prestige when the chief of the Secret Army, General Delestraint, came to visit one of its camps in the second half of April. Delestraint told Moulin what was happening there and persuaded him to supply arms and a special radio operator and transmitter to send messages directly to London from the Vercors. But London did not send the arms promised and the Vercors was unable to provide sufficient action to justify maintaining a transmitting station, so Moulin, after a time, pulled it out.

Frenay bitterly citicized the concept of the Vercors as conceived by Yves Farge and endorsed by Moulin. They saw it, he said, as a bastion of several thousand men sending out hit-and-run teams and being prepared to defend their entrenched camps from a German assault. Frenay insisted that no maquis, however strong, could stand up to a powerful regular army, particularly one as strong as the Germans', with armor and a full panoply of modern weapons. Frenay's idea was to set up individual maquis of about thirty men.

---

* Direction de Service et de Renseignements et de Sécurité Militaire.

"Fluidity, rapidity, and mobility were my three basic principles." He was utterly opposed to any fixed positions and to the bastion concept.

As commissaire for military affairs of the MUR, Frenay was a powerful voice in formulating strategy for the maquis. He put forward a plan for the structuring of a national maquis and proposed the name of Michel Brault (Jérome) to be the national chief, with Georges Rebattet and Robert Soulage as principal lieutenants. The Directing Committee ratified his plan and his nominations without controversy or delay.

Meanwhile, despite Moulin's objections, Frenay continued to work with Allen Dulles and the Americans. Frenay wrote later that Dulles had given him thirty-seven million francs, many times more than Moulin had furnished his movement. The Americans had also provided photographic equipment, sabotage material, and quantities of hard-to-get office supplies, such as typewriters. Frenay had used much of this money, equipment, and arms to send to the maquis, where it was urgently needed.

Then Frenay heard that Pierre de Leusse, Geneva-based agent of Fighting France, had gone to Berne to see the Americans and to ask them to break off contacts with Frenay's delegates. London feared an "American takeover of the French Resistance." Frenay rushed to tell Bertie Albrecht, his closest associate, shouting in a rage: "What the hell do they want us to do—drop dead?"

A few days later he received a message from his agents who said that Max Shoop, his main liaison to Dulles, had informed them that London had torpedoed their efforts and compromised relations with the Americans. Frenay, a tough and stubborn man, told his agents to go back to Dulles and tell him that they were still working together. He would not break off. He decided to take up this issue and many other points of conflict with de Gaulle's people in London. D'Astier and Jean-Pierre Lévy were already there and Frenay asked for a plane to go to join them.

Whatever trouble Frenay might stir up in London, Jean Moulin would be only too happy to see him go, for Moulin had his hands full consolidating his new position as chief of the CNR and delegate of the French National Council (CNF) in London. He also had to cope with a new police offensive against the Resistance. The Resistance was very hard hit in the month of April by a number of Gestapo raids that caught key men. Moulin's radio operator, Hervé (Joseph Monjaret), who had become his personal delegate to Franc-Tireur, was arrested on April 4 and many members of Franc-Tireur were picked up.

Monjaret said in a conversation in Paris in 1977 that he had been "betrayed" by a member of his movement. He was taken before the Gestapo chief in Lyon, Klaus Barbie, who beat him with a bullwhip, then tortured him for hours by holding his head down in a lavabo filled with water, pulling him up just before he drowned, then repeating the water torture over and over again. Finally, they fastened electrodes to his nipples and testicles and turned on the current in bursts. More dead than alive, Monjaret was thrown into prison in Lyon. Monjaret was then deported to Mauthausen concentration camp near Vienna, in a Night and Fog contingent. He survived and was liberated by Allied troops on April 29, 1945.

At the end of April, Frenay's movement was hit hard by the Gestapo. The key arrest was that of Jean Multon, who had only recently joined Combat and had become the right-hand man of Frenay's regional chief, Maurice Chevance (Bertin), one of his earliest recruits for Combat. Multon turned traitor as soon as he was arrested and made a deal with the Nazis to drop charges against him in return for his becoming a Gestapo agent. Since he knew the top men in the movement, their addresses, and the key letter boxes, he was responsible for the almost complete devastation of Combat. His worst treason would be to lead Victoire, Bertie Albrecht, into a Gestapo trap. Frenay has never forgotten his anguish when Bertie was arrested and deported to Germany, where she died. Multon, arrested after the liberation, was found guilty of treason and shot.

Jean Moulin went back north to meet with the military chiefs of the five principal movements in that zone. He took General Delestraint with him, for it would be necessary to reach agreement on the conditions governing the organization of the Secret Army in the north. Each of the movements had armed and trained men, already bloodied in skirmishes with the Germans. The OCM had the biggest contingent, about two hundred, with a potential of one thousand or more. The Communist armed forces were grouped in the Francs-Tireurs et Partisans Français, FTPF, which remained separate from the Secret Army.

Passy was present at the meeting and brought them up to date on a number of agreements that had been reached on April 1. The five movements would put their troops at the disposal of the general as soon as the Secret Army structures permitted him to absorb them. Orders would be issued by the Etats-Majors of the Secret Army, and Delestraint could select his officers without regard to membership in the movements. The first quota for the Secret Army in the north would be twenty thousand men. Its objectives and targets would be selected with respect to Allied landings in France.

Delestraint stated that he was satisfied with the agreements. He explained to the military chiefs that he had not only been appointed by de Gaulle to head the Secret Army in both zones, but had had long talks in London with Allied planners of the British general staffs, as well as with officers of the American general staff. They had all agreed that he should create, train, and arm a first force of fifty thousand men and then, insofar as possible, an additional force up to one hundred thousand more. The Secret Army would become the nucleus of a new French army of the future, as well as the striking force that would hit the enemy on D-day, in cooperation with the landing forces of the Allied armies.

The major point of controversy came from the Communists, and on a familiar issue: immediate action or waiting for D-day. Pierre Villon, Communist head of the Front National movement, insisted that "Hitler's war machine had to be hit and weakened bit by bit and day by day." Villon, today, almost forty years later, still bristles with indignation at the *"attentisme,"* the "waiting for D-day syndrome" of Moulin, Delestraint, and London. Front National itself, and the Communist party underground, kept up their attacks on German policemen, shooting at them in the streets or in German institutions such as the Soldatenheim social centers, rest homes, and other meeting places. They threw grenades and bombs, blew up troop trains, did what they could not only to bloody the Germans but to make them conscious that they were insecure in France. This differed mainly from the Groups Francs in its emphasis on killing Germans. The Groupes Francs of Renouvin and other commando leaders carried out acts of sabotage, rescued resistants from prison, attacked French collaborators, and only rarely killed German soldiers, mainly for fear of reprisals against French hostages.

Villon argued: "The Germans are trained to be an orderly people. Their soldiers are highly disciplined. They become neurotic and incompetent in a situation of disorder, of chaos and anarchy. That's what we had to create to throw them off balance. And we could not wait for D-day to do it." Villon was adamant on that point and said that he explained it to Moulin and Delestraint, letting them know that his people simply would not obey orders to wait for the landings before going on the attack. This issue would come to a head at the liberation of Paris. Passy told Moulin later that it was imperative to find some active missions to give an outlet to the combativity of Villon, or risk incoherent and possibly rash, ill-considered actions by his movement.

Moulin had to bring the CNR into being first by choosing and designating the men who would serve as its directors. He had to create the Secret Army of the north, which only existed in theory as a result of the agreements just reached, but did not yet have specific commanders named and troops assigned. He had to create new central services in the south to bring the Secret Army effectively under the command of Delestraint and not of Frenay. He had to overcome the hostility of the Resistance movements to the political parties. And he had to extend to the north certain agencies that had existed only in the south, such as the Comité General d'Etudes, the CGE.

Moulin decided to move the CGE to Paris and to increase its membership by delegates from the north so that it might be truly a manifestation of a national spirit in its mission of preparing democratic laws to be ready at the liberation of France. The original members, functioning in the south, were Paul Bastid, Robert Lacoste, Alexandre Parodi, and François de Menthon. In addition, Pierre-Henri Teitgen and René Courtin had been specialists for political and economic questions. Moulin now made Teitgen and Courtin full-fledged members. From the north he appointed the jurist Jacques Charpentier, the functionary Michel Debré, the industrialist Pierre Lefaucheux, and the diplomat René Brouillet. In addition, it was agreed that the CGE would publish henceforth a review called *Les Cahiers Politiques* as a platform for discussing the future laws and nature of a liberated French Republic.

While Moulin was busy consolidating his authority, creating a Secret Army, and encouraging discussion on the future of a liberated France, the Allied forces were striking hard on all fronts to push back the Axis and advance the day of liberation.

The Russians, having broken the back of von Paulus and his army at Stalingrad on February 2, went on the offensive with warm spring weather thawing the winter ice. Marshal Timoshenko led his troops on an advance in the sector of Lake Ilmen. In mid-April, the Red Army captured Rzhev, a strategic Nazi stronghold on the central front.

The RAF hit Berlin in the heaviest bombing raid of the war, on April 20, making Hitler and the Germans pay for the death tolls in London.

In the Pacific, in the month of April, the Anglo-American navies and air forces sank or disabled ten Japanese warships, sank twelve of their transports, and downed fifty-five Japanese fighters.

The RAF followed the Berlin raid by dropping one thousand tons of bombs on Essen.

The Allies were not underestimating German power. They had not forgotten the drive of the Nazis on March 15, recapturing Kharkov as a demonstration that the defeat of Marshal von Paulus had not pulled all the talons of the German eagle. However, the Soviets regrouped and fought their way back to Kharkov. The zigzags of battle would be composed more of zigs forward than zags backward by the Red Army. The Germans were on the defensive and falling back in Russia, despite isolated successes.

The Germans were also being routed in North Africa. On March 18, American troops captured Gafsa in Tunisia, and on March 23, the British breached Rommel's Mareth line defenses there. In a broadcast from London that greatly encouraged and surprised the Allied forces in North Africa, General de Gaulle announced that he would try again to seek new grounds for unity with General Giraud. De Gaulle had come to realize that he had to challenge Giraud and Murphy on the spot and not sulk in London.

On March 28 British bombers hit Berlin heavily, setting a new record for tonnage of bombs dropped, making it the biggest raid of the war so far. The RAF also struck hard at the Nazi U-boat base in Saint-Nazaire, while British pilots in Tunisia supported British ground troops and armor in the major breakthrough of the Mareth line. Nazi troops were reported to be fleeing under heavy air attack.

British planes, active on all fronts, dropped twelve tons of ammunition and medical supplies to the Franc-Tireur groups and other maquisards in the Alps of the Haute-Savoie.

Not all British air raids were applauded by the French, particularly not the unfortunate raid on the Longchamp racetrack in Paris. A low-flying British bomber, trying to hit a German antiaircraft gun in the Bois de Boulogne, hit an outdoor meeting at Longchamp that had attracted a large crowd. Some two hundred and fifty civilians were reported killed and seven hundred injured on April 4.

On April 5, the Nazis deported to a concentration camp in Germany former Premiers Edouard Daladier and Léon Blum, along with former Commander in Chief General Gamelin. They would join another former premier, Paul Reynaud, and Minister Georges Mandel in captivity in Germany.

American and British forces, striking from the east and the west, made a junction in Tunisia and planned new, joint, and final assaults on the Afrika Korps. They rapidly captured Sousse and Kairouan and drove Rommel's forces into the Carthaginian promontory on April 12.

American Lieutenant General "Tooey" Spatz, commanding the air force, announced that Allied planes controlled the air of North Africa. They had shot down 519 Axis planes and destroyed 1,000 on the ground, with a loss of only 175 planes for the Allies.

Allied submarines in the Mediterranean sank ten Axis supply ships the last week in April.

On May 16, the American OSS reported in Washington that French resistants had, in the first four months of 1943, killed 850 German officers and soldiers, wounded 2,500 others, destroyed 180 locomotives, and destroyed or damaged 2,000 railway cars. A group of Jewish partisans in Paris and the Paris region had blown up hotels requisitioned by the Germans, thrown grenades into buses transporting German soldiers, as well as into restaurants and German soldier recreation centers and movie halls. Hundreds of Jewish hostages had been shot and thousands of Jews deported. The Commissariat of Jewish Affairs announced that 35,000 Jews would be deported to Germany and that, by the end of 1943, all Jews would have been shipped out.

In Paris, German authorities began a census of all childless women between eighteen and twenty-five, who would be trained in French factories and then sent to work in Germany. The Vichy regime promised to furnish the Germans a new labor contingent of four hundred thousand workers by June 30. The pledge would lead to a massive influx of men into the maquis.

Anglo-American troops broke through German lines in Tunisia and reached the coastal plains, then spread out in an enveloping maneuver to prepare the final battle against the Germans. The next day, May 7, the capital city of Tunis and the principal port, Bizerte, were captured by the Allies. German troops fled in retreat toward Cape Bon. On May 10, twenty-five thousand Axis troops, fighting a rearguard action outside Bizerte, surrendered to the Allies.

Churchill flew into Washington as authorities announced that he had come to consult President Roosevelt on opening a second front in Europe, to squeeze Hitler between the Soviet and the Anglo-American forces.

Moulin, inside France, was working to plaster over his differences with the movement chiefs concerning organization and tactics. Essentially everyone had become convinced that it was impossible to prevent the Resistance from carrying out immediate actions. It could not be asked to keep its forces in check until D-day. Pierre Villon of Front National and the Communist leaders of the Francs-Tireurs et Partisans Français (FTPF), as well as the Jewish Partisans and other groups in the north and in the south, had been hitting the Germans hard, toughening and bloodying themselves in combat. They would be all the more effective on D-day for having been fighting all along.

General de Gaulle, demonstrating again his political perception and flexibility, promptly reversed previous instructions he had issued and drafted a new "personal and secret instruction" to General Delestraint, stating that "the principle of the necessity for immediate actions is accepted." He added that these actions would be launched on the initiative of the movements themselves. Delestraint was not to intervene tactically but was to issue broad directives, defining in general the categories of targets for attack, the zones of action, and the technical conditions of the attacks. Resistance leaders would be free to order their own actions in their own sectors.

More importantly, General de Gaulle decreed a major change in Delestraint's authority. He stated that since the army of the interior had not yet attained a definitive structure, Delestraint would have the status of an inspector general designated to take over active command "at the moment of the landings."

This decision by de Gaulle represented not only a victory for Passy but most particularly for Henri Frenay, who had made the same arguments in his confrontation with Moulin. Frenay rejoiced when he heard the news of the decisions taken in London. It helped relieve the anxiety he was suffering not only because of the arrests of his people but because he still had not been scheduled for a Lysander pickup, a fact he interpreted as a personal slur. Lysanders were coming in and out of France but none for Henri Frenay. Both d'Astier and Jean-Pierre Lévy were in London, while Frenay fretted in Mâcon, waiting for a plane.

Moulin was not upset by de Gaulle's decisions. He had himself suggested to London the change in policy on immediate action, and as for Delestraint, he would still be commander of the Secret Army on D-day and still held the highest rank as inspector general. Moulin's highest priority was to name the members of the Counseil National de la Résistance and hold the first official meeting. Once he had done that, the process would be irreversible. Frenay and others could complain, but they would have to fall in line, for unity would have been achieved in practice as well as in theory. That would be Moulin's triumph, the successful achievement of the difficult mission de Gaulle had given him when Moulin had flown into France on New Year's Day.

Moulin saw the leaders of the movements of the north as his biggest problem. He persuaded them to accept the creation of the CNR, on condition that he scrap the permanent Executive Committee idea and work through two coordinating committees in the north and in the south.

Moulin was able to send de Gaulle the good news on May 7 that everything had been agreed upon. He could not resist pointing out that Brossolette had predicted that he would not overcome the hostility of the north but that Brossolette had been proved wrong. He said he hoped to hold the first meeting of the CNR at the end of the month, and get it to take a strong position on North African affairs. He then attached to his message the proof of success: the names of the delegates to the CNR designated by the various parties to the agreement.

Most of the names were predictable.

The most important was Claude Bourdet, for Combat. It meant that Frenay had capitulated, had agreed to be represented on the CNR and by his own number-two man, a man respected by all the others. Franc-Tireur had named one of the founders of its movement, Antoine Avinin. Libération-Sud had named d'Astier's number-two man in the movement, Pascal Copeau. The Socialist party had named its most successful organizer in the Resistance, Daniel Mayer, another man respected by everyone. The Catholic Démocrates Populaires had made a logical and popular choice in Georges Bidault, who would soon be destined for an even greater role in the Resistance, and later for one of the most important posts in liberated France.

The Fédération Républicaine had named Louis Marin, on the extreme right wing of the Republican spectrum, to match Pierre Villon on the extreme left. This accorded with Daniel Mayer's formula of national union: "from Louis Marin to Maurice Thorez."

The one surprise designation was that of Maxime Blocq-Mascart by the OCM. Blocq-Mascart had been so marked in the scandal of the anti-Semitic article in the *Cahiers* of the OCM that he was certainly not the best possible choice for inclusion on the CNR.

Moulin informed de Gaulle that all the movements in both the north and the south favored an early de Gaulle-Giraud meeting in North Africa. The Resistance wanted the meeting to be a public one, between Frenchmen, meaning that the Allies must stop interfering and trying to impose Giraud as the leader of France. The Resistance, said Moulin, called for the creation in Algiers of a provisional French government with General de Gaulle as president and General Giraud as military commander in chief, and that, whatever the outcome of the negotiations in Algiers, General de Gaulle would remain the chief of the French Resistance.

In his war memoirs, General de Gaulle made special reference to Jean Moulin's report. It was sent not only to London, but to Algiers, where it was published in the press and broadcast by the French, British, and American radio stations. Its effect was "decisive." Immediately after its publication, Giraud sent a telegram asking de Gaulle to come to Algiers. De Gaulle replied on May 25 that he would come at the end of that week. He sent Moulin congratulations and a special message of encouragement for the delegates of the CNR.

Moulin set May 27 as the date for the first official meeting of the CNR, a great event in the modern history of France. It was an extremely difficult and dangerous meeting to arrange. First it was necessary to find in Paris an absolutely safe house in which so many top men of the Resistance could meet. What a catch for the Gestapo if they could have got wind of it! Then, the date had to be right for most of the delegates. Those who could not make it could, however, send deputies. And special arrangements had to be made to get everyone to the meeting. No one was given the actual address—it was the house of René Corbin in the Rue du Four. Instead, each delegate was given another, different address, where a guide would meet them and take them to the final address.

Most of the delegates were able to make it, but some, like Daniel Mayer, were in London, others were on mission or had other commitments. Blocq-Mascart finally did not come. He was replaced by J. H. Simon. Jacques Bedu-Bridel filled in for Louis Marin. Avinin was replaced by Jean-Pierre Lévy's number-two man in Franc-Tireur, Claudius-Petit. André Le Trocquer sat in for Daniel Mayer.

The meeting was a triumph for Jean Moulin. Its highlight was a motion by Georges Bidault, approved unanimously by all the delegates, stressing their approval of negotiations between de Gaulle and Giraud for national unity, underlining the presence of France on all the war fronts, and the commitment of the French to throw all their resources into the battle of liberation. To accomplish that, France needed a united and strong government, provisional, of course, until the French people could vote, but presided over at once by General de Gaulle, with Giraud at the head of the armed forces. This endorsed the position already taken by Jean Moulin.

Moulin had every justification to exult on the night of May 27, 1943. He had brought about a kind of miracle, uniting men of very different political views, of highly competitive ambitions and egos, working and fighting under constant stress, with their lives on the line in every meeting and every decision. He had done so against opposition that at times seemed insurmountable.

Moulin was not naïve or exalted. He knew perfectly well that if opposition and hostility had been overcome, these feelings had not been eradicated, and that the work of consolidation and execution was always needed. His mission had not ended. He had, however, made it possible to begin to work together on a national scale inside and outside France.

18
THE TRAGEDY OF JEAN MOULIN

If May 1943 was the month of triumph for Jean Moulin and his comrades of the Secret Army and the CNR, then June would be the month of tragedy. The first victim would be Charles Delestraint, newly redesignated as inspector general of the Secret Army.

Early in June, General Delestraint decided that he wanted to confer with René Hardy, chief of "Résistance-Fer," shorthand for Résistance Chemin de Fer; that is, the Resistance movement for the railways. René Hardy was a railway specialist and had developed for Henri Frenay a plan for the systematic and professional sabotage of the railway system. There was a controversy, similar to the argument about immediate action versus D-day action, over whether the plan should be put into effect at once or held back until the Allied landings, when it would be most useful in disorganizing the Germans' defenses.

Delestraint asked his chief of staff, Henri Aubry, to contact Hardy in Lyon and have him come to Paris on June 9 to meet Delestraint at the Muette station of the Métro line.

Aubry asked his secretary to handle the communication, and there the plot begins to thicken. Aubry's secretary sent the message to a Madame Dumoulin, who lived on the Rue Bouteille in Lyon. This was an official "letter box" of the Combat movement. However, it was known by most members that the letter box was "burned," that is, had come to the attention of the Gestapo, whose agents kept watch on it. Aubry knew it was burned. But did he know that his secretary would use it? Did she know it was burned? Why did she use it? Why did she send the message "in clear," instead of coding it? These questions have provoked bitter debate for years. All that can be said with certainty is that the message was sent in clear language to a burned letter box, an act of incredible negligence if not treason.

René Hardy claimed later that he never received the message. He knew the letter box was burned and had not gone there for weeks. But by an extraordinary coincidence, he did decide to go to Paris for an appointment on the same date, June 9, requested by Delestraint. Hardy had made an appointment for that day with Jean-Guy Bernard to discuss plans for extending to the northern zone the infiltration system of NAP. Bernard later confirmed the fact that he did have a meeting scheduled with Hardy for June 9. But Hardy never showed up for the meeting. The Gestapo had arrested him en route.

Hardy had a Wagon-Lit sleeping compartment reservation for the night of June 7–8. His tickets had been picked up for him by a liaison agent of the movement, and the sleeping berth had been reserved by his fiancée, Lydie Bastien. He himself had not gone to the station of the Wagons-Lits office as a security precaution, although he was traveling under his own name.

He got on the train, entered his compartment, and discovered he was sharing it with a Monsieur Cressol, a Vichy functionary. Well and good— a safe traveling companion. However, in the next compartment, unknown to Hardy, were two former resistants who had been arrested and turned into Gestapo agents: Jean Multon (Lunel) and Robert Moog (Boby). Multon was the Combat traitor who had trapped so many leaders of that movement, including Bertie Albrecht.

Multon and Moog had been dispatched to Paris by the Gestapo after its agents had read the message in the Dumoulin letter box. It would be their job to help the Paris Gestapo identify and arrest Delestraint and Hardy when they met at the Muette subway station. Neither knew that Hardy would be sleeping in the compartment next to theirs. No Hollywood scriptwriter could have invented a more successful device for a thriller.

Moog did not know Hardy personally, but Multon had seen him once a few months earlier, in a restaurant in Marseille. Hardy was lunching with a fellow resistant when Multon came into the bar of the station restaurant. Hardy's colleague knew Multon and nodded to him. Nodding back, Multon had taken notice of Hardy, and Hardy had also noted Multon.

After checking in with the conductor, and getting his ticket and berth validated, Hardy got off the train to get some fresh air on the station platform. It was at that moment that Multon arrived at the same railway car. Hardy recognized him, and to judge from Multon's facial reaction, he, too, had recognized Hardy. Multon was startled and frightened, for his treachery was known to Combat and he had to assume that all Combat members had been warned against him. And he was sure that Hardy had spotted him. Meanwhile, Moog, who had sharp eyes and the heightened senses of a double agent, had noted the "eye exchange" between Hardy and Multon. Hardy then caught sight of Lazare Rachline, a Special Operations agent of the British, walking toward the train. The Paris express that night seemed to be the "spy special." Hardy, suspecting he had been "fingered," strolled over to Rachline, asked him for a light, and whispered over his cigarette: "Tell de Bénouville that if anything happens to me, it's Lunel's fault."

All the spies and counterspies boarded the train and went to their sleeping compartments. Despite his fears, Hardy did not try to steal away. He went to his compartment. All agents were in bed when the train pulled into the station of Chalon-sur-Saône at one in the morning, all, that is, except Moog. He had left the train and summoned the German police, who arrested Hardy and the Vichy official who had the bad luck to be sharing his sleeping compartment. They also questioned Rachline, because he had been seen talking to Hardy on the quay. But he persuaded them that he was an innocent traveler who had given Hardy a light and exchanged some nonsensical words about the weather.

Hardy and Cressol, his fellow traveler, were put in jail in Chalon to be interrogated later. Multon and Moog got back on the train and continued on to their mission in Paris: the arrest of General Delestraint.

At nine in the morning of June 9, General Delestraint walked to the entrance of the Muette station. He was wearing a beret, the rosette of the Légion d'Honneur in his buttonhole, and was striding along at a brisk, snappy military pace. He was recognized at once by another French double agent, René Saumandre, a servant of the Abwehr.

Saumandre sidled up to Delestraint and whispered to him that Didot, fearing that the Muette station was being watched, wanted to change their meeting place, and he would guide him there. Delestraint, reassured by the ready recognition of his presence and the use of the code name Didot, suspected nothing and fell into step alongside the Abwehr spy. He told Saumandre that they had better hurry because he also had appointments at nine-thirty with two of his Secret Army comrades, Gastaldo and Theobald, at the Rue Pompe station. Saumandre grinned at his good luck: Now he would have three Secret Army men, not just one.

As the two men drew abreast of a parked Gestapo car, Saumandre grabbed Delestraint by the shoulders. The door flew open and Saumandre shoved Delestraint into the back seat. Other agents were sent to the Rue Pompe to grab Gastaldo and Theobald. All three were driven to Gestapo headquarters at 84 Avenue Foch. This beautiful, tree-lined avenue, one of Paris's most fashionable addresses, was a macabre choice for the torture chambers of the Gestapo.

Klaus Barbie, chief of the Gestapo in Lyon, granted an interview many years later to a Brazilian journalist, Edwardo Dantas-Ferreira. He spoke to him at length about Hardy, the arrest of General Delestraint on June 9, and the events that followed upon it. It would take more space than is available in this one-volume history of the Resistance to reproduce and analyze the Barbie declarations fully. For scholars interested in the affair, a full treatment can be found in volume three of the exhaustively detailed history of the French Resistance by Henri Noguères and Marcel Degliame-Fouché.

Point by point the writers refute Barbie's testimony, until not a shred of credibility remains. They completely reject Barbie's allegation that Hardy was a traitor working for him as a Gestapo agent, though they do not clear Hardy of the charge of treachery.

Hardy testified later that it was sometime on the tenth of June that Barbie came to Chalon to interrogate him. (Cressol, the Vichy functionary arrested with Hardy, confirmed that fact in separate testimony.) Barbie then escorted Hardy from Chalon to Gestapo headquarters in Lyon. There Hardy was interrogated by Barbie, and released, a compromising fact that naturally led to speculation that a deal might have been made. It led to many questions that would be posed years later when Hardy was brought to the bar in the first of two trials that would finally set him free as legally innocent.

Hardy's "legal innocence" has never ended the mystery and controversy over "l'Affaire Hardy." Legal innocence or guilt does not establish absolute innocence or guilt. Almost forty years after the tragic events of June 1943, Frenchmen today still argue about "l'Affaire Hardy."

The questions are many: Did Barbie discover in the interrogation of June 10 that Hardy was Didot? Saumandre had earlier referred to Hardy as Didot and must have told some Gestapo agents that fact. It is possible that the information had not yet worked its way up through channels to Barbie. But Barbie could have known. If he did know, why did he release Hardy that night? Was it because he had "turned" him into a Gestapo agent? A man close to Hardy, but who did not like him, testified to the contrary, convinced from a terrifying personal ordeal that the Gestapo did not know on June 10 that Hardy was Didot. The man is Max Heilbronn, a most reliable witness.

Max Heilbronn was born in Paris in 1902, making him at the time of the Hardy affair forty-one years old, a bit advanced in years for a militant resistant, particularly a Jew, more vulnerable than others to Nazi persecution. He had married the daughter of the owner of one of the great department stores of the world, the Galeries Lafayette of Paris, and was moving up in the administration of the store.

In 1939 Max was a reserve captain of the Fifth Regiment of Army Engineers, specializing in railway engineering. It was this army specialty in the railway system that led Max to become René Hardy's assistant when Hardy became chief of the NAP-Chemin de Fer, then Résistance-Fer.

During the war Captain Heilbronn was in charge of an engineering commando that blew up railway bridges, trestles, and switches from Maisons-Lafitte to Rouen, and then, during the retreat, from Orléans to Nantes along the Loire. He learned a lot about sabotage and how vital the rails were to the army. Heilbronn developed a number of techniques for railway sabotage which he incorporated in the plan that came to be called the *Plan Vert*, the Green Plan, so called, he says, because he and Hardy drafted it on green paper.

Max Heilbronn's code name, given to him by Frenay, was Harrel. He had had the idea for a plan of massive sabotage of the rail lines early in 1940, right after the fall of France. He was convinced that the Allies would land one day and that a French Resistance had to be ready to help the Allies by disrupting the Nazi railways. He had met an agent of de Gaulle, Honoré d'Estienne d'Orve, who approved the plan, and said he would arrange for Max to join de Gaulle in London. D'Estienne d'Orve was executed by the Nazis before anything could be arranged.

Heilbronn had been arrested at the same time, but he convinced the police that his travels around France were all for the Galeries Lafayette, as a purchasing agent. The police had no evidence against him other than his frequent travels, so they let him go, with a warning. Heilbronn went to Lyon, center of the Resistance, and obtained a position as engineer in the Rural Works of Vichy, a cover for Resistance activities. Father Chaillet, a Jesuit priest in the Témoignage Chrétien movement and an associate of Henri Frenay, introduced Max Heilbronn to René Hardy, who was recruiting engineers for the Resistance.

"It was dislike almost at first sight," Heilbronn recalled. "We worked together in a common cause but were hostile to each other. We were also highly competitive rivals. Hardy and his group of men were engineers of the SNCF, the national railways system, whereas I was an army engineer. Each thought of himself as better qualified than the other. Hardy also wanted us to launch large-scale sabotage of the railways long before the landings, while I thought we ought to wait for large-scale activities until the Allies needed us. It was the argument raging everywhere: now or later?"

Heilbronn had sent a first draft of the *Plan Vert* to London in March 1943, along with a manual he had composed, entitled *Le Manuel du Parfait Derailleur* (*The Handbook of the Perfect Derailer*), which, desipite its joking title, was a serious handbook on techniques for derailing trains. Heilbronn's work came to the attention of American agents, who offered him direct help and money if he would work for them. "I went at once to see Frenay to tell him about the American offer. It was in May, and I knew that Frenay was already in touch with the Americans, himself.

"I told Frenay that he would have to call a halt to the idiotic conflicts and arguments I had been suffering with Hardy. Either straighten Hardy out, and tell him to stop his jealous sniping at me and my plans, or I'd go off and work with the Americans."

About a week later, Father Chaillet told Harrel that Frenay had passed the problem on to Georges Bidault and that Bidault had talked to Hardy and had been assured that Hardy would work loyally and efficiently with Heilbronn. A meeting was arranged at a farm in the Cévennes where they shook hands and got down to work drafting a final version of the plan, which at first had been called the Plan A.

Hardy and Max met at a bistro in Lyon toward the end of May 1943. Hardy was nervous, Heilbronn remembers. "He kept looking around him and told me that he was being followed. He had a package with him and said it had to be delivered to a certain address. He asked me to take it for him, since he was being watched. Like an idiot, I agreed. I learned later the Germans were watching us—I might have guessed as much from what Hardy said and the way he acted. When he gave me the package, they followed me. Inside the package, Hardy had put the *Plan Vert* and the manual on how to derail trains! I delivered it and did not find out until much later that the Germans picked it up after I left. They did not want me to know I was being watched."

Heilbronn told Hardy that he had delivered his package and Hardy asked to meet him in a café in the Place Carnot. The date of the meeting was set for June 12, two days after the Gestapo had released Hardy from prison, an important point in Heilbronn's view. "You see, as soon as Hardy and I finished talking on June twelfth, and he had left me, the Gestapo came up and arrested me. They took me down to a cellar room and began punching and beating me. They kept asking me to admit that I was Didot. I was badly hurt, felt faint, and realized I had better fall down and pretend to pass out before I was crippled. I think they were glad to see me faint, for it was a very hot day and they were sweating profusely from beating me up.

"Someone came in and threw water on me. I moaned and pretended still to be semiconscious. I heard them speaking and understood every word, for I am fluent in German. I heard a key phrase: *'Es war der andere.'* ("It was the other guy.") I knew then that they were after Hardy and had thought that I was Hardy. This proved to me that Barbie did not know exactly who Hardy was when he interrogated him on June tenth. It proves to me, too, that Hardy had not been released as a double agent. I took a terrible beating on Hardy's account."

Heilbronn was kept in prison in Lyon for six months, then transferred and held secretly in Compiègne for two months. From there Max was sent to Buchenwald. Some functionary listed him as a political prisoner, giving him a uniform with a red triangle on it. It saved his life. They knew he was a Jew and could have pinned a yellow triangle upon him, the triangle that led to the gas chambers and the crematoria. Instead, he was assigned to the work force as an engineer. He worked there until July 4, 1944, when he was sent to Struthof and then on to Dachau, where he managed to survive until the liberation armies threw open the gates of the death camp.

"I had plenty of time to think of what had happened. I did not like Hardy personally. I thought he made many mistakes, but I could not believe that he was a traitor." Heilbronn testified to that effect before the Military Tribunal that tried Hardy in 1947.

One of the most damaging pieces of evidence against Hardy was the fact that when he was released from prison and rejoined his comrades, he did not tell anyone that he had been arrested and interrogated. His chief, Henri Frenay, was completely misinformed. He noted down and wrote later that René seemed neurotic because of his close escape; Frenay thought that Hardy had spotted Multon and had jumped off the train before it arrived at Chalon. Hardy lied to him and to all the others.

Hardy became very active after he was released by the Gestapo, meeting with a number of men in the movement, making certain that everyone knew that he was functioning vigorously. In addition to Max Heilbronn, he saw another close associate, René La Combe, as well as Jacques Baumel, Henri

Aubry, Claude Bourdet, Marcel Degliame-Fouché, and Pierre de Bénouville. René La Combe, a deputy of the National Assembly today, recalled in an interview at the Palais Bourbon that Hardy had told him that he had recognized the traitor Lunel and had jumped off the train near Mâcon to escape arrest, the same lie that he had told Frenay and all the others.

Hardy, in later testimony, argued that it was in his favor that he had seen all these important resistants and many others between June 10 and June 20. If he had been released by the Gestapo as a double agent, he would have been followed and all the people with whom he met would have been picked up. Since none of them was arrested by the Gestapo, it proved, Hardy argued, that he was not working for Barbie and the Nazis. It was a good argument, except for the counterargument that Barbie was looking for Jean Moulin, the top man, and did not want to alert him by moving in on lesser members.

Jean Moulin was one of the first to be alerted to a new danger. He received a call on June 12 from an aide whose mother had gone to see General Delestraint's wife and had learned of his arrest. Moulin was seriously alarmed, although not surprised by the news. He had felt for weeks that the Gestapo ring was closing in on him and his associates. He had sent through a report to that effect on May 7, telling London that the Vichy and Nazi secret services were hot on his trail. He blamed it on the poor security of certain elements of the Resistance, charging that only three days after an important report of the MUR was circulated, the Gestapo had a copy of it, according to one of his spies at Gestapo headquarters.

The sense of impending doom led Moulin to put more pressure on London to send over men designated to be his successors in case of his arrest. He pointed out that he would not be able to brief his successors fully unless they were sent soon. His pleas were partially answered on the night of June 16. The man who parachuted to a field in Saône-et-Loire that night had been General de Gaulle's chief administrative assistant for two and a half years. His code name was Scarpin, the name of the clever but rascally valet in Molière's Italianesque comedies, but he was anything but a rascal. He was the intelligent, patriotic Claude Bouchinet Serreulles, former liaison officer to the British army, who had left France aboard the *Massilia* en route to Morocco, hoping to go on to London.

On arriving in Morocco, Serreulles had gone to see General Noguès, whom he had known earlier. The general tried to persuade him to stay there, promising that the French army would soon be back in the war. Serreulles did not believe him. He knew the French army and navy would not get him to London.

Serreulles then met a group of Polish aviators who had fled France and were making their way to England. He told them that was what he wanted to do, but could not get official clearance. The Poles laughed and said they would take care of everything. They picked Serreulles up in a truck delivering food to a Polish navy ship scheduled to sail to Gibraltar. They hid

Claude in a potato sack. The ship's crane picked up some crates and Claude's sack from the quay and lifted him aboard, right over the heads of the military police.

Arriving some days later in Liverpool, Serreulles met a Gaullist officer who told him about Free France and wrote down de Gaulle's address at St. Stephen's House in London. The officer told Serreulles that a few men had already rallied to de Gaulle and mentioned some names. One of the names was Geoffrey de Courcel. Serreulles shouted: "Is he tall and skinny, with a nose curving down to his chin?" The officer laughed and said that was a good description. Serreulles was overjoyed: "He is my childhood friend. We grew up together."

De Gaulle was just getting ready to move to Carlton Gardens, with a bigger staff. He needed help and took Serreulles on at once. "I did so many things," Claude recalled as he reminisced in 1977, about the early de Gaulle days.

"For two and a half years, de Gaulle had me jumping from one crisis to another. It was exciting, trying, challenging, but I was bursting with impatience for action in the field. Courcel had already gone, in 1941, to the Middle East. De Gaulle had taken on a new aide, a civilian, Gaston Palewski, with the title of directeur de Cabinet. I told de Gaulle that he could spare me and that, having been so close to him, knowing all his policies, I could most usefully serve him inside France working with Jean Moulin."

Serreulles had won his wings as a parachutist and wanted to jump into France. He kept pestering de Gaulle, as much as he dared press his haughty and short-tempered leader. Then, in February 1943, Jean Moulin came to London and Serreulles went to see him to tell him of his plans. Moulin liked Serreulles, saw that he was not a stooge for Passy and Brossolette, and agreed to endorse his request.

Serreulles flew off in April, to jump over Château-Thierry, but his plane was hit by flak. Claude was wounded and had to return to London. He was then held up by bad weather and did not get his chance to jump until June 16.

"It had been so long," Serreulles recalled, "that Moulin had forgotten that he had asked for me and did not remember what he had planned for me to do. I told him I'd do anything he would assign me to. Moulin replied that he was badly in need of an assistant for military affairs, which were causing him great trouble even before the arrest of General Delestraint. I told him that I was well briefed on political questions, particularly in the northern zone, where I could be useful, but was ready and willing to help him as a military aide if that's where the priority was.

"'Moulin then told me that he was calling a meeting of all the top military leaders of the unified Resistance on June 21 and that the meeting would be held in a suburb of Lyon, Caluire. He did not know the address, of course, since security required that no one be told in advance. I would be informed later where to go to contact a guide to the meeting. We parted, with

Moulin telling me he wanted to see me again the next morning. I had got to Lyon on the nineteenth, after my jump, so my next date with Moulin was for the twentieth. I was very excited to be back in France and set out walking around Lyon reorienting myself."

That same day, the nineteenth, while Moulin was getting acquainted with his new deputy, Serreulles, Chief of Staff Henri Aubry came back to Lyon from a week's trip to Marseille, where he had visited his wife, who was in a clinic there. It was there he had heard about Delestraint's arrest. He had also heard that Moulin was complaining about his absence and needed him back for an important meeting—the meeting of the twenty-first. André Lassagne, a professor in Lyon, was designated to select the meeting place and make the necessary arrangements. Aubry found many letters and messages on his return, including several urgent calls from René Hardy.

Aubry gave Hardy an appointment to meet him at eleven-thirty the next morning, Sunday the twentieth, at the Pont Morand. He also told Gaston Deferre, a Socialist leader who wanted to see him, to meet him there before the eleven-thirty meeting. He plannd to lunch afterward with Hardy, whom he liked and whom he knew as a fellow member of the Frenay-de Bénouville team.

Aubry also had a note from Moulin who wanted to see him at 10 A.M., before the Monday meeting.

Later on Saturday, Aubry ran into Hardy, who was out walking with his fiancée. He told Hardy that he would not only meet him the next morning but take him with him to the Monday meeting that Moulin had called. This was a grave breach of security on Aubry's part. He had no business even informing Hardy of the Monday meeting and no right at all to decide by himself, without Moulin's knowledge, to invite someone to a meeting called by the chief of the CNR, particularly a meeting of military leaders in which Hardy had only a peripheral role to play. Coming on top of the terrible error of his secretary who had sent a clear message to a burned letter box, Aubry's new breach of security was almost criminally negligent.

Aubry was monumentally careless that day. He lunched with three other men, all good friends and comrades, men of whom he felt sure. But no matter how sure of them he was, there is no excusing the fact that Aubry told them about the Monday meeting of the military chiefs.

Aubry must have been nervous about that Monday meeting. He suspected that he would be severely blamed for the arrest of Delestraint. He knew, too, that Moulin was aware of the fact that Aubry was a close friend and spokesman of Henri Frenay. Frenay had finally found a plane and was in London, but de Bénouville had briefed Aubry on Frenay's policy positions on military questions and on the organization of the Secret Army. Aubry knew there would be a clash between him and Moulin. Aubry was the chief of staff of the Secret Army. Someone had to be named to replace Delestraint and Moulin would certainly not name a Frenay man like Aubry.

Weeks earlier Moulin had learned how to deal with Combat's

chief by persuading Franc-Tireur and Libération to side with him in any disagreements with Frenay. Jean-Pierre Lévy was no problem. He supported
Moulin and did not trust Frenay on any leadership issue or power play.
D'Astier was a bit more difficult but he, too, distrusted Frenay. And his second
in command, Pascal Copeau, was simply fed up with power struggles and
wanted to cooperate loyally with Moulin. So Frenay was most often outvoted.

Copeau felt very strongly, as did Serreulles, that Moulin had
acted wisely in bringing the Communist party into a unified Resistance and
persuading the Central Committee to declare publicly its allegiance to General
de Gaulle, at least for the duration of the war. Serreulles believes today that
Moulin's decision to bring the Communists into the fold prevented an outbreak of civil war in France at the liberation. "We might have become another
Greece," Serreulles commented during a discussion in the fall of 1977.

On Saturday night, the nineteenth of June 1943, Moulin met in
Lyon with Copeau and with Franc-Tireur's acting chief, Claudius-Petit, both
of whom assured him that they would back him up against Frenay's men.

The next morning, Sunday, Aubry met with Deferre, as agreed,
and the two strolled over to the Pont Morand to meet Hardy. As they got near
the bridge, they saw Hardy sitting on a bench next to someone whose face was
hidden by a widespread newspaper. Aubry gave Deferre another appointment
and signaled Hardy to come over to him. When Hardy crossed the street,
Aubry invited him to lunch. Deferre walked away, wondering who had been
sitting next to Hardy, hiding his face in a newspaper.

Later—too late—it would be learned that the man behind the
newspaper was none other than Gestapo chief Klaus Barbie. It would be a major
piece of evidence when Hardy was brought to trial in 1947.* Hardy would
deny that he saw Barbie there, or if he was there, Hardy did not recognize him.
But Barbie's bodyguard testified that Barbie was there on the bridge sitting next
to Hardy.

The important question that cannot be answered one way or the
other with any certainty, for there is no proof, is this: Did Hardy tell Barbie
about the meeting Moulin had called in Caluire on the twenty-first? Some
writers have jumped to the conclusion that Hardy must have told him, but other
French historians have refused to make that assumption based on circum-
stantial evidence. All agree, however, that Barbie's presence, almost knee to
knee with Hardy, and his pains to hide his face, are damaging to Hardy's plea
of innocence.

Moulin dined with Claude Serreulles that Sunday night, June 20,
in a little bistro on the Saône. Moulin told Serreulles that he had decided that
Serreulles could be most useful in handling military affairs. There were many
issues to be thrashed out: the selection of a new commander of the Secret Army

---

* Hardy was acquitted at this trial but was then brought on trial a second time when new
evidence proved he had lied to the first tribunal. He admitted he had lied when confronted
by the new evidence. The second trial ended in a hung jury.

and agreement for his functions; coordination of multiple military organizations; the creation and structuring of Etats-Majors. Moulin told Serreulles who the military chiefs would be at the next day's meeting, what their functions were, the order of the day, and what decisions he would try to bring out of the meeting. He told Serreulles he wanted to see him again on Monday morning before the afternoon meeting. He would look for him on the quays of the Rhône River.

The next morning, very early, the two men met and walked down the Rhône talking about plans for the afternoon meeting, until they met up with Moulin's next appointment, Raymond Aubrac of Libération. Aubrac and Serreulles shook hands and made a date to meet for dinner. Serreulles left, after being told to go that afternoon to the top of the funicular, where he would get a sign from a liaison agent whom he was to follow onto a tramway that would take them to the secret meeting place.

At ten o'clock Moulin met Aubry. They walked along under a heavy rain under umbrellas, engaged in a violent argument. Moulin had heard about a parachute drop of arms near Brive. There had been a prior agreement on where the arms were to be stocked, but Aubry's men, who picked them up, took them to a different place. Aubry had finally recovered the arms, but Moulin was furious about the lack of discipline in the ranks. Aubry tried to sound him out on Delestraint's successor, but Moulin would say nothing more than to wait for the afternoon meeting to discuss the question. They parted, with Aubry not saying a word to Moulin about his decision to bring Hardy to the meeting.

The meeting was set for 2 P.M., at the house of Dr. Dugoujon in Caluire, the suburb in the hills above Lyon. Strangely, particularly in view of the importance and number of the men called to attend, no provision was made for a Resistance armed security guard at the approaches and around the villa. It was an elementary and routine precaution that might have saved the day for Moulin.

André Lassagne was assigned to take Henri Aubry to the meeting. Jean Moulin would escort Raymond Aubrac and Colonel Schwartzfeld. Bruno Larat would come with Colonel Lacaze, and Serreulles would come with the guide he would meet atop the funicular.

When Lassagne met Aubry at the funicular station he was astonished to see Hardy with him. He told them he would go up alone and they should follow in the next funicular, and then take Tramway 33 to the Place Castellane, Dr. Dugoujon's address.

Aubrac was supposed to pass along directions to Serge Ravanal of Libération but arrived late and Ravanal left before he came. Ravanal never got to the meeting, a stroke of good luck for him.

Serreulles never got there either. Recalling that important day, he said with some embarrassment: "I had just flown in from England. I was not familiar with Lyon and the hills around it. Like an idiot I took the wrong funicular. When I got to the exit at the top, I sat and waited a good hour for my guide. Then I knew I had blown it and I felt terrible. As I made my way down and back into Lyon, I thought: My very first meeting and I miss it. What in the world will Max say about his new deputy?"

Aubry, Hardy, Lassagne, Lacaze, and Larat all found their way and arrived in time for the meeting. The maid, as instructed, took them up to a first-floor sitting room. The doctor was downstairs in his ground-floor office, across from the waiting room, where his regular patients were sitting.

But Jean Moulin, Aubrac, and Schwartzfeld were not there at 2 P.M. Aubry and the others were surprised. Moulin had an obsession about being on time. To this day, no one knows exactly why the three men were late, very late, arriving only at 2:45.

Aubrac remembers meeting Moulin at 2:15 at the foot of the funicular, then waiting another fifteen minutes for Schwartzfeld, who was late, but no one can recall why Moulin met him at 2:15 to go to a 2 o'clock meeting.

The question of the timing is important, for Moulin was not the only one who was forty-five minutes late. Klaus Barbie and the Gestapo raced up to the house, surrounded it, and burst in at 2:45, just after Moulin had arrived. Had the Gestapo arrived at 2 P.M., Moulin, being late, would have seen the police cars in front of the house and continued on his way without coming in. No one knows why Barbie arrived so late for the meeting, if, as he claimed, he had known about it in advance.

In any case, Barbie and his thugs broke into the house minutes after Moulin's arrival and before Moulin had actually joined the men on the first floor. The maid had mistaken him and his associates for patients of the doctor and had ushered them into the regular waiting room on the ground floor.

Hardy pulled a gun out of his pocket when he heard the police breaking in, but the others shouted at him to put it away. They could not win a shoot-out with the Gestapo. The police burst in, grabbing, slapping, and punching, knocking heads against the wall, and ordering them to put their hands behind their backs. Handcuffs were snapped on everyone but Hardy. One of the Germans shouted that they had run out of handcuffs, so they put a single chain on Hardy.

A little man came up to Aubry, laughed, and called him Thomas, the code name given him only a short time before by Frenay. Aubry was shocked at the little man's knowledge of his new alias. The little man was Klaus Barbie. Obviously he had agents inside Combat.

The Nazi police came downstairs and broke into the doctor's waiting room with the same violence and brutality used against those caught in the meeting room up on the first floor. They lined everyone up, face to the wall, hands behind backs, and snapped handcuffs on them all, including a number of the doctor's sick patients. Dr. Dugoujon came running out of his consulting room and was stopped by a soldier with a machine-pistol who kicked him in the stomach as a way of telling him to line up against the wall. As he walked past Moulin, Max whispered to him: "My name is Jean Martel."

Moulin had taken the precaution of having another doctor write out a letter telling Dr. Dugoujon that he was suffering from rheumatism and probably needed a specialist. He had the letter on him to show the police to prove he was a legitimate patient.

Suddenly shooting was heard outside the house, then three or four revolver shots. René Hardy had been taken out by the Gestapo, led to a Citroën and told to get into it. Hardy testified later that he had shoved his guard aside, forcing him to drop the chain attached to Hardy's wrist. He had then run across the square and, as soldiers shot at him, thrown himself into a ditch after taking out his gun and shooting back at the soldiers. The Germans had a dozen prisoners to watch, and abandoned the pursuit of Hardy, who got away by running down the hill through the woods down to the Saône River.

That is Hardy's version of what happened. None of the resistants there that day believed him. As soon as it happened they all thought that Barbie had set up a phony escape to permit Hardy, the only man not hand-cuffed, to get away. They were sure he had become a Gestapo agent. Raymond Aubrac had no doubts, particularly since there was a trained Nazi commando in front of the house, armed with a machine-pistol that he did not even fire at Hardy. Aubrac laughs at the notion that Hardy, not exactly a close-combat fighter, could have bowled over tough Gestapo guards and run away with such ease.

Hardy had nonetheless been wounded in the upper arm and was bleeding when he got down the hill. He hailed two cyclists and asked them to take him to the home of friends nearby. They did, but one of them also called the French police to report the wounded man. The police came and took Hardy to the Grange-Blanche hospital. After treatment he was transferred to the internment center of Antiquaille for further treatment and interrogation.

Lucie Aubrac, Raymond's wife and one of the leaders of Libéra-tion, received orders from Resistance authorities—she does not say who they were—to execute Hardy as a traitor. The method chosen was poison and she sent Hardy a small jar of jam, small enough so that he would not offer to share it with any other prisoner. It was spiked liberally with cyanide. The plan did not work, for Hardy anticipated it and asked his jailers to test all outside food in the laboratory.

Hardy managed to escape from the hospital by jumping out the window onto the roof of a garage, and climbing over the hospital gate. So he told his comrades of Combat when he found his way to Paris and a meeting with de Bénouville. Hardy had become the Houdini of the Resistance.

Meanwhile all the other resistants at Dr. Dugoujon's house were arrested, along with the doctor and his patients. Gestapo agents discovered soon enough who were resistants and who were genuinely sick patients. They had full files on the resistants and their own doctor to find out who was ill. Some-how—he never said how—Klaus Barbie discovered that his raid had netted a big prize: the famous Max, personal envoy of General de Gaulle, chief of the Resistance. Trouble was, Barbie did not know which of his prisoners was Max. There was one tried-and-true way to find out: Take a few resistants down to the torture chambers in the cellar of Gestapo headquarters and work them over until one cracked and identified Moulin. Barbie has never named the man who broke down and fingered Max, but by the afternoon of June 23, Barbie knew that Max was "Jean Martel," the "patient" who had come to consult the doctor about his "rheumatism."

On the night of the day Max was identified, Dr. Dugoujon caught sight of Moulin staggering down a corridor of the Gestapo interrogation rooms in Lyon, barely able to walk, his head swathed in bandages. Barbie had carried out his threat to use every means of torture to identify the top man of the French Resistance.

One of Marie-Madeleine's "animals," who was at the gathering in Ussel in 1977, told of one type of torture that he had suffered. He unfolded his hands and revealed twisted, scarred fingers. "It was the door torture," he said. They had shoved his fingers into the open space between the hinges of the door and the wall, a small space when the door was open. Then they slammed the door shut, breaking his fingers and crushing them. Open and shut, open and shut, until blood gushed out of his hand like a fountain and he blacked out.

Joseph Monjaret (Hervé), in his Paris office decades later, described the water torture, the drowning in a lavabo or tub; and the electrode torture.

Others had had hot needles shoved under their fingernails.

There were whips and clubs and screw-levered handcuffs that could be tightened until they bit through the flesh and broke through the bones of the wrist.

Barbie had all these means to make Max talk. But he did not know the kind of man he had taken prisoner. Other prisoners who saw Max during the interrogation have described his pitiful state. Trade unionist Christian Pineau, who had been arrested and imprisoned in the jail in Lyon, and who had a safety razor that the Nazis had let him keep, for he had been appointed the prison barber, was called out of his cell one day to shave another prisoner. He was taken to the courtyard where he saw a man stretched out on a bench, guarded by an armed soldier. The man was Moulin. Pineau described him in his book *La Simple Vérité*: "He was unconscious, his eyes dug in as though they had been punched through his head. An ugly blue wound scarred his temple. A mute rattle came out of his swollen lips."

The German guard shoved Pineau and made a motion indicating that he had to shave Moulin. Pineau asked for soap and water, stalling to gain time to clear his head. He was in a state of shock. He walked close to Moulin and felt his forehead and hands. They were glacial.

The guard came back with soap and water and Pineau lathered up Moulin's bruised face. The blade of his razor was dull and he had a difficult time shaving Moulin and avoiding the most swollen places on his face.

Suddenly Max opened his eyes and looked at Pineau. Pineau thought, but could not be sure, that Moulin recognized him.

"Water," he groaned.

Pineau turned to the guard and said in German: "*Ein wenig wasser.*"

The guard hesitated a moment, then carried the soapy bowl to the fountain, rinsed it, and filled it with fresh water.

Pineau bent over Moulin trying to whisper words of comfort. Moulin uttered five or six words in English that Pineau did not understand because Moulin's voice was hoarse and distorted, with blood and drool running out of the corner of his mouth.

The guard gave Pineau the bowl of water, which he held to Moulin's lips. Moulin managed to swallow a few mouthfuls and then he lost consciousness again.

Pineau sat next to his unconscious body until a guard came and ordered him back to his cell. He looked back over his shoulder for his last sight of Moulin, stretched out unconscious on the courtyard bench.

A few days later, in Gestapo headquarters on the Avenue Foch in Paris, General Delestraint and Henri Aubry were brought into an interrogation room. Stretched out on a chaise longue against the wall of the room was the body of a man in a coma. It was Jean Moulin.

Still later, in a villa in Neuilly, resistant André Lassagne was taken into a room. There on a divan was, again, the body of Jean Moulin. He was still alive but only barely so. His head was covered in bandages. His face was yellow and drawn. He breathed feebly and did not say a word. Only his eyes told Lassagne that he was aware. It was the last time that any Frenchman saw Moulin alive.

Sometime early in July Moulin was transferred to Germany. He died either en route or shortly after arriving; the details are not known. His body was brought back to Paris, to the crematorium of Père-Lachaise, where his ashes were buried. In 1964, the ashes of Jean Moulin were transferred to the resting place of many of the heroes of France, the Panthéon. The oration was delivered by André Malraux, who called Jean Moulin "the champion of the people of the night."

General Delestraint was deported to Dachau and there he was shot dead by the SS, on April 19, 1945, just a few hours before the Americans liberated the death camp. The two men who had been arrested with him in Paris, Gastaldo and Theobald, had both been deported. Gastaldo came back from Mauthausen but died soon thereafter. Theobald escaped from camp and joined the French Expeditionary Force. Resistance fighters Colonel Schwartzfeld, Bruno Larat, and André Lassagne were all deported to Germany. Only Lassagne came back, but the former law professor lived on for only a few years, dying of the sufferings he had endured in concentration camp.

The man left in charge of the CNR, to his own dismay, was Claude Serreulles. He was only a week out of London, he had had only two talks with Moulin, and had only the sketchiest notions of what the CNR was.

Serreulles, having missed the meeting of June 21, turned up that evening for his dinner date with Aubrac; but Aubrac was in prison with Moulin and the others. Checking with comrades, Serreulles heard about the raids. A man of character, Serreulles rose to the occasion, taking charge as de Gaulle's delegate for France. He sent a telegram to London announcing the arrest of Moulin and the military chiefs. He said he was taking over for the moment while awaiting new instructions from General de Gaulle. Serreulles then informed the various services of the delegation that they were now under his orders. He sent messages to the principal movements of the northern and southern zones. In a rapid series of meetings, Serreulles introduced himself to the chiefs of the movements in the south and then left for Paris. He knew that Barbie had destroyed Lyon as the capital of the Resistance in the south.

The Gestapo moved to carry out a series of new arrests, mainly in the Lyon area. There they caught the chief of London's most effective escape network, the Brandy network.

One of the leaders of this network, who was away that day, was called Mary, which the French pronounce as though it were spelled Marie. His name is Raymond Basset, and he was not only efficient as an escape guide, but became one of France's most skilled saboteurs.

Colonel Basset today looks nothing like the killer and saboteur that he was in the Resistance. He is a white-haired, soft-spoken gentleman who sells religious ornaments, bracelets, and necklaces in a loft in an ancient building of the Marais, in Paris. This is the man who took a group of Englishmen across the Pyrénées with a Basque guide in the cold of winter. When he heard the barking of police dogs, realizing the guide was leading them to the Germans for a reward, he lifted up a rock, bashed the guide's head open, and then choked him so that his death rattle would not expose their position. Then, alone, he took his people over the mountains and down into Spain. The Spanish threw him into a lice-infested cell, from which the British rescued him. They sent him on to London and he promptly parachuted back to France.

The Brandy network was not the only one crippled by the Gestapo in the terrible summer of 1943. Several other networks were also hit by the Nazis, including some reporting to the Gaullist BCRAM and to the British SOE.

While the Resistance was struggling to survive the heavy blows dealt it by the Gestapo, and while Serreulles was trying to pull together the remnants of the leadership, awaiting instructions from de Gaulle on how to replace Moulin and Delestraint, General de Gaulle had committed his future to a critical political competition. He had decided that the time had come to meet the challenge put to him earlier that year by Roosevelt and Churchill and to go to North Africa for the ultimate test of strength with General Giraud and his American backers.

19
POWER STRUGGLES AMONG THE ALLIES

General de Gaulle had refused the Churchill-Roosevelt proposal of a marriage between himself and General Giraud, made at the Casablanca conference in January 1943. De Gaulle argued that he had been the leader of Free France and Fighting France since his first call for resistance. Giraud was a latecomer, a soldier with no political experience and no following in France beyond former officers of the Armistice Army. The Resistance was unanimously behind de Gaulle and he felt that he alone was the valid leader of Fighting France.

General Eisenhower, concentrating on the war against the German army in North Africa, did not want to be distracted by French political quarrels, so he asked de Gaulle after the conference in Casablanca not to come to Algeria until all fighting there had ended. Robert Murphy had strongly urged Eisenhower to take that position, hoping that by the time the Battle of Tunisia had ended he would have been able to consolidate Giraud's position as commander in chief of the French forces and bolster Giraud for the political struggle ahead with de Gaulle.

De Gaulle was willing to play that game, for he needed to give time to Jean Moulin, in the winter and spring of 1943, to unify and consolidate the Resistance behind him. He calculated that a unified Resistance committed to him would swing the balance against Giraud and be more effective than all the American pressures against him. He knew that the Americans and the British were actively planning to invade Hitler's Europe and that they would need the French Resistance at the moment of the landings. If the Resistance were solidly Gaullist, the Americans would have to recognize de Gaulle as the French leader.

The winter and spring of 1942–1943 was thus a time of infighting among all the Allied forces, while the war with the Axis was turning to the Allied advantage on the war fronts of Russia and the Pacific. Gaullists and Giraudists were waging their own war in North Africa, as well as a competition inside France between their secret services, while the BCRAM was trying simultaneously to be friendly with both the Americans and the British while opposing their directives on an almost daily basis.

Nobody was free of the political quarrels, not even the two close Allies, the Americans and the British.

General "Wild Bill" Donovan was eager for his OSS to take a major part in intelligence activities in Europe. But the British secret service wanted no interference from the Johnny-come-lately Yanks, whom they saw as a bunch of eager-beaver amateurs. The British secret service had centuries of history behind it; the Americans, they felt, were a "gaggle of giggling virgins eager to be ravished."

Some time before the landings in North Africa, Donovan had found exactly the right man to head up his intelligence operations in London: an American aristocrat named David Kirkpatrick Este Bruce. Bruce was the son of a United States senator and had served as a Democrat in the legislatures of Maryland and Virginia. A millionaire in his own right, Bruce was married to one of the world's richest women, Ailsa Mellon, the daughter of Andrew Mellon, multimillionaire steel magnate and former Republican secretary of the treasury. Tall, lean, elegant, a connoisseur of fine wines, a good squash player, socially prominent, Bruce was highly acceptable to the upper-class snobs who ran Whitehall and the British Establishment. At forty-four, Bruce was no amateur, no giggling virgin, but rather a handsome, cultured representative of America's upper classes. He was a good match for the British.

In 1941, Bruce had represented the American Red Cross in London. Donovan recruited him at that time and brought him back to Washington. In 1942, Bruce returned to London as chief of the OSS. With him were a group of American bankers and college professors whom Donovan had chosen and instructed to make every effort to get along with the British for initial training and then to set up their own Intelligence Service for Europe.

Getting along with the British was not the easiest of tasks, for the British did not always get along even with themselves. The Americans found at the outset that they were caught in the middle of a traditional rivalry between two British services: MI-5, responsible for counterintelligence in Britain and the Commonwealth, and MI-6, the Secret Intelligence Service (SIS), responsible for both espionage and counterintelligence outside British territory.

Two American rivals moved quickly to take positions in Britain. J. Edgar Hoover, head of the FBI, established liaison with MI-5 and let it be known that counterintelligence was his turf and he would abide no incursions from any other American service. Donovan moved just as promptly as Hoover to preempt MI-6 for his OSS. Bruce established excellent relations with the SIS and the chiefs of that service were delighted to work with Donovan, who, they felt, had enough clout with President Roosevelt to balance off Hoover and his allies in MI-5.

Bruce set up parallel structures to the British for better coordination. He staffed a section of OSS called SI, the American Secret Intelligence counterpart of Britain's SIS. The chief of SI was Dr. William Maddox, a professor of political science. He was assisted by Russell D'Oench, another upper-class American, grandson of the founder of the Grace Lines. They worked hand in glove with the British and resisted Donovan's urgent directives to create an independent American network of secret agents inside Europe. Maddox argued that nothing should be done to endanger the close, friendly relations with the British, who were highly experienced, had a complete, professional network in operation, and were supplying a mass of invaluable information to the Americans. The British, jealous of their prerogatives, were opposed to any autonomous, independent American network operating on the Continent in competition with—and perhaps at cross-purposes to—the British networks.

In theory, an agreement had already been reached at the turn of the year 1942–1943 between the British Special Operations Executive, SOE, and the OSS on relations with the Resistance networks and movements in occupied Europe. SOE–France had already angered de Gaulle and his services by setting up their own British resistance networks inside France, independent of de Gaulle's BCRAM.

Colonel Passy, partly to offset the British, partly because the Americans were enormously powerful and rich, set about early in 1943 to cultivate Bruce and Maddox. In a talk about that period in his beautiful Georgetown house in Washington, shortly before his death in 1978, David Bruce reminisced about the conflicts of the forties. "Passy did try hard to make good contacts with us. He knew that Washington and the American diplomats in Algiers were anti-Gaullists. He knew, too, that he was under attack, accused of running a torture-chamber in the cellar of his headquarters in Duke Street. All kinds of lurid accusations were flying about—not a word of truth in them. Maddox and I were only too pleased to deal with him. After all, American troops would someday—soon, we hoped—be sent in to France to drive Hitler out, and we would need close and good relations with the French."

Bruce went over to the silver bucket where wine was cooling. He twirled the bottle, tested its temperature, then came back to his chair to continue his recollections. "Stewart Menzies, chief of MI-6, a professional soldier, was favorably disposed toward us, but his deputy, Claude Dansey, a crusty old curmudgeon who could not stand any interference or rivalry from the Americans—indeed, we could hardly do anything right in old Claude's eyes—was absolutely livid about Passy cozying up to the Yanks. He did everything he could—and it was quite a bit—to sabotage our relationship and our plans to set up American teams for France."

Donovan's Special Operations Branch, known as SO, since SOB seemed not exactly a comfortable acronym, was determined to avoid this kind of friction in its dealings with British SOE. However, the SO inherited the SOE's conflicts with Passy and the Gaullists. They would have liked to bypass the Gaullists or hold them down and control them, but the growth of the Resistance inside France in numbers, experience, and combativeness made it the major force inside the country. It was daily more and more apparent that Moulin was succeeding in consolidating the Resistance movements behind de Gaulle.

Jean Moulin and General Delestraint had made this clear to the British and Americans on their visit to London in February 1943. They needed Allied support, Allied funds, arms and coordination; they needed it now and would need it even more importantly when the hour of invasion would strike. But they insisted that the Allies stop meddling in French politics and finally accept the fact that it was de Gaulle and not Giraud who was supported inside France and with whom they would have to deal on planning the invasion. Their success later in France in firming up a Secret Army and a National Council of the Resistance (CNR) gave substance to their arguments.

General de Gaulle, strengthened by the support of the unified Resistance, decided early in May that the time had come for him to go to Algiers and begin his campaign to compete on the spot, man to man, with Giraud.

At the end of May, when fighting had ended on the North African fronts, General de Gaulle flew to Algiers. At that very moment at the Trident Conference being held in Washington, the Combined Chiefs of Staffs of the Allies took their first decision on the date for an Allied invasion of occupied France. They thought it might be possible to launch the invasion as early as May 1944. Bruce and Stewart Menzies, head of MI-6, informed of the plans for Overlord, the code name of the invasion of Europe, realized that they had to move swiftly to end Allied competition and set up a coordinated Allied intelligence service. On May 29, Menzies offered Bruce and the OSS a full partnership in European espionage operations in preparation for Allied landings in France.

On that same May 29, by an unhappy coincidence, Allied planes struck at German installations in Rennes, one of the principal cities of Brittany, killing more than two hundred local French citizens. Allied bombings in France were one of the most controversial and frustrating dilemmas of the war. The French would cheer Allied bomber fleets flying overhead on their way to hit Berlin, Dusseldorf, and other enemy targets in Germany. They also cheered when Allied planes struck at German naval fortifications and submarine bases on the Channel and Atlantic coasts, for the French knew that the Anglo-Americans had to destroy or weaken those bases if they were ever successfully to invade Hitler's fortress in Europe to liberate France. However, when Allied planes hit population centers like Rennes and Paris, even when there were German installations there, the loss of innocent French lives made the operations seem too costly for the value of the targets. Most importantly, the French bitterly resented Voice of America broadcasts praising the accuracy of "precision bombing" of American planes. Precision bombing was a propaganda phrase, not a reality. It did not fool the Germans, who knew how often our high-flying planes missed their targets, and it did not fool the French, whose list of victims of precision bombing was long and bloody.

On May 30, General de Gaulle, accompanied by French National Council Commissioners André Philip and René Massigli, arrived in Algiers. At the Cinéma Majestic, which had been rented for the occasion by his supporters, de Gaulle made a public appearance. Thousands of Frenchmen and women massed inside and outside the theater, waving French flags with de Gaulle's Cross of Lorraine sewed on. It was an impressive demonstration of popular support and it sent a message to Robert Murphy, who was still backing General Giraud and was still determined to hold de Gaulle's influence to a minimum.

On that day the War Department in Washington announced that United States armed forces totaled almost seven million men. By mid-May, when all fighting ended, the Allies under General Eisenhower had taken more than two hundred and ninety thousand German prisoners in North Africa. General Douglas MacArthur was appointed supreme commander for combined operations in the Pacific.

Although Murphy wanted to contain de Gaulle as much as possible, he knew that he could not exclude him from at least sharing power with Giraud. The support of the French people in France and of a number of officers in North Africa could not be ignored. On June 3, after only a few days of conferences in Algiers, a general agreement was reached for the constitution of a Comité Français de Libération Nationale (CFLN), a "single, central French power exercising sovereignty over all the territories outside of enemy occupation."

Co-presidents of the CFLN were Charles de Gaulle and Henri Giraud. From this point on, the co-presidents would engage in a daily contest to win dominance one over the other. Despite powerful support for Giraud from the Americans, it was not much of a contest. Giraud was simply no match for de Gaulle in brains, political perception, and determination. It would not take de Gaulle many weeks to demonstrate to all the members of the CFLN that he was their best bet to stand up to the Allies and restore an independent French Republic.

The members of the CFLN were men destined to play a major role in French life for the next ten years and more. They were Maurice Couve de Murville, finance commissioner, a future foreign minister and prime minister of France; Jean Monnet, commissioner of armaments, the future "Mr. Europe," creator of the Common Market; René Mayer, commissioner of communications, another future prime minister; René Pleven, commissioner of the colonies, future prime minister; René Massigli, commissioner for foreign affairs, future minister and parliamentary leader; and André Philip, commissioner of labor, another future minister of the Fourth Republic of France.

The later careers of these men demonstrated that General de Gaulle and the men around him in London and Algiers had received the political training and experience that enabled them to become the men who ruled France. The leaders of the Resistance inside France, living in the shadows underground, could not match them in a free, open arena. As commissioners in Algiers, the members learned their trade as ministers of an embryonic government. Resistance leaders learned how to fight and survive in a struggle against a foreign enemy, not in the political warfare of a democracy. There were exceptions, of course. Georges Bidault, a Resistance leader, became foreign minister and prime minister of the Fourth Republic. But most of the leaders of the Resistance movements either did not seek or could not win political power. That was the name of the game played in London and Algiers.

A famous power player came from London to Algiers on June 4 to play the game: Winston Churchill. A week earlier, Churchill had been in Washington conferring with President Roosevelt on plans for the assault on Hitler's Fortress Europa, the long-awaited second front. Russia, having suffered more than four million casualties in its desperate battles with the Nazi armies, had long been demanding a second front in Europe to draw off troops from the eastern to the western front. A powerful pro-Russian lobby in the United States, sympathetic to the valiant Red Army, particularly after its heroic and spectacular victory at Stalingrad, was putting Roosevelt under heavy pressure on the second front issue.

Churchill was exerting pressure of his own, with all his eloquent powers of persuasion, for a second front, not on the Normandy coast of France, the most direct route to Germany, the most logical place for the invasion, but rather in Italy. Churchill and his military spokesmen kept talking to reporters and to American leaders about the "soft underbelly of Europe." Those of us in the Allied armies, who were soon to be sent into Italy only to run into the series of almost insurmountable mountain barriers, a deadly obstacle course to any south-north advance, learned to curse Churchill and his "soft underbelly." But, toward the end of May 1943, he persuaded Roosevelt to go ahead, beginning first with the invasion of the island of Sicily, a major stepping stone toward Europe's "soft underbelly."

Having convinced Roosevelt to invade Italy, Churchill flew to Algiers on June 4 to see the man who would command the troops for the invasion of Europe, General Dwight D. Eisenhower. And, while there, Churchill decided to do what he could to bring to heel General de Gaulle, whose rivalry with Giraud and conflicts with Murphy were causing Churchill considerable concern. Eisenhower had complained to Churchill about his "protégé" de Gaulle, and so had Roosevelt. Since it was Churchill who had first recognized de Gaulle and supported him with money and arms, the Americans felt that he ought to be the one to discipline him and force him to cooperate with Allied directives and purposes.

According to a report sent to Washington by Robert Murphy (on file in the OSS archives as R&A report 1172) Churchill gave de Gaulle a verbal lashing in the presence of General Giraud. Churchill told de Gaulle flatly, all but ordering him to obey, that he must reach an understanding with the Americans and work loyally with them. General Giraud, Churchill said, had already reached such an agreement and it was imperative for de Gaulle to do the same.

De Gaulle told Churchill that he would, of course, cooperate loyally with all his allies, including the Americans, on all questions except those affecting French sovereignty and the interests of France. De Gaulle did not make the mistake of telling Churchill specifically what those questions might be, for any list would be limiting or subject to interpretation. De Gaulle knew exactly what he meant: Like any other leader—like Churchill himself, or Roosevelt or Stalin—he and his French associates would determine for themselves the interests of France. France, said de Gaulle, had a right and a duty to defend her high interests at all times against all threats. Churchill sighed deeply. He knew he could not force de Gaulle to do anything that the French general felt was incompatible with French interests and honor. Deep within him Churchill, as fiercely chauvinistic an Englishman as de Gaulle was a Frenchman, understood and sympathized with de Gaulle.

In mid-June, Supreme Commander Eisenhower called de Gaulle and Giraud into conference to explain to them his concern that a divided, quarreling French command would lead to insecurity in North Africa and to problems for French participation in the liberation campaign in Europe. He told the French generals that he assumed they would want the reconstituted divisions of the French army that had been fighting valiantly under General Juin in Tunisia to participate in the invasion of Italy and ultimately, of course, in the liberation of France. This would not be possible, Eisenhower made clear, unless there were a united, coherent French command. He asked them to work it out and to give him their assurances that there would be no important changes in the French command in North Africa.

De Gaulle and Giraud went into conference together after their meeting with Eisenhower on June 19. They knew the American general was right, and right or wrong, he was the supreme commander and the sole supplier of their weapons. They would have to meet his demands. They rapidly agreed to share the command of French troops. Giraud would be in charge of the French troops in North Africa, mostly led by conservative, ex-Vichy, anti-de Gaulle officers. De Gaulle would command all other French forces in the empire and in England. It was not exactly the united command that Eisenhower had asked for, but if they agreed to cooperate in their commands it ought to satisfy the supreme commander. Eisenhower, in fact, was not happy with their decision, but he felt that at that moment a truce between the quarreling French generals was better than nothing. He was determined to force the French into a single, unified command before assigning any important objectives to French divisions.

Eisenhower's orders to the two French generals did not have the result that the Americans had been hoping for, although at first it looked as though Giraud had stolen a march on de Gaulle. Giraud began concentrating on his duties as commander in chief of French forces in North Africa. It seemed to him and to his advisers that the armed forces were a key power base.

General de Gaulle, with his more subtle understanding of the power game, knew that at that moment the only real military power in North Africa was being wielded by Eisenhower. Eisenhower would use French troops but under his command only. Giraud would be a subordinate officer to the supreme commander. De Gaulle also understood that in the long range the ultimate prize is political leadership. In a democracy the political power, not the military power, is supreme. So de Gaulle concentrated on his duties as co-president of the CFLN, the embryonic government of France.

Slowly, steadily, ineluctably, General de Gaulle began to emerge as the sole political leader of Fighting France. General Giraud, who did not understand and actively disliked politics, stopped coming to CFLN meetings. He spoke derisively of being bored by questions of garbage disposal and post office deliveries, subjects that had come up at one of the early meetings he attended. So he stopped coming.

General de Gaulle attended every meeting and insisted on being addressed as "Monsieur le Président," his correct title at such meetings. Gradually all the commissioners began to think of him as the president of France. It soon became apparent to those of us working at headquarters in Algiers that in fact, if not yet officially, General de Gaulle was the sole president of the French Committee of National Liberation, with Giraud functioning as commander of the North African armed forces.

There were important developments on all fronts in that summer of 1943. The Germans, trying to rally from their defeats in Russia, launched a counteroffensive all along the eastern front in the first days of July. The newly confident and battle-toughened Soviet troops stopped the offensive with small gains and heavy German losses. There was no longer any doubt that the Germans had long since passed their high-water mark in Russia and that the Nazi tide was receding.

On July 10 the Allies landed in Sicily, first step toward the invasion and liberation of Europe. Roosevelt sent a message to Pope Pius XII, assuring him that the Allies intended to restore human rights to the people of Italy and destroy the evil Fascist regime. Roosevelt and Churchill sent a joint message to that effect to the Italian people, asking them whether they wanted to continue to die for Mussolini and Hitler, or were ready to take steps "to live for Italy and for civilization." It was a clear call for insurrection against Mussolini. Hitler, alarmed, rushed to meet with Mussolini in Verona on July 19, while Allied planes struck heavily at the marshaling yards of Rome.

In London in early August, General Giraud, on a tour of Allied capitals, consulted with Anthony Eden and Winston Churchill.

Henri Frenay was still in London, trying to get the British to clear a seat for him on a plane to Algiers, where he could confer with de Gaulle. While waiting to see de Gaulle, Frenay was delighted to get an opportunity to talk with Giraud. Giraud had just returned from a trip to Washington, where he had conferred with American military men on the needs of the French army, and had filled them in on his rivalry with de Gaulle. Roosevelt was still hoping that Giraud would prove to be a noble alternative to de Gaulle. Murphy's reports continued to encourage that belief, but FDR detected a less confident tone in his envoy's messages, and was reading other dispatches from some of Donovan's OSS agents who had come to believe that Giraud was a limited soldier and de Gaulle a true leader. The pendulum of power was beginning to swing to de Gaulle. Frenay was one of a number of Resistance leaders in London to whom Giraud granted a joint audience. He noted down the details of the meeting and described it in his memoirs.

"Like a sergeant looking over a bunch of rookies, he asked us our names, one by one, then shook our hands. Sitting very erect on the edge of an armchair, talking to everyone and to no one in particular, he said, 'Gentlemen, you have requested to see me. Why?'

"We told him how disappointed we were that de Gaulle had had to wait so long to go to Algiers. We pointed out that the CNR resolution had stated that de Gaulle was to take over the provisional government, and that he, Giraud, only the high command of the armed forces. Moreover, we knew that he had gone to Washington to procure arms for the divisions being levied in North Africa. Hence it seemed opportune to mention the scarcity of arms afflicting the Resistance.

" 'Arms, is it? Well, gentlemen, they are not indispensable, you know. One can get along without them.'

"We looked at one another dumbfounded.

"The general continued: 'Gentlemen, what is of the essence in modern warfare? Of course! Air power. If you can neutralize enemy air power, you immediately have the upper hand. And what do you need to neutralize an airfield? Pebbles!'

"We thought we had heard wrong, but no, the general continued his oration: 'To obstruct a hangar's sliding door and stop its aircraft from exiting all you need is a pebble. With another pebble you can block a plane's air shaft, causing it to turn over when it tries to land.'

"With the self-satisfaction of a nightclub magician, Giraud rose and concluded: 'You see, gentlemen, one can make war even without weapons!'

"And this was the man who was going to command our armies!"

Frenay and his friends could never quite decide whether Giraud was mocking them, putting them down, or whether he was quite mad. He had that effect on many who came into contact with him during some of his zanier moods.

Frenay, contemptuous of Giraud and his performance, became ever more committed to de Gaulle as the hope of a new, strong France. He renewed his pleas to the British for passage to Algiers and enlisted the help of Passy, who felt Frenay could help de Gaulle put down Giraud and his American backers. Passy had excellent connections with the British, and Frenay, at last, flew off to Algiers.

He met de Gaulle in his modest headquarters at the Villa Les Glycines. General Giraud had been installed by Murphy in the sumptuous Summer Palace, but the outward signs of superiority hid the reality of the power situation. It was de Gaulle, in his modest headquarters, who was already presiding over meetings of the National Committee, the CFLN.

Frenay told de Gaulle that relations "between your services and the Resistance are very bad." He explained that the Resistance was not receiving the funds and the arms it needed to continue to keep on fighting. As always, Frenay blamed this on Moulin. De Gaulle told him that he had received Moulin's report on this issue and on Frenay's getting funds from the Americans. De Gaulle told Frenay that he did not at all like Frenay's solution of "knocking on the Americans' door." He said: "They welcomed you only because they believed they could circumvent de Gaulle."

Frenay protested that this was untrue and that Allen Dulles and the Americans had not put any political pressure upon him and his envoys in Switzerland.

De Gaulle waved aside his protestations and told Frenay to be patient, that he would read his reports and proposals and meet him again to discuss them. Meanwhile, de Gaulle warned Frenay to be careful in Algiers. "This place is pestilential. Vichy and the Americans are still toying with that poor devil Giraud."

De Gaulle, despite his quarrels with Frenay, recognized the man's patriotism, courage, and extraordinary leadership in the Resistance. He called Frenay back to a meeting with his comrades of the Combat group in Algiers, and decorated him with the Cross of the Liberation, recognizing him as a "Compagnon de la Libération" of France, "in honor and through victory."

A few days later, at a meeting at Les Glycines, Frenay renewed his request for more money, arms, and a voice for the Resistance in the councils of Fighting France. To his relief and delight, General de Gaulle nodded his head and said that he believed it would be most useful to have some kind of a Resistance organization with whom his people could consult easily on a daily basis. De Gaulle did have his delegation in France, cooperating with the CNR. But radio transmissions between Algiers and London with France were slow and subject to breakdowns and sunspot static. De Gaulle was also baiting a well-camouflaged trap for the troublesome Frenay. By granting him his own organization, appealing to his ego, he would be keeping him outside of France, clearing the field for his own agents in the Resistance.

Frenay jumped for the bait and into the trap. He promptly proposed that a new consultative Resistance organization be set up in London, for that is where Passy and the BCRAM were still located, as well as the American and British secret services and governmental bodies in charge of treasury and armaments. De Gaulle agreed to this proposal. De Gaulle, however, warned Frenay that he was still unhappy about his delegation in Switzerland working with the Americans. "Whether you know it or not, it enables the Americans to get a wedge between us. You don't see what they're up to, but I do. Believe me, it's no thanks to them that I'm here in this office right now. Have you read the terms in which they recognized the CFLN?"

General de Gaulle was alluding to the fact that, a few days earlier the Soviet Union, alone among the Allied powers, had granted de Gaulle's CFLN full recognition as representing "the interests of state of the French Republic." The British had only recognized the CFLN as "the administrator of those territories that recognize its authority." They had, however, added an important clause, vital to de Gaulle, that the "CFLN is the organism qualified to conduct the French war effort." The Americans had held de Gaulle to the bare minimum possible, recognizing his committee only as "the administrator of territories that accepted its authority."

To the very bitter end the American government refused to grant General de Gaulle and the French National Committee any semblance of governmental authority. Washington kept insisting piously that only the French people, in freedom, after liberation, could bestow governmental authority on its leader—a somewhat sanctimonious policy that Washington did not bother to espouse in other cases when it would endow a dictator with all the authority, money, and arms he wanted. To this very day, the bitterness in French-American relations engendered by the conflicts between American officials and de Gaulle has never been fully dissipated.

Marie-Madeleine Fourcade, aware that Allied dissension was harmful to her cause, decided the time had come for her to join other Resistance leaders in London, in July 1943. She had been reluctant to leave her network even temporarily until she could find someone reliable to take her place. Commandant Léon Faye, Eagle, most qualified to do so, was busy in operational activities and did not want to assume the administrative burdens of network leadership. The Noah's Ark network had been badly hit and hurt by the Gestapo, as had the other movements. Faye was anxious for Marie-Madeleine to go to London to ask the British for arms and funds. He was also worried that Marie-Madeleine's luck would finally run out, as it did for almost everyone after a time.

Marie-Madeleine presided over a meeting of a dozen of her network comrades in Paris on July 16, two days before she was scheduled to leave for London. Eagle had been to Algiers, had seen Giraud and de Gaulle, and reported that they had reached a viable agreement. De Gaulle, Faye said, would handle the provisional government and Giraud would remain commander in chief of the French army, "which was really his only ambition." This was the arrangement demanded by the Resistance, which was working out in practice but was not yet official. Faye was premature in his report. Giraud had proposed that the Alliance network be "militarized," that is given military status and brought under his command. Faye had agreed personally and said he would put it to Marie-Madeleine and their comrades on his return to France. They all agreed to be "at the disposal" of the French military command—a vague term—while being loyal to de Gaulle in everything that involved politics. The Alliance network, however, would continue to serve the British but as a French network, integrated into the Allied command. With great tact and skill, Marie-Madeleine worked out successfully her delicate relationships with de Gaulle, Giraud, and the British. In practice, she continued to transmit information to the British.

The "animals" arranged to give Marie-Madeleine a farewell party at a fashionable bar in Paris run by Bernard de Billy, who worked closely with the Alliance. They sat on velvet banquettes in the midst of high-ranking German officers and officials, "the stuffiest, most affected of Germans, monocles screwed tightly in their eyes," Marie-Madeleine recalled in her memoirs. While sitting with the Germans, they greeted Jean Sainteny, Dragon, who arrived with his pockets stuffed with messages. They gave the messages to one of Marie-Madeleine's agents, Chinchilla, who left the bar, mounted her bicycle, and delivered the messages to their clandestine radio operators.

Eagle took Marie-Madeleine for a farewell walk along the Champs-Elysées, "in the golden haze at the end of the lovely day." Marie-Madeleine looked around her and breathed deeply of "the air, no longer polluted by traffic, sweet with the smell of leaves on the trees." The unaccustomed drinks "had induced a state of euphoria. We stopped at the Arc de Triomphe to look at the most beautiful view in the world. I gave the capital a big, conspiratorial good-bye smile; it answered with a scowl—the swastika flags cracking like whips in the twilight breeze."

On the morning of July 18, Marie-Madeleine did some last-minute shopping. Her plane was due to arrive at midnight. "Ant," her bodyguard, would pick her up at five in the afternoon at the corner of the Rue François Ier in a bicycle-taxi he had hired.

Marie-Madeleine got into the bicycle-taxi on schedule, and as it rounded the rond-point of the Champs-Elysées, she saw a hunchback staring at her with glittering eyes. It was her faithful Eagle, wishing her farewell.

The bicycle-taxi took her to the Gare de l'Est, where a faithful comrade, "Armadillo," was waiting. He would return to London with her, along with "Jack Tar," another of her most trusted agents.

They took the train to Nanteuil-le-Haudouin, where they were to meet a Dr. Gilbert, who would drive them to the rendezvous site.

The moon was full and bright as Dr. Gilbert drove them to the field to await their plane.

Then they heard it, "like a large, sputtering motorcycle." One of the agents, with a flashlight, sent out the Morse signal, M-M-M-. The Lysander flashed back R-R-R- with its position lights. The plane swooped in, a giant blackbird silhouetted against the moon. It taxied down the field and swung around into takeoff position. The rear cockpit opened up and three men shot out of it, hauling their luggage with them. They were "Petrel" and two new radio operators, "Nightingale" and "Stork," who had come up from Algiers to London and now to France. There was just time for Marie-Madeleine to hug them all and then she piled into the Lysander with Armadillo and Jack Tar. The door slammed shut and the Lysander began to roll for takeoff. Marie-Madeleine checked her watch. The entire operation, from landing to takeoff, had taken seven minutes, hugs and all. They were only twenty-five miles from Paris, in the middle of the German occupation. A few hours later and they were all in London.

Marie-Madeleine soon found herself embroiled in the political conflicts of London. Passy and the BCRAM criticized her and her network for sending their information directly to the British instead of to the Gaullists. Had the Gaullists received it first, they could have used it as a lever on the British. Marie-Madeleine had to remind them that Loustaunau-Lacau had originally been willing to work with de Gaulle but that de Gaulle had refused his collaboration. Then Marie-Madeleine discovered that the British were turning over all her network's intelligence information to General Giraud's secret service. When she asked "Uncle" Claude Dansey about it, she was told that, of course, the British had an exchange agreement with the French military, and Giraud was the commander in chief. Marie-Madeleine recalls how furious she was "to have our network, with all the dangers we were facing, all the men we were losing being used in a political power struggle." She was not hostile to Giraud, but she knew her messages were being used to build Giraud against de Gaulle and she wanted no part in that kind of game.

No one enjoyed the bitter political rivalries that set ally against ally, resistant against resistant, but the fight for power went on, not only in London and Algiers, but inside France, parallel to the fight against Vichy and the Germans.

20
NEW LEADERS
FOR THE RESISTANCE

Claude Serreulles was facing a tremendous challenge. The two top chiefs of the Resistance, General Delestraint and Jean Moulin, had to be replaced urgently. He must also substitute someone at the head of Railway-Sabotage for René Hardy, who was on the run and suspected of treason. Moulin's work in forging a united Resistance had been on the verge of success when he was captured, and it could all disintegrate rapidly now unless new leaders were found. That was more easily decided than accomplished.

Jean Moulin had worn three leadership hats at once: As president of the newly formed Conseil National de la Résistance (CNR) inside France, as member of the Conseil National Français (CNF) in London, and as de Gaulle's personal envoy in France. It seemed obvious to Serreulles that no one, not he nor anyone else, could replace Moulin in those three functions, or, indeed, in more than any one of them. Serreulles felt that the Gestapo arrests of Resistance leaders required a complete review and restructuring of the Resistance in its relationships both inside and outside of France.

First of all it required that he, as de Gaulle's man on the spot, make himself known to all the Resistance leaders in the north and south, and make certain that they remain loyal to de Gaulle and willing to follow his directives. This was an enormously difficult task for a young delegate inexperienced in the field and virtually unknown.

As a first step, Serreulles met with the leaders of Combat. In July 1943, in the absence of Henri Frenay, Combat was being run by Claude Bourdet. No one then suspected that weeks and months would go by and that Frenay would not return to France. Instead he would become deeply involved with the challenge of creating an independent French government. He finally accepted an appointment in de Gaulle's Cabinet, leaving Combat to be run by Bourdet, Pierre de Bénouville, and others. Frenay's absence was a bit of good luck for Serreulles, for Frenay, with his outsize ego, would have been almost impossible to deal with on any basis other than his own succession to Moulin. Bourdet and the others were more reasonable and flexible, more interested in uniting Resistance efforts than in their own leadership ambitions. Bourdet and de Bénouville readily agreed to accept Serreulles as interim chairman of the comité directeur of the MUR, one of the organs of the CNR, which Moulin had headed.

With Jean-Pierre Lévy and d'Astier de la Vigerie both still in London, their movements, Franc-Tireur and Libération, were headed temporarily by their associates. For Libération the key men were Pascal Copeau and young Pierre Hervé. Both of these men were impatient with the many quarrels provoked by Frenay and anxious to get on with the main mission of unifying their movements and preparing for the Allied landings. For Franc-Tireur the acting chief was Claudius-Petit, working closely with Antoine Avinin and Georges Altman. All of them appreciated the difficulty and urgency of the task that Serreulles was undertaking and endorsed him as the interim head of the Mouvements Unifiés de la Résistance, MUR.

"Although all went well in the south, where I met with the sympathy and help of all the Resistance leaders, I ran into a very different situation when I went north to meet with the leaders in Paris," Serreulles recalls today. The first challenge to Serreulles in the north came when he learned that the Resistance leaders there had sent messages to the three acting chiefs in the south, to Bourdet, Copeau, and Claudius-Petit, asking them to come to Paris to meet in common with their Coordinating Committee. They knew perfectly well that they were undercutting Serreulles. This was deliberate, for many of them had only accepted most grudgingly the creation of the CNR and the appointment of Jean Moulin to head that Resistance council. Having opposed Moulin, they were in no way reluctant to challenge his young, untried assistant.

From the very first days of the Resistance, in 1940, the men who created movements in the northern zone, under German occupation, at great personal risk, had resented de Gaulle and the men in London, who, they felt, had run away from France to join Allied forces. They felt that a true patriot should stay in France and fight the Nazi occupation of the motherland.

Serreulles accepted the challenge thrown at him. He sent out a message, in his function as president of the comité directeur, canceling a meeting that had been scheduled by the eight principal national movements. He called for another meeting, a day later and at a different address, at which he would preside as chairman. He was throwing his own challenge to the opposition, daring them to oppose openly the authority of his position. Unwilling to challenge him on the purely procedural question of where and when a meeting would be held and under whose chairmanship, they obeyed Serreulles's summons to a meeting of his own choosing.

Sitting in the chair at the meeting, Serreulles was able to steer the discussion along lines he had prepared in advance and had coordinated with the men he knew to be loyal to himself and de Gaulle. He stressed the importance of participating in the Allied landings, when only a completely unified French national force could maintain the independence of France and prevent Allied dominance of French affairs. Serreulles, a flexible and reasonable man, also knew that to maintain his basic principles and avoid a split he would have to yield on some points and help save the face of the northern leaders who had demanded the creation of their own Central Committee, parallel to the CNR directorate.

"It seemed to me," Serreulles explained, "that I could let them have their Central Committee in name and form, if I could keep the substance of authority in the control of the CNR and de Gaulle's delegation. I, therefore, agreed, to their relief, to the formation of a Central Committee. The Central Committee's mission would be to coordinate actions and activities that had been carried out in a disparate fashion in the north and in the south as a result of the years in which there had been a demarcation line between the zones. Now that there was no demarcation line, the zones had to disappear and a truly united, national Resistance function as such. With these views accepted and endorsed by all the chiefs present at the meeting, the Central Committee came into existence without splitting up the Resistance, but rather as a part of its unity."

Despite these internal power struggles, the war against the enemy was being fought successfully on all fronts. Every day German troops in France came under attack from Resistance forces, most particularly in Paris, where the Communist Francs-Tireurs et Partisans Français and the independent Jewish Partisans of Abraham Lissner were active in daily "terrorist" assaults, as their actions were characterized by the Gestapo and the collaborationist French press and radio. In the first week of June, six truckloads of German soldiers were attacked by Jewish Partisans armed with hand grenades. Partisans also attacked five marching groups of German soldiers in the streets of Paris. They threw grenades through the windows of German clubs and German military cinemas. One band of armed Jews cut off both ends of a street running into the Avenue de la Grande Armée, trapped a column of two dozen German soldiers in it, and then opened fire from doorways and rooftops, cutting the German column to ribbons.

Other armed Jews were active in central and southern France. Jacques Lazarus, known in the Resistance as Captain Jacquel, made contact with the Jewish Boy Scouts, the Eclaireurs Israélites de France, and their chief, "Castor." Until the summer of 1943, the Scouts had been active mainly in social work, helping supply food, money, and medical services to Jews. They then developed a successful system of forging false papers and establishing escape routes and safe-houses for Jews, working often with Catholic convents and anti-German priests. In the summer of 1943, the Scouts formed their first military units, which were incorporated, with the aid of Captain Jacquel, into the *Armée Juive*, the Jewish army, known as the AJ. The AJ formed a Scout maquis in a woods outside the village of La Malquière, near Vabre in south-central France. Its leader was known as Commandant Roger.

Jacquel and a brave young Jewish militant named Gilbert Bloch, who was killed in a fire fight with the Germans on August 8, 1944, were most active in 1943 setting up and training Jewish maquis groups. They also organized the first young Jewish paramilitary Scout group in Limoges, and a system of convoys to help Jews escape to Spain across the Pyrénées. More than five hundred Jews were saved from deportation to Germany by the armed convoys of the AJ and the Jewish Partisans.

Vichy and the Nazis, enraged by Jewish resistance, heightened their anti-Semitic terror and repression. On June 27, 1943, the *Vichy Journal* published a decree annulling all naturalizations of Jews in France since August 10, 1927. The chief of the Vichy Jewish Affairs Office, Darquier de Pellepoix, estimated that some one hundred thousand French Jews would lose their citizenship as a result of that decree. He also announced that at least one hundred thousand other Jews had emigrated from France since the defeat in 1940 and predicted that France "would solve its Jewish problem by eliminating the Jew."

Jewish partisans in Paris opened fire on German troops and shot Wehrmacht General Abt. They also derailed three German troop trains north of Paris. Captain Jacquel organized a group of Jewish resistants to raid arms arsenals and set up arms caches in the woods of the Cévennes in central France for the use of Jewish maquis groups. Himself a former captain of the French army, he began training young Jews in the use of weapons and in tactics, in preparation for joining forces with other maquis groups to harass the Germans and cut their communications as soon as the Allies would land in France.

One of the most effective of the Resistance groups in the summer of 1943, and the one that would prove most helpful to the Allies after the landings, were the Resistance teams of the SNCF, the Société Nationale des Chemins de Fer, the nationalized railways. They were known simply as the *cheminots,* the rail workers, and their movement as Résistance-Fer. Professional technicians ran this group separately from the similar group that had been headed by René Hardy but had lost effectiveness with his fall from grace. The *cheminots* provided the Allies and their Resistance comrades with invaluable, constant information on all German rail transport of men and matériel. Dispatchers of the SNCF knew what cars were carrying troops, or weapons, or medical supplies, gold or plundered art—anything the Nazis were sending back to Germany or into France. *Cheminots* were told which trains to derail, and often other Resistance groups would be called in to haul away the loot from the wrecked cars.

The *cheminots* were mainly members of Communist or Socialist unions and parties. Two or three men would walk the rails, as though checking the bolts, part of their duties. When advised by Resistance patrols that no French police or Germans were near, they would unscrew the bolts and lift out a section of rail. They had been informed by dispatchers of the exact time that a German train was due. They did not want to wreck innocent French passenger trains.

Sometimes the Germans, knowing that the *cheminots* tried to sabotage only their trains, hooked up their supply or troop cars to French passenger cars. The *cheminots* soon caught on. Rail experts would time a train's movements and call ahead to tell the saboteurs how long it took for the French cars to pass a given strip. Then, instead of unbolting the rails, special teams of sappers would plant dynamite under the tracks, with a carefully timed fuse attached. They became expert in setting off the charges as soon as the French cars had passed over their dynamite. There were so many miles of track that it was impossible for the Germans to patrol them all.

The success of the rail sabotage was so great that it became known as the Bataille du Rail. The railways had truly become a battlefield. By the time the Allies landed on the beaches of Normandy, almost two thirds of the railway system in the region had been sabotaged and was almost useless to the German army.

The leaders of the Resistance movements were aware of the risks their men and women were running and were determind to provide them and their families all the help they needed and merited. They set up commissions on food, supplies, medical services, and kept up a stream of urgent demands for funds and for arms. Claude Serreulles, sensitive to their needs and frustrations, knew how far removed Fighting France in Algiers and London was from those actually doing the fighting in the streets of Paris, Lyon, and Marseille.

Serreulles did everything he could to meet the legitimate needs of the movements, but also took care to maintain the authority of the provisional government of Algiers. There could be only one Executive power and it had to be de Gaulle, with the CNR loyal to him, not to the Comité Central of the Resistance movements. It was, therefore, imperative to find the right man as the new leader of the CNR to replace Jean Moulin. Serreulles had already decided that he could not be both the envoy of de Gaulle's CFLN and the head of the CNR.

"I knew that the true spirit and purpose of the CNR was for it to be the emanation, the very essence of the Resistance. It seemed to me that it could only be the true organ of expression of the Resistance if its chief was a man from the Resistance movements and not a man from London. And it had to be someone whom the leaders of the Resistance would elect themselves, not someone appointed by London or Algiers.

"I sent a number of messages to both London and Algiers to apprise Passy, Interior Commissioner André Philip, and General de Gaulle of my thinking. I never received a reply to any of my messages. I had to go ahead, make the decision and carry it out on my own.

"It soon became apparent to me that the ideal man to head

up the CNR was Georges Bidault. For almost a year, Bidault had worked closely and loyally with Jean Moulin. Moulin had chosen him as chief of the Bureau d'Information et de Presse. Bidault had worked for the Catholic paper *L'Aube* before the war. A lycée teacher of history, he was a liberal Christian Democrat, politically on the crossroads of the right and left political parties and movements of France. He was well known and liked in political circles but was not a professional politician. He had joined the Resistance early, as a militant in the ranks of both Combat and Front National, making him acceptable to both Frenay and the Communists, no mean stunt. I was certain that Bidault could win a majority of votes and provoke a minimum of frictions or jealousies."

Early in July, Serreulles began "talking up" Bidault to be the new president of the Conseil National de la Résistance. Bidault recalls the moment vividly today. In a talk in his apartment near the Etoile, Georges Bidault said: "It had never entered my mind that I might be called upon to head the CNR and I was astonished when friends began calling to tell me that Serreulles was 'electioneering' for me. I was honored and flattered and also a bit frightened. It was a grave responsibility, particularly at that moment, at the height of the de Gaulle-Giraud rivalry in Algiers. Also, the Resistance had been hard hit by the Gestapo and I knew we would have a very difficult time reorganizing and preparing for our maximum effort at the time of the Allied landings. If the others thought that I could lead them in that effort, I was willing to accept the challenge." Finally, in September, Bidault was elected president of the Conseil National de la Résistance.

During this period, Serreulles met d'Astier de la Vigerie, who had just returned from London and Algiers. He informed Serreulles that General de Gaulle had decided to create a Consultative Assembly in Algiers, as an embryonic House of Parliament for liberated France. Serreulles was astonished. Not a word had been sent to him from Algiers advising him of this important decision. Serreulles felt that a Consultative Assembly would be invalid unless there was a strong contingent that came from the Resistance movements inside France. So, on his own initiative, he began drawing up lists and consulting with Resistance leaders on the designation of representatives to the assembly. He sent urgent messages to London and Algiers calling for planes to take the representatives to Algiers. It was a time of maximum air activity, not only because of the superb summer weather, but because, at last, big, bimotor Lockheeds were being supplied by the Americans to supplement the valiant but small Lysanders. The Lysanders normally carried one or, in an emergency, two passengers and very rarely three. The Lockheeds could take a dozen passengers at least.

Serreulles felt that he had to tackle all his problems at once, including a restructuring of the delegation itself. Just as no one man could fulfill all Moulin's functions, Serreulles felt that no one man could be the single delegate of Algiers. "I sent messages to General de Gaulle every week throughout July and August," Serreulles recalls, "telling him that he ought to name several men to the delegation in France, to assist the chief delegate, and to have capable men on hand to step quickly into his post in case of arrest, instead of being caught short as we had been caught when the Gestapo captured Moulin."

Serreulles sighed deeply and pursed his lips. "Not a word, not one single word came back from de Gaulle! At first I could not understand it. Other messages were being sent from France to London and cleared through Passy and the BCRAM machine. But my messages did not get an answer. I began to suspect why I was getting the silent treatment, but I decided to ignore it and to go ahead with my work as I saw fit. After all, if they would not answer me, they could not criticize what I did."

Serreulles believed that de Gaulle was not answering him because Passy, who disapproved what he was doing, and who did not want Resistance delegates to flood into Algiers and dilute de Gaulle's control of all political institutions, was intercepting his messages and not passing them on to de Gaulle. It was also possible that de Gaulle disapproved his actions but did not want to go on record as saying so. It is easier not to answer embarrassing queries.

Serreulles also had to find a replacement for General Delestraint. Serreulles knew that de Gaulle had reduced Delestraint's title from commander of the Secret Army to that of chief of staff of the Secret Army. A commander might be needed at the time of the landings, but in the meanwhile what was needed was a planning chief, a chief of staff, without the authority to order action. The chiefs of the six regions of the south met under the chairmanship of Pierre de Bénouville, head of the military affairs committee of the MUR. They quickly reached agreement on a proven Resistance fighter, with long experience as a professional soldier, Colonel Dejussieu, code name Pontcarral, a member of the Combat group. De Bénouville put his name forward and it was immediately approved, a fact that delighted Henri Frenay when he heard the news in London. Frenay knew that, at last, one of his own men who shared his ideas on the tactics and strategy of the Secret Army, would be in charge. It was a clear victory for Frenay and ended the long quarrels he had been having with General Delestraint. Serreulles was only too happy to express his own pleasure at the appointment of Pontcarral, whose excellent reputation had impressed him, for it also meant one less internecine quarrel with which he would have to cope.

Serreulles took further steps to tighten and unify the Resistance on a national scale by moving the comité directeur of MUR, which had functioned exclusively in the south, into the north. "I felt strongly that maximum unity could be achieved only if that organization of the southern movements would move with me to Paris and work closely with the five major movements of the north."

While all this was going on, very little attention was being paid to the arrival in France of two men who had been parachuted in mid-June, just at the height of all the crises of the Gestapo raids on the Resistance. The two men were First Lieutenant Ernest F. Floage and Second Lieutenant André J. Bouchardon of the American army. They were the very first emissaries of General Donovan's Special Operations Branch, the SO, which had worked out its agreement in London with the British Special Operations Executive. Despite Claude Dansey's continuing efforts to prevent any independent American activities in the Resistance, the Yanks were coming. Very slowly, to be sure, but on the way to join up with Resistance movements. Their mission was to make contact with maquis groups, find out what arms and equipment they needed. The Americans would contact London, ask for drops, and then train and lead the French in sabotage operations, as well as longer-range tactics to help the Allied troops after landings in France.

A number of maquis were blossoming into existence all over France in that summer of 1943. There was no typical maquis and no typical way in which men joined or became leaders of maquis units. Each maquis, each chief, had its own story to tell. One of the most impressive of the men who became maquis leaders at that time was a worker named Robert Noireau. His hair is gray today, but his barrel chest and powerful arms are still heavily muscled and he is a man who radiates strength and a zest for life. At a luncheon meeting in the Café du Dôme, in Paris, he told the story of his life as a maquisard.

"I was a Communist, the foreman of a work team in Besseges, north of Paris. We knew that a good many trains were coming through our sector en route to Germany and we wanted a chance to sabotage the German transports. We needed an excuse to work at night so we could take advantage of the darkness, so we blew up the motor of a machine we used and volunteered to fix it at night. This gave us a chance to sneak into the freight yard and empty the grease from the gearboxes of trains scheduled for Germany. We also threw sand and gravel into the gearboxes and motors.

"After a week of sabotage, the Gestapo came sniffing around the yards and around our factory. My boss warned me that they were asking about me by name and he told me to take off. I left that night and discovered later that the Gestapo had come to get me at five A.M., just before dawn, their favorite hour to strike.

"Unfortunately, they guessed where I had taken refuge, and they turned up there and grabbed me. They took me to an SS casern and locked me up. I looked around and noticed a damp spot in the wall behind the toilet. Guessing that it might be a weak spot in the barrack walls, I kicked at it and pulled it until my foot went all the way through. It was a trapdoor in a drain-pipe system that I had found. I made my way through it to the courtyard and from there to a pine tree growing alongside the wall. I climbed the tree, got onto the wall, and crawled along on all fours until I came to a lamppost in the street, where I could get hold and drop down to freedom.

"It was about one A.M. I knew that my wife and daughter were living in a village about fifty miles away. I had to make as much mileage as I could before the sun came up, so I began running at a steady pace. I was in good shape and ran for almost twenty miles before it felt that my lungs would explode out of my chest. By then the sun was up anyway and I had to stop running so that I could hide and rest a bit.

"I saw a cornfield up ahead and the corn was high, so I crept into it, burrowed out into the middle of the field, and fell into a deep, exhausted sleep.

"When I woke up it was six o'clock. My hands were bleeding from wounds I had torn into them when I ripped away the planking back in the barracks. I was covered with sweat and dirt and was hungry as a lion.

"I made my way cautiously through the cornfield until I caught sight of a peasant's house. I crawled up to it and then burst in. I must have frightened the peasant and his family out of their wits. They gave me a bowl of hot soup and some bread, and led me to the barn where I could rest and hide until dark.

"Then I made my way to Aubain, where I found out that my wife had been arrested as soon as the Germans had found out I had escaped. I sent her word through a friend that I was all right and told her to go to her mother's in Paris as soon as she was released. I did not dare try to see her, for that is what the Gestapo thought I would do.

"Resistants in Aubain were preparing to move to a new camp in the Lot and they took me with them. It was in Figeac that I joined my first maquis unit. It was a part of Frenay's Secret Army, or at least that is what they said, although I learned later that Frenay was in Algiers and not commanding any Secret Army in France in August 1943. No matter, it was the unit set up by Combat, when Frenay was its chief.

"As men made their way into the woods, new units were formed. One day I was given the mission of organizing thirty men into a maquis fighting unit. We were not yet fighting in the summer and fall of 1943. We were training. But our chance for combat against the Germans was not far away."

There were a great many men, like Noireau, who joined the maquis in the summer of 1943, and by the time the Allies landed in France there were more than a hundred thousand armed Frenchmen behind the German lines ready to disrupt enemy communications and harass the German rear positions. Every heavily wooded region of France, particularly in Alsace and Lorraine, the Haute-Savoie and the Alps, the Haute-Vienne, the Dordogne, and all the villages of the Corrèze were alive with armed maquis groups awaiting what the Americans called D-day and the French called Le Jour J.

Not everyone was waiting for D-day. That was the role of the maquis, particularly because of all the inexperienced young men who came to the maquis to avoid the forced labor draft and who were not yet ready to do any effective fighting. But individual partisan attacks on the Germans went on day after day, as did acts of sabotage by railway and factory workers. And from time to time, generally on an important, symbolic holiday, masses of the French people would show where their hearts were. July 14, 1943, was such an occasion.

All over France, the forbidden tricolor flag of the Republic came out of hiding and went on display. Resistants openly distributed clandestine papers in the subway of Paris. The police reported that as many as fifty thousand people demonstrated in Marseille. And in Paris, the Communist movement FTPF celebrated Bastille Day by an audacious assault on a column of armed German soldiers near the Arc de Triomphe. They killed fifteen Germans and the only casualty they suffered was a light hand wound of one of their grenadiers.

On July 23, the Allies captured Palermo in Sicily and the next day came big news: In Rome the Grand Fascist Council adopted an order of the day reinstating constitutional powers for the government and the Parliament. The next day, July 25, Benito Mussolini, Duce of Italy, partner of Hitler in the Axis coalition, was arrested and imprisoned. Marshal Badoglio was appointed as the new head of government. He declared that "the war continues . . . ," but Allied representatives were already preparing to negotiate Italy's surrender.

On July 28, the Fascist party was dissolved. Five hundred Allied bombers left Naples in ruins, while on the eastern front Stalin, in an order of the day, announced that the German summer offensive had been smashed and that Red Army troops, who had recaptured 110 towns, were advancing all along the line. In the Place de Clichy, in Paris, a Jewish partisan, Joseph Clisa, led a grenade attack on a busload of Luftwaffe officers. Later, a Frenchwoman betrayed him to the Gestapo and Clisa, in a shoot-out, saved the last bullet for himself rather than fall into the hands of the Germans.

On August 17, the Allied armies captured Messina, completing the conquest of the island of Sicily. The way had been cleared for the invasion of Italy, first breach in Hitler's Fortress Europa.

Claude Serreulles was doubly cheered by the news of Allied victories and the decision of de Gaulle, at last, to send him a man to share responsibility with him. De Gaulle had accepted Serreulles's argument that no one man could be the single delegate-general of the CFLN, as Moulin had been. Two men were needed, one for the former southern zone, one for the former northern zone. Serreulles had established himself in Paris and needed an equal colleague for the southern zone. London told him that Jacques Bingen, a good friend of Serreulles's, had been chosen.

Bingen, thirty-five years old, was one of the top officials of Fighting France. A graduate of two elite schools, the Ecole des Mines and the Ecole des Sciences Politiques, he had become in the spring of 1942 chief of nonmilitary affairs of the BCRAM, after having directed the operations of the Merchant Marine for the National Committee. He would work hand in hand with Serreulles. Bingen flew in on a Lysander on the night of August 15–16, 1943. His code name was Necker.

It was at that moment that an old controversy became reheated: de Bénouville's contacts with Dulles and the American secret service agents in Switzerland. De Bénouville brought this issue to the attention of the newly arrived delegate, Jacques Bingen. He knew that Bingen was grateful to Frenay for having given him letters of introduction and commendation to the regional chiefs of Combat, which had greatly facilitated Bingen's first tour of inspection in the south. De Bénouville was also able to prove to Bingen that at that moment communications with London had all but broken down. The Resistance was not getting its messages through, was not getting answers from London, and was severely short of funds and arms. Switzerland and the Americans offered money and communications.

Bingen was grateful for the help of Combat and he knew that communications had indeed broken down, but he was hesitant to approve de Bénouville's plan to send all messages via the Americans' radio system in Switzerland. Nonetheless, he could not but accept the validity of the argument that Fighting France would be credited by the Allies with all the information passed on by the Americans. More importantly, it was argued that this would greatly facilitate the Allied war effort at a moment of planning for Overlord, the Allied invasion.

Bingen's task was eased by a number of helpful developments, which he reported to London. He was pleasantly surprised to find how genuine and widespread were the pro-Gaullist sentiments of the Resistance and how limited and grudging was the support for Giraud. Above all, he was delighted to report that, apart from some superficial and irrelevant criticism, the great majority of the Resistance chiefs enjoyed the closest and most favorable relations with Serreulles, who, in joint meetings, had demonstrated to Bingen "an astonishing authority." Bingen himself found it easy to work closely with Serreulles. There was, as he had expected, mistrust between the Resistance movements and the political parties, but he found that Georges Bidault, the new chief of the CNR, was adept at bridging those gaps.

While Bingen and Serreulles were busy putting together the new Resistance political structures, London was preparing to parachute in a number of agents assigned to create a new military structure for the Resistance, particularly oriented toward preparing close coordination with Allied troops after the landings. The new agents would be called "military delegates" and would institute a system that divided France into regions, with regional military chiefs to be appointed. They would work closely with Colonel Dejussieu, Pontcarral, who was highly popular with all the military leaders of the Resistance movements.

One of the biggest problems at the end of the summer of 1943 was the situation of the men in the maquis facing the approach of winter. Most of the young men had fled their homes to enter the maquis in the late spring and summer. They came wearing cotton trousers, thin sweaters, and shoes with wooden soles. They could not survive a winter in the woods in their condition. Some maquis leaders recommended sending them home for the winter season and then calling them back again. Michel Brault (Jérome), the national chief of the maquis, vetoed that suggestion, for he feared that the Germans would seize the young men and send them off to work in Germany. It would be safer to keep them in the maquis. Resistance chiefs would have to get them warm clothing.

Jérome and his deputies sent out appeals for help. A very warm response, in every sense of the word, came from the town of Mazamet in the Pyrénées. Mazamet is renowned throughout the world for its cold, clear, clean mountain water. Wool merchants send their fresh-cut clippings from their sheep ranches, from as far away as Australia, to be washed in the waters of Mazamet. It is an extraordinary experience to go to Mazamet when the sheepmen hold their international convention there. They are big, rangy men who drink and eat with both hands and roar out their greetings to each other like rams in rut. Mazamet has caught the spirit of the ranchers and is a generous, lively town. The men of Mazamet sent Michel Brault twenty thousand wool sweaters and jackets lined with sheepskin for his maquisards. A comrade in Paris obtained ten thousand pairs of wool stockings.

That solved one of the problems of how to survive the winter. It did not solve the agonizing problem of the boredom and sense of futility of young men hiding in forests with nothing to do. There were not enough weapons to arm them. Instructors were afraid to train them with machine guns because of the noise that might alert Vichy or German patrols. Even more frustrating was the news that kept coming in about Communist maquisards who did have arms and were actively engaged in running battles with the enemy in the early fall of 1943.

Serreulles and Bingen both kept sending urgent messages back to London to report on the crisis provoked by London's failure to drop arms to the maquis. "Not a day goes by," Serreulles reported, "that I am not set upon by the chiefs of some organization who bitterly complain about their inability to arm their militants." Bingen told London that the "situation is tragic." He asserted that it was a matter of keeping trust and "rescuing from starvation and enemy bullets these young men to whom we have given our word in your name."

Despite all these continuing political, financial, and material problems, the Resistance grew in strength and daring through the summer and fall of 1943. German repression and the forced labor draft sent thousands of new recruits into Resistance movements and maquis encampments. Resistance leaders, with new forces and experience in guerrilla warfare, stepped up their armed assaults on German bases and German troops. London's instructions to avoid direct confrontation until the Allied landings had been virtually a dead letter from the start, for the Communists had rejected it and others began to follow suit. By 1943 the Groupes Francs of every movement were engaged in combat to the point where their underground papers issued regular military communiqués on armed action against the enemy.

London and Algiers had no choice left but to approve the demands of Serreulles and Bingen. Arms drops were ordered for the Groupes Francs and the maquis. London finally understood that if the Resistance fighters were not armed they might not be around to help at the time of the landings. Colonel Passy finally yielded on the issue of Combat's arrangements to get money from the Americans in Switzerland and to use their radio communications. The transmitters in Switzerland were more powerful, and the radio operators were not caught and tortured by the Gestapo. It was a safe and sure channel, as Frenay had always argued.

Serreulles was delighted. Only four months after the arrests of Moulin and Delestraint, he had been able to replace them and restructure the Resistance High Command. There was a new chief of the CNR, Georges Bidault; a new chief of the Secret Army, Colonel Pontcarral; two delegates, north and south, to replace Moulin, who had been the overall delegate: Serreulles and Bingen. Money and arms were beginning to come in regularly and in increased amounts. There was still much to be done but, by September 1943, Serreulles's mission had made great progress, with every hope of successes ahead.

21
SABOTAGE, TERRORISM, AND THE WAR

Allied victories in Italy, Russia, and the Pacific, plus rumors that the invasion of France was imminent, encouraged the Resistance to step up its sabotage and armed action against the enemy.

The most active saboteurs continued to be the *cheminots*, the railway workers, who formed their own teams and also cooperated with the commandos, the Groupes Francs of the Resistance movements. In the month of August 1943, railway saboteurs set dynamite sticks under tracks in several busy sectors: Marseille, Saint-Amour, and Mâcon. They succeeded in blowing up ten long trains, including ammunition cars and troop transport cars, inflicting heavy casualties on the Germans. In Normandy, near the Channel ports, and in Alsace, on the German frontier, not a day went by without some sabotage of German transports.

Railway workers and engineers combined their efforts. They would put up red flags and red signals as they pretended to repair a line or dig a trench for new cables. As they went ahead with this "work," they would sabotage all existing cables. One day late in September, outside Lunéville, in eastern France, a railway team struck pure gold: While digging a ditch they uncovered a complex of thirty-eight cable lines that carried almost all of the German army communications from units in France back to headquarters in Berlin. Singing lustily as they swung their axes, they chopped the cables to slivers.

German engineers soon discovered the nature and extent of the sabotage and asked Berlin to send a large contingent of German technicians to supervise the French and keep an eye on their operations. Berlin complied, but it was impossible to keep an eye on all of France's vast, complex national network of communications. It was too easy for a saboteur to throw the wrong switch, to cut a cable, unbolt a strip of track, or drain oil from a gearbox.

Resistance teams of executioners shot down traitors and collaborators who had betrayed patriots to the Germans, and killed Germans who had tortured patriots. In Lyon a notorious collaborator was shot to death in the street outside his office. Gestapo agents, whether German or French, were the constant targets of attack. Even large German units came under assault by commandos of the Groupes Francs. In Toulouse, according to a communiqué of the MUR, twenty-four German military trucks, a number of construction cranes, a cement mixer, and a tugboat were all destroyed. Bombs blew up the homes of well-known collaborators, as well as the offices of the German Navy Ministry and the Feldgendarmerie, with six German casualties.

The most chilling series of assassinations were carried out from the fall of 1943 to the fall of 1944 by an American who became the "hit man" for a Resistance group in Paris. We will call him Tom Rodgers. His real name has the same American ring to it, although he is a most unusual American.

Tom was born in Paris, where his father was the chief executive of an American corporation doing business in France. His mother was French and she insisted that he be educated in French schools. Tom grew up more French than American. His French was, of course, perfect, learned in school up to and including his passing of the "bachot" at the end of his secondary education. Tom then went to college in America and soon was completely bilingual and bicultural, completely at home in American or French languages and customs. He was also bisexual, although his basic preference was homosexuality.

After Tom graduated from college and was wondering what he wanted to do in life, war broke out in Europe. Through his father, who had connections with the State Department, Tom offered his services as an undercover agent in France. No one was better qualified. Tom was given a commission in the army, sent to training schools and assigned to G-2, Army Intelligence. The United States was not yet in the war, but Tom suggested to superior officers that he be sent to the embassy in London, to work with the military attaché there and be on the spot to go into France as soon as needed.

The British were delighted to meet this cultured and completely "Gallicized" American. They persuaded American counterparts to release Tom on detached duty to them as a "liaison" officer, a device that was used more than once in that period. They trained Tom in sabotage and hand-to-hand combat and taught him a number of ways to kill a man without using a weapon. Two stiff fingers jabbed sharply under the rib cage and upward toward the heart was a favorite method taught, although of course it was not possible for a trainee to try the trick in practice. But Tom learned it and practiced it on a sack stuffed with grass. He never really expected to use it.

It was shortly after Pearl Harbor that Tom was told that he would be dropped into France. He went into training at a paratroop station outside London and showed a remarkable aptitude for jumping from a plane and landing safely. Tom would hit the ground in perfect position, knees flexed, his legs like springs. He looked forward to his jump back to France. They told him that his job would be to gather intelligence information on German positions and send it back. There was no hint of any combat assignment. That was the responsibility of the French Resistance and not of Allied officers at that point in the struggle.

Tom's plane ran into bad weather and poor visibility, but Tom was dropped anyway, despite the bad conditions. His target was a farm outside Paris where the Resistance had marked out a landing strip and a safe-house. But when Tom came floating down he found himself, to his horror, over the river Seine, near the Saint-Cloud Bridge, at the edge of the Bois de Boulogne. All around him were heavily populated, built-up areas, and he was sure that a thousand eyes were following his descent.

Tom tugged at his guide ropes and aimed for the woods, which seemed to offer him some shelter. He managed to land just inside a clump of trees near the Longchamp racetrack. He shucked off his parachute and made his way down tree-lined paths, away from Saint-Cloud and toward the Porte Maillot. He knew that he would have to find a place to hide during the day until he could make contact with his Resistance unit.

Tom thought back to all his friends and remembered that a boy he had been close to in the lycée lived near the Bois de Boulogne in Neuilly. He made his way to the exit at the Porte Maillot and into a café where he looked up his friend's name in the telephone book. He found it, at the old address, and put through his call. His friend answered the phone and expressed amazement that Tom was in Paris. Tom told him that he had parachuted in. He felt he had no choice, for he could not suddenly invent a story that would account for his presence and for the call after all the intervening years. His friend whistled his surprise and asked what Tom wanted from him. Tom told him that he needed a place to hide for a few hours or perhaps a night until he could get to his own unit. His friend told him to come around at three o'clock, when he would be free to receive him.

Tom went to the Trocadéro until it was two o'clock and then decided to reconnoiter his friend's block before entering his house. He knew he had made a wise decision as soon as he turned the corner. He could see black Citroën cars, the kind used by detective squads. And there were a number of men leaning on lampposts and fixedly reading the same page of their papers. Tom walked briskly past them, turned the next corner, and got out of the neighborhood as quickly as he could. He knew that his old school "friend" had turned him in to the police. A cold anger gripped him and he vowed he would come back to that street one day and settle the score with his betrayer.

Tom had an emergency number to call, and a code phrase to speak: "My car has broken down. I think it's a bearing." The code meant that he had missed the rendezvous and would call again later. He did and was able to arrange a pickup at the corner of the Avenue Gabriel and the Rue de l'Elysée.

Tom made contact with the Resistance at that pickup and was escorted to an apartment in Paris, which would, for the time being, be his safe-house. He was given an identity card and a working card, as an executive at an advertising agency. He was given information on the latest events in Paris and briefed on the essential functions of a citizen at that time.

He worked well with his unit, familiarizing himself with their routines, and nothing untoward or dramatic occurred until one day, when a handsome German officer came over to talk to him at a café. Tom knew at once that it was a homosexual approach. He had not thought much about sex under the stimulus of his exciting parachute drop and his work in the underground, but suddenly he felt a hot flush in his cheeks and a rapid beat of his pulse. He chatted with the German for a few minutes, then excused himself, saying he had to get back to work. He said he would be back at the café for lunch the next day.

Three days later Tom Rodgers and Hugo von Eckstadt were lovers. Hugo was a Berliner, a perfect picture of the Aryan model, tall, blond, blue-eyed, broad of shoulder, narrow at the waist, cultivated, intelligent, fluent in French. He was also a major in the Gestapo. Tom was captivated but nervous about his liaison. He finally felt that he had to tell his Resistance comrades what he was doing.

They were horrified when they heard the name of the German officer. He was in the unit assigned to track down members of the Paris Resistance. He had been responsible for a number of arrests and had participated in the torture of patriots. Tom's beautiful, cultured Aryan was a sadistic Nazi. He was told to break off at once and to keep far away from von Eckstadt and any other Gestapo officer.

Once again Tom felt a terrible, icy anger chill his blood, as he had the day his schoolboy friend had betrayed him. This time he determined he would act on his own and disobey orders.

He met von Eckstadt at their favorite café and made a date to spend the night with him. For the first time he was not afraid to reveal where he lived. He gave the German his address and asked him to come to his apartment.

When he returned home, Tom went to the kitchen, got an ice pick, and took it to the bedroom. He plunged the ice pick into the mattress under the headboard of the bed, forcing it deeply down. When he put his pillow back in place, he checked to make sure that the pick was not visible. He would have to get into bed before Hugo and take his position on the right side. To test his position, Tom stretched out, closed his eyes, and dropped his hand down behind the headboard, moving slowly as though falling asleep. His hand readily found the handle of the pick.

Early in the morning, with Hugo breathing heavily beside him in a deep sleep, Tom slid his hand down the headboard, grasped the ice pick, and pulled it slowly out of the mattress. He carefully shifted position so that he was facing Hugo, who was curled up on his left side, his back to Tom. Tom could see a white spot on Hugo's neck, just below his hairline, at the tip of the spine. He struck swiftly and surely, the ice pick piercing the skin, plunging downward into the body. Hugo grunted once, never moved. He was dead.

Tom lay paralyzed, his mind blank. "I had a feeling of unreality, as though I were spectator and a participant, at the same time, in a horror movie," Tom said as he described the scene more than thirty years later.

He left the body in his bed and reported to work as usual. Then, after a long, ghastly night of vigil with the dead body, he sighed with relief as a Resistance squad arrived just before dawn to carry out the corpse.

Tom is well known in Paris today, although only a few know the role he played during the occupation. Tom had gone back to America for a few years after the liberation. He grew back the moustache he had shaved off before parachuting. He gained back the twenty pounds he had carried on his frame before the war. He had lost his hair and looked nothing like the man he was when he killed Hugo and many others, including his old schoolmate.

"I became a skilled executioner. I suppose some might call me an assassin, but I never thought of myself in that role. I made few judgments on whom to kill, nor did I profit from the killings. I was given the name of a sadistic Nazi or a French traitor and told that the committee had decided that he must be killed. And I killed. Sometimes with the ice pick—it is a silent, swift killer—sometimes with my hands, with a jab to the heart or a stranglehold. My hands are strong. I never used a gun or a grenade. I did not trust them as weapons and I felt they would expose me to danger. I killed in private, quietly.

"The biggest problem and the greatest danger was not the killing itself. It was the disposal of the body. I worked with a team of young men, powerful men. They could pick up a body like a loaf of bread and all but tuck it under their arms, wrapped in sacking, or stuffed into an empty steamer trunk or a wooden crate. They'd pick it up early in the morning, in a panel van, with the name of a freight company painted on. We were never caught, never even suspected.

"How many? Almost twenty executions in a two-year span until the Allied landings. Unusual? Yes, I suppose so, for one man. But not at all unusual for the Resistance. I think that every group and movement had its executioners."

Resistance leaders of the principal movements say that they knew no one quite like Tom in their units. They do confirm, however, the policy of executing French traitors and vicious Gestapo agents. "One kills vermin, doesn't one?" a leader of a northern unit said when questioned on this issue. Although survivors today all insist on their right to execute traitors, I have found none willing to be quoted by name as having carried out or given execution orders, with the exception of Marie-Madeleine Fourcade, whose men carried out a British order to execute the traitor Bla.

All through the summer and fall of 1943, leaders bombarded General de Gaulle in Algiers and Passy in London with complaints about the inadequacy of their aid to the clandestine forces. One of the most articulate of these letters of criticism was sent by a Communist who would become a minister in de Gaulle's postliberation Cabinet: Charles Tillon, chief of the Francs-Tireurs et Partisans

Français, by far the largest, most combative and efficient of all the Resistance movements. In it, Tillon told de Gaulle that the Resistance was carrying out three missions of utmost importance to Fighting France and to the Allies: (1) preventing by every possible means the deportation of French citizens to Germany; (2) sabotaging the means of production and transport of the enemy; (3) creating in the ranks of the Germans and the French the kind of climate that would make the people "cooperate with you and your forces at the moment of liberation."

The Action Committee Against Deportation every week rescued and gave shelter to hundreds of young French dissidents who fled their homes rather than be sent to Germany to work. Commandos, Tillon told de Gaulle, were destroying enemy gas dumps, food depots, roads and waterways, bridges, freight trains, locomotives, electric and telephone lines. The sabotage of the rail lines was most effective and Tillon claimed that five times as many interruptions of the rail system were caused by derailings on the ground as by Allied bombings, and with much less danger to French citizens.

The FTPF claimed to have killed thousands of Germans and to have created a general atmosphere of insecurity, so that Germans could only move about in public in great numbers, heavily armed, instead of marching about singing as conquerors as they had done in 1940 and early in 1941. The Resistance demonstrated to French citizens that the Germans were not supermen, were not invulnerable. Armed action and executions of traitors discouraged collaboration and encouraged cooperation with the Resistance.

Tillon told de Gaulle that "the possibilities are great at the present moment." Deportation had angered the French people, as had German requisitions of French food resources, leaving austere rations for the people. Food controllers were being chased from the fields by peasants wielding pitchforks. So great and frequent were protests and demonstrations in Brittany that they amounted to insurrection. Mindful of de Gaulle's warnings that Communist assaults were exposing the French people to murderous reprisals, Tillon inserted a paragraph in his appeal to the effect that "no premature action should throw the French people against German machine guns. We are watchful against provocations."

But, Tillon insisted, the time had come to bring masses of young Frenchmen into guerrilla action. And that required arms. The FTPF were seriously short of the means needed to continue their attacks upon the enemy. Sometimes, wrote Tillon, "we are obliged to arm an entire group with one pistol." His men lacked identity papers, ration cards, and money to ensure their daily existence and that of their families. Tillon complained that he had often presented his needs to de Gaulle's delegates in France, who had promised to meet them, but nothing, or almost nothing had been provided. "Give us the arms and we will use them well, General," Tillon pleaded.

Tillon reprinted the full text of his letter in the book he later wrote about the Francs-Tireurs and noted dryly: "No response was received."

Although General de Gaulle and his staff did not supply the

Resistance with as many arms as leaders called for, there were, nonetheless, a number of parachute drops of small arms, grenades, explosives, machine-pistols, and submachine guns, as well as fuses and timing devices. In addition, London and Algiers were looking ahead to the kind of structures they wanted to see in place at the time of the Allied landings. It would be necessary to coordinate the military activities of the various Resistance groups and movements. Serreulles and Bingen were far too busy dealing with political, economic, financial, and social problems of the Resistance to exercise additional authority in the military sphere on a national scale. Pontcarral was busy training the Secret Army and had no time for other military operations. It was necessary to put in place for the ensemble of the territory a new military structure led by agents sent in from London. Bingen had been briefed on this plan before he left for France. On arrival he spread the word, so that Resistance leaders would not be surprised or resentful when the new military delegates arrived, as they began to do in the fall of 1943.

The Resistance, always jealous of its sovereignty, always suspicious of directives and controls from London, told Bingen that it would accept "military attachés," meaning simply liaison officers. Bingen had to make it clear that London's delegates would not be mere low-level messengers. Bingen recommended to London that the new agents be called "délégués militaires," the word delegate demonstrating that they were acting with power delegated to them by the highest authorities of Algiers.

By and large the new military delegates were well received in the zones and regions of their assignments. They were the channel to London and Algiers and to the inter-Allied command, the only hope of the Resistance to receive the increased funds and arms so badly needed. The military delegates soon grew close to the men to whom they were assigned, learned to respect and admire them, and to identify with their needs. There were, as in all human associations, friction and conflicts, and, in some regions, incompatibility of the delegates and the Resistance chiefs, but such splits were rare.

Even more rare—indeed there was only one example—was an outstanding case, an extraordinary fusion of functions in Region C, departments of eastern France. In that important French-German border region, so often fought over by the two traditional enemies, one man emerged as the sole commander of the region, as military chief of the Resistance and also as the military delegate of General de Gaulle. The man had several code names, which changed frequently, but the one by which he became best known, and which is his legal name today, is Gilbert Grandval.

Grandval was thirty-six years old in 1940, the commercial director of a company manufacturing fertilizer and chemical products. His name then was Gilbert Hirsch-Ollendorf. His grandfather, Paul Ollendorf, had been the publisher of the works of Guy de Maupassant. The family was of Jewish origin, solidly middle class and fiercely nationalistic, as so many families were in Alsace and in Lorraine. "I was sickened by the capitulation of Pétain and outraged at the brutality of the German occupation and then the annexation of Alsace-

Lorraine. I became a resistant immediately. My work as commercial director of a large firm enabled me to travel all over France. It was an excellent cover for my activities in searching out safe-houses for escape routes. But the Gestapo was on my trail. I moved out of my house in Saint-Cloud, the night before the Gestapo swooped down in a dawn raid. Pure luck, just luck, saved my life."

In was in June 1943 that he escaped the Gestapo raid, and from then on Grandval led a completely clandestine life, changing domiciles constantly, always on the run. He was a member of the movement Ceux de la Résistance, a middle- and upper-middle-class group that had been founded in Paris by Jacques Lecompte-Boignet. At that moment, Lecompte-Boignet was in London and the movement was being led by Jean de Vogüé, whom Grandval knew as Madelin. Grandval himself was known to him as Chancel.

Grandval became the military director of the Armée Secrète in the Paris region for Ceux de la Résistance. In that capacity he worked closely with the chief of the FTPF in Paris, Colonel Henri Rol-Tanguy, and with the military delegate of Region P, André Boulloche. Grandval was promoted to the job of regional commander and went on a tour of the Ardennes, the Vosges, and other districts in eastern France. He worked closely with the military delegate of Region C, André Schock. In January 1944, André Schock was betrayed by a resistant, André Vial, who had been arrested by the Gestapo and "turned" into an informer.

The arrest of the military delegate was a severe blow to the entire organization. Grandval, aided by resistants Maurice Bourges-Maunory and Jean Bertin, managed to find the code book of Schock and his file of messages to and from London. And on the very day of Schock's arrest, his deputy, "Axe," a specialist on Alsace, was parachuted into France. Unfortunately there was something wrong with Axe's code books and he proved unable to decipher or encipher messages from and to London. Grandval decided that he would use Schock's codes, although that was a violation of procedure following an arrest. He expected London to appoint someone to replace Schock. Axe was too green to play much of a role. Then, a few weeks later, Axe was picked up by the Gestapo, leaving Grandval without any delegation from London.

To his astonishment, an exchange of cables with London brought forth a directive naming him as the military delegate of General de Gaulle, in addition to his functions as military commander of the movement. No one else had received and no one else would receive this double designation. Grandval believes that one of the reasons London chose him was the fact that he got along very well with the leaders of the most effective movement, the Francs-Tireurs et Partisans Français, that is, the Communists, while making it very clear that he was a dedicated follower of General de Gaulle.

There developed a conflict over command of the FFI, the Forces Françaises de l'Intérieur, a new overall national command of all Resistance forces. The national commander, inside France, named by de Gaulle, was Jacques Chaban-Delmas. Pierre Villon of Front National, the Communist front, had put forward the candidacy of one of his own men, a Communist named Malleret, code name General Joinville, to be the chief of staff of the FFI.

Grandval said: "There was no doubt in my mind that we had to support de Gaulle and his principal commanders, General Pierre Koenig in London and Chaban-Delmas in France. As for myself, the intense activity of Region C made it impossible for me to come to Paris. I was delighted to avoid these byzantine quarrels. I let it be known that I felt that only one thing mattered, the liberation of France, and that we ought to devote ourselves fully to the combat against the enemy. Most of the resistants in my region agreed with me. We had a lot to do, for our battleground was vast, eight departments: the Ardennes, the Marne, Meurthe-et-Moselle, Meuse, Moselle, Bas-Rhin, Haut-Rhin, and Vosges. I had my hands full checking on the training of the men, the supply of the maquisards, the plans for D-day."

While Grandval and other Resistance leaders were meeting the challenges of new structures and new strategies, and trying to adjust to the many changes in the Conseil National de la Résistance and the delegation of General de Gaulle, the Allied forces won a major victory over the enemy. On September 8, Italy surrendered unconditionally. Roosevelt and Churchill had reaffirmed their commitment to the principle of unconditional surrender—no deal with the Fascists or the Nazis of Italy and Germany. Marshal Badoglio ordered Italian forces to cease all resistance to the Allies but "to resist all other attacks," that is, to resist the advance of Nazi troops rushing to replace the Italians.

The Germans, anticipating the Italian surrender, had sent the Wehrmacht into the cities of northern Italy and as far south as Rome. While the Allies were landing near Naples, the Nazis were occupying Rome, and in one of the most daring and spectacular coups of the war, Nazi Commando Otto Skorzeny knocked out Mussolini's guards at Gran Sasso and liberated the Fascist dictator. German parachutists dropped down in Saint Peter's Square, investing the Vatican. Badoglio then called upon Italian troops to join the Allies in the fight against Hitler and the Nazis.

Day by day the war news was broadcast by the BBC French Service from London and by the French Radio Service in Algiers. The French resistants listened spellbound and felt the day of liberation was fast approaching. They got, however, no special lift from the news that the Italians had joined the Allies. They mostly despised Italy as the country that had stabbed France in the back in 1940 and was now betraying its German ally in 1943. The defeat of Italy also brought about important changes inside France. The Italians had furnished the men for the occupation forces in the French Alps and in the southeastern regions of France. The Italian Secret Police, the OVRA, served in those regions as the Gestapo did elsewhere, and was every bit as cruel and vicious, but less efficient and thorough. The OVRA would be replaced by the dread Nazi Gestapo.

The biggest impact of the Italian defeat on French territory occurred on the island of Corsica, where some eighty thousand Italian troops were garrisoned along with the elite Sturmbrigade of the SS Reichsführer, a contingent of ten thousand men and one hundred tanks. The powerful German force had been sent in by the German High Command late in July to strengthen the backbone of the Italian forces. The Germans meant to hold on to Corsica for its psychological as well as its strategic value to the French and the Allied command.

Allied generals had signed the armistice convention with Italy at a secret meeting in Syracuse on September 3, but the Anglo-American High Command had not thought it necessary to inform either General de Gaulle or General Giraud. Giraud was getting messages from the Corsican Resistance asking for instructions and stating the readiness of the Front National forces, the dominant movement in Corsica (and a Communist one), to open hostilities against the Italian and German occupiers.

Early in the evening of September 8, Radio Algiers broadcast the news of the Italian capitulation, a broadcast heard in Ajaccio, Corsica, during a meeting of the Central Committee of Front National. The sudden news required a number of crisis decisions by the Resistance. If the Italians had surrendered, they could not attack Italian troops, assuming that the Italian garrisons in Corsica agreed to lay down their arms and, above all, release the many patriots they had imprisoned. But there was the question of the German forces. They had not and would not surrender. The Resistance would have to act quickly against the Germans, cut their communications, set up ambushes and road traps before they could muster their full force.

A huge crowd massed in the public square the next morning and marched into the prefecture, where leaders of the Resistance took over the office of the Vichy Prefect. Front National committeemen moved in on municipal offices throughout the island to take over the administration in the name of the Comité Français de Libération Nationale.

Most of the Italians stayed inside their barracks and did not move, although a diehard contingent of Fascist Black Shirts joined the Germans. General Kesselring ordered the German troops to control the east coast and cover the landings of the Ninetieth Panzer Division, which he was dispatching to Corsica from bases in Sardinia. Despite its brave words, the Resistance did not have the strength to fight against a powerful German force. Front National leaders had to send a message to Giraud, apprising him of the situation and calling for the intervention of the French army.

Giraud had a battle plan for landings in Corsica that had been drawn up months earlier. But it could not be put into action unless the Allied High Command provided him with the naval transport to carry his invasion troops to Corsica. The Allies, however, were not at all prepared to divert forces badly needed for the continuing campaign against the Germans in Italy. Giraud was turned down.

Giraud knew that he would have to face formidable forces in Corsica. If the Ninetieth Panzer landed with auxiliary troops, the Germans would have close to twenty-five thousand first-class soldiers in Corsica, backed up by Luftwaffe planes in Sardinia. Giraud felt nonetheless committed to go to the aid of the Corsicans and to demonstrate the combativity of the Merchant Marine, and told them his problem, asking them how many warships and transports, flying the French flag, could be put at his disposal to carry troops of the First Army Corps to Corsica. They told him that they could give him the naval cover and transport that he needed for the landings.

From the twelfth of September through the eighteenth, French cruisers, destroyers, and torpedo boats covered freighters and transports, as forces of the newly constituted First French Army landed on the beaches of Corsica and at the port of Ajaccio. General Henri Martin was in command of French liberation forces. The fighting began on September 18 and lasted until the first days of October. It was brutal and bloody right up to the end, when the French took Bastia and the Germans evacuated Corsica and sailed to reinforce the German troops in Italy. Corsica was freed on October 4.

The Corsican liberation was a triumph for General Giraud but further poisoned his relations with General de Gaulle, for it had been carried out without notifying de Gaulle. De Gaulle saw it as a deliberate plot to undercut his authority and bolster Giraud's, as it undoubtedly was. The Resistance in Corsica was almost totally dominated by the Communist-led Front National and the FTPF, which had formed an alliance of convenience with the secret service agents of General Giraud. The Communists knew, of course, that General Giraud was an extreme right-winger, and that, given a chance, he would throw them all in jail. But they were more anxious to put down the Gaullists, seeing in de Gaulle a more dangerous rival for ultimate power in France. Giraud saw an advantage in an alliance with the hated Communists, for the liberation of Corsica could greatly enhance his reputation as a fighting commander of France. And the Americans, still trying to keep de Gaulle out of power, made sure that Giraud got all the arms needed for the uprising in Corsica. Huge arms shipments had poured into Corsica in July and August, supplied by the OSS to Giraud's secret service, the DSR/SM. And, when Giraud got the signal on the twentieth of September that French troops were going into action in Corsica as planned, he flew there to be on hand in person for the campaign.

Incredibly, up until the day that Giraud flew out of Algiers to join the expeditionary force to Corsica, General de Gaulle knew nothing about the entire operation. He had not been consulted or informed either by Giraud or by the Americans while arms were being sent and plans were proceeding for a Corsican insurrection. When de Gaulle discovered what was happening he called a meeting of the CFLN and had a stormy session of recriminations with Giraud, after which Giraud flew off to Corsica, throwing his gauntlet right at de Gaulle.

De Gaulle, furious, called in his top staff people and ordered them to bring the Giraud secret service under control. He conferred with Commandant André Pelabon, a former police official whom he had named to head up the BCRA in Algiers; with General Cochet, the early resistant of the French army; and with a brilliant young scholar, Jacques Soustelle, who had joined the Gaullist ranks. Soustelle was an archaeologist and anthropologist who had written highly praised studies of the Aztecs of Mexico. De Gaulle was impressed with his fine mind and his driving energy. He had already made him chief of his propaganda services. He took advantage of the Giraud affair in Corsica to appoint him chief of a new intelligence service, Direction Générale des Services Spéciaux (DGSS). It would be the mission of these three men to discipline and then break up Giraud's secret service. Those of us in OSS and G-2 in Algiers found ourselves in the middle of an intense and dangerous French struggle for power.

A number of things happened in that period that strengthened General de Gaulle's hand. One was the unwise decision of America's OSS chief, General Donovan, to come out in the open and support Giraud against de Gaulle in joint Allied meetings. This gave the Gaullists a chance to reconfirm their charges that Giraud was a tool of the Americans. The nationalistic French officers and Resistance leaders were highly sensitive to such accusations.

At the same time, General Cochet was called to London to meet with American and British officials to discuss plans for an operation known as Sussex. Operation Sussex grew out of the general agreement that David Bruce, chief of the OSS, London, had reached on May 29, with the chief of Britain's secret service, MI-6, Stewart Menzies. On that date, after long quarrels and rivalries, Menzies had offered the Americans a "full partnership" in European espionage operations.

The Bruce-Menzies general agreement had to be carried out in practice by a detailed plan. That plan was drawn up by Claude Dansey, with great reluctance, since he was jealous of British supremacy in intelligence activities. It provided for Anglo-American supervision of fifty two-man intelligence teams to be parachuted into northern France in a region stretching from the Channel through Brittany and up to the Belgian border. Their mission would be to gather intelligence on German positions in advance of the Overlord landings. Washington, delighted with plans for Sussex, sent a special team to direct American participation in the operation.

In the fall of 1943, the British appointed a highly respected, much admired military hero, General Colin Gubbins, to be the head of their Special Operations Executive in London. General Donovan responded in kind by appointing as the new head of his Special Operations Branch in London a young, much-liked West Pointer, Colonel Joseph Haskell. His brother John was OSS chief in Italy and his father had been a regular army general. Haskell had top-level contacts and delighted the British by providing OSS London with two strategic bomber squadrons for transport of agents and supplies to the Resistance in France. Gubbins and Haskell soon overcame all of Claude Dansey's attempts to block the Americans out of continental operations.

Haskell, working on plans with his British opposite numbers of

SOE, came up with a new operational scheme, code-named Jedburgh, for the creation of an international Intelligence Service. The idea was to set up a "Jed team" to be composed of one American OSS officer or one British SOE officer, plus one French officer, plus one British or American enlisted man as radio operator, thus a trinational team, a truly united nations effort. These "Jeds" would be parachuted into France in uniform to join Resistance groups in the weeks following the Allied landings. It would be their mission to arm and train the underground fighters, to coordinate their activities and act as liaison with Allied troops. This would be, of course, in addition to the intelligence-gathering espionage operations of the Sussex teams, who would already be in place.

The difficulty with all these plans was of finding the men to staff the teams, particularly in the case of Operation Sussex, which called for the recruitment of Frenchmen by the Americans. French émigrés in the United States were either men who had come in 1940 and who were too out of touch with France to serve efficiently as spies, or who had come out of France recently with highly emotional political views and biases, making them unreliable as agents. After a few weeks, recruiters in the United States gave up the job and said they could not find the needed men.

Some fifty Americans fluent in French were needed for the United States component in the Jed teams. The task of finding them in training camps in America was given to a Wall Street attorney, George Sharp, chief of the western European desk of the Special Operations Branch in Washington. He worked well and had filled his entire quota of fifty American Jed officers by the end of November.

The OSS in London had to turn to Colonel Passy and the BCRAM to ask for help on Sussex, which needed Frenchmen for their teams. Passy passed the request on to his opposite number in Algiers, Colonel Pelabon. This gave Pelabon and de Gaulle a very important lever to use in their struggle for power with Giraud. It took two full months of wrangling before the plans could be carried out, but finally recruits began to come in. Then, in December, at the Cairo Conference, the Combined Chiefs of Staff committed themselves to Overlord and appointed General Eisenhower to be supreme commander of the cross-Channel operation, the historic Normandy landings. They sent out orders for every effort to achieve Allied cooperation to make those landings a success.

In view of the tremendous stakes in the landings, Allied officers put aside their personal quarrels and began to function as true teams. The Sussex plan was given a new tripartite command in January. Commander Kenneth Cohen of British Intelligence was named chairman; Colonel Francis Miller, a Virginian, was appointed to be the OSS representative; most importantly, Gilbert Renault-Roulier, the famous Colonel Rémy, one of the most brilliant espionage agents of the war and a dedicated Gaullist, was chosen to be the French representative on Sussex. Rémy persuaded de Gaulle to let them recruit agents directly from the ranks of the French army. From then on, Sussex had the agents it needed, and de Gaulle had his ultimate victory over Giraud and his arch-enemy Robert Murphy.

The final event of that eventful fall of 1943 was the decision in November to enlarge the membership of the Comité Français de Libération Nationale to include representatives of the Resistance. The internal Resistance ended up with a clear majority on the key Committee of Liberation and in a new Consultative Assembly. And most significantly, the name of General Henri Giraud had been dropped from the membership list. The Resistance delegates gave de Gaulle a big majority in Algiers. The infighting would continue for a few weeks. Neither Giraud nor his sponsor, Murphy, would give up easily, but give up they finally did, early in 1944, when it became apparent that the inter-Allied command needed the full cooperation and leadership of de Gaulle and the Resistance leaders for the landings, now scheduled for early June.

De Gaulle further strengthened his leadership inside France by completing the restructuring of the Resistance institutions that Serreulles and Bingen had done so much to bring about. Ultimate control of the Resistance by de Gaulle and the Liberation Committee was furthered by the appointment of a new delegate-general to replace Jean Moulin as the chief delegate to the CNR. Until then, Serreulles had functioned as delegate in the north and Bingen as delegate in the south. They each maintained their functions in those places as deputies to the new top authority, the delegate-general. He was Emile Bollaert, former prefect of the Rhône Department, the same rank that Moulin had held. Both Serreulles and Bingen, younger men of much lower rank, accepted Bollaert without protest as their chief.

Claude Bouchinet Serreulles, who had accomplished the most critical tasks at the most vital moment, to become a true hero of France, was called to Algiers by General de Gaulle, decorated with the Cross of the Liberation and proclaimed to be a "Compagnon de la Libération."

The year 1943 ended with good news on all fronts for the Allies. The Russians advanced all along the eastern fronts. In September they had captured Pavlograd, only forty miles from Dnepropetrovsk. On that same day, September 19, the Italian divisions in Sardinia obeyed Badolgio's appeal to come over to the Allied side, attacking the German garrisons and driving them off the island. Also on September 19, the United States Navy announced that it had built "the greatest sea power on earth," as the new U.S. fleets, for the first time, outnumbered and outgunned the British, who for so long had ruled the waves.

The Soviets drove the Nazis out of Smolensk and battled their way into the suburbs of Kiev at the end of September. In Paris, FTPF commandos executed Julius Ritter, chief of the Nazis' forced labor organization for France, shooting him down early one morning as his car came out of his garage on the Rue Petrarque.

On September 29 the British Eighth Army captured Foggia, the principal Nazi air base in Italy. American and Australian troops invaded New Guinea and the Solomon Islands. American paratroopers, in a mass drop over New Guinea, encircled twenty thousand Japanese troops and tightened the noose around them.

On October 21, the French Committee of National Liberation in Algiers reconfirmed its commitment to democracy and rebuked General Giraud. It restored into law the Crémieux decree of 1870, which had granted citizenship to Algerian Jews, a decree that Giraud had canceled when he took command after the Allied landings in 1942.

Partisans led by a man named Tito announced that they had captured Nazi strongholds in Yugoslavia and taken two thousand German prisoners. Greek partisans broke the assault of a German brigade of four thousand men, inflicting heavy casualties on the Germans. The Russians liberated Dnepropetrovsk on October 26.

On November 28, the three Allied leaders, Roosevelt, Churchill, and Stalin, met at Tehran.

As the year 1943 drew to an end, the Soviets broke the German lines all along the northern front and were in full pursuit of Nazi troops fleeing toward the Polish border, on their way out of Russia.

General de Gaulle and his *"compagnons"* celebrated the advent of the New Year, predicting that 1944 would be the year of their liberation and the restoration of the freedom and grandeur of France.

22

THE TWILIGHT OF OCCUPATION

Many would die before the year 1944 brought the light of liberation to France. Men who had been fighting in the shadows died in the shadows, often by their own hand for fear of talking under German torture. Jacques Bingen, arrested by the Gestapo, swallowed a poison pill, afraid that he might crack under torture. Others, like Colonel Touny, chief of the OCM, would die in concentration camp.

Jean-Pierre Lévy knew that as a Jew he would have almost no hope to survive, so he had no reason to celebrate New Year's Day, 1944. He was in prison, with little chance to live to see the dawn of liberation. He had been in prison ever since his arrest in October 1943, shortly after his return to France from London.

"I ran into trouble," Jean-Pierre recalls today, "when I went to Paris to confer with Resistance leaders there. They had assigned me the apartment of one of their agents, who was in London, not knowing that the apartment was under tight police surveillance.

"The concierge of the building was a police spy and she denounced me. I was arrested by special commandos of an antiterrorist police squad, directed by Commissaire David, a famed hunter of men. I was interrogated, however, by Inspector Portale, who had no use for the Nazis or for Vichy, and who was anxious to get good marks for himself with the Resistance to avoid reprisals after the liberation. He knew who I was, of course, but, instead of charging me with Resistance activities, which would have led to a severe sentence and deportation to a concentration camp—particularly since I was Jewish—he decided, instead, to charge me with being a black marketeer, and a vendor of false ration cards and false papers, in other words a common criminal, not a terrorist.

"I was sent to the Santé prison along with an assortment of thieves and thugs. My friends found a lawyer who became my liaison officer to the Groupes Francs, the Resistance commandos of the Paris region, and he brought me word that the commandos would strike and free me during my arraignment at the Palais de Justice, on January 19, 1944.

"The attack was swift and violent but badly planned. I had been told to run, as soon as I saw my friends pull out their guns, and make for the door at the end of the corridor. But they had not carefully studied the palais before the attack and they did not know or they failed to tell me that there were two different doors, one leading down the corridor to a guard, and one leading down to the street. As luck would have it, I ran down the corridor right into the arms of a Garde Républicaine. The others did get away, with some casualties, but I was caught.

"I was then transferred to a different judge in a different chamber, much tougher than the one I had been scheduled to face. He found me guilty and ordered me kept in a special security cell at the Santé prison. Another lawyer-contact did manage to see me there, however, and told me that another plan was being drawn up to free me from prison. We were all afraid that the Germans would learn my true identity. It was imperative to get me out. But I sent back word that this time I wanted to know every detail of the plan and to be sure that there would be no wrong door.

"The plan was simple enough, although based on a dangerous first step. That first step was to play sick, and to get a doctor working with us to confirm my sickness and to order me transferred to the infirmary in Fresnes prison, on the grounds that he lacked the facilities needed for treating me at the Santé. The real reason was simply to get me moved out of the security cell and into a police van for the transfer to Fresnes. The police van could be attacked en route. The danger, of course, was that if anything went wrong and I was not hijacked away from the police, that I would get to Fresnes, where it would be discovered that I was not sick. Besides, Fresnes was a way station to the concentration camps. I was risking all in a commando attack on the van.

"I was, you can imagine, nervous when I was handcuffed and led into an armored police car. I heard the motor start and the van began to roll. I sat there, sweating, waiting for the shock when the driver would hit the brakes, signaling to me inside that our commandos had struck.

"I did not have long to wait—perhaps ten, twelve minutes—when I heard shouting and was jolted and knocked down on the floor by the sudden braking of the police van. Three Citroën cars had tracked the police van from the Santé prison to the Porte d'Orléans at the outskirts of Paris. One of the Citroëns shot out and cut across the front of the police car, forcing the driver to stand on his brakes. Another commando car swung behind the police car and our men jumped out, pointing submachine guns to keep everyone away. The third car pulled up alongside the driver of the police car, pointed a machine-pistol at him, and said: 'Quick, hand over your keys or we'll kill you and blow the van up.' The driver threw his keys out of the window, the commandos opened the back door, took off my cuffs, shoved me into the Citroën guarding the rear, and we sped off. The whole operation took less than five minutes and I was free.

"The car I was in turned back into Paris and then pulled up in front of a café. I went in and was led into a rear room. There I saw the man who had arranged the whole affair, Benjamin Roux, who grabbed me in a big bear hug. There were four other men with him, whom I did not know. They grinned and stepped up to introduce themselves. One was a police commissioner, named Luciani, the other three were police inspectors, I don't recall their names. They saluted me and said, 'We are at your orders.' Roux winked at me, grinning from ear to ear. The police were coming over to our side. The tide had turned and the currents of liberation were running strong and deep."

The biggest frustration for the Resistance as hope of liberation grew was the lack of arms. Telegrams poured into headquarters in Algiers and London telling of the disastrous consequences of the Allied failure to send enough arms to the Resistance. Georges Rebattet, who had replaced Michel Brault as national maquis chief, sent a message to de Gaulle telling him of a "tragic situation for deportation-evaders." Every week, Rebattet said, "we lose a hundred men. And the Germans take no prisoners." Money, weapons, and munitions were needed immediately, "lest the evaders be forced into banditry or massacred."

Resistance delegates also sent through messsages telling of catastrophes like the Allied air raid on a ball-bearing plant in Annecy. "The planes overshot the plant at an altitude of five thousand meters. Civilian houses were destroyed. . . . The air raid wreaked terrible havoc." In sharp contrast, the week before, the Resistance, on the ground, sabotaged a number of transformers, destroyed rail lines, wiped out locomotive depots, and harassed enemy troops. "If you get us the arms," they wired Algiers, "our groups will knock out any target you want, without endangering civilians. We, on the ground, are more accurate than your planes bombing from high up. . . . To leave our men unarmed is a grave political and military error."

No man understood this better or was more determined to do something about it than Emmanuel d'Astier de la Vigerie. He was also in a key position to help. De Gaulle had made d'Astier commissaire de l'intérieur, the office in charge of all police and internal security affairs for the French National Committee (CFLN) in Algiers. Many were surprised that de Gaulle would give that key post to a man who was not a Gaullist at the outset and who had an evident taste for intrigue. But de Gaulle had every confidence in d'Astier's high sense of honor and integrity and he did not fear that d'Astier would conspire against him personally. He told Henri Frenay, who had expressed astonishment and dismay at the d'Astier appointment, that he needed someone able, firm yet flexible, and that d'Astier had those qualities.

D'Astier was fundamentally loyal to his chief, but he did not hesitate to go behind de Gaulle's back when he felt the issue involved the well-being of the Resistance and the overall strength of France. He felt, correctly, that in many areas he could accomplish more for de Gaulle's cause than de Gaulle himself.

The principal case in point was the Allied failure to provide arms and munitions. From his experience in London in 1943, D'Astier had learned that the British controlled all planes over France and that, therefore, they controlled the question of arms supplies to the maquis. He also knew that the British and American military were reluctant to give too many arms to French civilians, whom they did not trust. Above all, the military was worried about arming Communists who might strike for power after the landings. The Americans were almost as suspicious of the Gaullists as they were of the Communists. It was clear to d'Astier that the only way to assure the Resistance of the arms, munitions, and explosives that it needed was to win approval at the very top. If Churchill could be persuaded of the need to arm the Resistance, it would be done.

D'Astier's chance to approach Churchill came early in 1944. Churchill, who had been ill, was recuperating in the warm sun of Marrakech, in Morocco, one of his favorite wintering resorts. De Gaulle felt he had to pay him a visit and express his concern for his health. Churchill was no more pleased to receive de Gaulle than de Gaulle was to call upon him. Their relations were at one of their frequent low points; d'Astier's relations with Churchill, on the other hand, were excellent.

D'Astier arrived in Marrakech on January 13, in time for the parade that would be held the next day, when Churchill, convalescent, would don his uniform as marshal of the Royal Air Force and pass the troops in review in the presence of General de Gaulle. Churchill loved to review the troops and did so many times during the war, going up front on occasion to review troops just before an attack.

D'Astier was amazed to see Churchill, who had been gravely ill, his doctors fearful of a fatal pneumonia, stand up for a long thirty minutes and more as French units of the new First Army proudly marched past. He was not surprised to learn that nothing of any real importance had been discussed between Churchill and de Gaulle, each man icily correct but uncommunicative. D'Astier requested and was granted a private meeting with Churchill. He did not inform de Gaulle of his action, which went well beyond his portfolio as minister of the interior. He was invading the territory of the military and the diplomats, none of whom had accomplished anything.

When Churchill launched into a diatribe against de Gaulle, his xenophobia and his aggressive hostility toward Churchill and the British, d'Astier put the blame on Churchill himself. He said that Churchill had recognized all kinds of governments-in-exile—Greece, Yugoslavia, Poland—that were virtually puppet governments, but that the only government that was a strong and serious ally, the French government, was the one that he would not deal with.*

Churchill laughed and admitted the validity of d'Astier's charge. He conceded that de Gaulle was the true leader of France, but argued that he

---

* The description of the talks between d'Astier and Churchill appears in detail in Henri Noguères, *Histoire de la Résistance en France*, Tome 4 (Paris: Robert Laffant, 1976), pp. 298–311.

ought not to cause him constant trouble. He referred particularly to current moves in Algiers by de Gaulle to conduct a purge campaign against some men who had been helpful to the Allies. He said it was an embarrassment to him, notably "the cases of Boisson and Peyrouton." Pierre Boisson and Marcel Peyrouton had both been Vichy officials who had switched to the Allies at the last minute.

D'Astier pointed out to Churchill that it was not de Gaulle, but the Resistance that demanded severe punishment of these pro-Nazi criminals, just as they would eventually demand severe punishment of Pétain, Weygand, and others.

Churchill exploded and told d'Astier that the French could do what they liked with Pétain and the others. "Go ahead and shoot them if you wish." But Boisson and Peyrouton had persuaded French units not to resist Allied landings. These men had worked for the Allies, so it was, in effect, Roosevelt and Churchill whom de Gaulle was challenging in pursuing Boisson and Peyrouton. He warned d'Astier that if they went ahead with action against Boisson, "Roosevelt will break relations with you and I'll follow him."

D'Astier knew very well that Churchill felt that England's fate was in the hands of Roosevelt and the Americans. He was going to be Roosevelt's friend and partner at all costs, and he would side with Roosevelt in any quarrel with the French, especially with de Gaulle. Churchill had befriended de Gaulle, had given Free France its first status, its first monies, uniforms, and arms. But he was fed up.

D'Astier, seeing no sense in continuing any discussion on this point, hastily steered the talks where he wanted them to go: to the problem of arms for the Fighting French inside France.

Churchill, having made his point on the purges, immediately changed his mood and became an affable friend. He conceded that the supply of arms had been inadequate and he promised "the aid that you need."

D'Astier, not without some bitterness, replied that similar promises had been made to provide such aid eighteen months before, but nothing had happened.

Churchill promised that this time something would happen. But, he admonished d'Astier, "tell de Gaulle to stop sticking pins into me."

Churchill said that he would continue this talk with d'Astier in London. D'Astier told de Gaulle nothing about his meetings.

True to his word, Churchill granted d'Astier another meeting in London about a month later, but this time it was not a tête-à-tête. A representative of Roosevelt, named Reed, attended. It became evident to d'Astier that Churchill had him there so that he could report to Roosevelt on how diligently Churchill had argued on his behalf. Churchill was explicit about Roosevelt. He said: "Mr. Roosevelt and the American government have undertaken commitments in respect to Boisson and Peyrouton. In this matter, I declare my solidarity now and in the future with President Roosevelt."

D'Astier's riposte that Laval and Pétain could also win them-

Ruined village of the Vercors. (Carl Mydans,
Life Magazine © 1944 Time Inc.)

OPPOSITE TOP
*Resistant hanged and burned by Germans
in the Vercors. (Comité d'Histoire)*

OPPOSITE BOTTOM
Corpses in the Vercors massacre. (Comité d'Histoire)

BELOW
*Widows in the Vercors, August 1944.
(Robert Capa, Life Magazine © 1944 Time Inc.)*

OPPOSITE TOP
Ruins of church in the Vercors, sacked by Germans.
(Documentation Française)

OPPOSITE BOTTOM
The dead after the massacre in Oradour, July 1944.
(Comité d'Histoire)

General de Gaulle on bridge of a French naval craft
en route to landing in Normandy.
(ECPA, Army Photographic Service, Paris)

TOP

On D-Day, June 6, 1944, an American mortar crew
have gained a foothold on a beach in Normandy and
are about to fire into a Nazi position.
(U.S. Army Photograph)

BOTTOM

Soldiers of the 3rd Division, U.S. Seventh Army,
race up the Red Beach area on the first day of the
Allied landings in southern France, August 15, 1944.
(U.S. Army Photograph)

FFI soldier guarding a square in Chartres, July 1944. (Robert Capa, Life Magazine © 1944 Time Inc.)

Frenchwoman who consorted with a German, her head shaved, being paraded through the streets of Chartres, September 1944. (Robert Capa, Life Magazine © 1944 Time Inc.)

OPPOSITE TOP

The German commander of Paris, General von Choltitz, in scout car of French Second Armored Division, after his capture at his headquarters in the Hôtel Meurice, Paris, August 25, 1944. (Comité d'Histoire)

OPPOSITE BOTTOM, RIGHT

Colonel Rol-Tanguy (center, wearing cloak on shoulders), chief of the FFI for the Paris region. (Musée Carnavalet)

OPPOSITE BOTTOM, LEFT

Alexander Parodi, de Gaulle's delegate to the Resistance, Paris, July 1944. (Comité d'Histoire, courtesy M. Parodi)

BELOW

General Dwight D. Eisenhower, Supreme Commander of the Allied forces in Europe, with General de Gaulle. (U.S. Army Photograph)

RIGHT
*Resistants throwing incendiary bottles on German tanks, in front of Notre Dame Cathedral, August 1944.
(Musée Carnavalet, Doisneau-Rapho)*

BELOW
*Parisian children on the barricades, August 1944.
(Musée Canavalet)*

TOP
*Barricades on the Boulevard Saint-Germain at the
corner of the Rue Jacques, Paris, August 1944.
(Musée Carnavalet)*

BOTTOM
*Fighting on the Petit Pont, near Notre Dame,
August 1944. (Comité d'Histoire)*

OPPOSITE TOP

*General Leclerc being cheered on entry into liberated
Paris, August 25, 1944. (USIS)*

OPPOSITE BOTTOM

*A Second Armored Division tank, near the Place
de la Concorde, August 25, 1944. (USIS)*

BELOW

*Troops of Leclerc's division attacking German position
in Chamber of Deputies, Place du Palais Bourbon,
August 25, 1944. (Robert Capa, Life Magazine
© 1944 Time Inc.)*

ABOVE

*General de Gaulle addressing liberated Parisians from
the balcony of the War Department, Paris.
(Robert Capa, Life Magazine © 1944 Time Inc.)*

OPPOSITE TOP

*Generals de Gaulle, Leclerc, and Juin; at far right,
Colonel Rol-Tanguy, at Gare Montparnasse,
August 25, discussing arrangements for the German
surrender. (Archives Documentation Française)*

OPPOSITE BOTTOM

*General de Gaulle leading liberation parade,
August 26, 1944. (Comité d'Histoire)*

General de Gaulle's head emerging over crowd cheering
him at the Arc de Triomphe, August 26, 1944.
(Frank Scherschel, Life Magazine ©1944 Time Inc.)

selves favored treatment from the Allies by sparing some American lives in the impending invasion of France, was met, he wrote in his diary, by an "appreciable silence."

D'Astier, after Churchill had brought up the names of Boisson and Peyrouton several times, finally said that he would have to tell his comrades of the Resistance that Churchill wanted to drive a bargain with them: guns for the pardons of Boisson and Peyrouton.

Churchill hastily denied that he was offering that kind of a deal. He said he was willing to tell the French people that the British government had made commitments with Boisson and Peyrouton before there was any kind of a French government in existence. He wanted de Gaulle and the National Committee to make a gesture of friendship, of goodwill, of cooperation with the Allies. Then many things would become possible, many doors could open. He made it quite clear that the French ought to expel the two men from North Africa and turn them over to the Allies.

D'Astier warned Churchill that any measures the Allies took against the French would be counterproductive for the Allies. After all, more than a million Allied soldiers would be landing soon in France and they needed every bit of help the French could provide. He warned Churchill that the French Resistance would not tolerate any form of AMGOT, Allied Military Government, or any French military command not recognized by the French population. There could be clashes between the French and the American soldiers and this could turn a liberation into an occupation with catastrophic consequences for everyone.

Churchill assured d'Astier that the Allies were aware of such a danger and only had in mind a desire to help France regain her grandeur and her power. He told d'Astier that he would see to it that the Resistance got the aid it needed, and that this could be best arranged in another meeting with his top technicians present.

The meeting was held on January 27 in Churchill's office at 10 Downing Street. Churchill was assisted by three military aides and by Lord Selborne of the Ministry of Economic Warfare. General Mockle Ferryman of the SOE attended, along with Sir Charles Portal of the Air Ministry and Charles Mack of the Foreign Office, an impressive array of top-level British leaders. On the French side were two men: d'Astier and Georges Boris of the BCRAM.

Churchill opened the meeting saying its purpose was to provide arms to the French Resistance. He said that there were important conditions that had to be posed, notably that the French give assurances that the arms would be used only against the enemy and not in conflicts between the French themselves; that all political considerations be put aside and that the Resistance receiving the arms obey without question the orders of the supreme commander, General Eisenhower. Churchill said nothing about Boisson and Peyrouton.

D'Astier replied that the Resistance would, of course, obey inter-Allied orders.

Churchill expressed an interest in being informed about the men of the maquis. He asked for a map and wanted to see just where the maquis were, insisting that every effort be made to strengthen them, and said the guerrillas could become a great force from Lake Geneva to Toulon.

Churchill ordered two hundred supplementary sorties for the month of February. He specified, upon the counsel of d'Astier and Boris, that arms be dropped to the maquis of the Savoie, the Puy-de-Dôme in the Massif Central, and the region of Roanne, in west-central France. Further plans would be made to supply the maquis of Brittany and the Ardennes. He also accepted a suggestion of d'Astier that he increase the number of Lysander and Hudson flights and send over cadres of officers to train and lead the maquis. Churchill asked them to come back to see him on February 2, with completed plans for these projects.

D'Astier met with Churchill on that date at the War Office. Churchill asked him if he was now satisfied. D'Astier, thanking him for all he had done, was obliged nonetheless, he said, to point out that it was not enough. Churchill, surprised, said that if it was not enough, it certainly was considerable. After all, he had ordered the delivery of enough arms for about sixteen thousand men.

D'Astier told the prime minister that the figure of sixteen thousand was only theoretical. In reality, the aid laid on would arm only ten thousand resistants, not sixteen thousand. Theory was far from practice. He said that Churchill should order double the arms shipments of February for the month of March.

To d'Astier's delight, Churchill nodded his agreement and dictated a note to that effect to his aide, Major Morton, who, throughout the conversation, had endorsed everything that d'Astier said. Morton even went so far as to tell the prime minister that the French needed munitions and explosives as much as, perhaps even more than arms. D'Astier hastily added: "And concentrated foods." Churchill nodded his head and told Morton to add all that to the list.

The next day, Lord Selborne met with d'Astier's brother, General François d'Astier, chief of de Gaulle's military mission in London, and showed him a memo from Churchill scolding Selborne for not having sent enough arms for February, ordering that the deficiency of February be made up in March, plus larger orders for March itself. The memo stated that the prime minister attached great importance to the arming of the maquis and that he wanted all of his promises to the French to be kept, in the shipment of arms, munitions, and concentrated foodstuffs.

D'Astier's personal initiative had been a magnificent success. It came at a crucial moment. The maquis were under heavy attack and were almost bare of supplies. At the same time, the Germans had increased their quota of workers to be supplied by Vichy to a total of 2 million men, of whom three hundred thousand had to be dispatched at once in January. This meant that new floods of Frenchmen, fleeing the forced labor draft, flowed into the maquis and had to be clothed, fed, and armed.

If Churchill, looking at the map, saw instantly the importance of the maquis in the region of Lake Geneva and throughout southeastern France, the Germans were no less aware of the existence of this threat to their security behind their lines when they would have to face an invading Allied force. They had marked off on their maps the plateau of the Glières and the Vercors in the eastern Alps. All through January, German and pro-Nazi French militia troops carried out a series of raids of maquis encampments.

At that point, Colonel Donovan's OSS reports—urging him to begin an American role in helping the French Resistance, not to leave it entirely in British hands—began to make an impression upon General Eisenhower.

On January 4, the very first American sortie carrying arms to the Resistance flew over the Vercors to drop its containers. This early American effort, however, was immediately dwarfed by the mass drops that Churchill ordered following his talks with d'Astier. Some 150 airlifts were flown in February and 370 in March, delivering 150 tons of explosives, 30,000 machine guns, 25,000 handguns, ammunition, and tons of foodstuffs. Churchill had made good on his promise and had done so with no strings attached, no quid pro quo.

London would also come to the aid of the Resistance in some spectacular individual actions, notably the extraordinary attack on the prison of Amiens.

Dominique Ponchardier, chief of a small network, Sosies, in northern France, called for the operation, but the idea itself was the brainchild of a veteran fighter of the Spanish civil war, Pépé, who had become a refugee in France and then entered the French Resistance, operating both in the Sosies network and in the Francs-Tireurs et Partisans commandos in and around Paris.

One of Pépé's lieutenants, Jean Beaurin, was imprisoned in Amiens. Beaurin, only twenty years old, had carried out some of the most daring and effective exploits of the band, including five derailings of German trains. One of the trains was blown up on the Tréport-Abbéville line, a long train of troops and matériel en route to the Russian front. More than two hundred German soldiers were killed, four hundred wounded, and tons of arms destroyed when Beaurin blew the track from under the speeding train. It was also Beaurin who brought about the head-on collision of two trains on the Paris-Lille line, one a train of Wehrmacht troops coming down from Lille on leave, the other a train heading north, loaded with Panzers for the Russian front. Beaurin manipulated the switches and brought the trains together in a crash that killed a German division general, ninety officers, and one hundred noncoms and soldiers, all of them hated SS forces.

Pépé learned that Beaurin was going to be shot by an execution squad on February 20. Other members of the group were also in Amiens prison with Beaurin, scheduled for trial, and, very likely, for the execution squads, too. Pépé came to his chief, Ponchardier, and asked permission to work out a plan to break his men out of the prison.

Ponchardier agreed at once and set about informing London of the reasons for the request, sending through detailed data on the prison. One of the men to whom he sent the information on Amiens was Group Captain Charles Pickard, commander of a squadron of Mosquito bombers, a specialist on parachute operations and clandestine landings in occupied Europe. He was a much-decorated hero of the RAF, with three DSOs. Pickard had just taken over command of the Mosquito fighter-bomber squadron that the RAF had trained for low-level, ground-grazing attacks on the German launching pads for their new secret weapon.

The secret weapon was identified as the V-1 rocket, the terrible "buzz bombs" that hit London targets without warning. Their existence had been discovered by Marie-Madeleine Fourcade's team. Marie-Madeleine, in London, received the news of the rockets from Petrel, who informed her that the espionage information had been picked up by one of their most remarkable agents, Amniarix, Jeanne Rousseau, a brilliant linguist, fluent in five languages. She had infiltrated German communications and records, and had described the secret laboratories in Peenemünde, on the Baltic Sea, where the rockets were designed.

Pickard's squadron was one of some twenty that had been assigned to knock out the launching pads of the rockets. But, he had also been designated for "special operations." The prison at Amiens became one of those special operation targets when news came through that two British agents of the Intelligence Service had been caught and imprisoned at Amiens. It was now no longer a question of rescuing French resistants alone but also important British agents. This made it easier to justify assigning Pickard and his planes to the Amiens mission.

Messages were speedily exchanged laying on the operation for February 18. That morning, Ponchardier and some of his men took up positions in the woods and around the prison ready to break in when the moment came. Captain Pickard commanded two squadrons of Mosquitos, protected by four sections of American Mustang fighters, flown by veteran Canadian pilots with a long list of "kills" to their credit. They came down in a hawklike swoop over Amiens at noon. One of the squadrons peeled off to bomb the railway lines around Amiens. The other, led by Pickard, dive-bombed down on the prison to less than two hundred feet above the ground, dropping their bombs and pouring machine-gun fire into the north wing and the central section of the prison. In London, Pickard had built a maquette of the prison and had marked his targets on aerial photo maps.

Explosions rocked the prison. Flames and smoke shot up into the air. The first bomb blasted a huge hole in the central prison wall. Another scored a direct hit on the German guardhouse. Still another hit a munitions room, where cases of grenades had been stored, and they began exploding one after the other, like a Chinese New Year fireworks display gone mad.

Beaurin and his comrades had heard the planes as the church bells were striking noon. He had been told there would be a rescue attempt, but he knew no details of the attack. He ran to the window of his cell, saw a plane drop a bomb and then veer off, exposing the RAF emblem and colors on its wings. Beaurin began to cheer and to shout: "The British are here." The next thing he knew he was flat out on the ground, knocked down by a tremendous blast. The wall of his cell cracked and something flew through the air and hit him hard in the eye. As he looked around he saw his comrades bent over, spitting blood. His own head was exploding with pain and he grabbed a sheet, doubled it over, and bit into it to keep from screaming, as new shock waves hit his cell.

He saw his cell door fly open and he managed to pull himself up and to shout at the others to come with him. They rushed through the door on their way to freedom. Smoke was everywhere, clouding up the corridors. He coughed his way through the fog, hand in hand with Maurice Holleville, a fellow resistant scheduled to be shot by the Germans. They found their way to the front door. There was not a German to be seen. The guards had been killed by the early direct hit. They staggered into the open, gulping down the clean, fresh air, found their bearings, and made their way to a hiding place in which Ponchardier had, in advance, told them to hole up.

Ponchardier, himself, with a dozen commandos, had drawn their guns and burst into the prison, shooting any Germans they saw and rounding up prisoners, telling them to get out fast, promising to pick them up and get them away as quickly as possible before the Germans and the French Nazi militia could react. Outside, a Resistance truck was picking up prisoners as speedily as they came out, rescuing patriots and common criminals indiscriminately. The whole operation took some thirty minutes from the first bombs to the rescue of the prisoners. It had been called Operation Jericho, and the walls had, indeed, come tumbling down.

Jean Beaurin and more than a dozen other men condemned to death had been rescued, along with the British agents. But casualties had been terrible. Ninety-five prisoners, including many resistants, had been killed and eighty-seven more had been wounded in the raid. Valorous Group Captain Pickard had gone down to his death, with his longtime comrade-in-arms, Flight Lieutenant John Broadley, a twenty-two-year-old hero, who had won the DSO, the DFC, and the DFM, three of the most honored decorations of the British government. Their Mosquito and a Mustang had crashed.

The price paid for the rescue of the condemned men from Amiens was very high, many more men dying than would have been killed without the raid. Nonetheless, the leaders of the Resistance and of the RAF believed the raid had been necessary and successful. The Germans and their fellow-traveling French Nazis had to learn that they could not live in security and kill French and British patriots at will. The Germans had to pay and they did pay heavily in the Amiens raid. Moreover, there was a big dividend for the Resistance. The men who had been rescued from the prison all had important intelligence information in their possession. It was now possible to identify some sixty to seventy Gestapo agents and Nazi spies that had infiltrated the Resistance movements. They were all caught and killed, thus saving the lives of a number of resistants who would have been arrested as a result of German counter-espionage. Gestapo forces were shaken up and their effectiveness in that region sharply reduced.

The day after the attack on the Amiens prison, another prison revolt broke out, this time in the south, at the central prison of Eysses, one of the main prisons of the Vichy system. Being held in that prison were almost fifteen hundred resistants who had been tried and condemned by French tribunals. The inspection visit of a Vichy penitentiary official provided the occasion for the prison uprising.

A few arms had been smuggled to the inmates, who had organized their own internal "assault team" and had planned several different versions of a prison breakout. When the Vichy official came through on his inspection tour, and their cell doors had been opened, the assault squads pulled out their guns, surrounded the warden, the Vichy envoy, and all the guards in that cellblock. They then tried to force their way out of the front doors and across the courtyard of the prison. Unfortunately, they ran into heavily armed units of the Gardes Mobiles, who opened fire and drove them back into the prison. They had not planned any coordinated air attack or any Resistance commando attack from the outside. The mutineers were trapped inside the prison. There was no way out. On the other hand, the guards were outside and there was no way in except by an assault with machine guns and grenades that would surely overpower the prisoners but would result in the death of the prison director and the Vichy official. It was a standoff.

The news reached Vichy, where Pétain's ministers were convened to discuss strategy to cope with the Eysses revolt. The man chiefly concerned was the infamous Joseph Darnand, creator of the Milice, the armed militia that performed the functions of the German Gestapo and worked closely with the Gestapo. Darnand had been named Minister for the Maintenance of Order.

Darnand himself came to Eysses to negotiate with the mutinous prisoners. He told them that they had no chance to break out and win their freedom. They all knew that. But he promised them that there would be no sanctions against them, no reprisals of any kind if only they would release the warden and the Vichy official unharmed. He gave his "word of honor" that they could then return to their cells without punishment.

The prisoners' committee considered the proposals and finally agreed.

Two days later, Darnand set up court-martials to try the leaders of the prison revolt. Twelve resistants were put on trial, found guilty, condemned to death, and, on February 23, were shot by a firing squad. Every single one of the fifteen hundred resistants imprisoned at Eysses was then deported to Germany.

Hundreds upon hundreds of resistants were arrested, imprisoned, deported, or killed in the grim winter months of February and March 1944. One of the hardest blows of all was the aborted escape to London of Emile Bollaert, who had been named delegate-general to the Resistance, and of Passy's deputy at the BCRA, Pierre Brossolette. Both Bollaert and Brossolette had been trying for months to get out of France and report to de Gaulle in Algiers. They had finally taken passage on a small boat that the Resistance had bought and was using to take about twenty Allied airmen back to England, across the Channel. But in a storm the boat's engine failed and its mainmast splintered. The captain just managed to get back to the French shore and discharge his passengers. Brossolette and Bollaert were taken by car to a safe-house but arrived in the middle of a police ambush. Both were arrested and imprisoned in Rennes. Bollaert would survive deportation, but Brossolette, fearful of talking under pressure, threw himself out of a fifth-floor window and died in a coma in a hospital.

The Resistance and the Allies had, once again, to take steps to tighten command structures in anticipation of the landings in France. General Eisenhower, in March, assumed control of all secret service operations connected with the Overlord landings. All services were ordered to report to his headquarters, SHAEF, Supreme Headquarters Allied Expeditionary Forces. The joint special operations unit that had been created by OSS and SOE was cut away from those bodies and renamed Special Force Headquarters of SHAEF. Another group was formed to coordinate all Resistance and special force activities for a newly planned second front in France, in the south, called Operation Anvil. A number of us in Algiers were briefed on Anvil and received assignments on how to operate and coordinate with the Resistance when we were to land on a broad front along the Riviera from Toulon to Saint-Raphaël, after the Normandy landings.

As the dawn of liberation drew near, Giraudist and ex-Vichy reactionaries made their last and ill-fated attempt to challenge General de Gaulle. The leader in their mad scheme was none other than that wealthy right-wing conspirator, Jacques Lemaigre-Dubreuil, who had played such an important role in Operation Torch.

Lemaigre-Dubreuil and members of Giraud's DSR/SM secret service had made contact with an eccentric named Paul Dungler who claimed to be the leader of an independent, non-Gaullist Resistance movement in Alsace-Lorraine. Dungler was known to have good contacts with Marshal Pétain and his regime in Vichy. Pétain had, in the summer of 1943, sent Dungler to Algiers with offers of reconciliation addressed to Giraud and de Gaulle. Both generals angrily rejected the absurd proposals that Dungler had brought.

Dungler continued to hang around Algiers looking for something to do. He met an American named Henry Hyde, chief of the Secret Intelligence Branch of OSS and one of the very last diehard anti-Gaullists in Algiers. He also met with officers of the DSR/SM. Hyde and the Giraud secret service officers agreed to send Dungler back to France, with instructions to make contact in Nice with dissident German officers of Admiral Canaris's Intelligence Service, the Abwehr, the Army Intelligence rival of Heinrich Himmler's dread Gestapo.

     Neither the Americans nor the Giraudists bothered to inform Jacques Soustelle, the newly appointed chief of de Gaulle's DGSS, Direction Générale des Services Spéciaux, or Colonel Passy and his men of the BCRAM, both of whom were responsible for French intelligence operations. But, of course, Algiers being the sieve it was, where everything leaked, they soon found out about Dungler's "mission."

     They told de Gaulle and obtained from him a warrant to arrest Dungler. Warned by friends inside headquarters, Dungler fled to Lemaigre-Dubreuil's sumptuous villa to hide out. Then OSS men smuggled him out of Algiers to an American airfield and flew him to an area over Vichy where he parachuted down into France. De Gaulle and his men were furious and began to set in motion plans to destroy Giraud and his ridiculous band of schemers.

     Ever since his Corsican coup, General Giraud had been working with the Communists, strange bedfellows in his campaign against de Gaulle. So, at the same time that Dungler was flirting with the Abwehr, Giraud sent a Communist officer, Captain Larribère, to contact armed Resistance units in the Toulouse-Marseille area. Giraud, apparently totally unconcerned with any security rules, gave this agent the list of code phrases that would be used by the Allied radio at the moment of landing in southern France. Those phrases indicated, two to three days in advance of the landings, the exact place and time of the operations.

     Larribère had given this vital information to a number of men he contacted inside France. Had any one of them fallen into the hands of the Gestapo, the Germans would have had precise information on the Allied landings. Not a word about Larribère and his insane mission had been transmitted to General de Gaulle and his services. However Larribère, very proud of himself, called upon Jacques Soustelle on his return to Algiers. Soustelle exploded with rage and rushed to tell de Gaulle what had happened.

     Meanwhile, Dungler had contacted the Abwehr agents and was hoping to get information from them about a plot to assassinate Hitler, which he would then radio to Giraud in Algiers. He did not know that an angry de Gaulle had taken over the radio facilities of Giraud's secret service. Dungler tried to raise his contacts in Algiers and did not know why he failed to get through. Himmler, by then, had learned of the various plots and was delighted to seize the chance to score points against the rival Abwehr. He sent his agents to arrest Dungler, who confessed to his dealings with the Abwehr. Himmler ordered the agents to return to Germany for interrogation by the Gestapo.

     Armed by the facts of Giraud's incredible and dangerous schemes, de Gaulle rapidly persuaded the political leaders in Algiers to approve his decision, as sole president of the Comité Français de Libération Nationale, which they now considered to be the Provisional Government of the Republic, to dismiss General Giraud as commander in chief. To save what was left of his face, Giraud was given the empty title of inspector general and then placed on the army's reserve list. De Gaulle was now solely in command as chief executive and commander in chief of the French Provisional Government.

The Resistance moved to tighten up its own ranks. An important new top echelon of command had been agreed upon at the very end of 1943, on December 29, when Pontcarral, head of the Armée Secrète, on orders from London, had signed a new protocol of agreement between the Secret Army and the FTPF Communists. Article 1 of the protocol stated that the two organizations had agreed henceforth to merge into one command organism, the Forces Françaises de l'Intérieur, FFI, followed by a number of clauses detailing the creation and appointment of regional and departmental structures for the new organization. The Resistance chiefs all agreed to take orders from General Pierre Koenig, the head of the FFI in London.

The Communists were making every effort to take over key posts inside all command structures. Pierre Villon, who had made the Front National into a genuine national association of men from extreme right to extreme left, proposed a new action program for the CNR, which he called the Charter. It was adopted on March 15, 1944.

The Charter was a series of agreements designed to govern current action against Vichy and the Germans and, above all, to provide measures to install a new and just social order as soon as the national territory was liberated. In the spring of 1944, everyone sensed that the landings were imminent and would take place in the first spell of fine weather at the end of the spring or early summer. Therefore, all were concerned about the political power to be installed and the social programs to be followed in the wake of the liberating armies. The Comité d'Etudes inside France, with such men as Alexandre Parodi and Michel Debré, were working on these questions of the future Republic, as were law professors led by the Catholic resistant François de Menthon, in Algiers. Resistance leaders knew that Villon was a dedicated Communist and that Front National, for all its democratic and right-wing members, was controlled by Villon. That did not influence their judgment on his Charter, which they thought to be an excellent program.

The goals foreseen by all parties included the installation immediately after the liberation of a provisional government presided over by General de Gaulle; Allied military orders would be followed but there would be no Allied Military Government, no AMGOT; rapid trial and punishment of traitors and confiscation of their assets; reestablishment of democracy in every collectivity and every domain. Other issues were being debated such as direct or indirect universal or limited suffrage, and the timing and nature of elections to a constituent assembly to create a new Republic of France.

On the eve of the Allied landings, both the French and the Germans began a series of military moves, particularly in and around the maquis camp of the Plateau des Glières in the mountainous Haute-Savoie region of eastern France. The first dramatic battle took place in March. There was a fierce combat engagement by the newly formed Bataillon des Glières, which would lead to controversy and recriminations that have not ended today, some thirty-five years later.

Early in February, the leader of the maquis in that region, Théodose Morel, known as Tom, who was famed as a fighter, had attracted to his side several hundred new men. He already commanded a detachment of the Armée Secrète, several sections of Francs-Tireurs et Partisans, several dozen Spanish Republicans, and a whole host of men from right to left who had come to fight under his leadership, and under the slogan he had given his men: "Vivre Libre ou Mourir"—Live Free or Die.

Tom had been given the mission, by superior officers, of assembling in the wooded area of the Glières some 250 men whose assignment it was to clear a site for a drop zone for Allied supplies. The leaders of the Haute-Savoie had been informed of Churchill's promises to d'Astier and were expecting mass drops of arms and food. What Tom's superiors did not know was that that dynamic man had rallied to his side not 250 men but some 450 men, an exceptionally large and unwise concentration of men, unwise because a battalion-size unit could not function with the flexibility needed by guerrillas.

Tom was acting in accordance with orthodox military doctrine, which required a buildup from squad to platoon to company to battalion, all heavily armed and able to take up strong defensive positions. He was in a position to set up an entrenched camp, a kind of bastion. But that was in sharp contradiction to the tactics of the Resistance, which were based upon Frenay's doctrine of trentaines, that is, no group to be greater than thirty in order to be able to move quickly, to hit the enemy and run, in typical guerrilla fashion. Much later this guerrilla technique would prove very successful when the Vietminh used it against the French in Indochina, and the Vietcong against the Americans in Vietnam.

The expected British arms drops came as promised in mid-February, four planes dropping fifty-four containers, to be followed the next night by a second drop of thirty containers, loaded with guns and munitions. The Germans and their pro-Nazi French accomplices, the GMR, the Groupes Mobiles de Reserve, watched these planes fly over and dip down for the drop. They knew the maquisards were there and pinpointed their positions on their maps as they set up a circle of attack troops around the plateau.

At that moment, a young medical student left the maquis to buy pharmaceutical products in the valley and was caught by the police. Tom sent out a commando unit, which captured thirty GMR men. He then offered to exchange them for their captured student. Their colonel agreed, and Tom released his prisoners, but the GMR colonel did not return the young student. Tom, furious, led a new attack on the GMR command post. His commandos blasted their way in, won a quick victory over the GMR, and began to disarm their prisoners.

Major Lefèvre, commander of that post, demanded the traditional right of an officer to keep his pistol to maintain his honor. Tom asked him what his honor as a GMR was worth, since they had not kept their bargain to release the medical student. In a drunken rage, roaring that he had been insulted, Major Lefèvre drew his pistol and shot Tom through the heart. He was cut down at once by a burst from a machine-pistol from a maquis officer, but Tom was already dead.

The maquisards, blood in their eyes, renewed their attacks on the GMR and killed dozens of the pro-Nazi French, taking almost fifty prisoners back with them to the maquis deep inside the wooded plateau. The maquis had lost only three men, but the three were all key men: Tom, his deputy Georges Descours, and a former ski champion, Jo Frizon. They paid a terrible price for a small and dangerous victory over the GMR, dangerous because the Germans took careful note of what had happened and made their own plans.

The next day, the British came through again with a mass drop, a gigantic parachute operation, dropping almost ninety tons of arms and munitions, enough to arm four thousand men. The men of the Glières were completely overwhelmed. The arms were dropped over more than four hundred different sites, scattered all over the plateau. Some of the containers had buried themselves in deep snow and others fell into ravines that were very hard to reach. Although Tom had assembled too many maquisards for guerrilla fighting, there were not enough men to pick up all that had been dropped. And the men they did have were separated from one another over a wide area, looking for containers. They were no longer functioning as an efficient unit, but rather as foragers out hunting for supplies. The British had dropped more than they needed and more than they could collect. Meanwhile, overhead, a German spotter plane flew over the maquis, plotting their positions and relaying the information to Heinkel bomber pilots who came over, dropped bombs, and strafed the area with blazing machine guns.

The leaders of the maquis bands did not want to leave the containers, for fear the Germans would come to gather them up, and would then boast how the Resistance had armed the German troops. For the honor of the maquis, and to ensure further arms drops, it was felt necessary to search out all the containers. Day after day, hundreds of men scoured the fields, the woods, the snowbanks. The Germans waited, watched, and prepared to move against them.

General Julius Oberg, commander of an Alpine division of crack troops, conferred with commanders of the Luftwaffe and chiefs of the Gestapo. In addition, units of Darnand's Milice were asked to join the Germans in an all-out assault on the plateau. General Oberg had some fifteen thousand troops and two air squadrons at his disposal.

The opening assault began with a heavy artillery and bombing barrage on March 25. The next day, Oberg gave the order for a general assault on all fronts. Wave after wave of fire swept across the plateau of the Glières, turning trees into torches and the snowbanks into mounds coated with charred ash. The men in the maquis, hopelessly outnumbered, fifteen thousand to five hundred, fell back toward their entrenched camp, dug holes, hunkered down, and tried to survive the whirlwind of flame.

By nightfall of the twenty-sixth, the Germans had penetrated well into the plateau. Almost all the maquis officers were killed by the evening of the twenty-seventh. The maquisards could not hold any positions. They broke and ran, like rabbits fleeing a horde of foxes. The Germans began a systematic combing of the woods, determined to let no man escape. Few did: One hundred fifty-five maquisards were killed in combat, thirty were wounded and died later. One hundred sixty were taken prisoner and either executed on the spot or sent to concentration camps in Germany.

As soon as the facts were known, serious quarrels broke out among maquis leaders and other chiefs of the Resistance over the strategy and tactics of the affair. Some tried to put the best face upon it. One of the leaders of the Haute-Savoie region, Henri Romans-Petit, asserted that the battle resulted in a "defeat of arms but a victory of souls." His comment had a fine ring to it but it is difficult to accept. The slaughter of so many men, for no purpose at all, was one of the first but, alas, not the last of the tragedies played out by brave men of the maquis.

The lessons of the tragedy of the Glières were not learned, not accepted even in the days immediately following the massacre, let alone years later. Resistance leaders received orders from London and Algiers to create large maquis forces and bastions. Frenay and his maquis chief Jérome complained, to no avail. General de Gaulle's headquarters sent through a plan for the formation of such forces in the Massif Central region. Meanwhile, the Germans and Darnand's Milice pushed ahead on a wide-scale campaign against all the maquis, in the Alps of the Haute-Savoie and the Savoie, in the mountains of the Jura near the Swiss border, in the central forests of the Corrèze and the southwestern vineyards of the Dordogne. Darnand's Milice were joined by a vicious band of French killers, the Bonny-Lafont gang.

Lafont was the alias of a gangster named Henri Chamberlin. He had joined forces with a former commissioner of police, Pierre Bonny, who had helped him recruit the most savage killers, torturers, and sadists in the French underworld. Bonny and Lafont, charged with many horrible crimes, had been picked up by the Gestapo and recruited by the Nazis as auxiliary troops to search out and kill resistants.

Every maquis that the Germans located came under attack and not only those in entrenched camps as in the Glières. The records show that in almost every instance, men who dug into entrenched positions were overrun and slaughtered, while those who fought as guerrillas, lurking in the shadows, coming out only for a quick hit and a swift retreat, were the only ones who survived with minimum losses and maximum damage to the enemy.

All through the spring of 1944, pitched battles were fought by the Germans and bands of resistants all across France and particularly in the eastern, central, and southern regions, where the maquis groups were concentrated. The Germans and the pro-Nazi French, such as the Milice of Darnand and the Bonny-Lafont gang, fought side by side and engaged in punitive expeditions against villages and towns in reprisal for Resistance attacks upon the Germans. Citizens were massacred, shot down in the streets of Brantôme, hanged from lampposts in Nîmes. Northern France was not spared. One of the worst massacres bloodied the streets of Ascq, on the Lille-Tournai railway line. The Resistance had sabotaged and derailed a German troop train on that line, not far from Ascq. The Germans rounded up sixty men in the town, took them to a pasture facing the railway station, and machine-gunned them. Nazi patrols broke into houses inside Ascq and shot down twenty-six men in their own homes in front of their families. One of those shot down was a local priest who had rushed in to give the final sacraments to a dying man. The next day funeral services were held for the victims, and despite German threats, twenty thousand people came en masse to the ceremonies.

While fighting raged inside France, there was no end to political infighting among the Frenchmen at de Gaulle's headquarters in Algiers. By April, de Gaulle had at last rid himself of Giraud, but he still found himself in the middle of vexatious quarrels between rival leaders of police and intelligence forces, the commissioner of the Interior, d'Astier de la Vigerie, and the director of the DGSS, Jacques Soustelle, who was joined by Colonel Passy, chief of the BCRAM. Each was engaged in a contest to see who could get to France first and organize the forces inside France under his own command. De Gaulle ended that quarrel by deciding not to let any of them go on a special mission to France.

At that moment, de Gaulle welcomed Claude Serreulles to Algiers. Because of the two and a half years that he had served as chef de Cabinet to de Gaulle, Serreulles had been closer to him than anyone else. He was trusted by de Gaulle and not overawed by him. Thus, Serreulles could talk freely to the haughty leader of the Provisional Government of France.

"I wanted de Gaulle to know the whole truth about the intrigues and plots that had been carried on by Passy and by Brossolette to the detriment of the Resistance," Serreulles recalled in the course of several long interviews on his role in those days. "I knew that Passy had wanted Brossolette to replace Moulin and that he was furious with me for having changed the structures, bringing in Bidault as head of the CNR and separating London's 'delegation' from the Council of the Resistance. But they endangered the entire Resistance when they failed to answer my many messages and when they finally cut off all communications to the delegation."

Serreulles frowned as he recalled, "I discovered in talking with de Gaulle that he had not received a tenth of the reports that I had sent addressed to him personally over a period of almost nine months. I learned, too, that Passy had not passed my reports on to d'Astier. It was shameful and dangerous for our own secret services to sabotage our work in this fashion and

I told de Gaulle so quite frankly. My testimony came at a very bad time for Passy and for Soustelle, who were right in the middle of their struggle with d'Astier for power.

"It was, at that moment, most interesting for me to be in Algiers, for de Gaulle was on the point of making an important decision concerning the makeup of the Comité Français de Libération Nationale. Should he or should he not enlarge the CFLN to include members of the Communist party, and what posts should he give them? He put this question to me. It was, incidentally, one of the points in dispute between d'Astier, who favored inclusion of the Communists, and the Soustelle-Passy combine, which opposed it.

"I told de Gaulle, without hesitation, that the Communists were prominent in the Resistance, fighting as patriots for the liberation of our country. I reminded him that Jean Moulin, whom he honored, had insisted on bringing the Communists into the Conseil National de la Résistance. And I asked de Gaulle: 'How can they be fighting in the Resistance and not share in the responsibilities of government?' I said that the liberation of our country must not be aborted by any form of civil strife among the patriots who had fought so long side by side. Of course the Communists must be in the government."

Serreulles smiled and added: "I am quite sure that my words were not responsible for de Gaulle's decision to bring the Communists in. He had, I'm certain, already made up his mind to that effect. It was not that he trusted the Communists any more than any of us did, but it simply made sense to work with them when they were working, fighting, and dying with us."

Serreulles told de Gaulle that his delegation inside France was too small and too narrow at the top. He said that there could be one delegate-general to replace Bollaert but that he ought to be assisted by five or six delegates for different regions. He recommended highly a professional civil servant, a cool, efficient man, Alexandre Parodi, for the post of delegate-general. Parodi was known, respected, and liked by all the Resistance leaders. He was an able administrator, with no personal leadership ambitions. De Gaulle agreed with Serreulles, and Parodi was at once appointed delegate-general.

Serreulles, his large brown eyes moist as he thought back in 1977 to those days of the Resistance, went on to speak of his greatest disappointment, and of Passy's revenge upon him for having criticized him to de Gaulle.

"I flew to London to get passage back to France, to rejoin my comrades of the Resistance and to prepare for the great day of the Allied landings. I had been waiting for this moment ever since, way back in 1940, I had been pushed into a potato sack by the Poles in Morocco who smuggled me on the ship that took me to England to carry on the fight. But when I asked Passy for the seat in the plane back to France, he told me coldly that the British had refused to grant me passage. 'You know too much, are too informed of all our plans. The Gestapo is looking for you and it is too dangerous to let you go back to France.'

"I knew that Passy was lying. The British had said no such thing. It was Passy who did not want me to go back to France. Passy had excellent relations with the British and he could easily persuade them not to carry me. I was furious but I was blocked in London. When d'Astier came to London, I rushed over to tell him what Passy had done and he was enraged by Passy's blocking me after all that I had done in the Resistance. He had a first-class row with Passy, but, you see, Passy hated d'Astier even more than he was angered with me. D'Astier could not do a thing with him. We thought of appealing to de Gaulle, but it would do no good, for Passy would simply hide behind the British.

"D'Astier did go to the British to try to do something with them. But they sent us a letter stating that for technical reasons they could not bring me back to France until D-day."

Serreulles stopped in his narrative, grinned, and said: "The message cheered me up anyway. Just seeing the words D-day in that letter. All right, I would be patient. D-day could not be far away, and Passy would not stop me then. I would return to France with the liberating armies. Ah, that would be the day!"

PART SIX
LIBERATION

23
THE LANDINGS IN NORMANDY

It was almost a half hour before midnight on June 4, 1944, and on duty at FFI headquarters in London was a captain named Mamy. He had hurried to complete his security check of the office, looking at papers left on desks, testing locks on top-secret files, doing it as quickly as he could in order to get back to his desk to listen to the 11:30 P.M. broadcast of Personal Messages on the BBC, the coded messages that sent instructions to the Resistance.

Captain Mamy himself had participated in the coding for several top-level plans: the *Plan Vert*, the Green Plan for sabotaging rail lines in support of the Allied landings; the *Plan Bleu*, the Blue Plan for cutting off hydroelectric power lines; the Violet Plan, aimed at cutting or blocking the Germans' underground long-distance telephone lines; and, finally, the *Plan Tortue*, the Tortoise Plan, whose code name was then changed to Bibendum, whose mission it was to prevent German armored units from making their way to the Allied landing beaches.

Normally, these messages took up about four to six minutes of air time. Mamy checked his watch as the broadcast began. He heard some familiar phrases that brought a smile to his lips. "The doctor buries all his patients," a code sent by someone with a grudge against doctors. It signaled the dispatch of a boat to the coast of Finistère. Another message, coded by another planner with a sense of humor, announced: "I kiss you, darling, three times." It told a maquis group in the Ain that three planes would be coming over for an arms and matériel drop. The phrases came quickly and in great number on that broadcast of June 4, 1944: "The crocodile is thirsty"—"The raven has a red breast"—"The squirrel has a heavy tail"—"The bears have a thick coat"—"Kiou is kind"—"Baba calls to Coco."

Captain Mamy checked his watch. The broadcast was running well beyond six minutes. Suddenly, he heard the phrase: "It is hot in Suez." He tensed up immediately. That was the phrase for a general mobilization and a nationwide series of attacks by the Resistance in support of Allied landings.

Mamy did not have the key to the date and place, but he did know that the key signal had just been given; the landings must be imminent.

Then he heard: "The dice are cast." That, too, was a nationwide signal to all Resistance units of France for a general uprising. As he was puzzling over that disturbing signal—disturbing because he had been told that a nationwide uprising was too dangerous and had been dropped from the planning—he suddenly heard the words: "The arrow will not pierce." This was one of the key code phrases that he had worked on himself, calling on the Resistance specialists to launch the Green and Violet plans to cut rail and telephone lines. No doubt in his mind that the invasion was very near, Captain Mamy began to write out notes for the morning duty officer, who would have an urgent series of calls to make to staff officers.

General de Gaulle had arrived in London on that same day, June 4. The night before, the Consultative Assembly in Algiers had voted to change the title of the French National Committee of Liberation to the new title: Provisional Government of the French Republic, and thus de Gaulle considered that he was arriving as the president of France. No one else agreed with his position.

Churchill was polite to de Gaulle. He had sent his personal York plane to Algiers to pick up de Gaulle and bring him to London, an act which signaled the French leader that the landings were about to take place. Churchill had then sent a personal message to the desk of the Connaught Hotel to greet de Gaulle upon his arrival in London. It welcomed him "to these shores," and proclaimed that "great military events are about to take place." The letter invited de Gaulle to join Churchill on his train, which would then take them to General Eisenhower's headquarters in the countryside, and promised him a personal briefing from the supreme commander.

General de Gaulle went to see Churchill at lunchtime that day, as the letter had suggested, taking a number of aides with him; among them was General Koenig, commander of French regular forces and overall commander, too, of the internal Resistance, the FFI, Forces Françaises de l'Intérieur. They were picked up at their hotel by Anthony Eden, who escorted them to Churchill's train. Waiting with Churchill to receive the French were General Ismay, Field Marshal Smuts, and Labor party leader Ernest Bevin, the tough champion of England's stevedores.

The meeting was correct but the atmosphere definitely chilly. General de Gaulle was icily angry about a decision taken by the British some weeks earlier. British authorities had forbidden the French to communicate with each other between London and Algiers in coded messages, ordering that all messages be sent in the clear. This meant that the British could read every message exchanged by French authorities. It was a security order, designed to prevent the French in London from leaking any information to Algiers about invasion plans. De Gaulle took it as a personal affront, an expression of deep mistrust of the French. He ordered General Koenig to halt all cooperation between French liaison officers and the Allies. A breach of this magnitude in so important a sector as liaison between the French and the Allies on the eve of landing in France was highly dangerous to all concerned.

For General de Gaulle the stakes were enormous, nothing less than the independence and sovereignty of France, to say nothing of his own position as leader of the French. He feared that the Allied officers would try to put into effect Roosevelt's plans for Allied Military Government, treating France as a conquered and occupied nation instead of a free and sovereign state. De Gaulle had been informed by his representatives in the military missions, headed by his old friend Colonel Claude de Boislambert, that the Americans had actually printed "occupation money," French francs, in the form of dollar bills. De Gaulle fumed about American "counterfeit forgeries" for France.

De Gaulle's concern was clearly justified. Roosevelt had been talking about offering France a "secretaryship" in a new world organization that would be headed up by the four great powers: America, Britain, Russia, and China. De Gaulle was livid when that report was sent to him from Washington, and it led him to delay replying to a Roosevelt invitation to visit him in America.

Churchill, on the other hand, was fed up with de Gaulle's haughty manner and systematic obstructionism. On the eve of one of the greatest military adventures in history—the launching of an assault force of more than one hundred and fifty thousand Americans and Britons across the Channel in a direct attack on Hitler's Fortress Europa—he had no patience for de Gaulle's sensitive pride and stiff neck. It was the British navy that would have to carry those men to the beaches of France, and the RAF, principally, that would cover the naval armada.

Churchill had just finished reading the meteorological reports when de Gaulle's party came aboard his train. The reports were not good. While Churchill was greeting de Gaulle, General Eisenhower, at his command post, was consulting his principal advisers and operational commanders: Field Marshal Montgomery, Eisenhower's deputy commander, in charge of the landings; Admiral Ramsay, in charge of naval operations; Air Chief Marshal Leigh-Mallory; and his good friend, commanding American assault troops, General Omar Bradley, the soldier's soldier, beloved of all the GIs.

These were the men who would command the troops hitting the beaches on one of three possible invasion dates: June 5, 6, or 7, depending on weather conditions. These were the only three days for a period of two weeks when the tides would permit landings. Any delay of two weeks, or a month, at worst, would mean keeping one hundred and fifty thousand men locked up with the secret of the invasion, all the while maintaining them in a state ready for the assault. It was an almost impossible task. A delay would not only risk breaking secrecy and the morale of the troops, but would lessen the time available for widening of the bridgehead and the capture of a major port before the bad weather of the fall made it impossible. Too much delay could halt the invasion for another year.

Churchill plunged directly into the heart of the matter with de Gaulle, telling him that the landings were imminent, but not spelling out precisely where and when. This infuriated de Gaulle. Churchill told the French leader how deeply he and the Allied officers regretted the necessity for bombing French cities, towns, and villages. Even as Churchill and de Gaulle were lunching in London, Allied bombers were pounding rail centers, marshaling yards, airfields, road junctions, and gas depots all over France. A spokesman for General Eisenhower, in a broadcast to France, warned all French citizens to move away from all railway lines. A later broadcast told them to evacuate Paris, and a still later one told them to stay in Paris. Partly, the Allies were trying genuinely to warn the French, partly they were playing a war of nerves with the Germans.

All during their earlier luncheon, Churchill and de Gaulle had been able to hear the blasts and feel the shock waves of the tremendous air attacks on the Pas de Calais, an Allied effort to confirm the Germans in their intelligence estimate that it was in the Pas de Calais that the Allies would land. During the last days of May, there had been great casualties all through France in air raids: six hundred killed and five hundred wounded in Lyon; more than three hundred killed and four hundred wounded in Nice; almost two thousand dead and fifteen hundred wounded in Marseille. German attacks on the maquis multiplied, particularly in the Vercors, and thousands of Frenchmen and women, who had fought so hard and suffered so much, would die in the last hours before liberation. All this weighed heavily on the shoulders of the leaders lunching on June 4.

At lunch, each of the two men reacted in accordance with his own personality and national imperatives. Churchill kept pressing de Gaulle to accept Roosevelt's invitation to go to Washington to discuss the issue of the future government of France. De Gaulle sharply refused. His government, albeit provisional, existed whether Roosevelt recognized it or not, and there was no need to negotiate the issue of a French government with a foreign power, however friendly and allied. It was uniquely a question for the French to settle among themselves. Allied recognition was bound to follow.

Ernest Bevin exploded, exclaiming that a good many Englishmen and Americans were about to die to liberate France. To win the victory they needed full cooperation. He told de Gaulle that if he would not send his liaison officers, he would be committing a hostile act toward the Allies.

De Gaulle, completely unimpressed by the stevedores' union leader, told Bevin that he demanded the right to send coded messages to Algiers, that he would not tolerate American counterfeit money in France, and could not negotiate under that kind of intolerable pressure.

It was Churchill's turn to explode. Churchill told de Gaulle what he had already told him on an earlier trip to Algiers, that in any quarrel between de Gaulle and Roosevelt he would side with Roosevelt.

De Gaulle, with a twisted smile and a wave of his hand, dismissed Churchill's threat with a muttered: "Yes, to be sure."

Churchill then said, referring to the issue of administration of liberated French territory, that if de Gaulle expected to get the "title deeds" to France, he would be disappointed. The answer was no!

De Gaulle stood up. The conversation, if it could be described by so mild a term, had come to an end. Silently, if side by side, de Gaulle and Churchill made their way to General Eisenhower's headquarters.

At headquarters all went well. De Gaulle and Eisenhower respected one another and had a good rapport. Eisenhower, as always, went out of his way to be courteous and respectful of the leader of the French. He took de Gaulle to his war map and for twenty minutes went over all invasion plans in great detail, showing his complete trust in de Gaulle. Not only did he reveal all his plans, but in a shrewd masterstroke, the supreme commander asked the French leader deferentially whether he would give him his advice on the essential decision: whether to go ahead with the landings in the next two days, despite unfavorable weather reports, or to delay another two weeks, risking greater delays.

De Gaulle paused and considered the question with the deliberation that it merited. His eyes thawed out and smiled down on Eisenhower, as he told the supreme commander that as a "head of state" (a clear jab at Churchill, who refused to consider him as such) he wished to confer full freedom of action upon the military commander, in whom he had full confidence. Then he added, "I will only say this: that in your place I would make no postponement. The risk from weather seems to me less than the danger of several weeks' delay, which is bound to exacerbate the moral tension of the troops taking part and to compromise the secret." De Gaulle, the military analyst, had hit upon the precise points that were of concern to Eisenhower. Eisenhower thanked him, shook his hand, promised that all would be done to free France and defeat the common enemy. It was the only bright spot of warmth and friendship on that day of generally bad weather on all fronts. Unfortunately that moment would not last long.

Just before de Gaulle made ready to leave Eisenhower's command post, the supreme commander, looking a little embarrassed, handed de Gaulle a sheet of paper and said: "Oh, you will want to see this. It is the proclamation I will make on D-day to the people of western Europe."

General de Gaulle, keenly sensitive to every maneuver, picked him up on his remark and said: "This is what you propose to say to the people of France?" putting considerable stress on the word *propose*, subtly implying his right to amend Eisenhower's words. The supreme commander merely nodded.

General de Gaulle refused Churchill's invitation to ride back to London with him on his train. Churchill noted, in his memoirs, that de Gaulle "drew himself up and stated that he preferred to motor with his French officers separately." The chill was becoming a deep freeze.

Back at his office, General de Gaulle read Eisenhower's proclamation with dismay. It talked of instructions that would be given the French by the Allied military authorities but said not a word about the Provisional Government of the French Republic, not a word about de Gaulle or his delegates, not a word about any French authority. Eisenhower had not followed Roosevelt's instructions to make it clear that de Gaulle had no official status as a government leader, but if he did not disown de Gaulle, he certainly did not give him any recognition.

Eisenhower was aware of de Gaulle's sensitivities and would have liked to meet him at least halfway. The supreme commander knew that he would need help from the French on the landings and in the Battle of France. In his memoirs, *Crusade for Europe,* Eisenhower wrote: "We were depending on a considerable assistance from the insurrectionists in France. They were known to be particularly numerous in the Brittany area and in the hills and mountains of southeast France." He went on to add that he was anxious to have de Gaulle participate in the broadcasts to France on D-day. He felt de Gaulle could guide the French people and help avoid premature uprisings and useless sacrifices at noncritical points, marshaling their main efforts when and where help was needed in the fighting. (This was a strange comment from Eisenhower, since his own headquarters had already given the order for a general uprising all through France, a signal that would cause the loss of many lives in premature uprisings and useless sacrifices. Eisenhower did not seem to be aware of that signal.)

From his headquarters in London the next day, General de Gaulle sent Eisenhower his own version of what ought to be said in the D-day proclamation, greatly amending Eisenhower's original text. A brief note from Eisenhower thanked him for his suggestions but informed him that it was too late to make any changes, for the invasion was already wheeling into position, and the supreme commander's full attention was engaged. This exchange took place at the end of the morning of June 5.

On the afternoon of June 5 Charles Peake, British Foreign Office diplomat assigned to Free France, called upon de Gaulle with two requests: first, that he join in a series of broadcasts to occupied Europe on the following morning, when invasion troops would be fighting on the beaches; second, that he turn over to the Allied commanders the corps of French liaison officers who had been trained for months to participate in the landings and facilitate contacts between the Anglo-Americans and the French people, a vital, urgent mission.

General de Gaulle flatly turned down both requests. He felt that the broadcast precedence was an open insult to France. The order of broadcasts was: the king of Norway, the queen of Holland, the grand duchess of Luxembourg, the prime minister of Belgium, General Eisenhower, and then, in last position, separated from the other leaders by the supreme commander, de Gaulle.

On the issue of the liaison officers, de Gaulle was almost as adamant in his refusal. He did not refuse absolutely; he posed two conditions to the assignment of French liaison officers to the Allied command. First, he demanded freedom of communications between his offices in London and Algiers, that is, removal of the ban on coded messages that had been in effect since the end of April. No free communications for the French, no liaison with the Allies, de Gaulle asserted. The second condition was his outright demand that the Allies recognize officially the Provisional Government of the French Republic. De Gaulle argued that there had to be an authoritative governmental force in being during the liberation of France to avoid the real dangers of complete anarchy, or even a civil war.

The Allies, he asserted, could not provide governmental services; all that foreigners could do would be to occupy France. In that case the invasion would be a hostile act, not an act of liberation. Recognition was a sine qua non and he would not assign any liaison officers to any occupying forces. Either the Allies were true allies, friends, comrades-in-arms, or they were an occupying force that would meet with dangerous resistance from the French people and the Resistance movements. It was a stern warning from de Gaulle, and an arrogant one just hours before some one hundred and fifty thousand Americans and Englishmen were to risk their lives on the beaches of France.

Churchill was furious when he learned of de Gaulle's harsh refusals of cooperation at that critical moment. At two in the morning he summoned Pierre Viénot, de Gaulle's diplomatic representative in London, and delivered a blistering message to de Gaulle. At the very moment that Churchill was raging at the French, the first Allied commandos were hitting the beaches of Normandy, before dawn on June 6. Viénot delivered Churchill's cannonade to de Gaulle, who was completely unmoved by it. De Gaulle called his old friend and wartime comrade Claude de Boislambert, whom he had made head of France's Military Mission for Administrative Liaison (MMLA in French) and told him to stand fast and keep a tight rein on his 170 French officers, all chafing at restraints and straining to land in France.

Colonel de Boislambert agreed with de Gaulle—it would have done no good to disagree with him—but suggested that it would be in de Gaulle's interest, in the highest interests of France, that some liaison officers in French uniform show up in France as soon as possible.

Upon reflection, de Gaulle agreed that this might be wise. He thereupon instructed de Boislambert to inform the Allies that a limited contingent of twenty officers, under the command of Colonel Chandon, would sail for France on June 8. De Gaulle stipulated that they would not serve as liaison officers for civil affairs, for that would mean yielding to Allied pretensions to be in charge of French civil affairs, but would serve only as "general liaison officers and observers." Meanwhile, Resistance leaders were to be informed of developments, and those who had been named in advance by Algiers should move as soon as they could to serve as prefects and commissaires de la République. The Resistance would take over administration from Vichy according to advance planning, and present the Allies with a *fait accompli*: a liberated France under control of its own Provisional Government.

Both de Gaulle and the Allies were acutely aware of the fact that the Communists were highly organized in the Resistance and that they controlled key levers of direction in the councils of the Resistance. No one could be sure just how swiftly and efficiently all the men designated in advance would move or be able to move to take over administrative posts, or how loyal to de Gaulle they would be. There might well be a race between Gaullists and Communists, and the Communists might well win that race, with the gravest consequences for postliberated France. This question was on almost everyone's mind in Algiers, where those of us in inter-Allied headquarters were breathlessly following events, while preparing for our own invasion of southern France scheduled for some weeks later. But de Gaulle was prepared to accept any risks rather than to mortgage the independence of France by yielding any form of civil and political authority to foreigners, even those who were fighting and dying for France.

As for the D-day broadcast, nothing could induce or oblige de Gaulle to speak in last position after every other head of state of western Europe, including even the postage-stamp-size state of Luxembourg. Instead he spoke on D-day evening, hours after other leaders had spoken. All alone, a loneliness to which he had become accustomed in the four years since his original appeal for resistance, General Charles André Joseph Marie de Gaulle addressed the people of France.

"The supreme battle has begun," de Gaulle intoned in his own peculiar speech pattern, a deep, strong bass voice increasing in intensity and pitch until it cracked at the peak in a tremolo falsetto. "It is not only the Battle of France, it is France's battle!" Insistent upon his own view of the course of events, de Gaulle continued: "The orders given by the French government and the French leaders it has appointed must be implicitly obeyed." De Gaulle was deliberately challenging Eisenhower and all the Anglo-American commanders. He spoke only of French orders given by French leaders, although the Anglo-Americans would provide almost all the soldiers of the liberation campaign. The Fighting French, brave men all, were only a handful compared to the mass of more than a million Allied soldiers.

As de Gaulle was speaking, those Americans and Englishmen were fighting desperately to dig in on the five beachheads on the coast of Normandy that they had opened up early on that cloudy, stormy morning: Sword, Juno, and Gold for the British beachheads; Omaha and Utah for the Americans'. In addition the two airborne divisions, the 82nd, around Sainte-Mère-Eglise, and the 101st, around Carentan, were fighting to control traffic centers to prevent German reinforcements from reaching the bridgeheads.

The citizens of Saint-Lô could not hear de Gaulle, or anything else. Those who were still alive were deafened by the devastating bombings the Allies had unleashed upon them the day before the landings. Saint-Lô, once a citadel of Charlemagne, stood atop a hill overlooking the Vire Valley. It stood midway between the invasion coast and the west shore of the Cotentin Peninsula. It was the key road center of a junction vital to Marshal Rommel, the German commander. The attack on Saint-Lô by hundreds of bombers had begun at 8 P.M. on the night of June 5, just as the first, slowest boats in the invasion armada of five thousand vessels were setting sail into the Channel. The bombing lasted all through the night of June 5–6 and wiped out Saint-Lô. The population had taken to the countryside after the first wave of bombers struck. Some took refuge in a big cave behind the municipal hospital. When the raids ended, every building was down and a thousand dead bodies were buried under the ruins.

As de Gaulle was speaking, bombers were making their runs over Caen in the early evening of June 6, dropping blockbusters and phosphorous bombs. During and after de Gaulle's speech, the Allied bombers roared over Caen, a principal objective of the British.

Vire was almost completely destroyed on D-day and Coutances was hit heavily in two raids. Lisieux was almost totally destroyed. By a kind of miracle its famed cathedral was not hit, nor were its law courts, but the prison was destroyed along with most of the town. Falaise was hit again and again, on June 6, 7, 10, and 12, and all but wiped out.

Only one major town behind the invasion beaches was spared, with important consequences for de Gaulle and the Allies: the town of Bayeux. An important road junction and a subprefecture, Bayeux offered the Allied troops a convenient military and administrative center almost equidistant between the British and American armies. In fact, the invasion border drawn between Arromanches, in the British sector, and Saint-Laurent, in the American sector, ran right into Bayeux, principal town of the Bessin Valley.

The Bessin area of Normandy, scene of the landings, was in no way prepared to play so dramatic a role in a crusade for Europe. It was an agricultural area of rich soil and fat cows, one of the most prosperous areas of France. Because of Allied bombings and Resistance sabotage of railways and roads, the farmers of the Bessin had had great difficulty, in the weeks immediately preceding the invasion, in getting their produce to the Paris markets, with the result that much of their milk, butter, cheese, and eggs was consumed at home. The citizens of the Bessin and particularly at Bayeux were rosy-cheeked and plump, to the astonishment of British soldiers who thought they were liberating famished victims of the German occupation. In fact the only famished victims in Bayeux, long deprived of fresh milk, butter, and eggs, were the British soldiers themselves. A military correspondent for London's *Daily Mirror* sent back a dispatch that startled his British readers: "If you're short of anything, just ask the French people, there's a good chance they've got it."

The population of Bayeux was seven thousand. The town, known to the world only for its historic and beautiful tapestry of Queen Matilda and its eleventh-century cathedral, is surrounded by meadows that slope to the sea. All around are the famous hedgerows of Normandy that would give the Allied troops a terrible time. Over the centuries, the fields have been parceled out and divided by earthen walls, overgrown with thornbushes, with roots deeply implanted in the ground. The walls are as thick as a tank and all along them run deep drainage ditches, dangerous traps even for wide-tread tanks, and deadly for jeeps or other narrow-tire vehicles. The Allies had rigged up long iron lances on the front of their tanks to knock down the hedgerows, but it was slow, tough going, and had the Germans correctly judged that the landings would be well south of Calais, the Anglo-Americans could have been halted in the Normandy beachhead and thrown back into the Channel.

Happily, the Allies were completely prepared for everything they encountered in France, at least militarily, if not politically, while the Germans were not only caught off-guard, but kept off-guard for weeks by one of the most successful hoaxes ever played in the art of intelligence warfare.

The excellent preparation of the Allies was due mainly to the Resistance, which had thoroughly spied and mapped out every foot of German defenses from the North Sea beaches to the Channel beaches, and over and down to the beaches of Brittany and the Atlantic as far south as Bordeaux, in the six possible landing areas that had been originally considered by the High Command. The North Sea beaches, on the coasts of Holland and Belgium, and the Atlantic beaches of France, were rapidly discarded as possible landing sites because they were beyond the range of Allied fighter planes. That left two sets of beaches: on the coast of the Pas de Calais on the narrowest neck of the Channel, opposite the cliffs of Dover; and the Normandy beaches of the Bessin, from Caen to Cherbourg, with the great port of Cherbourg a most tempting target. Le Havre, at the mouth of the Seine, had been considered and discarded because the Allied troops would have been divided on either side of the Seine and would have had to fight separately against strong German forces.

Marie-Madeleine Fourcade's network, the Alliance, had key men in the area, for the Bessin was the homeland of Jean Sainteny, Dragon. As early as the fall of 1940, Sainteny had begun recruiting eyes and ears among his childhood friends, many of them sailors with detailed knowledge of shipping, supplies, and beach defenses. Among them was a draftsman, Maurice Dounin, art teacher of the lycée in Caen. He walked and bicycled up and down the coast, sketching every German fortification and taking copious notes for weeks and months. He sent his detailed information on to Sainteny. Then, one day in March 1944, Sainteny was amazed to receive from a courier a long, rolled-up canvas. When he unrolled it, it proved to be a more than fifty-foot map of the beaches and road nets from the mouth of the Dives to the Cotentin Peninsula. Every German gun, every beach obstacle, all military units and their strengths, the most complete, detailed military picture of what had already been selected as the landing sites, were on that map. It was a colossal achievement in espionage and Jean Sainteny was able to carry it out with him when he was picked up by a Lysander and flown to London on March 16.

It was one of the proudest moments in the life of Marie-Madeleine Fourcade when she brought the map to the British secret service chief, her friend Claude Dansey. The Allied officers planning the landings were overjoyed to receive the map. For the first time, in March 1944, they began to take the

French Resistance seriously. Later, in his memoirs, *A Soldier's Story*, General Omar Bradley, commanding the American landing forces, wrote that he had counted heavily on the Resistance to impede German reinforcements from reaching the beachheads, and that this was a key element in the Allies' ability to hold on to the beaches long enough to build up strength for a breakout.

The man who made the map, Dounin, was caught by the Gestapo, along with some fifteen other Resistance agents of the area, and imprisoned in Caen. On June 7, one day after the landings that his map had helped make a success, Dounin and his friends were executed by the Germans. One of the band, a fisherman named Thomine, escaped arrest and continued his invaluable espionage. He had noticed that whenever the Germans installed a new coastal battery, they scheduled a practice shoot-out over the Channel. In order to be able to shoot, they had to warn fishermen and ships' captains to keep them away from the practice area. Notices would be posted in the town halls along the coast. Thomine stole or copied those notices and fed them into the Resistance network. By his efforts, the Allied commanders knew the location of every German coastal gun.

All of these Resistance reports, plus aerial reconnaissance, gave the Allies as much information as the Germans themselves had about the beach defenses and the Wehrmacht units in the area. The Allies were encouraged to learn that German defenses were relatively thin behind the Normandy beaches and along the Cotentin Peninsula. Moreover, its defenses were manned by mediocre units. The Resistance had sent in a complete Order of Battle of German units, and Allied Intelligence thus knew the worth of each outfit. German defenses ran from moderate to weak. There was not a crack division in the immediate area. The worried Allied planners grew more confident as Resistance reports stressed these German weaknesses, and everyone in London had a rare laugh when they learned what had happened in their key target of Bayeux just a few days before the landings.

There had been a momentary tremor of fear when it was learned that Marshal Rommel, their old and feared adversary, the Desert Fox of Africa, now in charge of western France and the coastal defenses, had come on June 1 for an inspection tour of Bayeux. As it turned out, the inspection was routine, and not based on any knowledge of an impending invasion. It was one of those ghastly coincidences that give general officers fits on the eve of any great battle. There would be other such coincidences, some much more grave, on D-day itself. But on June 1, Rommel did little more than ride around to show himself, and in the process become the victim of a local deception practiced by his own German officers.

Those German officers had been ordered many weeks before to mine all the fields bordering on the beaches. French authorities had protested that if they mined the fields, the peasants would not be able to work them. It might lead to a serious drop in the production of local Camembert cheeses, for example, if the cows could not graze without danger of being blown up.

The German officers had grown comfortable in their occupation of this rich area of Normandy, and were very fond of the Camemberts and the Pont-l'Evêque cheeses of the region. So they put up signs everywhere warning of mines, but did not actually put in any mines. The farmers let their cattle graze in the "mined" fields. Just before Rommel was scheduled to arrive, German officers drove around to all the farms, warning the peasants to take the cattle out of the "minefields," lest Rommel force them to put in the mines. The farmers obligingly withdrew their cattle. Rommel drove off feeling there was no need to reinforce the sector.

The false minefields were helpful to the Allied cause, but nothing could compare to the massive deception the Allies themselves had been carrying out for months, aimed at persuading the Germans that the invasion would be launched from Dover, across the narrow neck of the Channel, to land on the beaches around Calais. A whole series of devices was used to carry out this deception.

General George Patton, commander of the American Third Army and a flamboyant officer who strode around with ivory-handled guns hanging on his hips, was known for his independence, his boasting, and his disrespect of higher authority. He was chosen to play a key role in the hoax. He was appointed chief of an army group that did not exist, whose false mission it was to land Allied troops on the beaches of the Pas de Calais. Patton rode up and down the roads of England, behind the white cliffs of Dover, telling everyone how he was going to blast his way through Hitler's Fortress Europa and make mincemeat of the Nazis. At dinner in a hotel he would roar out for all ears to hear that he would personally capture Rommel and stuff him down Hitler's throat as soon as he broke out of Calais.

While Patton was putting on an act that he loved to perform, his dramatic role was reinforced by a fake radio net that the Allies installed in his "staging area." It was a net that corresponded in size and in volume of traffic—all invented—to what a legitimate Army Group radio net would in fact carry. It was done in every detail, a brilliant job of deception, knowing that enemy spies were monitoring the net. Heavy guards were thrown around the staging area, to reaffirm the espionage observations that something big was going on behind the wire gates.

False landing plans were carelessly left on desks at night for spies to pick up. Photo reconnaissance planes made run after run over the Calais beaches. Two days before the landings the air force sent wave after wave of bombers over the Pas de Calais to soften up the German defenses for the landings. The Germans saw their spy information being confirmed by the bombings.

One of the most convincing of all their analyses was based upon dispatches they were receiving from a French colonel in Algiers who was an Abwehr spy. The French counterespionage agents had caught this traitor many months earlier. But they did not imprison or execute him, as his crime merited. Instead, they "turned him around" and used him as their own agent, to feed false information to Admiral Canaris's intelligence headquarters. They knew that Canaris and his analysts would check his reports out carefully and find out soon enough that they were false.

The Germans, as planned, did discover in only a few weeks' time that their French spy had been "turned." The French counted on their competence. They wanted to continue to use the German spy, knowing the Germans knew he was "blown." They expected the Germans to check his information against other spies', confirming that it was misinformation. They then took, with Eisenhower's enthusiastic endorsement, a great gamble: They gave the spy exact information to the effect that the landings would take place on June 5, 6, or 7, on the Normandy beaches, with major targets to be taken between Caen and Cherbourg. It was the D-day plan in its major elements.

The Germans swallowed the bait whole. Knowing that their spy had been turned, they were now convinced that the landings would take place anytime and anywhere except on June 5, 6, or 7 on the Normandy beaches. That was ruled out absolutely, for two reasons: Their "turned" spy, always wrong, had sent it through; their other spies, often right, were all sending through reports designating the Pas de Calais for mid-June as the main effort. So completely hoaxed were the Germans that they clung to their decision to defend the Pas de Calais for seven weeks, while the Allied armies were widening and deepening their bridgehead and destroying the German Seventh Army in Normandy.

General Bradley wrote that it was not until the war was over and German documents seized and analyzed that the Allies learned how complete their deception was. On the night of June 6, some twenty hours after thousands of American and British troops had landed on the beaches, German staff officers at Seventh Army headquarters were still studying reports of Allied activities. They had received their first signal at about two in the morning from LXXXIV Corps, which reported airborne landings from Caen to Cotentin. But Rommel's Army Group and Field Marshal Gerd von Runstedt's Western Command were still convinced that the main Allied attack would come through the Pas de Calais. They analyzed the Normandy landings as a ruse to deceive them and lead them away from the Calais area.

The German Seventh Army, which at first had seen the American airborne landings in the Cotentin as a threat to Cherbourg—which, indeed, was the target—changed its mind by the afternoon and sent reports to headquarters that the Allied landings had been smashed from the river Vire all the way to Bayeux. This was the sector of Omaha Beach where landing troops had run into great trouble because of one of those accidental coincidences of war. Instead of the area being held by the second and third-grade troops that Allied intelligence agents and the Resistance had correctly reported, Rommel had moved up one of his elite units, the combat-blooded and tough veterans of his 352nd Division, for field exercises.

The field exercises of the 352nd coincided with the landings of Lieutenant General Leonard Gerow's V Corps divisions. "Gee" Gerow's men ran into crack German troops and were halted in their attempt to break out of the beachhead. The 352nd sent back such glowing reports of their success to Seventh Army that its intelligence officers, anticipating events, informed Army Group that the Americans had been thrown back into the Channel and that the British were fighting on alone in their sector. American paratroopers were busy, with the help of the local Resistance, cutting wires and felling telephone poles and pylons across the Cotentin Peninsula. In the resultant confusion, the Germans did not receive any alarming messages from the troops defending Cherbourg, so they concluded that Cherbourg was not a target, and that the airborne landings were mere diversions, part of an Allied deceptive move designed to draw German strength away from the British attack near Caen.

By sunset the 352nd Division, under heavy American fire, hastily revised its boasts of having driven the Americans back to the water's edge. The Americans, in fact, were already driving inland, breaking through the defense lines of the 352nd. American troops were proving more than a match for one of Germany's best divisions.

Earlier in the day, Adolf Hitler had telephoned from his bunker in Berlin, to order von Rundstedt to hold his reserve divisions in check. "Await daylight to get a clearer view of the situation" was his advice to the commander of the western front.

Colonel General Alfred Jodl was not to be ignored. He telephoned from OKW headquarters ordering all available reserve forces to be thrown into the battle, thus contradicting Hitler's orders. Von Rundstedt, demanding clarification, was told that by "available reserves," the High Command meant only those in western France, and not the Fifteenth Army, the most powerful force, which was keeping a keen eye on the Channel and the cliffs of Dover. They were waiting for the "real attack," and would not be fooled by the "little diversion" in Normandy.

No French army units were among those which landed on the Normandy beaches. But Frenchmen were the very first Allied troops to hit the soil of France, some two full hours before the Anglo-American landings began. They were members of the Deuxième Régiment des Chasseurs Parachutistes (RCP), one of the finest units of all the French forces. They had been trained in English and Scottish camps, along with Allied paratroopers, and had excelled in many areas, setting inter-Allied records for marksmanship. They wore the red beret of the French paratroopers and the Cross of Lorraine.

The Deuxième RCP received the mission of jumping into Brittany before midnight on the fifth of June, in advance of the Normandy landings. Their "sticks" were divided into two groups, half of them to be dropped in the Côtes du Nord, half in the southern sector in the Morbihan. They were assigned to set up two bases, Agamemnon and Beatrice in the north, Charlotte and Dudule in the south. The paratroopers were to make contact with the local Resistance, which was large and aggressive throughout Brittany.

Brittany was one of the most densely occupied areas of France, with as many as one hundred and fifty thousand German troops stationed there. These troops were in a position to move rapidly north from Brittany and attack the Normandy bridgeheads from the rear, which could present a grave danger to the Allied troops. The French paratroopers, aided and guided by the Resistance, had the important mission of keeping those German troops bottled up inside Brittany and not in position to attack the Allies in Normandy.

German armored units in the Morbihan, in the region of Ploërmel-Guer, were the greatest threat to the Allied rear. The railways leading from their area to Normandy had to be blown up and cut in as many places as possible, as did the roads, which had to be made impassable for as long as possible. A half-dozen rail lines had to be attacked.

Leading the attack were two young officers: Lieutenant Marienne, who jumped with one "stick," and Lieutenant Deplante, who jumped with another. Both landed safely, Marienne right on target and Deplante about six miles off his objective. Within minutes of Marienne's landing, almost before he could get his parachute off, men and women came running across the fields to welcome him. The local Resistance leaders had received signals about his drop and had been waiting for him and his men. The paratroopers were the first French soldiers they had seen fighting in France since the terrible shame of the defeat and surrender of 1940. Not only Resistance members, but farmers, their wives, and their families came running across the fields to cheer the homecoming heroes of the liberation.

Bretons came by the thousands to rally behind Marienne and Deplante when they had set up their bases. The paratroop officers were able to send a signal back to London announcing that they were now thirty-five hundred strong, clamoring for weapons, above all heavy weapons, to go into action. Meanwhile, without delay, they had begun tearing up the track, mining the roads, setting ambushes, doing everything possible to keep the German troops from attacking the Allies in Normandy, as instructed. They had suffered one casualty, a Breton, Corporal Bouétard, killed in a skirmish, the first French soldier to die in the battle of liberation.

The Germans did not seem to know that French paratroopers had jumped and set up bases. There was considerable confusion in German headquarters in Brittany as intelligence analysts tried to understand what was happening in Normandy. If the main Allied attack really was in Caen, far to the north, it was out of immediate range for the Brittany-based troops.

All over France Resistance men were hearing the BBC reports. Among those reports—heard by FFI leader Grandval in eastern France, Colonel Georges (Robert Noireau) in the Ain, Pierre Bertaux in the mountains south of Toulouse—were two coded messages of specific import in each region. Grandval heard the code: "I will bring the eglantine," which meant that the landings were under way and that the *Plan Vert*, the plan for rail sabotage, was to be put into effect immediately. Colonel Georges and Pierre Bertaux heard: "Reeds must grow, leaves rustle," a signal for the *Plan Vert* in the central and southwestern sectors. Almost immediately there followed coded messages for the Violet, Blue, and Bibendum plans, to cut roads, telephone and power lines, and to prevent German armored units from moving freely.

Maquisards sprang into action across France, some with magnificent results, others with terrible losses.

Early in the morning of D-day the thirty-four maquisards of the Concieux camp in central France, having heard the messages, set off at dawn to attack the German garrison at Taintrux, nearest to their camp. They divided up into three sections of roughly ten men each. The first section, spotted by the Germans, came under fire, retreated, and got back to base without losses. The second section captured a dozen Germans but got caught in a German pincers counterattack. Four of them were killed on the spot. Five were captured, stripped, beaten, tortured, and executed the next day. The third section had a big success. It overran the German posts that were its objective, took forty-eight prisoners without a loss of life. But, the next morning, ten thousand Germans rushed into Taintrux, shot up the buildings, took leading citizens as hostages, and shot them as an example to any town in which the Resistance attacked a German garrison. Similar German terror and killings ravaged French towns and villages in the Ain, the Drôme, the Ardèche, Aveyron, Dordogne, Isère, and dozens of other regions. The list is long and tragic. The Allied signals calling for a general uprising long before it was needed, and before the Resistance had been fully armed and briefed, was one of those terrible errors that plague almost all big, complex enterprises.

Despite the tragedies and the bloody reprisals taken by Germans against helpless civilians, the Resistance achieved more than the Allied command ever hoped or understood was possible. Until the actual Battle of France, the Allies consistently underestimated the Resistance. In the first day after D-day, 180 German trains were derailed, some 500 railway lines were cut. In the first month of fighting, when the issue was still in doubt in the beachheads, the Resistance managed 3,000 cuts of railway lines. On June 7, for example, only the day after D-day, the Resistance in Burgundy, the famous eastern wine country of France, blew up so many rail lines that not a single train could move in a quadrilateral bounded by Lons-le-Saunier, Chalon, Dijon, and Besançon. In Dijon alone, the principal city of Burgundy, 37 cuts of rail lines were effected in one day, on June 7.

Every day, several times a day, reports from French rail workers flowed into Eisenhower's headquarters, sent over Resistance channels. The Anglo-American command knew every detail of time, place, and cargo of every single German supply and troop train in and around France. General Eisenhower later told this writer, at his headquarters in Saint-Germain, outside Paris: "I knew as much and probably more about German rail transport than Rommel or von Runstedt. The French Resistance was magnificent. The railway men not only kept us informed of all movements but, over and over again, they impeded the transport of German trains, holding them up as much as thirty-six hours, enough to help turn the tide of battle in our favor, particularly when we were still inside the beachheads of Normandy."

A German troop train, en route from Belgium across to Normandy to reinforce the 352nd Division, ran out of fuel after making only twenty miles. The trainmaster was baffled, since it had been fully fueled when it took off. He did not know that for every shovel of coal that went into the train's furnace, the fireman sent two shovels flying out of the cabin into the darkness of Flanders fields.

The Resistance had the audacity to use the private train of pro-Nazi French Premier Pierre Laval to carry its couriers and even to hide men in a false closet built into the water tank. Who would look into the water tank of Laval's own train? Who would know that Laval's engineer was a member of Résistance-Fer? They even dared to give their own *cheminot* caps, blue jeans, and badges to Allied airmen and to move them openly, disguised as workers, across France and down to the Pyrénées, where guides took them into Spain.

One of the greatest exploits of the Bataille du Rail was the Resistance attack on one of Rommel's elite combat units, the Das Reich Armored Division, which he called for urgently to use against the Allied beachheads in Normandy. The division was down south in the Dordogne, when, on June 7, at a critical moment in the battle, it received the order to head for Normandy. Had it arrived in the following days it might well have turned the battle against the Allies, for it had tremendous firepower and crack fighting units.

Resistance forces in the Dordogne were ordered into action against that German armored division. They attacked with bazookas, machine guns, and grenades as the division moved out of Souillac. German fire drove off the Resistance forces with ten casualties in the first assault. Further attacks were then launched from a woods in Cressanac, with more Resistance casualties. But the sacrifice was not in vain. The Das Reich Division was moving slowly, and on June 8 was still far from the beaches. At daybreak on June 9, as the division was crossing the Bretenaux Bridge over the Dordogne, FFI units again went on the attack. The fight lasted from six-thirty in the morning to ten-thirty, four hours, during which fifteen resistants were killed and two severely wounded. Men of the Resistance gave up their lives to slow up the Das Reich Division and slow it they did.

While fighting men of the Resistance were impeding the German armor, Resistance intelligence units were also hard at work. They had plotted on a map the route being taken by the Das Reich Division. They had monitored its radio net and read its signals. Then they had transmitted all the information over their secret radios to London. London turned over the data to the RAF and soon fighters and bombers were streaking across the skies of France and diving down on top of one of the most important targets of the day. They shot up the columns of the crack armored division, further delaying its movement and weakening its capability to damage the Allied beachheads.

Some of the maquis intelligence units plotted attacks in such a way as to force units of the German division to take a single-line railway on which they would be sitting-duck targets. One of the maquisards was a Resistance leader known as "Colonel Berger." Colonel Berger, in real life, was a writer named André Malraux, a future Nobel Prize winner and minister of cultural affairs for President de Gaulle many years later.

The main body of the Das Reich Division was delayed another six days. Rails and trains and roads were blown up by either RAF bombs or railway workers' explosives. Only a few tanks managed to get through to Normandy a week and more later, too late to have any influence on the battle. Not only did the Resistance mangle and frustrate the Das Reich Division, but when the division radioed news of its plight, the German High Command instructed other divisions heading north to circle around Dordogne. Two powerful forces, the Gross-Deutschland and the Goering divisions, detoured to avoid the FFI. They ran into FFI units anyway, for the Resistance was active everywhere. They, too, arrived too late for the battle of the beaches in Normandy.

French army estimates put the number of German divisions that the Resistance prevented from reaching the northwestern battlefields, or from escaping to the east toward Germany, at as many as ten to fifteen. Asked about this, General Omar Bradley told this correspondent: "I don't know how many divisions the Resistance shot up or bottled up. But I can tell you this: The French Resistance was worth a hell of a lot of divisions to us. We needed them, and they were there when needed."

The French, limited as their resources were, also managed to play a military role in the liberation of their country from the very first hours of D-day. Not only did the Chasseurs Parachutistes jump into Brittany some two hours before any Allied troops landed in France, but one of the very first units to land in Normandy, at Ouistreham, was a French contingent, a company of 180 men led by Captain Jean Kiefer. This company was attached to a British unit, Commando 4, whose mission it was to capture fortified villas overlooking the beach, converted by the Germans into blockhouses. Captain Kiefer and his men were the first troops on that beach and suffered very heavy casualties. A mortar shell fell on one platoon as it came out of the sea, killing many of the men and all of the officers. A sergeant took command and led the survivors in a charge across the beach. Within the hour, the French and British commandos had taken their objectives.

The French navy also flew its flag over the Channel, small as its numbers were. In all, 467 Allied warships made up the Overlord armada, guarding some 5,000 small vessels. France's contribution to the fleet was two 7,000-ton cruisers, the *Georges Leygues* and the *Montcalm,* and a 10,000-ton cruiser, the *Duquesne,* which was used as a supply ship. The *Georges Leygues* and the *Montcalm* led the way to the landings at Bayeux, while the objective of the destroyer *La Combattante* was the beach at Ouistreham. In addition, France contributed four new fast frigates to mount guard over convoys: the *Aventure, Découverte, Surprise,* and *Escarmouche.* Four corvettes, the *Estienne d'Orves,* the *Aconit,* the *Renoncule,* and the *Moselys,* were busy chasing German subs. Two old cargo ships were sunk on the coast for use as artificial harbors, and standing guard over them was a grand old lady of the French navy, the World War One battleship *Courbet,* which had also shelled German tanks in the Cotentin in the last days of the battle in 1940. It then sailed for England and became the first ship to fly the flag of Free France after de Gaulle's appeal for resistance on June 18, 1940. In command of the French naval forces on D-day was Rear Admiral Jaujard, the only French flag officer with a command on that historic day.

The French air force was also represented with one hundred planes in the Allied air fleet of nine thousand. There were three French fighter groups, Ile de France, Alsace, and Cigognes; two medium bomber groups, Lorraine and Berry; and two heavy bomber groups, Tunisie and Guyenne. The Lorraine group was given the honor of laying down the first smoke screen in front of the Allied landing forces on June 6. The bombers flew so low in their zeal that one of the planes snapped off its smoke pipe when it hit a chimney of a beachside villa. Other bombers dived down behind the smoke screen to hit German units moving up to oppose the landings.

So, on June 6, alongside American and British forces, French soldiers, sailors, and airmen were participating in the Normandy landings, while across France the Resistance harassed German forces. The promise that General de Gaulle had made to the people of France on June 18, 1940, that the power of the Allies would result in the liberation of France and the ultimate destruction of the common enemy was coming true almost exactly four years later.

24

MASSACRES AND LIBERATION

While French forces from the outside were hitting the enemy on the beaches of Normandy, the men of the internal Resistance went into high gear in support of the landings, carrying out orders for a general uprising in accordance with the messages sent on the BBC on June 4: "It is hot in Suez" and "The dice are cast."

General Pierre Koenig, de Gaulle's overall commander of French forces in London as well as chief of the FFI, was appalled to receive urgent messages from the Resistance for a mass drop of arms and supplies in support of nationwide uprisings. General Koenig did not know for four days that the signal for a general insurrection had been sent. Some radio operator had punched it out by mistake and no one had caught it. It was a calamitous error and had to be corrected at once to avert a terrible tragedy.

New messages were sent out advising FFI commanders to halt all abnormal operations and revert back to guerrilla tactics until further notice. Some of these messages did get through and prevented disaster in a number of areas, but in some sectors the new signals arrived too late to halt ongoing operations. Many Resistance units had gone into action against vastly superior German forces, thinking that they only had to hold out a short time before Allied forces would arrive. They were doomed to be destroyed.

One of the worst tragedies occurred on June 10, the very day that Koenig was sending out his new warning signals: the massacre at Oradour. A Resistance force near that southeastern town had attacked the Germans and been driven back. As a warning to all towns near Resistance forces, and an example to the Resistance of the consequences of their actions, the Germans selected Oradour to be a lesson of horror.

Two survivors of the massacre later told American investigators what had happened. Their testimony is on file in the National Archives in Washington, file 150140.

The first witness interrogated was Mathieu Borie.

"About two P.M. on June tenth, I saw five half-tracks arrive down the road from Limoges. They wheeled into skirmish formation and began to round up all the people in sight. I was working at Mercier's, the grocer, when a German officer entered and ordered us all out to the public square. We started to walk, but a few hung back. The officer pulled out his pistol and shot the laggards on the spot.

"As we walked along, we saw German soldiers kicking in doors, breaking into houses, smashing windows, and shouting to everyone to go to the main square. It took about half an hour for them to round everyone up.

"The Germans then ordered the men to step away from the women. The men were all lined up along the wall of the square. The women and children marched off toward the church.

"The German officer walked over to the mayor, behind whom I was standing. He demanded that Mayor Deshourteaux name fifty hostages. The mayor answered: 'I cannot name hostages.' They seized him and took him off to the town hall, returning with him about ten minutes later. This time he agreed to name hostages: 'I name myself,' said the mayor, 'and if that is not sufficient, I name all the members of my family.'

"The Germans said they were sure that a storage of arms existed in Oradour and that while searching for it they were going to place all the men in groups in the barns. They divided us into groups of forty to fifty each and drove us into the barns kicking at our rears, hitting us with the stocks of their guns. My group was led into a shed on the square, with armed German guards all around."

Borie managed to see other groups forced into barns and sheds and garages around the square. He assumed, correctly, that all were being treated the same way. They were kept under armed guard until about 4 P.M. when suddenly, without any warning, the Germans opened fire with machine guns, tommy guns, and rifles on the people packed into tight spaces.

"I let myself fall and all my comrades in misery were hit and wounded and several fell on top of me. The Germans turned savagely upon all their victims, prodding us with pitchforks and covering us with layers of straw and faggots of wood."

Borie, wounded in the left forearm and thigh, could see and hear all that was happening. His friends and neighbors were crying out, moaning, and somewhere he heard the loud music of a radio playing. Then, to his horror, the Germans came in carrying torches and set fire to the straw and faggots they had spread around. Borie crawled through the burning straw toward a hole in the barn wall and managed to push his way through. He made his way to a nearby series of rabbit hutches where he hid until nightfall. When he crept nervously out, he saw bodies all over the square and smelled burned flesh. He picked his way through the bodies, blinded by smoke, tears, and emotion, recognizing the corpses of friends and relatives. He swore out a statement that twenty-four members of his family had been massacred that day in Oradour.

Similar testimony was received from Madame Marguerite Rouf-fanche, the only woman to have survived the Oradour massacre. She had been herded into the church with her two daughters and grandson and many other citizens of Oradour. The Germans came into the church carrying a black box that they left behind as they turned and hurried out. Madame Rouffanche had hidden behind the altar. She felt the shock when the box exploded and black smoke billowed out. The women and children began chok-ing and coughing.

"I gathered up my children and took shelter behind the sacristy. The Germans burst in and began machine-gunning the interior of the church, some from inside, others shooting from outside the windows down into the church. There were screams of terror and pain and women and children fell where they were. My daughter was killed at my side.

"More Germans came in carrying straw trusses, chairs and benches and logs of wood. These caught fire from flames coming up from the basement. My dress and hair began to burn. I ran through the flames to get behind a high altar. By luck there was a small ladder there. I climbed up and got out of the church through a small window. I fell to the ground on a heap of brambles. At the same instant, a woman who had been near me sought to escape as I did, and she had a seven-month-old baby with her. She threw the baby out of the window, shouting to me to catch it. As she shouted, the Germans opened fire and killed her. Her name was Madame Joyeux.

"I don't know what happened to the baby. I was too far away to catch it. The Germans saw me and started to shoot. I was hit. A bullet fractured my shoulder blade, another pierced my thigh. My two legs were badly burned and then I was hit again in my right side. I fell down and played dead. I lay there for hours, sucking on the leaves of a patch of green peas to quench my thirst. At about five o'clock, people from a neighboring village, who had heard what happened, came by to look for any survivors and found me. Seven members of my family were killed in the massacre of Oradour."

The total of French civilians, men, women, and children mas-sacred by the SS troops at Oradour came to 642.

Many more would die in other regions of France in that first month of liberation, June 1944. Before General Koenig's warnings and orders against premature uprisings had been sent, and even afterward, members of the Resistance had gone into action all through France, and most particularly in two of the principal maquis regions: the Massif Central mountains near Clermont-Ferrand, and the plateau of the Vercors. in the Alpine Massif in eastern France near the Swiss border.

The first pitched battle fought by the French maquis against the German army was the Battle of Mont-Mouchet. Mont-Mouchet is located in the Margeride Mountains of the Massif Central, rising about a mile high in Auvergne in central France. Late in May 1944, the regional commander of the FFI in the Auvergne, Colonel Coulaudon, known as Gaspard, issued a general mobilization order. There were, at the time of his order, some twenty-five hundred maquisards already in place in the dense pine forests around the forestry lodge of Mont-Mouchet. By May 31, some ten thousand men had answered Gaspard's call to arms.

Gaspard and other Resistance leaders had received advance copies of a Koenig Plan, sent from FFI headquarters in London, providing three supporting forces that would enter into the battle at the side of the Forces of the Interior: Force A was designated as the French assault elements to assist the landings in the north; Force B consisted of French troops that would form the divisions of the First French Army, under General Jean de Lattre de Tassigny, for the landings in the south, on the Riviera; Force C would be airborne to the interior of France. It would liberate a zone that would enable General de Gaulle to install elements of the Provisional Government of the French Republic, in order to establish French sovereignty inside France, without waiting for the complete liberation of the country.

The plan to create Force C had been drawn up earlier in the spring by the members of COMAC, the Comité d'Action Militaire of the Resistance created by the CNR. It had been taken to London by Pierre de Bénouville, head of the military committee and a leader of the Combat movement, along with another founder of Combat, Maurice Chavance (Bertin). They had given the plan to FFI officers for clearance by the Allied Supreme Command. The FFI officers were enthusiastic about the plan. The Gaullists were fearful, indeed convinced, that the Allies were planning to install some form of Military Government in France, and that the Americans wanted to keep de Gaulle out of power. Force C would permit the Gaullists to fly their flag and begin administering French affairs. General Koenig approved the plan.

Supreme Headquarters saw Force C as a potential threat to the authority of Allied officers, for it might interfere with combat imperatives. Supreme Headquarters approved only Force A and Force B and canceled the plan for Force C. Although the plan had been approved by General Koenig, no one at FFI headquarters informed the Resistance that Force C had been canceled by the Allies. The leaders of the maquis went ahead under the impression that powerful Allied forces would come flying in to join them in the final liberation campaign against the Germans.

At the time that the plan for Force C was under discussion in London, Colonel Gaspard met an Englishman code-named Philippe who had parachuted in the Auvergne and made his way to his headquarters. From what Philippe said, Gaspard assumed that he was a top Allied officer with a command position for the region. In fact, Philippe was only one of the new Jedburgh liaison teams that were then jumping in to work with the maquis. He had no command position, but he was generally familiar with London's plans. He spoke enthusiastically of Force C and said he would do everything he could to get London to drop arms along with elements of Force C to join the maquisards of the Auvergne.

Gaspard, buoyed up by Philippe's encouragement and promises, went off late in May for a top strategy meeting with Resistance leaders of the region. He met with Henri Ingrand, who had been designated as commissaire of the Republic to establish a governmental authority as soon as the Germans were driven out. He also conferred with representatives of the principal movements: Combat, Libération, Franc-Tireur, and the Communist Francs-Tireurs et Partisan Français, the FTPF. Also present at these meetings were representatives of the Communist and Socialist parties. All of them agreed to support maquis camps and assault centers, all, that is, except the FTPF. They said they were studying their own plans at the moment and would probably come in later. In fact the Communists of the region were planning to seize the public buildings in the towns and villages and establish themselves in power in the urban centers while the Gaullists were fighting in the remote mountains and rural areas.

But even without the FTPF, Colonel Gaspard had enough men to put together a formidable force in the Massif Central, whose thick forests lent themselves admirably to guerrilla warfare. He could count on some fifteen thousand men in three redoubts. He established his headquarters at the forester's lodge at Mont-Mouchet, at the intersection of roads with good telephone communications. Several companies could be deployed almost invisibly, except from the air, in the pine forests around the lodge.

Gaspard had also recruited for his operations one of the most effective of the freewheeling commando groups that operated in the region. They called themselves Les Truands, a name that meant literally the Vagabonds, but had the strong connotation of "Outlaws." There were thirty of them, reputed to be tough, brave, and totally dedicated comrades-in-arms. They shared everything: their rations, their wine, and, it was said, their women—particularly the "gray mice" of the German army and French collaborationist female prisoners. In their initiation ceremonies, the Truands made a recruit drink non-stop a full quart of a potent blend of red wine, white wine, and brandy.

The commandos had already won important victories over the Germans. They had blown up 150 high-tension pylons of the Monistrol power plant that sent energy to German war factories in the Loire Valley and as far as the industrial belt around Paris. They had raided German garrisons and taken more than 100 prisoners. They agreed to be the tip of the lance for Gaspard, the shock troops of a planned attack on the Germans as soon as the Allies had flashed news of the landings and given the signals for the national insurrection.

Gaspard was further assured of London's endorsement of his plans when three officers of the SOE parachuted in to offer their assistance to him. These men had been in intensive training at isolated security camps. They were only vaguely aware of Allied plans, but their arrival confirmed Gaspard's belief that the plans to send him a special force were operative. One of them, a British actor named Denis who had been in France before, had been tortured by the Gestapo. The Nazis had broken his teeth, one by one, with a mallet, and then pulled his ankles out of joint. He had refused to reveal any information and the Gesapo had left his broken body on the floor of the interrogation room, convinced that no one in his condition could move. But Denis did and could. He dragged his body upright, blood running out of his mouth, his sprained ankles buckling under him and shooting flames of pain up his legs. But he crawled and dragged himself away and found help. Gaspard felt sure that London would not have sent him men of that caliber unless all had been agreed.

The maquisards organized raiding parties for supplies. One band of raiders traveled more than 150 miles to Montluçon, where they attacked a warehouse and loaded stolen trucks with ten tons of sardines for the maquis. Another foraging commando, the Laurent group, "liberated" six thousand leather jackets that had been manufactured on orders from Vichy. The packing cases were stamped with the legend "Manufactured for the marshal."

On June 2, four days before the Allied landings, an unexpected battle took place between the men of Mont-Mouchet and the Germans. An SS battalion of about eight hundred troops, armed with mortars, was stationed not far from Montluçon. Its commander had been informed that there was a small Resistance unit nearby. The Germans had no idea just how large and tough an enemy they were facing, for there were more than two thousand maquisards in the region.

Fighting was fierce and fast with casualties on both sides. The Germans were stopped and then hurt badly and forced to flee in retreat when the maquis forces made their way around to the German rear, catching the SS troops in a vise. The Germans concentrated their forces to break out of the trap, leaving many casualties bleeding in the snow. It was a heady victory for the maquis and misled them into overestimating their own strength and seriously underestimating the strength that the Germans would be able to bring to bear once German intelligence had properly evaluated the strength of the maquis.

The Germans sent their small observation plane, which the French had dubbed "Le Mouchard" or the Spy, over the forests, dipping low to get pictures of the maquis encampments. At night the Allies sent their own planes over, dropping arms to the maquis: handguns, rifles, bazookas, grenades, but not, unfortunately, the most important weapon for mountain fighting: the mortar.

"The dice are cast. The dice are cast."

The men of the maquis, huddled around their radios, burst out into a hearty cheer. This was the signal they had so long awaited. The Allies were landing in the misty dawn of June 6. Liberation was near. Now was the time to go into action to strike a blow for freedom.

The Germans had a radio, too. And they had spies throughout the region. They knew the Allies had landed and that the Resistance would gear up to attack them. So the Germans decided to go on the attack themselves to nip the Resistance in the bud. Gaspard checked his guerrillas' weapons, discussed tactics, and sent out patrols and spies to select German targets. While he was gearing up a full German division of twelve thousand troops, heavily armed, supported by armored cars, heavy artillery, mortar batteries, and spotter planes, launched a mass attack on June 10. The three thousand men of the maquis of Mont-Mouchet had only light arms, without mortars, heavy artillery, or airplanes. The maquisards kept looking up at empty skies for a Force C that would never arrive.

The maquisards fought heroically against greatly superior numbers. One company, led by Lieutenant Fred, attacked a German battalion, inflicted a number of casualties on the Germans, and held up their advance all through the day. By nightfall, Lieutenant Fred and twenty of his men were dead, but the Germans had not attained their objectives.

The maquisards, under cover of the early mountain nightfall, fell back on the only road still open, the southern road. They took their transport, their reserves in food and clothing and headed for a redoubt at Truyère, higher in the mountains. Messages from their spies and observers reported that the Germans had ordered up some four thousand to five thousand additional troops from the garrison at Clermont-Ferrand. Most of the three thousand men whom the Germans had attacked were able to fall back in good order. They left hundreds of dead Germans on the battlefield. Total German casualties in the Battle of Mont-Mouchet were fourteen hundred dead and seventeen hundred wounded. Although vastly superior German forces had driven the maquisards out of their positions and farther back into the woods, it was, nonetheless, the biggest victory the Resistance had achieved in direct combat with the German army. The French had lost only one hundred and sixty dead and another one hundred wounded, an astonishing triumph considering the disparity in numbers and firepower.

Gaspard sent desperate messages to London, calling for arms, ammunition, explosives, mortars, air support—and Force C. London could not take fighter or bomber support away from the Normandy beachheads, but it did redouble air drops of arms to the maquis. Gaspard had many men waiting for those arms in the redoubt of Truyère, a plateau in the mountain. With the new drops, Gaspard was able to put together thirty companies of armed men, totaling four thousand troops. But they had ammunition for only one day of heavy fighting. The terrain around Truyère was more suitable to tank action than it had been at Mont-Mouchet, and the Germans were moving up armor.

On June 20 the Germans, who had beefed up their forces to twenty thousand men, supported by tanks and dive bombers, launched a massive assault against the four thousand lightly armed maquisards. Once again the maquisards fought like lions, inflicting many more casualties on the Germans than they suffered themselves. They claimed that in the two pitched battles they fought at Mont-Mouchet and Truyère they knocked out three thousand five hundred Germans and lost only three hundred and fifty of their own men. But they once again were outnumbered and had to retreat to a higher massif at Mioran, burying themselves into a mountainous terrain where the Germans did not dare follow them.

The maquis of this area in central France had acquitted themselves well in pitched battles that they never should have fought. Colonel Gaspard never forgave the Allies for sending a signal for an uprising without any Force C to aid the maquis. He had learned his lesson; from then on he and other leaders in the region confined their activities to purely guerrilla hit-and-run tactics, as they should have done all along. They were lucky to have survived open battle with superior German forces.

Not so lucky were the maquisards of the biggest and most famous of all the maquis of France: the men of the Vercors.

The Vercors was theoretically the perfect model of what a maquis should be, the ideal fighting ground for partisan forces, nature's finest citadel. No Army Corps of Engineers could have designed and built a better redoubt for hit-and-run guerrillas than God had done in the Alps of eastern France.

The Vercors is a high plateau surrounded by a mountain wall of rock like the Great Wall of China. It is thirty miles deep from north to south, from Grenoble to Die, and twelve to fifteen miles wide, a quadrilateral with steep sides and fully wooded slopes. It has only one relatively weak point in its ramparts—Saint-Nizier, in the northeast corner, where the walls are lowest. Eight roads run through the Vercors. Two of them climb over passes three thousand to four thousand feet high, while the others run through tunnels in the rock or through cuttings. All the roads are easily defended, as are the twenty-odd mountain tracks. All these roads and tracks run through extensive Alpine forests of fir and ash. In these forests are villages where peasants have cleared some spaces for cattle breeding and potato growing. In the Middle Ages the Vercors was the lair of brigand chiefs who ruled as lords over the plateau. The king's soldiers were content to try to keep them bottled up inside and did not dare penetrate the Vercors themselves.

The Vercors had been the center of controversy from the day in 1942 that Yves Farge and the Franc-Tireur movement of the Dauphinois had selected it to become a bastion of the Resistance. Henri Frenay of Combat had denounced it as a dangerous trap for the Resistance. But others, such as architect Pierre Dalloz, saw the high plateau as an ideal reception and training area of the Resistance and a concentration zone for Allied airborne troops. Certainly it was ideal for such projects.

The five founders of the Vercors maquis were Pierre Dalloz of Grenoble; Dr. Martin, the Socialist mayor of Grenoble; Aimé Pupin, code-named Mathieu, a café owner in Grenoble; Dr. Eugène Ravalec, who raised the first Resistance groups in the Vercors; and "Clement," another café owner whose real name was Eugène Chavant, who recruited for the maquis. Along with them in the first days of the Vercors were the motley assembly of ordinary Frenchmen and women, the unheroic heroes of the Resistance. There was a bank manager and an accountant, a cabdriver, an ironmonger, a railway worker, a reporter, and a secretary. In one village of the Vercors where a unit was formed, the first two volunteers were the local parish priest and the town pimp.

In 1942 Pierre Dalloz met the painter and art critic Yves Farge, who was already prominent in Franc-Tireur. He told Farge about the Vercors and its natural advantages. Farge reported it to Jean Moulin, who approved the idea of building a center there and turned the project over to the then chief of the Secret Army, General Delestraint. Delestraint met Dalloz, took a copy of his map and sketch of the Vercors, along with photographs, on his trip to London. One night early in January 1943, listening on his radio to the BBC program of Personal Messages, Dalloz heard the phrase: "The Montagnards must continue to climb the peaks." It was the code signal agreed on in advance that informed him that London had accepted his "Montagnard" Plan to build up the maquis in the Vercors.

The plan aimed at an all-out attack on the Germans in support of Allied landings on the Mediterranean coast. The Vercors would be in the rear of Wehrmacht forces either trying to hold the Allies in the south or retreating toward Lyon to take up new positions in the northeast, in front of Alsace. It was not conceived by Dalloz as a permanent fortress, nor as the assembly point for large forces to engage the Germans in a pitched battle. Dalloz agreed with the judgment of Frenay and others who saw it only as a kind of bandit's lair for guerrilla fighters. His only difference with Frenay was his belief that a large force could come into action in coordination with Allied landings and hold the Germans off for a few days, just long enough for the Allies to join up with the maquis. That was the essential calculation and tragic error.

At first, all seemed clear and sensible. General Delestraint returned from London and carried with him the message that Vercors operations would be called for in the context of "general operations," meaning Allied landings. He said that the maquis of the Vercors would only have to fight a short if fierce battle, and that Allied airborne troops would be sent in support. The Vercors, Dalloz wrote in a memorandum on his plan, must attack "by surprise against a distressed and disorganized enemy." He made it clear that maquisards could not fight a pitched battle with German units at full strength and under orderly discipline. The attack must come in the rear of an enemy being hard hit by the Allies in a frontal assault.

As soon as the plan was drawn up things began to go wrong. A young group of raiders near Grenoble was caught by Italian police. Tortured by the OVRA, the Italian Gestapo, they broke down and talked. As a result their leader, Aimé Pupin, and his principal assistants were arrested by the Italians. One by one through 1943 Resistance leaders in the Vercors area were caught.

All through the winter and spring of 1944 the men of the Vercors engaged in raids on German installations and skirmishes with German troops in sectors nearby. It was foolhardy, for it could have goaded the Germans to a full-scale attack on the Vercors itself. But the maquisards were bored with training and planning and demanded action. In one of their raids they rescued Senegalese prisoners and brought them to the Vercors to join their combat units. In another raid they captured police uniforms and put them on. They continued to wear the uniforms in combat with the Germans, who were confused to find themselves fighting French policemen.

The Germans did conduct occasional raids on the maquis camps in the Vercors plateau. In January 1944, the Germans hit the Mallaval village of Narraques-en-Vercors and some of the houses of the plateau village of Rousset. The maquis of the Vercors suffered a number of dead in German attacks on Saint-Julien-en-Vercors in March and on La Chapelle in April. German attacks increased in strength and intensity through May as the time of the Allied landings approached. By June 6, when the Allies hit the beaches of Normandy, as many as a third of the Resistance cadres of the Vercors maquis had fallen in these German assaults.

On that day, most of the maquisards were busy blocking the roads and mining the approaches to the Vercors. The traffic tunnels of the city of Grenoble were mined by that city's public works technicians. Everyone did his job to help block off the Germans so that the maquis could hold out for the arrival of the Allied airborne troops—the force that would never come. Their faith was strengthened by Eugène Chavant, one of their leaders who had gone down to the southern coast, been picked up by a submarine and taken to Algiers, where he spent a week at headquarters. Chavant returned to the Vercors on June 5, the eve of the landings, to reassure everyone that the Supreme Command was going ahead with the Montagnard Plan. Algiers did not know that London had changed the plan.

As soon as the BBC messages were broadcast, the commanders of the Vercors moved to action. They sent out a call for all reserves and volunteers to report for duty. These poured in by the thousands from all the plains around the plateau. New companies were formed overnight. Several were moved into position on the slopes above Saint-Nizier, the weakest point in the mountain wall around the Vercors, where the Germans could debouch in strength. The Brisac company joined the Goderville company in defensive positions on those slopes. They halted the tramway that shuttled up and down from Saint-Nizier to Grenoble. The Germans understood at once that the FFI had occupied Saint-Nizier and began their plans for an assault on the position. The maquisards knew they had alerted the Germans and expected the attack; but they expected Allied paratroopers at any moment.

On the morning of June 13, the Germans launched their first big attack on the Vercors, on the road up the Saint-Nizier slope, just as expected. The Brisac company of the FFI, about one hundred fifty men strong, held the right side of the road, on top of the Vercors cliff at three thousand feet. The Goderville company, another one hundred fifty men, held the left side, just beyond a cemetery where many of the maquisards would ultimately be buried. The Germans, advancing along the front on the slope, were one thousand five hundred men strong.

The maquisards put up a good fight, firing down on the Germans, lobbing grenades into their lines as the Germans struggled up the slope. At a critical moment a platoon of the Chasseurs Alpins came running up to support the two companies and help drive the Germans back.

The Germans, suffering heavy casualties in a poorly conceived attack in mountainous terrain, had to beat a retreat. The maquisards had won a big victory with only ten men lost. The men of the maquis were further cheered by Allied planes that dropped them containers of machine guns. But they still had no mortars and there was still no sign of Force C.

The next day the Germans attacked again. This time, with better planning, they laid down artillery and mortar barrage on the maquis positions and sent three thousand men in behind cover of the barrage. The FFI companies were hit hard and had to break away and run for cover on higher ground.

The Germans dug in on the slopes around Saint-Nizier. They received orders to hold that ground but not to risk a fight with the maquisards in denser forests higher up, for the time being. Their job was to keep the Vercors bottled up at Saint-Nizier, to protect the approaches to Grenoble, until the situation clarified itself. The German High Command still did not know where the main thrust of the Allied landings would come.

With the Germans in static positions, more and more men came into the Vercors, until the total of volunteers in June and July reached four thousand. Yves Farge, who had been named commissaire de la République, set up a "République du Vercors." Engineers mined the roads. Telephone men strung wire and set up internal communications, as well as direct wireless relays to Algiers and London. Transport and medical services were organized. The BBC began to broadcast news about the heroes of the Vercors who had liberated their territory. But the Allies still did not send any mortars or airborne troops.

Lulled into a false sense of security by German inaction and by news of Allied advances out of the Normandy beachheads, the Vercors flew the *Tricolore* of France from all village buildings and celebrated the national holiday, July 14, as a day of liberation. At noon, during the height of their celebration, there appeared in the clear, bright sky eighty American planes. The people of the Vercors cheered and cheered as the American planes opened up their bomb bays and dropped red, white, and blue parachutes carrying containers of arms. An airdrop at high noon seemed to signal that the Germans were beaten and the Allies supreme.

But the Germans were far from beaten, and the Allies had mistakenly put on a big show for Bastille Day without understanding the consequences of their action. They did not know that the Germans had the Vercors surrounded; that the maquisards were badly outnumbered and outgunned and would not stand a chance if the Germans attacked en masse. At no time could guerrillas have stood off the troops of the regular German army launched in strength—perhaps not even with airborne troops.

The day after that Bastille Day show, the Germans sent bombers with incendiary shells over Vassieux and La Chapelle-en-Vercors. Smoke and flames rose over the trees of the Alpine redoubt. Wave after wave of bombers hit the village of the "République du Vercors." It was the beginning of the end.

On July 19 the Germans threw two divisions, totaling more than twenty thousand men, around the Vercors. They then sent them in assault waves, methodically, against all the entries through the mountain peaks into the plateau of the Vercors. The maquisards guarded each of these defiles and put up a strong fight. But they were no match for superior German numbers, bombs, and artillery. One by one the maquis guardposts were overrun, the guards killed.

Maquis leaders sent distress signals to London and Algiers, calling for help. At the Vassieux field, workmen were busy leveling the ground, preparing for the Force C airborne troops.

Suddenly, on July 21, the maquisards heard the roar of planes coming up from the south, from the direction of Algiers. They looked up. At last, at long last, they saw what they had been praying and pleading for: long lines of gliders, forty in all, with airborne troops swooping down from the sky, released by the bombers that had been towing them. Force C had arrived! Rescue and liberation were at hand!

The men of the maquis stood up next to their machine guns and waved their caps and berets in greeting to the gliders. Down came the gliders, faster and faster, lower and lower. The men on the ground could now see the fuselages clearly. No cocarde of the French air force, no RAF markings, no American stars or stripes. What was this? Where did those gliders come from? The awful truth burst upon them: The gliders were German. The Germans had known about their hopes and plans and knew there were no Allied planes in the air in that sector. They had launched a brilliant, deceptive, surprise attack right in the heart of the Vercors.

Too late, the men jumped to their machine guns. They shot one German glider down, but the others were already on the ground and German assault troops were jumping out and setting up heavy machine guns on the airstrip. Altogether more than five hundred crack SS commandos were brought in by those gliders, some of the best troops the Germans had. The SS men fanned out fast, occupying the village of Vassieux and the neighboring villages of Mure and Château. They set up machine-gun nests and mortar emplacements and began to bombard the French positions, knocking out the maquis machine guns rapidly.

The SS then ran amok among the villages, killing everything and everyone that moved: men, women, children, dogs, cats, and livestock. Human beings were hacked to pieces and impaled on hooks in butcher shops. Hour after hour, all day and all night for two days, the Germans poured troops into the breaches of the Vercors and broke through all its defenses. They put villages to the torch, sacked hospitals, and killed doctors and nurses along with the wounded.

The men of the maquis, three thousand five hundred to four thousand at the outset, were decimated by the assault of twenty thousand Germans. They had to break off the fight and run for high ground in the fir forests where the Germans, unable to bring their strength to bear, would not dare follow. They hid up in the high maquis for a month, until the French army landed in the south and marched up the Route Napoléon toward Grenoble, driving the Germans north. Then the remaining men of the Vercors could finally come down and join the French troops in the liberation campaign. But by then the Vercors was a morgue.

All through the eastern Alps and central mountains other maquis were still in existence, harassing the German attempts to retreat up the Rhône and to escape via Lyon to take up new positions in the Vosges and in Alsace. Hundreds of men fought in the maquis of the Oisans and Tireves in the Isère around Lyon. Thousands more fought successfully in the central Cévennes, throughout the Ain, in camps of the Massif Central, and down through Dordogne in the southwest to the foothills of the Pyrénées. They inflicted heavy losses on the Germans, prevented German units from attacking Allied positions at critical moments. They served the Allied cause well and made a strong contribution to the liberation of their homeland. And they fought as they should—as guerrillas, hit and run, in and out of the shadows.

The Allies estimated that they armed some one hundred and fifty thousand maquisards and that thousands more armed themselves with weapons captured from Vichy and German troops and arsenals. The official count of maquisards who died in battle was put at twenty-four thousand. The full count of those who died as partisans is probably double the official count.

While Frenchmen were fighting and dying in the southern and eastern maquis, and other Frenchmen were harassing the Germans in central France and in Brittany, General Charles de Gaulle was concentrating on what was for him the most important objective of the day: the establishment of French sovereignty in France. He did not have any fears about the tide of battle. De Gaulle had every confidence in the power of the Anglo-American invasion forces. But he also feared the Allies. He feared their plans for an Allied Military Government, for circulating their own currency. He was sure that Roosevelt had given Eisenhower strict orders not to let de Gaulle establish a French government in France. Finally, he felt the Allies did not sufficiently appreciate the danger that the Communists would be prepared to fill any vacuum of power in liberated France. For these reasons, and because he personally desired to cap his four years of struggle with the liberation of France, Charles de Gaulle was determined to establish his government, and Allies be damned.

De Gaulle's representative and spokesman, Maurice Schumann, had gone in on the invasion and had sent back reports on the early Allied occupation. On June 8 Schumann was in Bayeux, the first important provincial city to be liberated. Bayeux was a departmental subprefecture, an important political center. Schumann was disturbed to discover that the British had met with the Vichy-appointed subprefect, Pierre Rochat, and had decided to keep him on the job under their orders. The British liked Rochat and laughingly dubbed him "King of the Liberated Territories." De Gaulle's delegate, who had dreamed of the day he would come back to liberate France, did not find the confirmation of a Vichy "king" a laughing matter. A French *sous-préfet* is roughly equivalent to an American lieutenant governor of a state.

Rochat, although young, had a sense of the dignity of his office and was as patriotic a Frenchman, in his own view, as were the Gaullists or the men of the Resistance. He was an appointee of the collaborationist Vichy regime, to be sure, but someone had to administer France or the Germans would have taken over. He kept the Germans from governing his country and he meant to keep the Allies at arm's length, too. In that sense, Rochat's views did not differ from the views of Maurice Schumann or of the local chief of the Resistance, Raymond Triboulet, who would eventually replace him as subprefect.

Rochat began by telling the British that he would not permit American francs, "occupation money," to be used in his region. Even the Germans had at least made a show of respecting the integrity of French finances. Besides, his district had more than five million francs on hand in public funds and that was enough for all immediate needs. It was a quiet sector, low in crime, and the local police force could handle public order. It was a rich farming and dairy area, so there was no problem of feeding the population. Indeed, the Bessin could help feed the Allied armies—with proper payment of course, Rochat pointed out.

Maurice Schumann and de Gaulle's liason officer, Colonel Chandon, reported back to London the nature of the situation in Bayeux and urged de Gaulle to take steps speedily to implant his own authority. De Gaulle, of course, was thinking of nothing else. He had already taken steps to ask the Supreme Command to furnish him with transport to visit Bayeux and the date had been set: June 14.

De Gaulle had selected an imposing delegation to accompany him on the trip: General Pierre Koenig, hero of the Battle of Bir Hakeim, commander of the FFI; Colonel Claude Hettier de Boislambert, chief of the military liaison mission; Admiral Thierry d'Argenlieu, his naval officer; his military aide, General Marie Béthouart; his diplomatic representative, Ambassador Pierre Viénot; and his chief of Cabinet, Gaston Palewski. One other man was named to the delegation and given a private briefing by de Gaulle a day before departure: François Coulet, who had served as secretary-general of the prefecture in Corsica after the departure of the Germans and the Italians.

Coulet had been one of the first administrators of a liberated French territory and de Gaulle had chosen him for a delicate and vital mission. Coulet would be the new commissaire régional de la République in Bayeux, with orders to take over administration from the Vichy officials and to prevent the Allies from interfering in any way. It would be the first, critical test of de Gaulle's ability to implant his own men and his authority in newly liberated territories of mainland France, a test that could be decisive in determining the future government of the French Republic.

At dawn on the fourteenth, General de Gaulle and his party left London. By 10 A.M., they were on board *La Combattante*, which flew a tricolor bearing the Cross of Lorraine and the initials *CdeG*. De Gaulle, stretching six feet eight inches from his boots to the crown of his kepi, wrapped in a long leather tunic that accentuated his height, stood on the bridge, his eyes glued to binoculars, as he strained for the first sight of his beloved France. June 14 was a sad anniversary date, for it was on June 14, 1940, that the Germans had entered Paris. One of the staff officers walked over to de Gaulle and reminded him of that event. Still staring ahead, searching the horizon, General de Gaulle muttered: "Well, they were wrong. It was an error." He stood stiffly in the wind, feet spread against the swell. His staff fell silent. No one dared utter another word until they saw de Gaulle's figure relax, the glasses come down from his eyes. He turned and smiled at them. "Gentlemen, I give you France."

General de Gaulle landed and paid a courtesy call on General Montgomery. He had refused an invitation to lunch, telling an aide: "We have not returned to France to lunch with Montgomery."

Bayeux was de Gaulle's first target. De Gaulle, General Koenig, and Commissaire Coulet went directly to the office of the Vichy subprefect, Rochat. General de Gaulle questioned Rochat on the available supplies of money and food and the morale of the population under the bombings. He then ordered him to remove the portrait of Marshal Pétain hanging on the wall, symbolizing the Etat Français of Vichy. The removal of the portrait and the hanging of the *Tricolore* of the Republic symbolized the bloodless coup d'etat of Bayeux. The Republic had replaced the State. De Gaulle had replaced Pétain. De Gaulle was presenting the Allies with a *fait accompli*.

There followed the public demonstration that, for de Gaulle, legitimized his accession to power. For four years he had argued that Free France was the "legitimate" if not the legal power of France. Churchill and Roosevelt had refused to accord him and his CFLN governmental status. Now, he would take it and they would not stop him. On a platform before Rochat's office, de Gaulle held out his arms to the people of Bayeux and they cheered and embraced him. That was his investiture in office. As he had told Roosevelt at the Casablanca Conference, in January 1943, no one had ever elected Joan of Arc to leadership. She led and was acclaimed. So was Charles de Gaulle "elected" by a genuinely spontaneous acclamation in Bayeux on June 14, 1944.

General de Gaulle left Bayeux and toured Isigny and Grandcamp en route back to his ship off the beach of Courseulles. Everywhere he was acclaimed by people emerging from cellars and bomb shelters. The figure of de Gaulle symbolized liberation. For them the war had ended and the Republic had been restored.

Members of the local Resistance gathered around de Gaulle, told him of their clandestine radio transmitter, asked if there were new instructions. In Normandy the Resistance was Gaullist, not Communist. The general knew he would be challenged by the Communists along the way and most particularly and importantly in Paris, but, on June 14, he was among his own people in Normandy.

Just before embarking for his return to temporary governmental headquarters in England, President de Gaulle turned to François Coulet and told him that he was to stay behind and administer the region in the name of the Provisional Government. He was to issue a proclamation stressing the establishment of the new government and take all civil affairs in hand. "Do not interfere with or provoke the military, but do not let the Allied military interfere with you. Cooperate with the Resistance, but you are the law in this region now."

As soon as de Gaulle had left, Coulet went to see his aides. They drew up plans for taking over the region and for extending their authority as the armies advanced. They were determined that there be no vacuums into which the Allies or the Communists could step.

On the morning of June 15, the people living in and around the Normandy beaches read wall posters addressed to the "Liberated Population." It informed all that the Provisional Government of the French Republic had named François Coulet to the post of commissaire régional, "with the duty of exercising the rights of French sovereignty in the liberated territories of the Rouen region."

At that moment such a poster was completely illegal. Coulet had not been officially appointed by the Provisional Government in Algiers; he had merely been named in a private conversation with General de Gaulle. In fact, the Resistance had already earlier named a commissaire for that region, with the approval of Algiers: Bourdeau de Fontenay. At first, de Fontenay was angered by Coulet's "usurpation" of his post, but then he understood that instant action was called for, and he himself was still too far away to take over his post. As soon as practicable, de Fontenay did take over as planned. As for the decree issued in Algiers that finally named Coulet, after the fact, that document was issued by a self-appointed government that the Allies did not recognize as such. Thus, when Coulet issued his proclamation, in Bayeux on June 15, he had no real power behind him and no document to back him up in case of a challenge by Allied officers or military police.

Unabashed, Coulet at once informed the Vichy subprefect, Rochat, that he was dismissed and ordered him out of his office. In his place he installed Raymond Triboulet, a local landowner, a member of the local Resistance. Triboulet, with no administrative experience of any kind, was delighted to be named subprefect, even provisionally, and threw himself into his new duties. He walked in, nodded greetings to an anteroom full of supplicants, and then proceeded to interview them one by one, citizens and British officers alike, all who had some governmental problems to be solved. They accepted him as subprefect, for he was sitting in the subprefect's office.

Coulet was busy, too, acting as commissaire régional. On June 16 he issued a decree blocking all bank accounts. He based this decree on his earlier experience in Corsica. On June 17 he sequestered all newspapers, until the underground papers of the Resistance could emerge and be legalized. On June 18, the anniversary of de Gaulle's historic broadcast of 1940 calling on the

French to continue resistance to the enemy, François Coulet organized a mass public ceremony, expecting great enthusiasm.

Coulet was astonished and depressed when the bishop of Bayeux, Monseigneur Picaud, objected. The bishop said he was not a Gaullist and would not conduct a Te Deum in de Gaulle's name. Coulet had to plead with him until he finally, grudgingly consented, on the grounds that it would keep the Allies from imposing severe occupation regulations. Then the head of the Bayeux Committee of Liberation, created by the Resistance, told Coulet that he had never heard anything about a broadcast of June 18, and that the Resistance had not been created by de Gaulle. It took a combination of threats and persuasion to convince him to attend the ceremony in an official capacity. Gaullists were in the majority in Normandy and Brittany but not every official was a follower of de Gaulle.

Coulet's supreme test, the one in which the issue was finally joined and decided, came in his clash with British Civil Affairs officers, the clash that General de Gaulle had clearly foreseen.

The chief of Civil Affairs, General Lewis, on Montgomery's staff, angrily awaited a visit from the French who, he had been told, had installed themselves in office in Bayeux. He felt they had to report to him and seek his approval, which he had no intention of granting. As days went by and the French showed no signs of reporting to him, the general fumed and vowed to put the usurpers of power in their place. If they would not come to him, he would go to them and dress them down.

General Lewis and his aides strode into the subprefecture as though they were investing an enemy citadel. He walked into Coulet's office without knocking, sat down, and told him: "We have our plans for the liberated territories. We do not intend to deal with a French administration and we expect order to be maintained." He paused, looked sternly at Coulet, and added: "We know you are here without the agreement of our government. We will accept your presence but only provisionally and under our orders."

François Coulet, prepared for this onslaught, his answer well rehearsed in advance, did not at first react to the general's harsh tone. He replied calmly in a low but steady and cool voice. He expressed the gratitude of the French people to their allies for liberating Normandy. He talked of common war aims and the spirit of cooperation. Then, his body stiffening and his voice taking on a sharp edge, Coulet said: "But this country is ours, not yours, and we decide what will be done here." Coulet startled the Englishmen by banging his fist down on his desk and shouting at them: "My presence here has nothing to do with you. I have received the order to be here from General de Gaulle's government and I shall leave only upon his orders and act only upon his orders." With that, François Coulet, not in any way revealing how he was churning inside, stood up, signaling that the audience had come to an end.

Taken aback, General Lewis decided to beat a strategic retreat and think things over. He, too, arose. He glared at Coulet, opened his mouth, closed it, did an about-face, and stalked out. That was the end of it. Coulet had won. The Allies did not challenge him again.

Coulet's troubles were by no means over. The Allies, while not trying to move him out, went ahead with their plans to distribute their occupation francs. The canny Normans, who knew the money was worthless and would not long be distributed, accepted it in payment for their produce but rushed to turn it over to the tax collector in advance payment of their taxes, getting full credit in their own francs. Coulet called a meeting of French tax agents and Allied Civil Affairs officers and worked out an arrangement whereby the Allies, who had a large reserve of real francs, would exchange them for the false francs being given to the tax collectors. Finally Eisenhower, persuaded by arguments advanced by Colonel de Boislambert, whom he respected, canceled occupation francs in July.

Coulet then received an urgent message that the Allies had taken Cherbourg on June 27, the first major French port to be freed. Coulet drove like the wind to Cherbourg, where, to his relief, he found the people and clergy enthusiastically pro de Gaulle. He entered the port cheered by shouts of *"Vive de Gaulle; Vive la République!"* Coulet headed at once for the prefecture, where, as in Bayeux, he installed himself, ousted the Vichy officials, and proclaimed the sovereignty of the Provisional Government of the Republic.

Coulet fired collaborationist officers of the Maritime Prefecture, installing local patriots and resistants in their place. He far exceeded any kind of personal authority by dismissing magistrates and even managers and directors of private companies. He arrested notorious collaborators of the Nazis and suspended the laws of the Vichy State, particularly the odious laws of discrimination against Jews that the Nazis had imposed on Vichy. By applying strict official action and meting out immediate punishment, from fines to imprisonment to traitors, Coulet avoided personal vendettas and rioting. Even though he did not have any legal authority, he exercised a moral authority that maintained public order.

The dawn of liberation had first broken over the beaches of Normandy. But soon convoys began sailing slowly through the Mediterranean, from the ports of Italy and Algeria, heading for the beaches of the world's most beautiful resort coast, the Riviera. It was there, between Saint-Raphaël and Saint-Tropez, that the First French Army would come back from four years of exile to participate in the liberation of its homeland.

25

THE LANDINGS ON THE RIVIERA

Anglo-American forces were breaching Hitler's Atlantic Wall in Normandy; Soviet troops were liberating the Crimea and capturing Sevastopol, rolling up the Ukraine front; U.S. marines were fighting on Wake Island, while American and French forces were liberating Rome and driving the Germans northward toward Siena and Florence. And, in that climactic summer of 1944, another front was about to be opened in France: the southern front, with landings of French and American forces all along the Riviera between Cannes, on its easternmost landing line, and Cavalaire on the west. The operation, called Anvil when originally planned, had its name changed to Dragoon in the final weeks, to confuse German intelligence.

The original plan for the southern landing was agreed upon in the summer of 1943 at the Québec Conference, which, without specific detail, approved a proposal to open up a second front in western Europe. Later, in November and December 1943, at the Cairo and Tehran conferences, General Eisenhower had been appointed commander in chief for the second front, and the landing beaches had been agreed on.

At first, Anvil was thought of as a two-division assault in support of the Channel landings in Normandy. Even that small a force was immediately contested by Britain's General Montgomery and by Eisenhower's chief of staff, General Walter Bedell Smith. They were very worried about the forces that had been assigned to Overlord, deeming them insufficient for success, particularly in assigned naval craft. They wanted Anvil cut down to only one division and its "lift," that is, its naval support, diverted to the Channel invasion fleet. Eisenhower refused their request and maintained Anvil when he arrived at Supreme Headquarters in London in January 1944.

General Omar Bradley, commanding American troops in the Normandy landings, approved Eisenhower's decision, even though he could have used more support for his own forces. He explained his view on this issue in his war memoirs.

"Even though abandonment of the Anvil attack would have greatly eased my problems, I hoped desperately that it need not be ditched. For, as the air forces bit more deeply into the French transport system, it was apparent that we would have logistical troubles while advancing across France. In addition to cleaning the enemy out of southern France, Anvil would open up an additional line of supply from the port of Marseille, up the Rhône Valley to Alsace.

"During the winter and early spring of 1944, Anvil led a frenetic, on-again, off-again double life. Not only was it harassed by the Overlord shortage in craft, but Anvil was caught between opposing American and British views."

These opposing viewpoints were hotly contested at the end of May, just before the cross-Channel invasion. At that time, General Alphonse Juin, a Saint-Cyr classmate of General de Gaulle, and one of the few men besides de Gaulle's brothers who addressed him with the familiar *tu*, added to his already great prestige when his French Expeditionary Force in Italy scored impressive victories in the Allied breakthrough of the German lines. The U.S. Fifth Army captured Rome and the High Command granted Juin and the French Corps permission for a ceremonial march through Rome. Few shots had to be fired inside Rome as the Germans, in disorder, retreated rapidly north toward Florence to re-form on the Gothic line.

With this new situation, a number of general officers, including General Juin, saw a brilliant opportunity to break the German front in Italy, force a way through to Trieste, then north to Vienna, with a column flying east to Belgrade, rolling up the central European front. General Juin favored canceling Anvil, by then renamed Dragoon, and assigning to his expeditionary force the newly formed French Army B, commanded by General Jean de Lattre de Tassigny. That army, itself, would be renamed in August the First French Army. Juin was certain that with the addition of that powerful force, the French could swiftly seize Vienna, a tremendous prize of prestige as well as a strategic coup.

Winston Churchill instantly saw the great stakes involved in this controversy over strategy. He saw it not only as a military question, but, primarily, as a geopolitical issue. Churchill, the statesman, ever conscious of postwar aims and future power struggles, had long feared a Communist domination of eastern and central Europe if the Red Army of Russia liberated all that territory. He saw the proposals of Britain's General Harold Alexander and France's Alphonse Juin as his chance to beat Stalin to the prize. He called General Eisenhower to explain the need to cancel Dragoon. He also called the chairman of the Joint Chiefs of Staff, General George Marshall. Marshall, long an advocate of a second front in France, suspicious of Churchill's political gamesmanship, and mindful of his earlier touting of quick success in piercing "Italy's soft underbelly," was firmly opposed to any change of plans to satisfy Churchill's geopolitical objectives.

Churchill wasted no time arguing with General George Marshall, a man of complete integrity, impervious to any nonmilitary briefs. He went over Marshall's head, first to Harry Hopkins, Roosevelt's principal adviser, and then, with Hopkins's encouragement, to his friend and comrade-in-arms, Franklin Delano Roosevelt. Roosevelt, more than anyone, was aware of and alert to Churchill's political moves. Roosevelt, at that time, was still confident of his own ability to handle old "Uncle Joe," as he referred to the Soviet tyrant, Stalin. Roosevelt listened respectfully to Churchill but kept his own views to himself. He said he would think about it.

"We must not wreck one campaign for the sake of another," Churchill argued. "Both can be won."

Churchill insisted that Anvil, by depriving the Italian theater of the men and support it needed, would wreck that campaign. He cited reports from Generals Alexander, Montgomery, and Juin, who said that Anvil would condemn the Allied troops in Italy to a "passive role" at a moment when a great breakthrough could be achieved. General Juin, in answer to a letter from Churchill, had written: "A bad strategic orientation now risks grave consequences, and, it must be feared, the severe judgment of history."

Armed with these arguments from prestigious commanders, Churchill went back to Eisenhower to reopen the argument. But the supreme commander would not yield to Churchill. Eisenhower was utterly opposed to any attempt to advance north in Italy toward central and southeastern Europe. He knew that there were crack German troops there and that Hitler would order them to hold the line at all costs on the road to Vienna, which Hitler regarded as a German city. Eisenhower also agreed with the judgment of General Bradley, that it was vital to take Marseille as rapidly as possible. Marseille was little farther from the Saar and the German frontier than Brittany was, and could serve as an essential supply port. And Eisenhower needed the roads and railways of the Rhône Valley.

Eisenhower flatly refused to cancel Dragoon. However the long arguments, including the reluctance of Admiral Ernest King, naval commander in the Pacific, to release shipping from his own theater to provide craft for Dragoon, had complicated and delayed planning for the southern landings. Eisenhower, while refusing to cancel the assault, agreed that it would have to be postponed, and that it could not be launched simultaneously with the Normandy landings. A new date of August 15 was set for Dragoon, but, in compensation, its commanders would see their strength greatly expanded. Instead of the one division that Montgomery had tried to cut it down to, or the two divisions originally planned, Dragoon would be executed by two armies.

General Alexander Patch would command the U.S. Seventh Army, with General Lucian Truscott in command of VI Corps, to include the Thirty-sixth and Third U.S. divisions at the outset. Later, the southern force would be beefed up with the U.S. Forty-fifth and other divisions, and the command stepped up to Sixth Army Group under General Jacob Devers. On the French side, General Jean de Lattre de Tassigny had two divisions for the landings and five more in North Africa, to bring his French army in France eventually to seven combat divisions, two of them armored. His best armored division, the famed Deuxième Blindée, commanded by General Leclerc, had been assigned to Eisenhower for Normandy and would have the historic honor of liberating Paris.

Roosevelt had sat still and listened to all these arguments raging through May and June, consenting silently to the cancellation of the June 6 landing date for Dragoon. Then, at the end of June, on the twenty-ninth, he made his decision known to Churchill. Dragoon would not be canceled. Roosevelt told Churchill that he had taken a commitment at Tehran to Stalin to mount Anvil. He would not now abandon it without informing and consulting with Stalin. He would also have to consult with the French. Furthermore, Eisenhower had informed him that the southern French landings were of utmost importance. He could not make any changes for purely political considerations. Dragoon was on!

Churchill, the most dogged of men in pursuit of his objectives, did not give up even then. One week before Dragoon was scheduled to be launched, Churchill tried again. He proposed that Dragoon be shifted from the south to provide direct support for the Allied operations in the north, to help Eisenhower roll back the Germans in Brittany, or to land in the Bay of Biscay. He had, by then, abandoned his political arguments in support of central Europe. But Eisenhower was not to be swayed by last-minute games. There was no time to reschedule the thousands of orders cut for naval convoys in the Mediterranean. It would be impossible to change all the battle maps of all the unit commanders. It really was not a serious alternative, Eisenhower concluded in a message to Roosevelt.

FDR sent his final and definitive no to Churchill, who messaged back, "I pray God you may be right." Unconquerable and inimitable, Churchill, having fought Dragoon right up to the end, decided he wanted to be in on it. He flew to Italy, boarded a British destroyer, and sailed to the French coast, where he could observe from the bridge the operation he had tried so hard to kill. Skeptical to the last, he sent a message to the king assuring him that the landings were proceeding well but that he did not know how long it would take to capture Marseille and clear the Rhône Valley.

Among those who had impatiently awaited the campaign of liberation was the woman who had served its cause so well and had survived so many narrow escapes from capture and death: Marie-Madeleine Fourcade. Marie-Madeleine had been waiting in London for the day that she could return to France. So many of her "animals" had died in the long, cruel four years of underground fighting and dangerous espionage activities that she wanted to be with the living to celebrate the great moment of liberation. In London she had read with pride the detailed and frightening reports her agents sent through about new German secret weapons and their locations, vital information for the RAF, which pounded those sites and probably saved London from destruction.

From "Grand Duke," Capitaine le Comte des Isnards, had come

the warning: *"Boches* on point completing between Calais and Boulogne installations under bomb-proof cupolas firing rocket shells range one hundred miles stop one thousand guns concentrated on London."

From "Shad," Jean-Claude Thorel, came data on installations of self-propelled rockets in new excavations at Nesle, eight to twelve miles from Le Tréport, on the Channel..

"Urus," André Coindeau, learned of German plans for secret bomb attacks on London on Christmas 1943 or New Year's 1944.

"Osprey," Henri Fremendity, had discovered that the Germans had a new siege gun, a World War I "Big Bertha" type, the biggest artillery cannon ever built, capable of throwing a heavy shell two hundred miles, firing one round every fifteen minutes. Guns would start firing during a Christmas attack. They were dug in at the Watten forest in Eperlecques, seven miles northeast of Saint-Omer, inland from the Channel. He had seen two of the big guns being hauled on a railway flatcar, one of the guns being 140 feet long. Information had been passed on to Resistance sabotage teams to try to stop those guns.

Marie-Madeleine pleaded daily with her friend and boss, Sir Claude Dansey, to let her go back to join her network. He kept telling her that her cover had been blown too often, that the Germans would surely grab her soon after she returned, and that she knew too much to be allowed to fall into German hands.

Late in June, after the Allies had established their positions in Normandy and there was no longer any danger that they might be thrown back into the sea, Sir Claude called in Marie-Madeleine. He told her that the Gaullist Intelligence Service, which she had finally agreed to join, had pressured him into agreeing to send her back at last. He told her that if captured she should say that she was on a special mission for him, to spy out the strength of the French Communist party. He said the Gestapo would believe that cover story and spare her life. He gave her a rabbit's foot good luck charm.

Marie-Madeleine took off for France in a Hudson bomber early in July, flying over the flak at the mouth of the Loire. The plane banked quickly north to the Seine and a landing strip marked off by torches in the forest of Fontainebleau. As she stepped out of the Hudson, she heard a voice shout: "Hello, Marie-Madeleine!" She was startled. Her return was to have been incognito to prevent the Germans from intercepting any messages referring to her. It was her old comrade "Flying Fish," Raymond Pezet, a fighter pilot. Marie-Madeleine grinned and handed over a birdcage she was carrying with a homing pigeon inside.

"In the day of the V-1 rocket, we still communicate by pigeon," she laughed. She had promised Sir Claude Dansey to send back a message that she had landed safely. While her friends were making the traditional cracks about the pigeon being very tasty with green peas, she screwed into the ring on its leg the message: "With love and kisses, POZ."

She and Pezet then walked through the forest until they met a peasant in a cart and asked for a lift to the nearest hotel. Marie-Madeleine was carrying a suitcase and the peasant thought they were a couple on a black-market trip. He warned them that the area was infested with Germans and dropped her off at a hotel on the rim of the forest. German soldiers, coming in and out of the hotel, looked at them too often for Marie-Madeleine's peace of mind. She went to her room, washed, changed, and told Pezet that they had to leave at once, there was no time to rest.

They found a cab that took them to the rail station at Joigny. As they sat in the crowded station, German soldiers rushed in and shouted: "Papiers! Papiers!" Pezet and Marie-Madeleine slowly worked their way to the end of the platform, then quietly moved out of the station. There they saw a steam-truck and talked the driver into taking them with him. Three days and eleven vehicle changes later, they got on the Marseille train, which took them to their rendezvous in Aix, near Marseille, with Grand Duke, who had been running the network during the fifteen months of Marie-Madeleine's absence in London.

On the night of July 15–16, London dropped six tons of supplies —radios, batteries, handguns, grenades, dried foods, cigarettes—requested by Marie-Madeleine after conferences with Grand Duke and other network leaders. She was happy to be back at work, getting daily bulletins about progress of the Allied forces fighting in Normandy. She looked forward to the landings in the south, which she knew were scheduled for sometime in August. She had asked her coastal agents to redouble their efforts to get all possible information on German activities in that sector.

Grand Duke came to see her a few days after the big drop of supplies to ask where she had hidden the money and the mail, for he had been tipped off by the subprefect that the Germans were going to conduct a house-to-house search in Aix to ferret out the Resistance. They, too, were expecting Allied landings and wanted to protect the rear of their troops.

"The four million francs are in the crate of potatoes under the sink and I sewed the mail into the hassocks," Marie-Madeleine told Grand Duke. He went to get the money and documents to take to a better hiding place and said that she ought to come home with him. She said that she still had things to do and would leave the next morning, since the German raids were only scheduled for the next night. Grand Duke told her to be careful, and left.

She was in the kitchen, peeling tomatoes when she heard a loud noise at her door. She ran to shoot the bolt, but it was too late. Two dozen Germans in gray-green uniforms had burst in and engulfed her room like a tidal wave. Among them were four civilians, who screamed at her: "Where's the man? Where is he?"

Marie-Madeleine, white-faced and frightened, protested that she was a woman alone and that there was no man with her. One of the civilians said that a man had been seen in the courtyard. She protested that it led to more than one apartment. They told her that the man was tall and fair and known as Grand Duke and that he was a terrorist of the maquis, the leader of a big network called the Alliance. Marie-Madeleine's blood froze.

Marie-Madeleine pretended to be horrified by terrorism and promised to report to them if she had any information to help them find the terrorists. They had started to leave her room when suddenly one of the civilians, who had been watching her silently and suspiciously, got down on all fours in front of the sofa, where she had run to sit down after they had burst in. He looked under it, stretched his hand out, and then drew his arms back, standing up with a sheaf of papers. He glanced at them, smiled at Marie-Madeleine, whose pale face had suddenly flushed bright red, and, with a triumphant gesture, waved the papers under his colleagues' noses. They were Marie-Madeleine's messages to London. Her turn had come. Like Navarre and Eagle and Swift and all the others, POZ had been caught at last. "It was perfectly normal," Marie-Madeleine wrote later, "it was bound to happen to me as well. Anything else would have been unfair."

Her captors shouted abuse at her and demanded that she talk and tell all or that they would show her they could make her talk. Marie-Madeleine looked at them with scorn and said: "I'll only tell the Gestapo chief who I am. I haven't the right to tell you. You're too unimportant."

She was fighting for time and was relieved to hear that the chief of the Gestapo was not in town but would be back the next morning. She would be taken directly to him. She thought: "I must escape tonight, or Grand Duke will walk into a trap when he comes to get me tomorrow morning. The whole network must be warned. I must, I must escape tonight."

She was taken downstairs and moved off by car. She saw the street sign: Rue Rifle-Rafle. She breathed a sigh of relief, for there was an old prison there and a chance to break out. Then she heard her driver ask directions to the Miollis barracks. Even better, not a prison at all.

She was taken into a guardroom and then put into a punishment cell, usually used for soldiers who had broken discipline. The door was heavily bolted, no way out there. As she was looking around, the lights went out and she was left in darkness. Suddenly all her courage oozed away. She ran to the corner of the room and vomited. Then she pulled herself over to a bed, stinking of urine, squashed bedbugs, and coarse German-issue tobacco. She threw herself down and tried to sleep, wondering how she would face up to Gestapo torture on the morrow.

She awoke with a start and looked at her watch. It was midnight. She had a little more than five hours to escape. She could not stay in bed feeling sorry for herself.

She saw a faint gleam of light high in the wall of her room. It was a window, four-fifths covered over by a wooden board. Air was flowing through the opening, so there was no glass in the window. She pushed her bed under it, took the cell's washbowl and set it upside down on the bed, took off her shoes, and climbed up for a close look.

She was now level with the window and began gulping in the soft, fragrant night air of Provence in July. She reached out and found that

there was a space between the wooden board and the wall, but that there were
bars in the space. They were not prison bars, but rather the bars that are put
on ground-floor windows the world over. They were strong and deeply im-
bedded, not a chance to pry them or the boards loose. Her only chance would
be to force her body through the space left by the board and between the bars.

Marie-Madeleine climbed down again and decided to make the
attempt in the dead of night when chances were good that all her guards and
the outside world would be asleep. She had already seen that the window of
her cell was over the street running in front of the barracks.

When her watch told her it was three o'clock, Marie-Madeleine
got undressed. She remembered stories her father had told her about Indochinese burglars who worked naked covered with fat and grease. She had no
fat or grease but decided to work naked, too, and hold her bank notes and
batik dress in her teeth as she forced her way through the bars. She knew she
must carry nothing that would make a noise if dropped.

She climbed up to the window again and began testing the width
of the bars with her head. She was slim and was sure that her body could slip
through sideways, but the real trouble would be the bony head, which was not
flexible. One bar after the other was too narrowly spaced. Then, her head
popped through the next to last double bars. At that precise moment, a motor
convoy swirled into the street and braked in front of the barracks. It must be
the Gestapo returning, she guessed. Marie-Madeleine hung there in the void,
naked and pinned to the board like a beetle. She heard voices. The sentry
was giving instructions. It was not the Gestapo. A convoy had got lost in the
night. It pulled away.

Sweat poured out of Marie-Madeleine's body, helping to lubri-
cate it for the tight squeeze she was facing. She had forced her head through,
suffering lacerations and bleeding. Now was the turn of her hips. It was sheer
agony as she twisted to find an escape passage. The pain was terrible, but she
kept telling herself that if the head had gone through the rest of the body had
to pass. Besides, the pain was nothing compared with the Gestapo torture awaiting her if she did not make it through the bars.

There was a scrape, a shooting pain, a plop, and she was falling
through the air, landing on the pavement, mercifully only a short drop below
the ground-floor window. But it was enough of a drop for her body to make
a dull thud in the silent night.

The sentry heard it. He shouted: *"Wer da?"* and flashed his
torch. Marie-Madeleine had wrapped her dress around her head and was flat-
tened down on the pavement. The flashlight beamed well over her head, swept
the street, and then shut off. The sentry was silent, probably thinking it was a
stray cat.

Marie-Madeleine summoned up all her courage and last reserves
of strength. She could not lie there naked on the sidewalk. She had to get up
and make a run for it.

Praying that the sentry was looking down the other side of the barracks, Marie-Madeleine arose like a ghost and on all fours, not daring to stand upright, crawled as fast as she could, losing all the skin on her knees, across the public square. There she stood up, seeing nothing but dark open space ahead of her, and plunged into it, running as fast as her bleeding legs could take her. She ran and ran, fighting for breath, until she saw the whitish outlines of stone crosses in a cemetery. At last a hiding place, perhaps an open chapel until morning! She fell across a tombstone, catching her breath and wondering which direction it was to Grand Duke's farm.

Marie-Madeleine looked at her watch. She knew that Grand Duke would leave his farm at seven-thirty en route to his meeting with her at eight. He would walk right into a trap unless she stopped him. As she looked around, she realized with a tightening around her heart that she had run in the wrong direction. To get to Grand Duke's farm she would have to retrace her steps and walk right past the barracks from which she had just escaped. Each step back was like a step to death.

As she came upon the barracks everything was quiet, the sentry locked into his thoughts, glancing at her without interest. Had he looked closely he would have seen the lacerations on her face, dried-up bloodstains on her legs. But he hardly glanced at her at all. She walked past him boldly, her head up, moving quickly as though in a hurry for an appointment, indeed the truth.

Once around the corner, terror gripped her again. She ran and hid among some hollyhocks. Then, screwing her courage back up, she rapped on the door of a house, saying, when it opened, that she had become lost in the bombing raids during the curfew. A rheumy-eyed woman told her to clear off and not bother her or she'd call the police. Marie-Madeleine knew that in ten minutes the bugle would blow at the barracks, and soon they would find her empty cell and set out in pursuit with a band of dogs. She was horrified at the thought of dogs hunting her down.

She walked into town, stopped a woman in the street, said she was lost, and asked the way to the Vauvenargues Road, where Grand Duke's farm was located. She almost cried in relief when the woman said she was going that way and asked Marie-Madeleine to accompany her. She would be less conspicuous walking with another woman.

The woman led her past a church and then pointed out the way across the Torse River. How would she be able to get across? Wouldn't the bridge be guarded and her escape already discovered? These questions shot through her jangling nervous system.

Marie-Madeleine made her way down to the banks, saw peasant women gleaning corn and dandelions. She joined them, bent double, stealing glances at the bridge, where she saw soldiers stopping all women who crossed, checking their identities. Just as she had feared, her escape had been discovered and the bridge blocked.

She worked her way under the bridge with the gleaners, then slowly along the banks far beyond the soldiers, until she reached a place where she could ford the river. She hurried around a bend in the waters, another and still another. All the estates looked alike in their setting of olive trees and cypresses. It was almost seven o'clock and Marie-Madeleine was frantic. And then, she saw it—a hill away stood the farm, a stream to cross, two bends. She began to run, weary though she was, knowing that Grand Duke and his wife would bind her wounds.

She flew at the front door. It was unlocked! "How careless Grand Duke is," she thought as she rushed in and locked the door behind her.

"I rushed into the hall, called out, then ran to their bedroom door, and burst in upon them. They were up on their feet in a flash, naked, beautiful, healthy, their wide, staring eyes drinking me in.

"I shouted at them: 'I've just escaped! I've saved your lives!' Then everything around me became confused and I collapsed."

Grand Duke took Marie-Madeleine to a hideout he had had prepared for just such an emergency. Then, after a few days' rest, they set out to join the maquis in the hamlet of Claps, in the famous Sainte-Victoire Mountain, immortalized in the canvases of Cézanne. It had been the site of a historic battle in 102 B.C., when the Roman General Marius defeated the Teuton hordes. Marie-Madeleine told everyone that once again men would be coming from Rome to defeat the latest Teuton hordes infecting France. It was the end of July when she made that prediction and she would be proved right within two weeks.

Marie-Madeleine would not be there to see the second routing of the Teutons at Sainte-Victoire. London, looking ahead, had already ordered her to set up her network operations in the region of Nancy and Strasbourg, to be ready to furnish detailed data on all German positions and strengths to General George Patton when his Third Army would arrive to liberate Alsace and Lorraine.

Marie-Madeleine's "animals" were not the only spies operating successfully in southern France and along the Mediterranean coast. There were a number of daring and resourceful agents in the Marco Polo network. This network was founded by a submarine officer, Captaine de corvette Pierre Sonnéville. Sonnéville had been in Grenoble just after the Germans had crossed the demarcation line and occupied the free zone. He had recruited a number of local personalities, René Gosse; Dunoyer de Ségonzac; the former president of the Senate Jules Jeanneney; and others. He then extended the network from Grenoble down through the Vercors to the Mediterranean coast and gave its command over to his deputy, Guivante, also known as Paul and as Saint-Gast.

Saint-Gast recruited, among others, a remarkable couple, Albert and Sonja Haasz. Albert was a doctor and Sonja a lawyer. Both were Jews who had banded together with other Jews to fight in the Resistance. Many thousands of French and European Jews fought with courage and skill in the Resistance, but their stories are not well known, for they rarely identified themselves as Jews. Albert and Sonja, for example, were simply known as Hungarians, which gave them their opportunity to conduct espionage against the Nazis, whom they hated.

They worked in Arles and in Aix and then made contact with Resistance leaders in Nice: Captain Legrand and Madame Jotte Latouche, known as Emilie, the wife of the commander of the submarine *Surcouf*. Legrand and Emilie had organized a network of sabotage and espionage and escape routes to both Switzerland and Spain from the Riviera. They thought highly of the Haasz couple and arranged to send them to England by submarine for training and return to France. Saint-Gast met them, liked them, and assigned them to sabotage and espionage school in Sussex. They trained, parachuted into the Vercors in August 1943, and then made their way to Nice for their assignments.

In Nice, they were ordered to infiltrate the Todt Organization, which had built and was maintaining the German coastal fortifications. It was a daring and dangerous assignment, but they carried it off. Albert Haasz went to the German authorities, to the chief of the Feldkommandantur, and told him that he was being persecuted by the French because he was a Hungarian and had voiced his pro-German feelings openly. Haasz, who to this day speaks with a strong Hungarian accent—Hungarians never seem to lose it—was in fact French, born of French parents. But his parents had been living in Budapest, in the diplomatic service, when he was born. His father left his mother, who stayed on in Hungary. So Haasz was educated in Hungary, while holding French citizenship. His wife, Sonja, was Belgian.

There were a number of Hungarian and other eastern European Nazis in the area, so the Germans were not surprised by Haasz's story. He was an excellent doctor whose services they could use. And Sonja was a brilliant linguist and lawyer. The Nazis hired both of them. Haasz volunteered for service in the Todt Organization, which hired him promptly. And Sonja, to his horror, was taken on by the Gestapo of Nice, in the office of the local gauleiter Wilhelm Baumgartner.

Week after week, Albert and Sonja would pass on a mass of espionage information to Emilie and Legrand, through letter boxes set up for them and often changed. They pinpointed clubs and meeting places of the Gestapo and of Todt officers, which a man named André, a specialist of the network, promptly blew up. They sent in details of a powerful propaganda transmitter of Radio Monte Carlo being used by the Germans, and that, too, was blown up. But their biggest coup came when Sonja came home one night carrying a tissue-paper tracing of a map detailing the German fortifications from Genoa to Marseille. It was a major coup, but it led to their exposure and capture in February 1944.

The Germans discovered somehow that there were spies in their midst. They set up surveillance on their employees and interrogated dozens of their own spies and counterspies. One of those counterspies, who had infiltrated the Resistance, reported that he had heard talk of a Hungarian couple and something about a coup involving coastal fortifications. That was all the clue that the Gestapo needed. Albert and Sonja were arrested at once. They were cruelly tortured. The Gestapo interrogator gouged out Sonja's right eye. Then they were sent to Germany, Sonja to Auschwitz, Albert Haasz to Mauthausen, where he saved his life by becoming a camp doctor. Sonja, too, survived, by becoming a nurse and then head of the records department in Auschwitz. Albert, like Sonja, had been savagely beaten. He was strung up by his thumbs, while his torturers beat his kidneys with clubs. His toes were pierced to the quick by hot needles. He was then subjected to the dread torture of the *baignoire,* repeated drownings in a bathtub, his head held under water until his lungs almost burst.

Albert and Sonja are in New York at the time of this writing. Dr. Albert Haasz is a respected professor of thoracic medicine at the Howard Rusk Medical Center in Manhattan. Sonja has been helping him write his book, *Concentration Camp Doctor,* about his experiences in Mauthausen. Neither one has ever forgotten their experiences in the Marco Polo network of southern France, and they were delighted to learn that the map they had sent through had helped the Allied navy train its six hundred fifty big guns on the German coastal emplacements.

The Germans had, in all, about five hundred guns, which would be no match for the combined firepower of the Allied warships and, above all, the Allied bombers. The Germans had less than two hundred fifty planes in all categories against the Allied total of two thousand aircraft. The Kriegsmarine had only thirty surface vessels, all small craft, plus ten submarines, against an Allied fleet that would include two hundred fifty warships. The Allied Mediterranean armada was not as big by half as the greatest armada ever assembled, the one that crossed the Channel, but it was, by far, at some two thousand vessels, the biggest armada ever to sail the historic Mediterranean along routes used by Phoenicians, Carthaginians, and Romans who had set out to conquer ancient Gaul. The vessels, graded by their speed and assigned relevant sailing dates, the slowest first, were assembled in Taranto, Naples, various ports of Sicily, Corsica, and Oran in Algeria.

This writer was assigned to board one of the ships in the armada in Naples, a Liberty ship called the *John S. Cropper.* I had waited impatiently, a full year in Algiers, for assignment to the invasion of France. The assignment was a double one: I would function as radio combat correspondent with the First French Army and the American Seventh Army, broadcasting alternately in French and in English to the troops, informing them of the fighting in each army frontier; secondly, I had a military intelligence mission to perform. As I reported from the battlefronts of each army, I was to locate troublemakers, of whom there were all too many. "Troublemakers" were defined in my orders as all Americans who "hated the Frogs," that is, all anti-French Americans in key command positions who could do harm to the two armies. Also, of course, I was to look for all anti-American Frenchmen who expressed their dislike for *"les sales 'ricains."* Plenty of those, too.

I was promised by none less than General Walter Bedell Smith that no man named by me would in any way have his career injured or any demerits put next to his name. I would not have to act as a master snitch, doing men in for the opinions they expressed. I could not have carried out such a mission. General Smith told me that the "troublemakers," endangering the safety of the operations, would simply be transferred to another command where they would not be in front-line combat, or in support of combat, and, above all, would not have to deal with any officer of a different nationality.

Long before the landings, I called on General de Lattre and told him that I would be broadcasting to the troops, and that it would be my honor to tell the Americans on his frontiers about the magnificent exploits of his French army. De Lattre, a kind of combination French-style Patton and Mac-Arthur—flamboyant, intelligent, elegant, and egomaniacal—welcomed the news and made it clear to me that it would be a grand idea to keep the world's press informed of his army's exploits and not merely the troops themselves. We became firm friends. Our friendship was cemented before the landings by my open espousing in Algiers of the Anvil-Dragoon plans. The difficulty I faced was, that of all the troublemakers goading the Americans on his front, de Lattre de Tassigny himself was one of the worst. But I did not have to report that to General Smith. He was only too aware of the conflicts between de Lattre and Generals Patch and Devers.

De Lattre's first clash with Patch came on June 27. De Lattre had returned to Algiers from the secret training camp where he was whipping French Army B into shape. I had been there with him and was waiting for him when he came out of his meeting. He spoke warmly of Patch, whom he considered an honest, no-nonsense kind of an American, a soldierly general, like Bradley. But de Lattre was upset to have learned from Patch that the southern landings had not yet been confirmed by SHAEF. In answer to de Lattre's questions on the assignment of his army in the event that Anvil were to be canceled, Patch had replied that it would still be assigned to the American Seventh, probably in Italy, for a drive on Austria. De Lattre had stiffly informed Patch that this was flatly contrary to the instructions he had received from his head of government, General Charles de Gaulle. Patch had shrugged and said: "That's too bad."

General de Lattre, incensed, drove to de Gaulle's villa to inform him of the conversation. De Gaulle told him to go back to see Patch to tell him that the First French Army was not a satellite army of the American Seventh, and that de Gaulle did not intend for it to be used as such. De Gaulle was insistent upon Anvil and Patch was to inform his superiors to that effect.

De Lattre then sent a letter to British General Sir Henry Maitland Wilson, who had replaced Eisenhower as supreme commander of the Mediterranean theater, demanding an audience to discuss the use of his army. He received a curt, almost rude reply, not from Wilson, but from Wilson's chief of staff. He told de Lattre that Wilson could not give him an answer or meet with him at that time, and that when the moment for a decision came, the general would meet with General de Gaulle. So much for de Lattre! De Lattre, a proud and vain man, exploded.

The controversy cooled off quickly, however, a day later, when it was learned that Roosevelt had finally decided to reconfirm the southern landings. De Lattre was delighted. Now he could concentrate on his plans for the landings instead of fighting with his Allies. Indeed, he went so far as to send a confidential memorandum to his commanders, informing them that they must keep in mind that they were part of an Allied coalition; that, in the coalition, the French were completely dependent on the Anglo-Americans for supplies; that they would, for that reason, have to follow Allied military directives and orders; that, finally, this was "the price we have to pay to participate in the liberation of France."

General de Lattre, who had come in contact with the Resistance inside France when he was still serving in the Armistice Army, knew how important the Resistance could be in helping his troops on the landings. He was also concerned, as was de Gaulle, about the activities and the attitudes that would prevail among the Communists, who were the biggest, best disciplined military and political group in the south. De Lattre cooperated enthusiastically with an Allied group that had been set up to deal with the Resistance: the SPOC, the Special Projects Operation Center.

SPOC's mission was to send officers to take charge of R.2, the Resistance sector where Dragoon would take place. It included the Riviera coastal cities from Nice and Cannes in the east to Toulon and Marseille in the west. They would be in the first assaults. Then would come the backcountry inland from the Riviera, about fifty miles deep, including about seven departments of Provence. There were thought to be some fifteen thousand men of the Resistance in that area, "thought to be" because the Supreme Command in Algiers was never sure of the reliability of Resistance figures of strength. In fact, those figures were sometimes exaggerated, but not this time. There were far more than fifteen thousand members of the Resistance in that area. Unfortunately, less than five thousand were armed. The rest were calling for arms drops, which had never come. Finally in June and July, to win support for their own landings, the Allies dropped no less than one hundred thousand containers of arms and munitions to the Resistance of Provence. Before dropping them, however, plans were being made to make sure that they did not fall unduly into hands of the Communists, who represented more than a third of all the Resistance forces in the area.

SPOC parachuted in seven Jedburgh teams to carry out Allied orders and organize the Resistance. In theory all the special forces and intelligence agents had been gathered together under the banner of a new command created in June: the Etat-Major des Forces Françaises de l'Intérieur (EMFFI), which integrated General Koenig's FFI and Passy's BCRAM staffs and agents, along with the Special Forces Headquarters of the Anglo-Americans; that is, the British SOE and the American OSS of General Donovan, commanded by Colonel David Bruce.

In principle Donovan and Bruce were supposed to be at their desks in London supervising all American Intelligence activities in Europe, and preparing special studies and orders for the invasion of southern France. In fact neither man was in London. In defiance of orders they had left London and gone to the invasion fleet assembly area to find a friend who would take them on the landings in Normandy.

At dawn on June 6, Donovan and Bruce were aboard the cruiser *Tuscaloosa*. Several admirals had ordered Donovan off their ships, but he had found a sympathetic young skipper and was well across the Channel with Bruce before anyone knew where he was.

"I was pretty nervous about the whole affair," Bruce admitted months later in an interview in Paris. "Perhaps it was my nerves, or my own clumsiness, but I almost killed Donovan. A German plane came swooping down to strafe us, and trying to get away, I plunged right into Donovan, the edge of my steel helmet cutting him just below the jugular vein. He spouted blood and I thought he was a goner.

"Despite the blood pouring out, Donovan insisted it was only a superficial cut. He said we had to push inland and make contact with our agents. We got to an American battery captain who stopped us, but then saw Donovan's Congressional Medal of Honor ribbon, and waved us on. He was still bleeding.

"We saw no OSS agents, but we did run into a German machine-gun nest. We hit the dirt and burrowed in. Donovan told me that we could not be captured. We knew too much. He asked me whether I was carrying my poison pill. I admitted I was not. Donovan said that was all right, he had at least two on him and would give me one. But, when he searched his pockets, he could not find them. Then he remembered that he had left them in his medicine cabinet in the bathroom back at Claridge's Hotel in London. He said to me: 'David, if we get out of this alive, please call Gibbs, the hall porter, and tell him to warn everyone not to touch the medicine in my bathroom.'

"Then Donovan said: 'Ah well, no matter for the pills. If the Germans take us, I'll shoot you first, as your commanding officer, then I'll shoot myself, so there's nothing to worry about.'"

Bruce felt there was a good deal to worry about in escorting Donovan, who was reverting to the "Wild Bill" Donovan of his youth. But they escaped further trouble when Allied troops arrived and put down the German guns.

Despite the absence of Donovan and Bruce and the rivalry among the many Allied and French intelligence services, the invasion commanders had useful hard intelligence on German coastal strengths and weaknesses, and on German strategic planning. The Germans might have been able to muster enough strength to drive the Allies back into the sea, both in Normandy and in Provence, if they had massed all the troops at their disposal. The High Command of the Wehrmacht was keeping twenty-five divisions in the Baltic states and another eighteen in Norway. Had these troops, or most of them, been pulled out for the Battle of France, the Allies could have been overwhelmed. But Marshal Keitel at Hitler's headquarters told Rommel and von Rundstedt that they could get enough help from garrisons in southern, central, and western France. Keitel did not suspect the strength of all the Allied landings, nor did he have any idea that the FFI partisans could so disrupt communications that German reinforcements could not reach their objectives.

In all of southern France, the German High Command had only ten divisions. One of those divisions was headquartered in Bordeaux, with the mission of defending the Atlantic coast, from the mouth of the Loire to the Spanish frontier—a hopeless task for only one division. Of the remaining nine divisions, the Ninth Panzer, a powerful force, was pulled out of its positions in Arles just before the southern landings and sent to the northern front. Another division had been sent to the Alps during the battles of Mont-Mouchet and the Vercors, and was tied down fighting the maquis. That left the commander of the German Nineteenth Army, General Kurt Wiese, headquartered in Avignon, north of Marseille, with only seven divisions to fight off an invasion of the Mediterranean coast.

The German commander deployed three of his divisions east of the river Rhône, and four of them west of the Rhône, not knowing where the main Allied thrust would come. They were spread very thin from Marseille in the west to Menton in the east of the Riviera coast. They totaled only two hundred fifty thousand men. They did have coastal guns covering the beaches, but virtually no air cover at all. The Luftwaffe had been thoroughly beaten by the RAF, all but shot out of the skies. Air cover is an essential element of a seaborne invasion. When the moment came, the Allies would not only control the air and blast away the coastal guns, they would throw more than three hundred thousand fresh but battle-trained troops at the two hundred fifty thousand Germans. And the Allies could, as the invader, pick their spots, concentrate where they would, while the Germans, stretched thin, had to try to hold everywhere.

We were well briefed on our excellent chances for a speedy capture of the beaches, and it was with confidence that I went to Naples to board my invasion vessel. I first saw the *John S. Cropper* at the dock in Naples. I had left our Psychological Warfare office armed with an M-1 rifle, my training-camp marksman's medal, and a Hermes portable typewriter. On my head a steel helmet one size too big bobbed around on top of an inner helmet-liner one size too small. I had never been what one might call a spit-and-polish soldier. Back in Military Intelligence Training School at Camp Ritchie, Maryland, I was known as Sergeant Klutz. On that day in August 1944, wandering around the crowded docks of Naples trying to find my transport, my helmet slipping over my eyes, my knapsack sliding off my back, my canteen unhooked and swinging against my hip, clutching my gun in one hand and typewriter in the other, I certainly did not strike terror in the hearts of any watching German spy.

If there had been any spies on those docks—and there must have been a goodly number of Italian Fascists on the German payroll—they would not have had any trouble learning that an invasion was in progress. When I stopped a couple of dirty-faced urchins, shooting craps on the dock, to ask my way to the *Cropper*, one of them said: "You goin' to France? Got any gum?" I gaped at him and hurried away to question a group of stevedores farther on. I addressed them in impeccable academic Italian and they sprayed me with a burst of liquid Neapolitan and Sicilian, of which I could not understand a word. I finally found a British merchant seaman who told me where the *Cropper* was docked.

When I found my ship, an American naval rating with a scarlet face was bellowing at the top of his lungs at an Italian work crew that was looking at him with interested curiosity, as one would observe a boiler that was about to blow up. The seaman saw me, spotted my typewriter, and yelled over to me: "You talk Eyetie?" Why the typewriter indicated a knowledge of Italian, I did not understand, but, foolishly, I nodded my head and indicated that I could speak Italian. He came over, glared at me, and said: "You sailin' on the *Cropper*?" He looked carefully for officer's pips or bars, as I admitted that I was sailing with him, and seeing nothing ominous, he then said: "OK, get this crew to load the ship." Without waiting for my anguished refusal, he skipped up the gangplank and disappeared aboard. At that moment the captain appeared on the deck, looked down, and roared at me: "Get that crew moving, and fast!"

I looked at the Neapolitan dockworkers, their bare shoulders glistening with sweat under the burning sun. Their cheeks were sunken and emaciated, their eyes lusterless. I walked over to the mountain of cargo waiting to be loaded, ran my eyes over it, and found what I was looking for: crates of K rations. I pulled a carton off the pile, took my bayonet off my webbed belt, and cut it open. Then, slicing open the small K-ration packets, with their hard chocolate bars, and mini packs of three cigarettes, I held the treasures in my hands, let them see what I had, and shouted, hoping it was right and comprehensible: "*Uno per uno!*" holding my hands out to them. They came with a rush, but lined up one by one, as I wanted them to do, and I handed them each a K-ration pack. Then, half in Italian, half in French and with much sign language I got them to begin loading up their nets with crates and moving them up to the number-two hold waiting to be filled.

The crates held foodstuffs of all kinds: dehydrated potatoes, peaches in syrup, powdered eggs, and other loathsome army substitutes for real food. I had no idea how a ship was supposed to be loaded. It seemed to me that there must be some kind of a system, but what it might be eluded me. So, under that hot Naples sun, bathed in sweat under my army woolens—no summer uniforms had been available when I checked into Naples—I just wanted to get the job done. My crew grabbed whatever was near to hand and hauled it up. I could not imagine how the army cooks would ever make sense out of the mess. I had visions of my fellow soldiers eating peaches and mashed potatoes for days on end. I certainly had no intention of eating with them. I had other plans, knowing that the navy eats well, for it takes on fresh food at every port.

Aboard the *Cropper*, I reported in to the skipper and told him proudly that I had finished the loading. He grunted, unimpressed, and waved me off. I asked permission to speak and he looked up at me in surprise, his thick eyebrows raised in circumflex accents: ᐱ ᐱ. I took this to be permission and spoke out:

"Sir, we will be at sea, I know, for a week or more, waiting to hit the beaches. The soldiers are packed in tight in the holds. It's hot as hell. We need to keep up morale. I would like to be ship's news, entertainment, and morale officer."

The captain was interested. He puffed his pipe as a sign for me to go on.

I talked about boxing matches on deck and improvised Bingo games. And then I really caught his attention when I said: "I'm a news writer and broadcaster. I can monitor the BBC morning broadcast for ships at sea that gives the world news, particularly news from all the fighting fronts. Then, with your permission, I'll type up the broadcast—I'm a fast typist—cut a stencil, and run it off on the ship's mimeo machine. I'll put out a ship's newspaper with world news and ship's scuttlebutt, jokes, and gossip and it will be great for the troops and a good kind of annex to your daily log on this invasion run."

The captain blew out a cloud of smoke and shouted: "Done." He called in his first mate and told him to make all arrangements with me.

I told the mate I'd need a place to work, a kind of private office. When he said there was no private office aboard, I asked him if he had anyone locked up in the ship's padded cell, used for violent prisoners or lunatics who go berserk. He said that it was empty at the moment. I told him I'd like to work and sleep in the padded cell until another lunatic came along. Since I had volunteered to go on the invasion, I surely could qualify as a kind of lunatic. He agreed at once. From then on, I had luxurious private quarters on the *John S. Cropper*. And the mate arranged for me to eat in the navy mess when he saw the title of our ship's new newspaper. I had called it the *Crop O'Shit*. He thought that was great and merited fresh meat and eggs.

We cruised around the Mediterranean, zigging and zagging and shifting course to confuse German reconnaissance planes. Just before the landings, on August 14, the Admiral of the Fleet saw the German spy plane checking our positions some hours before dusk. He gave the order to swing the armada around to head toward Genoa. He wanted the Germans to think we were making a run around the Gothic line to attack the German troops from the rear. He let the spy plane take pictures and plot our course, and then, when night fell, the admiral swung us back around again and ordered full steam ahead toward the Riviera.

Just before dawn on August 15, 1944, American and French warships trained their big guns on the coast, from Cannes to Cavalaire, while bombers dived over the German positions, particularly around the principal ports of Toulon and

Marseille. As in Normandy, the first wave of attacks was launched mainly by American troops but once again the Supreme Command, alert to French sensitivities, gave French commandos the signal honor of being the very first troops to land on the soil of Provence. In an order of the day, the Allied fleet saluted Lieutenant Colonel Charles Bouvet and his men, spearheading the liberating forces on the night of August 14–15. American assault troops followed all through the fifteenth and then the bulk of the French divisions came rushing in on the sixteenth.

U.S. Navy Secretary James Forrestal, who had ordered his admirals not to take "Wild Bill" Donovan on the Normandy landings, exercised his own privilege of high office by boarding a warship to "watch the fun," as he told the captain. As soon as the beach and hinterland were secured, early on the seventeenth, Forrestal took a landing craft in and jumped out on the sands of one of the most beautiful beaches of the Riviera, at Saint-Raphaël.

Admiral Jean Lemonnier, the French flag officer of the fleet, joined Forrestal and arranged a celebration and a *vin d'honneur* in the public square. Forrestal and his aides were served enough champagne to float their ship. They were garlanded with honeysuckle and orange blossoms and thoroughly kissed by beautiful girls. Forrestal, the next day, sent a thank-you note to Admiral Lemonnier, saying: "When the war is over, I hope very much to return to your country and find you as mayor of Saint-Raphaël, so that you can find me a small but permanent sinecure in that delightful town. *A bientôt*." Poor Forrestal! When the war ended, he became secretary of defense, suffered the overload of work and anxieties of the cold war. He broke down under the strain and ended up committing suicide.

There are always those unlucky ones, in any human situation, who lose while others are harvesting the fruits of victory. Although our landings were almost unopposed, hundreds were wounded and died in early skirmishes. As I drove my jeep across the white sands of Saint-Tropez, a jeep just ahead and to the left of me hit a mine and blew up. The blast sent me into a skid, a stall, and a fright. But I switched my engine on again and made it up to the shore road. There I received my first, and happily last, wound of the war. Someone threw a bunch of grapes to me and cut my left eye. The army medic who dressed the cut refused to put me in for the Purple Heart.

The Supreme Command had assigned to the French the important mission and the honor of liberating Toulon and Marseille. The American planners had scheduled the liberation of Toulon for D-day plus 20 (September 4), of Marseille for D + 40 (September 24), and of Lyon for D + 90 (November 15). General de Lattre and his staff planners were determined to reach their objectives well before this timetable if they could. It all depended on how fast they could get their full complement of troops and weapons onto the beaches. On the first wave, the French brought in some fifteen thousand men, thirty tanks, and eighty artillery pieces. That was not nearly enough to defeat the Germans, well dug in at the naval base of Toulon, with twenty-five thousand men inside a system of thirty forts and hundreds of casemates. Toulon would be a tough nut to crack for the first major combat mission of the new First French Army.

I was one of the correspondents in whom de Lattre confided as he discussed his battle plans on August 18. He had decided to go in on the attack the very next day. De Lattre had already contacted the local Resistance through a naval officer who had been parachuted in two months before for the purpose of gathering intelligence to be used in the assault on the German positions. He told me about his reports.

"The Resistance has done a first-rate job in providing us with detailed maps of German positions and strengths. They also have about two thousand men ready to fight along with us, if I can get them the arms they need. I'm doing that now!" General de Lattre went on to say that the people of Toulon and the surrounding area had suffered under the Germans and were anxious to participate in the struggle for their liberation. There were many volunteers. Meanwhile, the buildup of forces on the beaches was continuing. De Lattre was sure he could start his attack without delay, knowing that reinforcements were on the way. He offered to keep me informed on every move in the battle for my radio broadcasts on army transmitters. When Toulon fell he would have the powerful base transmitter.

The next day, General de Lattre saw General Devers, then deputy supreme commander of the Mediterranean theater. Devers heard him out and gave approval for his battle plans, as did General Patch, commander of the U.S. Seventh Army. De Lattre returned to his command post and immediately issued orders for the assault on Toulon, to be launched the next day, on August 20. At the time he issued the orders, he had just received an important code signal from the colonel commanding an infantry regiment that had just taken the village of Le Revest, a suburb of Toulon. This action completed the investing of Toulon and cleared the way for the attack directly on the naval base itself.

The battle began at dawn on the twenty-first and lasted a full week of fierce fighting through the outer defenses, then street by street and house by house to the inner core of fortresses ringing the base. The men of the Resistance, in their FFI units, fought side by side with the regular army. De Lattre was both pleased and disturbed by the actions of the FFI. He told me: "The Resistance honors France and we are all proud of the FFI. But it is imperative that the FFI be integrated as rapidly as possible into the army. There can only be one French army, indivisible, disciplined, and responsible to the French government. The day of clandestine operations against an enemy of occupation is over. So, therefore, ends the day of irregular partisans. One Army, One Flag!" De Lattre had received instructions from de Gaulle to draft the resistants into the army. Some resistants joined at once and were given ranks from sergeant to general. Others, particularly the Communists, balked at being drafted. The struggle to absorb the FFI went on for months.

Meanwhile the battle raged on for Toulon, whose German forces, commanded by Admiral Karl Ruhfuss, had received orders from Hitler to fight to the death and to blow up the port facilities before going under. The Germans did fight hard but did not obey orders to fight to the death, and did not blow up the naval works as Hitler had demanded. Many thousands were taken prisoner, fort by fort, until the French broke through the last German defense lines on the twenty-seventh of August. Admiral Ruhfuss, commanding the citadel, held out through the day but finally surrendered just before midnight. The next morning, August 28, the last German combatants, eighteen hundred sailors, marched out of their fortified positions, hands on their heads. Toulon was liberated.

General de Lattre called in Admiral Ruhfuss and ordered him to produce a detailed map of all minefields and explosive charges. When the German admiral refused to answer, de Lattre told him that he and his men would answer with their lives for every Frenchman killed by a German mine or explosive charge. Admiral Ruhfuss capitulated and handed over the maps that de Lattre had demanded.

The Battle of Toulon had cost the French twenty-seven hundred killed and wounded. The Germans had lost some five thousand killed, and had left almost twenty thousand prisoners in French hands. Toulon had been liberated by D + 13, a week ahead of schedule.

The Battle of Marseille had begun on the same day that de Lattre had launched his orders to attack Toulon, August 20. General de Lattre, at the outset of the attack, had had a serious quarrel with one of his senior commanders, General Hubert de Goislard de Monsabert, a feisty little man, barely five feet tall, with a shock of thick white hair that he wore like a plume on a knight's helmet. Indeed there was something quite medieval about the general, beginning with his name. De Monsabert had made contact with the Resistance of Marseille, who had informed his unit commanders that they would stage an insurrection before the assault. He was certain that the population, particularly the tough dockworkers and the underworld gangsters of Marseille, would work with his troops. De Monsabert was convinced that in a surprise assault he could break into the very center of the port, throw the Germans into confusion, and force their surrender. De Lattre thought it a foolhardy scheme and refused to approve it.

This controversy almost cost me and two other American correspondents our lives.

On August 21, one of de Monsabert's officers informed me that his division was already inside Marseille. "We are mopping up and by nightfall the port will be liberated." There had been no word about this at our headquarters press camp. I was thrilled to be the first reporter to be tipped off on a really big story, the liberation of Marseille, at that date the biggest city of France to be freed.

I ran to get my driver and jeep and to round up the two civilian reporters assigned to go with me, two of the most able correspondents in our profession: Homer Bigart of the *New York Herald Tribune* and Robert Vermillion of the United Press.

We jumped into the jeep in camp at Aix and drove swiftly off to Marseille. As our jeep came down the hill into the city, we noticed French people looking at us in amazement, some waving hesitantly and some ducking back into doorways. It did not at all look like a city being liberated. As we drove deeper and deeper into Marseille, seeing no army units, our fears were confirmed: We were the only Allies in Marseille. My driver and I were the only soldiers there, not exactly a liberating force. As we turned into a street near the prefecture, toward which we had been heading, shots rang out all around our jeep. My driver jammed on the brakes and we jumped off the jeep and plunged into the nearest doorway.

There were two Frenchmen in the doorway, one very tall and thin, the other short and squat, and they were shouting at each other. They wore tricolor blue-white-red brassards of the FFI, and one of them held a rifle, while the other had cartridge belts slung across his shoulders and around his hips. The tall one was trying to get the gun from the short one, shouting that he would get the fascists shooting down at us from the rooftops. The squat one insisted he was the better shot and, in any case, had the gun. He demanded the cartridges held by the tall one.

Homer Bigart, whose stammer became worse when under strain, began to shout at them: "Luh-luh-luh-luh-listen, fuh-fuh-fuh-fellers." Since they could not understand a word of English, to say nothing of the stammer, Homer's message was not getting through. Vermillion was leaning against the wall, helpless from laughter. My driver, a tough American soldier, ran back to the jeep under a hail of bullets, recovered his rifle, got back to our doorway, and began shooting up at the roof. The short man then surrendered his rifle to the tall one, who loaded it and began his own fusillade. Whoever had been shooting at us—and the FFI men insisted it was a unit of local fascists of Marcel Déat's party—did not like our return fire. They stopped shooting.

After a quarter hour, we cautiously stuck our heads out and slowly made our way back to our jeep. We jumped on and started the motor, just as the snout of a German Tiger tank began to snake around the corner. We screamed at our driver to get the hell out as fast as he could. He pulled his steering wheel around and we took off on two wheels for the opposite corner. I shouted directions and in five minutes we saw the gates of the prefecture ahead of us. To our relief, a huge French flag was flying from the balcony.

Shouting "Vive la France!" at the top of our lungs to stop anyone from shooting at us on our way in, we drove at full speed toward the gates. They had already begun to swing open and we hurtled right into the main courtyard. There we saw a scene out of a Breughel painting. Men with bloody head-bandages were squatting on the cobblestones. Some were laid out on stretchers, with nurses working over them. Others hobbled about on makeshift crutches. Men with brassards were shouting orders. Armed men were seen in every window. Two machine guns were set up in the corners of the yard. The whole scene was illuminated by candles, oil lamps, and burning rags, although behind the glass doors and windows we could see electric light.

I jumped off the jeep, grabbed someone with a gun and brassard, told him who we were, and asked who his leader was. He beckoned us to follow him inside and he led us to an office in which a number of men and women were busy on telephones. One of them stepped forward and said he was the chief of the Resistance, in charge of the occupation of the prefecture. "The people of Marseille have risen up and we will liberate our city," he announced grandly. He said that he was Commandant Fouchet. Resistance headquarters later told me they had never heard of him. All kinds of last-minute "resistants" were turning up.

We soon discovered that the "tip" we had been given by de Monsabert's staff officer was somewhat exaggerated. A few of de Monsabert's units had penetrated into the suburbs and the perimeter of Marseille. De Monsabert had transmitted de Lattre's orders against a premature attack, but with a wink had added: "Of course, if you see a target of opportunity . . ." This had been understood to be a signal to break into Marseille, and somehow it had been given to me as a fact that Marseille was in the process of liberation. The prefecture and some minor buildings had been seized by the Resistance. The Germans could break in and take them back with no trouble if they decided it was necessary. We were trapped inside the prefecture and would have to stay there until de Monsabert's troops did break through.

The French finally did arrive, thirty-six hours later, and we became official liberators. Meanwhile, we had been harangued by the local Resistance inside the prefecture. They had treated us to a number of Marxist orations about "power to the people." We heard not a word about de Gaulle and began to understand de Gaulle's fear that the Communists would try to strike for power before the French government could establish itself in place.

At last, however, the men whom the real Resistance leaders had officially chosen to take over in the name of the Republic did reach the prefecture. One of them, very close to the Communists himself, was Raymond Aubrac from Libération, who had been named commissaire de la République for Marseille. Another was a Socialist party deputy, François Leenhardt, a member of the Comité de Libération, determined to prevent any illegal seizure of power. Both men cooperated loyally. They appointed a new prefect for the department, Flavien Veyren. Pierre Massenet, a civil engineer, was appointed deputy-prefect of Marseille.

Meanwhile, the First French Army troops fought their way into the center of Marseille. General de Monsabert, under cover of a flag of truce, called on the German commander and demanded his surrender, pointing out the hopelessness of his position and the utter futility of further fighting that could lead only to senseless killings on both sides.

At that first meeting of General de Monsabert and German General Curt Schaeffer, the German, under orders from Hitler to fight on, refused to surrender. Fighting continued, from that moment on August 23 through August 27, when the French troops invested the last principal fort still held by the Germans inside Marseille. French artillery was blasting holes into the thick walls of Fort Saint-Nicholas, when General Schaeffer, estimating that he had saved his honor by putting up a stiff fight, decided the time had come to disobey Hitler's fight-to-the-death order. He sent an emissary out under a white flag with a letter of surrender. The next morning, August 28, France's second largest city, Marseille, celebrated its liberation with a triumphant parade of the French army in its first victory over the Germans since the defeat and capitulation of June 1940.

French engineers went to work at once clearing the port of Marseille, whose harbor had been blocked by the hulls of eleven large ships sunk there. Almost two hundred wrecks were scattered around the port. All the quays had been blown up by two thousand mines. More than fifty thousand square meters of warehouses had been destroyed, along with railway and electrical installations. The transporter bridge had been blown up and two hundred fifty-seven cranes had collapsed.

French and American engineers worked miracles in Marseille. Two weeks after its liberation, nine Liberty ships sailed in through a cleared channel and discharged cargo on the repaired docks, while fifty other ships unloaded in the roads. Three thousand tons were put ashore, justifying the judgment of Eisenhower and Bradley in maintaining Operation Dragoon over Churchill's objections. In the months ahead more than twenty thousand tons of supplies would flow through the port of Marseille.

While the French were investing and liberating Toulon and Marseille, the Americans were racing up the Rhône and the slopes of the Alps, aiming at Lyon and Grenoble. It was on the way up the Rhône that I saw, across the river on its west bank, a French flag flying from the crenellated terraces of the ancient walled city of Tarascon. In the thirties, as a French teacher in New York, I had used, as a text, passages from Alphonse Daudet's classic tale of Tartarin de Tarascon. Expecting to go back to teaching when the war was over, I was burning to go to Tarascon, so that I could talk about it in class. I was nervous, however, for we had strict orders from Supreme Headquarters not to cross the Rhône.

I consulted with Eric Sevareid and Winston Burdette, the CBS correspondents with the Seventh Army. Eric thought it made no sense to go to Tarascon. He was right in context. But Winston agreed with me that literature and romance made a special sense of their own beyond the military. So we agreed to try to get to Tarascon.

I was in touch with the Resistance wherever we went, for I admired its brave men and women and knew them to be the only ones who could get anything done in the confusion of the campaign. Sure enough I found a resistant who had a rowboat and who agreed to row us across to Tarascon.

We were spotted coming across, so there was a delegation, headed by the mayor, wearing his tricolor sash of office, waiting to greet us at the gates of the town. We marched off to the *mairie*, followed by cheering crowds.

There the mayor broke open bottles of champagne to *"arroser la Libération."* Then he invited me to join him on the balcony overlooking the town square. The mayor delivered a proclamation of liberation, and then announced that the "personal representative of the illustrious supreme commander, General Eisenhower, would address the liberated people of Tarascon." I looked around until I realized he was referring to me.

I delivered a speech of greetings from the Allies. As I was addressing the crowd, I saw, to my dismay, a column of German armored cars coming into the far end of the square. Once again, I was finding myself trapped inside a "liberated" place that had not been liberated at all. The mayor, having earlier seen Allied troops across the river, and watched German units speeding out of town, had believed that the Americans were coming across the Rhône. He had hoisted the flag that we had seen, but in no way had Tarascon been liberated. The Germans, as I could plainly see, were there in force.

I finished my address, warning the people that our troops were still across the river, exhorting them to do nothing to provoke the Germans into violence against them. Then we all hastily stepped back off the balcony. We climbed to the roof and, using binoculars, watched the Germans. It soon became apparent that the Germans were only racing through Tarascon on their way out of southwestern France, heading back toward the northeast before being bottled up by Allied troops. Tarascon was safe if it would only sit by and watch quietly for a few days until the Germans had all left.

Burdette and I made our way back to the banks of the Rhône, where our rowboat and FFI guide awaited us. As we rowed away in a golden dusk men, women, and children came down to the bank and waded into the river, waving good-bye and asking us to come back one day. Then, knee-deep in the water, they all halted and began to sing "La Marseillaise." The music and lyrics of the national anthem of France never fail to move me, but that day I heard the most marvelous "La Marseillaise" ever, ringing out over the river Rhône.

On August 23 units of an American column, Task Force Butler, and several thousand men of the FFI who had invested Grenoble at the moment of the landings, broke through the last German defenses and liberated Grenoble. Butler's column, with little opposition, had raced up Alpine roads, along the historic Route Napoléon. Now the advancing forces of Dragoon and Overlord, pushing toward each other from the north and south, were moving to close a vise around the German First and Nineteenth armies. General Patton had sent powerful forces driving south toward Orléans and General Patch issued orders for an all-out push north toward Lyon to close the pincers.

The fight for Lyon began on August 22, only a week after our landings, mainly because the Germans retreated rapidly from the south. Ready to attack Lyon were units of Task Force Butler, a brigade of motorized cavalry, and the Thirty-sixth Texas Division, with strong forces of the FFI pointing the way.

Franc-Tireur, Combat, and Libération commandos had been active all through the departments of the Isère and the Drôme all around Lyon and Grenoble. The Resistance blew bridges, blocked roads, cut communication lines, and harassed the Wehrmacht every step of its way. The Germans had powerful forces in the sector, including the Eleventh Panzer Division with a full complement of Tiger and Mark V tanks. In counterattacks outside Lyon, German armor penetrated within three miles of Thirty-sixth Division headquarters before American armor was able to come up. The Germans were stopped at that critical point by strong contingents of the Communist Francs-Tireurs et Partisans Français, the FTPF. Resistance fighters held the Germans up inside Lyon for thirty-six hours, long enough for the Americans to bring their forces to full strength.

The Germans finally broke out and ran north. All along the way they were harassed and shot up by the Resistance and pounded mercilessly by the U.S. Army Air Force. By August 28, the German Nineteenth Army no longer existed as a fighting force. Scattered units, the remnants of the once-victorious army, were running north and east back toward Germany.

The Germans, thoroughly beaten, evacuated Lyon on September 2. Yves Farge, still a leader of the Resistance in that longtime capital of the Resistance despite the disaster in the Vercors, took over as commissaire de la République in Lyon on September 3. He received the thanks of General de Monsabert and General Lucian Truscott, American VI Corps commander, for the valiant fighting of the FFI, which had played a major role in the Battle of Lyon.

General de Gaulle flew into Lyon shortly after its liberation. His trip there had been arranged by the most loyal of his close associates, Claude Serreulles, who in July, after a long, impatient wait in London, had parachuted back into France as the delegate of the Provisional Government for southern France. Serreulles worked closely with a co-delegate, Jacques Maillet. Between them they laid down the condition for the re-creation of Republican law and order. They were in charge of installing in office the new authorities, the commissaire and the prefects.

On arrival in Lyon, General de Gaulle was greeted by Yves Farge, who told him that he would be meeting and dining with the leaders of the maquis and the principal agents of the Resistance.

General de Gaulle nodded assent and then asked: "But what about the authorities?"

Yves Farge smiled and replied: "They are all in jail, General."

By early September all three of France's principal cities, Paris, Lyon, and Marseille, had been liberated and the government of the Republic installed in office. There had been little difficulty in Marseille and in Lyon, where there was no significant challenge to the authority of General de Gaulle and the Provisional Government of the French Republic.

Paris was another story.

26
THE RACE FOR PARIS

In the summer of 1944, the heart of Paris was not young and gay. Many of its youth had fled south to the free zone in the early days of the occupation of the city, and more fled later, in a flood tide churned up by the mass deportations to Germany, and by the decrees of the forced labor draft that sent many Frenchmen into the maquis. Most of those who stayed behind in Paris had joined the Resistance. They lived for the day of revenge when they would arise, drive out the Germans, and make the collaborationists pay for their crimes.

The population of Paris was suffering from severe shortages of food and drugs. By mid-July Paris was facing a famine. Dr. Jean-Marie Muzy, Swiss delegate of the International Red Cross, wrote an official report in July 1944 on the distress of Paris. "Essentials are lacking and prices have risen fantastically. A minor official earns sixty francs a day, but a small slice of meat costs one hundred francs. For the poor, it is already black misery."

The normal prewar consumption of milk in Paris was a daily average of 1,200,000 liters. In July 1944, available milk in Paris was down to 225,000 liters a day, a shortage of almost one million liters, or almost one million American quarts. The Swiss doctor estimated that there were at least twenty-five thousand undernourished babies in Paris. Mothers had to wean their infants early and many mothers had no milk to give because of their own famished condition.

One could search all over Paris and not find a plate of the city's traditional *pommes frites*. Only 25 percent of the people received their rations of potatoes. Not a drop of wine could be bought in Paris after wine distribution was suspended in July. Parisians received only two eggs as a monthly ration, along with 3.2 ounces of cooking oil, and 2 ounces of margarine. A popular joke reported that the meat ration could be wrapped in a Métro ticket, provided it had not been used—otherwise the meat would fall through the punched hole. The one staple food in full supply in Paris was the rutabaga, a variety of turnip normally used for cattle fodder. "Coffee" was a bitter ersatz brew of crushed acorns. Paris was starving.

Taxis had long since disappeared. The "taxis" of July 1944 were *vélo-taxis*, bicycles with a wheeled trailer-seat attached. There were *super-taxis* composed of bicycles built for two or even three and four cyclists, who could haul a party of four people. They were pedaled by former professional champions who used to compete in the famous Tour de France national bike race. There were a few cars licensed by the Germans, but they burned wood, not gasoline, in giant boilers. They were called *gazogènes*. Gasoline was given only to trucks carrying vital supplies. The normal contingent of ten thousand supply trucks for Paris had been cut down by the Germans to twenty-five hundred. The subway ran a few hours a day. Otherwise, transportation was by bicycle. Those not strong enough to pedal through the day had to stay home. The only bright sight in Paris was a view of the beautiful, lean legs of Parisian women, their full skirts billowing behind them like sails as they pedaled down the boulevards.

The Germans kept a few famous restaurants and cabarets well supplied for their officers and the collaborationist elite. Maxim's was full every night. So was the Lido, Shéhérazade, and Suzy Solidor's. On weekends, the smart set could be found in the Bois de Boulogne, at the racetracks of Longchamps and Auteuil. The horses were thin but running. Luna Park, Paris's amusement center, advertised that it could be reached by only "ninety-nine strokes of your bike's pedals." The Moulin Rouge boasted standing room only for the nightly songs of Edith Piaf and her handsome young protégé, Yves Montand. Serge Lifar starred at the ballet and presented his own young protégés, who were the hit of the season: Roland Petit and Zizi Jeanmaire. The big theater-cinema, Gaumont Palace, France's popular music hall, kept its projectors running by a brace of bicycles generating pedal-power from four men pumping away at thirteen miles an hour, storing up enough current for two complete shows. The cinema advertised parking space for three hundred bicycles. The Vieux Colombier theater featured Jean-Paul Sartre's latest play, *Huis Clos*, which would later appear on Broadway as *No Exit*. While audiences watched his play, Sartre, in an attic bedroom a few blocks away, was writing Resistance tracts.

In the early evening, all of Paris was at home, particularly during the painfully brief thirty minutes when electric current was on. People huddled around their radio sets listening, through the static of German jamming, to the forbidden broadcasts of the BBC. They had cheered the news of the Allied landings in Normandy on June 6. They had cheered the news, suppressed by German censors, of the Allied liberation of Rome and the exploits of the French troops under General Juin. They had cheered the courage of the defenders of Stalingrad and their victory over the Germans. And sometimes, as on the night of August 3, 1944, a night of a beautiful, pink and almond-green sunset, a perfect summer night, the people of Paris had trembled as they heard about the burning of Warsaw, a disaster that would soon become a nightmare model for all Parisians.

With the Soviet Red Army only a brief march from the gates of

Warsaw, the Polish Resistance had come up out of the underground to stage an open insurrection, hoping to harass the Germans, distract them, and be able to hold out for a day or two until the liberating Russian armies broke through the German defenses around Warsaw. The German garrison troops, disciplined and well armed, under orders to hold Warsaw and delay the Russians as long as possible, turned savagely against the Resistance. The Poles, with only side-arms, knives, and clubs against German armor and firepower, never had the slightest chance. Moreover, the Russians, either stopped by German defenses, or deliberately holding back to let the Poles be slaughtered—the better to dominate Poland and bring it under Soviet control—did not break into Warsaw. There would be no Red Army rescue for the Polish Resistance. Two hundred thousand Poles died in the insurrection. Warsaw was put to flame by the Nazis. At the end of the battle, Warsaw was a pile of blackened ruins. When the Red Army then came in, not a house was left intact. Warsaw was not liberated, it was cremated.

A number of men, responsible for what would happen in Paris, wondered that night whether Paris might not be facing the same fate. One of these men was General Omar Bradley, commander of the U.S. Twelfth Army Group. Paris was on his direct line of advance. His forward units, in General George Patton's Third Army, swept east from Laval early in August and raced toward Le Mans, only 110 miles from Paris. They could have reached the French capital in a few days, except that these were not the battle plans.

Paris, wrote General Bradley in his wartime memoirs, had become tactically "meaningless." "Paris represented nothing more than an inkspot on our maps, to be bypassed as we headed toward the Rhine. Logistically, it could cause untold trouble, for behind its handsome facades there lived four million hungry Frenchmen. The diversion of so much tonnage to Paris would only strain further our already taut lines of supply. Food for the people of Paris meant less gasoline for the front."

Bradley was a soldier, not a sentimentalist, and he had, in any case, little personal commitment to Paris. When a group of newsmen came to see him to ask him that Paris be spared artillery and air bombardment to avoid the dread fate of Warsaw, Bradley noted: "Though lacking their affection for a city I had never seen, I assured them that we would not damage so much as a cobblestone in its streets. Instead of hammering down its west gates in a frontal attack, I explained, we would first pinch off Paris and thereafter enter it at our leisure." When reporters pressed him to say which division would get the honor of liberating Paris, Bradley laughed and made a joke of their question, suggesting that they had enough men in the correspondents corps to take Paris themselves and save him "a lot of trouble." He added: "For while I wouldn't want the French to know it, I might just as well tell you we're not at all anxious to liberate Paris right now."

The supreme commander, General Dwight D. Eisenhower, was wrestling with the very same problem that Bradley had already decided in his own mind. At his headquarters, just inland from the beach at Granville, in Normandy, Eisenhower had heard of the restlessness of the French commander of the Second Armored, Jacques-Philippe de Hautecloque, known by his Resistance name, General Leclerc. As far back as December 30, 1943, during a visit to Algiers, Eisenhower had discussed the liberation of Paris with General de Gaulle. De Gaulle had told him: "It is essential that French troops take the capital." Eisenhower, sensitive to France's psychological need to wipe out the memory of 1940, agreed at once with de Gaulle's request. Later, he further agreed to hold Leclerc's Second Armored in reserve and not use it in the assault on the beaches or in the battles en route to Paris.

General Koenig had explained to Eisenhower that de Gaulle wanted the people of Paris to see their very finest fighting division at the peak of its form, dashing liberators of Paris, chasing away the memory of the disheveled, defeated troops of June 1940. Eisenhower had balked at first at the thought of Americans and Englishmen fighting and dying in the crucial first weeks of the assault on Hitler's Fortress Europa, while Frenchmen held back in nice, clean uniforms, to make a good impression on Paris. But he finally understood how important it was to the French to regain their lost pride and honor and he consented.

Having broken out of the Normandy beachhead with heavy casualties, and being engaged in a costly fight with tough, battle-hardened German troops, General Eisenhower was having second thoughts in July about sending Leclerc, or anyone at all, to liberate Paris. The supreme commander had in front of him a twenty-four-page document in a blue manila cover marked "Top Secret—Post-Neptune Operations, Section II—Crossing of the Seine and Capture of Paris." It had been drawn up for him by a three-man planning committee of Supreme Headquarters. He had told the planners that he believed the Germans would put up a strong fight for Paris for reasons of prestige and morale. They could also tie up Allied forces in house-to-house fighting. He wanted to know what the planners thought might happen if he sent a division in to liberate Paris.

The report confirmed his worst fears. To dislodge the Germans, dug in in Paris, would require "prolonged and heavy street fighting, similar to that in Stalingrad." It would result in the "destruction of the French capital." Even worse, in Eisenhower's view, was the dire prediction that if the Allies were successful and were able to liberate Paris swiftly, without prolonged and heavy fighting, "Paris will become a serious limitation to our ability to maintain forces in operation. The capture of Paris will entail a civil affairs commitment equal to maintaining eight divisions in operation."

That last sentence shocked Eisenhower. Making a rapid calculation, the supreme commander realized that it meant dry fuel tanks for one fourth of the divisions that he had already landed in France, as the gas would be diverted to an army of trucks needed to bring food and drugs to the people of liberated Paris. Gasoline was in short supply that summer in France. His commanders, particularly Patton, kept calling for more and more gas for their insatiable tanks. Eisenhower had said: "I hurt every time I give up a gallon." Paris would cost him thousands and thousands of gallons. It would mean no hope of reaching and crossing the Rhine by early winter. It might well mean delaying the end of the war for a year, with many casualties and much suffering for all. This was a risk that Eisenhower was determined not to take.

He read and reread the figures in the report, for he knew he would have a hard time restraining Leclerc and explaining his decision to de Gaulle. The report estimated that Paris would require seventy-five thousand tons of food and medical supplies in the first two months of liberation, plus an additional fifteen hundred tons daily of coal for the public utilities. With Cherbourg the only big port available, in addition to the beaches, and with the French railway system in ruins, thanks to the Resistance, all this tonnage would have to be moved from Normandy to Paris by truck, on the already famous and overburdened "Red Ball Express" trucking system of the American army. That meant a 416-mile round-trip supply system. Eisenhower shuddered to think how many gallons of gas that would require. He suspected that the report's estimate that it would displace the equivalent of eight divisions might be modest.

The authors of the planning study recommended strongly that Eisenhower should avoid the commitment to liberate Paris as long as possible. Instead, they proposed another plan: a pincer movement north and south of Paris. This would allow the Allied troops striking north to roll up the launching sites of the V-1 and V-2 rockets causing so much damage in London. Montgomery's Twenty-first Army Group could send its left wing out to cross the Seine between the Oise and the sea, to liberate the port of Le Havre. When the group reached Amiens, Monty could break off two corps in a wheeling movement to the east, to get above and beyond Paris. At the same time Bradley would send the Twelfth Army Group across the Seine at Melun, south of Paris. He would strike for Reims, east of Paris, and then wheel north to meet the British coming down from the push beyond Amiens. When they met, they would form a gigantic vise around Paris, trapping all the Germans who might have stayed inside the bag. The experts estimated that the maneuver could be carried out between September 15 and October 1.

Eisenhower was impressed by the plan. It offered him three important advantages: (1) It avoided destructive, costly street fighting inside Paris; (2) it enabled him to push his troops, both British and American, through the best possible open tank country, north and south of Paris, terrain he could use to maximum advantage; and (3) it saved gasoline vitally needed to reach and breach the Siegfried line and throw a bridgehead across the Rhine before the onset of winter.

Only one thing could upset this plan: an unforeseen event such as an uprising in Paris. To forestall such an event, General Eisenhower sent strict instructions to General Koenig, head of the FFI, insisting that "no armed movements were to go off in Paris or anywhere else," without specific, written orders from Supreme Headquarters. Eisenhower knew it would be a strain on the impatient French Resistance forces to hold back and "to live with the Germans a little bit longer," as Eisenhower put it in a memo to his chief of staff, General Walter Bedell Smith. But, "their sacrifice may help us shorten the war," the supreme commander concluded.

Another general was studying the same situation and arriving at diametrically different conclusions. In the searing heat of the Algerian summer, General Charles de Gaulle pored over battle maps and pondered on the challenge of Paris. He saw two dangerous enemies barring his way to the restoration of a free and independent France with himself as chief of government. Neither one of the two enemies was German. He had once told this writer, in a conversation in Algiers: "I do not talk of Hitler and I do not fear Hitler, for Hitler is doomed. The powerful Red Army is sweeping across Europe from the east, while the Americans are racing across from the west. They will squeeze Germany to death, of this there is no doubt. The trouble is that the mighty Russian Bear will clutch all eastern Europe to its Communist bosom, while the American Eagle will drop millions of dollars and buy up the West. France, all Europe, will lose its independence if we do not liberate ourselves and regain our rank among the powers of the world," de Gaulle argued.

His conviction that the Americans threatened French independence and that the Communists threatened freedom and democracy was the cornerstone of de Gaulle's strategy. For almost all of the four years de Gaulle had been rejected by President Roosevelt as the leader of the French. As late as June 1944, after Roosevelt had honored de Gaulle with a personal invitation to visit him in the White House, the president sent a memo to General Marshall warning him against de Gaulle. "We should," the president wrote, in this memo of June 14, "make full use of any organization or influence that de Gaulle may possess that may be of advantage to our military effort, provided we do not by force of arms impose him on the French people as the government of France." In a memo to Eisenhower, Roosevelt instructed him to deal with the Comité Français de Libération Nationale, but "not to do anything that would constitute a recognition of the CFLN as the provisional government of France." This was a direct rejection of the decision of the French to drop the designation CFLN and to call de Gaulle's executive Cabinet the Provisional Government of the French Republic.

De Gaulle had these challenges uppermost in mind when he flew to Washington to see Roosevelt in July, while American troops were already fighting in France. His mood was not improved when he discovered that his mission was in the hands of his hated adversary, Robert Murphy. But Roosevelt and de Gaulle knew that each needed the other. Despite their hostility, they had to reach agreement to facilitate the battle being fought in France.

It was finally agreed that France would be divided into two zones: (1) a Zone of the Interior, in which administrative control would be turned over to the delegates of the CFLN, as territory was liberated; and (2) a Zone of Operations, where fighting was still in progress, in which Supreme Headquarters would have sole and complete control. General Eisenhower, as supreme commander, would decide the boundaries between the two zones and, in any emergency, would have the supreme authority.

This agreement did nothing to resolve fundamental disagreements between de Gaulle and the Americans. De Gaulle saw himself as the head of the Provisional Government of the French Republic, which represented French sovereignty in France. His authority, not Eisenhower's, was supreme in France, with the narrowest exception of the fighting fronts. For Eisenhower, however, all of France was a theater of military operations and everything inside that theater, the political and economic as well as the military, had to be fitted into the tactical and strategic needs and demands of the theater commanders. Furthermore, no provision was made, in the Washington agreements, for Paris.

Roosevelt had made it clear that he would not recognize or permit to be installed any French government until the war had ended and the French people could act in free elections. That being so, he considered that liberated Paris would remain in the American Zone of Operations until all Germans had been driven out of France. Then without constraints, the French could organize themselves for elections. Until then, the army would be the supreme authority.

General de Gaulle had no intention of accepting Allied authority in the liberated French capital. He was convinced that the future of France depended upon his installing the Provisional Government in Paris as rapidly as possible. If the Americans held him off, as they intended, then his worst enemies, the French Communists, would certainly rise up in Paris and move into the seats of power. The Communists would pay no attention to Allied directives, and Eisenhower might well find himself caught short by a political challenge from the extreme Left, for which he was totally unprepared. He might also find American authorities trapped in the middle of a French struggle for power, even a civil war, for control of Paris. The only way to avoid such a tragedy, de Gaulle believed, would be for one of his French army divisions, the Second Armored of General Leclerc, to get the green light to go into Paris as soon as possible to prevent the Communists from seizing power.

On June 14, the very day that FDR sent his memo to Marshall warning him about de Gaulle, de Gaulle sent orders to General Koenig in London to stop all arms drops in and around the Paris region. De Gaulle estimated that the Communists had about twenty-five thousand men in the Resistance in the Paris region, by far the largest group, and that they controlled the Comité d'Action Militaire, COMAC, as well as the CPL, the Comité Parisien de Libération. He did not want them to have enough arms for a successful insurrection. This had been a concern of de Gaulle's for almost a year, during which he tried to get the Allies to drop arms to the non-Communist Resistance movements, with a bare minimum to the Communists. He told every important Allied visitor that the Communists intended to install a "Red Commune," as socialists had done in the Franco-Prussian War. He derided many of the Resistance committees, which the Communists had come to dominate, as committees of Public Safety modeled on the revolutionary committees of Robespierre's terror.

Whether the Americans understood this danger enough to act was unclear to de Gaulle. So he decided, as usual, to take matters into his own hands. He sent a secret message to General Koenig telling him that, with or without American approval, General Leclerc should make ready to break into Paris. He, de Gaulle, would follow Leclerc, as soon as he had entered Paris, so that de Gaulle could personally install his government. It would be the most daring gamble of his life. But it was the culmination of the gamble he had already taken four years earlier.

While the Allies and de Gaulle were quarreling over their respective authority, a number of men in Paris—French, Germans, and a Swede—were also aiming to control the course of events. Representatives of General de Gaulle inside Paris were keeping a watchful eye on their Communist comrades of the Resistance movement. A young man of twenty-nine, Jacques Chaban-Delmas, had been named the chief national liaison officer of the Provisional Government to the Resistance. This made him the military parallel authority to Alexandre Parodi, who was the chief political delegate of the Provisional Government. He had been given the rank of brigadier general.

Before the war, Chaban-Delmas had served as a deputy inspector of finance, an elite post in the French civil service. Tall, strikingly handsome, he was an outstanding athlete. He played three-quarter wing on the national Rugby team. It was Chaban-Delmas who, early in August 1944, received a secret order from London to retain absolute control of the Resistance in Paris and under no circumstances to permit an insurrection to break out without de Gaulle's direct authorization.

Allied with Chaban-Delmas were two other followers of General de Gaulle with top-flight jobs inside France: Georges Bidault and Alexandre Parodi. Bidault, who had taken over Jean Moulin's position as president of the Conseil National de la Résistance, was committed to working closely with all members of the Resistance, including the Communists. He was equally committed to preventing the Communists from any premature uprising or seizure of power. Unfortunately, Bidault's authority as president of the CNR did not count for much in Paris, where the Communists were the most powerful, best organized force in the Resistance, with a strong, assertive representation inside the CNR.

Although Bidault had come to Paris, he would not play a major role there. But Alexandre Parodi would. Parodi, a prewar high official of the Ministry of Labor, was a calm, cool, highly organized executive. He had risen in the ranks of the Resistance and had been appointed to fill one of the other main posts that had been held by Jean Moulin: general delegate of the Provisional Government. Late in July 1944 Parodi, like Chaban-Delmas, received strict instructions to contain the Communists. His instructions came directly from General de Gaulle, who wrote: "You are the representative of the government. That is to say that your orders must, in the last analysis, be obeyed. . . . The State stands above all organizations and activities."

The orders given to Parodi and to Chaban-Delmas would be extremely difficult to carry out, for the leaders of the Resistance in Paris did not agree that the "State stands above all organizations and activities." They understood that de Gaulle was acting as "the State," but for them he was only the leader of the exterior Resistance, their ally to be sure, even their titular head. His leadership had been accepted when Moulin had restructured the CNR and had brought into it the political parties, including the Communist party and its fighting groups. But de Gaulle was not "the State," above all things and all activities, at least not for the Communists. The internal Resistance, which had been leading the fight against Vichy and the Germans for four long years of sacrifice, with tens of thousands of its people deported or dead, accepted no master. No one, certainly not de Gaulle or the Allied armies, would be permitted to dictate the policies and actions of the Resistance.

On paper, the Resistance was headed by the Executive Committee of the CNR, with Georges Bidault as titular president. But Bidault had no more authority than his own one vote. The men who wielded real power in the Paris Resistance were either Communists or close allies of the Communists. They commanded the most loyal troops. COMAC, the military action committee, was completely dominated by Communists. There were three voting members on COMAC. The key man, because of his forceful personality and his membership in both COMAC and the CNR, was the leader of the Front National, Pierre Villon. Working closely with Villon was the militant Communist Valrimont. A prewar union leader, Valrimont was a skilled, tireless debater and dialectician. The third man, Count Jean de Vogüé, was not a Communist but he was a great admirer of both Villon and Valrimont and became their willing fellow-traveler. Vogüé's code name was Vaillant. The three Vs—Villon, Valrimont, and Vaillant—were known as the Three Musketeers of Paris, with Villon playing the role of the dashing leader, Captain d'Artagnan.

Under COMAC came the national general staff of the FFI, headed up by a Communist who had been given the rank of general: Alfred Malleret, code name Joinville. General Malleret-Joinville would not himself play a decisive role in the events that would take place in Paris, but he was able to give the full authority of his position to a Communist comrade who did play the key role. This man was a young but battle-toughened veteran of war and revolution, Henri Tanguy, known in the Resistance as Colonel Rol, and thereafter as Henri Rol-Tanguy, preserving his Resistance name as so many did. Rol-Tanguy came right after Malleret-Joinville in the hierarchy, and held the title of chief of the regional staff, which made him chief of the FFI for the Paris region.

Rol-Tanguy was thirty-six years old, a prewar metallurgical worker in various factories, such as the Citroën, Renault, and Bréguet auto and airplane plants, from which jobs he was fired in turn because of his Communist propaganda activities. He had fought in Spain in the International Brigade and then in the French army in the Battle of France, in which he had fought with courage and been severely wounded. He was tall, blond, strong, and handsome, a man of action and of few words—a man, like Villon, with strong personality and leadership qualities. Above all, Rol-Tanguy was a man of daring, with little concern about the cost of his actions just so long as he was convinced of the justice of his cause—which he was all of the time. As regional chief of the Ile-de-France, he commanded the FFI of all departments in the Paris region. His was a position of great power. Since the Communists contributed by far the largest contingents in this region, Rol-Tanguy virtually commanded his own loyal troops and was not constrained to obey the orders of Chaban-Delmas, Parodi, Bidault, or General de Gaulle. Rol-Tanguy saw de Gaulle as the enemy, the potential dictator of France. He was criticized for his toughness and over-heated radicalism, but even his most severe critics agreed that he was honest and loyal, qualities highly prized in the Resistance.

Parallel to the FFI military structure was its political counterpart, the CPL, the Comité Parisien de Libération. Its mission was to infiltrate the public administration and prepare to seize the city hall and local municipal offices and services in order to administer Paris until new elections could be held. Among its other duties was the mission of recruiting, arming, and training members of the Patriotic Militia to provide security forces for the local authorities. There were six members of the CPL, three of them Communists and three of them Liberals or Moderates.

One of the key men on the committee was a native-born Parisian, a thirty-six-year-old lawyer, Léo Goldenberg, known in the Resistance and thereafter by his clandestine name, Léo Hamon, representing the moderate movement Ceux de la Résistance. Hamon was cool and subtle. Friends called him The Eel, enemies The Snake, for his ability to glide smoothly in and around all barriers and problems. If he was smooth and flexible, it was nonetheless with the toughness of steel wire. His heart was as big as his brain, and by the force of that brain and an assertive personality, he would play a role greater than the modest forces of his movement would normally generate.

All of the leaders of the Paris Resistance agreed on one basic imperative: There had to be an uprising by the people of Paris. The capital would have to participate actively in its own liberation, for Paris was the symbol, the quintessence of France, and if Paris did not fight for its freedom, it would be as though France had not fought. On this all were of one mind. Where the unanimity cracked, and where the most serious quarrels broke out, concerned the tactics of liberation.

When should an insurrection be launched? Who should lead it? How would it be coordinated with the Allies and with the troops of the new French army? Who should occupy which buildings and in the name of what authority? These and many other questions went to the heart of the fundamental issue: Who would seize and wield the power in liberated Paris? That was the issue that would be fought over by General Chaban-Delmas, by de

Gaulle's delegate Alexandre Parodi, by Colonel Rol-Tanguy, and Léo Hamon, to say nothing of General Leclerc and the most directly interested and powerful of all men in Paris: the German military governor, General Dietrich von Choltitz.

Major General von Choltitz was a Prussian, although he did not look the part. He was not tall, lean, stiffly erect, with a dueling scar burning on his tight, white face. He was short and fat and his oily face showed sweat at the least exertion. His one "Prussian" feature was the monocle he was continually screwing into his right eye. But this little, fat man was one of the terrors of the Wehrmacht, his name a synonym for brutality and the destruction of cities.

In May 1940, as a lieutenant colonel, von Choltitz had commanded the German forces in Holland, and when the Dutch refused to surrender the port of Rotterdam, rejecting his ultimatum, von Choltitz had carried out his threat to bomb the city "mercilessly." According to the Dutch, he destroyed the port, wounding almost eighty thousand people and killing almost one thousand—this in an attack upon a country against which Germany had not even declared war. When asked whether this did not bother his conscience, von Choltitz blandly replied: "Why?"

Von Choltitz's greatest and bloodiest victory, in which he reconfirmed his reputation for cruelty, came in his capture of the Black Sea port of Sevastopol. At the beginning of the siege of that port, he had four thousand eight hundred men in his regimental command. On the day he took the port, only three hundred forty-seven of those men were still alive. They took few prisoners. Tens of thousands of Russians were massacred. Later, promoted to division commander, von Choltitz had to cover the retreat of the German army on his sector of the Russian front. In his wake he left nothing but the ashes of a scorched earth and burned-out cities and villages. He would later tell the Swedish consul in Paris: "It has been my fate to cover the retreat of our armies and to destroy the cities behind them." This was the man chosen in August 1944—just before the retreat of the western armies of Germany—to cover Paris for them.

Von Choltitz had been commanding a unit on the Normandy front when, on July 20, a plot to kill Hitler had failed. Implicated in the plot was the Wehrmacht's senior officer in France, General Karl Heinrich Stülpnagel, who tried to kill himself when the plot failed. Blinded and gravely wounded, he had been taken to Berlin, where he lay half-dead in the Plotzensee prison. His commander for *Gross Paris*, General Hans von Boineburg-Lengsfeld, was considered to be a dilettante, without the authority or the courage to face the difficult decisions that would have to be made in Paris as the Allied armies approached. Hitler decided that Paris had to be defended at all costs. He wanted a military governor for Paris who would be completely loyal and would carry out all orders faithfully. Von Choltitz had been recommended to him as exactly that kind of man, and he had ordered von Choltitz to report to him personally at his command post, the "Wolfsschanze," the Wolf's Lair, in the Rastenburg forest of eastern Germany.

Von Choltitz had met Hitler one year earlier in Russia, outside the strategic center of Dnepropetrovsk, in the Ukraine. The Prussian aristocrat had been shocked by the vulgar table manners of the Bavarian peasant, but von Choltitz had also been favorably impressed by the electric vibrations of energy and confidence radiating out of Hitler.

But in August 1944 von Choltitz was not facing the same man he had met a year before. Hitler was now an old and beaten man. His eyes were dull and glazed over. A little spittle dribbled out of the corner of his mouth. Hitler cradled his left hand in his right to hide its trembling. And his once powerful voice, which had hypnotized all Germany, was now the cracked voice of a senile man, barely above a whisper.

Hitler began by telling von Choltitz how he had founded the Nazi party and how he had rebuilt Germany's armed strength. Then, his voice gathering up an echo of its old power, he began to orate about the victories he was planning and the secret weapons that would crush the Allies in the west and in the east. His voice became a shriek, the voice of a madman, screaming of vengeance against the Prussian generals who had tried to kill him. Then, suddenly, like a balloon that had been blown too big, he seemed to burst in upon himself. The tirade was over and his voice again sank to the level of a whisper as he told von Choltitz that Paris must become a front-line city, a veritable fortress. Von Choltitz would be named the "Befehlshaber," the fortress commander of Paris, bearing personal authority from Hitler himself. He was to stamp out without pity any act of terrorism and to defend his positions there by blowing up every bridge, fighting street by street and house by house.

Dietrich von Choltitz got on the train to return to his new command in Paris knowing that he had been appointed and instructed by a madman. Despite his loyal temperament and his professional tradition of obedience to his superiors, von Choltitz was shaken in his belief and faith in his new mission. He could not see the sense of a house-to-house defense of Paris, which would destroy one of the world's greatest legacies of architecture and history, bringing down upon Germany a universal and perhaps eternal hatred. What military purpose, beyond delaying a few Allied divisions a few days, could such a horror justify? Would he carry out Hitler's orders to fight in Paris at all costs and to the bitterest of ends? For the first time in his military career, von Choltitz was not sure what he would finally decide to do.

Installed at his new headquarters in the luxurious Hôtel Meurice, overlooking the Tuileries and the Louvre, von Choltitz pondered on what steps to begin to take to forestall trouble in Paris. He knew that Paris had a long revolutionary history, which every Parisian had learned to revere in school. The cobblestones of Paris were a constant reminder of the barricades erected throughout history, just as its broad and beautiful avenues were in fact fields of fire, cleared away by nervous governments, fearful of the people of Paris.

Von Choltitz, assuming his new command on August 10, had every reason to be concerned about his ability to maintain order in Paris. He had inherited from von Stülpnagel a staff of dissident, anti-Hitler officers not willing to carry out any further High Command orders, interested only in saving their own skins and avoiding arrest by the Gestapo, which was conducting a purge following the July 20 plot. The German defenses were built upon thirty-two positions inside Paris, staffed by mediocre troops who had been cast off by front-line commanders and assigned to occupation duties. Many of his "soldiers" were clerks and military bureaucrats or men who had been severely wounded and were unfit for combat. Von Choltitz did have a few combat-ready SS troops at his disposal, men well trained in street fighting.

Von Choltitz, in his logs, claimed to have only four tanks at his command, although Parisians had seen many tanks, sometimes four at a time, in various locations patrolling the city. General Leclerc would later claim that he had captured fifty-nine German tanks, but his figures were just as exaggerated upward as von Choltitz had downgraded his own numbers: Each general was trying to justify his own record. In fact, von Choltitz was not strong enough to stand up to a full Allied attack, but he certainly had enough strength to wipe out the Resistance in any prolonged pitched battle.

As von Choltitz took over this command with misgivings on August 10, a messenger brought him the news that the Paris railway workers had gone on strike. The rail lines had been in disarray and not a single passenger train had functioned for several weeks. But on the tenth all traffic had come to a halt. German railwaymen and German troops had to be assigned to keep a minimum of supply trains moving. It was a warning to von Choltitz of things to come.

Concerned about where the next strike might break out and worried that the Paris police represented a source of arms inside the city, von Choltitz gave orders for a swift, surprise disarmament of the Paris police, to be carried out early on the morning of August 13. He knew that the police were, by and large, a conservative corps and had a record of close collaboration with the Germans. It was thought by his intelligence officers that policemen were unlikely to go over to the Resistance. But von Choltitz, knowing that the tide was turning against the Germans, suspected that there could be a last-minute rush to the Allied and patriotic bandwagon, and he did not doubt that the police would be ready to jump.

In fact, the Paris police had already been infiltrated by the Resistance. The organization NAP, Noyautage de l'Administration Publique, had long ago set about recruiting policemen. There were three Resistance groups established at the Prefecture of Police. The group Honneur de la Police had been originally created in 1943 by the MLN, the Mouvement de Libération Nationale, and was loyal to General de Gaulle. It had about one thousand five hundred members, the largest single contingent of resistants in the police. Second in importance was the "Front National de la Police" with about one thousand two hundred men, controlled by Communists. Finally, there was a small but militant unit called Police et Patrie, affiliated to Libération-Nord, with some two hundred adherents. The activities of the three groups were co-ordinated by the chief of NAP for Paris, Yves Bayet. Bayet was in touch with Alexandre Parodi, de Gaulle's chief delegate, and was ready to carry out his orders to install, at the right moment, the man designated by the government to be the prefect of police for liberated Paris: Charles Luizet. Luizet had won respect for the admirable way he had taken over as the first prefect of liberated Corsica.

At first thought, the number of policemen in the Resistance seems small, only some three thousand men out of a total force of some twenty thousand. But a militant, organized 10 to 15 percent was, in fact, a significant minority, particularly since it could be expected that at the time of an uprising the bulk of the police would sense that the Germans were doomed and would have little or no reason to oppose a Resistance coup. There had been Nazi collaborationists in the police, responsible for savage crimes, but sadistic brutes are found in every police force. The Paris police had been passive collaborators, or, more simply, men accustomed to carrying out the orders of the government to maintain public security. It would not be difficult for an active 10 percent to take over the police of Paris.

The German raids following von Choltitz's orders to disarm the Paris police had alerted the Resistance, which immediately began calling all precincts, telling the men on duty to spread the word to hide their weapons. They were warned against any individual resistance against German soldiers, and to await the call to collective action. The word was spread rapidly and a great many weapons were successfully hidden from the Germans.

The next day, August 14, the representatives of the three Re-sistance groups met in an apartment on the Rue Chapon, near the Rue du Temple, in one of the most densely inhabited regions of Paris. Yves Bayet, chief of Honneur de la Police, presided as overall leader of the police Re-sistance. Representing the FFI was the fiery Communist revolutionary, Colonel Rol-Tanguy. The men rapidly agreed to form a Comité de Libération of the police to coordinate their efforts, with Bayet as the chief. Then Rol-Tanguy, always impatient with planning and structures, called for immediate action, proposing the first strike in the history of the Paris police. He conceded that the decision was not his to take, for he could only speak in the name of the FFI and not for the police themselves. It was up to them to make their own decision, but he wanted them to know that the FFI would approve and would back them. Bayet realized that he would have to plan the strike and control its timing to keep the Communists from taking over leadership.

The very next morning, August 15, as the BBC was broadcasting the news that French and American troops were landing on the southern beaches of France, Bayet felt the right moment had come. He gave the order and the Paris police walked off their beats. Less than three hundred clerks showed up in the otherwise empty, huge building of the Prefecture of Police. The Prefecture was located on the Ile de la Cité between the Saint-Michel

Bridge and the parvis of the Cathedral of Notre Dame. In posts at the prefecture, in the commissariats of police, and at the precinct stations throughout Paris, the strike was 99 percent effective.

The Vichy-appointed prefect of police, Amadée Bussière, who had tried to win the support of his men by obtaining for them wage increases and extra cigarette rations, discovered that he had no authority left at all. His appeals to the police to come back to duty went unanswered. He then tried to win them over by announcing that he had dismissed the director of the municipal police, a notorious pro-Nazi and a stern disciplinarian whom the men hated. But that gesture, too, had come too late. The police stayed out, Bussière tried once more to placate the Resistance. On the sixteenth, he opened the gates of three prisons, the Tourelles, the Roquette, and the Santé, releasing all political prisoners and keeping in their cells only common-law criminals. But the police stayed out. Von Choltitz protested sharply to Bussière and called in two unit commanders to start planning defenses of key positions in Paris if a rebellion broke out. He did not have the manpower to replace the police.

On the seventeenth, the temperature in Paris went up in both politics and climate. A hot August sun was baking Parisians when more than one thousand civil servants walked off their jobs and marched to the Hôtel de Ville to demonstrate. They shouted *"Pain! Pain!"* (Bread! Bread!) and sang "La Marseillaise." The municipal authorities were powerless to handle the crowd, for they had no police to call upon; besides, it is difficult to disperse a crowd pleading for bread in a famished city. As for the Germans, they had started to pull out of Paris. All but essential military services and last-ditch defensive units were on the run.

French crowds on the Faubourg Saint-Honoré, one of Paris's most fashionable boulevards, gathered at the Place Beauvau, on the corner of the Palais de l'Elysées, the French White House, where the president of the Republic resides. They were not looking for the chief of state. Marshal Pétain was in Vichy, about to be taken away by the Germans. The crowd was peering into the Rue des Saussaies, where Gestapo torture chambers were located: They were watching Gestapo agents burning their papers in a big bonfire in the middle of the street.

Across the Seine, on the Left Bank, at the Hôtel Matignon, residence of the prime minister, the pro-Nazi chief of government, Pierre Laval, was soaking in a marble tub, all his valises packed. It would be his last bath and his last day in France until he was brought back from Germany to be tried and executed for treason. All over Paris collaborationists and their Nazi masters were on the run.

Jacques Chaban-Delmas, the National Military Delegate, had flown to London on August 11 to inform the top command that there was a danger of a premature insurrection in Paris, launched by the Communists, which could lead to the destruction of the city in a heavy-handed German counterattack with tanks and planes. He saw General Koenig, chief of the

FFI, and General Sir Hastings Ismay, chief of the British Imperial Staff, Churchill's right-hand man. He begged them all to intervene with General Eisenhower and obtain his agreement to send Allied divisions swiftly to Paris before the Communists could launch their insurrection.

Ismay expressed his sympathy for the problem but said he could do nothing to help. Eisenhower could not divert his troops from the first priority of defeating the German army and getting into Germany and Berlin before winter made it impossible. He could not be swayed by what was essentially a political problem for the French. "Can't you control your own people?" was the blunt question that Ismay put to Chaban-Delmas. Chaban had to admit that he had no control over the Communists. Ismay shrugged his shoulders in response.

General Koenig said that he would send orders to Paris not to take any premature action without a specific signal from him. He knew that the Communists would very likely ignore his injunction and that Chaban-Delmas had no control over them. Nonetheless, he told Chaban-Delmas to see Rol-Tanguy on his return and do everything he could to persuade him against an uprising that would almost certainly lead to the destruction of Paris in street fighting with von Choltitz's units. Then he and Chaban-Delmas worked out a contingency plan on what he should do to prevent Communist control of Paris if the Communists insisted on going ahead. Koenig gave Chaban-Delmas a code signal that would be sent over the BBC when the time came for action.

The Communists were the most feverish of all Parisians when matters came to a boil on the seventeenth of August 1944. On that Thursday, three separate meetings of Resistance leaders had been scheduled, by the Paris liberation committee (CPL), the military action committee (COMAC), and the national resistance council (CNR), all on the identical and vital question: Should there be an insurrection in Paris?

At the CNR meeting, the head of de Gaulle's political delegation, Alexandre Parodi, who had received word to do everything to prevent the insurrection, denounced talk of an insurrection as certain to lead to tens of thousands of deaths and widespread destruction without a hope of success. He told the council members that the Allies would not be coming to Paris before early September. That would mean that the Resistance would have to hold out for two weeks without sufficient arms, gas, medical supplies, or food. The Germans had some twenty to twenty-five thousand rearguard troops left in Paris against less than five thousand lightly armed partisans. German divisions, retreating before the Allies, would be fleeing through Paris and would be brutal if threatened in any way. An insurrection, Parodi argued, was madness. It was suicide. Parodi proposed, instead, that the Resistance maintain and control the strikes that had already been launched. The strikes would impede and frustrate the Germans without provoking bloodshed and destruction.

Georges Bidault, president of the CNR, then spoke and endorsed the arguments of Parodi. He felt, however, that it would be impossible to control the strikes, which had begun to get out of hand. First the railway workers had gone out, then the police, then the post office and the civil service. It was like sparks in a dry forest, spreading swiftly into a wildfire. He agreed, nonetheless, that the council had to work with the strikers, to try to contain them, and if that proved impossible, to take over leadership, for the Resistance could not, at this ultimate stroke before midnight, lose contact with the masses. As for an insurrection, he felt the same way. Try to contain it; if not, lead it.

The Communist leader on the CNR and COMAC, Pierre Villon, arose to deliver a fiery oration in favor of launching an immediate insurrection. For four long years, he shouted, they had been fighting the war in the shadows, emerging from time to time from their hiding holes to hit the enemy and then to bolt back into the underground. They had fought with courage and had made blood sacrifices, all aimed at the day when, as free men, they could rise up and drive the enemy out of the capital. That day was now at hand.

Were they to sit still, to do nothing, to wait for Americans and Englishmen to liberate them? Was that to be the ultimate end of the Resistance? Villon asked. The Communist leader, who was and is a fervent French patriot, insisted that the French give the Allies a demonstration of their willingness to fight for their own freedom and for their independence. Finally, he argued, if Paris did not stand up and fight, how could they expect any city between Paris and the Rhine to join in the struggle for liberation? And if they did not stand and fight, how would they prevent more massacres like Oradour? The council meeting broke up with no agreement other than to meet again to discuss the issue further.

The Communist-dominated Action Committee then met and voted promptly for insurrection.

At the meeting of the Paris liberation committee, the CPL, Léo Hamon emerged in his role as principal adversary of the Communists. A man of the Left, Hamon was not a militant anti-Communist. He respected the Communists for their courage and the efficiency of their organization. He felt that as free Frenchmen they had a right to their opinions and a right to fight for leadership of the nation just so long as they stayed within the rules of the Republic. But he meant to beat them if he could. He would fight fair, by the rules, as he demanded of them, but he would fight to prevent a Communist take-over.

In his surprisingly country-style house in the heart of urban Montparnasse, Hamon said recently that he did not then and does not now believe that the Communists sought to use the insurrection as a coup to seize power, as the Gaullists believed. "No, that was not true," Hamon said in an interview. "They did intend to play a major role in a new Republic. They probably wanted to put a Communist at the head of the Prefecture of Paris and also of the Prefecture of Police, perhaps, too, to have a Communist as mayor of Paris. They felt they could demand that much if they liberated Paris. They would also demand equal representation, at least, in any new government, when it came time to distribute Cabinet posts. And they would want to win a big representation in Parliament and reshape the social and economic policies of France. All these were legitimate goals and I believe that those were their goals. But I thought them mad to seek to achieve those goals by an insurrection that could destroy Paris and kill as many as two hundred thousand people in a German bloodbath. This is why I fought against them."

Hamon challenged the hotheaded president of the CPL, Communist André Tollet. He shot question after question at him. How many men do you have and how many do the Germans have? How many machine guns? How many stens? He charged that an insurrection at that moment was madness. He warned Tollet to take no action without getting the approval of the CNR. He won the first round of the argument on the seventeenth, when Tollet agreed to do nothing until they met again the next day.

The next day, August 18, brought surprise news: The Resistance leaders learned that Premier Laval, in one of his last acts, had secretly brought one of Parliament's prewar leaders to Paris, the Radical party leader Edouard Herriot, who had been in prison. Laval had a scheme for calling a meeting of Parliament to set up a negotiating team to work out a deal with the Allies. His scheme had failed when Herriot raised a number of objections and imposed a series of conditions that Laval could not meet. Then Laval and Herriot had both been taken from Paris to Germany by a German escort as potential pawns for later use. At the same time most of the French propagandists for the collaborationist radio and press had closed up shop and were fleeing Paris. The post office strike had closed down all mail and telegraph delivery and thrown an almost intolerable strain on telephone communications. The administration of Vichy was crumbling, providing new fuel to Communist arguments that the time had come to take over.

Meanwhile, wall posters were sprouting up all over Paris, replacing newspapers as a source of public information and communication. Without consulting anyone the Communist FTPF had posted an order calling for a general mobilization of the people of Paris. The Communists falsely invoked orders of COMAC and the CNR, orders that had not been issued. They told all Parisians that they should consider themselves drafted and report to the FFI and/or the Patriotic Militia units of their neighborhood or factory. They would be armed and could then attack the enemy everywhere, in the streets, in his command posts and his supply stores, while setting up protective units to guard the municipal services of water, gas, and electricity. The order ended with an alleged citation of General de Gaulle to stand up and fight, for victory was near, an appeal that de Gaulle had not addressed to the people of Paris. The poster was an unauthorized fake that caused a great deal of confusion and brought many people into the streets, putting themselves in grave danger without purpose.

In the morning of that same August 18, another poster contained an appeal for insurrection signed by prewar parliamentarians of the Communist party. It called upon all Parisians to do their duty and to obey the orders they would get from the FFI to arm themselves by seizing arms from the Germans, and to participate in the insurrection of liberation, in accordance with directives of the Comité Parisien de Libération. This poster was affixed to the walls of Paris well before the liberation committee meeting where André Tollet had promised Léo Hamon he would debate the issue before any action would be taken.

A third poster was put up by Rol-Tanguy's FFI staff, proclaiming, as the FTPF poster had, a general mobilization of the people of Paris.

Finally, a fourth poster was distributed by the major trade unions, the Communist-dominated CGT and the left-Catholic CFTC, calling on all workers to launch a general strike to paralyze the region, and to stay out until further order.

Chaban-Delmas, furious, rushed in to a COMAC meeting and told the members that they were heading for total destruction. He gave them a detailed military briefing on German strength and on the decision of the Allies not to come into Paris before September 1 at the earliest. There was no way that an insurrection could succeed, he warned. Villon told him that the Germans were already retreating, they could be seen in the streets of Paris, running with their loot. Von Choltitz's troops were demoralized and mediocre. If hundreds of thousands of Parisians answered the call of insurrection, as they would, he was sure, the Germans could not put it down. Losses could be heavy, he conceded, but the ultimate victory would be a triumph for Paris and ensure a better future for all.

A violent quarrel broke out at the CPL meeting on that Friday, August 18. Hamon accused the Communists of bad faith in putting out the mobilization posters without even waiting for the meeting to take place. Rol-Tanguy was there and he brushed aside Hamon's complaints, announcing that the hour of insurrection had struck. "If you do not march with us, we will march alone," was the challenge he threw at Hamon.

"With what arms will you fight? With how many men?" was Hamon's answer to his challenge.

"We have about six hundred to seven hundred fifty men ready to go," Rol-Tanguy replied.

"You're mad," shouted Hamon. "You don't rise up in Paris against a German army with only six hundred men."

Rol-Tanguy finally agreed, under constant pressure from Hamon, to meet on the morrow with the members of the CNR, and he promised that the insurrection would not be launched until after that meeting. "We will then go ahead, whether the meeting agrees or not," was the parting shot of

Rol-Tanguy. It hold Hamon clearly that the Gaullists would have to move first to take the initiative from the Communists.

None of these men arguing about the need or viability of an insurrection was aware of the fact that General von Choltitz had been keeping a close check on events and drawing up a plan to meet the challenge.

The Vichy-appointed mayor of Paris, and member of the famous champagne family, Pierre Taittinger, also saw the tragedy approaching. He had urgently requested a meeting with the commander of *Gross Paris*. Von Choltitz told him he would receive him at his headquarters in the Hôtel Meurice on Thursday, August 17. Von Choltitz, icily cold, flanked by a number of general officers in full uniform, began the meeting by warning Taittinger that he was prepared to take drastic measures against any violence by Parisians. For example, if a single shot was fired against his soldiers from a house on the Avenue de l'Opéra, near the Rue des Pyramides, "I shall have all the houses on that block burned down and I shall shoot all the inhabitants."

Then General von Choltitz told Taittinger: "I have at my disposal twenty-two thousand men, mostly SS, one hundred Tiger tanks, and ninety bombers." He then added that he would increase the zone of punishment if any act more serious than a single shot were fired. In other words, he was warning Taittinger that Paris would suffer the fate of Warsaw if there was an uprising by the Resistance.

Taittinger told von Choltitz that Paris "is one of the few great cities of Europe that remain intact; you must help me to save it."

Von Choltitz, thawing out, said that he did not want to destroy Paris. He pointed out to Taittinger that he had not surrounded his headquarters in the Hôtel Meurice with machine guns, but only with white, wooden barriers. He took Taittinger by the arm and led him to his balcony, overlooking the Tuileries. He pointed to a group of children, with their mothers, playing at a sandpit. "I like to see the people moving freely here under my windows," von Choltitz said.

Sensing his change of mood, Taittinger said: "Generals rarely have the power to build, they more often have that of destroying." Taittinger then asked von Choltitz to imagine that one day he would return after the war to the hotel as a tourist (an eventuality that did, indeed, come about) and that he would walk out on the same balcony. "You look to the left, at the Perrault colonnade, with the great Palais du Louvre on the right, then the Palais de Gabriel and the Place de la Concorde. And among these splendid buildings, each one charged with history, you are able to say: 'It was I, von Choltitz, who, on a certain day, had the power to destroy them, but I saved them for humanity.' General, is that not worth all a conqueror's fame?"

Von Choltitz pondered on Taittinger's eloquent words, which had clearly impressed him. After a long pause, he said this: "There is one thing on which I absolutely insist, there must be no attacks on the five posts defended by the army: my headquarters in the Hôtel Meurice; the Avenue Foch; the Place de l'Opéra; the Palais du Luxembourg; and the barracks in the Place de la République. As for the rest, I'm prepared to close my eyes to individual acts—I say individual advisedly—and I put my faith in the good sense of the population of Paris."

Then, von Choltitz put his hand on Taittinger's shoulder. "You're a good advocate for Paris, Monsieur Taittinger; you're doing your duty very well, indeed. But I have my duty as a German general. I shall go as far as I can to respond to your appeal concerning the destruction of strategic buildings and the shooting of hostages. . . . We shall do the best we can to live in harmony during the few days we have still to spend together."

Taittinger left the Meurice bemused by von Choltitz's last words: "the few days we have still to spend together." Did the commander of *Gross Paris* really believe it would all be over in only a "few days"? Taittinger found that a most encouraging thought.

As Taittinger and von Choltitz discussed the fate of Paris and the Resistance committees argued about forcing that fate, one of the men most concerned with their actions was setting out on the most critical mission of his life. On August 17, 1944, General Charles de Gaulle was climbing aboard his command aircraft, a small two-engined Lockheed Lodestar, on the airstrip of Algiers.

Ever since receiving messages from General Koenig and General Chaban-Delmas about the dangers of a Paris insurrection and the refusal of Eisenhower to move up the timetable for the liberation of the capital, de Gaulle had decided that he had to take control of that situation. He had sent a message to Eisenhower stating his desire to visit the fighting front in France, stressing that it was only a visit. He knew the Americans would move to block him if they thought he had come to stay and to direct French operations, as indeed he secretly intended to do.

American air authorities in the Mediterranean were aghast at the thought of de Gaulle trying to make the trip to France in the tiny Lockheed. They insisted that he take a Flying Fortress, which the Air Command would send to Algiers from Corsica to pick up de Gaulle. De Gaulle agreed, but only on condition that the Americans paint the French colors and the Cross of Lorraine on their plane. Otherwise he would not fly in it.

Muttering to themselves, the Americans grudgingly painted their Flying Fortress as de Gaulle had demanded. Then, on landing in Algiers, the Fort skidded badly and damaged itself so that it could not be used.

De Gaulle, getting his own way as always, then flew in his own plane to the next stop, Casablanca. There the Americans, undaunted, and just as stubborn as de Gaulle, sent him another Flying Fortress. De Gaulle, not wishing to endanger his mission by a petty fight, got into the American machine for the next leg, to Gibraltar. But he ordered his pilot to fly just behind them in the Lockheed.

On landing in Gibraltar, the Flying Fortress burst a tire, while the Lockheed came down to a perfect landing. De Gaulle, brooking no further arguments, got into his Lockheed for the final lap to Normandy. The Fort took off after him, carrying his staff and his aides, including one of his senior commanders, the hero of the Italian campaign, General Juin.

The Fort got lost in a storm, was tossed off course, lost its radio, and almost crashed. It landed, finally, in Cherbourg, some three hours after de Gaulle had arrived in the little Lockheed. De Gaulle, himself, had had a narrow escape. His pilot had got lost in the same violent storm. He finally landed at a small fighter base, near Cherbourg, with only twenty seconds of flying time left in the gas tanks. It was only one of almost two dozen close brushes with death in de Gaulle's perilous career.

De Gaulle, wasting no time, went promptly to "Shellburst," code name for General Eisenhower's headquarters at Granville, at the base of the Cotentin Peninsula. Eisenhower knew why he had come and was determined not to give him what he wanted. Eisenhower had just been informed about widespread strikes in Paris. He was, as he later wrote, "damned mad" about the French defying his orders to lie low and not provoke the Germans. He did not intend to let de Gaulle use the situation in Paris as an excuse to get him to send troops there earlier than he had planned and before he could spare them.

Eisenhower greeted de Gaulle warmly, then led him to the briefing room where, without delay, he used his pointer to show de Gaulle where the troops were and how he was sending them north and south of Paris to close in a pincers around the Germans well east of Paris. It should take some two weeks, from September 1 to September 15, to conclude the whole operation, and he could not change that timetable.

General de Gaulle went right to his point. There was a serious Communist threat in Paris. An uprising could create havoc in the city and it might well bring about a disruptive situation that could represent a real danger to the Allied effort. The Allies, he argued, must strike for Paris before the Communists sparked an insurrection.

General Eisenhower politely but firmly demurred. It would be premature to try to break into Paris now. The Germans could bring several divisions to bear upon the defense of the French capital and force slow, destructive, and useless house-to-house street fighting that would delay the entire Allied advance and destroy Paris without any legitimate military objective to be gained. Eisenhower put deliberate stress on the word *military*, letting de Gaulle know that he believed de Gaulle's concern to be political. Ironically, de Gaulle thought that Eisenhower's decision was political. He was convinced that the Americans were still worried about his seizing power and wanted to keep him out of Paris. There was truth in both analyses.

General de Gaulle, stiff-backed, grim of face, had listened to Eisenhower's final refusal to advance his timetable for Paris. He then said quietly that Paris was of transcendental national importance to France. If necessary, therefore, he might be obliged to withdraw Leclerc's Second Armored Division from Eisenhower's command and send it to Paris on his own authority. It would mean rupturing Allied unity, de Gaulle knew, precipitating a grave crisis with unknown consequences, but de Gaulle felt that the stakes were so high that Paris was worth any risk.

The two generals, who had frequently been in conflict, but who deeply respected and even liked one another—each of them would become president of his country at another critical hour a decade later—separated on a cold note. Later, Eisenhower would say that he had smiled and said not a word when de Gaulle had threatened him with the withdrawal of the Second Armored. "I was convinced that Leclerc couldn't have moved that division a mile if I didn't want it to. It drew all its ammunition and food and gas from Allied stores. It simply could not move against orders." Eisenhower, for all his experiences with the French, simply did not appreciate how resourceful they could be—in pursuit of a French national goal.

De Gaulle, his face tight with emotion, climbed into his Lockheed Lodestar and said to his aide: "Where is Leclerc?" He flew back to his headquarters in Rennes, in Brittany, to await news of Leclerc.

Leclerc was standing in a Norman apple orchard hidden by a black, moonless night. He was talking in whispers to a tall young French officer who held tightly on to a briefcase made from the skin of a katambouru, the native antelope of Chad. Chad was one of the first territories in French Africa to be liberated in the name of de Gaulle and Free France by the man who called himself Leclerc. In that briefcase, which he had given his officer, was a map and in its center, circled in black grease pencil, was Paris.

Even before getting de Gaulle's desperation order to march on Paris alone and against Allied orders, Leclerc had prepared himself to do exactly that. Eisenhower had been quite wrong to think that he could not move a mile without his permission. In Chad four years before, Leclerc had sworn that one day he would liberate Paris. He meant to keep that promise. Leclerc's fuel trucks had demanded a double ration at the army gas pumps, stating that they had a supply mission for French towns and villages trapped by war without food and drugs. His commanders had illegally failed to report their vehicle losses to the army command, so he could draw gas for cars and tanks that no longer existed. The night before, some of his men had deliberately got drunk with American soldiers at the supply dump, on crocks of Calvados, the potent applejack of Normandy. While the French and Americans laughed and drank together, other French soldiers stole into the dumps and took all the fuel and munitions they could grab. Leclerc calculated that he had stolen enough supplies to keep his two thousand vehicles and six thousand men in action for a week to ten days, enough time to liberate Paris.

Leclerc knew that he was committing a grave breach of discipline. But he counted on de Gaulle being able to handle Eisenhower. Leclerc, in any case, was not worried. He was pledged to liberate the capital under the flag of Free France. He meant to get there before the Communists could take it over, or to take it away from the Communists if they beat him to the first punch. Paris was now the prize in a threatened civil war between Communists and Gaullists. Leclerc sent a courier ahead with a message to de Gaulle about his plans. He might defy the Americans, but he would not move into Paris without de Gaulle's order to do so.

De Gaulle's representatives inside Paris were making their plans to block a Communist seizure of power. Alexandre Parodi already knew that there was no way he could stop the Communists from launching an insurrection, and after the stormy meetings of the seventeenth and eighteenth and the wall posters calling for mobilization, he was sure the signal would be given on the nineteenth.

Late in the afternoon of the eighteenth, Parodi called a meeting of the Délégation Générale at his command post in an apartment at 35 Avenue de Ségur near the Eiffel Tower. Among the delegates who came to that meeting was a mysterious figure all in black, with black curly hair, deep black eyes, peering out from under heavy black horn-rimmed glasses. He was a man no one there knew except Parodi. He had only just arrived in Paris. It was Charles Luizet, a Gaullist "of the first hour," who had been administrator in Tangiers in 1940 and had declared himself at once for General de Gaulle and his call to resist the Germans. He had become de Gaulle's prefect in liberated Corsica. Now he had come to Paris to be ready to take over his assignment as prefect of police. He had to seize that post before the Communists could.

Luizet had flown into France on August 11 and had worked his way to Paris on the seventeenth. On arrival, he had gone to a barbershop to freshen up, and it was from the barber that the future prefect of police learned that the police had gone on strike. Luizet hurried out to make contact with Parodi, for he sensed that the strike was the signal for him to take over the prefecture. His instructions from London to Parodi were orders to avoid an open confrontation with the Communists that would split the Resistance, but to try to keep a step or two ahead of the Communists in moving to control key posts in Paris.

Parodi and Luizet agreed that the man who could win the day for them was Yves Bayet, chief of the liberation committee of the Paris police and head of its largest Resistance unit, Honneur de la Police. Bayet, a loyal Gaullist, well aware of the threat of the Communists, was just the man to beat the Communists to the punch. They called him, arranged a meeting for that evening. At the meeting, they told Bayet that the next morning, the nineteenth, the CNR and the CPL were holding separate and then joint meetings. Parodi told him: "There is not the slightest doubt that agreement will be reached to launch a general uprising tomorrow. I can't hold them back any longer. The meeting will begin at half-past nine. By noon the die will have been cast. In fact I would not be surprised, in view of the posters calling for action, if fighting breaks out in the streets tomorrow morning. You'll have to make your move early."

With those words Parodi himself was calling for an insurrection, without awaiting word from General Koenig. Events were moving too rapidly in Paris for its leaders to await consultation with London. Paris was on its own. All it could do, and Chaban-Delmas did do it that night, was to send an urgent, pleading cable to Koenig, warning him that the fighting was due to start and that he had to make one more effort to get Eisenhower to send troops in. Chaban-Delmas and Parodi had no idea that General Leclerc was about to receive orders from de Gaulle clearing him for action.

Yves Bayet had to run to get into his command post before the 9 P.M. curfew closed down the streets of Paris and made it difficult for messages to be carried to his principal agents. He managed to contact by telephone the deputy commander of his Resistance unit to instruct him to spread the word rapidly that his men should assemble the next morning "near the prefecture." His agent, whose Resistance name was Anthoine, was on the phone most of the night calling policemen and asking each of them to spread the word to friends. Many, knowing their friends had no phones, would go out into the street, defying the curfew, and, moving quietly in the shadows, would dash from doorway to doorway to deliver messages. By midnight more than two thousand policemen had been notified to assemble at 7 A.M. on the Place du Parvis, between the prefecture and Notre Dame.

When Communist leaders Rol-Tanguy and André Tollet arose the next morning and got out their bicycles to go to the meetings at the house of a friend of Georges Bidault in the Rue de Bellechasse, they could already hear sporadic sounds of shooting in the streets. They hoped that a few hotheads would not provoke the Germans until their partisans had been sent off to capture key buildings and organize the uprising. Hotheaded as they were themselves, they knew that individual acts would be suicidal and that an organized attack was the only chance to succeed. They were determined to make the morning meetings move quickly to a decision. Time had just about run out.

The CNR and the CPL began their meetings as scheduled. Louis Saillant, a leader of the Communist-dominated CGT trade union, told the members that his union had, that morning, officially launched an order for a general strike. Everyone present understood that this was the signal for the insurrection. Colonel Rol-Tanguy then announced that the FFI had decided to call the insurrection into action later that day. He appealed to all members of the CNR and the CPL to close ranks and vote unanimous approval.

Suddenly they heard a fusillade of shots in the street below their windows. The non-Communist members knew at once that the insurrection that they were supposed to be discussing and voting on had already broken out, just as Communist André Tollet had warned them. None of this came as a surprise to Alexandre Parodi. That was why, the night before, he had given the green light to Bayet to seize the Prefecture of Police. He knew they were all risking the destruction of Paris, but he tried to take some comfort from the thought that it was the Communists, not he, who had precipitated the insurrection.

Parodi knew that he and his friends would have to do as Rol-Tanguy had asked, to close ranks now that the fatal decision had been taken. He turned to Georges Bidault, who was presiding over the meeting, and said: "I vote for the insurrection." He had been instructed to avoid a split in the Resistance if he could not hold the Communists in check. By his vote, he was maintaining unity with a heavy heart.

The vote was unanimous. All committee members then agreed on the terms of an appeal to the people of Paris. As they sat down to draft it, they opened the windows and heard the strains of "La Marseillaise." The voices were coming from the Ministry of National Education, nearby. The insurrection was under way even before the leaders could draft their appeal.

The Communists laughed and hastened away to send their troops into action. Rol-Tanguy pedaled slowly in the heat toward the Boulevard Saint-Michel. He was heading for one of his main targets, the Prefecture of Police. He was sure that his commandos of the Front National would have no trouble seizing the building.

But Yves Bayet and his men had done their work well the night before. By 7 A.M. some two thousand Gaullist policemen were crowded into the square in front of Notre Dame Cathedral. Bayet had told his section chiefs to get the men there and to keep them available for orders that he would obtain from the CNR and the CPL. But his section and platoon chiefs had had bad experiences in the past few days with orders to await orders. Communications were uncertain in strikebound Paris. Bayet's men had made up their minds what they were going to do if orders did not come in soon. They were not going to be caught shuffling around the square in front of the prefecture. At any moment the Germans might take note of their mass assembly and read its message correctly. They did not want to get caught in the open.

The prefect of police, Amadée Bussière, opened his eyes as his valet, Georges, touched his shoulder lightly. The blind had been lifted and the bright August sun was pouring into the bedroom. As Georges brought him his breakfast tray, Bussière asked casually: "Anything new this morning, Georges?" The valet, imperturbable as the most royal of English butlers, nodded his head and calmly replied: "*Oui*, Monsieur le Préfet, they are back."

Bussière bounded out of bed, electrified by the reply. "They" meant to him his policemen. It meant—what a joy!—that the strike was over. Wondering why Georges had not told him that great news at once, Bussière ran to the window and looked out. To his astonishment and dismay what he saw were several hundred policemen in the vast courtyard of the prefecture, brandishing pistols, guns, and grenades and wearing tricolor brassards. In the center of the excited police was a black Citroën and standing next to it was a tall, blond man, also wearing a brassard, and haranguing the crowd.

The tall blond saw several policemen looking up at the windows. He turned, looked up himself, and saw the prefect, in a dressing gown, looking down at them openmouthed. The tall blond grinned, and shouted: "In the name of the Republic and of Charles de Gaulle, I take possession of the Prefecture of Police."

Yves Bayet had accomplished his mission. He immediately left the prefecture to go to the Café des Deux Magots, where a man with black curly hair and black eyes under black glasses waited for the news. Bayet grinned as he said to Luizet: "Monsieur le Préfet, your office and your men await you." He threw him a smart salute and escorted Luizet to the Citroën that would take them back to the prefecture.

A cyclist was pedaling past the prefecture at that moment. He heard a lusty "La Marseillaise" being belted out by hundreds of voices. And he saw a tricolor flag of the Republic being unfurled upon the staff. The cyclist stopped, listened, looked, and then rushed toward the entrance gates. There he was stopped by guards who shoved pistols at him and told him to move on. They were waiting for the new prefect and no one could come in until Luizet had taken office.

The cyclist mounted his velo, fuming, and, despite the sun burning him, raced with all his strength to his own headquarters. Rol-Tanguy had been totally caught off-guard by the Gaullists. He had not had the slightest suspicion that they would take over one of the key posts, perhaps the most vital tactical lever of power in Paris, before he had acted himself. The Gaullists had won an all-important first round. But the battle for Paris had only just started.

No one could be sure, on that overheated morning of Saturday, August 19, whether Paris would be liberated intact or in ashes. Only one thing was sure: The insurrection had begun.

27
THE INSURRECTION OF PARIS

Sporadic fighting had broken out all over Paris following the orders posted on August 18 by the Francs-Tireurs et Partisans Français and by the elected officials of the Communist party. FFI commandos in groups of three, six, up to twelve, were on the attack, some stopping and commandeering German vehicles, others firing on German patrols, attacking guardposts, seeking out arms. They were more interested in stripping German soldiers of their weapons than in holding them prisoner, although they knew it would be wise to take some German prisoners in order to be able to threaten counteraction if the Germans announced that they were going to shoot hostages.

At his underground headquarters, Colonel Henri Rol-Tanguy had set in motion his overall insurrectional plans. Communist partisans were already carrying out his orders to seize police commissariats. The Gaullists held the central Prefecture of Police, but the Communists struck to take over the precincts throughout the twenty *arrondissements* or districts of Paris. They had orders to seize as many public buildings as possible: post office branches, city halls, municipal hospitals, which would be needed for the wounded, and, for reasons that were not quite clear, the city morgue, the slaughterhouse, and the Comédie Française. Everywhere flags of the Republic began to fly from balconies and the staffs of public buildings. They had not been seen for four years.

The greatest concentration of German barracks and offices was in the suburb of Neuilly, in villas bordering on the Bois de Boulogne. It was the most luxurious, the richest neighborhood of the Paris region. In Neuilly could be found the greatest number of French collaborators. It was quiet and safe, so the Germans had quartered some five thousand troops in Neuilly. Yet it was in Neuilly that the Resistance would provoke the first violent confrontation of that first day of insurrection, August 19.

André Caillette, an FFI officer in charge of the sector, led a unit of sixty-five men to the *mairie*, the town hall, of Neuilly. In seconds they had taken over all three floors of the town hall, surprising the Vichy officials and clerks, who did nothing to resist them. Indeed, most of them applauded the FFI and announced that they had been waiting for the Republic to be restored.

Within minutes of the FFI take-over, the Germans began to organize a counterattack. German tanks rolled up to the doors and began firing shells into the building. The men inside never had a chance.

At the Prefecture of Police in Paris, a young law student, Edgar Pisani, was trying frantically to work the switchboard. He threw a key, listened, and then shouted: "The Germans are storming the *mairie* of Neuilly." The men inside Neuilly's town hall had managed to put a call through to the prefecture to appeal for help. It was a futile call, for the Prefecture of Police was hardly in a position even to help itself. The premature attack in Neuilly was a disaster. Many resistants were killed, others wounded and taken prisoner.

Meanwhile, a German truck was hit by an incendiary bullet outside the Prefecture of Police and exploded. German soldiers running for cover were hit by police marksmen shooting from the windows. But the illusion of winning a skirmish was soon lost when an explosive shell from a tank burst into the iron gates of the prefecture and blew them open. The explosion was so violent that Pisani was lifted up out of his chair and thrown into the opposite corner of the room under a cloud of dust and plaster.

The shell had been launched by a Tiger tank that had just clanked into the square between the prefecture and Notre Dame, with a Renault tank just behind it. The police, crouching behind sandbags, with only pistols and a few obsolete submachine guns, were no match for tanks. Many of the men who had taken the prefecture that morning were still unarmed, milling about the courtyard. They panicked and ran for the entrance to the subway station inside the prefecture, a private entrance for the use of the police.

A police sergeant named Armand Fournet, appalled at the rush to escape, ran to the entrance, blocked it, and waved his pistol in the air, shouting that he would shoot any man who tried to walk past him. "We must stand together, fight together; it is our only hope to survive," he told the policemen pressing toward the station. They stopped, ashamed, paused for one critical moment, then turned around and went back to the courtyard and to their posts.

Pisani had picked himself up from the floor, run back to the communications system, and pressed the button signaling a general alarm to all Paris police stations. At the same time he sent a message on the Teletype machine informing all precincts that the Germans were attacking the prefecture. All help available was needed to counterattack the Germans from the rear; the men in the prefecture would meet their frontal attack.

Among the men preparing to meet the attack was a slim, quiet scientist, one of the great atomic pioneers of the world, Frédéric Joliot-Curie.

In his laboratory in the Collège de France he had demonstrated, before the war, that when an atom splits, a chain reaction takes place. It was a giant step toward uncloaking the mystery of the atom and ushering in the atomic age. But Joliot-Curie, on that August 19, was engaged in a cruder experiment: He was in the cellar of the prefecture manufacturing Molotov cocktails. Joliot-Curie was a Communist.

Earlier that morning, Joliot-Curie had carried two valises into the prefecture. The valises contained bottles of sulfuric acid and several flasks of potassium chlorate. He had brought them over from the laboratory where his father-in-law and mother-in-law, Pierre and Marie Curie, had discovered radium. He took his materials down to the cellar where he and some assistants began pulling corks from bottles of champagne. They refilled the empty bottles with gas and acid, then recorked them and wrapped them in rags or paper soaked in potassium chlorate. A team of couriers ran the deadly bottles up to the roof of the prefecture.

As the tanks shot more explosive shells at the building, policemen on the roof began lofting the Molotov cocktails in an arc toward the tanks. Suddenly one of the improvised bottle-bombs scored a direct hit, landing right in the middle of a turret carelessly left open by the tank commander. A violent explosion racked the square. Flames shot up from inside the tank and in seconds it was a furnace, burning the men trapped within. There was a cheer from the roof, then screams as another tank sent an 88mm artillery shell crashing through the facade of the prefecture.

The fighting had broken out at about half-past three. By five, as the suffocating heat of the day began to cool off, a chill struck the men in the prefecture. Joliot-Curie had run out of sulfuric acid and the police had almost run out of ammunition. They had barely a few rounds left for a couple of dozen guns. They were defenseless, just as Chaban-Delmas and Léo Hamon had warned them they would be during the arguments of the seventeenth and the eighteenth.

Hamon was inside the prefecture at that moment. He remembers, and will never forget, his anguish for his comrades and his fury at their foolishness. "I knew that an uprising was needed for the honor of Paris. We had to participate in our own liberation. But only in coordination with the Allies, within at most a day of their arrival, not a week or two weeks of fighting alone. I rushed out of the prefecture to report to Parodi. I found him at his command post in the Avenue de Ségur, in discussion with Chaban-Delmas. Chaban-Delmas was berating him for having agreed to go ahead with the insurrection and Parodi was explaining that he had no choice, for Rol-Tanguy and Tollet had already given the order under instructions from the Communist party.

"I asked Parodi to give me an order to evacuate the police idiots from the prefecture and try to save their lives. He wrote out an order for me. I could not get back to the prefecture, but I telephoned through. Pisani was still wrestling with the switchboard. He told me to hold on, then he came back and said that the police refused to leave. I told him they would all be massacred and he replied coolly, 'Very likely.' And then he hung up. What a mess!"

It was more than a "mess." Dead bodies of Frenchmen and Germans were strewn about the boulevards and squares. But, under the Pont Saint-Michel, oblivious to all the shouting and shooting, a number of men and women in underwear or bathing suits were bronzing in the sun, as on any normal summer day.

For General von Choltitz there was nothing normal about the sight of six German soldiers dead in a pool of their blood in front of the Gare d'Orsay, on the left bank of the Seine. They had been caught in an FFI ambush and shot down, just as, around the corner on the Rue Solférino, three partisans lay stiffly, riddled by German bullets.

At his headquarters in the Hôtel Meurice after his inspection tour, von Choltitz flushed red with anger as he read a casualty report: More than fifty of his men had been killed and more than a hundred wounded in the day's fighting, and the sun had not yet set. The night might prove to be even more dangerous for the German garrison of Paris.

Von Choltitz, after consulting his staff, decided that the way to put down the uprising was to crush thoroughly the heart of the insurrection: the Prefecture of Police. He would call in a company of tanks and then, to be sure, and to give the Parisians a demonstration of what they could expect if they continued, he would order the Luftwaffe to dive-bomb the prefecture before the tanks moved in to demolish it. He would show them German firepower.

He looked at his watch. It was almost six in the evening. A dusk attack was not advisable. By the time the tanks moved in, after the air attack, it would be night, and the police could slip away under cover of darkness. Besides, his tanks would be vulnerable in the darkness of the Paris streets, and he did not know that the police had run out of Molotov cocktails. He gave the order to attack the next day at sunrise. The Luftwaffe would not dare take to the air save at dawn and at dusk, for fear of Allied fighters. So, first light it would be. Sunrise the next day, August 20, would come at 5:51 A.M. Paris time.

While von Choltitz was planning to crush the insurrection the next morning, various groups of the Resistance were proceeding with their mission of liberating Paris. Local representatives of neighborhood committees of liberation would walk into a mairie, unarmed, and ask the bureaucrats to turn it over to them in the name of the Republic. They would meekly do so. The men and women in the mairies were mainly clerks, ready to follow passively any government power. There were no hard-core collaborationists in the mairies of the arrondissements.

In some cases young FFI militants, overexcited by the act of liberation, armed with a pistol or two, would break into the mairie like conquering commandos, making a big scene. They would arrest collaborationists or women accused of sleeping with Germans, shave off their hair, and paint swastikas on their skulls or breasts in Mercurochrome or iodine. Excesses were committed in Paris and throughout France. The wonder is not that there were excesses but that there were so few after four years of a cruel occupation.

In the confusion of that first day of insurrection, a number of individual initiatives were taken. A group of guards from a barracks decided to march on the presidential palace, the Elysée, and take it over for the Republic. They walked into an empty palace, without opposition, and installed themselves after running up the *Tricolore* of the Republic on the courtyard staff.

A number of men went to various ministries and took over the buildings in the name of the Provisional Government. Other buildings were seized in the name of the Comité Parisien de Libération. A Communist named André Willard, designated by the CNR to be secretary-general of the Ministry of Justice, walked over to the ministry on the Place Vendôme and watched the Germans evacuating the Hôtel Ritz next door. Then, quietly, so as not to provoke the armed Germans, he and other resistants made their way into the ministry and occupied it, while the Germans were piling into cars and trucks in front of the Ritz.

Léo Hamon recalls what he now admits was the most imprudent act of his life. After having criticized the police, characterizing them as idiots for taking over the prefecture prematurely, Hamon decided that it was necessary, for political and psychological reasons, to occupy the Hôtel de Ville, the city hall of Paris.

"I gathered together a 'commando force' of sixty men at dawn. It was a unique commando force, for we did not have a single weapon. Nothing at all. We marched out a little before six A.M. on the morning of the twentieth and then marched right up to the main doors of the Hôtel de Ville. Guards opened the doors and asked who we were. I replied that we were Resistance partisans, ordered by the government of General de Gaulle to establish the Republic at the center of political sovereignty in Paris, the Hôtel de Ville. My knees were trembling, and although the sun was not yet high, I was covered in sweat. But we had no problem. The guards saluted, opened the doors, and we walked in and installed ourselves. We found the prefect of the Seine at his post, and we arrested him. The mayor of Paris, Pierre Taittinger, had not yet arrived at his office."

Taittinger had no intention of resuming his duties as mayor that day. He had already done his duty for the Paris that he loved and had sworn to protect. He had impressed von Choltitz with his arguments against destroying Paris, and then had again talked with the German commander on the phone on the morning of the nineteenth, advising him to deal with the representatives of de Gaulle's government. "They are not terrorists," Taittinger had told von Choltitz. "They are the men of Algiers, of the government, French patriots, and if you were a Frenchman you would be with them. I beg you to deal with them."

Taittinger had made an impression upon von Choltitz. The German was still pondering his advice that afternoon when he received a visit from the Swedish consul, Raoul Nordling, who was becoming the key intermediary between the Germans and the French. Nordling had been busy all during the nineteenth persuading Vichy officials to write out orders to Paris prison wardens for the immediate release of all political prisoners. He was fearful that the Germans, in retreat, might either take political prisoners with them to Germany or execute them as excess baggage, or in reprisal for Resistance attacks on Germans. He had finally obtained the signed orders he needed and then, at the end of the afternoon, had made his way to the head-quarters of von Choltitz.

Nordling found von Choltitz on his balcony, looking down on the Tuileries and watching a young Parisienne, her legs and thighs exposed, her skirt billowing behind her, as she rode her bicycle through the gardens. Nordling was dismayed to hear von Choltitz say: "I like those pretty Parisiennes. It would be a tragedy to have to kill them and destroy their city."

Like Taittinger, Nordling told him that the destruction of Paris would be a crime that history would never forgive and the name of von Choltitz would go down as one of the barbarians of Germany.

At that moment, a burst of gunfire rang out from behind the Louvre. Von Choltitz's face reddened and his jaw muscles twitched. "I'll blast them out of that prefecture. I'll bomb them out of it."

Nordling was in a state of shock.

"Bombs? In the heart of Paris? Do you realize that any near-miss would fall on Notre Dame and the Sainte-Chapelle, the precious heritage of Western civilization?"

Von Choltitz shrugged. He was a soldier. He had orders to hold Paris and to put down any insurrection without mercy. He would not be stopped by the most historic and beautiful of buildings. The responsibility fell on the French. If they did not call off their insurrection and evacuate the prefecture, he had no choice but to act. If it was a crime, it was the French who were guilty.

Nordling had come to von Choltitz with a plan to save the day. He had already received a call from the prefecture, informing him that they were out of ammunition, pleading for his help. He had immediately formulated a scheme in his own mind. Now he tried it on von Choltitz. "Why not agree to a temporary cease-fire to pick up the dead and wounded?" Nordling was hoping that a temporary cease-fire could gradually be extended from a few hours to a day, then more days of respite. He was fighting for time.

General von Choltitz had never in his career asked for a cease-fire. But, considering the suggestion, he saw advantages in it. It would let him, without losing face, call off the Luftwaffe air attack scheduled for dawn. He knew that if the attack was launched there would be no turning back. It would provoke conflict with an enraged Parisian population. Even lightly armed, a few million angry citizens could be very dangerous. He did not have enough men to police an infuriated Paris. He turned to Nordling and said: "All right. If they demonstrate during a one-hour trial period that the FFI officers can control their men," he would accept a temporary truce.

Nordling, greatly relieved, telephoned the Prefecture of Police with the good news. The news was then relayed to the Hôtel de Ville.

From his new headquarters at the Hôtel de Ville, Léo Hamon was able to have his men use banks of telephones and call directly all the *mairies* of the Paris districts and announce a truce. He instructed everyone to say that it was the Germans who asked for the truce to pick up the dead and dying. He did not want any of the Communist militants to accuse him or Luizet, at the Prefecture of Police, of yielding to the Germans.

Rol-Tanguy and Tollet were, indeed, wild with anger. Once again, as in the prefecture take-over, decisions had been made without them. Alexandre Parodi and Jacques Chaban-Delmas had given Hamon their approval and he had discussed the truce at length with Nordling. Parodi was not looking forward to facing Rol-Tanguy and Tollet. He felt he was in a stronger position this time, although he knew it would be difficult to hold the Communists off for long. But every hour gained was another hour that Paris lived.

Parodi presided over a meeting of the Délégation Générale, London's political liaison agency to the CNR, along with Chaban-Delmas, at seven in the morning of Sunday, August 20. Chaban-Delmas, the National Military Delegate, had received a message from London naming him as temporary military governor of Paris, giving him new specific authority for the capital. The next day General Koenig would be designated as military governor of Paris, but he would not arrive for a week, and Chaban remained in his place until then.

Parodi's assistant for the region, Roland Pré, came to the meeting and informed him that the Germans had agreed to send truce negotiators to Nordling's consular offices at 11 A.M. The CNR was scheduled to hold a plenary session at nine o'clock. Parodi and Chaban did not have much time to work out their strategy and impose their point of view. Parodi had in hand a document that Hamon had brought to him after an early-morning meeting with Nordling. It was a proclamation to be made public giving the conditions of a truce, if a truce was agreed upon.

Parodi was lucky that morning. Only six of the sixteen members of the Conseil National de la Résistance were able to come to the meeting, and only one of them was a Communist. It was Pierre Villon, a formidable debater, but he was all alone. He would fight hard against the truce, calling it appeasement if not treason. He argued they would lose their momentum, permit the Germans to regain their balance. Patriots who had arisen would be slaughtered, claimed Villon, trying to reverse the arguments that had been thrown against the Communists, who were accused of risking a massacre of the Resistance by their premature uprising.

General Chaban-Delmas used his rank and his new authority as military governor of Paris to give the CNR members a military briefing. He stressed the overwhelming superiority of the Germans. He told them that the men in the prefecture had run out of ammunition and had only been able to arm less than five hundred of the more than two thousand policemen who had seized the building. He informed them, as he had been informed by Nordling, that Hitler had ordered von Choltitz to destroy Paris, that Eisenhower had rejected de Gaulle's plea to advance the Allied arrival in Paris, and that no help could be expected for at least a week.

Parodi then explained the conditions of the truce. There were four points proposed by Nordling:

1. The Germans would agree to recognize the FFI as regular troops, and if they were captured, they would be treated as prisoners of war, under Geneva rules;
2. The FFI could remain in public buildings already occupied;
3. The Germans would have free access to designated routes for their troop movements;
4. The FFI would refrain from any further attacks on German strongpoints in the city.

Parodi argued, finally, that to sign a truce with one of the most powerful armies in the world, on behalf of a Resistance that had virtually no arms and had only just barely opened fire, was a disgrace for the Germans, if anyone, and certainly not for the Resistance, which had got by far the better of the deal.

The briefs of Parodi and Chaban-Delmas were much more rational than the angry tirades of Villon. In any case, the other members present were all non-Communists. They voted five to one in favor of a truce and agreed to send a three-man negotiating team to the eleven o'clock meetings at the office of the Swedish consul. The three men selected for the mission were Roland Pré, Resistance name Oronte, deputy to Parodi; General Chaban-Delmas; and Léo Hamon. All three mounted their bicycles and pedaled off to the most important meeting of their lives. An impatient Nordling ushered them in, ten minutes late, saying he had just been able to keep the Germans waiting.

Raoul Nordling was a remarkable mediator. "He was the perfect diplomat, the tactful and unflappable negotiator," said Léo Hamon when recalling the meeting. "The Germans, to show good faith, offered to let us have a load of meat for the people of Paris, meat that had been held up at the slaughterhouse of La Villette. We stood on our dignity and refused. We wanted no gift from the Germans. Nordling immediately proposed that the Germans send the meat to him and he would then turn it over to us. It was so agreed.

"Swiftly, all the points of the draft we had already studied were agreed upon. The Germans would evacuate Paris by the external boulevards without interference from us. They would let us stay, without attack, in the prefecture, the Hôtel de Ville, the various mairies and commissariats we had already occupied. We, on the other hand, would not attack the Germans in their five vital command posts as designated earlier in von Choltitz's meeting with Taittinger. The Hôtel Meurice would, of course, be ruled off-limits for the FFI, along with a quadrilateral of streets formed by Rivoli, Castiglione, Saint-Honoré, and Saint-Florentin. The truce was agreed upon by all present, drafted, and signed. It was a great moment for us. Paris had been saved." Hamon paused and added: "At least for another day. Now, we would have to make sure that the Communists would live up to it."

Fighting was still going on. It was difficult, in the shattered communications of a Paris in insurrection, to make contact with the FFI chiefs, Colonels Rol-Tanguy and Lize. They finally got the message, agreed to send out cease-fire orders, but demanded another meeting to discuss the truce and its extent.

Meanwhile, Parodi had been driving through Paris en route to another meeting when a German patrol stopped his car in a routine check. He was riding with two aides who had brought with them a number of secret documents detailing German positions in Paris. Even worse, they had guns and, in their briefcases, a proclamation calling for a general uprising in Paris. It bore that day's date and had been drawn up by the Communists. The Germans promptly arrested all three men. By the most extraordinary of circumstances, a young woman who happened to be one of the three men's fiancée, walked past them as they were being dragged, in handcuffs, down the Avenue Henri Martin. She gasped and rushed to phone Resistance headquarters.

While Resistance aides to Parodi learned that he had been arrested, General von Choltitz was on the phone with the Military Tribunal of Saint-Cloud being told that they had arrested three men who claimed to be "ministers of de Gaulle." They had compromising documents on them and were bearing arms. The general had issued orders to shoot all civilians bearing arms. Should they shoot these three men?

"Yes, of course, shoot them!" von Choltitz curtly replied.

Then, just before hanging up, von Choltitz had a second thought. "No, send them around to me first before we execute them. I want to see them." It had occurred to him that if these men were, indeed, ministers of de Gaulle they might help him impose the truce and restore order to Paris.

As he waited for the prisoners to be brought to him at his hotel, von Choltitz was surprised to see a panting, excited Raoul Nordling rush into his room. Nordling apologized for coming over without a call or an appointment, but it was on a vital matter, he said. He had been informed that a minister of de Gaulle, named Alexandre Parodi, had been arrested. It was imperative that the man be found and not killed by the Gestapo. Parodi and the other two men with him were the men with whom Nordling had discussed the truce only the night before. If they were killed, leadership in Paris would pass totally into Communist hands, with disastrous results. Something had to be done quickly.

The German commander smiled at the Swede and said: "Your Excellency, it seems that those are the three gentlemen for whom I am waiting now. They have been found."

When Parodi was in front of him, von Choltitz became the stern

Prussian commander of *Gross Paris*. He told Parodi that he was a fool to go driving around Paris with compromising documents and arms on him. He warned him that the fighting, still going on, must be stopped at once, or he would unleash his forces with the most tragic consequences for Paris and its people.

Parodi will never forget that moment. "Inside me, I was seething with anxiety, but I knew I could not let von Choltitz see it. I replied coldly that whereas he commanded a disciplined army with radio communications, I did not command and control the Resistance nor did we have reliable communications. I said that I had approved the truce and would work in good faith to carry it out, but I could give no guarantees."

Von Choltitz questioned Parodi closely about the incendiary proclamation found on him. He did not believe the explanation that it had been prepared for the day before and that the date was a typing error. Von Choltitz was unhappy about Parodi's attitude, but he was reluctant to take action against him, mindful of Nordling's warning that if he had Parodi shot the Communists would take over the Resistance. He finally decided: "Since these men were arrested after the truce had been agreed upon, I will turn them over to Nordling's custody."

Von Choltitz, to ease the situation, asked Parodi if he was an officer. Parodi, stiff-necked, replied: "In the reserves." Von Choltitz smiled and said: "No matter, you are an officer, and it is permitted between officers to shake hands." He held out his hand as he finished the phrase. Parodi turned away. He would not take his hand. Nordling rushed in to seize it and to thank von Choltitz effusively for his generous decision to turn the prisoners over to him. The day, and possibly Parodi's life, was saved by Nordling's tact.

It was after six in the evening when Parodi left the Hôtel Meurice. Fighting was still going on; there had been no letup by Rol-Tanguy's troops all through the day of the truce. Rol-Tanguy had been informed of the truce agreement at about four in the afternoon. He had replied that so long as there were Germans in Paris his men would fight them. At the same time the members of the action committee, COMAC, were being contacted and informed. Later that night they would meet and denounce the truce.

Parodi put his own plans into action. While the Communists had sent commandos to seize the commissariats of police and the district town halls, Parodi intended to seize the main national government buildings for de Gaulle. He sent one of his top aides, Yvon Morandat, to take over the Hôtel Matignon, the residence of the prime minister. Laval had already fled, but his personal guard had stayed on in the building. Morandat, wearing only a brassard as a sign of rank, proclaimed himself to be the representative of the Provisional Government of the Republic, who had come to take possession. The guard snapped to attention, saluted, and announced: "I have always been a fervent Republican." This from the guard of a fascist dictator.

Morandat, suppressing a smile, walked in and took over the prime minister's seat of office. He slept in the bed of the chief of government. Out of his element, he tossed all night. Everyone slept an uneasy sleep on the night of that first day of an uncertain truce. And the next morning, the twenty-first, everyone arose early to try to consolidate favorable positions for whatever might be ahead that day.

Morandat took a detachment with him across the Seine over the bridge of Alexandre III, then over to the Faubourg Saint-Honoré where he went to take possession of the Ministry of the Interior, on the Place Beauvau, opposite the Elysée Palace. He had no trouble taking over, but he did run into difficulty when he asked the majordomo to arrange a dinner for twelve for that evening. The majordomo sighed sadly and said that he had lived through many Cabinet crises and had always been able to manage, but not this time: The Vichy minister who had fled the day before had taken all the silverware with him!

Rol-Tanguy was busy that morning. With his top assistants he made his way to the Water and Sewers Administration. There, he and his men dropped through a trapdoor and down into his new command post in the historic sewers of Paris. He had literally become an underground warrior. There were three hundred miles of sewers and catacombs underneath Paris, with their own electric and telephone systems. It was from that secret hideout, communicating by phone to two hundred and fifty posts of the Water and Sewers Administration, that Rol-Tanguy would conduct his campaign of insurrection. He did not intend to accept the conditions of a truce.

All night long, while others slept, a number of groups of men had been at work. Overjoyed, they sang at their work. They were the reporters, editors, and printers of the clandestine press. At last the underground press was coming into the open. On Sunday the twentieth the editors, already designated by the CNR, took over the collaborationist newspaper sites that had been reassigned to them. The papers *Ce Soir*, *Front National*, and *Libération* moved into the plant of the collaborationist *Paris-Soir*. *Combat*, *Franc-Tireur*, and *Défense de Paris* took over *L'Intransigeant*. *Le Populaire*, the official organ of the Socialist party, and *Humanité*, the official organ of the Communist party, would reappear the next morning for the first time in four years. On almost all of them, in giant type on page one, was the headline that Rol-Tanguy and Pierre Villon had sent to them on orders of the liberation committees: "AUX BARRICADES!"

The people of Paris have always been stirred by a barricade and a call to fight for their freedom. They fell to with gusto in the morning of the twenty-first in answer to the headline appeals of the Resistance papers. They tore up streets to use the cobblestones, as their fathers and forefathers had done through the ages. One enterprising group tore down an iron *pissoir*. It had a bad smell, but it made an excellent metal shield atop their barricade. The actors and actresses of the Comédie Française were inspired. They raided the scenery storeroom and grabbed what they could. Then they painted signs with death-head skull and bones and the warning "ACHTUNG MINEN!" Not a single German tank dared test their bluff about mines.

Rol-Tanguy, burrowed into his sewer command post, read the headlines and received reports on the barricades with satisfaction. The Gaullists could not stop him now. One of his emissaries, Roger Cocteau, known by his Resistance name, Gallois, had at that moment made his way through the German lines, out of Paris, and through the suburbs to the village of Pussay, some sixty miles west of Paris, where the lead American units had just arrived. He ran to an American soldier and said he had a message for Eisenhower. The GI, unimpressed, kept munching his C ration. It took Gallois some time to get directions to the supreme commander's headquarters farther west. Gallois had been sent by Rol-Tanguy to tell Eisenhower about the insurrection and to plead for arms. Gallois had, however, changed his mind about the wisdom of the insurrection and planned, instead, to beg Eisenhower to send in the Allied troops to save Paris. Rol-Tanguy did not know this.

General de Gaulle was at the prefecture in the city of Rennes. There he received messages from the clandestine radio transmitters being used by Alexandre Parodi and Jacques Chaban-Delmas, one after the other pleading for help from the armies. Sitting in front of an eighteenth-century desk General de Gaulle, like a character of the same century, took his pen in hand and drafted an ultimate appeal to General Eisenhower. He all but begged for the dispatch of Allied troops to Paris, adding the words, "even if it could produce fighting and damage in the interior of the city." Eisenhower would understand the urgency of the appeal if a patriot like de Gaulle would accept the threat of destruction inside Paris.

De Gaulle gave the letter to General Juin and asked him to hand deliver it. He knew that Eisenhower admired the tough French general. He told Juin that if Eisenhower refused to act, he should tell him orally that de Gaulle would feel compelled to withdraw the Second Armored from the Allied command and send it into Paris, a decision that in any case de Gaulle had already taken.

He then picked up his pen again and drafted a message for the Second Armored commander, General Leclerc. In it, he told Leclerc to prepare to put himself under de Gaulle's orders rather than Eisenhower's and to be ready to move on signal toward Paris. De Gaulle did not know that Leclerc had already made such a decision on his own.

Meanwhile a young giant, code-named Fabri, whose real name, Paul Delouvrier, would become well known in postwar France as delegate-general to Algeria at the height of the native and colonial insurrections there, was hunkered down in his command post in the dense woods of Darvaux, in the Fontainebleau forest. His command post, with arms for five thousand men, was deep in the forest, but less than fifty miles from Paris. He had been given instructions by Chaban-Delmas to listen carefully to his radio for a very special signal that might come any day: *"As-tu bien déjeuné, Jacquot?"* (Did you lunch well, Jacquot?) It would mean that a small plane was coming in for a landing at a clearing in the woods. Aboard that small plane would be General de Gaulle. Two limousines were hidden near the clearing for de Gaulle and his party, to take them to Paris. A platoon of one hundred commandos was assigned to guard the cars and to see to it that de Gaulle got away without interference from the Germans. On August 21, Fabri put his men through a drill on procedure for the big event.

Alexandre Parodi at that moment was in the prime minister's office at the Hôtel Matignon, presiding over a meeting of the men who had been designated to be *secrétaires-généraux* of the various ministries, that is, chief administrative officers, ordered to install themselves as representatives of the Provisional Government. After giving them final instructions, Parodi left to attend another meeting of the CNR. Instead of only a half-dozen members, as at the earlier meeting before the insurrection, there were now twenty men in the room, including the National Military Delegate, General Chaban-Delmas. Parodi knew it would be a stormy session when, upon arrival, Pierre Villon refused to shake hands with him and accused him of breaking the back of the insurrection and endangering the Resistance by accepting a truce.

Chaban-Delmas asked Villon just what he thought the FFI could do against 150 Tiger tanks.

Villon, in a rage, shouted that "Chaban-Delmas talks like a coward."

Parodi got to his feet, reached for his hat, put it on, and told Villon: "You will, at once, apologize to Chaban-Delmas, or I walk out and we split right now." Chaban, himself, said nothing.

Villon, red-faced with anger, his eyes flashing, bit his lips and clenched his fists, fighting to get himself under control. He could not bring himself to yield to a demand for an apology, but he just managed to snap out the words: "I did not call him a coward. I only meant to say that he was talking like a coward."

Parodi exploded at the tactless explanation, which was no apology at all. He started to put on his coat and shouted at Villon asking him just who in the hell he thought he was talking to. Everyone joined in the shouting match. Georges Bidault, president of the CNR, finally shouted them all down and rapped for order.

Villon, after his explosion, knew he had acted badly, and went over to Chaban-Delmas, at last, to apologize. He said he had been up all night, was tired and overwrought, and did not know what he was saying.

The meeting resumed and Bidault finally persuaded them to agree on a compromise proposal: The truce would be denounced but only at five in the afternoon of the next day, August 22. He, like Parodi, was fighting for time, hour by hour, day by day, hoping the Allies would, at last, turn up.

Rol-Tanguy and the Communists accepted the compromise at the meeting but paid no attention to it once they left the meeting room. They continued to order their forces to put up barricades. And they sent out orders for a new FFI offensive to be launched the next morning, not waiting for the truce to be denounced in the afternoon.

Parodi had no faith in the Bidault compromise, for he had seen the wrath of Villon. On the way out of the meeting, his voice choked with emotion, Parodi whispered to Villon: "My God, Paris will be destroyed." Villon stared at him coldly and replied: "Better to die like Warsaw than to live another 1940."

Citizens of Paris, listening to the BBC later that night, heard General Koenig pleading with them to end an insurrection that could accomplish nothing, "except useless sacrifice of French lives."

In the darkness of the night, still intolerably hot from the baking of the day, standing naked to the waist on his balcony overlooking the Tuileries, General von Choltitz listened to the gunfire and saw flashes across the city. Sweat dripped from his chest. The truce, he knew, had failed. He had not carried out orders of his High Command or of his Führer. His orderly world was collapsing around him. For the first time in his army career, he was in a state of insubordination and at a loss on where to turn or what to do. He knew that if he carried out his orders, he would destroy Paris and kill hundreds of thousands to no avail in the last days of a war already lost. He did not want to have to live with that the rest of his life, assuming he would have a rest of a life to live, for he was certain that the Allies would hang him in the ashes of Paris if he burned it down.

On the morning of the twenty-second, General von Choltitz awoke red-eyed. He had slept badly in the hot night. Morning did not bring any resolution to his dilemma, and the morning reports showed that the Communists were not obeying the truce. What should he do?

On that same morning, another general awoke. He was clear-eyed and his troops were winning the war, but he, too, was pondering a dilemma. General Eisenhower had said no, firmly, to de Gaulle a few days before, but after de Gaulle left he continued to go over the argument in his own mind. He had a high regard for de Gaulle. As an American patriot, he understood how a French patriot might put all other interests aside when considering the liberation of his capital and the restoration of democratic government.

Eisenhower had received de Gaulle's latest written plea. He read it and reread it, then scrawled a note on it: "It looks as though we shall be compelled to go to Paris." He sent the letter with the note to his chief of staff, General Walter Bedell Smith. He then sent a cable to his superior officer, General George C. Marshall, in Washington. He told Marshall he might have to move on to Paris sooner than planned or desirable. He added that de Gaulle would be allowed to come in later, "under some joint Allied setup." Eisenhower, despite all his experience with de Gaulle, still underestimated his man. It was folly for Eisenhower to think that de Gaulle would ask any foreigner when he could go into Paris or that he would enter under some "Allied setup."

De Gaulle moved out of the prefecture in Rennes and went to another, more discreet command post. From August 22 on, de Gaulle would be unavailable to the Allies. His aides were told to evade any pressing questions as to his whereabouts. He would remain free and flexible of all restraints until the moment had come for him to drive into Paris.

Sporadic fighting continued in Paris all through the twenty-second, but with the end of the truce that afternoon, the Communists felt no restraints of any kind and ordered renewed attacks. Violent fighting broke out all over Paris on August 23. André Tollet, the Communist union leader who had first called for the insurrection, had gone to the Hôtel de Ville, which Hamon and his men had already taken. Hamon had no arms, but Tollet and his men did have some. Tollet was not going to let the Gaullists hold both the Prefecture of Police and the Hôtel de Ville. So, with a group of Communist youths, most of them teen-agers, he commandeered city hall. As he was trying to teach some of the youngsters how to handle their revolvers, four German tanks wheeled into the square and began shelling the building. Shooting out of the window, Tollet saw a young woman, a bottle in her hand, run fearlessly up to the tank and smash her bottle against its turret. Flames shot up in the tank as she ran away from it. Suddenly she staggered and fell. A bullet had cut her down. But the tank blew up and the other three tanks turned and clattered off. She had saved the Hôtel de Ville.

Von Choltitz, informed of the new and more violent fighting, called in Nordling. He pointed out that the three men he had released into his custody had done nothing to reinforce a truce. Nordling replied that the FFI would obey no one but de Gaulle himself. The Swedish consul was then astounded to hear the German commander of Paris say dryly: "Well, then, let someone go and see de Gaulle."

Nordling could hardly believe his own ears when he then heard von Choltitz say that very soon he would have to carry out Hitler's orders to destroy Paris and blow up all the bridges, unless, of course, the Allies arrived before he had acted. Nordling blinked and asked whether he would put such a suggestion in writing. Nordling feared that Allied commanders would not believe him if he came to them with such a remarkable story. Von Choltitz would not, of course, commit any such thought to writing. But he did immediately write out an order that stated: "The commanding general of *Gross Paris* authorizes the consul general of Sweden, R. Nordling, to leave Paris and its line of defense." He signed it, stamped it, and handed it over to Nordling.

Neither Nordling nor von Choltitz could possibly have known at that moment what a miracle it was that the name written on the pass was R. Nordling. Just before leaving his consular office in Paris to seek out American officers, Raoul Nordling turned purple in the face, gasped for breath, and fell to the floor, clutching his chest and moaning. He had suffered a heart attack.*

---

* Raoul Nordling recovered from his heart attack and resumed his activities, but only after the liberation.

The man who took his pass and left in his place was his brother, Rolf Nordling, identified correctly as "R. Nordling" in the pass.

On an airstrip west of Paris, General Leclerc was pacing back and forth, accompanied by Rol-Tanguy's emissary, Gallois. Rol-Tanguy would have been enraged to know that Gallois had not asked for arms as he had been instructed to do, but had pleaded with the Americans to send troops to take over the insurrection of Paris. Gallois had pleaded eloquently, just as Leclerc had done, just as de Gaulle had done in his letter. Leclerc was waiting for the outcome of Eisenhower's final conference on the issue with Omar Bradley, commander of the Twelfth Army Group, which was responsible for Paris.

A tiny Piper Cub came winging over the field and down to a swift landing. Out of it jumped one of Eisenhower's aides, General Edwin Siebert. He waved at Leclerc and shouted: "You've won. On to Paris."

A few minutes later another Cub came down from the skies. It was Omar Bradley, himself. The group commander walked over to Leclerc and Gallois. He waved a warning finger at them: "I don't want any fighting in Paris itself. . . . No heavy fighting there. Now, get your orders from corps commander."

Leclerc saluted, ran to his own plane, overjoyed. He jumped out of his plane on landing and raced to his command post, shouting the order: *"Mouvement immédiat sur Paris."* As Leclerc gave orders to pack up and move out, similar orders were being issued to the U.S. Fourth Infantry Division. Leclerc would be given the honor of commanding the first troops into Paris, but the Americans wanted to be sure he had enough backup strength in reserve outside Paris to make it stick, so they gave him one of their best divisions, with orders to stay close up. At the same time, Army Commander General Courtney Hodges told his staff to take a couple of artillery battalions away from the attacking divisions. "I don't want them to get the idea they can beat up Paris with a howitzer every time a machine gun gets in their way." The Americans by then were more concerned about not destroying Paris than many of the French were.

While Leclerc and the Fourth Division were preparing for a frontal assault on the gates of Paris from the southeast, General George Patton had already swung a left and right punch at the Germans north and south of Paris. Patton's left wing was rolling past Mantes after having crossed the Seine on the twentieth. It was pushing back Germans who might have been able to swing down against Leclerc. His right wing pushed past Sens and was heading for a rendezvous east of Paris with the left wing after it broke through Dreux. Patton planned to close Paris inside a pincers, while Leclerc broke through the Porte d'Orléans. It was hoped that Patton would by then have driven off all the German troops around Paris, leaving Leclerc only the garrison inside Paris to overcome. It was felt he could do that with a minimum of heavy shelling and virtually no major destruction of historic monuments and buildings.

Rolf Nordling used his pass time and time again to go through German checkpoints around Paris. Each time the pass was examined suspiciously, sometimes by Gestapo officers who did not owe allegiance to the Wehrmacht generals. It took twelve long and desperate hours for Nordling's party to pass through the German lines and reach the command post of General Bradley.

Bradley listened with increasing concern as Nordling told him that von Choltitz had waited as long as he could to carry out Hitler's orders to destroy Paris. Unless Allied troops came quickly to capture von Choltitz and liberate Paris, the capital would be wiped out. When he had finished, Bradley told him that the decision had already been taken to intervene in Paris but that orders would now be issued to make all possible speed in the operation. As they were talking, on the morning of August 23, a new message was delivered to von Choltitz from Hitler's headquarters. The orders stressed the military and political importance of Paris and ended with these words: "Paris must not fall into the hands of the enemy, or, if it does, he must find nothing but a field of ruins."

Everything needed to turn Paris into a "field of ruins" had already been done by teams of German sappers. Two tons of explosives had been wired in under the Invalides, enough to blow up the military offices and Napoleon's Tomb. Mine emplacements were being dug in under the Senate in the Palais du Luxembourg. More than five tons of TNT were stored in the palace's cellars. The other house of Parliament, the Chambre des Députés, on the Seine opposite the Place de la Concorde, and all of its office buildings behind the Palais Bourbon, had been mined. The Hôtel Talleyrand on the Rue Saint-Florentin and its beautiful neighbor, the Ministère de la Marine, on the Place de la Concorde, were also heavily mined. The Eiffel Tower had not yet been wired for destruction but that very day the order had come from Berlin to blow up "the symbol of Paris." German engineers went to examine the four steel supports for its tower as sun was setting on August 23.

While Paris was preparing to go to sleep on mattresses of dynamite, and while advance units of the French Second Armored were racing to the rescue, the citizens of London and of New York were singing, laughing, dancing in the streets, shouting: "Paris is free!" A French officer in London, Colonel André Vernon, fearful that the Allies would not come to the rescue of Paris, had deliberately released a false news bulletin to the BBC, announcing the liberation of Paris. He reasoned that once the Allied peoples had fervently celebrated the liberation of Paris General Eisenhower would be obliged to make the liberation come true. He did not know that a well-known American correspondent, Charles Collingwood of CBS News, fearful that bad communications might delay his dispatches once Paris was liberated, had recorded an advance description of the liberation of Paris and sent it to London. As soon as the CBS London office heard the BBC bulletin about Paris being liberated, CBS put Collingwood's "eye-witness" description on the air.

New York went wild. French opera star Lily Pons sang "La Marseillaise" in front of a cheering, weeping, laughing crowd of thousands at Rockefeller Center. Church bells called all the faithful to celebratory masses. Bars handed out free drinks and French restaurants broke open their stocks of champagne. People danced around Times Square and Piccadilly Circus. President Roosevelt and King George sent messages of congratulations to General de Gaulle. From his hospital bed, the great American hero of the First World War, General John J. Pershing, hailed this "great step on the road to victory."

General de Gaulle was conferring on the plans for liberation with Leclerc at the Château de Rambouillet on that twenty-third of August. Leclerc laid down his battle plan for de Gaulle. He had completely changed the original plan that had been filed with and approved by his corps commander. Once again he was a French officer reporting to his French commander in chief. The Americans would not decide his battle tactics. General de Gaulle studied his maps, nodded his head, and offered his hand to the man who had carried his Cross of Lorraine from the jungles of Africa to the beaches of Normandy. "Go! Go swiftly!" de Gaulle ordered Leclerc.

Leclerc sent an urgent message to Jacques Chaban-Delmas, informing him that he was on his way, urging him to make every effort to keep control in Gaullist hands until he could break through. Overjoyed, hopeful that the news would give the Communists pause, Chaban-Delmas raced over to a meeting of COMAC, the action committee, where he found Rol-Tanguy, Pierre Villon, and other Communist leaders. He found them confusedly discussing the BBC report that Paris had been liberated.

The Communists were brought up short with the news that Leclerc was on the march. As Frenchmen, as patriots, they were cheered by the realization that they were on the eve of freedom after four long, cruel years of Nazi occupation. As Communists, as resistants who had fought bravely and lost so many men in the underground war, they felt that they would be cheated of final victory, honor, and power if Leclerc broke through before they, themselves, had liberated Paris. They left their meeting to contact all Resistance units for a last, desperate effort to bring the insurrection to a peak of victory.

28

THE LIBERATION OF PARIS

Resistance spies in every town and village between Paris and the Allied armies called in daily, sometimes hourly reports on troop movements. They reported to the Allies on German positions and to the Paris Resistance on Allied moves. They kept a particularly close watch on General Leclerc and his Second Armored Division, for by then, all knew that he had been assigned the honor of liberating Paris.

The news that General Leclerc was on the way was a spur to the Communist-led FFI. Rol-Tanguy ordered an immediate all-out attack. He knew he had one day at best to establish his FFI as a liberating force before the army arrived. He wanted to welcome Leclerc and de Gaulle into a Paris already liberated by his men. Despite their hopes that the Communists might back off, the Gaullist leaders were ready with countermoves. They had decided to consolidate their hold on all government buildings and to see to it that the liberation press did not get only Communist-written communiqués and descriptions of events.

On August 23, Gaullist and Communist leaders of the Resistance all headed for the Hôtel de Ville, symbol of political sovereignty in Paris. Rol-Tanguy paced the corridors with Georges Bidault, president of the CNR, a Communist and a Catholic united against the Germans, but rivals for power. Chaban-Delmas and Parodi wondered whether de Gaulle would come in right behind Leclerc and where he would set up his office. Pierre Villon hoped that de Gaulle would come first to the Hôtel de Ville, where the Communists had massed in strength. They would give him a hero's welcome, but as their "guest," not as their leader or liberator.

While these political preoccupations boiled over at the Hôtel de Ville, the FFI were engaged in heavy fighting at two strongpoints in Paris: the Buttes-Chaumont tunnel, where a number of trains were parked, and the Prince-Eugène barracks of the German army on the Place de la République. The barracks was one of the vital centers that von Choltitz had warned Nordling must not be attacked without provoking terrible destruction by shelling and bombing.

FFI units attacked both sides with their last rounds of ammunition. They rapidly overran German guards at the Buttes-Chaumont, taking more than 125 prisoners, many arms and munitions. The fighting in the Place de la République was more severe and lasted all through the day and night.

The Second Armored of Leclerc moved at dawn on the twenty-fourth through the forest of Rambouillet, toward Paris twenty miles away. General Leclerc split his units into three columns along a front about seventeen miles wide. The Americans had ordered him to attack directly on the shortest line, from Rambouillet to Versailles, but he had changed the battle plans. He sent only one column, the smallest, toward Versailles, with orders to strike for the Porte de Sèvres, a northwestern gate, firing all their guns and making a big show, to persuade the Germans that theirs was the main thrust. He then sent a second column some five miles to the southeast through the valley of the Chevreuse and toward an entry into Paris by the Porte de Vanves. His main thrust, which he himself would use for his own entry into Paris, was entrusted to Colonel Pierre Billotte. Billotte would slip south, through Longjumeau and Fresnes and then break into Paris by the southern gateway, the Porte d'Orléans.

Late at night on the twenty-fourth, while the FFI was launching its ultimate effort to liberate Paris before de Gaulle's force could arrive, the first tanks of the Second Armored, commanded by Captain Raymond Dronne, entered Paris at the Orléans gateway. Dronne, a tough, redheaded tank commander, was the tip of the lance. He had only three Sherman tanks under his command. Admonished by Leclerc to make all haste, Dronne had outrun the division and burst into Paris. It was a dangerous move, for he would be no match for German Tigers that outnumbered him. But Leclerc gambled that when the Germans heard the news that Sherman tanks had entered Paris, they would assume that the full armored division was on the way in. They would then, he hoped, either prepare a retreat or take up defensive positions around their headquarters. He was sure they would not guess that only three tanks had led the way. He hoped that the Communists would also assume that the entire Second Armored was there and step back to let him take over.

People went mad when they saw the first French tanks, with the Cross of Lorraine and the tricolor blue-white-red of the Republic. Dronne's tanks were surrounded and he had to force his way through, open his turret, and plead with the people to fall back. He wanted to get to the Prefecture of Police and the Hôtel de Ville.

He finally made his way out of the crowd and slipped through streets of startled Parisians who looked at them in amazement. Finally he reached the Seine and saw ahead of him the Renaissance facade of the Hôtel de Ville. Dronne drove into the square and called a halt. His men braked, opened their turrets, and stared out at wrecked tanks and trucks in the square and flags of the Republic draped from the balconies of the Hôtel de Ville. Radio reporter Pierre Crenesse came running over to one of the tanks, named the Champaubert. He rushed over to the red-eyed, weary gunner leaning out of the turret. He held up his microphone to the soldier and shouted to his audience: "You will now hear the voice of the first French soldier, the first ordinary French soldier to arrive in Paris. Tell us, who are you and where are you from?"

The soldier grinned down at him and shouted back: "I'm Private Firmian Pirlian and I'm from Constantinople." De Gaulle and Leclerc may have defied the Americans in order to have a native Frenchman liberate Paris, but the Gods of War had fated otherwise. Captain Dronne and his unit stayed briefly at the Hôtel de Ville, then, assured of its safety, went to the Prefecture of Police, to await the division's arrival in the morning.

While Georges Bidault was composing a liberation proclamation at the Hôtel de Ville, Major General Dietrich von Choltitz, in a freshly pressed uniform and highly polished boots, his monocle screwed into his eye, stepped briskly into the dining room of the Hôtel Meurice for what he knew would be his last dinner at the hotel. If he was still alive the next day, he knew it would be as a prisoner of the Allies. He would surrender to an Allied officer, even a French officer, but he was determined not to surrender to the FFI, to die fighting rather than be taken by "the terrorists," as he still called all units of the Resistance.

General de Gaulle, waiting in Rambouillet, was thinking about his own relations with the Resistance that last night of the German occupation of Paris. He had received a message that the leaders of the Resistance were looking forward to receiving him at the Hôtel de Ville, where they would all hail the liberation of Paris and the restoration of the Republic. De Gaulle had been expecting just such a message. He understood that it was a power play. The Resistance, installed at the town hall, would assume the role of liberating authorities and "turn Paris over to him." He would not permit that to happen. He was the president of the Provisional Government of the Republic. His tanks had liberated Paris. He would, therefore, go immediately to the Ministry of War, to his old office, which he had left in June 1940. That office was the symbol of Republican authority. Himself a symbol for four years, General de Gaulle valued highly the power of symbolism. He would receive the Resistance leaders; they would not receive him. De Gaulle went to bed in Rambouillet, and would leave for Paris as soon as Leclerc sent him the all-clear signal.

The next morning, August 25, Leclerc's Second Armored Division entered Paris.

Colonel Paul de Langlade rode in the lead tank of his column and crossed the Paris city line in the west at the Porte de Saint-Cloud, a heavily populated residential area. Tens of thousands of Parisians, alerted by telephone calls from suburbanites who had seen the column heading toward the gates, were out in the streets shouting, cheering, laughing, crying. Women and children climbed up on the tanks, while men ran alongside brandishing clubs or guns, acting as infantry for the armored vehicles. The assault was becoming a parade.

Colonel Billotte's column had broken up into half-brigades. One took up defensive positions around the Porte d'Orléans. The other entered the Porte d'Orléans, where Leclerc would make his own entry later. On entering that gate, the troops raced toward the Gare Montparnasse to capture that important rail terminal. It dropped a few tanks off to hold the station and then headed for the Invalides sector, where the War Office was located. Its tanks seized the German barracks at the Avenue de la Tour-Maubourg without any opposition. Its unit commanders then attacked light German forces, routed them swiftly, and captured the Foreign Office on the Quai d'Orsay and the important symbol of parliamentary democracy, the Palais Bourbon, site of the Chamber of Deputies. Citizens of Paris rushed into the streets, set up barricades to prevent German counterattacks, and dashed into the buildings under cover of the tanks to take possession and run up the tricolor flag of the Republic.

A suicide squad of Germans surprised the liberators who tried to enter the Foreign Office, which they thought they had captured. A fusillade of gunfire drove the French back. Heavy fighting broke out at the corner of the Esplanade des Invalides and the Rue de l'Université, at the rear entrance of the Ministry of Foreign Affairs. The tanks had to shell the German positions and set fire to the ministry. One of Leclerc's tanks blew up and a number of civilians were killed before the Germans were wiped out.

The liberating forces ran into fierce opposition at the Ecole Militaire, behind the Eiffel Tower. SS units, sworn to fight to the death, resisted for five hours. Fifty Germans out of a garrison of two hundred fifty were killed before Leclerc's forces broke in and forced the surrender of the garrison.

Commandant Jacques Massu, a powerful six-foot-three brawler in de Langlade's column, led his men to Gestapo headquarters in the Hôtel Majestic, just off the Etoile. He personally led the charge into the German headquarters, burst into a room full of Nazi officers, shouting *"Heraus! Heraus!"* at the top of his lungs. The Germans, startled by the French giant bellowing at them in German, raised their hands in the air and surrendered.

Massu and his men secured the Majestic and then went to seize the Arc de Triomphe, pull down the Nazi swastika and run up the flag of France. From all the streets and wide avenues circling the Etoile, Parisians came running. Church bells were pealing out the signal of liberation, café owners were pulling out hidden caches of wines. On every balcony shouting Parisians were waving flags.

Shortly after noon, the *Tricolore* was flying from the Eiffel Tower. Leclerc's men all seemed to be bleeding from face wounds, but it was only smears of lipstick. Soldiers were handing notes to the crowd, asking people to call their mothers, fathers, friends. One young tank officer, Second Lieutenant Bureau, jumped off his tank, dashed into a café, and called his father, who cried for joy to hear his voice. One hour later, Bureau was killed in the attack on the Foreign Ministry.

With all the joy, there was sorrow on Liberation Day for many families. One hundred twenty-seven French—soldiers and civilians—died on the day of freedom. Seven hundred fourteen were wounded. Twenty-seven Germans were killed and 233 wounded on August 25. Counting the fighting during the insurrection, the total casualty list for the liberation of Paris mounted to 901 FFI and 582 civilians killed, against 2,788 Germans killed and 4,911 wounded.

General von Choltitz sat at his desk in the Meurice, staring at a map of Paris marked up with red grease-pencil crosses showing the penetration and spread of Leclerc's forces. It was noon and he had thrown away his marking pencil, knowing that the red blotches would spread as rapidly as a fever, too fast for him to keep up. He was living his last hours as commander of *Gross Paris*

He pushed away from his desk and made his way down to the dining room. He had eaten his last dinner there the night before. Perhaps it might be fitting to have a last glass of wine with his officers. At that moment a German tank, guarding the approaches to the hotel, swung into the Rue de Rivoli. One of the Second Armored Division tanks, the Douaumont, was also moving down that avenue toward the Meurice. Its commander saw the German Panzer a split second before the Panzer saw the Sherman. The Sherman's 75mm cannon roared and hurled a shell right at the German tank. The Panzer blew up and the explosion knocked the windows out of the Meurice and shook the cutlery off the table in the dining room.

General von Choltitz sipped some wine, wiped his lips, and said: "Gentlemen, our last combat has begun." He spoke quietly to his staff for a minute, wished them luck, and walked slowly out of the room and to his office. There he wrote a brief note of thanks to Raoul Nordling for all he had done. He then called in a staff officer and told him that they should be prepared to fight to the end if the FFI partisans tried to capture them. But, if regular army troops arrived, they should surrender. He arose, left his office, and entered a small room in the interior courtyard, where he would await his fate.

A few hours later, fate arrived in the person of a young French officer, Lieutenant Henri Karcher. Karcher had wanted to be one of the first men into Paris. In his pocket he had a photo of his wife and a little boy whose picture he had received a few weeks ago. It was his four-year-old son, born just after he had fled France. He was eager to see the son he did not know. He would tell his son that he had just captured the German commanding general of Paris. He walked in, took von Choltitz's gun as the symbol of his surrender, and said: "Follow me."

As von Choltitz was marched away, General Leclerc, his conqueror, who had been on combat alert since dawn, was sitting down to a late lunch in the Prefecture of Police. It was his first moment of rest in almost seven hours of tense activity. A hot August sun was burning into the room. It made Leclerc think of another hot sun that had burned down on him on another August 25, four years before, almost to the minute. He was then in a native dugout canoe, a pirogue, in Cameroun, deep in the heart of Africa. Three French officers were with him. All four men had answered the call of Charles de Gaulle to keep on fighting in the empire. Cameroun would be the first French colony reconquered by Leclerc. When he raised the flag of Free France in Cameroun, Leclerc had sixteen men with him. On August 25, 1944, when he carried the Cross of Lorraine into Paris, he had sixteen thousand men with him.

Leclerc took Cameroun away from Vichy officers. He took Paris from the Germans, for, at that moment, his men came into the prefecture with Leclerc's prisoner, General von Choltitz. Von Choltitz, close-shaven, scrubbed, and immaculate in his dress uniform and his medals, looked at the dusty Frenchman, with stubble on his cheeks and bread crumbs on a rumpled khaki uniform and mud-caked GI American boots. Leclerc's only insignia were two stars pinned askew on his shoulder panels. At first glance one could have mistaken the conqueror for the conquered.

As Leclerc and von Choltitz were reading a draft of the surrender document, there was a commotion at the door. In stormed Henri Rol-Tanguy, chief of the FFI of the Paris region, and his Communist comrade, Valrimont, head of Comité, both of them in a temper. Rol-Tanguy shouted that the FFI had been fighting the Germans all alone for six long days and was now not even informed of the surrender of the Germans. He demanded the right to witness the surrender ceremony. Valrimont further insisted that Rol-Tanguy should be given the honor, in the name of the Resistance, to add his name and signature to the surrender document. The Resistance had been fighting the Germans, hand to hand, much longer than the French army had.

Leclerc listened to their outburst. His jaw muscles twitched and his face reddened as the tirade grew long. He held up his hand and said crisply: "Enough! I have heard you. I agree. You have fought and fought well as Frenchmen. So you will sign. Now stop shouting."

Orders were given for a cease-fire, while Leclerc and von Choltitz left the prefecture and drove to Leclerc's headquarters at the Gare Montparnasse, where the formal surrender ceremony would take place. Leclerc would not accept the surrender at the Prefecture of Police, it had to be at his divisional headquarters. General de Gaulle had drilled it into him that it was the army that would accept the German surrender and not the Resistance.

At four-thirty in the afternoon of August 25, General Charles de Gaulle, who had left Paris in June 1940 as an obscure brigadier general, returned to a hero's welcome from tens of thousands of cheering Parisians. De Gaulle, defying snipers and the stray bullets still whistling through Paris, rode through the Porte d'Orléans in an open Hotchkiss. He had instructed his aide to find him a car of French manufacture. He would not ride into Paris in an American jeep. He waved to the roaring crowds. It was the beginning of his investiture as chief of government by acclamation, his final triumph over Roosevelt and the Americans who had done everything they could to block his way to power.

The cheering crowds were also his answer to Rol-Tanguy, Valrimont, Villon, and the leaders of the Communist party. Charles de Gaulle, not the Communist party, would wield power in Paris and in all of France. The Communists, waiting to receive him at the Hôtel de Ville, would wait a long time. De Gaulle instructed his driver to head first toward the Gare Montparnasse. He would witness the German surrender to Leclerc, his officer.

Thousands of Parisians filled the square on the Boulevard Montparnasse in front of the station. "De Gaulle! De Gaulle! De Gaulle!" the crowd chanted in unison. De Gaulle stretched his arms high and wide, converting his giant figure into a huge V sign. The crowd loved it and began roaring again. The general walked into the station and smiled as he saw another figure as tall as himself, if somewhat slimmer and younger. It was his son, Philippe, a naval officer, in charge of an armed unit, conducting a German major to the Chamber of Deputies to call for the surrender of the garrison there.

Leclerc saluted and handed de Gaulle the surrender document. De Gaulle's eyes blazed with anger when he saw Rol-Tanguy's signature. He upbraided Leclerc, reminding him that Rol-Tanguy, although FFI, not regular army, had accepted the rank of colonel in the army, making him Leclerc's subordinate. "One does not need the signature of a subordinate," de Gaulle snapped at Leclerc. He calmed down, however, when he learned that Leclerc had accepted the German surrender in the name of the Provisional Government of the French Republic. It was the first time in the war, and it would be the only time, that an Allied officer, in General Eisenhower's command, had failed to accept a surrender or capture an objective in the name of the Allies.

De Gaulle knew perfectly well that not an inch of France could have been liberated by the French themselves. It was the Allies, the Americans and the British in the west, the Russians in the east, who were defeating the Germans. The French were honorable but minor participants in the struggle, a fact that de Gaulle could chew on but could not bring himself to swallow.

De Gaulle's gorge had already risen, along with his hair-trigger temper, when he had read a proclamation, published and posted earlier that day by the Conseil National de la Résistance. It hailed the liberation of Paris, "in the name of the French nation," on behalf of the CNR, without any mention of General de Gaulle or the Provisional Government of the French Republic. Infuriated, General de Gaulle stalked out of the station, told Leclerc to take care of the routine formalities, and then ordered his chauffeur to take him to his old office in the Ministry of War. He would not go to the Hôtel de Ville where the Resistance waited to receive him.

The people of Paris, unaware of the bitter confrontations separating the men who had fought to liberate them, were out in the streets celebrating their liberation. After four years of repression, they were at last free. Unmindful of fighting still going on around them, they danced through the streets and also joined in the fight. They grabbed German helmets, clamped them on their heads, and joined French soldiers closing in on German strongholds still holding out. Hundreds of soldiers and civilians fell dead or wounded on that day of liberation. While some fell and some died, millions sang and embraced each other and the soldiers, sharing the joy of liberation with their liberators.

Those who lived through that wild day in Paris will never forget it, not only those dancing in the streets while some fought and died around the corner from the celebration, but even the sick and wounded in the hospitals, who threw off their pains and shouted with joy. Marie-Claire Scamaroni, courier for the Resistance, sister of the martyred Fred, who was tortured and killed in Corsica, was in intensive care with a raging fever from septicemia, which was threatening her life. She heard the shooting and the shouting and knew it was the moment of liberation, the moment she had fought and prayed for for four years. She shrieked with joy. Nurses and doctors came running to her bed, sure that she was delirious and in her last throes.

OSS chief David Bruce, in a jeep commandeered by Ernest Hemingway, who had jumped press camp and joined the Resistance after the landings, rode in over the Saint-Cloud Bridge. Hemingway sped through the Bois de Boulogne, out to the Champs-Elysées and straight to the Place Vendôme. There was a big Resistance contingent massed in the square. Hemingway, wearing colonel's insignia, self-appointed, took command and shouted: "Follow me." Into the Hôtel Ritz he marched his motley company.

The director, elegantly attired in a cutaway and wing collar, greeted them inside the main door. He welcomed Hemingway, an old friend, and asked what he would like. Hemingway glanced back at his band, winked at Bruce, and said: "Seventy-three dry martinis." To the bar they marched. Hemingway did not write a dispatch that day.

CBS correspondent Charles Collingwood, whose premature description of the liberation of Paris had been inadvertently released two days earlier, was arm-deep in girls in Pigalle. He was not about to describe the scene again. Collingwood had come a long way with the French from the day he reported the assassination of Admiral Darlan in Algiers. He had done his duty well and was going to enjoy the liberation of Paris.

Ed Ball, a colleague of America's most famous and most beloved combat correspondent, Ernie Pyle, wrote in his dispatch: "Describing Paris in words today is like trying to paint a desert sunset in black and white."

As the sun began to set on August 25, all heavy firing came to an end. Here and there a sniper's bullet whined through a street, but the fighting had ended. Some twenty thousand Germans had been taken prisoner. Forty-two men of the Second Armored had been killed and seventy-seven had been wounded. It is terrible to see anyone die in war, at any time, in any kind of fighting, but to fall in battle one minute before the end, that is not only tragic, but grotesque. Hundreds of people mourned their dead and wounded in liberated Paris that night.

In his office at the Ministry of War, General de Gaulle received the visit of his personal political representative in Paris, the man who had carried the main burden of responsibility in the tense week of insurrection, his delegate-general Alexandre Parodi, who had stood up to the Communist challenge almost naked and empty-handed. Parodi logically expected de Gaulle's thanks. What he received was a storm of criticism. "I admit," Parodi recalls wryly, "that I was somewhat taken aback."

Parodi, still trying to carry out his orders to avoid a split of the Resistance and an all-out confrontation with the Communists, had gone along with the proclamation of the twenty-fourth hailing the liberation of Paris. He knew that it made no reference to de Gaulle or to the Provisional Government, but he felt that if he signed it, his name, as delegate, would evoke the name of de Gaulle. That was not de Gaulle's view of the matter. Parodi was stunned by de Gaulle's vehemence, not only about his signature on the document, but de Gaulle's reiterated insistence that the CNR, COMAC, the FFI—all the forces of the Resistance—were under complete Communist rule. Parodi knew that they were not. The Communists were powerful but not absolute masters of Paris. He also was shocked to hear de Gaulle say that the CNR, which had many non-Communist, pro-Gaullist members, was nothing but a tool of the Communist party. It would be no pun to say that de Gaulle, in his anger, saw nothing but red.

De Gaulle told Parodi that he would not accept being received by the CNR or the CPL in the Hôtel de Ville. That building was the symbol of municipal authority. As chief of government, General de Gaulle would receive the Resistance in a national government building. Parodi, dismayed by de Gaulle's bitterness and hostility toward the Resistance, fearing that wartime unity would split apart and make it impossible to govern France peacefully, begged de Gaulle to reconsider. But he did not know de Gaulle well and had no influence upon him. In desperation, Parodi turned to a man whom de Gaulle did know and to whom he would perhaps listen, his prefect of police, Charles Luizet.

Luizet agreed with Parodi and came running around to talk de Gaulle into changing his plans. After a prolonged discussion, Luizet finally persuaded de Gaulle to go to the Hôtel de Ville. He won him over by telling him that it was not only the Resistance that was waiting for him there, but that tens of thousands of Parisians were waiting in the square and along the banks of the Seine to cheer their liberator, Charles de Gaulle.

De Gaulle relented. He agreed to go to the Hôtel de Ville, but only after he had first gone, as he had planned, to the Prefecture of Police.

The Prefecture of Police was a national government building and it had been occupied by pro-Gaullist policemen. There he would issue orders for another ceremony, the only one that really mattered to de Gaulle: his personal "investiture" by the people of Paris in his own formal and official "entry" into the capital. He would parade from the Tomb of the Unknown Soldier, down the Champs-Elysées and then on to the Cathedral of Notre Dame. He would show the CNR and all the Communist-run commands of the Resistance who was the choice of the people, who was the master of Paris and of France.

Georges Bidault, who would become President de Gaulle's minister of foreign affairs in the postwar government of the Republic, was not happy with de Gaulle at that moment. With the sun setting and the day of liberation ending, de Gaulle had still not shown up at city hall. A messenger brought Bidault the information that de Gaulle had gone first to the Prefecture of Police. Bidault was livid. The former history teacher, a devout and militant Catholic and democrat, would not tolerate the insult to the Resistance and to the principle of democracy itself. "This is the House of the People," Bidault proclaimed, sweeping his arms in an arc, encompassing the rooms of the Hôtel de Ville. "The prefecture," he said with contempt—"why, that is *'la maison des flics.'*" Why had de Gaulle gone to the house of the "cops" instead of to the people? The police for four years had been collaborating, arresting patriots and resistants. Bidault felt that de Gaulle was wrong in thinking that the Communists were plotting a coup and even more wrong to dump the entire Resistance into a toolbox of the Communists.

Bidault and other democratic resistants were right and de Gaulle was wrong. It was a slap in the faces of many patriots to honor the police first, indeed to honor the police at all. De Gaulle feared the leaders of the people, democrats as well as Communists. De Gaulle meant to rule without challenge.

At dusk, a roar from the crowd alerted Bidault and all the leaders of the Resistance that the great man had, at last, arrived. De Gaulle strode into the main hall of the Hôtel de Ville, towering over all around him, looking all the more impressive for the austerity of his simple khaki uniform, wearing only the red-and-blue badge of Fighting France and the Cross of Lorraine on his tunic pocket. He shook hands with everyone and then made a brief speech. His key phrase was this: "Our national unity is a necessity."

Bidault made his own speech of welcome and then asked de Gaulle if he would go out on the balcony and proclaim the Republic. No, said de Gaulle, with a stony face, "The Republic had never ceased to exist."

As Bidault glared at him, General de Gaulle then stepped out on the balcony and opened wide his arms to embrace the people of Paris, overflowing the square, the Rue de Rivoli, and the banks of the Seine. "De Gaulle! De Gaulle! De Gaulle!" The chant, all over Paris, was a vote of confidence in the leader of the French. The Communists, looking over his shoulders and listening to the roar of the crowd, knew they could not beat him, assuming that they ever really harbored such ambition. They were astute politicians and knew that France was far from being ready to become a Communist state. They were sure their time would come one day, but it would not be on August 25, 1944, or anywhere in the foreseeable future of that day of liberation.

The brilliant day faded slowly away into the flame red and lime green of a summer twilight in Paris. Then it was dark, as it had been for the past five years, the darkness of blackout, the darkness of war and occupation. Some people began to wonder if the day had only been a magnificent dream. Then suddenly, without warning, lights flashed on. They came to life all over Paris. Arc lights illuminated the Eiffel Tower and presented it center-stage to the theater that is Paris. The Palais de Chaillot, Les Invalides, Notre Dame, its gargoyles grinning in the lights, the Sacré-Coeur, atop Montmartre, a bright, white wedding cake at the feast of liberation, all leaped out of the night.

La Ville Lumière had been reborn, and everyone knew that it was all true, that it had not been a dream, that Paris had been liberated. Its engineers and electricians had squeezed out the last watt of available energy to light up their beloved city for the first time since the blackout of September 3, 1939, when war had been declared.

What followed the next day, even the fantastic parade of General de Gaulle, with Bidault and the other Resistance leaders at his side, with all of Paris lining the streets, was anticlimax. Paris had been liberated on August 25 and its liberation was illuminated by the glorious lights of a free capital. August 25 was and will always be the most revered date in the centuries-old history of Paris. August 25 is the feast day of Saint-Louis, the patron saint of Paris. What more appropriate day for the liberation of the city that belongs to France and to the world?

The next day may have been an anticlimax, but what an extraordinary anti-climax it was. The French have a flair for theater, but they outdid themselves on August 26. General de Gaulle ordered Leclerc to line up the Second Armored along his route of march. He wanted the people of Paris and the Communists to see the force at his command. He needed the troops, too, to provide security. Paris was still in a state of anarchy and disorder. For de Gaulle and his closest supporters, as well as all the leaders of the Resistance, to march together, all bunched up in a compact target, was a foolhardy act in an unstable city. He did not consult the Allied command, keeping Leclerc's division under his command without Allied permission.

The American corps commander, General Leonard Gerow, had sent a stern order to Leclerc directing him to "disregard" de Gaulle's orders for the parade. Leclerc, knowing that Gerow was within his rights, could not bring himself to disobey de Gaulle, certainly not in the wake of the liberation of Paris. He resolved to face the consequences of his insubordination later but to follow de Gaulle that day.

General de Gaulle went to the Etoile, preparing to lay a wreath on the Tomb of the Unknown Soldier and then to rekindle the eternal light.

He looked around at the men who had gathered to march with him. He saw the leaders of all the Resistance organizations, his adversaries and his supporters, Communists Henri Rol-Tanguy, André Tollet, and Pierre Villon, Gaullists Alexandre Parodi, Jacques Chaban-Delmas, and his top generals, Pierre Koenig, Alphonse Juin, and Jacques Leclerc. Charles de Gaulle, standing high above all of them, looked down at them and smiled. "Gentlemen," he said, "one step behind me." Then he strode forward.

Hundreds of thousands of Parisians cheered as de Gaulle led the parade down the Champs-Elysées. Then, as he entered into the Place de la Concorde, a shot rang out. Civilians and soldiers hit the pavements and sought shelter behind vehicles of the Second Armored. De Gaulle, erect, walked slowly to an open car waiting to take him to Notre Dame Cathedral. As his car entered the parvis in front of the cathedral, more shots rang out. De Gaulle slowly emerged from his car, seemingly oblivious to the shooting. He took a bouquet of flowers offered him by two little girls in Alsatian costumes. Then, calmly, majestically, de Gaulle walked into the cathedral to celebrate a Te Deum.

Earlier, Alexandre Parodi, to avoid any embarrassing incident, had gone to Notre Dame to arrange for the ceremony and to make sure that the archbishop of Paris, Cardinal Suhard, be kept out of the cathedral during the ceremony. The archbishop had been a collaborationist of Vichy and of the Germans. He had received Marshal Pétain and had even celebrated a mass for General von Choltitz, as well as having presided over the obsequies of Philippe Henriot, the most notorious pro-Nazi propagandist of the Vichy State Radio and Information Service. De Gaulle preferred to be received by the curate of Notre Dame, not its cardinal.

De Gaulle walked slowly down the central aisle to the head of the transept and to his seat of honor at the left of the main aisle. He stood erect, hymnbook in hand, as the firing continued. Then, over the din, one could hear his strong voice intoning each phrase of the Magnificat! But the shots continued to ring out. It was impossible to celebrate the Te Deum. It had become too dangerous for all. General de Gaulle left Notre Dame, with the cries of the crowd covering his departure: *"Vive de Gaulle! Que la Vierge le protége!"*

No one has ever discovered who fired the fusillade. De Gaulle was bemused by the fact that he did not hear the whistle of bullets around him and he did not see any sparks fly from the pavements or the walls. He concluded that someone had been firing in the air, and since his obsession was the Communists, he concluded that it was the Communists who were trying to create a climate of insecurity in Paris. An investigation did establish that the police, the army, and the FFI had all been trigger-happy that day and had fired wildly at windows and rooftops as soon as they heard shots. Most of the shots that rang out had come from security troops and not from enemies. There were fascist militiamen still in Paris and some German snipers. They might have started it. No one will know with any certainty what happened other than the result: It enhanced de Gaulle's already huge reputation for courage and for luck. Napoleon had once said: "Give me a lucky general!"

Charles de Gaulle quickly established himself as the leader of France in liberated Paris. One of his first decisions was to dissolve the CNR and all the other Resistance organizations, including the fighting men of the Forces Françaises de l'Intérieur, the FFI. He gave orders to incorporate the FFI immediately into the regular army, confirming orders he had earlier given to General de Lattre of the First French Army. De Gaulle had his quartermaster ask the Americans urgently for fifteen thousand khaki uniforms to clothe his new soldiers.

Despite his quarrels with the Americans and his determination to liberate Paris with French troops alone, de Gaulle knew that he needed American troops to ensure the safety of Paris. He had to ask Eisenhower for help. It must have been galling for the proud French general to have to admit that he could not trust his own people and needed to be covered by foreigners, but de Gaulle was so frightened by the specter of a Communist coup that he had swallowed his pride.

In a letter to Eisenhower on August 27, de Gaulle stated that he had to keep the Second Armored in Paris until order had been fully restored. Then, in a second communication the next day, General de Gaulle asked General Eisenhower to parade an American division, with all its awesome firepower, right through Paris to demonstrate to everyone Allied strength and Allied support for General de Gaulle. That request must have been the most bitter pill that General de Gaulle ever had to swallow. It was the ultimate admission that he had not established his own authority.

Eisenhower, astonished, but sympathetic and uneasy about any trouble behind his lines, agreed to furnish de Gaulle the parade he wanted. He kept the Fourth Division in reserve outside Paris and assigned the Twenty-eighth Infantry Division to parade through Paris in full battle array on August 29. The full battle array was not ordered to impress the people of Paris. The division was marching to engage the Germans east of the capital. For the first time in military history, a combat division, in full battle dress, paraded through the heart of a city and out the other end to hurl themselves upon the enemy.

Parisians gaped in awe as the Americans, in battle dress, unshaved, tough-looking, combat-hardened, came down the Champs-Elysées. They remembered the Germans four years earlier, clean-shaven, blond gods, with shining boots, the Aryan conquerers, seemingly invincible. Now the Americans, in dull khaki and reverse-leather shoes, unsmiling, confident without swagger. Long lines of jeeps rolled along with self-propelled cannon, while hundreds of planes flew overhead. This was mighty America, arsenal of democracy, whose factories were turning out the guns and planes that were crushing Hitler's once-invincible men.

As the ranks of the Twenty-eighth rolled by, the French snapped out of their silent awe and began to cheer thunderously. *"Vive les Américains! Vive Roosevelt!"* Some were shouting, "God bless America." Communist leaders watched quietly. De Gaulle stayed in his office. He needed but feared American power. The Communists knew that their hopes of coming to power in France were at best remote. They had not been able to prevent de Gaulle's coming to power, but they had not completely reconciled themselves to his leadership of France.

There are some American students of French affairs who still insist that it was an error, with the most costly consequences to the French and to the Allies both, to have let Leclerc "liberate" Paris and to send an American division in with a show of strength to consolidate de Gaulle's grip on the French. It is not that they subscribe to Roosevelt's argument that we should not have "imposed" a leader upon the French. What the dissenters were upset about was the dangerous psychological illusion of self-liberation.

In fact the French did not liberate themselves. Leclerc was allowed by Eisenhower to be the first division into Paris. But he could not have gone in without the U.S. Twenty-eighth Infantry right behind him, and without all the power of the United States and all the troops of the American and British armies. Leclerc's entry created the myth of self-liberation, just as the earlier uprising by the FFI created a rival myth that the Resistance and the people of Paris had liberated the capital. They did fight for it, bravely, but they did not liberate it. It is understandable that a proud people, once one of the ruling powers in the world, would need to believe it had liberated itself. The shame of 1940 had to be erased. What better way than to liberate Paris?

But the illusion of self-liberation led to the further illusion, fostered by Charles de Gaulle, that France was again a great world power, center of a mighty empire. That illusion led the French into the horrors and the terrible cost in blood and treasure in the wars in Indochina and the war of Algeria. For fifteen years, from the end of World War II to the end of the Algerian War, France was constantly at war. Victory in Europe, in May 1945, did not bring peace to France. Fifteen more years of war did not preserve the empire. After World War II, we were all living in a postcolonial world dominated by Russia and America. France's traditional foreign policy could not be maintained. France had to see itself, as it is slowly and painfully doing these days, as a European nation, not a world power. Europe, a united Europe of 250 million people, with vast resources and skills, can rival Russia, America, or China. France, the hexagon, all alone, cannot. De Gaulle could not see this, or could not tolerate the sight. Only now is this new direction becoming apparent to a new French generation.

In this sense, the liberation of Paris was a grand illusion, the last grand illusion of imperial France.

There were other myths generated in this period of liberation, not only in Paris but all through Normandy, Brittany, the cities and towns of the southwest, Bordeaux, Toulouse, Pau, and in each department east and west of the Rhône as our armies chased the Germans out of France. It was the myth of a "phony Resistance" spread by foreign correspondents, most of whom could not speak French and knew little or nothing of French politics. It grew out of the sudden appearance in the wake of our armies of loud-talking superpatriots wearing FFI brassards, brandishing guns, requisitioning cars and gas and food, many of whom were completely unknown to Resistance leaders.

True resistants, contemptuous of these bandwagoneers, called them derisively the RDM, Résistants de la`Dernière Minute. Correspondents with the armies soon heard talk about these "Resistants of the Last Minute." They also heard another term of ridicule, the "Résistants de Septembre." It is true that a good many fence-sitters, even collaborationists, sought to gain glory or whitewash guilt by becoming bandwagon patriots. Hundreds of thousands did try to jump aboard in the wake of victory, leading some correspondents to the false impression that the Resistance had sprung up in the last weeks of the war. This was a sad injustice to the tens of thousands of men and women who, since 1940, had fought and died in the Resistance, and the hundreds and thousands more who had fought and survived after terrible suffering and extraordinary bravery.

Beyond all these myths and illusions remains an honorable reality. The people of France did fight for their own liberation, even if they did not accomplish it alone. They fought with courage and paid a heavy price in blood. The courage and selflessness of the men and women in the Resistance is one of the most glorious chapters in the long, dramatic history of France. The most glorious battles and victories of Napoleon are less glorious than even the defeats of the Resistance. The men and women of the Resistance were soldiers without uniforms and almost without arms, fighting for freedom and democracy, not for empire.

Claude Bouchinet Serreulles, who risked his own life for long years in the Resistance, recently paid tribute to his fellow countrymen in a commemorative speech at a meeting of veterans of the Resistance in Paris. "The people, just ordinary people, were there when we needed them. Without them, there would have been no Resistance. Not everyone can pick up a gun and fight. Not everyone can leave his home and his family and go underground. I do not criticize those who did not follow us actively into the Resistance. I am grateful to the many patriots who did take risks to help us. We could not have gone on without them and they were millions."

Among the millions were Jean Vinzant's maid who risked her life to hide his illegal radio set, laughing at the Gestapo agents who searched for it in vain. Among them were the nuns who hid Jewish children in their convents. And three old ladies who gave their fields to the Free French as landing sites and hid resistants and Allied soldiers on their estate. Among them were Germaine Tillion, Jean-Pierre Lévy, Marie-Madeleine Fourcade, and Henri Frenay. These were the soldiers without uniform, the soldiers of the night who wrote one of the finest chapters in French history.

OUT OF
THE SHADOWS

They came out of the shadows of oppression into freedom. They saw men and women cheering and parading, wearing the tricolor brassards of the Republic and de Gaulle's Cross of Lorraine. They saw uniformed soldiers wearing helmets covered with fishnet and driving a machine called a jeep. American uniforms and an American machine, but the soldiers were speaking French. They were their soldiers, the soldiers of the liberator, Charles de Gaulle.

They heard the familiar notes of Beethoven's Fifth, which they had listened for so eagerly for four long years, the identity signal of the BBC in London. They had heard it at low volume, hunched over their sets so that the police or Vichy spies could not catch them listening to the forbidden radio. But in August 1944 they heard the BBC loud and clear, blaring out of open windows. They were free.

Not free everywhere in France. Last-ditch German defenders were still holed up in pockets in Brittany, Bordeaux, and Alsace. General Patton, slashing across France in pursuit of the enemy, finally ran out of gas in eastern France and could not go into Germany. Eisenhower's fear that the early liberation of Paris might divert too much fuel to the capital and halt his advance had been realized. Patton ranted and raved but Eisenhower did not. It was not Ike's style to rant. He merely said that what was done had to be done.

General Bradley's fear that once the French army got into Paris he would not be able to get it out again was not confirmed. Some French units did stay in Paris as security troops and General de Gaulle did install his government and devote himself immediately to consolidating his political position. But General Leclerc led his Second Armored Division east for combat, just as General de Lattre ordered the First French Army to maintain contact with the enemy and follow orders of the Allied Supreme Command. Having broken ranks for Paris, the French were eager to show Eisenhower that they could follow orders and fight in the common cause.

At the same time, de Lattre ordered all authorities in liberated territories to register all men between eighteen and thirty. He also conferred with FFI commanders and local Resistance leaders on the procedure for integrating the Groupes Francs and all armed Resistance units and individuals into the regular armed forces. He ordered all partisans and guerrillas to turn in their guns to the army. He made it clear that he would not tolerate any irregular armed men in liberated France.

There was a good deal of grumbling and opposition to these orders, but most of the Resistance leaders knew that the orders were justified. Many men and women who had lived for years with their guns near or on them would not give them up, but did not dare say so. They covered them with grease, packed them in oilcloth, and buried them and then declared that they had no weapons. Many joined the new combat forces. Others were appointed to administrative or political posts in the liberated areas. Claude Serreulles was named commissaire of the Republic in Paris, Gilbert Grandval in Alsace, Yves Farge in Lyon, Pierre Bertaux in Toulouse, Raymond Aubrac in Marseille. Some made their way home to try to return to their careers and a new life in a new France.

Their hopes and dreams had been articulated in underground papers all through the war. They had clearly perceived the reasons for the fall of France: the weakness of the governments that rose and fell like the tides in a divided Parliament where it was impossible for any one man or any one party to command a majority for more than a few months; the power of the trusts and the monopolies; the corruption of the press; the hatred of the Right for the Left, of Capital for Labor; the fragmentation of French society. There would have to be changes made and they vowed to make those changes. They saw all this clearly as they fought in the shadows; ironically their vision was blinded by the full light of freedom.

The key weakness of France's political system resided in its system of parliamentary government.

The parliamentary system can work well in a two-party society, or even a three-party polity, provided that there are at least two strong parties and a general sense of a national consensus. It has worked well in Britain, even in the absence of a consensus; it is viable just so long as the swing of power remains inside a general pact of commitment to basic democratic principles. But when there is no one party or two parties that can obtain a strong majority and when there are strong forces fundamentally opposed even to the democratic principles of a republic, disaster constantly threatens.

France was a fragmented society when the war ended in 1945. The multiplicity of political parties and splinter groups that had weakened the Third Republic were all still alive. The multiplicity of newspapers and magazines that could not live on their own circulation and advertising revenues and were, therefore, obliged to seek subsidies from special interests, losing their independence and objectivity, had not changed. But the men and women of the Resistance failed to see this reality.

They forgot how difficult it had been to win unity even under occupation. The Communists emerged from the Resistance in strength, claiming they had demonstrated that they were a patriotic French national party. But they, still Communists, took orders from Moscow and viewed bourgeois notions of democracy with contempt. The right-wingers of France, who also despised democracy, were still there, waiting for their chance to whitewash themselves and try a comeback in the struggle for power.

The men and women who had led the fight against the Germans in both the interior and exterior Resistance conferred on the procedures leading to a new Republic all through the early months of liberation of the national territory, from the landings in Normandy in June 1944, through the day of Victory in Europe, May 1945, when the German generals signed the documents of unconditional surrender in the building known as the Little Red Schoolhouse in Reims. They finally reached agreement to hold a referendum on a constitution for a new Republic and simultaneous elections to an assembly.

On October 21, 1945, the French people voted overwhelmingly in favor of a new constitution and the election of a constituent assembly to draft it. The affirmative vote was 96 percent of the electorate. By a smaller 60 percent margin the assembly was limited to a life of seven months.

The different margin was a result of Communist opposition. The Communists felt certain they would win the greatest number of seats in that legislature, and they wanted to extend their tenure in office as long as possible.

The overwhelming affirmative vote for a new constitution gave a legal mandate immediately to the legislators who were elected to the Constituent Assembly on that same date, October 21, 1945. Communist expectations of victory in the elections were fully realized as their candidates rolled up the highest total of votes:

Communist party	5,005,000
Socialist party	4,561,000
Catholics (MRP)	4,780,000

The Catholic party, called Mouvement Républicain Populaire (MRP), was a new party that had not existed under that name in the previous Republic, although there had been strong Catholic political and trade union groups. The MRP was the only major new movement to come out of the Resistance. It was created and led by the courageous Catholic professors of history and law who had resisted the surrender to the Germans from the very first minute, men like lycée history professor Georges Bidault, who had become president of the CNR; law professor François de Menthon, founder of Liberté, who had merged his movement with Frenay's Combat; Edmond Michelet, who had survived a Nazi concentration camp; Pierre-Henri Teitgen, professor of law; and two brothers who were also distinguished legal scholars, the Coste-Floret twins, Alfred and Paul.

The Catholic party did exceptionally well for a new party, coming in second to the Communist party and just ahead of the Socialists. It did so partly because of the Resistance record of its founders but mainly because it declared that it was a new, progressive, democratic grouping of the Left. Everyone was a "leftist" in liberated France, for the traditional Right had totally discredited itself.

Of some nineteen million votes cast for the Constituent Assembly, a little more than fourteen million had gone to the "Big Three" parties that had been most active in the Resistance, the Communists, the Socialists, and the Catholics. The remainder was divided between two small groups, the Radicals and the Conservatives, parties on the right of center. The embryo of the body politic of the Fourth Republic was thus a misshapen monster, with a shriveled right wing, a shrunken middle, and a huge, swollen left wing. Most seriously, this body politic soon became separated from the head of the Republic when the Communists split openly and sharply with General Charles de Gaulle.

In November, the Constituent Assembly met to select its chief executive as the new prime minister of France. Catholic Pierre-Henri Teitgen and Socialist Vincent Auriol arose in turn to propose the name of Charles de Gaulle. All eyes then turned to the tiny, roly-poly Communist delegation chief in the Assembly, Jacques Duclos. Duclos grinned at them, stood up, and stated that the Communists, of course, would vote with their "Resistance partners to preserve Republican unity." The words, carefully chosen, and the smile, wry and sly, gave the message. They were not voting for de Gaulle but for Republican unity. It was a first-round victory for de Gaulle, but only a first round and everyone knew it.

The next round began when Premier de Gaulle called in party leaders to discuss formation of his Cabinet.

De Gaulle told the Communists that he would be happy to allocate posts to them but, he said, not one of the three key Cabinet portfolios: Interior (which controls the police), Foreign Affairs, and National Defense.

The number-one man in the Communist party was Maurice Thorez, the man who had fled from his army unit to escape the police repression of the Communist party during the "phony war." After spending the war years in Moscow Thorez had been brought back to France, cleared of charges, in a deal that de Gaulle had made with Stalin in return for Soviet support for Free France. Thorez and de Gaulle were, to say the least, not easy allies.

Thorez blew up and accused de Gaulle of trying to cancel out the votes of the French people. "We are the first party of France," he told de Gaulle, "and we merit and demand a fair share of governmental responsibility on democratic terms."

De Gaulle, unimpressed, replied coolly that, as chief executive, he had to exercise his mandate and choose his Cabinet ministers as he thought best.

Thorez, a tough coal miner from the northern fields, hardened by hundreds of political battles in his rise to the top of the Communist party, did not stand in awe of Charles de Gaulle. He told the premier that the Communist party would not accept his dictation and would not join his government unless it had its share of the key posts.

General de Gaulle, an autocrat, with neither the experience nor the taste for the give-and-take of democratic government, faced his first dilemma as a democratic leader. He was unwilling to entrust the police, the army, or the diplomacy of France to a party that he considered to be the agent of a foreign power. But he could not form a Cabinet if the largest party in France refused to participate in it. De Gaulle, a power virtually unto himself as leader of Free France during the war, despising politicians and the political process, demonstrated his disgust by sending a letter to the Speaker of the Assembly, Socialist Félix Gouin, announcing his resignation as premier. Thus France had a Cabinet crisis before it even had a constitution. The fragile unity of the Resistance, forged with utmost difficulty over four years by the bonds of a common fight against the enemy, could not survive the first six months of peace.

Vincent Auriol, who became president of the Republic later, played a major role in the fight between de Gaulle and the Communist party. He was the architect of the Socialist party doctrine of that day: It would join a government without de Gaulle, if he sulked on the sidelines, but only a three-party coalition of the Resistance: Socialists, Catholics, and Communists. Auriol refused what he called "the trap" of a Marxist coalition, a merger of the Socialists and Communists, in which his party might be swallowed up by the larger, more militant Communists, while France would be torn by class warfare between the Marxists and the anti-Communists.

Auriol persuaded the party leaders to go to see de Gaulle and seek a compromise. The Communist party refused. It demanded the premiership for one of its members. The Socialists said they would vote for a Communist premier if the Catholics went along to preserve the unity of the Resistance. Georges Bidault and his Catholic comrades refused to vote for a Communist. The shape of the future of French politics took on the aspects of the specter of the past: a divided France always in political crisis, with governments rising and falling with the four seasons.

The Socialist party leaders and the Catholic party leaders met privately. They soon came to an understanding of their roles. They were dedicated to democracy and to the Republic. They would not support either Communism or Caesarism. They would force the two extremes of Thorez and de Gaulle to compromise their differences. They would not support the far Left or the far Right. If no compromise could be reached, they would try to rally enough forces to their side to form a government themselves. This, in fact, eventually became the pattern of politics in the Fourth Republic, a coalition of social democrats and Christian democrats with a bare majority supplied by smaller groups clustered around the center.

At first, General de Gaulle withdrew his resignation and reached a compromise with the Communist party. De Gaulle held firm on not turning over the police and the diplomatic service to the "men of Moscow." But, in a Solomon-like decision, he cut the key Ministry of National Defense into two: a Ministry of the Armed Forces, which he gave to Catholic leader Edmond Michelet; and a Ministry of Armaments to which he appointed a leader of the

Communist Resistance, Charles Tillon. Thus the Communist party had a face-saving voice in national defense but did not have its hands directly on the armed forces. The "compromise" solved nothing and satisfied no one for very long, but it saved the day, saved faces, and provided time to get ahead with drafting the constitution of the Fourth Republic.

That new constitution, despite every effort by de Gaulle to give more power to the chief executive, gave all power, once again, as in the ill-starred Third Republic, to the sovereign Parliament. All the old politicians, sensing their chance, came rushing back to the political arena and to the political intrigues at which they were masters. Edouard Daladier, who had failed so miserably as premier during the phony war, made his political comeback as a deputy and then as a minister. Paul Reynaud, who had brought Pétain into his Cabinet, and had lacked the courage to take the government to North Africa to continue the fight, came back, too, to play a prominent role in the new-old Republic.

Collaborationists came crawling out of their holes to join reconstituted parties of the Right and even joined the Catholic party, singing the praises of de Gaulle as a means of absolving their sins. The old, corrupt, weak, and inefficient institutions began to creak again. The dream of Jean-Pierre Lévy of a France free of the economic tyranny of capitalism and the political tyranny of communism, free of discord, united in new pure, social, and democratic France, turned rapidly into a nightmare.

Henri Frenay was neither surprised nor disappointed. He had argued repeatedly and heatedly with Jean Moulin and with Charles de Gaulle against taking the Communists and the political parties into the Conseil National de la Résistance. He had warned that the Communist party would strike for power in postwar France. Frenay was, if not surprised, thoroughly frustrated. His own leadership had been rejected, even by the Executive Committee of Combat, which had voted against him on critical issues. He had no personal following, was not a member or a leader of any political group or party. His moment of greatness had been lived. He had no future in the new France.

Claude Serreulles was also not surprised, although he was disappointed. "I hoped against hope that the conflicting forces would overcome their hostilities in the interests of rebuilding our war-torn country. I still think that what we did in the Resistance was right. Without that unity, we might have had not a Cabinet crisis but a civil war. The fault was not to be laid only at the door of the Communist party. De Gaulle was too rigid, too inflexible, unable to function in a political democracy."

Serreulles, with no taste for politics himself, resigned as commissaire of the Republic and went back to the Foreign Service that he had left in 1940. He served as a diplomat until 1952, when he entered private life. He is today chief administrative officer of the morning paper *Le Parisien Libéré*, a most appropriate position and title for the man who had been chief administrative officer for General de Gaulle and who had done so much to bring about the liberation of Paris.

Navarre, Commandant Georges Loustaunau-Lacau, who would not work for de Gaulle in the Resistance, entered politics and was elected to the Assembly as a Conservative independent. Alhough a man of the Right, he was committed to democratic principles and to the Republic. He was a foe of both de Gaulle and the Communist party.

Marie-Madeleine Fourcade remained faithful to her "animals" of Noah's Ark. She created a veterans' organization for her network and devoted herself thereafter and until today to fighting for jobs, pensions, and medical care for her agents and their families. Marie-Madeleine, once the *bête noire* of the Nazis, has been for more than thirty years the terror of French bureaucrats. She storms the corridors and offices of the ministries of Paris fighting for every advantage that she can get for the survivors of the Resistance.

Jean-Pierre Lévy had as little taste for politics as Marie-Madeleine. He, too, has remained faithful to his comrades of the Resistance, serving as a member of the Order of Liberation, appearing at congresses and reunions of the movements, helping the survivors in every way that he can, while working as a high official of the Ministry of Health. He helped nurse back to health his wife, who had been a member of his movement and had just barely survived years in concentration camp. She weighed seventy pounds when she was rescued at the end of the war.

Emmanuel d'Astier de la Vigerie, who adored politics and intrigues of all kinds, threw himself into the political quarrels wracking the Constituent Assembly. To give himself a strong voice and a freewheeling position, d'Astier founded the morning paper *Libération*, the public version of the underground paper put out by his Libération movement in the Resistance. Until his death in the mid-fifties, d'Astier was a political celebrity on the Paris scene and remained faithful to his Resistance role as a close ally of the Communist party.

The most politically active of the Resistance leaders were the Communists and the Catholics. Pierre Villon, chief of Front National, became a Communist deputy to the Assembly and one of the most militant and articulate of Communist spokesmen from 1945 through today.

Villon was only one of many deputies who fought constantly against de Gaulle. Many democratic representatives resented de Gaulle's executive actions, taken without consulting the Assembly. The constant political frictions irritated de Gaulle. In January 1947 he once again resigned as premier. The Resistance leaders joined together and formed a coalition Cabinet, but that coalition burst apart in a dispute over a colonial revolt in Indochina. Socialists and Catholics wanted to vote to send soldiers and arms to Indochina. The Communist party opposed them.

Most leaders of the Resistance, who fought so bravely for their own independence, could not understand that other peoples were ready to fight for theirs. They did not understand that World War II had undermined the foundations of the British and French empires and that peoples everywhere would cast off the bonds of colonialism. Liberating American forces landing in

North Africa may have come to free the French from the Germans, but our message of freedom was heard and cheered by the indigenous peoples. Thomas Jefferson once wrote about the "infectious disease of freedom." This "disease" infected all the subject peoples of the world.

One Frenchman did see this clearly, the man whom journalists dubbed "Mr. Europe," Jean Monnet. Monnet was the man who conceived the Coal and Steel Community of western Europe, the Atomic Energy Community, and, his greatest achievement, the Economic Community, popularly known as the Common Market. All these projects brought together the western European democracies in "pools" whose aim was to eliminate barriers to trade and production, leading, eventually, to the concept of a federal United States of Europe, roughly similar to our own federal United States of America.

General de Gaulle could not tolerate the thought of seeing his France, once one of the big powers of the world, diminished to the status of a province of Europe. Resistance leaders Georges Bidault, François de Menthon, Michel Debré, d'Astier de la Vigerie, Pierre Villon, Henri Frenay, Marie-Madeleine Fourcade, Jean-Pierre Lévy, all of whom had fought so hard and risked so much to restore French independence, felt as de Gaulle did that France could not become a mere member state of a larger union. This refusal to abandon France's world role led the French to try to cling to imperial positions that could not be held. When Britain granted freedom and independence to India, French Indochina was doomed, but the leaders of France were dazzled by their vision of French grandeur.

Vietnamese leader Ho Chi Minh offered the French a ten- to twenty-year progressive evolution to independence for his country. The French government turned him down and sent troops to Saigon and Hanoi to put down his "rebellion." Fighting broke out in December 1946 and continued to grow in intensity year after terrible year until the final crushing defeat of the French in the now historic Battle of Dien Bien Phu, when the Viets overran the garrison and took ten thousand prisoners. That was too much for the French people to tolerate. The government had to pull its troops out and negotiate peace with the Vietnamese in the Geneva Conference of 1954. The French lost billions in francs and tens of thousands of men, their best professional soldiers, including almost all the elite cadets who graduated as officers each year from Saint-Cyr.

General de Gaulle watched this tragedy in deep gloom in his family retreat in eastern France, in the village of Colombey-les-Deux-Eglises. From time to time, he would come to Paris, to his headquarters on the Rue Solférino, to see political allies and friends. He had refused to form a traditional political party when he had resigned in disgust with the traditional parties in 1947. Instead he created a political "movement" that he called the Rassemblement du Peuple Français, the RPF, the Rally of the French People. It was, in fact, a party in all but name and structure.

De Gaulle was the sole leader of the RPF, but it did run candidates for office. They won huge votes and the biggest single bloc of seats in Parliament. This was not enough for de Gaulle. He would not return unless he had an absolute majority with a sure margin; otherwise he would again have to deal with the hated politicians. De Gaulle would not govern, he would only rule. And since he did not have the majority for rule, he retreated again to his home in Lorraine and sulked in his study.

The gloom that enveloped de Gaulle and most of his compatriots deepened when the native peoples of Algeria began to revolt against French imperial dominance soon after the defeat in Indochina. It was inevitable from the start: If the colonial peoples of Indochina could defeat France's best professional troops, so could other peoples in other imperial territories. Undoubtedly men as learned and bright as Georges Bidault could see this. They did. But they could not abide the sight before their eyes. Georges Bidault, in a talk during this period, paced the floor in front of the Medici fireplace in the French Foreign Office, balling up his fists as he proclaimed: "Ours will not be the generation that abandoned the heritage of our fathers."

His misplaced pride did him, his comrades, and the French people grievous harm. Once again their sons were sent to war. Short of fighting men after Indochina, the French instituted the draft and sent conscript soldiers into a battle that many did not understand and that many more bitterly rejected. We Americans can understand the anguish that tore France apart as we were torn apart in a similar tragedy in Vietnam. In the case of France, it brought down the Fourth Republic, whose government resigned. The politicians begged de Gaulle to return on his own terms.

De Gaulle came back in 1958. He thought that he could turn the tide in Algeria, but he could not. He saw the inevitable end and decided not to prolong the agony. He was as much of a nationalist as Bidault and the colonialists. He was as conscious of the heritage of his fathers and as committed to keeping it as they were. But de Gaulle was also a realist and a statesman. He could risk all for true glory but not for vainglory. The freedom and independence of France was worth fighting for against all odds in 1940. The retention of Algeria against all odds was not worth fighting for in 1960. De Gaulle understood that the imperial world was dead. But he fell just short of understanding that France, alone, was no longer a world power. He did not fully see how the world had changed.

Today, at long last, the French are aware of their changed role in a changed and still changing world. France is simply too small to rival the giant powers of the world, America, Russia, and China. Even those giants must take into account the emergence of new forces in Asia and Africa. America is reeling from the blows to its economy delivered by the Arabs and other oil-rich members of OPEC. For France to play any kind of an important role in world affairs, France must proceed with plans to unify the 250 million people of western Europe.

In a united Europe, France would assume a vital role as spokesman for all the quarter billion people of western Europe. Germany would certainly be the industrial and economic power of a united Europe, but France would just as certainly be the political power, for the simple reason that no one, including the Germans, could trust the Germans to be the political power and spokesman for a Europe so devastated by the Germans. Thus, paradoxically, as only a province of Europe, France would be more influential than she could be as a separate nation-state of her own.

Marie-Madeleine Fourcade, Jean-Pierre Lévy, Michel Debré, and many others active in the Resistance see this now. There are still controversies over whether a united Europe should be a federal United States, one supernation with one government, or whether it should be a kind of confederation of sovereign states, each retaining its own government and identity but coordinated as tightly as possible. It will be years before this controversy works itself into a new formula accepted by a large majority.

But the essence of what the Resistance fought for has already been achieved and guaranteed for as far ahead as one can look in a volatile political world. Nazism was defeated and democracy, triumphant. Communism has long passed its peak threat in western Europe. It remains strong in Italy and France but mainly because of democracy's failures, not because of its own magnetism. France's intellectuals, long enchanted by Marxism and communism, have long since been disenchanted. The French have their problems today as yesterday, but what people do not?

Many of the men and women of the Resistance feel that their long dark nights were in fact the brightest moments of their lives. For Henri Frenay it was the moment that he fell in love, fathered a child, and gave of the very best of himself in a noble cause. For Jean-Pierre Lévy, former salesman of hemp, it was the period when he discovered who and what he was and rose above himself. Marie-Madeleine broke all the traditional French taboos about the proper role of a woman. All of them would agree with the thought voiced recently by Jean-Pierre Lévy:

We lived in the shadows as soldiers of the night but our lives were not dark and martial. We were young and we were gay. We loved and we made love and we laughed perhaps more than we do today. There were arrests, torture, and death for so many of our friends and comrades, and tragedy awaited all of us just around the corner. But we did not live in or with tragedy. We were exhilarated by the challenge and rightness of our cause. It was in many ways the worst of times and in just as many ways the best of times, and the best is what we remember today.

GLOSSARY OF ALPHABETICAL SYMBOLS

AMGOT	*Allied Military Government for Occupied Territories*
AS	*Armée Secrète*—the Secret Army of the Resistance
BBC	*British Broadcasting Corporation*
BCRA	*Bureau Central des Recherches et d'Action*—the name of the same organization as below, adopted in August 1942
BCRAM	*Bureau Central de Renseignements et d'Action Militaire*—the name of the Intelligence Service of Free France, created in January 1942
BIP	*Bureau d'Information et de Presse*—the information agency of the unified Resistance
CDLL	*Ceux de la Libération*—a Resistance movement of the occupied northern zone
CDLR	*Ceux de la Résistance*—a Resistance movement of the occupied northern zone
CDM	*Camouflage du Matériel*—a French Armistice Army secret organization to camouflage war matériel
CFLN	*Comité Française de Libération Nationale*—French Committee of National Liberation, often refered to by Americans as "the National Committee," a Cabinet headed by General de Gaulle in Algiers
CFTC	*Confédération Française des Travailleurs Chrétiens*—French Confederation of Christian Workers, a major trade union organization
CGT	*Conféderation Générale du Travail*—the Communist-led trade union
CNF	*Conseil National Français*—the French National Council in London; an embryonic government-in-exile cabinet for de Gaulle, especially in the early years of the war
CNR	*Conseil National de la Résistance*—National Council of the Resistance; the unified directorate of the Resistance
COI	Coordinator of Information—U.S. Agency, a 1942 precursor to the OSS intelligence agency
COMAC	*Comité d'Action Militaire*—a Resistance military action committee
CPL	*Comité Parisien de Libération*—Paris Committee of Liberation
DGSS	*Direction Générale des Service Speciaux*—de Gaulle's Secret Service in Algiers
DSR/SM	*Direction de Service et de Renseignements et de Sécurité Militaire*—the intelligence source created by General Giraud in Algiers

DST	*Direction de la Surveillance du Territoire*—French counterespionage and internal security agency
EM	*Etat-Major*—general staff
FFI	*Forces Françaises de l'Intérieur*—official name of Resistance movements in 1944
FT	*Franc-Tireur*—name of a democratic Resistance movement operating mainly in the southern zone of France before and after its occupation
FTPF	*Franc-Tireurs et Partisans Français*—official name of the Communist party's Resistance movement, operating nationally
GESTAPO	*Geheime Staats Polizei*—Nazi Secret Police
GF	*Groupes Francs*—name given the commando and assault units of Resistance movements
GMR	*Groupes Mobiles de Réserve*—pro-Nazi Vichy armed mobile troops
JC	*Jeunesse Communiste*—youth movement of the Communist party
MI-5	*Military Intelligence*—branch of the British government, in charge of internal affairs
MI-6	*Military Intelligence*—external affairs, British
MLF	*Mouvement pour la Libération Française*—a merger of Frenay's Resistance movement, MLN, with left Catholics
MLN	*Mouvement de Libération Nationale*—a democratic Resistance movement created by Captain Frenay
MMLA	*Military Mission for Administrative Liaison*—General de Gaulle's liaison agency to the Allies in London and then in France
MRP	*Mouvement Républicain Populaire*—political party founded by Catholic resistants
MRU	*Mouvements de Résistance Unis*—a coalition of Resistance movements
MUR	*Mouvements Unis de la Résistance*—same as above
NAP	*Noyautage de l'Administration Publique*—infiltration and sabotage of the public administration
OCM	*Organisation Civile et Militaire*—a major Resistance movement of the army
OKW	*Oberkommandantur der Wehrmacht*—the German army High Command
ORA	*Organisation de Résistance de l'Armée*—a French army Resistance movement
OSS	*Office of Strategic Services*—U.S. intelligence agency
OWI	*Office of War Information*—U.S. propaganda agency
PC	*Command Post*
PWB	*Psychological Warfare Branch*—an Allied propaganda agency in Algiers
RAF	*Royal Air Force, British*
SAP	*Section Atterrissages et Parachutages*—parachute jumping and air supply unit of the Resistance
SHAEF	*Supreme Headquarters Allied Expeditionary Forces*—General Eisenhower's headquarters
SI	*Secret Intelligence*—American intelligence agency
SIS	*Secret Intelligence Service*—British intelligence agency
SNCF	*Société Nationale des Chemins de Fer*—French national railway

SOAM   *Service des Opérations Aériennes et Maritimes*—air and sea unit of
         the Resistance
SOE   *Special Operations Executive*—British intelligence and subversive ac-
         tivities agency
SPOC   *Special Projects Operation Center*—an Allied agency for special mili-
         tary operatives
STO   *Service du Travail Obligatoire*—forced labor draft for Germany

Bibliographical Notes

There is a vast and still fast-growing literature of World War II books, but, despite the thousands of titles available in English, there is an important gap. There are only a few books on the French Resistance, and, above all, no single, comprehensive one-volume history of that important and exciting war within the war, although there are a number of books in English on individual Resistance movements, as well as memoirs by Resistance leaders.

Among the memoirs, one of the best is the story of the Alliance, called Noah's Ark by the Gestapo. Its story is told by its chief, Marie-Madeleine Fourcade, and it was published by E. P. Dutton, under the title *Noah's Ark*.

The most controversial but important memoir is the work of Henri Frenay, chief of the biggest of the democratic movements, Combat. Frenay's view of what the Resistance did, and who did what to whom, is highly colored by his own role and his own subjective views, often contested by other writers. It appeared in English translation under the title *The Night Will End*, published by McGraw-Hill.

Is Paris Burning? by Larry Collins and Dominique Lapierre is a detailed, dramatic account of the insurrection and liberation of Paris and the extraordinary role played in those events by the Paris resistants. It was published by Simon & Schuster.

One of the most readable books about a single movement of the Resistance, one of the rare books written in English, is *The Vildé Affair*, by an American military historian, Martin Blumenson. It tells the story of the Musée de l'Homme and was published by Houghton Mifflin.

I want to recommend another book written in English that deserves the widest possible audience of Americans who are concerned about the health of our democratic institutions. It is *OSS—The Secret History of America's First Central Intelligence Agency*, by R. Harris Smith. It tells of America's activities in espionage, subversion, and dirty tricks in Europe, Africa, and Asia. It was originally published by the University of California Press and then republished, in paper, by the Dell Publishing Company, as a Delta book.

The most complete collection of source materials on the French Resistance is in French and may be found at the offices of the Comité d'Histoire de la Deuxième Guerre Mondiale in Paris. There are some five thousand titles of books, articles, monographs, and treatises. It is a principal resource for scholars of the subject.

The most comprehensive history was written by a journalist who was himself a Resistance fighter, Henri Noguères, with the collaboration of Marcel Degliame-Fouché and Jean-Louis Vigier. Four volumes of their works have already appeared under the title *Histoire de la Résistance en France,* covering the period June 1940 through May 1944. A fifth is scheduled to appear but no date has been set at this time. It will conclude the study by covering events through the final victory of the Allies and the establishment of the Fourth Republic of France in 1945. The series has been published by Robert Laffont.

Noguères's history is exhaustive and encyclopedic. There are few rigorously objective and scholarly works on the Resistance. French scholars, subjective on most subjects, are particularly so on this one.

One of the most prolific scholars of the period is Henri Michel. As director of the Comité de l'Histoire de la Deuxième Guerre Mondiale, Michel has had primary access to the files of that organization. He has written a dozen books on various aspects of the Resistance. His most useful work is a one-volume study: *Histoire de la Résistance Française.* It ran to five editions, the last of which was published in 1969 by the Presses Universitaires de France. It is a difficult book for Americans, for it assumes a great deal of background knowledge of France and French affairs.

The most objective work of scholarship was written by a young historian, Dominique Veillon. Entitled *Le Franc-Tireur,* it is a study of the movement and was prepared as a doctoral dissertation. The dissertation was received with honors and then published for the public by Flammarion, in 1978.

Most of the books on the Resistance come in the form of memoirs by Resistance fighters. Many are highly readable, exciting, firsthand accounts of events. The writers see these events through the prisms of their own personal visions and are not always accurate or reliable, but they do serve to cross-check one another and are a source for scholars.

The movement Libération, like Combat and Franc-Tireur, has its memorialists: its founder and chief, Emmanuel d'Astier de la Vigerie, and one of its brightest and most courageous militants, Lucie Aubrac. D'Astier's book is entitled *Sept fois sept jours* and was published by the Editions de Minuit. Aubrac's work is simply named *La Résistance.* It was published by Robert Lang. Both books reflect the colorful personalities and fierce partisanship of their authors.

The most prolific memorialist of all—indeed, he has made a career of it for the past thirty-five years—is the man the British praised as the greatest secret agent of the war, the legendary Colonel Rémy, who, in his former life, was Gilbert Renault, producer and writer of films. Rémy has written more than a dozen books and dozens more articles and movie scripts about the Resistance. They are all interesting, although some tend toward the fictional. He seems always to write with a movie in mind. One of the best of his books is entitled *Memoires d'un agent secret de la France Libre,* published by France-Empire.

Jean Moulin, chief of the CNR, tragic martyr of the Resistance, the man whom André Malraux praised as "the champion of the people of the night," left behind his own sadly aborted story, *Premier Combat,* published by the Editions de Minuit. His successor as CNR chief, Georges Bidault, who has lived through his own tragedy, argues his case in a book entitled *D'une Résistance à l'Autre.* In it he recounts his service to his country and to the cause of freedom in his resistance to the Nazis and also the reversal of that role as a leader of a French colonial resistance to the granting of freedom and independence to Algeria.

Among the many memoirs that tell the story of the Resistance in different regions of France are a few that are worthy of special mention:

■ *Libération de l'Est de la France* by Gilbert Grandval and A. J. Collin, published by Hachette. Grandval was the FFI chief of some seven departments of eastern France near the German border in the ancient provinces of Alsace-Lorraine.

■ *Libération de Toulouse et de sa région* by Pierre Bertaux, published by Hachette.

■ *Le Temps des Partisans* by Robert Noireau (Colonel Georges), published by Flammarion. Noireau's story is particularly interesting, for he was a militant Communist before and during the Resistance but was expelled from the Communist party after the liberation. He claims that he was expelled, as many were, because he fought in a non-Communist movement.

■ *Le Temps des Passions* by Francis Louis Closon, published by Presses de la Cité. Closon held a high rank in the Free French movement of de Gaulle in London. He is one of the most objective of the Gaullists.

■ *Souvenirs* was written by the least objective and most controversial of the leaders of Free France, Colonel Passy, chief of de Gaulle's Intelligence Service. His book is valuable as a source on the political infighting of the Resistance and is hotly contested by others in the Resistance. It was published by Editions Raoul Solar.

■ *Témoignages sur le Vercors* by Joseph La Picirella. This rare, almost unknown book was published privately by Joseph La Picirella, who was one of the maquis fighters in the deathtrap of the Vercors. He has created a Museum of the Vercors, called *Le Musée de la Résistance,* in the village of Vassieux-en-Vercors. His book is a series of eyewitness accounts of the battle of the Vercors, precious raw material.

The best combination of serious scholarship and high drama can be found in the brilliant work of historian Adrien Dansette, a distinguished member of the Institut Français. His book, *Histoire de la Libération de Paris,* set publishing records in France. Its first edition was printed in May 1946. The edition that I have in my library was its sixty-seventh, published in October 1966. I dare say there have been still more.

One of the least told and one of the most poignant stories of the Resistance is the drama of the French Jews who, more than any others, risked torture, deportation, and a horrible death at the hands of the Nazis. There are two rare books that tell this story:

■ *La Résistance Juive en France* by Anny Lévy Latour, published by Stock. Madame Latour took her degree in history. She is a careful researcher and a good writer as well as a dedicated champion and fighter for freedom and for the persecuted Jewish people. Her book should be a must on the list of any student of modern French history.

■ *Les Jeux de la Mort et de l'Espoir,* printed by the Jewish Federation. This is the story of and by Henri Bulawko, a Jew who fought the Nazis, was arrested, and sent to the death camp at Auschwitz, one of the 230,000 French Jews consigned to concentration camps. Only 30,000 returned at the liberation and some 10,000 of them died within a year or two.

INDEX

Quality MERIDIAN BOOKS of Special Interest

(0452)

☐ **WALLACE by Marshall Frady. Revised Edition.** "One of the best political biographies of any year . . . The biographer has brilliantly evoked an image of George Corley Wallace that is Faulknerian in its chilling similarity to Flem Snopes."—*The New Republic*   (00442X—$3.95)

☐ **THE TRANSFORMATION OF SOUTHERN POLITICS: Social Change and Political Consequence Since 1945 by Jack Bass and Walter DeVries.** A thorough examination of southern political attitudes and developments that looks at each state as an individual political entity as well as part of a collective political group.   (004705—$5.95)

☐ **THE CRIME SOCIETY: Organized Crime and Corruption in America edited by Francis A. J. Ianni and Elizabeth Reuss-Ianni.** This volume presents the most notable work of leading scholars, crime experts, and government commissions in learning the truth about organized crime in America, offering an unrivaled overview of organized crime as both a historical and vital segment of the American economy
(004500—$5.95)

☐ **TRANSCENDENTAL MEDIATION by Maharishi Mahesh Yogi.** According to Maharishi, "the natural state of man is joy." Here, in his own words, Maharishi Mahesh Yogi opens the path to that blessed state through the simple technique of deep meditation. (25115X—$3.95)

In Canada, please add $1.00 to the price of each book.

Buy them at your local bookstore or use coupon on
next page for ordering.

You'll Enjoy These MERIDIAN Books

(0452)

☐ **REVOLUTIONARIES by E. J. Hobsbawm.** A brilliant investigation of the theory and practice of revolution in the twentieth century. It traces the course of revolutionary ideology and action throughout the world—from Russia to Vietnam, from Spain to Cuba—describing and assessing goals, methods, successes, and failures, whether of political action, guerrilla warfare, or the individual act of violence.
(00425X—$3.95)

☐ **THE NATIONALIZATION OF THE MASSES: Political Symbolism and Mass Movements in Germany from the Napoleonic Wars through the Third Reich by George L. Mosse.** One of the most thought-provoking examinations of the roots of Nazism and modern fascism.
(004640—$4.95)

☐ **JAPAN: The Fragile Superpower by Frank Gibney.** A brilliant description of Japan's post-war economic miracle in this revealing close-up of its business, society, politics, and culture . . . "No one else I know has the author's combination of long and deep study of Japan, varied and intimate business experience in Japan, and lively writing skill."
—Edwin O. Reischauer, former U.S. Ambassador to Japan
(005930—$5.95)

☐ **REACHING JUDGMENT AT NUREMBERG by Bradley F. Smith.** Using newly revealed courtroom documents, here is the untold story of how the Nazi war criminals were judged and a superlative study of the nature of human justice . . . "Solid history . . . succeeds most admirably in clarifying the ideals and practical purposes of the trial."
—*The New York Times* (005035—$5.95)

In Canada, please add $1.00 to the price of each book.

Buy them at your local bookstore or use this convenient
coupon for ordering.

THE NEW AMERICAN LIBRARY, INC.
P.O. Box 999, Bergenfield, New Jersey 07621

Please send me the PLUME and MERIDIAN BOOKS I have checked above.
I am enclosing $_____(please add $1.50 to this order to cover postage and handling). Send check or money order—no cash of C.O.D.'s. Prices and numbers are subject to change without notice.

Name_____

Address_____

City_____State_____Zip Code_____

Allow at least 4-6 weeks for delivery.
This offer is subject to withdrawal without notice.